GLOBAL  STUDIES

JAPAN AND THE PACIFIC RIM

FOURTH EDITION

Dr. Dean W. Collinwood

Weber State University

University of Utah

Dushkin/McGraw-Hill Company
Sluice Dock, Guilford, Connecticut 06437

Visit us on the internet—http://www.dushkin.com/

Japan and the Pacific Rim

R
952
G51
4th ed.
1997

OTHER BOOKS IN THE GLOBAL STUDIES SERIES

- Africa
- China
- India and South Asia
- Latin America
- The Middle East
- Russia, the Eurasian Republics, and Central/Eastern Europe
- Western Europe

Cataloging in Publication Data
Main Entry under title: Global Studies: Japan and the Pacific Rim. 4th ed.
    1. East Asia—History—20th century–. 2. East Asia—Politics and government—20th century–. I. Title: Japan and the Pacific Rim. II. Collinwood, Dean W., *comp*.
ISBN 0–697–37423–8

©1997 by Dushkin/McGraw-Hill Companies, Guilford, Connecticut 06437.

Fourth Edition

Printed in the United States of America

Japan and the Pacific Rim

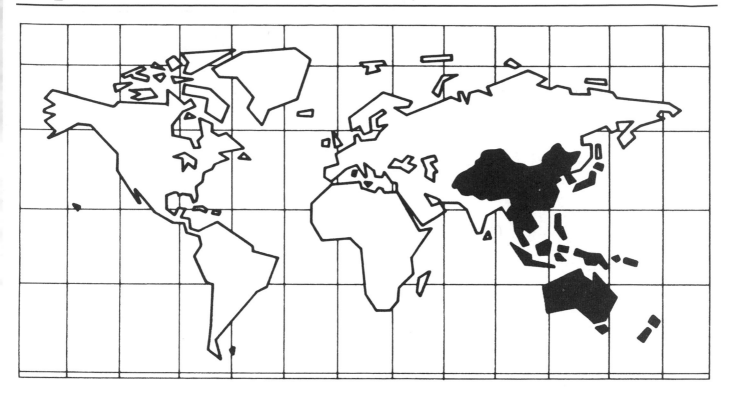

AUTHOR/EDITOR

Dr. Dean W. Collinwood

The author/editor of *Global Studies: Japan and the Pacific Rim* received his Ph.D. from the University of Chicago, an M.Sc. in international relations from the University of London, and a B.A. in political science with a minor in Japanese from Brigham Young University. He was a Fulbright scholar at the University of Tokyo and Tsuda College in Japan and has conducted research in East Asia, South and Southeast Asia, and the Pacific. Dr. Collinwood is currently professor of sociology at Weber State University and director of the U.S.–Japan Center of Utah, which administers the Japan Industry and Management of Technology Training Program for the U.S. government. He is also executive director of UCON—the Utah Asian Studies Consortium—and an adjunct professor of management at the University of Utah. He currently serves on the board of directors of the Western Conference of the Association for Asian Studies and is the author of books on Japan, Korea, and other countries.

SERIES CONSULTANT

H. Thomas Collins
PROJECT LINKS
George Washington University

STAFF

Ian A. Nielsen	Publisher
Brenda S. Filley	Production Manager
Lisa M. Clyde	Developmental Editor
Roberta Monaco	Editor
Charles Vitelli	Designer
Cheryl Greenleaf	Permissions Coordinator
Lisa Holmes-Doebrick	Administrative Coordinator
Shawn Callahan	Graphics
Lara M. Johnson	Graphics
Laura Levine	Graphics
Michael Campbell	Graphics
Joseph Offredi	Graphics
Juliana Arbo	Typesetting Supervisor

Selected World Wide Web Sites for Japan and the Pacific Rim

(Some Web sites continually change their structure and content, so the information listed here may not always be available.—Ed.)

GENERAL SITES

CNN Online Page—**http://www.cnn.com**—U.S. 24-hour video news channel. News is updated every few hours.

C-SPAN ONLINE—**http://www.c-span.org/**—See especially C-SPAN International on the Web for International Programming Highlights and archived C-Span programs.

International Network Information Center at University of Texas—**http://inic.utexas.edu**—Gateway has pointers to international sites, including Japan, China, and Taiwan.

I-Trade International Trade Resources & Data Exchange—**http://www.i-trade.com/**—Monthly exchange-rate data, U.S. Document Export Market Information (GEMS), U.S. Global Trade Outlook, and World Fact Book.

Political Science RESOURCES—**http://www.keele.ac.uk:80/depts/po/psr.htm**—Dynamic gateway to sources available via European addresses. Listed by country name. Includes official government pages, official documents, speeches, elections, political events.

ReliefWeb—**http://www.reliefweb.int**—UN's Department of Humanitarian Affairs clearinghouse for international humanitarian emergencies. Has daily updates, including Reuters, VOA, PANA.

Social Science Information Gateway (SOSIG)—**http://sosig.esrc.bris.ac.uk/**—Project of the Economic and Social Research Council (ESRC). It catalogs 22 subjects and lists developing-countries URL addresses.

United Nations System—**http://www.unsystem.org/**—The official Web site for the United Nations system of organizations. Everything is listed alphabetically. Offers: UNICC; Food and Agriculture Organization.

UN Development Programme (UNDP)—**http://www.undp.org/**—Publications and current information on world poverty, Mission Statement, UN Development Fund for Women, and more. Be sure to see Poverty Clock.

UN Environmental Programme (UNEP)—**http://www.unchs.unon.org/**—Official site of UNEP. Information on UN environmental programs,1996/97, products, services, events, search engine.

U.S. Agency for International Development (USAID)—**http://www. info.usaid.gov/**—Graphically presented U.S. trade statistics with Japan, China, Taiwan, and other Pacific Rim countries are available at this site.

U.S. Central Intelligence Agency Home Page—**http://www.odci.gov/cia**—This site includes publications of the CIA, such as the 1996 World Fact Book, 1995 Fact Book on Intelligence, Handbook of International Economic Statistics, 1996, and CIA Maps.

U.S. Department of State Home Page—**http://www. state. gov/index.html/**—Organized by categories: Hot Topics (i.e., 1996 Country Reports on Human Rights Practices), International Policy, Business Services.

World Bank Group-**www.worldbank.org/html/Welcome. html/**—News (i.e., press releases, summary of new projects, speeches), publications, topics in development, countries and regions. Links to other financial organizations.

World Health Organization (WHO)—**http://www.who.ch/**—Maintained by WHO's headquarters in Geneva, Switzerland, uses Excite search engine to conduct keyword searches.

World Trade Organization—**http://www.wto.org/**—Topics include foundation of world trade systems, data on textiles, intellectual property rights, legal frameworks, trade and environmental policies, recent agreements, etc.

ASIA

Asia-Yahoo—**http://www.yahoo.com/Regional/Regions/Asia/**—Specialized Yahoo search site permits keyword search on Asian events, countries, or topics.

South-East Asia Information—**http://sunsite.nus.sg/asiasvc.html/** —Excellent gateway for country-specific research. Information on Internet Providers and Universities in Southeast Asia, links to Asian online services.

CHINA

Chinese Society Home Page—**http://members.aol.com/mehampton/ chinasec.html/**—Information is listed under Chinese Military Links, Data Sources on Chinese Security Issues, Key Newspapers and News Services, and Key Scholarly Journals and Magazines.

Information Office of State Council of People's Republic of China—**hhtp://www.cityu.edu.hk/HumanRights/index. htm/**—Official site of China's government contains policy statements by the government related to human rights.

Inside China Today—**http://www.insidechina.com/**—This Web site is part of the European Information Network. Recent information on China is organized under Headline News, Government, and Related Sites, Mainland China, Hong Kong, Macau, and Taiwan.

JAPAN

Japan Ministry of Foreign Affairs—**http://www.mofa.go.jp/**—"What's New" lists events, policy statements, press releases. Foreign Policy section has speeches; Foreign Policy archive; information under Countries and Region, Friendship.

Japan Policy Research Institute (JPRI)—**http://www.nmjc.org/jpri/**—Headings include "What's New" and Publications before 1996.

We recommend that you check out our Web site, which can be reached at *http://www.dushkin.com/*

Contents

Global Studies: Japan and the Pacific Rim, Fourth Edition

Pacific Rim   Page 7

Pacific Islands   Page 13

Japan   Page 31

Selected World Wide Web Sites **v**
Introduction **viii**
Canada Statistics and Map **x**
U.S. Statistics and Map **xi**
Global Map **xii**

3 **The Pacific Rim: Diversity and Interconnection**
Map: Pacific Rim **2**

13 **The Pacific Islands: Opportunities and Limits**

20 **Japan: Driving Force in the Pacific Rim**
Map: Japan   **18**
Japan Statistics **19**

36 **Country Reports**

Australia (Commonwealth of Australia)	**36**
Brunei (Negara Brunei Darussalam)	**41**
Cambodia (Kingdom of Cambodia)	**43**
China (People's Republic of China)	**46**
Hong Kong	**52**
Indonesia (Republic of Indonesia)	**56**
Laos (Lao People's Democratic Republic)	**59**
Macau	**62**
Malaysia	**64**
Myanmar (Burma) (Union of Myanmar)	**67**
New Zealand (Dominion of New Zealand)	**71**
North Korea (Democratic People's Republic of Korea)	**75**
Papua New Guinea (Independent State of Papua New Guinea)	**79**
Philippines (Republic of the Philippines)	**82**
Singapore (Republic of Singapore)	**86**
South Korea (Republic of Korea)	**89**
Taiwan (Republic of China)	**93**
Thailand (Kingdom of Thailand)	**97**
Vietnam (Socialist Republic of Vietnam)	**102**

106 **Articles from the World Press**
Annotated Table of Contents for Articles   **106**
Topic Guide to Articles

108

Japan and the Pacific Rim: Articles

1. Recipe for Asian Unity, Itt Kenichi, *Japan Echo,* Winter 1995.   **110**
2. Global Forces Shape Asia, John Naisbitt, *Far Eastern Economic Review,* 50th Anniversary Issue, October 1996.   **114**
3. Asia on the Brink, Jim Rohwer, *Across the Board,* January 1996.   **116**
4. Pacific Insecurity: Emerging Threats to Stability in East Asia, Jonathan D. Pollack, *Harvard International Review,* Spring 1996.   **120**
5. Vital and Vulnerable, Gary Silverman, *Far Eastern Economic Review,* May 23, 1996.   **124**
6. Rock Solid, Simon Elegant and Margot Cohen, *Far Eastern Economic Review,* December 5, 1996.   **128**

Introduction

THE GLOBAL AGE

As we approach the end of the twentieth century, it is clear that our future will be considerably more international in nature than was ever believed possible in eras past. Each day, print and broadcast journalists make us aware that our world is becoming increasingly smaller and substantially more interdependent.

The energy crisis, world food shortages, nuclear weaponry, and regional conflicts that threaten to involve us all make it clear that the distinctions between domestic and foreign problems are all too often artificial, that many seemingly domestic problems no longer stop at national boundaries. As Rene Dubos, the 1969 Pulitzer Prize recipient, stated: "[I]t becomes obvious that each [of us] has two countries, [our] own and planet Earth." As global interdependence has become a reality, it has become vital for the citizens of this world to develop literacy in global matters.

THE GLOBAL STUDIES SERIES

It is the aim of the Global Studies series to help readers acquire a basic knowledge and understanding of the regions and countries in the world. Each volume provides a foundation of information—geographic, cultural, economic, political, historical, artistic, and religious—that will allow readers to better understand the current and future problems within these countries and regions and to comprehend how events there might affect their own well-being. In short, these volumes attempt to provide the background information necessary to respond to the realities of our global age.

Author/Editor
Each of the volumes in the Global Studies series is crafted under the careful direction of an author/editor—an expert in the area under study. The author/editors teach and conduct research and have traveled extensively through the regions about which they are writing.

In this *Japan and the Pacific Rim* edition, the author/editor has written regional essays on the Pacific Rim and the Pacific Islands, and country reports for each of the countries covered, including a special report on Japan. In addition, he has been instrumental in the selection of the world press articles that appear in this volume.

Contents and Features
The Global Studies volumes are organized to provide concise information and current world press articles on the regions and countries within those areas under study.

Regional Essays
For *Global Studies: Japan and the Pacific Rim, Fourth Edition,* the author/editor has written narrative essays focusing on the religious, cultural, sociopolitical, and economic differ-

(United Nations/Yutaka Nagata)
The global age is making all countries and all peoples more interdependent.

ences and similarities of the countries and peoples in the region. The purpose of the regional essays is to provide readers with an effective sense of the diversity of the area as well as an understanding of its common cultural and historical backgrounds. Accompanying the essays are maps showing the boundaries of the countries within the region.

Country Reports
Concise reports are written for each of the countries within the region under study. These reports are the heart of each Global Studies volume. *Global Studies: Japan and the Pacific Rim, Fourth Edition,* contains 20 country reports, including the lengthy report on Japan.

The country reports are composed of five standard elements. Each report contains a small, semidetailed map visually positioning the country among its neighboring states; a detailed summary of statistical information; a current essay providing important historical, geographical, political, cultural, and economic information; a historical timeline, offering a convenient visual survey of a few key historical events; and four graphic indicators, with summary statements about the country in terms of development, freedom, health/welfare, and achievements.

A Note on the Statistical Reports
The statistical information provided for each country has been drawn from a wide range of sources. (The most frequently referenced are listed on page 215.) Every effort has been made to provide the most current and accurate information available. However, occasionally the information cited by these sources differs to some extent; and, all too often, the most current information available for some countries is dated. Aside from these difficulties, the statistical summary of each country is generally quite complete and up to date. Care should be taken, however, in using these statistics (or, for that matter, any published statistics) in making hard comparisons among countries. We have also provided comparable statistics for Canada and the United States, which follow on the next two pages.

World Press Articles
Within each Global Studies volume is reprinted a number of articles carefully selected by our editorial staff and the author/editor from a broad range of international periodicals and newspapers. The articles have been chosen for currency, interest, and their differing perspectives on the subject countries. There are 29 articles in *Global Studies: Japan and the Pacific Rim, Fourth Edition.*

The articles section is preceded by an annotated table of contents as well as a topic guide. The annotated table of contents offers a brief summary of each article, while the topic guide indicates the main theme(s) of each article. Thus, readers desiring to focus on articles dealing with a particular theme, say, environment, may refer to the topic guide to find those articles.

WWW Sites, Glossary, Bibliography, Index
An annotated list of selected World Wide Web sites can be found on page v in this edition of *Global Studies: Japan.*

At the back of each Global Studies volume, readers will find a glossary of terms and abbreviations, which provides a quick reference to the specialized vocabulary of the area under study and to the standard abbreviations (NIC, ASEAN, etc.) used throughout the volume.

Following the glossary is a bibliography, which lists general works, national histories, and current events publications and periodicals that provide regular coverage on Japan and the Pacific Rim.

The index at the end of the volume is an accurate reference to the contents of the volume. Readers seeking specific information and citations should consult this standard index.

Currency and Usefulness
This fourth edition of *Global Studies: Japan and the Pacific Rim,* like other Global Studies volumes, is intended to provide the most current and useful information available necessary to understand the events that are shaping the cultures of the region today.

We plan to revise this volume on a regular basis. The statistics will be updated, essays rewritten, country reports revised, and articles replaced as new information becomes available. In order to accomplish this task, we will turn to our author/editor, our advisory boards, and—hopefully—to you, the users of this volume. Your comments are more than welcome. If you have an idea that you think will make the volume more useful, an article or bit of information that will make it more current, or a general comment on its organization, content, or features that you would like to share with us, please send it in for serious consideration for the next edition.

(United Nations, 89730)
Understanding the issues and lifestyles of other countries will help make us literate in global matters.

Canada

GEOGRAPHY

Area in Square Kilometers (Miles):
9,976,140 (3,850,790) (slightly larger
than the United States)
Capital (Population): Ottawa
(980,000)
Climate: from temperate in south to
subarctic and arctic in north

PEOPLE

Population
Total: 28,820,670
Annual Growth Rate: 1.09%
Rural/Urban Population Ratio: 23/77
Major Languages: English; French
Ethnic Makeup: 40% British Isles
origin; 27% French origin; 20% other
European; 1.5% indigenous Indian
and Eskimo; 11.5% mixed

Health
Life Expectancy at Birth: 76 years
(male); 83 years (female)
Infant Mortality Rate (Ratio):
6.8/1,000
Average Caloric Intake: 127% of
FAO minimum
Physicians Available (Ratio): 1/464

Religions
46% Roman Catholic; 16% United
Church; 10% Anglican; 28% others

Education
Adult Literacy Rate: 97%

COMMUNICATION

Telephones: 18,000,000
Newspapers: 96 in English; 11 in
French

TRANSPORTATION

Highways—Kilometers (Miles):
849,404 (530,028)
Railroads—Kilometers (Miles):
78,148 (48,764)
Usable Airfields: 1,386

GOVERNMENT

Type: confederation with
parliamentary democracy
Independence Date: July 1, 1867
Head of State/Government: Queen
Elizabeth II; Prime Minister Jean
Chrétien
Political Parties: Progressive
Conservative Party; Liberal Party;
New Democratic Party; Reform

Party; Bloc Québécois
Suffrage: universal at 18

MILITARY

Number of Armed Forces: 88,000
*Military Expenditures (% of Central
Government Expenditures):* 1.6%
Current Hostilities: none

ECONOMY

Currency ($U.S. Equivalent): 1.35
Canadian dollars = $1
Per Capita Income/GDP:
$22,760/$639.8 billion
Inflation Rate: 0.2%
Natural Resources: petroleum; natural
gas; fish; minerals; cement; forestry
products; fur
Agriculture: grains; livestock; dairy
products; potatoes; hogs; poultry and
eggs; tobacco
Industry: oil production and refining;
natural-gas development; fish
products; wood and paper products;
chemicals; transportation equipment

FOREIGN TRADE

Exports: $164.3 billion
Imports: $151.5 billion

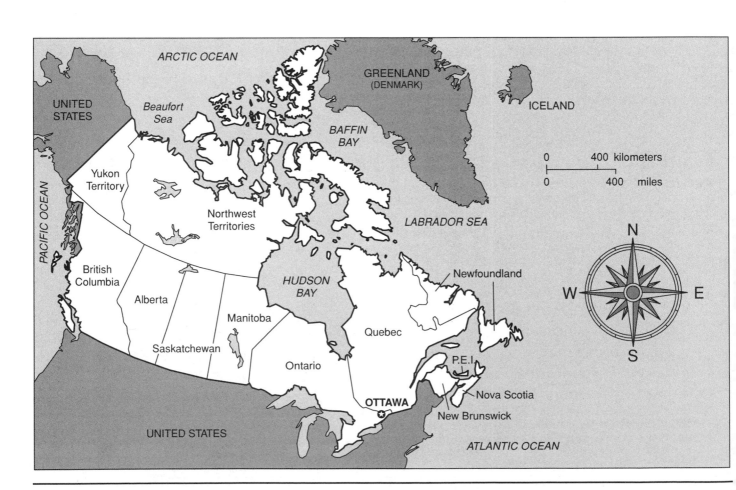

The United States

GEOGRAPHY

Area in Square Kilometers (Miles):
9,578,626 (3,618,770)
Capital (Population): Washington,
D.C. (567,100)
Climate: temperate

PEOPLE

Population
Total: 265,562,700
Annual Growth Rate: 1.02%
Rural/Urban Population Ratio: 25/75
Major Languages: English; Spanish;
others
Ethnic Makeup: 80% white; 12%
black; 6% Hispanic; 2% Asian,
Pacific Islander, American Indian,
Eskimo, and Aleut

Health
Life Expectancy at Birth: 73 years
(male); 80 years (female)
Infant Mortality Rate (Ratio):
7.8/1,000
Average Caloric Intake: 138% of
FAO minimum
Physicians Available (Ratio): 1/391

Religions
55% Protestant; 36% Roman
Catholic; 4% Jewish; 5% Muslim
and others

Education
Adult Literacy Rate: 97.9% (official)
(estimates vary widely)

COMMUNICATION

Telephones: 182,558,000
Newspapers: 1,679 dailies;
approximately 63,000,000 circulation

TRANSPORTATION

Highways—Kilometers (Miles):
6,243,163 (3,895,733)
Railroads—Kilometers (Miles):
240,000 (149,161)
Usable Airfields: 15,032

GOVERNMENT

Type: federal republic
Independence Date: July 4, 1776
Head of State: President William
("Bill") Jefferson Clinton
Political Parties: Democratic Party;

Republican Party; others of minor
political significance
Suffrage: universal at 18

MILITARY

Number of Armed Forces: 1,807,177
*Military Expenditures (% of Central
Government Expenditures):* 4.2%
Current Hostilities: none

ECONOMY

Per Capita Income/GDP:
$25,800/$6.738 trillion
Inflation Rate: 2.6%
Natural Resources: metallic and
nonmetallic minerals; petroleum;
arable land
Agriculture: food grains; feed crops;
oil-bearing crops; livestock; dairy
products
Industry: diversified in both capital-
and consumer-goods industries

FOREIGN TRADE

Exports: $513 billion
Imports: $664 billion

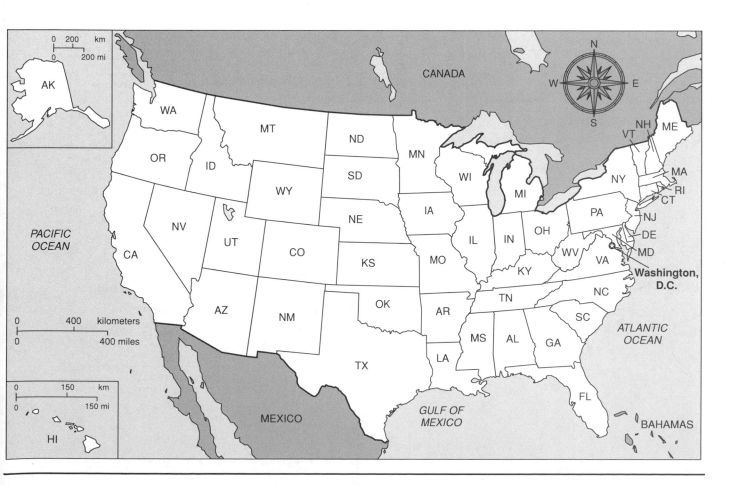

This map is provided to give you a graphic picture of where the countries of the world are located, the relationships they have with their region and neighbors, and their positions relative to the superpowers and power blocs. We have focused on certain areas to illustrate these crowded regions more clearly.

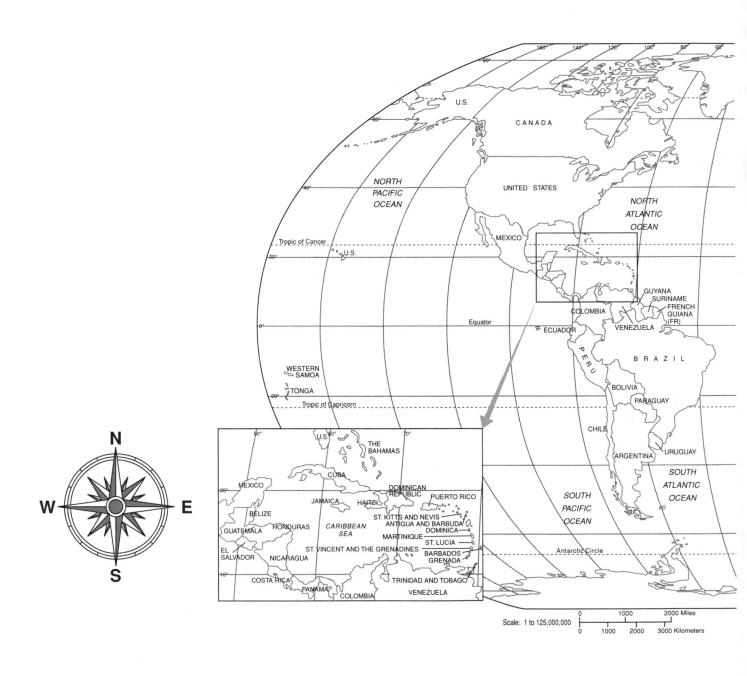

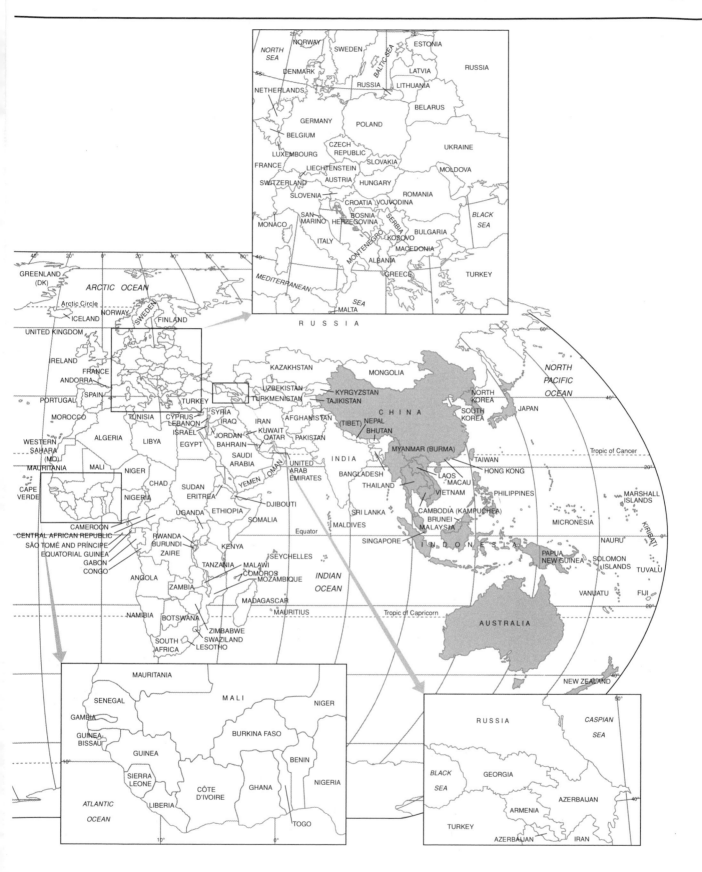

Pacific Rim Map

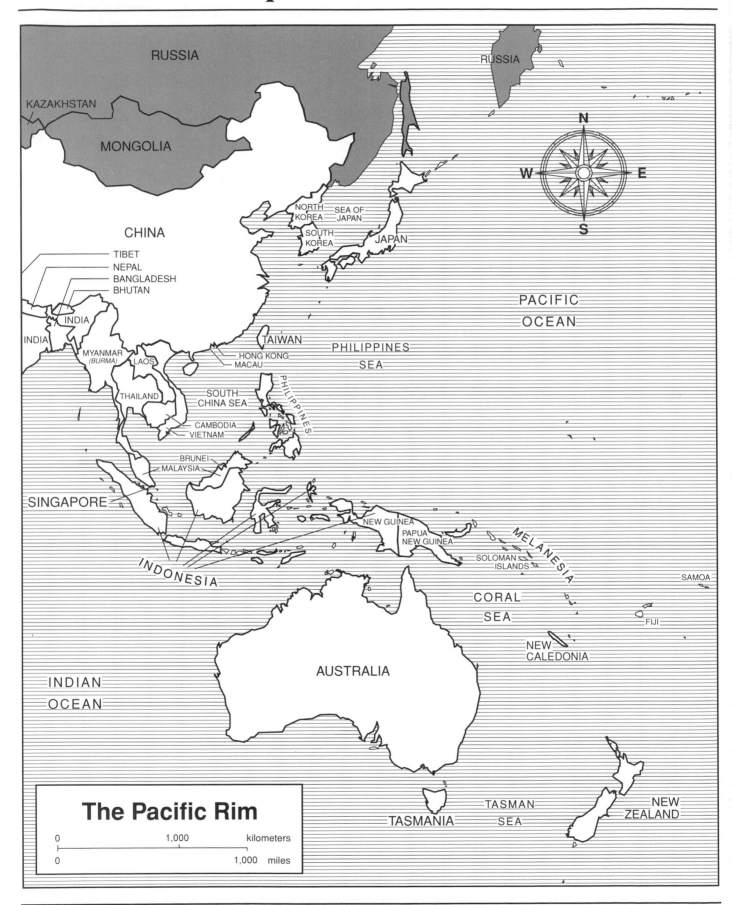

RUSSIA

KAZAKHSTAN

MONGOLIA

RUSSIA

N

W   E

S

CHINA

NORTH
KOREA

SEA OF
JAPAN

SOUTH
KOREA

JAPAN

PACIFIC

OCEAN

TIBET
NEPAL
BANGLADESH
BHUTAN

INDIA

INDIA

MYANMAR
(BURMA)

LAOS

TAIWAN

PHILIPPINES

HONG KONG
MACAU

SEA

THAILAND

SOUTH
CHINA SEA

PHILIPPINES

CAMBODIA
VIETNAM

BRUNEI
MALAYSIA

SINGAPORE

INDONESIA

NEW GUINEA

PAPUA
NEW GUINEA

MELANESIA

SOLOMAN
ISLANDS

SAMOA

CORAL

SEA

FIJI

NEW
CALEDONIA

INDIAN

OCEAN

AUSTRALIA

TASMAN

NEW

TASMANIA

SEA

ZEALAND

The Pacific Rim

0   1,000   kilometers

0   1,000   miles

The Pacific Rim: Diversity and Interconnection

WHAT IS THE PACIFIC RIM?

The term *Pacific Rim,* as used in this book, refers to 20 countries or administrative units along the Asian side of the Pacific Ocean, plus the numerous islands of the Pacific. Together, they are home to 30 percent of the world's population and produce 20 percent of the world's gross national product (GNP). It is not a simple matter to decide which countries to include in a definition of the Pacific Rim. For instance, if we were thinking geographically, we might include Mexico, Chile, Canada, the United States, Russia, and numerous other countries that border the Pacific Ocean, while eliminating Myanmar (Burma) and Laos, since they are not technically on the rim of the Pacific. But our definition, and hence our selected inclusions, stem from fairly recent developments in economic and geopolitical power that have affected the countries of Asia and the Pacific in such a way that these formerly disparate regions are now being referred to by international corporate and political leaders as a single bloc.

Most people living in the region that we have thus defined do not think of themselves as "Pacific Rimmers." In addition, many social scientists, particularly cultural anthropologists and comparative sociologists, would prefer not to apply a single term to such a culturally, politically, and sociologically diverse region. It is true that many, but certainly not all, of the countries in question have shared similar cultural influences, such as Buddhism and rice cultivation. But commonalities have not prevented the region from fracturing into dozens of societies, often very antagonistic toward one another.

Today, however, something is arising from the region itself that could have the effect of uniting the area in an entirely new way. If current trends continue, the entire Pacific Rim may one day share a common economic system (free market/state capitalism) and some common lifestyle values (materialism and mass consumption). There will also be a common awareness of the value of peaceful interdependence of the various nations to guarantee a steady improvement in the standard of living for all and the capacity of the region to, for the first time in history, supply the basic survival needs of its inhabitants.

What are the powerful forces that are fueling these trends? There are many, including nationalism and global communications. But the one that for the past 2 decades has stood out as a defining force in the region is the yen—the Japanese currency—and its accompanying Japanese business strategy. For more than 20 years, Japanese money has been flowing throughout the Pacific Rim in the form of aid and investment, while Japan's high-tech, export-oriented approach to making money has been facilitating development and helping other regional countries to create their own engines of economic growth in a way that none of them had experienced before. The tenacious Japanese recession of the 1990s has temporarily reduced the intensity of Japanese regional investment, allowing other high-growth countries, such as South Korea, Taiwan, and Hong Kong, to play a relatively larger role in the area. Japan's multibillion-dollar investments, however, will have effects that will be measured in decades, maybe even in centuries. Moreover, the other high-growth countries owe much of their success to the Japanese model, which they have successfully copied.

In the 1960s, when the Japanese economy had completely recovered from the devastation of World War II, the Japanese looked to North America and Europe for markets for their increasingly high-quality products. Japanese business continues to seek out markets and resources globally; but, in the 1980s, in response to the movement toward a truly common European economic community as well as in response to free trade agreements among North American countries, Japan began to invest more heavily in countries nearer its own borders. The Japanese hoped to guarantee themselves market and resource access should they find their products frozen out of the emerging European and North American economic blocs. The unintended, but not unwelcome, consequences of this policy were the revitalization of many Asia–Pacific economies and the solidification of lines of communication between governments and private citizens within the region. Recognizing this interconnection has prompted many people to refer to the countries we treat in this book as a single unit, the Pacific Rim.

TROUBLES IN THE RIM

The current preponderance of media images of billionaire Japanese businesspeople and chauffeur-driven Hong Kong Chinese has overshadowed the hard realities of life for most people in the Rim. For the most part, Pacific Rim countries have not met the needs of their peoples. Whether it is the desire of affluent Japanese for larger homes and two-car garages, or of rice farmers in Myanmar (Burma) for the right to sell their grain for personal profit, or of Chinese students to speak their minds without repression—in these and many other ways, the Pacific Rim has failed its peoples. In Vietnam, Myanmar, Laos, and Cambodia, for example, life is so difficult that thousands of families have risked their lives to leave their homelands. Some have swum across the wide Mekong River on moonless nights to avoid detection by guards, while others have sailed into the South China Sea on creaky and overcrowded boats (hence the name commonly given such refugees: "boat people"), hoping that people of goodwill, rather than marauding pirates, will find them and transport them to a land of safety. Despite the cut-off of refugee-support funds from the United Nations (UN), thousands of refugees remain unrepatriated, languishing in camps in Thailand, Malaysia, and other countries. Thousands of villagers driven from their homes by the Myanmar army await return, while the number of defectors from North Korea has been increasing steadily. Between 1975 and 1994, almost 14,000 Indochinese refugees reached Japan by boat, along with 3,500 Chinese nationals who posed as refugees in hopes of being allowed to live outside China. These examples, and many more not mentioned here, stand as tragic evidence of the social and political instability of many Pacific Rim nations and of the intense ethnic rivalries that divide the people of the Rim.

Warfare

Of all the Rim's troubles, warfare has been the most devastating. Not only have there been wars in which foreign powers like the United States and the former Soviet Union have been involved, but there have been and continue to be numerous battles between peoples of different tribes and races and religions. In Japan and China alone, an estimated 15.6 million people died as a result of World War II.

The potential for serious conflict remains in most regions of the Pacific Rim. Despite intense diplomatic efforts, the outlawed Khmer Rouge continues to wage guerrilla war against the elected government of Cambodia; Japan remains locked in a dispute with Russia over ownership of islands to the north of Hokkaido; Taiwan and China still lay claim to each other's territory, as do the two Koreas; and it was not long ago that Vietnam and China were engaged in battle over their mutual boundary. The list of disputed borders, lands, islands, and waters in the Pacific Rim is very long; indeed, there are some 30 unresolved disputes involving almost every

country of Asia and some of the Pacific Islands. Of growing concern is a 340,000-square-mile area of the South China Sea. When the likelihood of large oil deposits near the rocks and reefs of the Spratly Islands was announced in the 1970s, China, Taiwan, Vietnam, the Philippines, Malaysia, and Brunei instantly laid claim to the area. By 1974, the Chinese Air Force and Navy were bombing a South Vietnamese settlement on the islands; by 1988, Chinese warships were attacking Vietnamese transport ships in the area. Both China and Vietnam have granted nearby oil-drilling concessions to different U.S. oil companies, so the situation remains tense, especially because China claims sovereignty over almost the entire South China Sea and has been flexing its muscles in the area by stopping, boarding, and sometimes confiscating other nations' ships in the area. In addition to these national disputes, ethnic tensions—most Asian nations are composed of hundreds of different ethnic groups with their own languages and religions—are sometimes severe. In Fiji, it is the locals versus the immigrant Indians; in Southeast Asia, it is the locals versus the Chinese or the Muslims versus the Christians; in China, it is the Tibetans and most other ethnic groups versus the Han Chinese.

With the end of the cold war, many Asian nations have found it necessary to seek new military and political alliances.

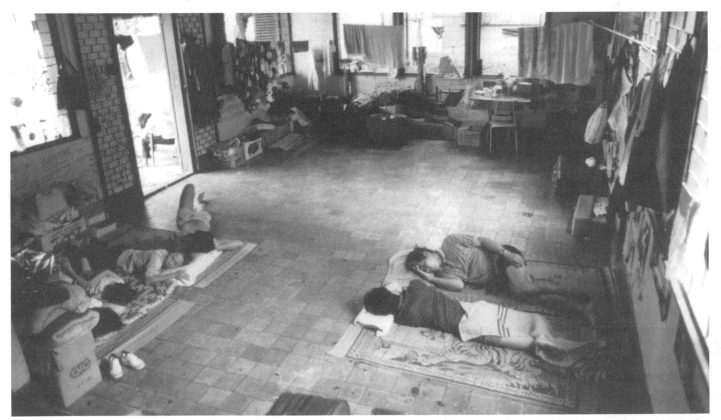

(UN photo by J. M. Micaud)

In areas of the Pacific Rim such as Vietnam, Laos, and Cambodia, conditions are so grim that thousands of people have elected to leave their homelands and become homeless refugees, trusting that they will find a better place to live. The people pictured above are living at the Hawkings refugee camp in Singapore. In some refugee camps, the living conditions are barely survivable.

Forced to withdraw from Vietnam and from its large naval base in the Philippines, the United States has been encouraging its ally Japan to assume a larger military role in the region. However, the thought of Japan re-arming itself causes considerable fear among Pacific Rim nations, almost all of which suffered defeat at the hands of the Japanese military only half a century ago. Nevertheless, Japan has acted to increase its military preparedness, within the narrow confines of its constitutional prohibition against re-armament, and now has the second-largest military budget in the world (its actual expenses are huge because its economy is so large, but Japan spends only about 1 percent of its budget on defense).

In response, China has also increased its purchases of military equipment (some $2 billion of air and naval purchases from 1992 to 1994), especially from cash-strapped Russia. As a result, whereas the arms industry is in decline elsewhere, it is big business in Asia. Four of the nine largest armies in the world are in the Pacific Rim. Thus, the tragedy of warfare, which has characterized the region for so many centuries, could continue unless governments manage conflict very carefully and come to understand the need for mutual cooperation.

In some cases, mutual cooperation is already replacing animosity. Thailand and Vietnam are engaged in sincere efforts to resolve fishing-rights disputes in the Gulf of Thailand and water-rights disputes on the Mekong River; North and South Korea have agreed to allow some cross-border visitation; and even Taiwan and China have amicably settled issues relating to fisheries, immigration, and hijackings. Yet greed and ethnic and national pride are far too often just below the surface; when left unchecked, they could catalyze a major confrontation.

Overpopulation

Another serious problem is overpopulation. There are well over 2 billion people living in the Pacific Rim. Of those, approximately 1.2 billion are Chinese. Even though China's government has implemented the strictest family-planning

(UN photo by Shaw McCutcheon)

The numbers of elderly people in China will triple by the year 2025. Even with the strict enforcement of limiting each family to only one child, China will be faced with the increasing need of caring for retirement-age citizens. This group of elderly men in a village near Chengdu represents just the tip of an enormous problem for the future.

TYPES OF GOVERNMENTS IN SELECTED PACIFIC RIM COUNTRIES

PARLIAMENTARY DEMOCRACIES
Australia*
Fiji
New Zealand*
Papua New Guinea

CONSTITUTIONAL MONARCHIES
Brunei
Japan
Malaysia
Thailand

REPUBLICS
Indonesia
The Philippines
Singapore
South Korea
Taiwan

SOCIALIST REPUBLICS
China
Laos
Myanmar (Burma)
North Korea
Vietnam

OVERSEAS TERRITORIES/COLONIES
Hong Kong†
French Polynesia
Macau†
New Caledonia

Australia and New Zealand have declared their intention of becoming republics by the year 2000.

†*Hong Kong and Macau revert to Chinese control in 1997 and 1999, respectively.*

policies in world history, the country's annual growth rate is such that more than 1 million inhabitants are added *every month*. This means that more new Chinese are born each year than make up the entire population of Australia. The World Health Organization (WHO) reports, however, that about 217 million people in East Asia use contraceptives today, as compared to only 18 million in 1965. Couples in some countries, including Japan, Taiwan, and South Korea, have been voluntarily limiting family size. Other states, such as China and Singapore, have promoted family planning though government incentives and punishments. The effort is paying off. The United Nations now estimates that the proportion of the global population living in Asia will remain relatively unchanged between now and the year 2025, and China's share will decline. In fact, in some countries, especially Japan, South Korea, and Thailand, single-child families and an aging population are creating problems in their own right.

Still, so many children have already been born that Pacific Rim governments simply cannot meet their needs. For these new Asians, schools must be built, health facilities provided, houses constructed, and jobs created. This is not an easy challenge for many Rim countries. Moreover, as the population density increases, the quality of life decreases. In crowded New York City, for example, the population is about 1,100 per square mile, and residents, finding the crowding to be too uncomfortable, frequently seek more relaxed lifestyles in the suburbs. Yet in Tokyo, the density is approximately 2,400 per square mile; and in Manila, it is 51,000! Demographers predict that, by the year 2000, many of the world's largest cities will be in the Pacific Rim: Shanghai, China, is projected to have about 12 million people; Jakarta, Indonesia, will have well over 13 million; Manila, the Philippines, will be home to approximately 11 million; and Bangkok, Thailand, will have nearly 11 million. Migration to the cities will continue despite miserable conditions for many (in some Asian cities, 50 percent of the population live in slum housing). One incredibly rapid-growth country is the Philippines; home to only about 7 million in 1898, when it was acquired by the United States, it is projected to have 130 million people in the year 2020.

Absolute numbers alone do not tell the whole story. In many Rim countries, 40 percent or more of the population are under age 15. Governments must provide schooling and medical care as well as plan for future jobs and housing for all these children. Moreover, as these young people age, they will require increased medical and social care. Scholars point out that, between 1985 and 2025, the numbers of old people will double in Japan, triple in China, and quadruple in Korea. In Japan, where replacement-level fertility was achieved in the 1960s, government officials are already concerned about the ability of the nation to care for the growing number of retirement-age people while paying the higher wages that the increasingly scarce younger workers are demanding.

Political Instability

One consequence of the overwhelming problems of population growth, urbanization, and continual military or ethnic conflict is disillusionment with government.

In many countries of the Pacific Rim, people are challenging the very right of their governments to rule or are demanding a complete change in the political philosophy that undergirds governments. For instance, despite danger of death, torture, or imprisonment, college students in Myanmar have demonstrated against the current military dictatorship. In some Rim countries, opposition groups armed with sophisticated weapons donated by foreign nations roam the countryside, capturing towns and military installations. In less than a decade, the government of the Philippines endured six coup attempts; elite military dissidents want to impose the old Marcos-style patronage government, while armed rural insurgents want to install a Communist government. Thousands of students have been injured or killed protesting the governments of South Korea and China. Thailand has been beset by numerous military coups, the former British colony of Fiji recently endured two coups, and half a million residents of Hong Kong took to the streets to oppose Great Britain's decision to turn over the territory to China in 1997. Military takeovers, political assassinations, and repressive policies have been the norm in most of the countries in the region. Millions of people have spent their entire lives under governments they have never agreed with, and unrest is bound to continue because those now alive are showing less and less patience with imposed government.

Part of the reason is that the region is so culturally fractured, between countries and, especially, within countries. In some states, dozens of different languages are spoken, people practice very different religions, families trace their roots back to many different racial and ethnic origins, and wealth is distributed so unfairly that, while some people are well educated and well fed, others nearby remain illiterate and malnourished. Under these conditions, it has been difficult for the peoples of the Rim to agree upon the kinds of government that will best serve them; all are afraid that their particular language, religion, ethnic group, and/or social class will be negatively affected by any leader not of their own background.

Identity Confusion

A related problem is that of confusion about personal and national identity. Many nation-states in the Pacific Rim were created in response to Western pressure. Before Western influences came to be felt, many Asians, particularly Southeast Asians, did not identify themselves with a nation but, rather, with a tribe or an ethnic group. In many cases, national unity has been difficult, because of the archipelagic nature of some countries or because political boundaries have changed over the years, leaving ethnic groups from adjacent countries inside the neighbor's territory. The experience of colonialism has left many people, especially those in places like Singapore, Hong Kong, and the Pacific islands, unsure as to their roots; are they European or Asian/Pacific, or something else entirely?

Indonesia illustrates this problem. People think of it as an Islamic country, as overall its populace are 87 percent Muslim. But in regions like North Sumatra, 30 percent are Protestant; in Bali, 94 percent are Hindu; and in East Timor, 49 percent are Catholic and 51 percent are animist. The Philippines is another example. With 88 different languages spoken, its people spread out over 12 large islands, and a population explosion (the average age is 16), it is a classic case of psychological (and economic and political) fragmentation. Coups and countercoups rather than peaceful political transitions seem to be the norm because the people have not yet developed a sense of unified nationalism.

Uneven Economic Development

While the Japanese are wrestling with how best to invest their savings (an average of $45,000 in savings per person, when all banked savings are divided by the population), Laotians and others are worrying about where their next meal will come from. Such disparity illustrates another major problem afflicting the Pacific Rim: uneven economic development.

Many Asians, especially those in the Northeast Asian countries of Japan, Korea, and China, are finding that rapid economic change seems to render the traditions of the past meaningless. For instance, almost all Japanese will state that Japan is a Buddhist country, yet few today claim any actual religious affiliation. Moreover, economic success has produced a growing Japanese interest in maximizing investment returns, with the result that Japan (and, increasingly, South Korea, Taiwan, Singapore, and Hong Kong) is successfully searching out more ways to make money, while resource-poor regions like the Pacific islands lag behind.

The *developed nations* are characterized by political stability and long-term industrial success. Their per capita income is comparable to Canada, Northern Europe, and the United States, and they have achieved a level of economic sustainability. These countries are closely linked to North America

(UN photo by John Isaac)
Some of the Pacific Rim nations are resource-rich, but development has been curtailed by political instability and a strong traditional culture. This worker is farming as his ancestors did with techniques that have not changed for hundreds of years.

economically. Japan, for instance, exports one third of its products to the United States.

The *newly industrializing countries* (NICs) are currently capturing world attention because of their rapid growth. Hong Kong, for example, has exported more manufactured products per year for the past decade than did the former Soviet Union and Central/Eastern Europe combined. Taiwan, famous for cameras and calculators, has had the highest gross national product growth in the world for the past 20 years. South Korea is tops in shipbuilding and steel manufacturing and is the tenth-largest trading nation in the world.

The *resource-rich developing nations* have tremendous natural resources but have been held back economically by political and cultural instability and by insufficient capital to develop a sound economy. An example of a country attempting to overcome these drawbacks is Malaysia. Ruled by a coalition government representing nearly a dozen race-based parties, Malaysia is richly endowed with tropical forests and large oil and gas reserves. Developing these resources has taken years (the oil and gas fields began production as recently as 1978) and has required massive infusions of investment monies from Japan and other countries. As of 1994 more than 3,000 companies were doing business in Malaysia, and the country was moving into the ranks of the world's large exporters.

Command economies lag far behind the rest, not only because of the endemic inefficiency of the system but because military dictatorships and continual warfare have sapped the strength of the people. Significant changes in some of these countries are now emerging. China and Vietnam, in particular, are eager to modernize their economies and institute market-based reforms. Historically having directed its trade to North America and Europe, Japan is now finding its Asian/Pacific neighbors—especially the socialist-turning-capitalist ones—to be convenient recipients of its powerful economic and cultural influence.

Many of the *less developed countries* (LDCs) are the small micro-states of the Pacific with limited resources and tiny internal markets. Others, like Papua New Guinea, have only recently achieved political independence and are searching for a proper role in the world economy.

Environmental Destruction and Social Ills

Environmental destruction in the Pacific Rim is a problem of mammoth proportions. For more than 20 years, the former Soviet Union dumped nuclear waste into the Sea of Japan; China's use of coal in industrial development has produced acid rain over Korea and Japan; deforestation in Thailand, Myanmar, and other parts of Southeast Asia and China has destroyed many thousands of acres of watershed and wildlife habitat. On the Malaysian island of Sarawak, for example, loggers work through the night, using floodlights, to cut timber to satisfy the demands of international customers, especially the Japanese. The forests there are disappearing at

---

WHERE DOES ALL THAT HEROIN COME FROM?

Governments around the world have attempted to stem the tide of illegal drugs, but still the contraband finds its way to desperate consumers. Where does it come from? Officials estimate that 59 percent of the world's opium, from which heroin is made, is produced in Myanmar (Burma), while the rest comes from Laos, Thailand, China, Afghanistan, and Pakistan. Shipped through international airports in Vietnam, Cambodia, Laos, and Myanmar, the drugs enter Europe and North America via Istanbul and other "clearinghouse" cities. Attempts to stop the drug business have included such measures as the execution of drug dealers (China), the burning of tons of heroin (Thailand), and the offering of trade incentives to countries that participate in drug-eradication programs. But the world's supply of heroin—and the number of addicts—is increasing, and experts predict that the global opium supply will double every 5 years.

---

a rate of 3 percent a year. Highway and hydroelectric-dam construction in many countries in Asia has seriously altered the natural environment. But environmental damage is perhaps most noticeable in the cities: mercury pollution in Jakarta Bay has led to brain disorders among children in Indonesia's capital city; air pollution in Manila is among the world's worst, while not far behind are Bangkok and Seoul; water pollution in Hong Kong has forced the closure of many beaches.

While conservationists are raising the alarm about the world's declining green spaces, medical professionals are expressing dismay at the speed at which serious diseases such as AIDS are spreading in Asia. In 1994, the Thai government reported that, by 1997, 2.4 million Thais (most of them between the ages of 15 and 44) would be HIV-positive. WHO officials, meeting in Japan in 1994, reported that the epidemic of AIDS was growing faster in Asia and Africa than anywhere else in the world.

GUARDED OPTIMISM

Warfare, overpopulation, political instability, identity confusion, uneven development, and environmental and social ills would seem to be an irresolvable set of problems for the people of the Pacific Rim, but the end of the twentieth century also gives reason for guarded optimism.

Unification talks continue off and on between North and South Korea, as do talks between Japan and Russia on the Northern Territories dispute. Other issues are also under discussion all over the region, and the UN peacekeeping effort in Cambodia seems to have paid off—at least there is a legally elected government in place, and most belligerents have put down their arms.

ECONOMIC DEVELOPMENT IN SELECTED PACIFIC RIM COUNTRIES

Economists have divided the Rim into five zones, based on the level of development, as follows:

DEVELOPED NATIONS
Australia
Japan
New Zealand

NEWLY INDUSTRIALIZING COUNTRIES (NICs)
Hong Kong
Singapore
South Korea
Taiwan

RESOURCE-RICH DEVELOPING ECONOMIES
Brunei
Indonesia
Malaysia
The Philippines
Thailand

COMMAND ECONOMIES*
Cambodia
China
Laos
Myanmar (Burma)
North Korea
Vietnam

LESS DEVELOPED COUNTRIES (LDCs)
Papua New Guinea
Pacific Islands

China, Vietnam, and, to a lesser degree, North Korea are moving toward free market economies.

Most heartening of all news is the flood of reports on the growing economic strength of many Pacific Rim countries. Typical was the *CIA World Fact Book 1996–1997,* which reported high growth in gross national product (GNP) per capita for most Rim countries: South Korea, 9.0 percent; Hong Kong, 5.0 percent; Indonesia, 7.5 percent; Japan (due to recession), 0.3 percent; Malaysia, 9.5 percent; Singapore, 8.9 percent; and Thailand, 8.6 percent. By comparison, the U.S. growth rate was 2.1 percent; Great Britain, 2.7 percent; and Canada, 2.1 percent. Other reports on the Rim compare 1990s investment and savings percentages with those of 20 years earlier; in almost every case, there has been a tremendous improvement in the economic capacity of these countries.

The rate of economic growth in the Pacific Rim has indeed been astonishing. In 1987, for example, the rate of real gross domestic product (GDP) growth in the United States was only 3.5 percent over the previous year. By contrast, in Hong Kong, the rate was 13.5 percent; in Taiwan, 12.4 percent; in Thailand, 10.4 percent; and in South Korea, 11.1 percent. In 1992, economic growth throughout Asia averaged 7 percent, as compared to only 4.8 percent for the rest of the world. Countries like China were expected to grow an average of 10 to 12 percent per year throughout the 1990s.

The significance of these data is that they reveal a shift in the source of development capital, from North America to Asia. Historically, the economies of North America were regarded as the engine behind Pacific Rim growth; and yet today, annual growth in the United States and Canada trails far behind many of the Rim economies. This anomaly can be explained, in part, by the hard work and savings ethics of Pacific Rim peoples and by their external market–oriented development strategies. But hard work and clever strategies without venture capital and foreign aid would not have produced the economic dynamo that the world is now witnessing. This is why Japan's financial contributions to the region, coming in chunks much larger than those of the United States, are so crucial. This is also why we consider that Japan and Japanese investment and aid are central to our definition of the Pacific Rim as an identifiable region. Some subregions are also emerging. There is, of course, the Association of Southeast Asian Nations (ASEAN) trading unit; but the one that is gaining world attention is the informal region that people are calling "Greater China," consisting of the emerging capitalist enclaves of the People's Republic of China and of Hong Kong and Taiwan. Copying Japanese strategy and aided by a common written language and culture, this region has the potential of exceeding even the mammoth U.S. economy in the not-too-distant future. For now, however, Japan remains the major player because it is in a position to lend such large amounts of money to other countries.

Japan has been investing in the Asia/Pacific region for several decades. However, growing protectionism in its traditional markets as well as changes in the value of the yen and the need to find cheaper sources of labor (labor costs are 75 percent less in Singapore and 95 percent less in Indonesia) have raised Japan's level of involvement so high as to give its actions the upper hand in determining the course of development and political stability for the entire region. This heightened level of investment started to gain momentum in the mid-1980s. Between 1984 and 1989, Japan's overseas development assistance to the ASEAN countries amounted to $6.1 billion. In some cases, this assistance translated to more than 4 percent of a nation's annual national budget and nearly 1 percent of GDP. Private Japanese investment in ASEAN countries plus Hong Kong, Taiwan, and South Korea was $8.9 billion between 1987 and 1988. In recent years, the Japanese government or Japanese business has invested $582 million in an auto-assembly plant in Taiwan, $5 billion in an iron and steel complex in China, $2.3 billion in a bullet-

(UN photo by Nichiro Gyogyo)

This Japanese factory ship is a floating cannery that processes salmon harvested from the Pacific.

train plan for Malaysia, and $530 million in a tunnel under the harbor in Sydney, Australia. Japan is certainly not the only player in Asian development (Japan has "only" 21 projects under way in Vietnam, for example, as compared to 80 for Hong Kong and 39 for Taiwan), but the volume of Japanese investment is staggering. In Australia alone, nearly 900 Japanese companies are now doing business. Throughout Asia, Japanese is becoming a major language of business.

Although Japan works very hard at globalizing its markets and its resource suppliers, it has also developed closer ties with its nearby Rim neighbors. In a recent year, out of 20 Rim countries, 13 listed Japan as their first- or second-most-important trading partner, and several more put Japan third. Japan receives 42 percent of Indonesia's exports and 26 percent of Australia's; in return, 23 percent of South Korea's imports, 29 percent of Taiwan's, 30 percent of Thailand's, 24 percent of Malaysia's, and 23 percent of Indonesia's come from Japan. Pacific Rim countries are clearly becoming more interdependent—but simultaneously more dependent on Japan—for their economic success.

JAPANESE INFLUENCE, PAST AND PRESENT

This is certainly not the first time in modern history that Japanese influence has swept over Asia and the Pacific. A major thrust began in 1895, when Japan, like the European powers, started to acquire bits and pieces of the region. By 1942, the Japanese were in control of Taiwan, Korea, Manchuria and most of the populated parts of China, and Hong Kong; what are now Vietnam, Laos, and Cambodia; Thailand; Burma (now Myanmar); Malaysia; Indonesia; the Philippines; part of New Guinea; and dozens of Pacific islands. In effect, by the 1940s, the Japanese were the dominant force in precisely the area that they influence in the 1990s and which we are calling the Pacific Rim.

The similarities do not end there, for, while many Asians of the 1940s were apprehensive about or openly resistant to Japanese rule, many others welcomed the Japanese invaders and even helped them to take over their countries. This was because they believed that Western influence was out of place in Asia and that Asia should be for Asians. They hoped that the Japanese military would rid them of Western rule, and it did: After the war, very few Western powers were able to regain control of their Asian and Pacific colonies.

Today, many Asians and Pacific islanders are apprehensive about excessive Japanese financial and industrial influence in their countries, but they welcome Japanese investment anyway because they believe that it is the best and cheapest way to rid their countries of poverty and underdevelopment. So far, they are right—by copying the Japanese model of economic development, and thanks to Japanese trade, foreign aid, and investment, the entire region—some countries excepted—is gaining such a reputation for economic strength that many people believe the next 100 years will be called the "Pacific Century," just as the previous 100 years were called the "American Century." It would not be farfetched to call it the "Japanese Century" and to rename the Pacific Rim the "Yen Bloc," as some observers are already doing.

It is important to note, however, that many Rim countries, such as Taiwan, Hong Kong, and South Korea, are strong challengers to Japan's economic dominance; in addition, Japan has not felt comfortable about its position as head of the pack, for fear of a backlash. For example, Japan's higher regional profile has prompted complaints against the Japanese military's World War II treatment of civilians in Korea and China and has forced Japan to pledge $1 billion to various Asian countries as a symbolic act of apology.

Why have the Japanese re-created in the 1990s a modern version of the old Greater East Asian Co-Prosperity Sphere of the imperialistic 1940s? We cannot find the answer in the propaganda of wartime Japan—fierce devotion to emperor and nation and belief in the superiority of Asians over all other races are no longer the propellants in the Japanese economic engine. Rather, Japan courts Asia and the Pacific today to acquire resources to sustain its civilization. Japan is about the size of California, but it has 5 times as many people and not nearly as much arable land. Much of Japan is mountainous; many other parts are off limits because of active volcanoes (one tenth of all the active volcanoes in the world are in Japan); and, after 2,000-plus years of intensive and uninterrupted habitation, the natural forests are long since consumed, as are most of the other natural resources—most of which were scarce to begin with.

In short, Japan continues to extract resources from the rest of Asia and the Pacific because it is the same Japan as before—environmentally speaking, that is. Take oil. In the early 1940s, Japan needed oil to keep its industries (as well as its military machine) operating, but the United States wanted to punish Japan for its military expansion in Asia, so it shut off all shipments to Japan of any kind, including oil. That may have seemed politically right to the policymakers of the day, but it did not change Japan's resource environment; Japan still did not have its own oil, and it still needed as much oil as before. So Japan decided to capture a nearby nation that did have natural reserves of oil—in 1941, it attacked Indonesia and obtained by force the resource it had been denied through trade.

Japan has no more domestic resources now than it did half a century ago, and yet its needs—for food, minerals, lumber, paper—are greater. Except for fish, you name it—Japan does not have it. A realistic comparison is to imagine trying to feed half the population of the United States from the natural output of the state of Montana. As it happens, however, Japan sits next to the continent of Asia, which is rich in almost all the materials it needs. For lumber, there are the forests of Malaysia; for food, there are the farms and ranches of New Zealand and Australia; and for oil, there are Indonesia and Brunei, the latter of which sells 50 percent of its exports to Japan. The quest for resources is why Japan is flooding its neighbors with Japanese yen—and that, in turn, is creating the interconnected trading bloc of the Pacific Rim.

Catalyst for Development
In addition to the need for resources, Japan has turned to the Pacific Rim in an attempt to offset the anti-Japanese import or protectionist policies of its historic trading partners. Because so many import tariffs are imposed on products sold directly from Japan, Japanese companies find that they can avoid or minimize tariffs if they cooperate on joint ventures in Rim countries and have products shipped from there. The result is that both Japan and its host countries are prospering as never before. Sony Corporation, for example, assembles parts made in both Japan and Singapore to construct videocassette recorders at its Malaysian factory, for export to North America, Europe, and other Rim countries. Toyota Corporation intends to build its automobile transmissions in the Philippines and its steering-wheel gears in Malaysia, and to build the final product in whichever country intends to buy its cars.

So helpful has Japanese investment been in spawning indigenous economic powerhouses that many other Rim countries are now reinvesting in the region. In particular, Hong Kong, Singapore, Taiwan, and South Korea are now in a position to seek cheaper labor markets in Indonesia, Malaysia, the Philippines, and Thailand. In recent years, they have invested billions of dollars in the resource- and labor-rich economies of Southeast Asia, increasing living standards and adding to the growing interconnectivity of the region. An example is a Taiwanese company that has built the largest eel-production facility in the world—in Malaysia—and ships its entire product to Korea and Japan.

Eyed as a big consumer as well as a bottomless source of cheap labor is the People's Republic of China. Many Rim countries, such as South Korea, Taiwan, Hong Kong, and Japan, are working hard to increase their trade with China. In 1990, two-way trade between Taiwan and China was more than $4 billion; between Hong Kong and China, it was $50 billion. Japan was especially eager to resume economic aid to China in 1990 after temporarily withholding aid because of the Tiananmen Square massacre. For its part, China is establishing free-enterprise zones that will enable it to participate more fully in the regional economy. Already the Bank of China is the second-largest bank in Hong Kong.

Japan and a handful of other economic powerhouses of the Rim are not the only big players in Rim economic development. The United States and Canada remain major investors in the Pacific Rim (in computers and automobiles, for example), and Europe maintains its historical linkages with the region (such as in oil). But there is no question that Japan is the main catalyst for development in the region, and its level of investment is likely to continue for at least the next decade because Japan is awash in investment monies seeking a home. Almost all of the top 20 banks in the world are Japanese, and the volume of the Japanese stock market is the biggest in the world. Many of the world's wealthiest business executives are Japanese, and they are eager to find places to invest their capital.

Not everyone is pleased with the way Japan is giving aid or making loans. Particularly in the Pacific Rim, money invested by the Japan International Development Organization (JIDO) is usually connected very closely to the commercial interests of Japanese companies. For instance, commercial loan agreements often require that the recipient of low-interest loans purchase Japanese products.

Nevertheless, it is clear that many countries would be a lot worse off without Japanese aid. In a recent year, JIDO aid around the world was $10 billion. Japan is the dominant supplier of foreign aid to the Philippines and a major investor; in Thailand, where U.S. aid recently amounted to $20 million, Japanese aid was close to $100 million. Some of this aid, moreover, gets recycled from one country to another within the Rim—Thailand, for example, receives more aid from Japan than any other country, but in turn, it supplies major amounts of aid to other nearby countries. Thus we can see the growing interconnectivity of the region, a reality now recognized formally by the establishment of the Asia Pacific Economic Cooperation Council (APEC).

During the militaristic 1940s, Japanese dominance in the region produced antagonism and resistance. However, it also gave subjugated countries new highways, railways, and other infrastructural improvements. Today, while host countries continue to benefit from infrastructural advances, they also get quality manufactured products. Once again, Northeast Asian, Southeast Asian, and South Pacific peoples have begun to talk about Japanese domination. The difference is that this time, few seem upset about it; most people no longer believe that Japan has military aspirations against them, and they regard Japanese investment as a first step toward becoming economically strong themselves. Many people are eager to learn the Japanese language; in some cities, such as Seoul, Japanese has displaced English as the most valuable business language. Nevertheless, to deter negative criticism arising from its prominent position in the Rim, Japan has increased its gift giving, such that now it has surpassed the United States as the world's most generous donor of foreign aid.

POLITICAL AND CULTURAL CHANGES

Although economic issues are important to an understanding of the Pacific Rim, political and cultural changes are also crucial. The new, noncombative relationship between the United States and the former Soviet bloc means that special-interest groups and governments in the Rim will be less able to rely on the strength and power of those nations to help advance or uphold their positions. Communist North Korea, for instance, can no longer rely on the Soviet bloc for trade and ideological support. North Korea may begin to look for new ideological neighbors or, more significantly, to consider major modifications in its own approach to organizing society.

Similarly, ideological changes are afoot in Myanmar, where the populace are tiring of life under a military dictatorship. The military can no longer look for guaranteed support from the crumbling socialist world.

In the case of Hong Kong, the British government shied away from extreme political issues and agreed to the peaceful annexation in 1997 of a capitalist bastion by a Communist nation, China. It is highly unlikely that such a decision would have been made had the issue of Hong Kong's political status arisen during the anti-Communist years of the cold war. One must not get the impression, however, that suddenly peace has arrived in the Pacific Rim. But outside support for extreme ideological positions seems to be giving way to a pragmatic search for peaceful solutions. This should have a salutary effect throughout the region.

The growing pragmatism in the political sphere is yielding changes in the cultural sphere. Whereas the Chinese formerly looked upon Western dress and music as decadent, most Chinese now openly seek out these cultural commodities and are finding ways to merge these things with the Communist polity under which they live. It is also increasingly clear to most leaders in the Pacific Rim that international mercantilism has allowed at least one regional country, Japan, to rise to the highest ranks of world society, first economically and now culturally and educationally. The fact that one Asian nation has accomplished this leap fosters hope that others can do so also.

Rim leaders also see, however, that Japan achieved its position of prominence only because it was willing to change traditional mores and customs and accept outside modes of thinking and acting. Religion, family life, gender relations, recreation, and many other facets of Japanese life have altered during Japan's rapid rise to the top. Many other Pacific Rim nations—including Thailand, Singapore, and South Korea—seem determined to follow Japan's lead in this regard. Therefore, we are witnessing in certain high-growth Rim economies significant cultural changes: a reduction in family size, a secularization of religious impulses, a desire for more leisure time and better education, and a move toward acquisition rather than "being" as a determinant of one's worth. That is, more and more people are likely to judge others' value by what they own rather than what they believe or do. Buddhist values of self-denial, Shinto values of respect for nature, and Confucian values of family loyalty are giving way slowly to Western-style individualism and the drive for personal comfort and monetary success. Formerly close-knit communities, such as those in American Samoa, are finding themselves struggling with drug abuse and gang-related violence, just as in the metropolitan countries. These changes in political and cultural values are at least as important as economic growth in projecting the future of the Pacific Rim.

The Pacific Islands: Opportunities and Limits

PLENTY OF SPACE, BUT NO ROOM

There are about 30,000 islands in the Pacific Ocean. Most of them are found in the South Pacific and may be classified into three mammoth regions: Micronesia, composed of some 2,000 islands with such names as Palau, Nauru, and Guam; Melanesia, where 200 different languages are spoken on such islands as Fiji and the Solomon Islands; and Polynesia, composed of such islands as Hawaii, Samoa, and Tahiti.

Straddling both sides of the equator, these territories are characterized as much by what is *not* there as by what *is*—that is, between every tiny island lie hundreds and often thousands of miles of open ocean. A case in point is the Cook Islands. Associated with New Zealand, this 15-island group contains only 92 square miles of land but is spread over 714,000 square miles of open sea. So expansive is the space between islands that early explorers from Europe and the Spanish lands of South America often unknowingly bypassed dozens of islands that lay just beyond view in the vastness of the 64 million square miles of the Pacific—the world's largest ocean.

However, once the Europeans found and set foot on the islands, they inaugurated a process that irreversibly changed the history of island life. Their goals in exploring the Pacific were to convert islanders to Christianity and to increase the power and prestige of their homelands (and themselves) by obtaining resources and acquiring territory. They thought of themselves and European civilization as superior to others and often treated the "discovered" peoples with contempt. An example is the discovery of the Marquesas Islands (from whence came some of the Hawaiian people) by the Peruvian Spaniard Alvaro de Mendana. Mendana landed in the Marquesas in 1595 with some women and children and, significantly, 378 soldiers. Within weeks, his entourage had planted three Christian crosses, declared the islands to be the possession of the king of Spain, and killed 200 islanders. Historian Ernest S. Dodge describes the inhumanity of the first contacts:

> The Spaniards opened fire on the surrounding canoes for no reason at all. To prove himself a good marksman one soldier killed both a Marquesan and the child in his arms with one shot as the man desperately swam for safety.... The persistent

(UN photo by Nagata Jr.)

In the South Pacific area of Micronesia, some 2,000 islands are spread over an ocean area of 3 million square miles. There remain many relics of the diverse cultures found on these islands; these boys are walking between the highly prized stone discs that were used as money on the islands of the Yap District.

13

Marquesans again attempted to be friendly by bringing fruit and water, but again they were shot down when they attempted to take four Spanish water jars. Magnanimously the Spaniards allowed the Marquesans to stand around and watch while mass was celebrated. . . . When [the islanders] attempted to take two canoe loads of . . . coconuts to the ships half the unarmed natives were killed and three of the bodies hung in the rigging in grim warning. The Spaniards were not only killing under orders, they were killing for target practice.

—Islands and Empires; Western Impact on the Pacific and East Asia

All over the Pacific, islanders were "pacified" through violence or deception inflicted on them by the conquering nations of France, England, Spain, and others. Rivalries between the European nations were often acted out in the Pacific. For example, the Cook Islands, inhabited by a mixture of Polynesian and Maori peoples, were partly controlled by the Protestant Mission of the London Missionary Society until the threat of incursions by French Catholics from Tahiti persuaded the British to declare the islands a protectorate of Britain. New Zealand eventually annexed the islands, and it controlled them until 1965.

Business interests frequently took precedence over islanders' sovereignty. In Hawaii, for instance, when Queen Lili-uokalani proposed to limit the influence of the business community in island governance, a few dozen American business leaders, without the knowledge of the U.S. president or Congress and with the unauthorized help of 160 U.S. Marines, overthrew the Hawaiian monarch, installed Sanford Dole (of Dole Pineapple fame) as president, and petitioned Congress for annexation as a U.S. territory.

Whatever the method of acquisition, once the islands were under European or American control, the colonizing nations insisted that the islanders learn Western languages, wear Western clothing, convert to Christianity, and pay homage to faraway rulers whom they had never seen.

This blatant Eurocentrism ignored the obvious—that the islanders already had rich cultural traditions that both pre-dated European culture and constituted substantial accomplishments in technology, the arts, and social structure. Islanders were skilled in the construction of boats suitable for navigation on the high seas and of homes and religious buildings of varied architecture; they had perfected the arts of weaving and cloth-making, tattooing (the word itself is Tahitian), and dancing. Some cultures organized their political affairs much as had early New Englanders, with village meetings to decide issues by consensus, while others had developed strong chieftainships and kingships with an elaborate variety of rituals and taboos (a Tongan word) associated with the ruling elite. Island trade involving vast distances brought otherwise disparate people together; and, although reading and writing was not known on most islands, some evidence of an ancient writing system has been found.

Despite these cultural attributes and a long history of skill in interisland or intertribal warfare, the islanders could not withstand the superior force of European firearms. Within just a few generations, the entire Pacific had been conquered and colonized by Britain, France, Holland, Germany, the United States, and other nations.

CONTEMPORARY GROUPINGS

The Pacific islands today are classified into three racial/cultural groupings. The first, Micronesia, with a population of approximately 352,000 people, contains seven political entities, three of which are politically independent and four of which are affiliated with the United States. Guam is perhaps the best known of these islands. Micronesians share much in common genetically and culturally with Asians. The term *Micronesia* refers to the small size of the islands in this group.

The second grouping, Melanesia, with a population of some 5.5 million (if New Guinea is included), contains six political entities, four of which are independent and two of which are affiliated with colonial powers. The best known of these islands is probably Fiji. The term "Melanesia" refers to the dark skin of the inhabitants, who, despite appearances, apparently have no direct ties with Africa.

Polynesia, the third grouping, with a population of 530,000, contains 12 political entities, three of which are independent, while the remaining six are affiliated with colonial powers. *Polynesia* means "many islands," the most prominent of which is probably Hawaii. Most of the cultures in Polynesia have some ancient connections with the Marquesas Islands or Tahiti.

Subtracting the atypically large population of the island of New Guinea leaves about 2.2 million people in the region that we generally think of as the Pacific islands. Although it is possible that some of the islands may have been peopled by or had contact with ancient civilizations of South America, the overwhelming weight of scholarship places the origins of the Pacific islanders in Southeast Asia, Indonesia, and Australia.

Geologically, the islands may be categorized into the tall, volcanic islands, which are well endowed with water, flora, and fauna and are suitable for agriculture; and the dry, flat, coral islands, which have fewer resources (though some are rich in phosphate). It also appears that the farther away the island is from the Asian or Australian continental landmass, the less varied and plentiful the flora and fauna.

THE PACIFIC COMMUNITY

During the early years of Western contact and colonization, maltreatment of the indigenous peoples and diseases such as measles and influenza greatly reduced their numbers and their cultural strength. Moreover, the carving up of the Pacific

THE CASE OF THE DISAPPEARING ISLAND

It wasn't much to begin with, but the way things are going, it won't be anything by the year 2000. Nauru, a tiny 8½-square-mile dot of phosphate dirt in the Pacific, is being gobbled up by the Nauru Phosphate Corporation. Made of bird droppings (guano) mixed with marine sediment, Nauru's high-quality phosphate has a ready market in Australia, New Zealand, Japan, and other Pacific Rim countries, where it is used in industry, medicine, and agriculture.

Many Pacific islanders with few natural resources to sell to the outside world envy the 4,500 Nauruans. The Nauruans pay no taxes, yet the government, thanks to phosphate sales, is able to provide them with free health and dental care, bus transportation, newspapers, and schooling (including higher education if they are willing to leave home temporarily for Australia, with the trip paid for by the government). Rent for government-built homes, supplied with telephones and electricity, costs about $5 a month. Nor do Nauruans have to work particularly hard for a living, since most laborers in the phosphate pits are imported from other islands; most managers and other professionals come from Australia, New Zealand, and Great Britain.

Phosphate is Nauru's only export, and yet the country makes so much money from it that, technically speaking, Nauru is the richest country per capita in the world. Unable to spend all the export earnings (even though it owns and operates five Boeing 737s, several hotels on other islands, and the tallest skyscraper in Melbourne, Australia), the government puts lots of the money away in trust accounts for a rainy day.

It all sounds nice, but the island is being mined away. Already there is only just a little fringe of green left along the shore, where everyone lives, and the government is debating what should happen when even the ground under people's homes is mined and shipped away. Some think that topsoil should be brought in to see if the moonlike surface of the excavated areas can be revitalized. Others think that moving away makes sense—with all its money, the government could just buy another island somewhere and move everyone (an idea that Australia suggested years ago, even before Nauru's independence in 1968). Of course, since the government owns the phosphate company, it could just put a halt to any more mining. But if it does, what would Nauru be to anybody? On the other hand, if it doesn't, will Nauru *be* at all?

by different Western powers superimposed a cultural fragmentation on the region that added to the separateness created by distance. Today, however, improved medicines are allowing the populations of the islands to rebound, and the withdrawal or realignment of European and American political power under the post–World War II United Nations policy of decolonization has permitted the growth of regional organizations.

First among the postwar regional groups was the South Pacific Commission. Established in 1947, when Western powers were still largely in control, many of its functions have since been augmented or superseded by indigenously created organizations such as the South Pacific Forum, which was organized in 1971 and has since spawned numerous other associations, including the South Pacific Regional Trade and Economic Agency and the South Pacific Islands Fisheries Development Agency. These associations handle, through the executive body (the South Pacific Bureau for Economic Cooperation), such issues as relief funds, the environment, fisheries, trade, and regional shipping. These organizations have produced a variety of duty-free agreements among countries and yielded joint decisions about regional transportation and cultural exchanges. As a result, regional art festivals and sports competitions are now a regular feature of island life. And a regional university in New Zealand attracts several thousand island students a year, as do universities in Hawaii.

Some regional associations have been able to deal forcefully with much more powerful countries. For instance, when the regional fisheries association set higher licensing fees for foreign fishing fleets (most fleets are foreign, because island

fishermen usually cannot provide capital for such large enterprises), the Japanese protested vehemently. Nevertheless, the association held firm, and many islands terminated their contracts with the Japanese rather than lower their fees. In 1994, the Cook Islands, the Federated States of Micronesia, Fiji, Kiribati, the Marshall Islands, Nauru, Niue, Papua New Guinea, the Solomon Islands, Tonga, Tuvalu, Vanuatu, and Western Samoa signed an agreement with the United States to establish a joint commercial commission to foster private-sector businesses and to open opportunities for trade, investment, and training. Through this agreement, the islands hope to increase the attractiveness of their products to the U.S. market.

An increasingly important issue in the Pacific is the testing of nuclear weapons and the disposal of toxic waste. Island leaders, with the occasional support of Australia and the strong support of New Zealand, have spoken out vehemently against the continuation of nuclear testing in the Pacific by the French government (Great Britain and the United States also tested hydrogen bombs on coral atolls for years but have now stopped) and against the burning of nerve gas stockpiles by the United States on Johnston Atoll. In 1985, the 13 independent or self-governing countries of the South Pacific adopted their first collective agreement on regional security, the South Pacific Nuclear Free Zone Treaty. Encouraged by New Zealand and Australia, the group declared the Pacific a nuclear-free zone and issued a communique deploring the dumping of nuclear waste in the region. Some island leaders, however, see the storage of nuclear waste as a way of earning income to compensate those who were affected by the nuclear testing on Bikini and Enewetak Islands. The Marshall Islands, for example, are interested in storing nuclear waste on already contaminated islands, although the nearby Federated States of Micronesia, which were observers at the Nuclear Free Zone Treaty talks, oppose the idea and have asked the Marshalls not to proceed.

In 1982, world leaders met in Jamaica to sign into international law the Law of the Sea. This law, developed under the auspices of the United Nations, gave added power to the tiny Pacific island nations because it extended the territory under their exclusive economic control to 12 miles beyond their shores or 200 miles of undersea continental shelf. This put many islands in undisputed control of large deposits of nickel, copper, magnesium, and other valuable metals. The seabed areas away from continents and islands were declared the world's common heritage, to be mined by an international company, with profits channeled to developing countries. The United States has negotiated for years to increase the role of industrialized nations in mining the seabed areas; if modifications are made to the treaty, the United States will likely sign the document.

COMING OF AGE?

If the Pacific islands are finding more reason to cooperate economically and politically, they are still individually limited by the heritage of cultural fragmentation left them by their colonial pasts. Western Samoa, for example, was first annexed by Germany in 1900, only to be given to New Zealand after Germany's defeat in World War I. Today, the tiny nation of mostly Christian Polynesians, independent since 1962, uses both English and Samoan as official languages and embraces a formal governmental structure copied from Western parliamentary practice. Yet the structure of its hundreds of small villages remains decidedly traditional, with clan chiefs ruling over large extended families, who make their not particularly profitable living by farming breadfruit, taro, yams, bananas, and copra.

Political independence also has not been easy for those islands that have embraced it nor for those colonial powers who continue to deny it. Two military coups toppled the elected government of Fiji (a former British colony) in 1987, and anticolonial unrest continues on many of the other islands (especially the French islands). Concern over economic viability has led most islands to remain in some sort of loose association with their former colonial overseers. After the defeat of Japan in World War II, the Marshall Islands, the Marianas, and the Carolines were assigned by the United Nations to the United States as a trust territory. The French Polynesian islands have remained overseas "departments" of France. In such places as New Caledonia, however, there has been a growing desire for autonomy, which France has attempted to meet in various ways while still retaining sovereignty. The UN decolonization policy has made it possible for

most Pacific islands to achieve independence if they wish, but many are so small that true economic independence in the modern world will never be possible.

Indeed, no amount of political realignment can overcome the economic dilemma of most of the islands. Japan, the single largest purchaser of island products, as well as the United States and others, are good markets for the Pacific economies, but exports are primarily of mineral and agricultural products (coffee, tea, cocoa, sugar, tapioca, coconuts, mother-of-pearl) rather than of the more profitable manufactured or "value-added" items produced by industrial nations. In addition, there will always be the cost of moving products from the vastness of the Pacific to the various mainland markets.

Another problem is that many of the profits from the island's resources do not redound to the benefit of the islanders. Tuna, for example, is an important and profitable fish catch, but most of the profits return to the Taiwanese, Korean, Japanese, and American fleets that ply the Pacific. Similarly, tourism profits largely end up in the hands of the multinational hotel owners. Eighty percent of visitors to the island of Guam since 1982 have been Japanese (over half a million annually)—seemingly a gold mine for local Guamanians, since each traveler spends more than $2,000. Close inspection of those expenditures, however, reveal that the Japanese tend to purchase their tickets on Japanese airlines and book rooms in Japanese-owned or -managed hotels. Thus, of the $92 million spent in 1992 by Japanese tourists in connection with their Guam vacations, well over 60 percent never made it into the hands of the Guamanians.

The poor economy, especially in the outer islands, has prompted many islanders to move to larger cities (about 1 million islanders now live in the Pacific's larger cities) to find work. Indeed, there is currently a tremendous mixing of all of the islands' peoples. Hawaii, for example, is peopled now with Samoans, Filipinos, and many other islanders; pure Hawaiians are a minority, and despite efforts to preserve the Hawaiian language, it is used less and less. Similarly, Fiji is now populated by more immigrants from India than by native Fijians. New Caledonians are outnumbered by Indonesians, Vietnamese, French, and others. And, of course, whites have long outnumbered the Maoris on New Zealand. Guam is peopled with islanders from all of Micronesia as well as from Samoa and other islands. In addition to interisland migration, many islanders emigrate to Australia, New Zealand, the United States, or other countries and then send money back home to sustain their families. Those remittances are important to the economies of the islands, but the absence of parents or children for long periods of time does considerable damage to the social fabric. In a few cases, such as in the Cook Islands and American Samoa, there are more islanders living abroad than remain on the islands. Those who leave often find life abroad quite a shock, for the island culture, influenced over the decades by the missionary efforts of Mormons, Method-

THIS IS LIBERATION?

In 1994, the people of the U.S. Territory of Guam celebrated the 50th anniversary of their liberation by U.S. Marines and Army Infantry from the occupying troops of the Japanese Army. During the 3 years that they controlled the tiny, 30-mile-long island, the Japanese massacred some of the Guamanians and subjected many others to forced labor and internment in concentration camps.

Their liberation, therefore, was indeed a cause for celebration. But the United States quickly transformed the island into its military headquarters for the continuing battle against the Japanese. The entire northern part of the island was turned into a base for B-29 bombers, and the Pacific submarine fleet took up residence in the harbor. Admiral Nimitz, commander-in-chief of the Pacific, made Guam his headquarters. By 1946, the U.S. military government in Guam had laid claim to nearly 80 percent of the island, displacing entire villages and hundreds of individual property owners.

Since then, some of the land has been returned, and large acreages have been handed over to the local civilian government—which was to have distributed most of it, but has not yet done so. The local government still controls about one third of the land, and the U.S. military controls another third, meaning that only one third of the island is available to the residents for private ownership. Litigation to recover the land has been bitter and costly (more than $40 million in legal expenses since 1975). The controversy has prompted some local residents to demand a different kind of relationship with the United States, one that would allow for more autonomy. It has also spurred the growth of nativist organizations such as the Chamorru Nation, which promotes the Chamorru language (the language of the original Malayo–Polynesian inhabitants; spelled *Chamorro* by the Spanish) and organizes acts of civil disobedience against both civilian and military authorities.

Guam was first overtaken by Spain in 1565. It has been controlled by the United States since 1898, except for the brief Japanese interlude. Whether the local islanders, who now constitute a fascinating mix of Chamorro, Spanish, Japanese, and American cultures, will be able to gain a larger measure of autonomy after 430 years of colonization by outsiders is difficult to predict, but the ever-present island motto, *Tano Y Chamorro* ("Land of the Chamorros"), certainly spells out the objective of many of those who call Guam home.

---

ists, Seventh-day Adventists, and especially the London Missionary Society, is conservative, cautious, and personal. Metropolitan life, by contrast, is considered by some islanders to be wild and impersonal. Some young emigrants respond to the "cold" environment and marginality of big-city life by engaging in deviant behavior themselves, such as selling drugs and joining gangs.

Island society itself, moreover, is not immune from the social problems that plague larger societies. Many islands report an increasing number of crimes and suicides. Young Samoans, for example, are afflicted with many of the same problems—gangs, drugs, and unemployment—as are their U.S. inner-city counterparts. Samoan authorities now report increases in incidences of rape, robbery, and other socially dysfunctional behaviors. In addition, the South Pacific Commission and the World Health Organization are now reporting an alarming increase in AIDS and other sexually transmitted diseases. Out of 22 Pacific island groupings, 13 reported cases of HIV or AIDS as of 1994—a 500 percent increase since 1989.

For decades, and notwithstanding the imposition of foreign ways, islanders have shared a common culture—everyone knows how to raise bananas, coconuts, and yams, how to roast pigs and fish, and how to make breadfruit, tapioca, and poi. But much of island culture has depended on an identity shaped and preserved by isolation from the rest of the world. Whether the essence of island life—and especially the identity of the people—can be maintained in the face of increasing integration into a much larger world remains to be seen.

Japan Map

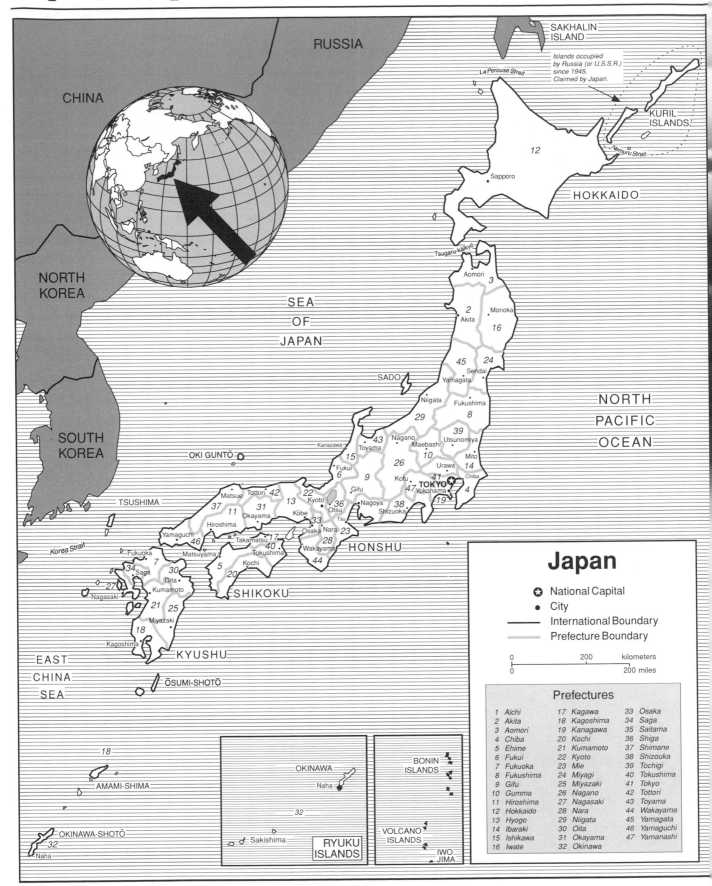

RUSSIA

SAKHALIN ISLAND

Islands occupied by Russia (or U.S.S.R.) since 1945. Claimed by Japan.

La Perouse Strait

KURIL ISLANDS

CHINA

Nemuru Strait

12

Sapporo

HOKKAIDO

NORTH KOREA

Tsugaru-kaikyo

Aomori

3

SEA
OF
JAPAN

2
Akita

Morioka

16

45

24

Sendai

Yamagata

SADO

Niigata

Fukushima

NORTH

SOUTH KOREA

29

8

PACIFIC

OKI GUNTŌ

43

Nagano

Utsunomiya

39

OCEAN

Kanazawa

Toyama

Maebashi

15

10

Mito

26

Urawa

14

Fukui

Kofu

Chiba

6

9

41

TOKYO

TSUSHIMA

Matsue

Tottori

42

22

Kyoto

Gifu

47

Yokohama

4

37

11

31

13

Nagoya

38

19

Okayama

Kōbe

36

Otsu

Shizuoka

Korea Strait

Hiroshima

33

Tsu

HONSHU

Yamaguchi

46

Takamatsu

17

Osaka

Nara

23

Fukuoka

Matsuyama

40

28

7

5

Tokushima

Wakayama

34

30

Kochi

20

44

Saga

27

Oita

SHIKOKU

Nagasaki

Kumamoto

21

25

EAST

Miyazaki

CHINA

18

SEA

Kagoshima

KYUSHU

ŌSUMI-SHOTŌ

Japan

⭐ National Capital
● City
— International Boundary
··· Prefecture Boundary

0   200   kilometers
0   200 miles

Prefectures

1 Aichi	17 Kagawa	33 Osaka
2 Akita	18 Kagoshima	34 Saga
3 Aomori	19 Kanagawa	35 Saitama
4 Chiba	20 Kochi	36 Shiga
5 Ehime	21 Kumamoto	37 Shimane
6 Fukui	22 Kyoto	38 Shizouka
7 Fukuoka	23 Mie	39 Tochigi
8 Fukushima	24 Miyagi	40 Tokushima
9 Gifu	25 Miyazaki	41 Tokyo
10 Gumma	26 Nagano	42 Tottori
11 Hiroshima	27 Nagasaki	43 Toyama
12 Hokkaido	28 Nara	44 Wakayama
13 Hyogo	29 Niigata	45 Yamagata
14 Ibaraki	30 Oita	46 Yamaguchi
15 Ishikawa	31 Okayama	47 Yamanashi
16 Iwate	32 Okinawa	

18

AMAMI-SHIMA

OKINAWA

Naha

BONIN ISLANDS

OKINAWA-SHOTŌ

32

Sakishima

32

Naha

RYUKU ISLANDS

VOLCANO ISLANDS

IWO JIMA

Japan (Nippon)

GEOGRAPHY

Area in Square Kilometers (Miles):
377,835 (145,882) (slightly smaller
than California)
Capital (Population): Tokyo
(8,300,000)
Climate: tropical in south to cold in north

PEOPLE

Population
Total: 125,507,000
Annual Growth Rate: 0.32%
Rural/Urban Population Ratio: 23/77
Ethnic Makeup: 99.4% Japanese; 0.6%
others (mostly Korean)
Major Language: Japanese

Health
Life Expectancy at Birth: 77 years
(male); 82 years (female)
Infant Mortality Rate (Ratio): 4.3/1,000
Average Caloric Intake: 124% of FAO
minimum
Physicians Available (Ratio): 1/588

Religions
96% Shinto; 76% Buddhist; 13%
Christian and others (most Japanese
observe both Shinto and Buddhist rites,
so the percentages add up to more than
100%)

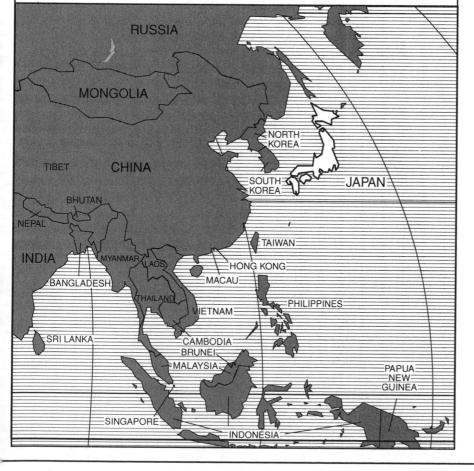

Education
Adult Literacy Rate: 99%

COMMUNICATION

Telephones: 64,000,000
Newspapers: 124

TRANSPORTATION

Highways—Kilometers (Miles):
1,111,974 (690,536)

Railroads—Kilometers (Miles): 27,327
(16,943)
Usable Airfields: 175

GOVERNMENT

Type: constitutional monarchy
Independence Date: May 3, 1947
(constitutional monarchy established)
Head of State/Government: Emperor
Akihito; Prime Minister Ryutaro
Hashimoto
Political Parties: Liberal Democratic
Party; Social Democratic Party; New
Frontier Party; New Harbinger Party;
Japan Communist Party; Komeito
Party; others
Suffrage: universal at 20

MILITARY

Number of Armed Forces: 292,600
*Military Expenditures (% of Central
Government Expenditures):* 1% of the
budget
Current Hostilities: none

ECONOMY

Currency ($ U.S. Equivalent): 122.9
yen = $1
Per Capita Income/GDP:
$20,200/$2.527 trillion
Inflation Rate: 0.7%
Natural Resources: negligible oil and
minerals
Agriculture: rice; sugar beets;
vegetables; fruit; animal products
include pork, poultry, dairy and eggs,
fish
Industry: metallurgy; engineering;
electrical and electronics; textiles;
chemicals; automobiles; fishing

FOREIGN TRADE

Exports: $395.5 billion
Imports: $274.3 billion

7–11 HUSBANDS

The official business day in Japan for most companies is 9:00 A.M. to
5:00 P.M., but most workers would feel disloyal to their companies—or
would not make enough money to live comfortably—if they spent such
a short amount of time on the job. Employees often stay at work or
participate in business dinners or other formal socializing until 9:00 P.M.
or later. The commute home in Tokyo averages about 1½ hours. This
means that workers arrive home at about 11:00 P.M. and leave the next
morning at about 7:00 in order to be to work on time, thus giving rise
to the popular term "7–11 husbands." Although most men say that they
would like to spend more (but not much more) time with their families,
88 percent of wives surveyed said that they prefer spending their leisure
time away from their husbands and feel more relaxed at home when
their husbands are not there.

Japan: Driving Force in the Pacific Rim

HISTORICAL BACKGROUND

The Japanese nation is thought to have begun about 250 B.C., when ancestors of today's Japanese people began cultivating rice, casting objects in bronze, and putting together the rudiments of the Shinto religion. However, humans are thought to have inhabited the Japanese islands as early as 20,000 B.C. Some speculate that remnants of these or other early peoples may be the non-Oriental Ainu people (now largely Japanized) who still occupy parts of the northern island of Hokkaido. Asiatic migrants from China and Korea and islanders from the South Pacific occupied the islands between 250 B.C. and A.D. 400, contributing to the population base of modern Japan.

Between A.D. 300 and 710, military aristocrats from some of the powerful clans into which Japanese society was divided established their rule over large parts of the country. Eventually, the Yamato clan leaders, claiming divine approval, became the most powerful. Under Yamato rule, the Japanese began to import ideas and technology from nearby China, including the Buddhist religion and the Chinese method of writing—which the elite somewhat awkwardly adapted to spoken Japanese, an entirely unrelated language. The Chinese bureaucratic style of government and architecture was also introduced; Japan's first permanent capital was constructed at the city of Nara between the years 710 and 794.

As Chinese influence waned in the period 794–1185, the capital was relocated to Kyoto, with the Fujiwara family wielding real power under the largely symbolic figurehead of the emperor. A warrior class controlled by *shoguns,* or generals, held power at Kamakura between 1185 and 1333 and successfully defended the country from invasion by the Mongols. Buddhism became the religion of the masses, although Shintoism was often embraced simultaneously. Between 1333 and 1568, a very rigid class structure developed, along with a feudalistic economy controlled by *daimyos,* feudal lords who reigned over their own mini-kingdoms.

In 1543, Portuguese sailors landed in Japan, followed a few years later by the Jesuit missionary Francis Xavier. An active trade with Portugal began, and many Japanese (perhaps half a million), including some feudal lords, converted to Christianity. The Portuguese introduced firearms to the Japanese and perhaps taught them Western-style techniques of building castles with moats and stone walls. Wealthier feudal lords were able to utilize these innovations to defeat weaker rivals; by 1600, the country was unified under a military bureaucracy, although feudal lords still retained substantial sovereignty over their fiefs. During this time, the general Hideyoshi attempted an unsuccessful invasion of nearby Korea.

The Tokugawa Era

In the period 1600 to 1868, called the Tokugawa Era, the social, political, and economic foundations of modern Japan were put in place. The capital was moved to Tokyo, cities began to grow in size, and a merchant class arose, which was powerful enough to challenge the hegemony of the centuries-old warrior class. Strict rules of dress and behavior for each of the four social classes (samurai, farmer, craftsman, and merchant) were imposed, and the Japanese people learned to discipline themselves to these codes. Western ideas came to be seen as a threat to the established ruling class. The military elite expelled foreigners and put the nation into 2½ centuries of extreme isolation from the rest of the world. Christianity was banned, as was most trade with the West. Even Japanese living abroad were forbidden from returning, for fear that they might have been contaminated with foreign ideas.

During the Tokugawa Era, indigenous culture expanded rapidly. Puppet plays and a new form of drama called *kabuki* became popular, as did *haiku* poetry and Japanese pottery and painting. The samurai code, called *bushido,* along with the concept of *giri,* or obligation to one's superiors, suffused Japanese society. Literacy among males rose to about 40 percent, higher than most European countries of the day. Samurai busied themselves with the education of the young, using teaching methods that included strict discipline, hard work, and self-denial.

During the decades of isolation, Japan grew culturally strong but militarily weak. In 1853, a U.S. naval squadron appeared in Tokyo Bay to insist that Japan open up its ports to foreign vessels needing supplies and desiring to trade. Similar requests had been denied in the past, but the sophistication of the U.S. ships and their advanced weaponry convinced the Japanese military rulers that they no longer could keep Japan isolated from the outside.

The Era of Modernization: The Meiji Restoration

Treaties with the United States and other Western nations followed, and the dislocations associated with the opening of the country to the world soon brought discredit to the ruling shoguns. Provincial samurai took control of the government. The emperor, long a figurehead in Kyoto, away from the center of power, was moved to Tokyo in 1868, beginning the period known as the Meiji Restoration.

Although the Meiji leaders came to power with the intention of ousting all the foreigners and returning Japan to its former state of domestic tranquillity, they quickly realized that the nations of the West were determined to defend their newly won access to the ports of Japan. To defeat the foreigners, they reasoned, Japan must first acquire their knowledge and technology.

Thus, beginning in 1868, the Japanese leaders launched a major campaign to modernize the nation. Ambassadors and scholars were sent abroad to learn about Western-style government, education, and warfare. Implementing these ideas resulted in the abolition of the feudal system and the division of Japan into 43 prefectures, or states, and other administrative districts under the direct control of the Tokyo government. Legal codes that established the formal separation of society into social classes were abolished; and Western-style dress, music, and education were embraced. The old samurai class turned its attention from warfare to leadership in the

(Japan National Tourist Organization)

The Japanese emperor has long been a figurehead in Japan. In 1926, Hirohito, pictured above, became emperor and ushered in the era named *Showa*. He died on January 7, 1989, having seen Japan through World War II and witnessed its rise to the economic world power it is today. He was succeeded by his son, Akihito, who named his reign *Heisei*, meaning "Achieving Peace."

government, in schools, and in business. Factories and railroads were constructed, and public education was expanded. By 1900, Japan's literacy rate was 90 percent, the highest in all of Asia. Parliamentary rule was established along the lines of the government in Prussia, agricultural techniques were imported from the United States, and banking methods were adopted from Great Britain.

Japan's rapid modernization soon convinced its leaders that the nation was strong enough to begin doing what other advanced nations were doing: acquiring empires. Japan went to war with China, acquiring the Chinese island of Taiwan in 1895. In 1904, Japan attacked Russia and successfully acquired Korea and access to Manchuria (both areas having been in the sphere of influence of Russia). Siding against Germany in World War I, Japan was able to acquire Germany's Pacific empire—the Marshall, Caroline, and Mariana Islands. Western nations were surprised at Japan's rapid empire-building but did little to stop it.

The Great Depression of the 1930s caused serious hardships in Japan because, being resource-poor yet heavily populated, the country had come to rely on trade to supply its basic needs. Many Japanese advocated the forced annexation of Manchuria as a way of providing needed resources. This was accomplished easily, in 1931. With militarism on the rise, the Japanese nation began moving away from democracy and toward a military dictatorship. Political parties were eventually banned, and opposition leaders were jailed and tortured.

WORLD WAR II AND THE JAPANESE EMPIRE

The battles of World War II in Europe, initially won by Germany, promised to re-align substantially the colonial empires of France and other European powers in Asia. The military elite of Japan declared its intention of creating a Greater East Asia Co-Prosperity Sphere—in effect, a Japanese empire created out of the ashes of the European empires in Asia that were now dissolving. In 1941, under the guidance of General Hideki Tojo and with the tacit approval of the emperor, Japan captured the former French colony of Indochina (Vietnam, Laos, and Cambodia), bombed Pearl Harbor in Hawaii, and captured oil-rich Indonesia. These victories were followed by others: Japan captured all of Southeast Asia, including Burma (today officially but not commonly called Myanmar), Thailand, and Malaya, the Philippines, and parts of New Guinea; and expanded its hold in China and in the islands of the South Pacific. Many of these conquered peoples, lured by the Japanese slogan of "Asia for the Asians," were initially supportive of the Japanese, believing that Japan would rid their countries of European colonial rule. It soon became apparent, however, that Japan had no intention of relinquishing control of these territories and would go to brutal lengths to subjugate the local peoples. Japan soon dominated a vast empire, the constituents of which were virtually the same as those making up what we call the Pacific Rim today.

In 1941, the United States launched a counteroffensive against the powerful Japanese military. (American history books refer to this offensive as the Pacific Theater of World War II, but the Japanese call it the *Pacific War*. We use the term *World War II* in this text, for reasons of clarity and consistency.) By 1944, the U.S. troops had ousted the Japanese from most of their conquered lands and were beginning to attack the home islands themselves. Massive firebombing of Tokyo and other cities, combined with the dropping of two atomic bombs on Hiroshima and Nagasaki, convinced the Japanese military rulers that they had no choice but to surrender.

This was the first time in Japanese history that Japan had been conquered, and the Japanese were shocked to hear their emperor, Hirohito—whose voice had never been heard on radio—announce on August 14, 1945, that Japan was defeated. The emperor cited the suffering of the people—almost 2 million Japanese had been killed—devastation of the cities brought about by the use of a "new and most cruel bomb,"

On December 7, 1941, the Japanese entered World War II by bombing Pearl Harbor, in Hawaii. This photograph, taken from an attacking Japanese plane, shows Pearl Harbor and a line of American battleships.

and the possibility that, without surrender, Japan as a nation might be completely "obliterated." Emperor Hirohito then encouraged his people to look to the future, to keep pace with progress, and to help build world peace by accepting the surrender ("enduring the unendurable and suffering what is insufferable").

This attitude smoothed the way for the American Occupation, led by General Douglas MacArthur. Defeat seemed to inspire the Japanese people to adopt the ways of their more powerful conquerors and to eschew militarism. Under the Occupation forces, the Japanese Constitution was rewritten in a form that mimicked that of the United States. Industry was restructured, labor unions encouraged, land reform accomplished, and the nation as a whole demilitarized. Economic aid from the United States, as well as the prosperity in Japan that was occasioned by the Korean War in 1953, allowed Japanese industry to begin to recover from the devastation of war. The United States returned the governance of Japan back to the Japanese people by treaty in 1951 (although some 60,000 troops still remain in Japan as part of an agreement to defend Japan from foreign attack).

By the late 1960s, the Japanese economy was more than self-sustaining and the United States was Japan's primary trading partner (it remains so today, with 34 percent of Japanese exports purchased by Americans and 30 percent of Japanese food imports coming from the United States). Japan's trade with its former Asian empire, however, was minimal, because of lingering resentment against Japan for its wartime brutalities. (In the late 1970s, for example, anti-Japanese riots and demonstrations occurred upon the visit of the Japanese prime minister to Indonesia.)

Nevertheless, between the 1960s and 1990s, Japan experienced an era of unprecedented economic prosperity. Annual economic growth was 3 times as much as in other industrialized nations. Japanese couples voluntarily limited their family size so that each child born could enjoy the best of medical care and social and educational opportunities. The fascination with the West continued, but eventually, rather than "modernization" or "Americanization," the Japanese began to speak of "internationalization," reflecting both their capacity for and their actual membership in the world community, politically, culturally, and economically.

The Japanese government as well as private industry began to accelerate the drive for diversified markets and resources in the mid-1980s. This was partly in response to protectionist trends in countries in North America and Europe with which Japan had accumulated huge trade surpluses, but it was also due to changes in Japan's own internal social and economic conditions. Japan's recent resurgence of interest in its neighboring countries and the origin of the bloc of nations we are calling the Pacific Rim can be explained by both external protectionism and internal changes. This time, however, Japanese influence—no longer linked with militarism—is being welcomed by virtually all nations in the region.

DOMESTIC CHANGE

What internal conditions are causing Japan's renewed interest in Asia and the Pacific? One change involves wage structure. For several decades, Japanese exports were less expensive than competitors' because Japanese workers were not paid as well as workers in North America and Europe. Today, however, the situation is reversed: Average manufacturing wages in Japan are now higher than those paid to workers in the United States. Schoolteachers, college professors, and many white-collar workers are also better off in Japan. These wage differentials are the result of successful union activity and demographic changes.

Whereas prewar Japanese families—especially those in the rural areas—were large, today's modern household typically consists of a couple and only one or two children. As Japan's low birth rate began to affect the supply of labor, companies were forced to entice workers with higher wages. An example is McDonald's, increasingly popular in Japan as a fast-food outlet. Whereas young people working at McDonald's outlets in the United States are paid at or slightly above the legal minimum wage of $4.75 an hour, McDonald's employees in Japan are paid as much as $7.10 an hour, simply because there are fewer youths available (many schools prohibit students from working during the school year). The cost of land, homes, food—even Japanese-grown rice—is so much higher in Japan than in most of its neighbor countries that employees in Japan expect high wages (household income in Japan is higher even than in the United States).

Given conditions like these, many Japanese companies have found that they cannot be competitive in world markets unless they move their operations to countries like the Philippines or Singapore, where an abundance of laborers keeps wage costs 75 to 95 percent lower than in Japan. Abundant, cheap labor (as well as a desire to avoid import tariffs) is also the reason why so many Japanese companies have been constructed in the economically depressed areas of the U.S. Midwest and South.

Another internal condition that is spurring Japanese interest in the Pacific Rim is a growing public concern for the home environment. Beginning in the 1970s, the Japanese courts handed down several landmark decisions in which Japanese companies were held liable for damages to people caused by

(United Motor Manufacturing)

As the economy of Japan developed, manufacturing wages rose to a point where Japanese products were less competitive in world markets. In response, Japanese industry began to build manufacturing facilities abroad in partnership with foreign companies. These American workers are busy in a Toyota–General Motors plant in the United States.

chemical and other industrial wastes. Japanese industry, realizing that it no longer had a carte blanche to make profits at the expense of the environment, began moving some of its smokestack industries to new locations in developing-world countries, just as other industrialized nations had done. This has turned out to be a wise move economically for many companies, as it has put their operations closer to their raw materials. This, in combination with cheaper labor costs, has allowed them to remain globally competitive. It also has been a tremendous benefit to the host countries, although environmental groups in many Rim countries are also now becoming active, and industry in the future may be forced to effect actual improvements in their operations rather than move polluting technologies to "safe" areas.

Attitudes toward work are also changing in Japan. Although the average Japanese worker still works about 6 hours more per week than does the typical North American worker, the new generation of workers—those born and raised since World War II—are not so eager to sacrifice as much for their companies as were their parents. Recent policies have eliminated weekend work in many industries, and sports and other recreational activities are becoming increasingly popular. Given these conditions, Japanese corporate leaders are finding it more cost effective to move operations abroad to countries like South Korea, where labor legislation is weaker and long work hours remain the norm.

MYTH AND REALITY OF THE ECONOMIC MIRACLE

The Japanese economy, like any other economy, must respond to market as well as social and political changes to stay vibrant. It just so happens that, for several decades, Japan's attempt to keep its economic boom alive has created the conditions that, in turn, are furthering the economies of all the countries in the Asia/Pacific region. If a regional "Yen Bloc" (so called because of the dominance of the Japanese currency, the yen) is created in the process, it will simply be the result of Japan doing what it calculates it has to do to remain competitive in the world market.

Outsiders today are often of the impression that whatever Japan does—whether targeting a certain market or reorienting its economy toward regional trade—turns to gold, as if the Japanese possess some secret of success that others do not. But there is no such secret that other nations could not understand or employ themselves. Japanese success in business, education, and other fields is the result of hard work, advance planning, persistence, and outside help.

However, even with those ingredients in place, Japanese enterprises often fall short. In many industries, for example, Japanese workers are less efficient than are workers in other countries. Japan's national railway system was once found to have 277,000 more employees on its payroll than it needed. At one point, investigators revealed that the system was so poorly managed for so many years that it had accumulated a

total public debt of $257 billion. Multimillion-dollar train stations had been built in out-of-the-way towns, for no other reason than that a member of the *Diet* (the Japanese Parliament) happened to live there and had pork-barreled the project. Both government and industry have been plagued by bribery and corruption, as occurred in the Recruit Scandal of the late 1980s, which caused many implicated government leaders, including the prime minister, to resign.

Nor is the Japanese economy impervious to global market conditions. Values of stocks traded on the Tokyo Stock Exchange took a serious drop in 1992; investors lost millions of dollars, and many had to declare bankruptcy. Moreover, the tenacious recession that hit Japan in the early 1990s forced Japanese companies to reduce overtime work and slow down expansion plans.

THE COMMANDMENTS OF JAPAN'S ECONOMIC SUCCESS

Still, the success of modern Japan has been phenomenal, and it would be helpful to review in detail some of the bases of that success. We might call these the 10 commandments of Japan's economic success:

1. Some of Japan's entrenched business conglomerates, called *zaibatsu*, were broken up by order of the U.S. Occupation commander after World War II; this allowed competing

(Sony Corporation of America)

A contributing factor in the modern economic development of Japan was investment from the Agency for International Development. The Sony Corporation is an example of just how successful this assistance could be. These workers are assembling products that will be sold all over the world.

businesses to get a start. Similarly, the physical infrastructure—roads, factories—was destroyed during the war. This was a blessing in disguise, for it paved the way for newer equipment and technologies to be put in place quickly.

2. The United States, seeing the need for an economically strong Japan in order to offset the growing attraction of Communist ideology in Asia, provided substantial reconstruction aid. For instance, Sony Corporation got started with help from the Agency for International Development (AID)—an organization to which the United States is a major contributor. Mazda Motors got its start by making Jeeps for U.S. forces during the Korean War. Other Rim countries that are now doing well can also thank U.S. generosity: Taiwan received $5.6 billion and South Korea received $13 billion in aid during the period 1945–1978.

3. Japanese industry looked upon government as a facilitator and received useful economic advice as well as political and financial assistance from government planners. (In this regard, it is important to note that many of Japan's civil servants are the best graduates of Japan's colleges and universities.) Also, the advice and help coming from the government were fairly consistent over time, because the same political party, the Liberal Democratic Party, remained in power for almost the entire postwar period.

4. Japanese businesses selected an export-oriented strategy that stressed building market share over immediate profit.

5. Except in certain professions, such as teaching, labor unions in Japan were not as powerful as in Europe and the United States. This is not to suggest that unions were not effective in gaining benefits for workers, but the structure of the union movement—individual company unions rather than industry-wide unions—moderated the demands for improved wages and benefits.

6. Company managers stressed employee teamwork and group spirit and implemented policies such as "lifetime employment" and quality-control circles, which contributed to group morale. In this they were aided by the tendency of Japanese workers to grant to the company some of the same level of loyalty traditionally reserved for families. In certain ways, the gap between workers and management was minimized.

7. Companies benefited from the Japanese ethic of working hard and saving much. For most of Japan's postwar history, workers labored 6 days a week, arriving early and leaving late. The paychecks were carefully managed to include a substantial savings component—generally between 15 and 25 percent. This guaranteed that there were always enough cash reserves for banks to offer company expansion loans at low interest.

8. The government spent relatively little of its tax revenues on social-welfare programs or military defense, preferring instead to invest public funds in private industry.

9. A relatively stable family structure (i.e., few divorces and substantial family support for young people, many of whom remained at home until marriage at about age 27), produced employees who were reliable and psychologically stable.

10. The government as well as private individuals invested enormous amounts of money and energy into education, on the assumption that, in a resource-poor country, the mental energies of the people would need to be exploited to their fullest.

Some of these conditions for success are now part of immutable history; but others, such as the emphasis on education, are open to change as the conditions of Japanese life change. A relevant example is the practice of lifetime employment. Useful as a management tool when companies were small and *skilled* laborers were difficult to find, it is now giving way to a freer labor market system. In some Japanese industries, as many as 30 percent of new hires quit after 2 years on the job. In other words, the aforementioned conditions for success were relevant to one particular era of Japanese and world history and may not be relevant to other countries or other times. Selecting the right strategy for the right era has perhaps been the single most important condition for Japanese economic success.

CULTURAL CHARACTERISTICS

All these conditions notwithstanding, Japan would never have achieved economic success without its people possessing certain social and psychological characteristics, many of which can be traced to the various religious/ethical philosophies that have suffused Japan's 2,000-year history. Shintoism, Buddhism, Confucianism, Christianity, and other philosophies of living have shaped the modern Japanese mind. This is not to suggest that Japanese are tradition-bound; nothing could be further from the truth, even though many Westerners think "tradition" when they think Japan. It is more accurate to think of Japanese people as imitative, preventive, pragmatic, obligative, and inquisitive rather than traditional. These characteristics are discussed in this section.

Imitative
The capacity to imitate one's superiors is a strength of the Japanese people; rather than representing an inability to think creatively, it constitutes one reason for Japan's legendary success. It makes sense to the Japanese to copy success, whether it is a successful boss, a company in the West, or an educational curriculum in Europe. It is true that imitation can produce conformity; but, in Japan's case, it is often conformity based on respect for the superior qualities of someone or something rather than simple, blind mimicry.

Once Japanese people have mastered the skills of their superiors, they believe that they have the moral right to a style of their own. Misunderstandings on this point arise often when East meets West. One American schoolteacher, for example, was sent to Japan to teach Western art to elementary-school children. Considering her an expert, the children did their best to copy her work to the smallest detail. Misunderstanding that this was at once a compliment and the first step toward creativity, the teacher removed all of her art samples from the classroom in order to force the students to paint something from their own imaginations. Because the students found this to be a violation of their approach to creativity, they did not perform well, and the teacher left Japan believing that Japanese education teaches conformity and compliance rather than creativity and spontaneity.

There is a lesson to learn from this episode as far as predicting the future role of Japan vis-à-vis the West. After decades of imitating the West, Japanese people are now beginning to feel that they have the skills and the moral right to create styles of their own. We can expect to see, therefore, an explosion of Japanese creativity in the near future. Some observers have noted, for example, that the international fashion industry seems to be gaining more inspiration from designers in Tokyo than from those in Milan, Paris, or New York. And, as of the mid-1980s, the Japanese have annually registered more new patents with the U.S. Patent Office than has any other nation except the United States. The Japanese are also now winning more Nobel prizes than in the past.

Preventive

Japanese individuals, families, companies, and the government prefer long-range over short-range planning, and they greatly prefer foreknowledge over postmortem analysis. Assembly-line workers test and retest every product to prevent customers from receiving defective products. Store clerks plug in and check electronic devices in front of a customer to prevent bad merchandise from sullying the good reputation of the store. Insurance companies do a brisk business in Japan, and even though Japanese citizens are covered by the government's national health plan, many people buy additional coverage—for example, cancer insurance—just to be safe.

This concern with prevention trickles down to the smallest details. At train stations, multiple recorded warnings are given of an approaching train to commuters standing on the platform. Parent–teacher associations send teams of mothers around the neighborhood to determine which streets are the safest for the children. They then post signs designating certain roads as "school passage roads" and instruct children to take those routes even if it takes longer to walk to school. The Japanese think that it is better to avoid an accident than to have an emergency team ready when a child is hurt. Whereas Americans say, "If it ain't broke, don't fix it," the Japanese say, "Why wait 'til it breaks to fix it?"

Pragmatic

Rather than pursue a plan because it ideologically fits some preordained philosophy, the Japanese try to be pragmatic on most points. Take drugs as an example. Many nations say that drug abuse is an insurmountable problem that will, at best, be contained but probably never eradicated, because to do so would violate civil liberties. But, as a headline in the *Asahi Evening News* proclaimed a few years ago, "Japan Doesn't Have a Drug Problem and Means to Keep It That Way." Reliable statistics support this claim, but that is not the whole

(Dean Collinwood)
Social problems such as drugs and homelessness are minimal in Japan. Neither the state nor the culture condones poverty, and there are few places in Japan that could be called a slum. Homeless people are a rare, albeit increasing, sight in Japan.

story. In 1954, Japan had a serious drug problem, with 53,000 drug arrests in one year. At the time, the authorities concluded that they had a big problem on their hands and must do whatever was required to solve it. The government passed a series of tough laws restricting the production, use, exchange, and possession of all manner of drugs, and it gave the police the power to arrest all violators. Users were arrested as well as dealers: It was reasoned that if the addicts were not left to buy the drugs, the dealers would be out of business. Their goal at the time was to arrest all addicts, even if it meant that certain liberties were briefly circumscribed. The plan, based on a do-what-it-takes pragmatism, worked; today, Japan is the only one of the industrialized countries without a widespread drug problem. In this case, to pragmatism was added the Japanese tendency to work for the common rather than the individual good.

This approach to life is so much a part of the Japanese mind-set that many Japanese cannot understand why the United States and other industrialized nations have so many unresolved social and economic problems. For instance, when it comes to the trade imbalance, it is clear that one of the West's most serious problems is a low savings rate (making money scarce and interest rates high); another is inferior-quality products. Knowing that these are problems, the Japanese wonder why North Americans and Europeans do not just start saving more and working more carefully. They think, "We did it; why can't you?"

Obligative

The Japanese have a great sense of duty toward those around them. There are thousands of Japanese workers who work late without pay to improve their job skills so that they will not let their fellow workers down. Good deeds done by one generation are remembered and repaid by the next, and lifelong friendships are maintained by exchanging appropriate gifts and letters. North Americans and Europeans are often considered untrustworthy friends because they do not keep up the level of close, personal communications that the Japanese expect of their own friends; nor do the Westerners have as strong a sense of place, station, or position.

Duty to the group is closely linked to respect for superior authority. Every group—indeed, every relationship—is seen as a mixture of people with inferior and superior resources. These differences must be acknowledged, and no one is disparaged for bringing less to the group than someone else. However, equality is assumed when it comes to basic commitment to or effort expended for a task. Slackers are not welcome. Obligation to the group along with respect for superiors motivated Japanese pilots to fly suicide missions during World War II, and it now causes workers to go the extra mile for the good of the company.

That said, it is also true that changes in the intensity of commitment are becoming increasingly apparent. More Japanese than ever before are beginning to feel that their own personal goals are more important than those of their companies or extended families. This is no doubt a result of the Westernization of the culture since the Meiji Restoration, in the late 1800s, and especially of the experiences of the growing number of Japanese—approximately half a million in a given year—who live abroad and then take their newly acquired values back to Japan. (About half of these "away Japanese" live in North America and Western Europe.)

Inquisitive

The image of dozens of Japanese businesspeople struggling to read a book or newspaper while standing inside a packed commuter train is one not easily forgotten, symbolizing as it does the intense desire among the Japanese for knowledge, especially knowledge of foreign cultures. Nearly 6 million Japanese travel abroad each year (many to pursue higher education), and for those who do not, the government and private radio and television stations provide a continuous stream of programming about everything from Caribbean cuisine to French ballet. The Japanese have a yen for foreign styles of dress, foreign cooking, and foreign languages. The Japanese study languages with great intensity. Every student is required to study English; many others study Chinese, Greek, Latin, Russian, Arabic, and other languages, with French being the most popular after English.

Observers inside and outside of Japan are beginning to comment that the Japanese are recklessly discarding Japanese culture in favor of foreign ideas and habits, even when they make no sense in the Japanese context. A tremendous intellectual debate, called *Nihonjin-ron*, is now taking place in Japan over the meaning of being Japanese and the Japanese role in the world. There is certainly value in these concerns, but, as was noted previously, the secret about Japanese tradi-

(AP Wirephoto by Elaine Kurtenbach)
The Japanese take education seriously. Half of the children start kindergarten at the age of three, and early on they are instilled with respect for authority.

tions is that they are not traditional. That is, the Japanese seem to know that, in order to succeed, they must learn what they need to know for the era in which they live, even if it means modifying or eliminating the past. This is probably the reason why the Japanese nation has endured for more than 2,000 years whereas many other empires have long since fallen. In this sense, the Japanese are very forward-looking people and, in their thirst for new modes of thinking and acting, they are, perhaps, revealing their most basic and useful national personality characteristic: inquisitiveness. Given this attitude toward learning, it should come as no surprise that formal schooling in Japan is a very serious business to the government and to families. It is to that topic that we now turn.

SCHOOLING

Probably most of the things that the West has heard about Japanese schools are distortions or outright falsehoods. We hear that Japanese children are highly disciplined, for example; yet, in reality, Japanese schools at the elementary and junior high levels are rather noisy, unstructured places, with children racing around the halls during breaks and getting into fights with classmates on the way home. Many readers may be surprised to learn that Japan has a far lower percentage of its college-age population enrolled in higher education than is the case in the United States—35 percent as compared to 50 percent. Moreover, the Japanese government does not require young people to attend high school (they must attend only until age 15), although 94 percent do anyway. Given these and other realities of school life in Japan, how can we

Doing well in school is seen by students as fulfilling their obligation to their families. Education is held in high regard and is seen as an important element in achieving a better life; it is supported very strongly by parents.

explain the consistently high scores of Japanese on international tests and the general agreement that Japanese high school graduates know almost as much as college graduates in North America?

Structurally, schools in Japan are similar to those in many other countries: There are kindergartens, elementary schools, junior high schools, and high schools. Passage into elementary and junior high is automatic, regardless of student performance level. But admission to high school and college is based on test scores from entrance examinations. Preparing for these examinations occupies the full attention of students in their final year of both junior high and high school, respectively. Both parents and school authorities insist that studying for the tests be the primary focus of a student's life at those times. For instance, members of a junior high soccer team may be allowed to play on the team only for their first 2 years; during their last year, they are expected to be studying for their high school entrance examinations. School policy reminds students that they are in school to learn and to graduate to the next level, not to play sports. Many students even attend after-hours "cram schools" (*juku*) several nights a week to prepare for the exams.

Time for recreational and other nonschool activities is restricted, because Japanese students attend school 240 days out of the year (as compared to about 180 in U.S. schools), including most Saturday mornings. Summer vacation is only about 6 weeks long, and students often attend school activities during most of the vacation period. Japanese youth are expected to treat schooling as their top priority over part-time jobs (usually prohibited by school policy during the school year, except for the needy), sports, dating, and even family time.

Children who do well in school are generally thought to be fulfilling their obligations to the family. The reason for this focus is that parents realize that only through education can Japanese youths find their place in society. Joining the army is generally not an option, opportunities for farming are limited because of land scarcity, and most major companies will not hire a new employee who has not graduated from college or a respectable high school. Thus, the Japanese find it important to focus on education—to do one thing and do it well.

Teachers are held in high regard in Japan, partly because, when mass education was introduced, many of the high-status samurai took up teaching to replace their martial activities. In addition, in modern times, the Japan Teacher's Union has been active in agitating for higher pay for teachers. As a group, teachers are the highest-paid civil servants in Japan.

They take their jobs very seriously. Public-school teachers, for example, visit the home of each student each year to merge the authority of the home with that of the school, and they insist that parents (usually mothers) play active supporting roles in the school.

Some Japanese youths dislike the system, and discussions are currently under way among Japanese educators on how to improve the quality of life for students. Occasionally the pressure of taking examinations (called "exam hell") produces such stress that a desperate student will commit suicide rather than try and fail. Stress also appears to be the cause of *ijime,* or bullying of weaker students by stronger peers. In recent years, the Ministry of Education has worked hard to help students deal with school stress, with the result that Japan's youth suicide rate has dropped dramatically. Despite these and other problems, most Japanese youths enjoy school and value the time they have to be with their friends, whether in class, walking home, or attending cram school. Some of those who fail their college entrance exams continue to study privately, some for many years, and take the exam each year until they pass. Others travel abroad and enroll in foreign universities that do not have such rigid entrance requirements. Still others enroll in vocational training schools. But everyone in Japan realizes that education, not money, name, or luck, is the key to success.

Parents whose children are admitted to the prestigious national universities—such as Tokyo and Kyoto Universities—consider that they have much to brag about. Other parents are willing to pay as much as $35,000 on average for 4 years of college at the private (but usually not as prestigious) universities. Once admitted, students find that life slows down a bit. For one thing, parents typically pay more than 65 percent of the costs, and approximately 3 percent is covered by scholarships. This leaves only about 30 percent to be earned by the students; this usually comes from tutoring high school students who are studying for the entrance exams. Contemporary parents are also willing to pay the cost of a son's or daughter's traveling to and spending a few months in North America or Europe either before college begins or during summer breaks—a practice that is becoming de rigueur for Japanese students, much as taking a "grand tour" of Europe was expected of young, upper-class Americans at the turn of the century.

College students may take 15 or 16 courses at a time, but classes usually meet only once or twice a week, and sporadic attendance is the norm. Straight lecturing rather than class discussion is the typical learning format, and there is very little homework beyond studying for the final exam. Students generally do not challenge the professors' statements in class, but some students develop rather close, avuncular-type relationships with their professors outside of class. Hobbies, sports, and club activities (things the students did not have time to do while in public school) occupy the center of life for many college students. Equally important is the cementing of friendships that will last a lifetime and be useful in one's career and private life.

THE JAPANESE BUSINESS WORLD

Successful college graduates begin their work careers in April, when most large companies do their hiring. They may have to take an examination to determine how much they know about electronics or stocks and bonds, and they may have to complete a detailed personality profile. Finally, they will have to submit to a very serious interview with company management. During interviews, the managers will watch their every move; the applicants will be careful to avoid saying anything that will give them "minus points."

Once hired, individuals attend training sessions in which they learn the company song and other rituals as well as company policy on numerous matters. They may be housed in company apartments (or may continue to live at home), permitted to use a company car or van, and advised to shop at company grocery stores. Almost never are employees married at this time, and so they are expected to live a rather spartan life for the first few years.

Employees are expected to show considerable deference to their section bosses, even though, on the surface, bosses do not appear to be very different from other employees. Bosses' desks are out in the open, near the employees; they wear the same uniform; they socialize with the employees after work; even in a factory, they are often on the shop floor rather than sequestered away in private offices. Long-term employees often come to see the section leader as an uncle figure (bosses are usually male) who will give them advice about life, be the best man at their weddings, and provide informal marital and family counseling as needed.

Although there are cases of abuse or unfair treatment of employees, Japanese company life can generally be described as somewhat like a large family rather than a military squad; employees (sometimes called *associates*) often obey their superiors out of genuine respect rather than forced compliance. Moreover, competition between workers is reduced because everyone hired at the same time receives more or less the same pay and most workers receive promotions at about the same time. Only later in one's career are individualistic promotions given.

Employees are expected to work hard, for not only are Japanese companies in competition with foreign businesses, but they also must survive the fiercely competitive business climate at home. Indeed, the Japanese skill in international business was developed at home. There are, for example, some 580 electronics companies and 7,000 textile enterprises competing for customers in Japan. And whereas the United States has only four automobile-manufacturing companies, Japan has nine. All these companies entice customers with deep price cuts or unusual services, hoping to edge out unprepared or weak competitors. Many companies fail. There were once, for instance, almost 40 companies in Japan that manu-

(Reuters/Bettmann)

In the Japanese business world, one's job is taken very seriously and is often seen as a lifelong commitment. These workers have jobs that, in many ways, may be more a part of their lives than are their families.

factured calculators, but today only six remain, the rest victims of tough internal Japanese competition.

At about age 27, after several years of working and saving money for an apartment, a car, and a honeymoon, the typical Japanese male worker marries. The average bride, about age 25, will have taken private lessons in flower arranging, the tea ceremony, sewing, cooking, and perhaps a musical instrument like the *koto,* the Japanese harp. She probably will not have graduated from college, although she may have attended a specialty college for a while. If she is working, she likely is paid much less than her husband, even if she has an identical position (despite equal-pay laws). She may spend her time in the company preparing and serving tea for clients and employees, dusting the office, running errands, and answering telephones. When she has a baby, she will be expected to quit—although more women today are choosing to remain on the job.

Because the wife is expected to serve as the primary caregiver for the children, the husband is expected always to make his time available for the company. He may be asked to work weekends, to stay out late most of the week (about four out of seven nights), or even to be transferred to another branch in Japan or abroad without his family. This loyalty is rewarded in numerous ways: Unless the company goes bank-

rupt or the employee is unusually inept, he may be permitted to work for the company until he retires, usually at about age 55 or 60, even if the company no longer really needs his services; he and his wife will be taken on company sightseeing trips; the company will pay most of his health-insurance costs (the government pays the rest); and he will have the peace of mind that comes from being surrounded by lifelong friends and workmates. His association with company employees will be his main social outlet, even after retirement; upon his death, it will be his former workmates who organize and direct his Buddhist funeral services.

THE FAMILY

The loyalty once given to the traditional Japanese extended family, called the *ie,* has now been transferred to the modern company. This is logical from a historical perspective, since the modern company once began as a family business and was gradually expanded to include more workers, or "siblings." Thus, whereas the family is seen as the backbone of most societies, it might be more accurate to argue that the *kaisha,* or company, is the basis of modern Japanese society. As one Japanese commentator explained, "In the West, the home is the cornerstone of people's lives. In Tokyo, home is just a place to sleep at night. . . . Each family member—husband, wife, and children—has his own community centered outside the home."

Thus, the common image that Westerners hold of the centrality of the family to Japanese culture may be inaccurate. For instance, father absence is epidemic in Japan. It is an unusual father who eats more than one meal a day with his family. He may go shopping or to a park with his family when he has free time from work, but he is more likely to go golfing with a workmate. Schooling occupies the bulk of the children's time, even on weekends. And with fewer children than in earlier generations and with appliance-equipped apartments, many Japanese women rejoin the workforce after their children are self-maintaining.

Japan's divorce rate, while rising, is still considerably lower than in other industrialized nations, a fact that may seem incongruent with the conditions described above. Yet, as explained by one Japanese sociologist, Japanese couples "do not expect much emotional closeness; there is less pressure on us to meet each other's emotional needs. If we become close, that is a nice dividend, but if we do not, it is not a problem because we did not expect it in the first place."

Despite these modifications to the common Western image of the Japanese family, Japanese families do have significant roles to play in society. Support for education is one of the most important. Families, especially mothers, support the schools by being actively involved in the parent–teacher association, by insisting that children be given plenty of homework, and by saving for college so that the money for tuition is available without the college student having to work.

Another important function of the family is mate selection. Somewhat less than half of current Japanese marriages are arranged by the family or have occurred as a result of far more family involvement than in North America. Families sometimes ask a go-between(an uncle, a boss, or another trusted person) to compile a list of marriageable candidates. Criteria such as social class, blood type, and occupation are considered. Photos of prospective candidates are presented to the unmarried son or daughter, who has the option to veto any of them or to date those he or she finds acceptable. Young people, however, increasingly select their mates with little or no input from parents.

Finally, families in Japan, even those in which the children are married and living away from home, continue to gather for the purpose of honoring the memory of deceased family members or to enjoy one another's company for New Year's Day, Children's Day, and other celebrations.

WOMEN IN JAPAN

Ancient Confucian values held that women were legally and socially inferior to men. This produced a culture in feudal Japan in which the woman was expected to walk several steps

(UN photo by Jan Corash)
In Japan, not unlike in many other parts of the world, economic well-being often requires two incomes. Still, there is strong social pressure on women to stop working once they have a baby. All generations of family members take part in childrearing.

behind her husband when in public, to eat meals only after the husband had eaten, to forgo formal education, and to serve the husband and male members of the family whenever possible. A good woman was said to be one who would endure these conditions without complaint. This pronounced gender difference can be seen today in myriad ways, including in the preponderance of males in positions of leadership in business and politics, in the smaller percentage of women college graduates, and in the pay differential between women and men.

Given the Confucian values noted above, one would expect that all top leaders would be males. However, women's roles are also subject to the complexity of both ancient and modern cultures. Between A.D. 592 and 770, for instance, of the 12 reigning emperors, half were women. In rural areas today, women take an active decision-making role in farm associations. In the urban workplace, some women occupy typically pink-collar positions (nurses, clerks, and so on), but many women are also doctors and business executives; 28,000 are company presidents.

Thus, it is clear that within the general framework of gender inequality imposed by Confucian values, Japanese culture, especially at certain times, has been rather lenient in its application of those values. There is still considerable social pressure on women to stop working once they marry, and particularly after they have a baby, but it is clear that many women are resisting that pressure: one out of every three employees in Japan is female, and nearly 60 percent of the female workforce are married. An equal-pay law was enacted in 1989 that makes it illegal to pay women less for doing comparable work (although it may take years for companies to comply fully). And the Ministry of Education has mandated that home economics and shop classes now be required for both boys and girls; that is, both girls and boys will learn to cook and sew as well as construct things out of wood and metal.

In certain respects, Japanese women seem more assertive than women in the West. For example, in a recent national election, a wife challenged her husband for his seat in the House of Representatives (something that has not been done in the United States, where male candidates usually expect their wives to stump for them). Significantly, too, the former head of the Japan Socialist Party was an unmarried woman, Takako Doi. Women have been elected to the powerful Tokyo Metropolitan Council and awarded professorships at prestigious universities such as Tokyo University. And, while women continue to be used as sexual objects in pornography and prostitution, certain kinds of misogynistic behavior, such as rape and serial killing, are less frequent in Japan than in Western societies. Indeed, Western women visiting Japan often report that they felt free to walk outside alone at night for the first time in their lives.

Recent studies show that many Japanese women believe that their lives are easier than those of most Westerners. With their husbands working long hours and their one or two children in school all day, Japanese women find they have more leisure time than Western women. Gender-based social divisions remain apparent throughout Japanese culture, but modern Japanese women have learned to blend these divisions with the realities and opportunities of the contemporary workplace and home.

RELIGION/ETHICS

There are many holidays in Japan, most of which have a religious origin. This fact, as well as the existence of numerous shrines and temples, may leave the impression that Japan is a rather religious country. This is not true, however. Only about 15 percent of the Japanese people claim any active

(The Bettmann Archive)

Religion in Japan, while not having a large active affiliation, is still an intricate part of the texture and history of the culture. This temple in Kyoto was founded in the twelfth century.

religious affiliation, although many will stop by a shrine occasionally to ask for divine help in passing an exam, finding a mate, or recovering from an illness.

Nevertheless, modern Japanese culture sprang from a rich religious heritage. The first influence on Japanese culture came from the animistic Shinto religion, from whence modern Japanese acquired their respect for the beauty of nature. Confucianism brought a respect for hierarchy and education. Taoism stressed introspection, and Buddhism taught the need for good behavior now in order to acquire a better life in the future.

Shinto was selected in the 1930s as the state religion and was used as a divine justification for Japan's military exploits of that era, but most Japanese today will say that Japan is, culturally, a Buddhist nation. Some new Buddhist denominations have attracted thousands of followers. The rudiments of Christianity are also a part of the modern Japanese consciousness, but few Japanese have actually joined Christian churches.

Most Japanese regard morality as springing from within the group rather than pronounced from above. That is, a Japanese person may refrain from stealing so as not to offend the owner of an object or bring shame upon the family, rather than because of a divine prohibition against stealing. Thus we find in Japan a relatively small rate of violent—that is, public—crimes, and a much larger rate of white-collar crimes such as embezzlement, in which offenders believe that they can get away with something without creating a public scandal for their families.

THE GOVERNMENT

The Constitution of postwar Japan became effective in 1947 and firmly established the Japanese people as the ultimate source of sovereignty, with the emperor as the symbol of the nation. The national Parliament, or Diet, is empowered to pass legislation. The Diet is divided into two houses: the House of Representatives, with 511 members elected for 4-year terms; and the House of Councillors, with 252 members elected for 6-year terms from each of the 47 prefectures (states) of Japan as well as nationally. The prime minister, assisted by a cabinet, is also the leader of the party with the most seats in the Diet. Prefectures are governed by an elected governor and an assembly, and cities and towns are governed by elected mayors and town councils. The Supreme Court, consisting of a chief judge and 14 other judges, is independent of the legislative branch of government.

Japan's Constitution forbids Japan from engaging in war or from having military capability that would allow it to attack another country. Japan does maintain a well-equipped self-defense force, but it relies on a security treaty with the United States in case of serious aggression against it. In recent years the United States has been encouraging Japan to assume more of the burden of the military security of the Asian region, and Japan has increased its expenditures in absolute terms. But until the Constitution is amended, Japan is not likely to initiate any major upgrading of its military capability. This is in line with the general wishes of the Japanese people, who, since the devastation of Hiroshima and Nagasaki, have become firmly committed to a pacifist foreign policy. Moreover, Japanese leaders fear that any significant increase in military capability would re-ignite dormant fears about Japanese intentions within the increasingly vital Pacific Rim area.

This tendency toward not wanting to get involved militarily is reflected in one of Japan's most recent performances on the world stage. The Japanese were slow to play any significant part in supporting military expenditures for the Persian Gulf War, even when the outcome had a direct potential effect on their economy. The Iraqi invasion of Kuwait in August 1990 brought on the wrath—against Japan—of a coalition of countries led by the United States in January 1991, but it generated an initial commitment from Japan of only $2 billion (later increased to $9 billion, still a small fraction of the cost) and no personnel of any kind. This meager support was criticized by some foreign observers, who pointed out that Japan relies heavily on Gulf oil.

In 1992, the Japanese government announced its intention of building its own F-16–type jet-fighter planes; and subsequently, amid protests from the public, the Diet voted to send as many as 1,800 Japanese soldiers—the first to go abroad since World War II—to Cambodia to assist in the UN–supervised peacekeeping effort. Countries that had experienced the full force of Japanese domination in the past, such as China and Korea, expressed dismay at these evidences of Japan's modern military capability, but the United States welcomed the moves as an indication of Japan's willingness to share the costs of providing military security to Asia.

The Japanese have formed numerous political parties to represent their views in government. Among these have been the Japan Communist Party, the Social Democratic Party, and the New Frontier Party. For nearly 40 years, however, the most powerful party was the Liberal Democratic Party (LDP). Formed in 1955, it guided Japan to its current position of economic strength, but a series of sex and bribery scandals caused it to lose control of the government in 1993. A shaky coalition of eight parties took control for about a year but was replaced by an even more unlikely coalition of the LDP and the Japan Socialists—historic enemies who were unable to agree on most policies. Eventually, the LDP was able to regain some of its lost political clout; but, with some half a dozen changes in the prime ministership in the 1990s and party realignments in 1994 and 1996, it would be an understatement to say that Japan's government is in flux.

Part of the reason for this instability can be explained by Japan's party faction system. Party politics in Japan has always been a mixture of Western-style democratic practice and feudalistic personal relationships. Japanese parties are really several parties rolled into one. That is, parties are divided into several factions, each comprised of a group of loyal younger members headed by a powerful member of the

Prepottery, paleolithic culture 20,000–4,500 B.C.	Jomon culture with distinctive pottery 4,500–250 B.C.	Yayoi culture with rice agriculture, Shinto religion, and Japanese language 250 B.C.–A.D. 300	The Yamato period; warrior clans import Chinese culture A.D. 300–700	The Nara period; Chinese-style bureaucratic government at the capital at Nara 710–794	The Heian period; the capital is at Kyoto 794–1185	The Kamakura period; feudalism and shoguns; Buddhism is popularized 1185–1333	The Muromachi period; Western missionaries and traders arrive; feudal lords control their own domains 1333–1568	The Momoyama period; feudal lords become subject to one central leader; attempted invasion of Korea 1568–1600

Diet. The senior member has a duty to pave the way for the younger members politically, but they, in turn, are obligated to support the senior member in votes and in other ways. The faction leader's role in gathering financial support for faction members is particularly important, because Diet members are expected by the electorate to be patrons of numerous causes, from charity drives to the opening of a constituent's fast-food business. Because parliamentary salaries are inadequate to the task, outside funds, and thus the faction, are crucial. The size and power of the various factions are often the critical elements in deciding who will assume the office of prime minister and who will occupy which cabinet seats. The role of these intraparty factions is so central to Japanese politics that attempts to ban them have never been successful.

The factional nature of Japanese party politics means that cabinet and other political positions are frequently rotated. This would yield considerable instability in governance were it not for the stabilizing influence of the Japanese bureaucracy. Large and powerful, the career bureaucracy is responsible for drafting more than 80 percent of the bills submitted to the Diet. Many of the bureaucrats are graduates from the finest universities in Japan, particularly Tokyo University, which provides some 80 percent of the senior officials in the more than 20 national ministries. Many of them consider their role in long-range forecasting, drafting legislation, and implementing policies to be superior to that of the elected officials under whom they work. They reason that, whereas the politicians are bound to the whims of the people they represent, bureaucrats are committed to the nation of Japan—to, as it were, the *idea* of Japan. Thus, government service is considered a higher calling than are careers in private business, law, or other fields.

In addition to the bureaucracy, Japanese politicians have leaned heavily on big business to support their policies of postwar reconstruction, economic growth, and social reform. Business has accepted heavy taxation so that social welfare programs such as the national health plan are feasible, and they have supported political candidates through substantial financial help. In turn, the government has seen its role as that of facilitating the growth of private industry (some critics claim that the relationship between government and business is so close that Japan is best described not as a nation but as "Japan, Inc."). Consider, for example, the powerful Ministry of International Trade and Industry (MITI). Over the years, it has worked closely with business, particularly the Federation of Economic Organizations (Keidanren) to forecast potential market shifts, develop strategies for market control, and generally pave the way for Japanese businesses to succeed in the international marketplace. The close working relationship between big business and the national government is an established fact of life in Japan, and, despite criticism from countries with a more laissez faire approach to business, it will undoubtedly continue into the future, because it has served Japan well.

THE FUTURE

In the postwar years of political stability, the Japanese have accomplished more than anyone, including themselves, thought possible. Japan's literacy rate is 99 percent, 99 percent of Japanese households have telephones, 99 percent have color televisions, and 75 percent own automobiles. Nationalized health care covers every Japanese citizen, and the Japanese have the highest life expectancy in the world. With only half the population of the United States, a land area about the size of Great Britain, and extremely limited natural resources (it has to import 99.6 percent of its oil, 99.8 percent of its iron, and 86.7 percent of its coal), Japan has nevertheless created the second-largest economy in the world. Where does it go from here?

When the Spanish were establishing hegemony over large parts of the globe, they were driven in part by the desire to bring Christianity to the "heathen." The British, for their part, believed that they were taking "civilization" to the "savages" of the world. China and the former Soviet Union were once strongly committed to the ideals of communism, while the United States has felt that its mission is that of expanding democracy and capitalism.

What about Japan? For what reason do Japanese businesses buy up hotels in New Zealand and skyscrapers in New York? What role does Japan have to play in the world in addition to spawning economic development? What values will guide and perhaps temper Japan's drive for economic dominance?

These are questions that the Japanese people themselves are attempting to answer; but, finding no ready answers, they are beginning to encounter more and more difficulties with the world around them and within their own society. Animosity over the persistent trade imbalance in Japan's favor continues to simmer in Europe and North America as well as in some countries of the Pacific Rim. To deflect these criticisms, Japan has substantially increased its gift-giving to foreign governments, including allocating money for the stabilization or growth of democracy in Central/Eastern Europe and for easing the foreign debt burden of Mexico and other countries.

What Japan has been loathe to do, however, is remove the "structural impediments" that make it difficult for foreign

The Tokugawa Era; self-imposed isolation from the West **1600–1868**	The Meiji Restoration; modernization; Taiwan and Korea are under Japanese control **1868–1912**	The Taisho and Showa periods; militarization leads to war and Japan's defeat **1912–1945**	Japan surrenders; the U.S. Occupation imposes major changes in the organization of society **1945**	Sovereignty is returned to the Japanese people by treaty **1951**	The newly merged Liberal-Democratic Party wins control of the government **1955**	Japan passes the threshold of economic self-sustainability **1960s**	Student activism; the Nuclear Security Treaty with the United States is challenged **late 1960s**	The ruling party is hit by scandals but retains control of the government; Emperor Hirohito dies; Emperor Akihito succeeds **1980s**	**1990s**

Japan reacts to protectionism in major markets by turning its attention to the Pacific Rim

Japan sends troops to maintain peace in Cambodia; Japan remains the second-largest economy in the world

The Liberal Democratic Party loses control of the government after 38 years in power but recovers power in 1996

A devastating earthquake in Kobe kills more than 5,000 people

companies to do business in Japan. For example, 50 percent of the automobiles sold in Iceland are Japanese, which means less profit for the American and European manufacturers who used to dominate car sales there. Yet, because of high tariffs and other regulations, very few American and European cars have been sold in Japan. Beginning in the mid-1980s, Japan reluctantly began to dismantle many of these trade barriers, and it has been so successful that it now has a lower overall average tariff on nonagricultural products than the United States—its severest critic in this arena.

But Japanese people worry that further opening of their markets may destroy some fundamentals of Japanese life. Rice, for instance, costs much more in Japan than it should, because the Japanese government protects rice farmers with subsidies and limits most rice imports from abroad. The Japanese would prefer to pay less for rice at the supermarket, but they also argue that foreign competition would prove the undoing of many small rice farmers, whose land would then be sold to housing developers. This, in turn, would destroy more of Japan's scarce arable land and weaken the already shaky traditions of the Japanese countryside—the heart of traditional Japanese culture and values.

Today, thousands of foreign firms do business in Japan; some of them, like Polaroid and Schick, control the Japanese market in their products. Foreign investment in Japan has grown about 16 percent annually since 1980. In the case of the United States, the profit made by American firms doing business in Japan (nearly 800 of them) in a single year is just about equal to the amount of the trade imbalance between Japan and the United States. Japanese supermarkets are filled with foreign foodstuffs, and the radio and television airwaves are filled with the sounds and sights of Western music and dress. Japanese youth are as likely to eat at McDonald's or

Kentucky Fried Chicken outlets as at traditional Japanese restaurants, and many Japanese have never worn a kimono nor learned to play a Japanese musical instrument. It is clear to many observers that, culturally, Japan already imports much more from the West than the West does from Japan.

Given this overwhelming Westernization of Japan as well as Japan's current capacity to continue imbibing Western culture, even the change-oriented Japanese are beginning to ask where they, as a nation, are going. Will national wealth, as it slowly trickles down to individuals, produce a generation of hedonistic youths who do not appreciate the sacrifices of those before them? Will wealthy Japanese people be satisfied with the small homes and tiny yards that their forebears had to accept? Will there ever be a time when, strapped for resources, the Japanese will once again seek hegemony over other nations? What future role should Japan assume in the international arena, apart from economic development? If these questions remain to be answered, circumstances of international trade have at least provided an answer to the question of Japan's role in the Pacific Rim countries: It is clear that, for the next several decades, Japan will continue to shape the pace and nature of economic development, and thus the political environment, of the entire Pacific Rim.

DEVELOPMENT

Japan is now entering a post-smokestack era in which primary industries are being moved abroad, producing a hollowing effect inside Japan and increasing the likelihood of rising unemployment. Nevertheless, prospects for continued growth are excellent.

FREEDOM

Japanese citizens enjoy full civil liberties, and opposition parties and ideologies are seen as natural and useful components of democracy. Certain people, however, such as those of Korean ancestry, have been subject to both social and official discrimination—an issue that is gaining the attention of the Japanese.

HEALTH/WELFARE

The Japanese live longer on average than any other people on earth. Every citizen is provided with inexpensive medical care under a national health-care system, but many people still prefer to save substantial portions of their income for health emergencies and old age.

ACHIEVEMENTS

Japan has achieved virtually complete literacy. Although there are poor areas, there are no slums inhabited by a permanent underclass. The gaps between the social classes appear to be less pronounced than in many other societies. The country seems to be entering an era of remarkable educational and technological achievement.

Australia (Commonwealth of Australia)

GEOGRAPHY

Area in Square Kilometers (Miles):
7,686,850 (2,867,896)
Capital (Population): Canberra (310,000)
Climate: generally arid to semiarid;
temperate in the south and east;
tropical in the north

PEOPLE

Population

Total: 18,322,000
Annual Growth Rate: 1.31%
Rural/Urban Population (Ratio): 15/85
Ethnic Makeup: 95% European ancestry;
4% Asian; 1% Aboriginal and others
Major Languages: English;
indigenous languages

Health

Life Expectancy at Birth: 75 years
(male); 81 years (female)
Infant Mortality Rate (Ratio): 7.1/1,000
Average Caloric Intake: 118% of
FAO minimum
Physicians Available (Ratio): 1/438

Religions

26% Anglican; 26% Roman Catholic;
24% other Christian; 24% other or
no affiliation

A LAND OF HEAT AND HARD WORK

Some people immigrate to Australia hoping that the relatively inexpensive land
and strong economy will easily provide them with a high standard of living.
But in character, many parts of Australia are like the American Wild West of
the 1870s: Sweaty and persistent hard work and luck are the only keys to
success. For example, cattle ranches in parts of Australia can have as many as
70,000 head of cattle to be cared for over a 5-million-acre spread. Just providing
water in the arid climate is a formidable task; dozens of wells must be dug to
reach the water table lying far below the earth's surface. Ranchers must also
contend with daily temperatures above 100°F and brush fires that destroy hundreds of acres of grassland and roast sheep and cattle alive. In 1994, some 155
wildfires destroyed thousands of homes and nearly 2 million acres, including
98 percent of the Royal National Park near Sydney. In the summer (February)
of 1993, temperatures in southern and eastern Australia hit 113°F, while in
1995, persistent drought reduced agricultural production by 20 percent.

Education

Adult Literacy Rate: 98%

COMMUNICATION

Telephones: 8,700,000
Newspapers: 143

TRANSPORTATION

Highways—Kilometers (Miles):
837,872 (51,948)

Railroads—Kilometers (Miles):
40,478 (25,096)
Usable Airfields: 439

GOVERNMENT

Type: federal parliamentary state
Independence Date: January 1, 1901
Head of State/Government: Queen
Elizabeth II, represented by Governor
General William Deane; Prime
Minister John Howard
Political Parties: Australian Labour
Party; Liberal Party; National Party;
Australian Democratic Party
Suffrage: universal and compulsory
at age 18

MILITARY

Number of Armed Forces: 68,300
*Military Expenditures (% of Central
Government Expenditures):* 2.4%
Current Hostilities: none

ECONOMY

Currency ($ U.S. Equivalent): 1.31
Australian dollars = $1
Per Capita Income/GDP:
$20,720/$374.6 billion
Inflation Rate: 0.8%
Natural Resources: bauxite;
diamonds; coal; copper; iron; oil;
gas; other minerals
Agriculture: beef; wool; mutton;
wheat; barley; sugarcane; fruit
Industry: mining; industrial and
transportation equipment; food
processing; chemicals; steel; motor
vehicles

FOREIGN TRADE

Exports: $50.4 billion
Imports: $51.1 billion

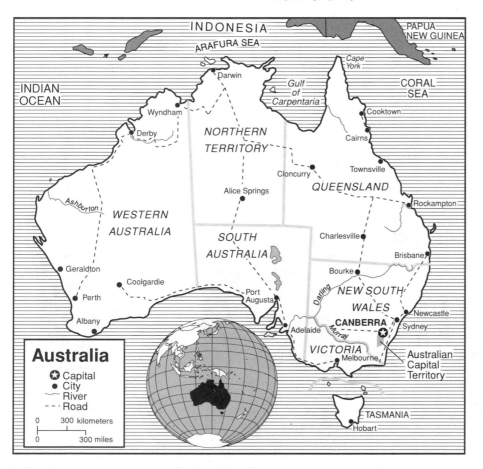

Australia
- ✪ Capital
- ● City
- River
- --- Road

0 300 kilometers
0 300 miles

THE LAND NO ONE WANTED

Despite its out-of-the-way location, far south of the main trading routes between Europe and Asia, seafarers from England, Spain, and the Netherlands began exploring parts of the continent of Australia in the seventeenth century. The French later made some forays along the coast, but it was the British who first found something to do with a land that others had disparaged as useless: They decided to send their prisoners there. The British had long believed that the easiest solution to prison overcrowding was expulsion from Britain. Convicts had been sent to the American colonies for many years, but after American independence was declared in 1776, Britain began to send prisoners to Australia.

Australia seemed like the ideal spot for a penal colony: It was isolated from the centers of civilization; it had some good harbors; and, although much of the continent was a flat, dry, riverless desert with only sparse vegetation, the coastal fringes were well suited to human habitation. Indeed, although the British did not know it in the 1700s, they had come across a huge continent endowed with abundant natural resources. Along the northern coast (just south of present-day Indonesia and New Guinea) was a tropical zone with heavy rainfall and tropical forests. The eastern coast was wooded with valuable pine trees, while the western coast was dotted with eucalyptus and acacia trees. Minerals, especially coal, gold, nickel, petroleum, iron, and bauxite, were plentiful, as were the many species of unique animals: kangaroos, platypus, and koalas, to name a few.

The British chose to build their first penal colony in what is now Sydney. By the 1850s, when the practice of transporting convicts stopped, more than 150,000 prisoners, including hundreds of women, had been sent there and to other colonies. Most of them were illiterate English and Irish from the lower socioeconomic classes. Once they completed their sentences, they were set free to settle on the continent. These individuals, their guards, and gold prospectors constituted the beginning of Australian society. Today, despite more than 18 million inhabitants, Australia remains a sparsely populated continent.

RACE RELATIONS

Convicts certainly did not constitute the beginning of human habitation on the continent. Tens of thousands of Aborigines (literally, "first inhabitants") inhabited Australia and the nearby island of Tasmania when Europeans first made contact. Living in scattered tribes and speaking hundreds of entirely unrelated languages, the Aborigines, whose origin is unknown (some scholars see connections to Africa, the Indian subcontinent, and the Melanesian Islands), survived by fishing and nomadic hunting. Succumbing to European diseases, violence, forced removal from their lands, and, finally, neglect, thousands of Aborigines died during the first centuries of contact. Indeed, the entire Tasmanian race (originally 5,000 people) is now extinct.

Most Aborigines eventually adopted European ways, including Christianity. Today, they live in the cities or work for cattle and sheep ranchers. Others reside on reserves (tribal reservations) in the central and northern parts of Australia. Modernization has affected even the reservation Aborigines—some have telephones, and some dispersed tribes in the Northern Territories communicate with one another by satellite-linked video conferencing—but in the main, they continue to live as they have always done, organizing their religion around plant or animal sacred symbols, or totems, and initiating youth into

(San Diego Convention and Visitors Bureau)

Australia has a number of animals that are, in their native form, unique in the world. The koala is found only in the eastern coastal region, where it feeds very selectively on the leaves of the eucalyptus tree. It is a marsupial and bears its young every other year. Pictured above is a very rare baby albino koala with its mother.

adulthood through lengthy and sometimes painful rituals.

Whereas the United States began with 13 founding colonies, Australia started with six, none of which felt a compelling need to unite into a single nation until the 1880s, when other European powers began taking an interest in settling the continent. It was not until 1901 that Australians formally separated from Great Britain (while remaining within the British Commonwealth with the Queen of England as head of state). Populated almost entirely by whites from Britain or Europe (people of European descent still constitute about 95 percent of Australia's population), Australia has maintained close cultural and diplomatic links with Britain and the West, at the expense of ties with the geographically closer nations of Asia.

Reaction against Polynesians, Chinese, and other Asian immigrants in the late 1800s produced an official "White Australia" policy, which remained intact until the 1960s and effectively excluded nonwhites from settling in Australia. During the 1960s, the government made an effort to relax these restrictions and to restore land and some measure of self-determination to Aborigines. In the 1990s, Aborigines successfully persuaded the federal government to block a dam project on Aboriginal land that would have destroyed sacred sites. The federal government sided with the Aborigines against white developers and local government officials. In 1993, despite some public resistance, the government passed laws protecting the land claims of Aborigines and set up a fund to assist Aborigines with land purchases. Evidence of continued racism can be found, however, in such graffiti painted on walls of highrise buildings as "Go home Japs!" (in this case, the term "Jap," or, alternatively, "wog," refers to any Asian, regardless of nationality). The unemployment rate of Aborigines is 4 times that of the nation as a whole, and a 1995 survey revealed substantially higher rates of chronic health problems and death by infectious diseases among this population.

ECONOMIC PRESSURES

Despite lingering discriminatory attitudes against nonwhites, events since World War II have forced Australians to reconsider their position, at least economically, vis-à-vis Asia and Southeast Asia. Australia has never been conquered by a foreign power (not even by Japan during World War II), but the impressive industrial strength of Japan now allows its people to enjoy higher per capita income than that of Australians, and Singapore is not far behind. Moreover, since Australia's economy is based on the export of primary goods (for example, minerals, wheat, beef, and wool) rather than the much more lucrative consumer products manufactured from raw resources, it is likely that Australia will continue to lose ground to the more economically aggressive and heavily populated Asian economies.

This inexorable alteration in socioeconomic status will be a new experience and difficult for Australians, whose standard of living has been the highest in the Pacific

(Australian Information Service photo)

When Europeans first landed on Australia, they found the continent inhabited by Aborigines, who had survived for millennia by fishing and nomadic hunting. With the Europeans came disease, violence, and neglect. Most Aborigines eventually adapted to the newcomers' customs, but some continue to live in their traditional ways on tribal reservations.

European exploration of the Australian coastline begins **1600s**	British explorers first land in Australia **1688**	The first shipment of English convicts arrives **1788**	The gold rush lures thousands of immigrants **1851**	Australia becomes independent within the British Commonwealth **1901**

Rim for decades. Building on a foundation of sheep (imported in the 1830s and now supplying more than a quarter of the world's supply of wool), mining (gold was discovered in 1851), and agriculture (Australia is nearly self-sufficient in food), the country has developed its manufacturing sector such that Australians are able to enjoy a standard of living equal in most respects to that of North Americans.

But as the year 2000 approaches, Australians look warily at the growing tendency to create mammoth trading blocs, such as the North American Free Trade Association, consisting of the United States, Canada, Mexico, and others; the European Union (formerly the European Community), eventually including, perhaps, parts of Central/Eastern Europe; the ASEAN nations of Southeast Asia; and an informal "yen bloc" in Asia, headed by Japan. These blocs might exclude Australian products from preferential trade treatment or eliminate them from certain markets altogether. Beginning in 1983, therefore, the Labour government of then–prime minister Robert Hawke began to establish collaborative trade agreements with Asian countries, a plan that seemed to have the support of the electorate, even though it meant reorienting Australia's foreign policy away from its traditional posture Westward.

In the early 1990s, under Labour prime minister Paul Keating, the Asianization plan intensified. The Japanese prime minister and the governor of Hong Kong visited Australia, while Australian leaders made calls on the leaders of South Korea, China, Thailand, Vietnam, Malaysia, and Laos. Trade and security agreements were signed with Singapore and Indonesia, and a national curriculum plan was implemented whereby 60 percent of Australian schoolchildren will be studying Japanese and other Asian languages by the year 2010. The Liberal Party prime minister, John Howard, elected in 1996, has also moderated his views on Asian immigration and now advocates a nondiscriminatory immigration policy rather than the restrictive policy he promoted in the 1980s.

Despite such initiatives (and a few successes: Japan now buys more beef from Australia than from the United States), the economic threat to Australia remains.

Even in the islands of the Pacific, an area that Australia and New Zealand generally have considered their own domain for economic investment and foreign aid, new investments by Asian countries are beginning to winnow Australia's sphere of influence. U.S. president Bill Clinton, in a 1996 visit to Australia, promised Australian leaders that they would not be left out of the emerging economic structures of the region, but years of recession and an unemployment rate over 8.5 percent in 1996, with nearly 2 million people living in poverty, leave Australians rather wary of their economic future.

THE AMERICAN CONNECTION

By any standard, Australia is a democracy solidly embedded in the traditions of the West. Political power is shared back and forth between the Labour Party and the Liberal-National Country Party coalition, and the Constitution is based on both British parliamentary tradition and the U.S. model. Thus, it has followed that Australia and the United States have built a warm friendship as both political and military allies. A military mutual-assistance agreement, ANZUS (for Australia, New Zealand, and the United States), was concluded after World War II (New Zealand withdrew in 1986). And just as it had sent troops to fight Germany during World Wars I and II, Australia sent troops to fight in the Korean War in 1950 and the Vietnam War in the 1960s—although anti–Vietnam War sentiment in Australia strained relations somewhat with the United States at that time. Australia also joined the United States and other countries in 1954 in establishing the Southeast Asia Treaty Organization, an Asian counterpart to the North Atlantic Treaty Organization designed to contain the spread of communism.

In 1991, when the Philippines refused to renew the lease on U.S. military bases there, there was much discussion about transferring U.S. operations to the Cockburn Sound Naval Base in Australia. Singapore was eventually chosen for some of the operations, but the incident reveals the close relationship of the two nations. U.S. military aircraft already land in Australia, and submarines and other naval craft call at Australian ports. The Americans also use Australian territory for surveillance fa-

cilities. There is historical precedence for this level of close cooperation: Before the U.S. invasion of the Japanese-controlled Philippines in the 1940s, the United States based its Pacific-theater military headquarters in Australia; moreover, Great Britain's inability to lead the fight against Japan forced Australia to look to the United States.

A few Australians resent the violation of sovereignty represented by the U.S. bases, but most regard the United States as a solid ally. Indeed, many Australians regard their country as the Southern Hemisphere's version of the United States: Both countries have space and vast resources, both were founded as disparate colonies that eventually united and obtained independence from Britain, and both share a common language and a Western cultural heritage.

There is yet another way that Australia is, or would like to be, like the United States: It wants to be a republic. A little less than half the population say that they can see no reason to remain a constitutional monarchy, with the king or queen of England as the head of state. Therefore, in 1993, the prime minister met with Queen Elizabeth II to announce his intention of turning Australia into a republic (within the British Commonwealth) by the year 2001. The queen indicated that she would respect the wishes of the people, but what the people want is still not clear—in 1996, they chose a new antirepublic leader, John Howard of the Liberal Party, who enthusiastically swore allegiance to the queen upon his inauguration as prime minister.

Unlike New Zealand, which has distanced itself from the United States by refusing to allow nuclear-armed ships to enter its ports and has withdrawn from ANZUS, Australia has joined with the United States in attempting to dissuade South Pacific states from declaring the region a nuclear-free zone. Yet it has also maintained good ties with the small and vulnerable societies of the Pacific through its leadership in such regional associations as the South Pacific Commission, the South Pacific Forum, and the ever-more-influential Asia–Pacific Economic Cooperation Group (APEC). It has also condemned nuclear bomb testing programs in French-controlled territories.

Australia is threatened by Japan during World War II
1940s

Australia proposes the South Pacific Commission
1947

Australia joins New Zealand and the United States in the ANZUS military security agreement
1951

Australia joins the South East Asian Treaty Organization
1954

Relations with the United States are strained over the Vietnam War
1960s

The Australian Labour Party wins for the first time in 23 years; Gough Whitlam is prime minister
1972

After a constitutional crisis, Whitlam is replaced by opposition leader J. M. Fraser
1975

Australia begins to strengthen its economic ties with Asian countries

Depletion of the ozone layer is believed to be responsible for a rapidly rising incidence of skin cancer among Australians
1980s

1990s

After six terms, the Labour Party is defeated by Liberal Party leader John Howard

Australia condemns nuclear testing in the Pacific; recalls French ambassador

AUSTRALIA AND THE PACIFIC

Australia was not always possessed of good intentions toward the islands around it. For one thing, white Australians thought of themselves as superior to the brown-skinned islanders; and for another, Australia preferred to use the islands' resources for its own economic gain, with little regard for the islanders themselves. At the end of World War I, for example, the phosphate-rich island of Nauru, formerly under German control, was assigned to Australia as a trust territory. Until phosphate mining was turned over to the islanders in 1967, Australian farmers consumed large quantities of phosphate but paid just half the market price. Worse, only a tiny fraction of the proceeds went to the people of Nauru. Similarly, in Papua New Guinea, Australia controlled the island without taking significant steps toward its domestic development until the 1960s, when, under the guidance of the United Nations, it did an about-face and facilitated changes that advanced the successful achievement of independence in 1975.

In addition to forgoing access to cheap resources, Australia was reluctant to relinquish control of these islands because it saw them as a shield against possible military attack. It learned this lesson well in World War II. In 1941, Japan, taking advantage of the Western powers' preoccupation with Adolf Hitler, moved quickly to expand its imperial designs in Asia and the Pacific. The Japanese first disabled the U.S. Navy by attacking its warships docked in Pearl Harbor, Hawaii. They then moved on to oust the British in Hong Kong and the Gilbert Islands, and the Americans in Guam and Wake Island. Within 5 months, the Japanese had taken control of Burma, Malaya, Borneo, the Philippines, Singapore, and hundreds of tiny Pacific islands, which they used to create an immense defensive perimeter around the home islands of Japan. They also had captured part of New Guinea and were keeping a large force there, which greatly concerned the Australians. Yet fighting was kept away from Australia proper when the Japanese were successfully engaged by Australian and American troops in New Guinea. Other Pacific islands were regained from the Japanese at a tremendous cost in lives and military hardware. Japan's defeat came only when islands close enough to Japan to be attacked by U.S. bomber aircraft were finally captured. Japan surrendered in 1945, but the colonial powers had learned that possession of small islands could have strategic importance. This experience is part of the reason for colonial Europe's reluctance to grant independence to the vast array of islands over which they have exercised control. Australia is now faced with the question of whether or not to grant independence to the 4,000 inhabitants of Christmas Island who recently voted to become a self-ruling territory within Australia.

There is no doubt that stressful historical episodes such as World War II drew the English-speaking countries of the South Pacific closer together and closer to the United States. But recent realignments in the global economic system are creating strains. When the United States insists that Japan take steps to ease the billowing U.S.–Japan trade imbalance, Australia sometimes comes out the loser. For instance, both Australia and the United States are producers of coal, and, given the nearly equal distance between those two countries and Japan, it would be logical to expect that Japan would buy coal at about the same price from both countries. In fact, however, Japan pays $7 a ton more for American coal than for Australian coal, a discrepancy directly attributable to Japan's attempt to reduce the trade imbalance with the United States. Resentment against the United States over such matters is likely to grow, and managing such international tensions will no doubt challenge the skills of the leadership of Australia well into the next century.

DEVELOPMENT

Mining of nickel, iron ore, and other metals continues to supply a substantial part of Australia's gross domestic product. In recent years, Japan has become Australia's primary trading partner rather than Great Britain. Seven out of 10 of Australia's largest export markets are Asian countries.

FREEDOM

Australia is a parliamentary democracy adhering to the ideals incorporated in English common law. Constitutional guarantees of human rights apply to all of Australia's 18 million citizens. However, social discrimination continues, and, despite improvements since the 1960s, the Aborigines remain a neglected part of Australian society.

HEALTH/WELFARE

Like New Zealand, Australia has developed a complex and comprehensive system of social welfare. Education is the province of the several states. Public education is compulsory. Australia boasts several world-renowned universities. The world's first voluntary euthanasia law passed in Northern Territory in 1996, but legal challenges prevent its use.

ACHIEVEMENTS

The vastness and challenge of Australia's interior lands, called the "outback," have inspired a number of Australian writers to create outstanding poetry and fictional novels. In 1973, Patrick White became the first Australian to win a Nobel Prize in Literature. Jill Ker Conway, Thomas Keneally, and Colleen McCullough are other well-known Australian authors.

Brunei (Negara Brunei Darussalam)

GEOGRAPHY

Area in Square Kilometers (Miles): 5,770 (2,228) (slightly larger than Delaware)
Capital (Population): Bandar Seri Begawan (51,000)
Climate: tropical

PEOPLE

Population

Total: 292,300
Annual Growth Rate: 2.77%
Rural/Urban Population (Ratio): n/a
Ethnic Makeup: 64% Malay; 20% Chinese; 16% others
Major Languages: Bahasa Melayu; English; Chinese; Iban; native dialects

Health

Life Expectancy at Birth: 70 years (male); 73 years (female)
Infant Mortality Rate (Ratio): 24.7/1,000
Average Caloric Intake: n/a
Physicians Available (Ratio): 1/2,176

Religions

63% Muslim; 15% indigenous beliefs; 14% Buddhist; 8% Christian

Education

Adult Literacy Rate: 77%

COMMUNICATION

Telephones: 33,300
Newspapers: 1

A LITTLE-KNOWN HAVEN

Brunei's capital—and its main center of population—is Bandar Seri Begawan, previously known as Brunei Town. Located approximately 10 miles from the mouth of the Brunei River, the town boasts pleasant sightseeing opportunities for travelers, including nearby beaches, the Hassanal Bolkiah Aquarium, and the Sultan Omar Ali Saifuddin Mosque, considered one of the most impressive examples of modern Islamic architecture in Southeast Asia. Visitors to the country are treated warmly, even when passing through immigration and customs; yet, due to its healthy reserves of foreign exchange earned from oil and gas revenues, the government has not actively pursued tourism. The British influence is palpable (English is one of the two official languages, and even the city museum is named after Winston Churchill) but wooden houses built on stilts over the water's edge clearly bespeak Bandar's Malay heritage.

TRANSPORTATION

Highways—Kilometers (Miles): 1,090 (676)
Railroads—Kilometers (Miles): 13 (8)
Usable Airfields: 5

GOVERNMENT

Type: Constitutional sultanate
Independence Date: January 1, 1984
Head of State: Sultan and Prime Minister Paduka Seri Baginda Sultan Haji Hassanal Bolkiah Mu'izzaddin Waddaulah
Political Parties: Brunei National United Party (inactive); Brunei National Democratic Party (the first legal party now banned)
Suffrage: none

MILITARY

Number of Armed Forces: 4,250
Military Expenditures (% of Central Government Expenditures): 6.2%
Current Hostilities: none

ECONOMY

Currency ($ U.S. Equivalent): 1.45 Bruneian dollars = $1
Per Capita Income/GDP: $16,000/$4.43 billion
Inflation Rate: 2.5%
Natural Resources: oil; gas; forest products
Agriculture: rice; vegetables; arable crops; fruits
Industry: oil (the prime industry, employing 7% of population); rubber; pepper; sawn lumber; gravel; animal hides

FOREIGN TRADE

Exports: $2.2 billion
Imports: $1.2 billion

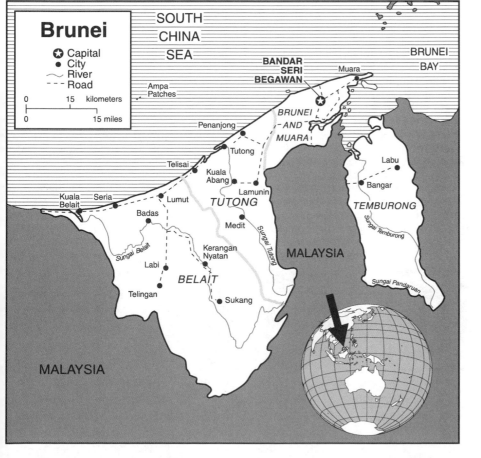

Brunei is first visited by Europeans
A.D. 1521

Brunei is known as haven for pirates
1700

Briton James Brooke is given Sarawak as reward for help in a civil war
1800s

The island of Labuan is ceded to Britain
1847

Britain attacks and ends pirate activities in Brunei
1849

The remainder of Brunei becomes a British protectorate
1888

The first Brunei Constitution is promulgated
1959

Brunei rejects confederation with Malaysia
1963

Brunei gains its independence
1984

1990s

The sultan of Brunei, Hassanal Bolkiah, is said to be the richest person in the world, with assets of $37 billion

Foreign workers are "imported" to ease the labor shortage

Brunei joins the International Monetary Fund

A WEALTHY COUNTRY

Home to only 292,300 people, Brunei rarely captures the headlines. But perhaps it should, for, despite its tiny size, the country boasts one of the highest living standards in the world. Moreover, the sultan of Brunei, with assets of $37 billion, is considered the richest person in the world. The secret? Oil. First exploited in Brunei in the late 1920s, today oil and natural gas almost entirely support the sultanate's economy, which has an economic growth rate of nearly 7 percent per year. The government's annual income is nearly twice its expenditures, despite the provision of free education and medical care, subsidized food and housing, and the absence of income taxes. Currently, Brunei is in the middle of a 5-year plan designed to diversify its economy and lessen its dependence on oil revenues, but 98 percent of the nation's revenues continues to depend on the sale of oil and natural gas. Japan purchases more than 60 percent of Brunei's exports; the other nations of the Asia Pacific purchase most of the remainder. Brunei's imports come primarily from Asia, especially Japan, and from the United States.

Muslim sultans ruled over the entire island of Borneo and other nearby islands during the sixteenth century. Advantageously located on the northwest coast of the island of Borneo, along the sea lanes of the South China Sea, Brunei was a popular resting spot for traders; and, during the 1700s, it became known as a haven for pirates. In the 1800s, the sultan then in power agreed to the kingdom becoming a protectorate of Britain in order to safeguard his domain from being further whittled away by aggressors bent on empire-building. The Japanese easily overtook Brunei in 1941,

when they launched their Southeast Asian offensive in search of oil and gas for their war machine. Today, the Japanese Mitsubishi Corporation has a one-third interest in the Brunei gas company.

In the 1960s, it was expected that Brunei, which is cut in two and surrounded on three sides by Malaysia, would join the newly proposed Federation of Malaysia; but it refused to do so, preferring to remain under British control. The decision to remain a colony was made by Sultan Sir Omar Ali Saifuddin. Educated in British Malaya, the sultan retained a strong affection for British culture and frequently visited the British Isles. (Brunei's 1959 Constitution, promulgated during Sir Omar's reign, reflected this attachment: It declared Brunei a self-governing state, with its foreign affairs and defense remaining the responsibility of Great Britain.)

In 1967, Sir Omar abdicated in favor of his son, who became the 29th ruler in succession. Sultan (and Prime Minister) Hassanal Bolkiah Mu'izzaddin Waddaulah (a shortened version of his name) oversaw Brunei's gaining of independence, in 1984. Not all Bruneians are pleased with the sultan's control over the political process, but opposition voices have been silenced. There are, in effect, no operative political parties in Brunei, and there have been no elections in the country since 1965, despite a constitutional provision for them.

Brunei's largest ethnic group is Malay, accounting for 64 percent of the population. Indians and Chinese constitute sizable minorities, as do indigenous peoples such as Ibans and Dyaks. Despite Brunei's historic ties with Britain, Europeans make up only a tiny fraction of the population.

Brunei is an Islamic nation with Hindu roots. Islam is the official state religion, and in recent years, the sultan has proposed bringing national laws more closely in line with Islamic ideology. Modern Brunei is officially a constitutional monarchy, headed by the sultan, a chief minister, and a Council; in reality, however, the sultan and his family control all aspects of state decision making. The Constitution provides the sultan with supreme executive authority in the state. In late 1995, Brunei joined with other ASEAN countries in declaring their region a nuclear-free zone.

In recent years, Brunei has been plagued by a chronic labor shortage. The government and Brunei Shell (a consortium owned jointly by the Brunei government and Shell Oil) are the largest employers in the country. They provide generous fringe benefits and high pay. Non-oil private-sector companies with fewer resources find it difficult to recruit in-country and have, therefore, employed many foreign workers. One third of all workers today in Brunei are foreigners. This situation is of considerable concern to the government, which is worried that social tensions between foreigners and residents, as is happening in other countries, may flare up in Brunei.

DEVELOPMENT

Brunei's economy is a mixture of the modern and the ancient: foreign and domestic entrepreneurship, government regulation and welfare statism, and village tradition. Chronic labor shortages are managed by the importation of thousands of foreign workers.

FREEDOM

Although Islam is the official state religion, the government practices religious tolerance. The Constitution provides the sultan with supreme executive authority, which he has used to suppress opposition groups and political parties.

HEALTH/WELFARE

The country's massive oil and natural gas revenues support wide-ranging benefits to the population, such as subsidized food, fuel, and housing, and free medical care and education. This distribution of wealth is reflected in Brunei's generally favorable quality-of-life indicators.

ACHIEVEMENTS

An important project has been the construction of a modern university accommodating 1,500 to 2,000 students. Since independence, the government has tried to strengthen and improve the economic, social, and cultural life of its people.

Cambodia (Kingdom of Cambodia)

GEOGRAPHY

Area in Square Kilometers (Miles):
181,040 (69,881) (slightly smaller than Oklahoma)
Capital (Population): Phnom Penh 800,000 (est.)
Climate: tropical

PEOPLE

Population

Total: 10,561,400
Annual Growth Rate: 2.83%
Rural/Urban Population (Ratio): 88/12
Ethnic Makeup: 90% Khmer (Cambodian); 5% Chinese; 5% others
Major Languages: Khmer; French

Health

Life Expectancy at Birth: 48 years (male); 51 years (female)
Infant Mortality Rate (Ratio): 109.6/1,000
Average Caloric Intake: 85% of FAO minimum
Physicians Available (Ratio): 1/27,000

Religions

95% Theravada Buddhist; 5% others

EDUCATION FOR A LAWLESS SOCIETY

Decades of chaos caused by civil war have produced a lawless society in Cambodia. Bandits and poorly paid soldiers stop travelers on highways to demand passage money, while the payment of bribes to government officials has become a necessary part of business. Lawlessness reaches down into the school system as well. When some 10,000 children took their high school entrance exams in 1996, cheating was so rampant that more than 100 police officers had to form a protective ring around each school offering the exam; the officers were there to prevent older siblings from slipping onto the schools grounds and calling out the answers to students inside. Parents and older siblings tried to thwart police by throwing rocks through open windows—rocks with answers attached (they learned some of the questions by bribing teachers) or by yelling out the answers from outside the grounds. Families also bribed the police to let them scale the school walls and whisper the answers through open windows. When all else failed, they bribed the test-graders to pass their children.

Education

Adult Literacy Rate: 35%

COMMUNICATION

Telephones: 7,315
Newspapers: 16

TRANSPORTATION

Highways—Kilometers (Miles): 34,100 (21,278)
Railroads—Kilometers (Miles): 655 (409)
Usable Airfields: 22

GOVERNMENT

Type: people's republic
Independence Date: November 9, 1949
Head of State/Government: King Norodom Sihanouk; First Premier Prince Norodom Ranariddh, Second Premier Hun Sen
Political Parties: Royalist Party (Funcinpec); Cambodian People's Party; Buddhist Liberal Democratic Party; Khmer Nation Party (declared illegal)
Suffrage: universal at 18

MILITARY

Number of Armed Forces: 56,500
Military Expenditures (% of Central Government Expenditures): 1.4%
Current Hostilities: border disputes with Vietnam and civil war

ECONOMY

Currency ($ U.S. Equivalent): 2,470 riels = $1
Per Capita Income/GDP: $630/$6.4 billion
Inflation Rate: 250%–300%
Natural Resources: timber; gemstones; iron ore; manganese; phosphates; hydropower potential
Agriculture: rice; rubber; maize; beans; soybeans
Industry: rice processing; fishing; wood and wood products; rubber; cement; gem mining

FOREIGN TRADE

Exports: $283.6 million
Imports: $479.3 million

Cambodia
- ✪ Capital
- ● City
- ～ River
- --- Road

0   50 kilometers
0   50 miles

A LAND OF TRAGEDY

In Khmer (Cambodian), the word *Kampuchea,* which for a time during the 1980s was the official name of Cambodia, means "country where gold lies at the foothill." But Cambodia is certainly not a land of gold, nor of food, freedom, or stability. Despite a new Constitution, massive United Nations aid, and a formal cease-fire, the horrific effects and the fighting of Cambodia's bloody Civil War continue.

Cambodia was not always a place to be pitied. In fact, at times it was the dominant power of Southeast Asia. Around the fourth century A.D., India, with its pacifist Hindu ideology, began to influence in earnest the original Chinese base of Cambodian civilization. The Indian script came to be used, the name of its capital city was an Indian word, its kings acquired Indian titles, and many of its Khmer people believed in the Hindu religion. The mile-square Hindu temple Angkor Wat, built in the twelfth century, still stands as a symbolic reminder of Indian influence, Khmer ingenuity, and the Khmer Empire's glory.

But the Khmer Empire, which at its height included parts of present-day Myanmar (Burma), Thailand, Laos, and Vietnam, was gradually reduced both in size and power until, in the 1800s, it was paying tribute to both Thailand and Vietnam. Continuing threats from these two countries as well as wars and domestic unrest at home led the king of Cambodia to appeal to France for help. France, eager to offset British power in the region, was all too willing to help. A protectorate was established in 1863, and French power grew apace until, in 1887, Cambodia became a part of French Indochina, a conglomerate consisting of the countries of Laos, Vietnam, and Cambodia.

The Japanese temporarily evicted the French in 1945 and, while under Japanese control, Cambodia declared its "independence" from France. Heading the country was the young King Norodom Sihanouk. Controlling rival ideological factions, some of which were pro-West while others were pro-Communist, was difficult for Sihanouk, but he built unity around the idea of permanently expelling the French, who finally left in 1955. King Sihanouk then abdicated his throne in favor of his father so that he could, as premier, personally enmesh himself in political governance. He took the title Prince Sihanouk, by which he is known to most people today, although in 1993 he declared himself, once again, king of Cambodia.

From the beginning, Sihanouk's government was bedeviled by border disputes with Thailand and Vietnam and by the incursion of Communist Vietnamese soldiers into Cambodia. Sihanouk's ideological allegiances were (and remain) confusing at best; but, to his credit, he was able to keep Cambodia officially out of the Vietnam War, which raged for years (1950–1975) on its border. In 1962, Sihanouk announced that his country would remain neutral in the cold war struggle.

Neutrality, however, was not seen as a virtue by the United States, whose people were becoming more and more eager either to win or to quit the war with North Vietnam. A particularly galling point for the U.S. military was the existence of the so-called Ho Chi Minh Trail, a supply route through the tropical mountain forests of Cambodia. For years, North Vietnam had been using the route to supply its military operations in South Vietnam, and Cambodia's neutrality prevented the United States, at least legally, from taking military action against the supply line.

All this changed in 1970, when Sihanouk, out of the country at the time, was evicted from office by his prime minister, General Lon Nol, who was supported by the United States and South Vietnam. Shortly thereafter, the United States, then at its peak of involvement in the Vietnam War, began extensive military action in Cambodia. The years of official neutrality came to a bloody end.

THE KILLING FIELDS

Most of these international political intrigues were lost on the bulk of the Cambodian population, only half of whom could read and write, and almost all of whom survived, as their forebears had before them, by cultivating rice along the Mekong River valley. The country had almost always been poor, so villagers had long since learned that, even in the face of war, they could survive by hard work and reliance on extended-family networks. Most farmers probably thought that the war next door would not seriously alter their lives. But they were profoundly wrong, for, just as the United States had an interest in having a pro–U.S. government in Cambodia, the North Vietnamese desperately wanted Cambodia to be pro-Communist.

North Vietnam wanted the Cambodian government to be controlled by the Khmer Rouge, a Communist guerrilla army led by Pol Pot, one of a group of former students influenced by the left-wing ideology taught in Paris universities during the 1950s. Winning control in 1975, the Khmer Rouge launched a hellish 3½-year extermination policy, resulting in the deaths of between 1 million and 3 million fellow Cambodians—that is, between one fifth and one third of the entire Cambodian population. The official goal was to eliminate anyone who had been "polluted" by prerevolutionary thinking, but what actually happened was random violence, torture, and murder.

It is impossible to fully describe the mayhem and despair that engulfed Cambodia during those years. Cities were emptied of people. Teachers and doctors were killed or sent as slaves to work in the rice paddies. Despite the centrality of Buddhism to Cambodian culture (Hinduism having long since been displaced by Buddhist thought), thousands of Buddhist monks were killed or died of starvation as the Khmer Rouge carried out its program of eliminating religion. Some people were killed for no other reason than to terrorize others into submission. Explained Leo Kuper in *International Action Against Genocide* (Report No. 53, 1984, p. 8):

Those who were dissatisfied with the new regime were . . . "eradicated," along with their families, by disembowelment, by beating to death with hoes, by hammering nails into the backs of their heads and by other cruel means of economizing on bullets.

Persons associated with the previous regime were special targets for liquidation. In many cases, the executions included wives and children. There were summary executions too of intellectuals, such as doctors, engineers, professors, teachers and students, leaving the country denuded of professional skills.

The Khmer Rouge wanted to alter the society completely. Children were removed from their families, and private ownership of property was eliminated. Money was outlawed. Even the calendar was started over, at year 0. Vietnamese military leader Bui Tin explained just how totalitarian the rulers were:

[In 1979] there was no small piece of soap or handkerchief anywhere. Any person who had tried to use a toothbrush was considered bourgeois and punished. Any person wearing glasses was considered an intellectual who must be punished.

It is estimated that, before the Khmer Rouge came to power in 1975, Cambodia had 1,200 engineers, 21,000 teachers, and 500 doctors. After the purges, the country was left with only 20 engineers, 3,000 teachers, and 54 doctors.

A kind of bitter relief came in late 1978, when Vietnamese troops (traditionally

France gains control of Cambodia A.D. **1863**	Japanese invasion; King Norodom Sihanouk is installed **1940s**	Sihanouk wins Cambodia's independence of France **1953**	General Lon Nol takes power in a U.S.–supported coup **1970**	The Khmer Rouge, under Pol Pot, overthrows the government and begins a reign of terror **1975**	Vietnam invades Cambodia and installs a puppet government **1978**	**1990s**

Vietnam withdraws troops from Cambodia; a Paris cease-fire agreement is violated by the Khmer Rouge

1993 elections result in a new Constitution, reenthronement of Sihanouk as king, and establishment of dual premiership

A 1994 coup attempt is unsuccessful

Cambodia's enemy) invaded Cambodia, drove the Khmer Rouge to the borders of Thailand, and installed a puppet government headed by Hun Sen, a former Khmer Rouge soldier who defected and fled to Vietnam in the 1970s. Although almost everyone was relieved to see the Khmer Rouge pushed out of power, the Vietnamese intervention was almost universally condemned by other nations. This was because the Vietnamese were taking advantage of the chaos in Cambodia to further their aim of creating a federated state of Vietnam, Laos, and Cambodia. Its virtual annexation of Cambodia eliminated Cambodia as a buffer state between Vietnam and Thailand, destabilizing the relations of the region even more.

COALITION GOVERNANCE

The United States and others refused to recognize the Vietnam-installed regime, instead granting recognition to the Coalition Government of Democratic Kampuchea. This entity consisted of three groups: the Communist Khmer Rouge, led by Khieu Samphan and Pol Pot and backed by China; the anti-Communist Khmer People's National Liberation Front, led by former prime minister Son Sann; and the Armee Nationale Sihanoukiste, led by Sihanouk. Although it was doubtful that these former enemies could constitute a workable government for Cambodia, the United Nations granted its Cambodia seat to the coalition and withheld support from the Hun Sen government.

Vietnam had hoped that its capture of Cambodia would be easy and painless. Instead, the Khmer Rouge and others re-

sisted so much that Vietnam had to send in 200,000 troops, of which 25,000 died. Moreover, other countries, including the United States and Japan, strengthened their resolve to isolate Vietnam in terms of international trade and development financing. After 10 years, the costs to Vietnam of remaining in Cambodia were so great that Vietnam announced it would pull out its troops.

It soon became apparent that the Khmer Rouge faction of the coalition was once again gaining control of important parts of the countryside. In late 1991 and early 1992, strenuous diplomatic efforts by United Nations officials and others resulted in a breakthrough. The warring groups agreed to a cease-fire, signed in Paris, that also permitted UN troops to establish a massive peacekeeping force in the country of some 22,000 troops, including Japanese troops—the first Japanese military presence outside Japan since the end of World War II. By 1993, the cost to the United Nations had reached nearly $2 billion.

The Paris agreement, signed by 17 nations, called for the release of political prisoners; inspections of prisons; and voter registration for national elections, to be held in 1993. Most important, the warring factions, consisting of some 200,000 troops, including 25,000 Khmer Rouge troops, agreed to disarm under UN supervision.

Unfortunately, the Khmer Rouge, although a signatory to the agreement, refused to abide by its provisions. With revenues gained from illegal trading in lumber and gems with Thailand, it launched new attacks on villages, trains, and even the UN

peacekeepers, and it refused to participate in the elections of 1993, although it had been offered a role in the new government if it would cooperate.

Despite a violent campaign, 90 percent of the people voted in elections that, after some confusion, resulted in a new Constitution, the reenthronement of Sihanouk as king, and the appointment of Sihanouk's son, Prince Norodom Ranariddh of the Royalist Party as first premier and Hun Sen of the Cambodian People's Party as second premier.

After the elections, the new Parliament outlawed the Khmer Rouge and ordered military operations against it. These actions, plus defections of key Khmer Rouge leaders and their followers, have reduced Khmer Rouge control to about 10 percent of the country. Several Khmer Rouge–controlled towns have been returned to government control.

DEVELOPMENT

In the past, China, the United States, and others built roads and industries in Cambodia, but the country remains an impoverished state whose economy rests on fishing and farming. Continual warfare for 2 decades has prevented industrial development. The economy is sustained primarily by massive foreign aid.

FREEDOM

Few Cambodians can remember political stability, much less political freedom. Every form of human-rights violation has been practiced in Cambodia since even before the arrival of the barbaric Khmer Rouge. Suppression of dissent continues: Journalists have been killed, and opponents of the government—including the king's brother—have been expelled from the country.

HEALTH/WELFARE

Almost all of Cambodia's doctors were killed or died during the Khmer Rouge regime, and warfare disrupted normal agriculture. Thus, disease was rampant, as was malnutrition. The few trained international relief workers in Cambodia today are hard-pressed to make a dent in the country's enormous problems.

ACHIEVEMENTS

Despite violence and intimidation, 90% of the Cambodian people voted in the 1993 elections, restoring an elected government, a limited monarchy, and acceding to a new Constitution. The new government has successfully weakened, but not eliminated, the influence of the Khmer Rouge.

China (People's Republic of China)*

GEOGRAPHY

Area in Square Kilometers (Miles):
9,572,900 (3,696,100) (slightly larger
than the contiguous United States)
Capital (Population): Beijing
(6,900,000)
Climate: extremely diverse

PEOPLE

Population

Total: 1,203,097,000
Annual Growth Rate: 1.04%
Rural/Urban Population Ratio: 73/27
Ethnic Makeup: 92% Han Chinese;
8% minority groups (the largest
being Chuang, Hui, Uighur, Yi, and
Miao)
Major Languages: Standard Chinese
(Putonghua) or Mandarin; Yue
(Cantonese); Wu (Shanghainese);
Minbei (Fuzhou); Minuan (Hokkien-
Taiwanese); Xiang; Gan; Hahka

Health

Life Expectancy at Birth: 67 years
(male); 69 years (female)
Infant Mortality Rate (Ratio):
52.1/1,000
Average Caloric Intake: 104% of
FAO minimum
Physicians Available (Ratio): 1/646

Religions
officially atheist; but Taoism,
Buddhism, Islam, Christianity, ancestor
worship, and animism do exist

Education
Adult Literacy Rate: 73%

COMMUNICATION
Telephones: 20,000,000
Newspapers: 852

THE TEACHINGS OF CONFUCIUS

Confucius (550–478 B.C.) was a Chinese intellectual and minor political figure. He was not a religious leader, nor did he ever claim divinity for himself
or divine inspiration for his ideas. As the feudalism of his era began to collapse,
he proposed that society could best be governed by paternalistic kings who set
good examples. Especially important to a stable society, he taught, were respect
and reverence for one's elders. Within the five key relationships of society
(ruler and subject, husband and wife, father and son, elder brother and younger
brother, and friend and friend), people should always behave with integrity,
propriety, and goodness.

The writings of Confucius—or, rather, the works written about him by his
followers and called the *Analects*—eventually became required knowledge for
anyone in China claiming to be an educated person. However, rival ideas such
as Legalism (a philosophy advocating authoritarian government) were at times
more popular with the elite; at one point 460 scholars were buried alive for
teaching Confucianism. Nevertheless, much of the hierarchical nature of Asian
culture today can be traced to Confucian ideas.

TRANSPORTATION

Highways—Kilometers (Miles):
1,029,000 (639,009)
Railroads—Kilometers (Miles):
65,780 (41,047)
Usable Airfields: 204

GOVERNMENT

Type: one-party Communist state
Independence Date: October 1, 1949
Head of State/Government: President
Jiang Zemin; Premier Li Peng
Political Parties: Chinese Communist
Party; several small and politically
insignificant non-Communist parties
Suffrage: universal at 18

MILITARY

Number of Armed Forces: 12,710,000
on active duty; 8,580,300 in People's
Militia
*Military Expenditures (% of Central
Government Expenditures):* n/a
Current Hostilities: none

ECONOMY

Currency ($ U.S. Equivalent): 8.32
yuan = $1
Per Capita Income/GDP:
$2,500/$2.97 trillion
Inflation Rate: 15%
Natural Resources: coal; oil;
hydroelectric sites; natural gas; iron
ores; tin; tungsten
Agriculture: food grains; cotton; oil
seeds; pigs; tea
Industry: iron and steel; coal;
machinery; light industry; armaments

FOREIGN TRADE

Exports: $121.0 billion
Imports: $115.7 billion

*Note: Because of the rapid change in China, ac-
curate statistics are difficult to find.

China

⊕ National Capital
—— International Boundary
▨▨▨ Provincial Boundary
- - - Disputed Boundary

0 —— 500 kilometers
0 —— 500 miles

CHINA

The first important characteristic to note about China is its age. Human civilization appeared in China as early as 20,000 years ago, and the first documented Chinese dynasty, the Shang, began about 1523 B.C. Unproven legends suggest the existence of an even earlier Chinese dynasty (about 2000 B.C.), making China one of the oldest societies with a continuing cultural identity. Over the centuries of documented history, the Chinese people have been ruled by a dozen imperial dynasties; have enjoyed hundreds of years of stability and amazing cultural progress; and have endured more hundreds of years of chaos, military mayhem, and hunger. Yet China and the Chinese people remain intact—a strong testament to the tenacity of human culture.

A second major characteristic is that the People's Republic of China (P.R.C.) is very big. It is the third-largest country in the world, accounting for 6.5 percent of the world's landmass. Much of China—about 40 percent—is mountainous; but large, fertile plains have been created by China's numerous rivers, most of which flow toward the Pacific Ocean. China is blessed with substantial reserves of oil, minerals, and many other natural resources. Its large size and geopolitical location—it is bordered by Russia, Kazakhstan, Pakistan, India, Nepal, Bhutan, Myanmar, Laos, Vietnam, North Korea, and Mongolia—have caused the Chinese people over the centuries to think of their land as the "Middle Kingdom": that is, the center of world civilization.

However, its unwieldy size has been the undoing of numerous emperors who found it impossible to maintain its borders in the face of outside "barbarians" determined to possess the riches of Chinese civilization. During the Ch'in Dynasty (221–207 B.C.), a 1,500-mile-long, 25-foot-high wall, the so-called Great Wall, was erected along the northern border of China, in the futile hope that invasions from the north could be stopped. Although China's national boundaries are now recognized by international law, recent Chinese governments have found it necessary to "pacify" border areas by settling as many Han Chinese there as possible (for example, in Tibet), to prevent secession by China's numerous ethnic minorities.

A third important characteristic of modern China is its large population. With 1.2 billion people, China is home to about 20 percent of all human beings alive today. About 92 percent of China's people are Han, or ethnic, Chinese; the remaining 8 percent are divided into more than 50 separate minority groups. Many of these ethnic groups speak mutually unintelligible languages, and although they often appear to be Chinese, they derive from entirely different cultural roots; some are Muslims, some are Buddhists, some are animists. As one moves away from the center of Chinese civilization in the eastern provinces, the influence of the minorities increases. The Chinese government has accepted the reality of ethnic influence and has granted a degree of limited autonomy to some provinces with heavy populations of minorities.

In the 1950s, Chairman Mao Zedong encouraged couples to have many children, but this policy was reversed in the 1970s, when a formal birth control program was inaugurated. Urban couples today are permitted to have only one child and are penalized if they have more. Penalties include expulsion from the Chinese Communist Party (CCP), dismissal from work, or a 10 percent reduction in pay for up to 14 years after the birth of the second child. The policy is strictly enforced in the cities, but it has had only a marginal impact on overall population growth because some 73 percent of China's people live in rural areas, where they are allowed more children in order to help with the farmwork. In the city of Shanghai, which is expected to have a population of 13.3 million people by the year 2000, authorities have recently removed second-child privileges for farmers living near the city and for such former exceptional cases as children of revolutionary martyrs and workers in the oil industry. Despite these and other restrictions, it is estimated that 15 million to 17 million new Chinese will be born each year until the end of the century.

Over the centuries, millions of people have found it necessary or prudent to leave China in search of food, political stability, or economic opportunity. Those who emigrated a thousand or more years ago are now fully assimilated into the cultures of Southeast Asia and elsewhere and identify themselves accordingly. More recent émigrés (in the past 200 years or so), however, constitute visible, often wealthy, minorities in their new host countries, where they have become the backbone of the business community. Ethnic Chinese constitute the majority of the population in Singapore and a sizable minority in Malaysia. Important world figures such as Corazon Aquino, the former president of the Philippines, and Goh Chok Tong, the prime minister of Singapore, are part or full Chinese. The Chinese constituted the first big wave of the 6.5 million Asian Americans to call the United States home. Thus the influence of China continues to spread far beyond its borders.

Another crucial characteristic of China is its history of imperial and totalitarian rule. Except for a few years in the early part of this century, China has been controlled by imperial decree, military order, and patriarchal privilege. Confucius taught that a person must be as loyal to the government as a son should be to his father. Following Confucius by a generation or two was Shang Yang, of a school of governmental philosophy called Legalism, which advocated unbending force and punishment against wayward subjects. Compassion and pity were not considered qualities of good government.

Mao Zedong, building on this heritage as well as that of the Soviet Union's Joseph Stalin and Vladimir Lenin, exercised strict control over both the public and private lives of the Chinese people. Dissidents were summarily executed (generally people were considered guilty once they were arrested), the press was strictly controlled, and recalcitrants were forced to undergo "reeducation" to correct their thinking. Religion of any kind was suppressed, and churches were turned into warehouses. It is estimated that, during the first 3 years of CCP rule, more than 1 million opponents of Mao's regime were executed. During the Cultural Revolution (1966–1976), Mao, who apparently thought that a new mini-revolution in China might restore his eroding stature in the Chinese Communist Party, encouraged young people to report to the authorities anyone suspected of owning books from the West or having contact with Westerners. Even party functionaries were purged if it were believed that their thinking had been corrupted by Western influences.

Historically, authoritarian rule in China has been occasioned, in part, by China's mammoth size; by its unwieldy, mostly illiterate population; and by the ideology of some of its intellectuals. The modern Chinese state has arisen from these same pressures as well as some new ones. It is to these that we now turn.

ORIGINS OF THE MODERN STATE

The Chinese had traded with such non-Asian peoples as the Arabs and Persians for hundreds of years before European contact. But in the 1700s and 1800s, the British and others extracted something new from China in exchange for merchandise from the West: the permission for foreign citizens to live in parts of China without being subject to Chinese authority. Through this process of granting extraterritoriality to foreign powers, China slowly began to lose control of its sovereignty. The age of European expansion was not, of course, the first time in China's long history that its ability to rule itself was challenged; the armies of Kublai Khan successfully captured the Chinese throne in the 1200s, as did the Manchurians in the 1600s.

But these outsiders, especially the Manchurians, were willing to rule China on-site and to imbibe as much Chinese culture as they could; eventually they became indistinguishable from the Chinese.

The European powers, on the other hand, preferred to rule China (or, rather, parts of it) from afar as a vassal state, with the proceeds of conquest being drained away from China to enrich the coffers of the European monarchs. Aggression against Chinese sovereignty increased in 1843 when the British forced China to cede Hong Kong Island. Britain, France, and the United States all extracted unequal treaties from the Chinese that gave them privileged access to trade and ports along the eastern coast. By the late 1800s, Russia was in control of much of Manchuria, Germany and France had wrested special economic privileges from the ever-weakening Chinese government, and Portugal controlled Macau. Further affecting the Chinese economy was the loss of many of its former tributary states in Southeast Asia. China lost Vietnam to France, Burma (today, Myanmar) to Britain, and Korea to Japan. During the violent Boxer

Rebellion of 1900, the Chinese people showed how frustrated they were with the declining fortunes of their country.

Thus weakened internally and embarrassed internationally, the Manchu rulers of China began to initiate reforms that would strengthen their ability to compete with the Western and Japanese powers. A constitutional monarchy was proposed by the Manchu authorities but was preempted by the republican revolutionary movement of Western-trained Sun Yat-sen. Sun and his armies wanted an end to imperial rule; their dreams were realized in 1912, when Sun's Kuomintang (Nationalist Party, or KMT), took control of the new Republic of China.

Sun's Western approach to government was received with skepticism by many Chinese who distrusted the Western European model and preferred the thinking of Karl Marx and the approach of the Soviet Union. In 1921, Mao Zedong and others organized the Soviet-style Chinese Communist Party (CCP), which grew quickly and began to be seen as an alternative to the Kuomintang. After Sun's death, in 1925, Chiang Kai-shek assumed control of the Kuomintang and waged a campaign to rid the country of

Communist influence. Although Mao and Chiang cooperated when necessary—for example, to resist Japanese incursions into Manchuria—they eventually came to be such bitter enemies that they brought a ruinous civil war to all of China.

Mao derived his support from the rural areas of China, while Chiang depended on the cities. In 1949, facing defeat, Chiang Kai-shek's Nationalists retreated to the island of Taiwan, where, under the name Republic of China (R.O.C.), they continued to insist on their right to rule all of China. The Communists, however, controlled the mainland (and have done so for more than 4 decades) and insisted that Taiwan was just a renegade province of the People's Republic of China. These two antagonists are officially (but not in actuality) still at war. Sometimes tensions between Taiwan and China reach dangerous levels. In the 1940s, the United States had to intervene to prevent an attack from the mainland. In 1996, U.S. warships once again patrolled the 150 miles of ocean called the Taiwan Strait to warn China not to turn its military exercises, including the firing of missiles in the direction of Tai

(UN photo/John Issac

In China today, urban couples are permitted to have only one child, and they can be severely penalized if they dare to have a second or if they marr before the legal ages of 22 for men and 20 for women.

wan, into an actual invasion. China used the blatantly aggressive actions as a warning to the newly elected Taiwanese president not to take any steps toward declaring Taiwan an independent nation.

For many years after World War II, world opinion sided with Taiwan's claim to be the legitimate government of China. Taiwan was granted diplomatic recognition by many nations and given the China seat in the United Nations. In the 1970s, however, many nations, including the United States, came to believe that it was dysfunctional to withhold recognition and standing from such a large and powerful nation as the P.R.C. Because both sides insisted that there could not be two Chinas, nor one China and one Taiwan, the UN proceeded to give the China seat to mainland China, and dozens of countries broke off formal diplomatic relations with Taiwan in order to establish a relationship with China.

PROBLEMS OF GOVERNANCE

The China that Mao came to control was a nation with serious economic and social problems. Decades of civil war had disrupted families and wreaked havoc on the economy. Mao believed that the solution to China's ills was to wholeheartedly embrace socialism. Businesses were nationalized, and state planning replaced private initiative. Slowly, the economy improved. In 1958, however, Mao

decided to enforce the tenets of socialism more vigorously so that China would be able to take an economic "Great Leap Forward." Workers were assigned to huge agricultural communes and were denied the right to grow crops privately. All enterprises came under the strict control of the central government. The result was economic chaos and a dramatic drop in both industrial and agricultural output.

Exacerbating these problems was the growing rift between the P.R.C. and the Soviet Union. China insisted that its brand of communism was truer to the principles of Marx and Lenin and criticized the Soviets for selling out to the West. As relations with (and financial support from) the Soviet Union withered, China found itself increasingly isolated from the world community, a circumstance worsened by serious conflicts with India, Indonesia, and other nations. To gain friends, the P.R.C. provided substantial aid to Communist insurgencies in Vietnam and Laos, thus contributing to the eventual severity of the Vietnam War.

In 1966, Mao found that his power was waning in the face of Communist Party leaders who favored a more moderate approach to internal problems and external relations. To regain lost ground, Mao urged young students called Red Guards to fight against anyone who might have liberal, capitalist, or intellectual leanings. He called it the Great Proletarian Cultural

Revolution, but it was an *anti*cultural purge: Books were burned, and educated people were arrested and persecuted. In fact, the entire country remained in a state of domestic chaos for more than a decade.

Soon after Mao died, in 1976, Deng Xiaoping, who had been in and out of Communist Party power several times before, came to occupy the senior position in the CCP. A pragmatist, he was willing to modify or forgo strict socialist ideology if he believed that some other approach would work better. Despite pressure by hard-liners to tighten governmental control, he nevertheless was successful in liberalizing the economy and permitting exchanges of scholars with the West. In 1979, he accepted formalization of relations with the United States—an act seen as a signal of China's opening up to the world.

China's opening has been dramatic, not only in terms of its international relations but also internally. During the 1980s, the P.R.C. joined the World Bank, the International Monetary Fund, the Asian Development Bank, and other multilateral organizations. It also began to welcome foreign investment of almost any kind and permitted foreign companies to sell their products within China itself. Trade between Taiwan and China (still legally permitted only via a third country) was nearly $6 billion by the early 1990s. And while Hong Kong was investing some $25 bil-

(UN/photo by A. Holcombe)
During Mao Zedong's "Great Leap Forward," huge agricultural communes were established, and farmers were denied the right to grow crops privately. The government's strict control of these communes met with chaotic results; there were dramatic drops in agricultural output.

The Shang Dynasty is the first documented Chinese dynasty 1523–1027 B.C.	The Chou Dynasty and the era of Confucius, Laotze, and Mencius 1027–256 B.C.	The Ch'in Dynasty, from which the word *China* is derived 211–207 B.C.	The Han Dynasty 202 B.C.–A.D. 220	The Three Kingdoms period; the Tsin and Sui Dynasties A.D. 220–618	The T'ang Dynasty, during which Confucianism flourished 618–906	The Five Dynasties and Sung Dynasty periods 906–1279	The Yuan Dynasty is founded by Kublai Khan 1260–1368	The Ming Dynasty 1368–1644	The Manchu or Ch'ing Dynasty 1644–1912

lion in China, China was investing $11 billion in Hong Kong. More Chinese firms were permitted to export directly and to keep more of the profits. Special Economic Zones—capitalist enclaves adjacent to Hong Kong and along the coast into which were sent the most educated of the Chinese population—were established to catalyze the internal economy. In coastal cities, especially in south China, construction of apartment complexes, new manufacturing plants, and roads and highways began in earnest. Indeed, the south China area, along with Hong Kong and Taiwan, seemed to be emerging as a mammoth trading bloc—"Greater China"—which economists began to predict would exceed the economy of Japan by the year 2000 and eclipse the economy of the United States by 2012. Stock exchanges opened in Shanghai and Shenzhen. Dramatic changes were implemented even in the inner rural areas. The collectivized farm system imposed by Mao was replaced by a household contract system with hereditary contracts (that is, one step away from actual private land ownership), and free markets replaced most of the system of mandatory agricultural sales to the government. New industries were established in rural villages, and incomes improved such that many families were able to add new rooms onto their homes or to purchase two-story and even three-story homes.

Throughout the country a strong spirit of entrepreneurship took hold; and many people, especially the growing body of educated youth, interpreted economic liberalization as the overture to political democratization. College students, some of whom had studied abroad, pressed the government to crack down on corruption in the Chinese Communist Party and to permit greater freedom of speech and other civil liberties.

In 1989, tens of thousands of college students staged a prodemocracy demonstration in Beijing's Tiananmen Square. The call for democratization received wide international media coverage and soon became an embarrassment to the Chinese leadership, especially when, after several days of continual protest, the students constructed a large statue in the square similar in appearance to the Statue of Liberty in New York Harbor. Some party leaders seemed inclined at least to talk with the students, but hard-liners apparently insisted that the prodemocracy movement be crushed in order that the CCP remain in control of the government. The official policy seemed to be that it would be the Communist Party, and not some prodemocracy movement, that would lead China to capitalism.

The CCP leadership had much to fear; it was, of course, aware of the quickening pace of Communist party power dissolution in the Soviet Union and Central/Eastern Europe, but it was even more concerned about corruption and the breakdown of CCP authority in the rapidly capitalizing rural regions of China, the very areas that had spawned the Communist Party under Mao. Moreover, economic liberalization had spawned inflation, higher prices, and spot shortages, and the general public was disgruntled. Therefore, after several weeks of pained restraint, the authorities moved against the students in what has become known as the Tiananmen Square massacre. Soldiers injured thousands and killed hundreds of students; hundreds more were systematically hunted down and brought to trial for sedition and for spreading counterrevolutionary propaganda.

In the wake of the brutal crackdown, many nations reassessed their relationships with the People's Republic of China. The United States, Japan, and other nations halted or canceled foreign assistance, exchange programs, and special tariff privileges. The people of Hong Kong, anticipating the return of their British colony to P.R.C. control in 1997, staged massive demonstrations against the Chinese government's brutality. Foreign tourism all but ceased, and foreign investment declined abruptly.

The withdrawal of financial support and investment was particularly troublesome to the Chinese leadership, as it realized that the economy was far behind other nations. Even Taiwan, with a similar heritage and a common history until the 1950s, but having far fewer resources and much less land, had long since eclipsed the mainland in terms of economic prosperity. The Chinese understood that they needed to modernize (although not, they hoped, to Westernize), and they knew that large capital investments from such countries as Japan, Hong Kong, and the United States were crucial to their economic reform program. Moreover, they knew that they could not tolerate a cessation of trade with their new economic partners. By the end of the 1980s, about 13 percent of China's imports came from the United States, 18 percent from Japan, and 25 percent from Hong Kong. Similarly, Japan received 16 percent of China's exports, and Hong Kong received 43 percent.

Fortunately for the Chinese economy, the investment and loan-assistance programs from other countries have been reinstated in most cases as the repercussions of the events of 1989 wane. China was even able to close a $1.2 billion contract with McDonnell Douglas Corporation to build 40 jetliners; and U.S. President Bill Clinton, as a result of a decision to separate China's human-rights issues from trade issues, has repeatedly renewed China's "most favored nation" trade status. Still, enormous problems exist, not the least of which is copyright violations by Chinese companies. Some have estimated that as much as 88 percent of China's exports of CDs consists of illegal copies. A 1995 copyright agreement is having some effect, but still, much of China's trade deficit with the United States, which is now higher than Japan's, comes from illegal products.

Improved trade notwithstanding, the Tiananmen Square massacre and the continuing brutality against citizens have convinced many people, both inside and outside China, that the Communist Party has lost not necessarily its legal, but certainly its moral, authority to govern. Amnesty International's 1996 report claimed that human rights violations in China occur "on massive scale" and noted that torture is used on political prisoners held in *laogai*, Chinese gulags similar to those in the former Soviet Union. Increasing international attention is turning to Tibet, which China invaded in 1959 and where Chinese officials have been purging monks and others who resist Beijing's authority.

THE SOCIAL ATMOSPHERE

Many believe that when the aging Communist Party leadership is replaced by younger leaders, China might once again broach the question of democratization and liberalization. In 1997, the aged Deng Xiaoping died and was replaced by Jiang Zemin. Where China will go under this new leadership is unclear. In the meantime, it is evident that the CCP has effected a major change in Chinese society,

Trading rights
and Hong Kong
Island are
granted to Britain
1834

The
Sino-Japanese
War
1894–1895

Sun Yat-sen's
republican
revolution ends
centuries of
imperial rule; the
Republic of
China is
established
1912

The Chinese
Communist
Party is
organized
1921

Chiang Kai-shek
begins a long
civil war with the
Communists
1926

Mao Zedong's
Communist Army
defeats Chiang
Kai-shek
1949

A disastrous
economic reform,
the Great Leap
Forward, is
launched by Mao
1958

The Cultural
Revolution;
Mao dies
1966–1976

Economic and
political
liberalization begins
under Deng
Xiaoping; the P.R.C.
and Britain agree to
return Hong Kong
to the Chinese
1980s

China expands its
relationship with
Taiwan; the
Tiananmen Square
massacre
provokes
international
outrage

1990s

Crackdowns on
dissidents and
criminals result in
hundreds of
arrests and
executions;
tensions begin to
ease

Economists
predict that
"Greater China's"
economy will
eventually
surpass those of
Japan and the
United States

Deng Xiaoping
dies; Jiang
Zemin becomes
president

Historically, the loyalty of the masses of the people was placed in their extended families and in feudal warlords, who, at times of weakened imperial rule, were nearly sovereign in their own provinces. Communist policy has been to encourage the masses to give their loyalty instead to the centrally controlled Communist Party. The size of families has been reduced to the extent that "family" as such has come to play a less important role in the lives of ordinary Chinese.

Historical China was a place of great social and economic inequality between the classes. The wealthy feudal lords and their families and those connected with the imperial court and bureaucracy had access to the finest in educational and cultural opportunities, while around them lived illiterate peasants who often could not feed themselves, let alone pay the often heavy taxes imposed on them by feudal and imperial elites. The masses often found life to be bitter, but they found solace in the teachings of the three main religions of China (often adhered to simultaneously): Confucianism, Taoism, and Buddhism. Islam, animism, and Christianity have also been significant to many people in China.

The Chinese Communist Party under Mao, by legal decree and by indoctrination, attempted to suppress people's reliance on religious values and to reverse the ranking of the classes; the values of hard, manual work and rural simplicity were elevated, while the refinement and education of the urban elites were denigrated. Homes of formerly wealthy capitalists were taken over by the government and turned into museums, and the opulent life of the capitalists was disparaged. During the Cultural Revolution, high school students who wanted to attend college had first to spend 2 years in manual labor in factories and on farms to help them learn to relate to the peasants and the working class. So much did revolutionary ideology and national fervor take precedence over education that schools and colleges were shut down for several years during the 1960s and 1970s and the length of compulsory education was reduced.

One would imagine that, after 40 years of communism, the Chinese people would have discarded the values of old China. However, the reverse seems to be true. When the liberalization of the economy began in the late 1970s, many of the former values also came to the fore: the Confucian value of scholarly learning and cultural refinement, the desirability of money, and even Taoist and Buddhist religious values. Religious worship is now permitted, with restrictions, in China.

Thousands of Chinese are studying abroad with the goal of returning to China to establish or manage profitable businesses. Indeed, some Chinese, especially those with legitimate access to power, such as ranking Communist Party members, have become extremely wealthy. Along with the privatization of state enterprises has come the unemployment of hundreds of thousands of "redundant" workers (2 million workers lost their jobs in one province in a single year in the early 1990s). Many others have had to settle for lower pay or unsafe work conditions as businesses strive to enter the world of competitive production. Demon-

strations and more than 300 strikes by angry laborers exploded in early 1994. Even those with good jobs were finding it difficult to keep up with inflation, which in recent years has been as high as 22 percent, and is still a dizzying 15 percent. Nevertheless, those with an entrepreneurial spirit were finding ways to make more money than they had ever dreamed possible under an officially communist country. Some former values may help revitalize Chinese life, while others, once suppressed by the Communists, may not be so desirable. For instance, Mao attempted to eradicate prostitution, eliminate the sale of women as brides, and prevent child marriages. Today some of those customs are returning, and gender-based divisions of labor are making their way into the workplace.

Predicting the future is difficult, but it is very unlikely that the economic reform process begun in 1978 will be slowed by political problems. The economy seems to be taking on a life of its own, and, once a solid middle class has developed, it is likely that political changes will follow, for that has been the history of the world. China, despite its size and longevity, cannot realistically expect to bypass the natural history of social change.

DEVELOPMENT

the early years of Communist control, authorities stressed the value establishing heavy industry and collectivizing agriculture. More recently, China has attempted to reduce its isolation by establishing trading relationships with the United States, Japan, and others and by constructing free enterprise zones. The world's largest dam is currently under construction, despite the objections of environmentalists.

FREEDOM

Until the late 1970s, the Chinese people were controlled by Chinese Communist Party cadres who monitored both public and private behavior. Some economic and social liberalization occurred in the 1980s. However, the 1989 Tiananmen Square massacre reminded Chinese and the world that despite some reforms, China is still very much a dictatorship.

HEALTH/WELFARE

The Communist government has overseen dramatic improvements in the provision of social services for the masses. Life expectancy has increased from 45 years in 1949 to 68 years (overall) today. Diverse forms of health care are available at low cost to the patient. The government has attempted to eradicate such diseases as malaria and tuberculosis.

ACHIEVEMENTS

Chinese culture has, for thousands of years, provided the world with classics in literature, art, pottery, ballet, and other arts. Under communism the arts have been marshaled in the service of ideology and have lost some of their dynamism. Since 1949, literacy has increased dramatically and now stands at 73 percent—the highest in Chinese history.

Hong Kong*

GEOGRAPHY

Area in Square Kilometers (Miles):
1,062 (658) (about 1⅓ times the size
of New York City)
Capital: Victoria
Climate: subtropical

PEOPLE

Population
Total: 5,542,900
Annual Growth Rate: 0.12%
Rural/Urban Population Ratio: 9/91
Ethnic Makeup: 98% Chinese
(mostly Cantonese); 2% European
and Vietnamese
Major Languages: Cantonese; other
Chinese dialects; English

Health
Life Expectancy at Birth: 77 years
(male); 84 years (female)
Infant Mortality Rate (Ratio):
5.8/1,000
Average Caloric Intake: n/a
Physicians Available (Ratio): 1/1,000

Religions
90% a combination of Buddhism and
Taoism; 10% Christian

Education
Adult Literacy Rate: 77%

HONG KONG'S RESTLESS PEOPLE

As recently as 1989, Chinese student protesters fleeing the massacre in
China's Tiananmen Square were smuggled across the border to safety in
Hong Kong. Ironically, while these exiles were finding refuge in Hong
Kong, thousands of earlier refugees from Chinese oppression, some now
quite wealthy, were packing their bags to leave Hong Kong before its return
to China in 1997. Still others—in this case, some of the 20,000 Vietnamese
refugees languishing in detention camps—were resorting to desperate measures to stay in Hong Kong rather than be repatriated to Vietnam, as required
before the 1997 Chinese takeover. Some were organizing violent demonstrations and burning houses and cars; others were making daring escapes
from the camps; still others were paying as much as $10,000 each to marry
a Hong Kong resident in order to obtain permanent residency in Hong
Kong. Obviously, the value of Hong Kong as a place of refuge depends on
what the alternatives are. For many years, however, Hong Kong has been
populated by restless and weary refugees. Will that change under Chinese rule?

COMMUNICATION

Telephones: 3,000,000
Newspapers: 69

TRANSPORTATION

Highways—Kilometers (Miles): 1,100
(683)
Railroads—Kilometers (Miles): 35 (22)
Usable Airfields: 2

GOVERNMENT

Type: colonial (British Crown colony)
Independence Date: Chinese sovereignty
to be reestablished on July 1, 1997

Head of State/Government: Queen
Elizabeth II; Governor Christopher
Patten (appointed by Great Britain)
to be replaced in July 1997 by Tung
Chee-hwa
Political Parties: United Democrats
of Hong Kong; Liberal Democratic
Federation; Hong Kong Democratic
Federation; Association for
Democracy and People's Livelihood;
Progressive Hong Kong Society
Suffrage: residents over age 21 who
have lived in Hong Kong for at least
7 years

MILITARY

Number of Armed Forces: foreign
relations and defense the responsibility
of British Armed Forces, 12,000 of
whom are stationed in Hong Kong
*Military Expenditures (% of Central
Government Expenditures):* 0.2%
Current Hostilities: none

ECONOMY

Currency ($ U.S. Equivalent): 7.74
Hong Kong dollars = $1
Per Capita Income/GDP:
$24,530/$136.1 billion
Inflation Rate: 8.5%
Natural Resources: none
Agriculture: vegetables; livestock
(cattle, pigs, poultry); fish
Industry: light—textiles and clothing;
electronics; clocks and watches; toys;
plastic products; metalware; footwear
heavy—shipbuilding and ship
repairing; aircraft engineering

FOREIGN TRADE

Exports: $168.7 billion
Imports: $160 billion

Note: Some of this information may change with
the reversion of Hong Kong to Chinese control.

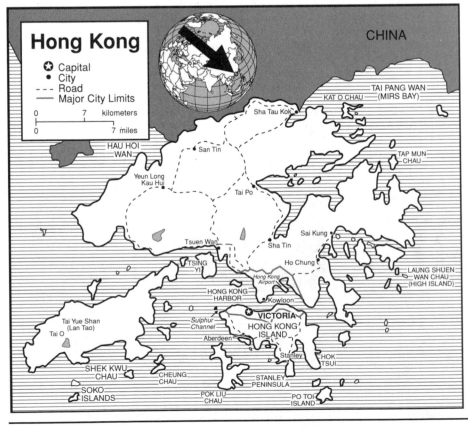

HONG KONG'S BEGINNINGS

Opium started it all for Hong Kong. The addictive drug from which such narcotics as morphine, heroin, and codeine are made, opium had become a major source of income for British merchants in the early 1800s. When the Chinese government declared the opium trade illegal and confiscated more than 20,000 large chests of opium that had been on their way for sale to the increasingly addicted residents of Canton, the merchants persuaded the British military to intervene and restore their trading privileges. The British Navy attacked and occupied part of Canton. Three days later, the British forced the Chinese to agree to their trading demands, including a demand that they be ceded the tiny island of Hong Kong (meaning "Fragrant Harbor"), where they could pursue their trading and military business without the scrutiny of the Chinese authorities.

Initially, the British government was not pleased with the acquisition of Hong Kong; the island had been annexed without the foreknowledge of the authorities in London, and development on the island consisted of nothing more than a small fishing village. Shortly, however, the government found the island's harbor a useful place to resupply ships and to anchor military vessels in the event of further hostilities with the Chinese. The harbor turned out to be one of the finest natural harbors along the coast of China. On August 29, 1842, China reluctantly signed the Treaty of Nanking, which ended the first Opium War and gave Britain ownership of Hong Kong Island "in perpetuity."

Twenty years later, a second Opium War caused China to lose more of its territory; Britain acquired permanent lease rights over Kowloon, a tiny part of the mainland facing Hong Kong Island. By 1898, Britain had realized that its miniscule Hong Kong naval base would be too small to defend itself against sustained attack by French or other European navies seeking privileged access to China's markets. The British were also concerned about the scarcity of agricultural land on Hong Kong and Kowloon. In 1898, they persuaded the Chinese to lease them more than 350 square miles of land adjacent to Kowloon. Thus, Hong Kong consists today of Hong Kong Island (as well as numerous small, uninhabited islands nearby), the Kowloon Peninsula, and the agricultural lands that came to be called the New Territories.

From its inauspicious beginnings, Hong Kong has grown into a dynamic, modern society, wealthier and more densely populated than its promoters would have ever dreamed in their wildest imaginations. Hong Kong is now home to 5.5 million people, nearly 14,000 people per square mile. Most of the New Territories are mountainous or are needed for agriculture, so the bulk of the population is packed into about one tenth of the land space. This gives Hong Kong the dubious honor of being one of the most densely populated human spaces ever created. Millions of people live stacked on top of one another in 30-story-high public tenement buildings. Even Hong Kong's excellent harbor has not escaped the population crunch: Approximately 10 square miles of former harbor have been filled in and now constitute some of the most expensive real estate on earth.

Why are there so many people in Hong Kong? One reason is that, after occupation by the British, many Chinese merchants moved their businesses to Hong Kong, under the correct assumption that trade would be given a freer hand there than on the mainland. Eventually, Hong Kong became the home of mammoth trading conglomerates. The laborers in these profitable enterprises came to Hong Kong,

(Photo credit United Nations/J. K. Isaac)

Hong Kong has enormous economic inequalities, with some of the richest people in the world living in close proximity to some of the poorest, a disparity largely caused by the constant influx of refugees. The contrast is illustrated above, with newly arrived Vietnamese shown against a prosperous city backdrop.

for the most part, as political refugees from mainland China in the early 1900s. Another wave of immigrants arrived in the 1930s upon the invasion of Manchuria by the Japanese, and yet another influx came after the Communists took over China in 1949. Thus, like Taiwan, Hong Kong became a place of refuge for those in economic or political trouble on the mainland.

Overcrowding plus a favorable climate for doing business have produced extreme social and economic inequalities. Some of the richest people on earth live in Hong Kong, as do some of the most wretchedly poor, notable among whom are recent refugees from China and Southeast Asia (more than 300,000 Vietnamese have sought refuge in Hong Kong since 1975), some of whom have joined the traditionally poor boat peoples living in Aberdeen Harbor. Although they are surrounded by poverty, many of Hong Kong's economic elites have not found it inappropriate to indulge in ostentatious displays of wealth, such as riding in chauffeured, pink Rolls-Royces or wearing full-length mink coats.

Workers are on the job six days a week, morning and night, yet the average pay for a worker in industry is only about $4,800 per year. With husband, wife, and older children all working, families can survive; some even make it into the ranks of the fabulously wealthy. Indeed, the desire to make money was the primary reason why Hong Kong was settled in the first place. That fact is not lost on anyone

who lives there today. Noise and air pollution, traffic congestion, and dirty and smelly streets do not deter people from abandoning the countryside in favor of the consumptive lifestyle of the city.

Yet materialism has not wholly effaced the cultural arts and social rituals that are essential to a cohesive society. Indeed, with 98 percent of Hong Kong's residents hailing originally from mainland China, the spiritual beliefs and cultural heritage of China's long history abound. Some residents hang small eight-sided mirrors outside windows to frighten away malicious spirits, while others burn paper money in the streets each August to pacify the wandering spirits of deceased ancestors. Business owners carefully choose certain Chinese characters for the names of their companies or products, which they hope will bring them luck. Even modern skyscrapers are designed, following ancient Chinese customs, so that their main entrances are in balance with the elements of nature.

Buddhist and Taoist beliefs remain central to the lives of many residents. In the back rooms of many shops, for example, are erected small religious shrines; joss sticks burning in front of these shrines are thought to bring good fortune to the proprietors. Elaborate festivals, such as those at New Year's, bring the costumes, art, and dance of thousands of years of Chinese history to the crowded streets of Hong Kong. And, of course, the British

legacy may be found in the cricket matches, ballet troupes, philharmonic orchestras, English-language radio and television broadcasts, and the legal system under which capitalism has flourished.

THE END OF AN ERA

Britain was in control of this tiny speck of Asia for nearly 160 years. Except during World War II, when the Japanese occupied Hong Kong for about 4 years, the territory was governed as a Crown colony of Great Britain, with a governor appointed by the British sovereign. In 1997, China recovered control of Hong Kong from the British. In 1984, British prime minister Margaret Thatcher and Chinese leader Deng Xiaoping concluded 2 years of acrimonious negotiations over the fate of Hong Kong upon the expiration of the New Territories' lease in 1997. Great Britain claimed the right to control Hong Kong Island and Kowloon forever—a claim disputed by China, which argued that the treaties granting these lands to Britain had been imposed on them by military force. Hong Kong Island and Kowloon, however, constitute only about 10 percent of the colony; the other 90 percent was to return automatically to China at the expiration of the lease. The various parts of the colony having become fully integrated, it seemed desirable to all parties to keep the colony together as one administrative unit. Moreover, it was felt that Hong Kong Island and Kowloon could not survive alone.

The British government had hoped that the People's Republic of China would agree to the status quo, or that it would at least permit the British to maintain administrative control over the colony should it be returned to China. Many Hong Kong Chinese felt the same way, since they had, after all, fled to Hong Kong to escape the Communist regime in China. For its part, the P.R.C. insisted that the entire colony be returned to its control by 1997. After difficult negotiations, Britain agreed to return the entire colony to China as long as China would grant important concessions. Foremost among these were that the capitalist economy and lifestyle, including private-property ownership and basic human rights, would not be changed for 50 years. The P.R.C. agreed to govern Hong Kong as a Special Administrative Region (SAR) within China and to permit British and local Chinese to serve in the administrative apparatus of the territory. The first direct elections for the 60-member Legislative Council were held in September 1991, while the last British governor, Chris Patten,

(Photo credit United Nations/S. Jackson)
Hong Kong's freewheeling approach to business and commerce drew millions of people and the possibility of work. This in turn put enormous strains on housing in a geographically limited area. This apartment building in Aberdeen is typical of how the population crunch has been handled.

| The British begin to occupy and use Hong Kong Island; the first Opium War A.D. 1839–1842 | The Treaty of Nanking cedes Hong Kong to Britain 1842 | The Chinese cede Kowloon and Stonecutter Island to Britain 1856 | England gains a 99-year lease on the New Territories 1898 | The Boxer Rebellion 1898–1900 | Sun Yat-sen overthrows the emperor of China to establish the Republic of China 1911 | The Japanese attack Pearl Harbor and take Hong Kong 1941 | The Communist victory in China produces massive immigration into Hong Kong 1949 | Great Britain and China agree to the return of Hong Kong to China 1980s | Mass demonstrations in Hong Kong against the Tiananmen Square massacre |

1990s

China resumes control of Hong Kong on July 1, 1997; Tung Chee-hwa becomes chief executive

attempted to expand democratic rule in the colony as much as possible before the 1997 Chinese takeover—reforms that the Chinese threatened to dismantle after 1997.

The Joint Declaration of 1984 was drafted by top governmental leaders, with very little input from the people of Hong Kong. This fact plus fears about what P.R.C. control would mean to the freewheeling lifestyle of Hong Kong's ardent capitalists caused thousands of residents, with billions of dollars in assets in tow, to abandon Hong Kong for Canada, Bermuda, Australia, the United States, and Great Britain. Surveys found that as many as one third of the population of Hong Kong wanted to leave the colony before the Chinese takeover. In the year before the change to Chinese rule, so many residents—16,000 at one point—lined up outside the immigration office to apply for British passports that authorities had to open up a nearby sports stadium to accommodate them. About half of Hong Kong residents already held British citizenship, but many of the rest, particularly recent refugees from China, wanted to secure their futures in case life under Chinese rule became suppressive. Immigration officials received more than 100,000 British passport applications in a single month in 1996!

Emigration and unease over the future have unsettled, but by no means ruined, Hong Kong's economy. According to the World Bank, Hong Kong is home to the world's eighth-largest stock market, the fifth-largest banking center and foreign-exchange market (and the second largest in Asia after Japan), and its economy is the sixth richest in the world. Close to 9,000 multinational corporations have of-

fices in Hong Kong, while some of the world's wealthiest billionaires call Hong Kong home. Moreover, over the objections of the Chinese government, the outgoing British authorities have embarked on several ambitious infrastructural projects that should allow Hong Kong to continue to grow economically in the future. Chief among these is the airport on Chek Lap Kok Island. At a cost of $21 billion, the badly needed airport is one of the largest construction projects currently under way in the Pacific Rim. Opinion surveys show that despite fears of angering the incoming Chinese government, most Hong Kong residents appear to support efforts to improve the economy and to democratize the government by lowering the voting age and allowing direct election rather than appointment of more officials.

These kinds of reports might lead outsiders to conclude that everyone in Hong Kong is unequivocally opposed to the departure of the British. However, although there are large British and American communities in Hong Kong, and although English is the language of government, many residents have little or no contact with the Western aspects of Hong Kong life and feel very little, if any, loyalty to the British Crown. They assert that they are, first and foremost, Chinese, and that as such they can govern themselves without the involvement of any Western power. This, of course, does not amount to a popular endorsement of China's claim to govern Hong Kong, but it does imply that some residents of Hong Kong, if they have to be governed by others, would rather they be Chinese. Moreover, some believe that the Chinese government may ac-

tually help rid Hong Kong of financial corruption and allocate more resources to the poor.

Hong Kong's natural links with the P.R.C. have been expanding steadily for years. In addition to a shared language and culture there are in Hong Kong thousands of recent immigrants with strong family ties to the People's Republic. And there are increasingly important commercial ties. Hong Kong has always served as south China's entrepôt to the rest of the world for both commodity and financial exchanges. For instance, for years Taiwan has circumvented its regulations against direct trade with China by transshipping its exports through Hong Kong. Commercial trucks plying the highways between Hong Kong and the P.R.C. form a bumper-to-bumper wall of commerce between the two regions. Already, 43 percent of Hong Kong's imports comes from China (16 percent from Japan), while 25 percent of its exports goes to China (24 percent to the United States). The P.R.C. realizes that Hong Kong needs to remain more or less as it is—therefore, the transition to Chinese rule may be less jarring to residents than is expected. Most observers believe that, even after the transition to Chinese rule, Hong Kong will remain, along with Tokyo, one of the major financial and trading centers of Asia and of the world.

DEVELOPMENT

Hong Kong is one of the financial and trading dynamos of the world. Hong Kong annually exports billions of dollars worth of products. Hong Kong's political future may be uncertain after 1997, but its fine harbor as well as its new $21 billion airport, currently under construction, are sure to continue to fuel its economy.

FREEDOM

Hong Kong has been an appendage to one of the world's foremost democracies for some 150 years. Its residents have enjoyed the civil liberties guaranteed by British law. After 1997, a new Basic Law—currently being implemented with the consent of the Chinese government—will take full effect.

HEALTH/WELFARE

Schooling is free and compulsory in Hong Kong through junior high school. The government has devoted large sums for low-cost housing, aid for refugees, and social services such as adoption. Housing, however, is cramped and inadequate for the population.

ACHIEVEMENTS

Hong Kong has the capacity to hold together a society where the gap between rich and poor is enormous. The so-called boat people have been subjected to discrimination, but most other groups have found social acceptance and opportunities for economic advancement.

Indonesia (Republic of Indonesia)

GEOGRAPHY

Area in Square Kilometers (Miles):
1,919,440 (740,903) (nearly 3 times
the size of Texas)
Capital (Population): Jakarta
(8,800,000)
Climate: tropical; hot, humid; more
moderate in highlands

PEOPLE

Population
Total: 203,584,000
Annual Growth Rate: 1.56%
Rural/Urban Population Ratio: 69/31
Ethnic Makeup: 45% Javanese; 14%
Sudanese; 7.5% Madarese, 7.5%
coastal Malays, 26% others
Major Languages: Bahasa
Indonesian; English; Dutch; Javanese;
many others

Health
Life Expectancy at Birth: 59 years
(male); 63 years (female)
Infant Mortality Rate (Ratio):
65/1,000
Average Caloric Intake: 105% of
FAO minimum
Physicians Available (Ratio): 1/7,427

Religions
87% Muslim; 9% Christian; 2%
Hindu; 2% Buddhist and others

Education
Adult Literacy Rate: 77%

COMMUNICATION

Telephones: 1,122,100
Newspapers: 252

EXPLOSIVE ISLANDS

Located in an area that geologists call "the belt of fire," Indonesia has
more volcanoes per square mile than any other country in the world.
Out of 500 volcanoes, 128 are active and 65 more are considered
dangerous. An eruption of Krakatau in 1883 killed 35,000 people.
Mount Kelud, 390 miles east of Jakarta, erupted in 1990, spewing lava
on nearby towns and dumping ash on towns as far as 30 miles away.
Kelud has erupted 8 times since 1811, claiming the lives of nearly 6,000
people. Its most recent explosion killed 15, injured 48, and required the
evacuation of 4,000 villagers.

TRANSPORTATION

Highways—Kilometers (Miles):
119,500 (74,000)
Railroads—Kilometers (Miles): 6,964
(4,318)
Usable Airfields: 450

GOVERNMENT

Type: republic
Independence Date: December 27,
1949
Head of State: President Suharto
Political Parties: Golkar Party
(quasi-official); Indonesia Democracy
Party; Muslim United Development
Party; Democratic People's Party
(unauthorized)
Suffrage: universal at age 17 and
married persons regardless of age

MILITARY

Number of Armed Forces: 279,000
Military Expenditures (% of Central

Government Expenditures): 1.5%
Current Hostilities: none

ECONOMY

Currency ($ U.S. Equivalent): 2,378
Indonesian rupiahs = $1
Per Capita Income/GDP:
$3,090/$619.4 billion
Inflation Rate: 9.3%
Natural Resources: oil; minerals;
forest products
Agriculture: subsistence food
production; rice; cassava; peanuts;
rubber; cocoa; coffee; copra; other
tropical products
Industry: petroleum; textiles, mining;
cement; chemical fertilizer; timber;
food; rubber

FOREIGN TRADE

Exports: $41.3 billion
Imports: $31.4 billion

A KALEIDOSCOPIC CULTURE

Present-day Indonesia is a kaleidoscope of some 300 languages and more than 100 ethnic groups. Beginning about 5000 B.C., people of Mongoloid stock settled the islands that today constitute Indonesia in successive waves of migration from China, Thailand, and Vietnam. Animism—the nature-worship religion of these peoples—was altered substantially (but never completely lost) about A.D. 200, when Hindus from India began to settle in the area and wield the dominant cultural influence. Five hundred years later, Buddhist missionaries and settlers began converting Indonesians in a proselytizing effort that produced strong political and religious antagonisms. In the thirteenth century, Muslim traders began the Islamization of the Indonesian people; today, 87 percent of the population claim the Muslim faith—meaning that there are more Muslims in Indonesia than in any other country of the world, including the countries of the Middle East. Commingling with all these influences were cultural inputs from the islands of Polynesia.

The real roots of the Indonesian people undoubtedly go back much further than any of these historic cultures. In 1891, the fossilized bones of a hominid who used stone tools, camped around a fire, and probably had a well-developed language were found on the island of Java. Named *Pithecanthropus erectus* ("erect ape-man"), these important early human fossils, popularly called Java Man, have been dated at about 750,000 years of age. Fossils similar to Java Man have been found in Europe, Africa, and Asia.

Modern Indonesia was sculpted by the influence of many outside cultures. Portuguese Catholics, eager for Indonesian spices, made contact with Indonesia in the 1500s and left 20,000 converts to Catholicism, as well as many mixed Portuguese–Indonesian communities and dozens of Portuguese "loan words" in the Indonesian-style Malay language. In the following century, Dutch Protestants established the Dutch East India Company to exploit Indonesia's riches. Eventually the Netherlands was able to gain complete political control; it reluctantly gave it up in the face of insistent Indonesian nationalism only as recently as 1950. Before that, however, the British briefly controlled one of the islands, and the Japanese ruled the country for 3 years during the 1940s.

Indonesians, including then-president Sukarno, initially welcomed the Japanese as helpers in their fight for independence from the Dutch. Everyone believed that the Japanese would leave soon. Instead, the Japanese military forced farmers to give food to the Japanese soldiers, made everyone worship the Japanese emperor, neglected local industrial development in favor of military projects, and took 270,000 young men away from Indonesia to work elsewhere as forced laborers (fewer than 70,000 survived to return home). Military leaders who attempted to revolt against Japanese rule were executed. Finally, in August 1945, the Japanese abandoned their control of Indonesia, according to the terms of surrender with the Allied powers.

Consider what all these influences mean for the culture of modern Indonesia. Some of the most powerful ideologies ever espoused by humankind—supernaturalism, Islam, Hinduism, Buddhism, Christianity, mercantilism, colonialism, and nationalism—have had an impact on Indonesia. Take music, for example. Unlike Western music, which most people just listen to, Indonesian music, played on drums and gongs, is intended as a somewhat sacred ritual in which all members of a community are expected to participate. The instruments themselves are considered sacred. Dances are often the main element in a religious service whose goal might be a good rice harvest, spirit possession, or exorcism. Familiar musical styles can be heard here and there around the country. In the eastern part of Indonesia, the Nga'dha peoples, who were converted to Christianity in the early 1900s, sing Christian hymns to the accompaniment of bronze pot gongs and drums. On the island of Sumatra, Minang Kabau peoples, who were converted to Islam in the 1500s, use local instruments to accompany Islamic poetry singing. Communal feasts in Hindu Bali, circumcision ceremonies in Muslim Java, and Christian baptisms among the Bataks of Sumatra all represent borrowed cultural traditions. Thus, out of many has come one rich culture.

But the faithful of different religions are not always able to work together in harmony. For example, in the 1960s, when average Indonesians were trying to distance themselves from radical Communists, many decided to join Christian faiths. Threatened by this tilt toward the West and by the secular approach of the government, many fundamentalist Muslims resorted to violence. They burned Christian churches, threatened Catholic and Baptist missionaries, and opposed such projects as the construction of a hospital by Baptists. Indonesia is one of the most predominately Muslim countries in the world, and the hundreds of Islamic socioreligious and political organizations intend to keep it that way.

A LARGE LAND, LARGE DEBTS

Unfortunately, Indonesia's economy is not as rich as its culture. About 75 percent of the population live in rural areas; more than half of the people engage in fishing and small-plot rice and vegetable farming. Forty percent of the gross national product comes from agriculture. The average income per person is only $3,090 a year (based on gross domestic product), and inflation consumes about 9 percent of that annually. A 1993 law increased the minimum wage in Jakarta to $2.00 *per day.*

Also worrisome is the level of government debt. Indonesia is blessed with large oil reserves (Pertamina is the state-owned oil company) and minerals and timber of every sort (also state-owned), but to extract these natural resources has required massive infusions of capital, most of it borrowed. In fact, Indonesia has borrowed more money than any other country in Asia and must allocate 40 percent of its national budget just to pay the interest on loans. Low oil prices in the 1980s made it difficult for the country to keep up with its debt burden.

To cope with these problems, Indonesia has relaxed government control over foreign investment and banking, and it seems to be on a path toward privatization of other parts of the economy. Still, the gap between the modernized cities and the traditional countryside continues to plague the government.

Indonesia's financial troubles seem puzzling, because in land, natural resources, and population, the country appears quite well-off. Indonesia is the second-largest country in Asia (after China). Were it superimposed on a map of the United States, its 13,677 tropical islands would stretch from California, past New York, and out to Bermuda in the Atlantic Ocean. Oil and hardwoods are plentiful, and the population is large enough to constitute a viable internal consumer market. But transportation and communication are problematic and costly in archipelagic states. Indonesia's national airline, Garuda Indonesia, has launched a $3.6 billion development program that will bring into operation 50 new aircraft stopping at 13 new airports. New seaports are also under construction. But the cost of linking together the 6,000 inhabited islands is a major drain on the economy. Moreover, exploitation of Indonesia's amazing panoply of resources is drawing the ire of more and more people around the world who fear the destruction of the world's ecosystem.

Indonesia's population of 203.5 million is one of the largest in the world, but 23 percent of adults cannot read or write. Only about 600 people per 100,000 attend college, as compared to 3,580 in nearby

Java Man lived here **1.7 million years** B.C.	Buddhism gains the upper hand **A.D. 600**	Muslim traders bring Islam to Indonesia **A.D. 1200**	The Portuguese begin to trade and settle in Indonesia **1509**	Dutch traders begin to influence Indonesian life **1596**	The Japanese defeat the Dutch **1942**	Indonesian independence from the Netherlands; President Sukarno retreats from democracy and the West **1949–1950**	General Suharto takes control of the government from Sukarno and establishes his New Order, pro-Western government **1966**	Anti-Japanese riots take place in Jakarta **1974**	Indonesia annexes East Timor **1975**

1990s

Economic reforms aim to increase foreign investment and employment opportunities

Oil revenues slump; the rupiah is devalued

Earthquakes kill 2,500 Indonesians in 1992 and injure 1,500 in 1994

Philippines. Moreover, since almost 70 percent of the population reside on or near the island of Java, on which the capital city, Jakarta, is located, educational and development efforts have concentrated there, at the expense of the communities on outlying islands. Many children in the out-islands never complete the required 6 years of elementary school. Some ethnic groups, on the islands of Irian Jaya (New Guinea) and Kalimantan (Borneo), for example, continue to live isolated in small tribes, much as they did thousands of years ago. By contrast, the modern city of Jakarta, with its classical European-style buildings, is predicted to have a population of more than 13 million by the year 2000. Social problems have been ameliorated somewhat by Indonesia's strong economic growth (an average of 6 percent over the past 20 years), which has reduced the official poverty rate (from 60 percent in 1970 to 15 percent in 1990).

With 3 million new Indonesians entering the labor force every year and 50 percent of the population under age 20, serious efforts must be made to increase employment opportunities. For the 1990s, the government earmarked millions of dollars to promote tourism. Nevertheless, the most pressing problem was to finish the many projects for which World Bank and Asian Development Bank loans had already been received.

MODERN POLITICS

Establishing the current political and geographic boundaries of the Republic of Indonesia has been a bloody and protracted task. So fractured is the culture that many people doubt whether there really is a single country that one can call Indonesia. During the first 15 years of independence

(1950–1965), there were revolts by Muslims and pro-Dutch groups, indecisive elections, several military coups, battles against U.S.–supported rebels, and serious territorial disputes with Malaysia and the Netherlands. In 1966, nationalistic President Sukarno, who had been a founder of Indonesian independence, lost power to Army General Suharto. (Many Southeast Asians had no family names until influenced by Westerners; Sukarno and Suharto have each used only one name.) Anti-Communist feeling grew during the 1960s, and thousands of suspected members of the Indonesian Communist Party (PKI) and other Communists were killed before the PKI was banned in 1966. In 1975, ignoring the disapproval of the United Nations, President Suharto invaded and annexed East Timor, a Portuguese colony. Although the military presence in East Timor has since been reduced, separatists were beaten and killed by the Indonesian Army as recently as 1991; and in 1993, a separatist leader was sentenced to 20 years in prison. In late 1995, Amnesty International accused the Indonesian military of raping and executing human-rights activists in East Timor, while the 20th anniversary of the Indonesian takeover was marked by Timorese storming foreign embassies and demanding asylum and redress for the kidnapping and killing of protesters. In 1996, antigovernment rioting in Jakarta resulted in the arrest of more than 200 opposition leaders and the disappearance of many others. The rioters were supporters of the Indonesian Democracy Party and its leader, Megawati Sukarnoputri, daughter of Sukarno.

Suharto's so-called New Order government rules with an iron hand, suppressing student and Muslim dissent and control-

ling the press and the economy. In 1994, Suharto was reelected (in an uncontested election) to his sixth 5-year term, and his Golkar Party continues to hold a solid political majority.

In 1974, upon the visit of the prime minister of Japan, antigovernment and anti-Japanese riots broke out in Jakarta. Many believed that Suharto and the Japanese were in collusion to exploit the Indonesian economy. While the aim may not have been exploitation, it is true that Indonesia and Japan have established very close economic ties. Indonesia sends 42 percent of its exports to Japan and buys 23 percent of its imports from Japan. And Japanese investment money continues to flow into Indonesia, as elsewhere in the Pacific Rim. Japan's Toyota Corporation spent millions of yen in 1993 to purchase stock in Indonesia's PT ASTRA International automobile company. Many of the country's planned tourist-industry expansions are financed by Japanese banks. Taiwan, South Korea, Germany, and the United States are also heavy investors. Indonesia may try to become a better political neighbor, as the country is feeling the need for more integration into the world economy. In 1995, Indonesia signed a security agreement with Australia, and it hosted the Asia–Pacific Economic Cooperation meeting in 1994.

DEVELOPMENT

Indonesia continues to be hamstrung by its heavy reliance on foreign loans, a burden inherited from the Sukarno years. Current Indonesian leaders speak of "stabilization" and "economic dynamism."

FREEDOM

Demands for Western-style human rights are frequently heard, but only the army has the power to impose order on the numerous and competing political groups, many imbued with religious fervor.

HEALTH/WELFARE

Indonesia has one of the highest birth rates in the Pacific Rim. Many children will grow up in poverty, never learning even to read or write their national language, Bahasa Indonesian.

ACHIEVEMENTS

Balinese dancers' glittering gold costumes and unique choreography epitomize the "Asian-ness" of Indonesia. Despite its heavy debt, Indonesia continues to pay its bills on schedule.

Laos (Lao People's Democratic Republic)

GEOGRAPHY

Area in Square Kilometers (Miles):
236,800 (91,400)
Capital (Population): Vientiane
(377,000)
Climate: tropical monsoon

PEOPLE

Population

Total: 4,837,300
Annual Growth Rate: 2.84%
Rural/Urban Population (Ratio):
81/19
Ethnic Makeup: 50% Lao; 20% tribal
Thai; 15% Phoutheung (Kha); 15%
Meo, Hmong, Yao, and others
Major Languages: Lao; French;
English

Health

Life Expectancy at Birth: 51 years
(male); 53 years (female)
Infant Mortality Rate (Ratio):
99.2/1,000
Average Caloric Intake: 94% of FAO
minimum
Physicians Available (Ratio): 1/6,495

Religions

85% Buddhist; 15% traditional
indigenous and others

Education

Adult Literacy Rate: 84%

WHAT'S FOR DINNER?

When the first entity that could be called the nation of Laos was formed
in the fourteenth century A.D., the country's name was Lang Xang, meaning
"Land of a Million Elephants." One of the founders of Laos was said in
legend to have been sent by God and to have arrived on Earth riding on
an elephant. Elephants are still used as beasts of burden in Laos, but other
animals, such as water buffalo, oxen, horses, chickens, and ducks, are more
important to Laotian daily life. Animals are often tied up underneath Laotian
houses, which are built up on stilts. Many animals end up on the dinner
table: Quail, snakes, deer, wild chickens, and fish add protein to the rice-
based Laotian diet. North American cultural sensitivities have been offended
by Laotian Hmong immigrants' culinary preferences; when the Hmong (a
mountain people who were severely persecuted by the Communists and
who subsequently emigrated from Laos *en masse*) settled in the United
States, city dwellers complained that the Hmong were catching rats in city
parks and cooking them for dinner.

COMMUNICATION

Telephones: 7,400
Newspapers: n/a

TRANSPORTATION

Highways—Kilometers (Miles):
14,130 (8,817)
Railroads—Kilometers (Miles): —
Usable Airfields: 52

GOVERNMENT

Type: Communist state
Independence Date: July 19, 1949
Head of State/Government: President
Nouhak Phoumsavan; Prime Minister
(General) Khamtai Siphandon
Political Parties: Lao People's
Revolutionary Party
Suffrage: universal at 18

MILITARY

Number of Armed Forces: 53,100
*Military Expenditures (% of Central
Government Expenditures):* 8.1%
Current Hostilities: none

ECONOMY

Currency ($ U.S. Equivalent): 717
new kips = $1
Per Capita Income/GDP: $850/$4.0
billion
Inflation Rate: 6.5%
Natural Resources: timber;
hydropower; gypsum; tin; gold;
gemstones
Agriculture: rice; potatoes;
vegetables; coffee; sugarcane; cotton
Industry: tin mining; timber; electric
power; agricultural processing

FOREIGN TRADE

Exports: $227 million
Imports: $528 million

THE REALITY
OF LAOTIAN LIFE

Laos seems a sleepy place. Almost everyone lives in small villages where the only distraction might be the Buddhist temple gong announcing the day. Water buffalo plow quietly through centuries-old rice paddies, while young Buddhist monks in saffron robes make their silent rounds for rice donations. Villagers build their houses on stilts for safety from annual river flooding and top them with thatch or tin. Barefoot children play under the palm trees or wander to the village Buddhist temple for school in the outdoor courtyard. Mothers stay home to weave brightly colored cloth for the family and to prepare meals—on charcoal or wood stoves—of rice, bamboo shoots, pork, duck, and snakes seasoned with hot peppers and ginger.

Below this serene surface, however, Laos is a nation divided. Although the name Laos is taken from the dominant ethnic group, there are actually about 70 ethnic groups in the country. Over the centuries, they have battled one another for supremacy, for land, and for tribute money. The constant feuding has weakened the nation and served as an invitation for neighboring countries to annex portions of Laos forcibly or to align themselves with one or another of the Laotian royal families or generals for material gain. China, Burma (today called Myanmar), Vietnam, and especially Thailand—with which Laotian people share many cultural and ethnic similarities—have all been involved militarily in Laos.

Historically, a cause of unrest was often palace jealousies that led one member of the royal family to fight against a kinsman for dominance. More recently, Laos has been seen as a pawn in the battle of the Western powers for access to the rich natural resources of Southeast Asia or as a "domino" that some did and others did not want to fall to communism. Former members of the royal family continue to find themselves on the opposite sides of many issues.

The results of these struggles have been devastating. Laos is now one of the poorest countries in the world. There are few industries in the country, so most people survive by subsistence farming, raising just what they need to eat rather than growing food to sell. In fact, some "hill peoples" (about two thirds of the Laotian people live in the mountains) in the long mountain range that separates Laos from Vietnam continue to use the most ancient farming technique known, slash-and-burn farming, an unstable method of land use that only allows 3 or 4 years of good crops before the soil is depleted and the farmers must move to new ground.

Even if all Laotian farmers used the most modern techniques and geared their production to cash crops, it would still be difficult to export food (or, for that matter, anything else) because of Laos's woefully inadequate transportation network. There are no railroads, and muddy, unpaved roads make many mountain villages completely inaccessible by car or truck. Only one bridge, the Thai-Lao Friendship Bridge near the capital city of Vientiane, spans the famous Mekong River in Laos. Moreover, Laos is landlocked. In a region of the world where wealth flows toward those countries with the best ports, having no access to the sea is a serious impediment to economic growth. In addition, for years the economy has been strictly controlled. Foreign investment and trade have not been welcomed, and tourists were not allowed until 1989. But the economy was opening up by the early 1990s, and the government's new "Socioeconomic National Development Plan" was calling for foreign investment in all areas and an annual economic growth rate of 8 percent.

Some progress has been made in the past decade. Laos is once again self-sufficient in its staple crop, rice, and electricity generated from dams along the Mekong River is sold to Thailand to earn foreign exchange. Laos imports various commodity items from Thailand, Singapore, Japan, and other countries, and it has received foreign aid from the Asian Development Bank. Exports to Thailand, China, and the United States include teakwood, tin, and various minerals. Despite its 1995 "certification" by the United States that it is a cooperating country in the world antidrug effort, Laos is also the source of many controlled substances such as opium and heroin, much of which finds its way to Europe and the United States. The Laotian government is now trying to prevent hill peoples from cutting down valuable forests for opium-poppy cultivation.

HISTORY AND POLITICS

The Laotian people, originally migrating from south China through Thailand, settled Laos in the thirteenth century A.D., when the area was controlled by the Khmer (Cambodian) Empire. Early Laotian leaders expanded the borders of Laos through warfare with Cambodia, Thailand,

(UPI/Bettmann)

Laos is one of the poorest countries in the world. With few industries, most people survive by subsistence farming. These fishermen spend their days catching tiny fish, measuring 2 to 5 inches, that must suffice to feed their families.

The first Laotian nation is established A.D. 1300s	Vietnam annexes most of Laos **1833**	Laos comes under French control **1885**	The Japanese conquer Southeast Asia **1940s**	France grants independence to Laos **1949**	South Vietnamese troops, with U.S. support, invade Laos **1971**	Pathet Lao Communists gain control of the government **1975**	Laos signs military and economic agreements with Vietnam **1977**	The government begins to liberalize some aspects of the economy **1980s**

1990s

The Pathet Lao government maintains firm control over the country

Laos and Thailand make moves toward improved relations

The first bridge across Mekong River to Thailand opens

Burma, and Vietnam. Internal warfare, however, led to a loss of autonomy in 1833, when Thailand forcibly annexed the country (against the wishes of Vietnam, which also had designs on Laos). In the 1890s, France, determined to have a part of the lucrative Asian trade and to hold its own against growing British strength in Southeast Asia, forced Thailand to give up its hold on Laos. Laos, Vietnam, and Cambodia were combined into a new political entity, which the French called Indochina. Between these French possessions and the British possessions of Burma and Malaysia lay Thailand; thus, France, Britain, and Thailand effectively controlled mainland Southeast Asia for several decades.

There were several small uprisings against French power, but these were easily suppressed until the Japanese conquest of Indochina in the 1940s. The Japanese, with their "Asia for Asians" philosophy, convinced the Laotians that European domination was not a given. In the Geneva Agreement of 1949, Laos was granted independence, although full French withdrawal did not take place until 1954.

Prior to independence Prince Souphanouvong (who died in 1995 at the age of 82) had organized a Communist guerrilla army, with help from Ho Chi Minh and the Vietnamese Communist Viet Minh. This army called itself the Pathet Lao (meaning "Lao Country"). In 1954, it challenged the authority of the government in Vientiane. Civil war ensued, and by 1961, when a cease-fire was arranged, the Pathet Lao had captured about half of Laos. The Soviet Union supported the Pathet Lao, whose strength was in the northern half of Laos, while the United States supported a

succession of pro-Western but fragile governments in the south. A coalition government consisting of Pathet Lao, pro-Western, and neutralist leaders was installed in 1962, but it collapsed in 1965, when warfare once again broke out.

During the Vietnam War, U.S. and South Vietnamese forces bombed and invaded Laos in an attempt to disrupt the North Vietnamese supply line known as the Ho Chi Minh Trail. Americans flew nearly 600,000 bombing missions over Laos (many of the small cluster bombs remain unexploded in fields and villages and present a continuing danger). Communist battlefield victories in Vietnam encouraged and aided the Pathet Lao Army, which became the dominant voice in a new coalition government established in 1974. The Pathet Lao controlled the government exclusively by 1975. In the same year, the government proclaimed a new "Lao People's Democratic Republic." It abolished the 622-year-old monarchy and sent the king and the royal family to a detention center to learn Marxist ideology.

Vietnamese Army support and flight by many of those opposed to the Communist regime have permitted the Pathet Lao to maintain control of the government. The ruling dictatorship is determined to prevent the democratization of Laos: In 1993, several cabinet ministers were jailed for 14 years for trying to establish a multiparty democracy.

The Pathet Lao government was sustained militarily and economically by the Soviet Union and other East bloc nations for more than 15 years. However, with the end of the cold war and the collapse of the Soviet Union, Laos has had to look

elsewhere, including non-Communist countries, for support. In 1992, Laos signed a friendship treaty with Thailand to facilitate trade between the two historic enemy countries. In 1994, the Australian government, continuing its plan to integrate itself more fully into the strong Asian economy, promised to provide Laos with more than $33 million in aid. In 1995, Laos joined with ASEAN nations to declare the region a nuclear-free zone.

Trying to teach communism to a devoutly Buddhist country has not been easy. Popular resistance has caused the government to retract many of the regulations it has tried to impose on the Buddhist Church (technically, the *Sangara,* or order of the monks—the Buddhist equivalent of a clerical hierarchy). As long as the Buddhist hierarchy limits its activities to helping the poor, it seems to be able to avoid running afoul of the Communist leadership.

Intellectuals, especially those known to have been functionaries of the French administration, have fled Laos, leaving a leadership vacuum. As many as 300,000 people are thought to have left Laos for refugee camps in Thailand and elsewhere. Many have taken up permanent residence in foreign countries. The exodus has imposed a significant drain on Laos's intellectual resources.

DEVELOPMENT

Communist rule after 1975 isolated Laos from world trade and foreign investment. The planned economy has not been able to gain momentum on its own. In 1986 the government loosened restrictions so that government companies could keep a portion of their profits. A goal is to integrate Laos economically with Vietnam and Cambodia.

FREEDOM

Laos is ruled by the political arm of the Pathet Lao Army. Opposition parties and groups as well as opposition newspapers and other media are outlawed. Lack of civil liberties as well as poverty have caused many thousands of people to flee the country.

HEALTH/WELFARE

Laos is typical of the least developed countries in the world. The birth rate is high, but so is infant mortality. Most citizens eat less than an adequate diet. Life expectancy is low, and many Laotians die from illnesses for which medicines are available in other countries. Many doctors fled the country when the Communists came to power.

ACHIEVEMENTS

The original inhabitants of Laos, the Kha, have been looked down upon by the Lao, Thai, and other peoples for centuries. But under the Communist regime, the status of the Kha has been upgraded and discrimination formally proscribed.

Macau

GEOGRAPHY

Area in Square Kilometers (Miles):
16 (6) (about one tenth the size of
Washington, D.C.)
Capital (Population): Macau
(478,000)
Climate: subtropical

PEOPLE

Population
Total: 491,000
Annual Growth Rate: 1.25%
Rural/Urban Population Ratio: 0/100
Ethnic Makeup: 95% Chinese; 3%
Portuguese; 2% others
Major Languages: Portuguese;
Cantonese

Health
Life Expectancy at Birth: 77 years
(male); 82 years (female)
Infant Mortality Rate (Ratio):
5.4/1,000
Average Caloric Intake: n/a
Physicians Available (Ratio): 1/2,470

THE LEGEND OF A-MA

Every May, the people of Macau celebrate the Feast of A-Ma, a Chinese
goddess after whom the Portuguese named Macau. During the course
of the festival, the entire fishing fleet comes to port to honor this
patroness of fishermen and seamen at the temple that bears her name,
located at the entrance of the Inner Harbor.

According to legend, A-Ma was a poor girl looking for a passage to
Canton. She was refused by the wealthy junk owners, but a lowly
fisherman took her aboard. Soon a storm wrecked all the boats but the
one carrying A-Ma. When it landed in Macau, she disappeared, only to
reappear later as a goddess at the spot where the fisherman built her a
temple.

Religions
46% unaffiliated; 45% Buddhist; 7%;
Roman Catholic; 1% Protestant; 1%
other

Education
Adult Literacy Rate: 90%

COMMUNICATION

Telephones: 55,643
Newspapers: 8

TRANSPORTATION

Highways—Kilometers (Miles): 42 (26)
Railroads—Kilometers (Miles): none
Usable Airfields: none

GOVERNMENT

Type: Chinese territory under
Portuguese administration; scheduled
to revert to China in 1999
Independence Date: —
Head of State/Government: President
(of Portugal) Mário Alberto Soares;
Governor Vasco Joachim Rocha Vieira
Political Parties: Association to
Defend the Interests of Macau;
Macau Democratic Center; Group to
Study the Development of Macau;
Macau Independent Group
Suffrage: universal at 18

MILITARY

Number of Armed Forces: defense is
the responsibility of Portugal
*Military Expenditures (% of Central
Government Expenditures):*
responsibility of Portugal
Current Hostilities: none

ECONOMY

Currency ($ U.S. Equivalent): 8.03
patacas = $1
Per Capita Income/GDP:
$10,000/$48 billion
Inflation Rate: 7.7%
Natural Resources: fish
Agriculture: rice; vegetables
Industry: clothing; textiles; toys;
plastic products; furniture; tourism

FOREIGN TRADE

Exports: $1.8 billion
Imports: $2.0 billion

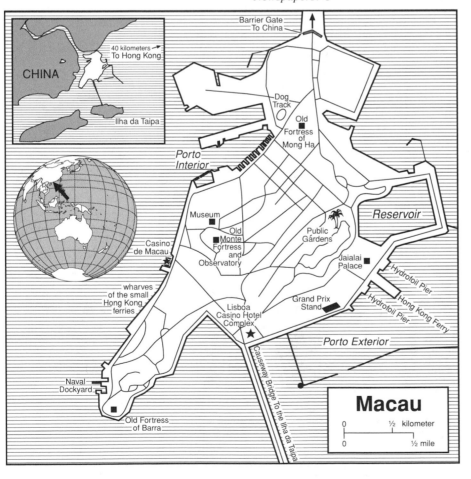

| A Portuguese trading colony is established at Macau A.D. 1557 | Portugal declares sovereignty over Macau 1849 | China signs a treaty recognizing Portuguese sovereignty over Macau 1887 | Immigrants from China flood into the colony 1949 | Pro-Communist riots in Macau 1967 | Portugal begins to loosen direct administrative control over Macau 1970s | Macau becomes a Chinese territory but is still administered by Portugal 1976 | China and Portugal sign an agreement scheduling the return of Macau to Chinese control 1987 | 1990s |

50,000 illegal Chinese immigrants seek permanent residency status in Macau

Macau will revert to Chinese control in 1999

MACAU'S HISTORY

Just 17 miles across the Pearl River estuary from British Hong Kong is another speck of foreignness on Chinese soil: the Portuguese territory of Macau (sometimes spelled Macao). The oldest permanent outpost of European culture in the Far East, Macau has the highest population density of any political entity in the world: Although it consists of only about 6 square miles of land, it is home to nearly half a million people, crowded onto the peninsula and two small islands. Some 95 percent of these are Chinese, and Cantonese is universally spoken, although Portuguese is still the official language. Macau's population has varied over the years, depending on conditions within China. During the World War II Japanese occupation of China, for instance, Macau's Chinese population is believed to have doubled, and more refugees streamed in when the Communists took over China in 1949.

Macau was frequented by Portuguese traders as early as 1516, but it was not until 1557 that the Chinese agreed to Portuguese settlement of the land; it did not, however, acknowledge Portuguese sovereignty. Indeed, the Chinese government did not recognize the Portuguese right of "perpetual occupation" until 1887.

In 1987, after 9 months of negotiation, Chinese and Portuguese officials, meeting in Beijing, signed an agreement that will end European control of the first and last colonial outpost in China. The Portuguese will have administered the tiny colony of Macau for close to 450 years; the transfer to Chinese control is scheduled for December 20, 1999.

The agreement is similar to that signed by Great Britain and China over the fate of Hong Kong. China agreed to allow Macau to maintain its capitalist way of life for 50 years, to permit local elections, and to allow its residents to travel freely without Chinese intervention. Unlike Hong Kong residents, who have staged massive demonstrations against future Chinese rule or have emigrated from the colony, Macau residents—some of whom have been openly pro-Communist—have not seemed bothered by the new arrangements. In fact, plans are under way to bolster the economy in preparation for 1999 by constructing an airport in the territory, and President Mario Soares of Portugal, on an official visit in 1993, indicated that plans for the reversion to China were going smoothly. Indeed, businesses in Macau and Hong Kong were contributing to a de facto merging with the mainland by investing more than $20 billion in China in 1994.

Since it was established in the sixteenth century as a trading colony with interests in oranges, tea, tobacco, and lacquer, Macau has been heavily influenced by Roman Catholic priests of the Dominican and Jesuit orders. Christian churches, interspersed with Buddhist temples, abound. The name of Macau itself reflects its deep and enduring religious roots; the city's official name is "City of the Name of God in China, Macau, There Is None More Loyal." Macau has perhaps the highest density of churches and temples per square mile in the world. Buddhist immigrants from China have reduced the proportion of Christians in the population.

A HEALTHY ECONOMY

Macau's modern economy is a vigorous blend of light industry, fishing, tourism, and gambling. Revenues from the latter two sources are impressive, accounting for 25 percent of gross domestic product. There are five major casinos and many other gambling opportunities in Macau, which, along with the considerable charms of the city itself, attract more than 5 million foreign visitors a year, more than 80 percent of them Hong Kong Chinese with plenty of money to spend. Macau's gambling industry is run by a syndicate of Chinese businesspeople operating under the name Macau Travel & Amusement Company, which won monopoly rights on all licensed gambling in Macau in 1962.

Export earnings derived from light-industry products such as textiles, fireworks, plastics, and electronics are also critical to the colony. Macau's leading export markets are the United States, China, Germany, France, and Hong Kong; ironically, Portugal consumes only about 3 percent of Macau's exports.

As might be expected, the success of the economy has a downside. In Macau's case, the hallmarks of modernization—crowded apartment blocks and bustling traffic—are threatening to eclipse the remnants of the old, serene Portuguese-style seaside town.

DEVELOPMENT

The development of industries related to gambling and tourism (tourists are primarily from Hong Kong) has been very successful. Most of Macau's foods, energy, and fresh water are imported from China; Japan and Hong Kong are the main suppliers of raw materials.

FREEDOM

Under the 1987 agreement, China will acquire full sovereignty over Macau in 1999, but local elections will be permitted, as will the capitalist way of life. The governor is currently appointed by the president of Portugal, while the 17 members of the Legislative Assembly are elected directly by the people of Macau.

HEALTH/WELFARE

Macau has very impressive quality-of-life statistics. It has a low infant mortality rate and very high life expectancy for both males and females. Literacy is 90 percent. In recent years, the unemployment rate has been a low 2 percent.

ACHIEVEMENTS

Considering its unfavorable geographical characteristics, such as negligible natural resources and a port so shallow and heavily silted that oceangoing ships must lie offshore, Macau has had stunning economic success. Its annual economic growth rate is approximately 5 percent.

Malaysia

GEOGRAPHY

Area in Square Kilometers (Miles):
329,750 (121,348) (slightly larger
than New Mexico)
Capital (Population): Kuala Lumpur
(1,000,000)
Climate: tropical

PEOPLE

Population

Total: 19,723,600
Annual Growth Rate: 2.24%
Rural/Urban Population Ratio: 62/38
Ethnic Makeup: 59% Malay and
other indigenous; 32% Chinese; 9%
Indian and Pakistani
Major Languages: Peninsular
Malaysia: Bahasa Malaysia, English,
Chinese dialects, Tamil; Sabah:
English, Malay, numerous tribal
dialects, Mandarin and Hakka
dialects; Sarawak: English, Malay,
Mandarin, numerous tribal dialects,
Arabic, others

Health

Life Expectancy at Birth: 67 years
(male); 73 years (female)
Infant Mortality Rate (Ratio):
24.7/1,000
Average Caloric Intake: 117% of
FAO minimum
Physicians Available (Ratio): 1/2,638

Religions

Peninsular Malaysia: Malays nearly
all Muslim, Chinese predominantly
Buddhist, Indians predominantly
Hindu; Saba: 33% Muslim, 17%
Christian, 45% others; Sarawak: 35%
traditional indigenous, 24% Buddhist
and Confucian, 20% Muslim, 16%
Christian, 5% others

Education

Adult Literacy Rate: 78% overall

COMMUNICATION

Telephones: 1,579,634
Newspapers: n/a

TRANSPORTATION

Highways—Kilometers (Miles):
29,026 (17,996)
Railroads—Kilometers (Miles): 1,801
(1,116)
Usable Airfields: 115

GOVERNMENT

Type: constitutional monarchy
Independence Date: August 31, 1957
Head of State: Prime Minister Datuk
Mahathir bin Mohamad; Paramount
Ruler (King) Jaafarbin Abdul Rahman
Political Parties: Peninsular
Malaysia: National Front
Confederation and others; Sabah:
Berjaya Party and others; Sarawak:
coalition Sarawak National Front and
others
Suffrage: universal at 21

MILITARY

Number of Armed Forces: 119,900
*Military Expenditures (% of Central
Government Expenditures):* 5%
Current Hostilities: dispute over the
Spratly Islands with China, the
Philippines, Taiwan, and Vietnam;
Sabah is claimed by the Philippines

ECONOMY

Currency ($ U.S. Equivalent): 2.55
ringgit = $1
Per Capita Income/GDP:
$8,650/$1668 billion
Inflation Rate: 2.9%
Natural Resources: oil; natural gas;
bauxite; iron ore; copper; tin; timber;
fish
Agriculture: rubber; palm oil; rice;
coconut; pepper; timber
Industry: rubber and palm oil
manufacturing and processing; light
manufacturing; electronics; tin
mining and smelting; logging and
processing timber; petroleum
production and refining; food
processing

FOREIGN TRADE

Exports: $56.6 billion
Imports: $55.2 billion

PHONING FOR FISH IN MALAYSIA

Malaysia is having trouble keeping its telephones. In 1996, according to the
Associated Press, Telekom Malaysia received hundreds of complaints about
missing handsets at public phone booths on the island of Borneo. To the
dismay of officials, some 900 had disappeared in a single year. An investigation revealed that fishermen were the culprits. They were connecting the
stolen handsets to high-powered batteries, lowering them into the water and
using the resulting high-pitched sounds to attract fish into their nets.

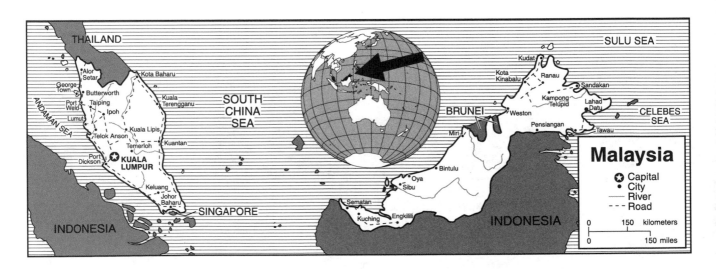

A FRACTURED NATION

About the size of Japan and famous for its production of natural rubber and tin, Malaysia sounds like a true political, economic, and social entity. But Malaysia, although it has all the trappings of a modern nation-state, is one of the most fragmented nations on Earth.

Consider its land. West Malaysia, wherein reside 86 percent of the population, is located on the Malay Peninsula between Singapore and Thailand; but East Malaysia, with 60 percent of the land, is located on the island of North Borneo, some 400 miles of ocean away.

Similarly, Malaysia's people are divided along racial, religious, and linguistic lines. Fifty-nine percent of the population of nearly 20 million are Malays and other indigenous peoples, many of whom adhere to the Islamic faith or animist beliefs; 32 percent are Chinese, most of whom are Buddhist, Confucian, or Taoist; and 9 percent are Indians and Pakistanis, some of whom follow the Hindu faith. Bahasa Malaysia is the official language, but English, Arabic, two forms of Chinese, Tamil, and other languages are also spoken. Thus, although the country is called *Malaysia* (a name adopted only 30 years ago), most people living in Kuala Lumpur, the capital, or in the many villages in the countryside do not think of themselves first and foremost as Malaysians.

Malaysian culture is further fragmented because each ethnic group tends to replicate the architecture, social rituals, and forms of etiquette peculiar to itself. The Chinese, originally imported in the 1800s from south China by the British to work the rubber plantations and tin mines, have become so economically powerful that their cultural influence extends far beyond their actual numbers.

Malaysian history is equally fragmented. Originally controlled by numerous sultans who gave allegiance to no one or only reluctantly to various more powerful states in surrounding regions, Malaysia first came to Western attention in 1511, when the prosperous city of Malacca, founded on the west coast of the Malaya Peninsula about A.D. 1400, was conquered by the Portuguese. The Dutch took Malacca away from the Portuguese in 1641. The British seized it from the Dutch in 1824 (the British had already acquired an island off the coast and had established the port of Singapore). By 1888, the British were in control of most of the area that is now Malaysia.

However, British hegemony did not mean total control, for each of the many sultanates—the origin of the 13 states that constitute Malaysia today—continued to act more or less independently of the British, engaging in wars with one another and maintain-

ing an administrative apparatus apart from the British. And some groups, such as the Dayaks, an indigenous people living in the jungles of Borneo, remained more or less aloof from the various intrigues of modern state-making and developed little or no identity of themselves as citizens of any modern nation.

It is hardly surprising, then, that Malaysia has had a difficult time emerging as a modern nation. Indeed, it is not likely that there would have been an independent Malaysia had it not been for the Japanese, who defeated the British in Southeast Asia during World War II and promulgated their alluring doctrine of "Asia for Asians."

After the war, Malaysian demands for independence from European domination grew more persuasive; Great Britain attempted in 1946 to meet these demands by proposing a partly autonomous Malay Union. However, ethnic rivalries and power-sensitive sultans created such enormous tension that the plan was scrapped. In an uncharacteristic display of cooperation, some 41 different Malay groups organized the United Malay National Organization (UMNO) to oppose the British plan. In 1948, a new Federation of Malaya was attempted. It granted considerable freedom within a framework of British supervision, allowed sultans to retain power over their own regions, and placed certain restrictions on the power of the Chinese living in the country.

Opposing any agreement short of full independence, a group of Chinese Communists, with Indonesian support, began a guerrilla war against the government and against capitalist ideology. Known as "The Emergency," the war lasted more than a decade and involved some 250,000 government troops. Eventually, the insurgents withdrew.

The three main ethnic groups—Malayans, represented by UMNO; Chinese, represented by the Malayan Chinese Association, or MCA; and Indians, represented by the Malayan Indian Congress, or MIC—were able to cooperate long enough in 1953 to form a single political party under the leadership of Abdul Rahman. This party demanded and received complete independence for the Federation in 1957, although some areas, such as Brunei, refused to join. Upon independence, the Federation of Malaya (not yet called Malaysia), excluding Singapore and the territories on the island of Borneo, became a member of the British Commonwealth of Nations and was admitted to the United Nations. In 1963, a new Federation was proposed that included Singapore and the lands on Borneo. Again, Brunei refused to join. Singapore joined but withdrew in 1965. Thus, what is known as Malaysia acquired its current form in 1966.

It is regarded today as a rapidly developing nation that is attempting to govern itself according to democratic principles.

Political troubles stemming from the deep ethnic divisions in the country, however, remain a constant feature of Malaysian life. With nine of the 13 states controlled by independent sultans, every election is a test of the ability of the National Front (Barisan Nasional), a multiethnic coalition of 11 different parties that has a two-thirds majority in Parliament, to maintain political stability. Particularly troublesome has been the state of Sabah (an area claimed by the Philippines), many of whose residents have wanted independence or, at least, greater autonomy from the federal government. In 1994, however, the National Front was able to gain a slight majority in Sabah elections, indicating the growing confidence that people have in the federal government's economic development policies.

ECONOMIC DEVELOPMENT

The single most important reason why Malaysia has been able to maintain stability has been its steady economic growth. Although it has had to endure the cyclical fluctuations of market demand for its products, the economy has grown at about 5 to 8 percent a year since the 1970s. Malaysia is among the world's top 20 exporters/importers, and the manufacturing sector has been developed to such an extent that it accounts for nearly 70 percent of exports. Malaysia continues to be known for its abundance of raw materials, especially timber (Malaysia produces half of the world's timber exports), tin, and petroleum. Rice, coconut oil, and pepper are also important exports.

This amazing transformation of the economy did not happen accidentally; it has been the result of proactive government planning, directly modeled after Japan's export-oriented strategy and using massive amounts of Japanese investment money. Unlike North Korea or Myanmar (Burma), which have resisted integration into the global economy, Malaysia launched a New Economic Policy (NEP) in the 1970s that welcomed foreign direct investment and sought to diversify the economic base. Japan, Taiwan, and the United States invested heavily in Malaysia. So successful has this strategy been that economic growth targets set for the mid-1990s were actually achieved several years early. In 1991, the government replaced NEP with a new plan, now generally called "Vision 2020." Its goal is to bring Malaysia into full "developed nation" status by the year 2020. Sectors targeted for growth include the aerospace industry, biotechnology, microelectronics, and information and energy technol-

The city of Malacca is established; it becomes a center of trade and Islamic conversion **A.D. 1403**	The Portuguese capture Malacca **1511**	The Dutch capture Malacca **1641**	The British obtain Malacca from the Dutch **1824**	Japan captures the Malay Peninsula **1941**	The British establish the Federation of Malaya; a Communist guerrilla war begins, lasting for a decade **1948**	The Federation of Malaya achieves independence under Prime Minister Tengku Abdul Rahman **1957**	The Federation of Malaysia, including Singapore but not Brunei, is formed **1963**	Singapore leaves the Federation of Malaysia **1965**	Malaysia attempts to build an industrial base; Datuk Mahathir bin Mohamad becomes prime minister **1980s**

1990s

The NEP, proclaimed a success, comes to an official end

The NEP is replaced with Vision 2020

Economic relations are strained with some Western nations

ogy. The government has expanded universities and encouraged the creation of some 170 industrial and research parks, including "Free Zones," where export-oriented businesses are allowed duty-free imports of raw materials. Some of Malaysia's most ambitious projects include the development of what Malaysians hope to be the world's largest offshore financial center (on Labuan Island) and the construction of a $6 billion hydroelectric dam—a project strongly opposed by environmentalists.

Despite Malaysia's economic successes, serious social problems remain. These problems stem not from insufficient revenues (Malaysia was blessed with an annual budget surplus until 1990) but from inequitable distribution. The Malay portion of the population in particular continues to feel economically deprived as compared to the wealthier Chinese and Indian segments. (At one time these upper-class households received, on average, 16 times the income of the poorest Malay families.) Furthermore, most Malays are farmers, and rural areas have not benefited from Malaysia's economic boom as much as urban areas have.

In the 1960s and 1970s, riots involving thousands of college students were headlined in the Western press as having their basis in ethnicity. This was true to an extent, but the core issue was economic inequality. Included in the economic master plan of the 1970s were plans (similar to affirmative action in the United States) to change the structural barriers that prevented Malays from fully enjoying the benefits of the economic boom. Under the leadership of Prime Minister Datuk Mahathir bin Mohamad, plans were developed that would assist Malays until they held a 30 percent interest in Malaysian businesses. In 1990, the government announced that the figure had already

reached an impressive 20 percent. Unfortunately, many Malays have insufficient capital to maintain ownership in businesses, so the government has been called upon to acquire many Malay businesses in order to prevent their being purchased by non-Malays. In addition, the system of preferential treatment for Malays has created a Malay elite, detached from the Malay poor, who now compete with the Chinese and Indian elites; interracial goodwill is still difficult to achieve. Nonetheless, social goals have been attained to a greater extent than most observers have thought possible. Educational opportunities for the poor have been increased, farmland development has proceeded on schedule, and the poverty rate has dropped to 17 percent.

THE LEADERSHIP

In a polity so fractured as Malaysia's, one would expect rapid turnover among political elites. But Prime Minister Mahathir, a Malay, has continued to receive the support of the electorate for more than a decade. His primary challenger has been the Chinese Democratic Action Party (DAP), which has sometimes reduced Mahathir's majority in Parliament but has not been able to top his political strength. The policies that have sustained Mahathir's reputation as a credible leader include the NEP, with its goals of economic diversification, privatization, and wealth equalization, and his nationalist—but moderate—foreign policy. Malaysia has been an active member of ASEAN and has worked hard to maintain good diplomatic relations with the Western nations, while simultaneously courting Japan and other Pacific Rim nations for

foreign investment and export markets (Mahathir's "Look East" policy). Anticipating negative economic consequences from the growing strength of the European Union and the North American Free Trade Agreement, Mahathir promoted a plan to create an Asian-free trade zone that would exclude the United States and other Western nations. Failing in that, he refused to attend the Asia-Pacific Economic Cooperation group meetings held in 1993 in the United States, at which more than a dozen regional leaders discussed economic cooperation. Rocky economic relations between Malaysia and some Western nations, which resulted in the canceling of airport- and dam-construction projects, were improved somewhat in 1996 by the visit of the Australian prime minister to Prime Minister Mahathir.

Malaysia's success has not been achieved without some questionable practices. The government seems unwilling to regulate economic growth, even though strong voices have been raised against industrialization's deleterious effects on the teak forests and other parts of the environment. Moreover, the blue-collar workers who are the muscle behind Malaysia's economic success are prohibited from forming labor unions, and outspoken critics have been silenced. Charges of government corruption are becoming more frequent and more strident.

DEVELOPMENT	FREEDOM	HEALTH/WELFARE	ACHIEVEMENTS

Malaysia continues to struggle to move its economy away from agriculture. Attempts at industrialization have been successful: Malaysia is the third-largest producer of semiconductors in the world, and manufacturing now accounts for 30% of the gross domestic product.	Malaysia is attempting to govern according to democratic principles. Ethnic rivalries, however, severely hamper the smooth conduct of government and limit such individual liberties as the right to form labor unions.	City dwellers have ready access to educational, medical, and social opportunities, but the quality of life declines dramatically in the countryside. Malaysia has one of the highest illiteracy rates in the Pacific Rim. Malaysia still spends only a small percentage of its GDP on education.	Malaysia has made impressive economic advancements. The government's New Economic Policy has achieved a measure of wealth redistribution to the poor. Since the 1970s, the economy has grown at an impressive 5% to 8% annually. Malaysia has also made impressive social and political gains.

Myanmar (Union of Myanmar; commonly known as Burma)

GEOGRAPHY

Area in Square Kilometers (Miles):
678,500 (261,901) (slightly smaller than Texas)
Capital (Population): Yangon (previously Rangoon) (2,459,000)
Climate: tropical monsoon and equatorial

PEOPLE

Population

Total: 45,104,000
Annual Growth Rate: 1.84%
Rural/Urban Population Ratio: 75/24
Ethnic Makeup: 68% Burman; 9% Shan; 7% Karen; 4% Rakhine; 3% Chinese; 8% Mon, Indian, and others
Major Languages: 60% Burmese; various minority languages

Health

Life Expectancy at Birth: 58 years (male); 63 years (female)
Infant Mortality Rate (Ratio): 65.7/1,000
Average Caloric Intake: 106% of FAO minimum
Physicians Available (Ratio): 1/3,389

Religions

89% Buddhist; 4% Muslim; 4% Christian; 3% animist and others

Education

Adult Literacy Rate: 81%

COMMUNICATION

Telephones: 73,545
Newspapers: 1

BUDDHISM

Most people in Myanmar are Buddhists, and the Buddhist hierarchy of priests, called the *Sangha,* has been a powerful opponent of the military dictatorship. This is a rather unusual position for Buddhists, who have generally preferred a passive attitude toward "worldly" issues.

Detachment from the world was the philosophy of Buddhism's founder, Siddhartha Gautama. He was born about 563 B.C. in what is today Nepal. Raised in luxury and expected to follow in his father's footsteps as a ruler and warrior, Gautama instead abandoned his wife, children, and riches to lead the life of a poor wanderer in search of life's meaning. At about age 35, while meditating under a tree, he experienced a spiritual insight that earned him the title of *buddha,* meaning the "awakened" or "enlightened one." From that experience he came to believe that life would be full of pain for everyone unless they renounced their attachment to greed and the other selfish desires of the world.

TRANSPORTATION

Highways—Kilometers (Miles): 27,000 (16,740)
Railroads—Kilometers (Miles): 3,991 (2,474)
Usable Airfields: 80

GOVERNMENT

Type: military government
Independence Date: January 4, 1948
Head of State: General Than Shwe
Political Parties: National League for Democracy; National Coalition of Union of Burma; National Unity Party; more than 100 others
Suffrage: universal at 18

MILITARY

Number of Armed Forces: 280,000 plus 85,000 paramilitary personnel
Military Expenditures (% of Central Government Expenditures): 40%
Current Hostilities: internal strife

ECONOMY

Currency ($ U.S. Equivalent): 5.86 kyats = $1
Per Capita Income/GDP: $930/$41.4 billion
Inflation Rate: 38%
Natural Resources: crude oil; timber; tin; antimony; zinc; copper; tungsten; lead; coal; marble; limestone; precious stones; natural gas
Agriculture: teak; rice; corn; oilseed; sugarcane; pulses
Industry: agricultural processing; textiles; footwear; wood and wood products; petroleum refining; copper, tin, tungsten, and iron mining; construction materials; pharmaceuticals; fertilizer

FOREIGN TRADE

Exports: $674 million
Imports: $1.2 billion

THE CONTROLLED SOCIETY

For more than 3 decades, Myanmar (as Burma was officially renamed in 1989) has been a tightly controlled society. Telephones, radio stations, railroads, and many large companies have been under the direct control of a military junta that has brutalized its opposition and forced many to flee the country. For many years, tourists were allowed to stay only 2 weeks (for a while the limit was 24 hours), had to stay at military-approved hotels, and could visit only certain parts of the country. Citizens too were highly restricted: They could not leave their country by car or train to visit nearby countries because all the roads were sealed off by government decree and rail lines terminated at the border. Even Western-style dancing was declared illegal. Until a minor liberalization of the economy was achieved in 1989, all foreign exports—every grain of rice, every peanut, every piece of lumber—though generally owned privately, had to be sold to the government rather than directly to consumers.

Observers attribute this state of affairs to military commanders who overthrew the legitimate government in 1962, but the roots of Myanmar's political and economic dilemma actually go back to 1885, when the British overthrew the Burmese government and declared Burma a colony of Britain. In the 1930s, European-educated Burmese college students organized strikes and demonstrations against the British. Seeing that the Japanese Army had successfully toppled other European colonial governments in Asia, the students determined to assist the Japanese during their invasion of the country in 1941. Once the British had been expelled, however, the students organized the Anti-Fascist People's Freedom League (AFPFL) to oppose Japanese rule.

When the British tried to resume control of Burma after World War II, they found that the Burmese people had given their allegiance to U Aung San, one of the original student leaders. He and the AFPFL insisted that the British grant full independence to Burma, which they reluctantly did in 1948. So determined were the Burmese to remain free of foreign domination that, unlike most former British colonies, they refused to join the British Commonwealth of Nations, an economic association of former British colonies. This was the first of many decisions that would have the effect of isolating Burma from the global economy.

Unlike Japan, with its nearly homogeneous population and single national language, Myanmar is a multiethnic state; in fact, only about 60 percent of the people speak Burmese. The Burman people are genetically related to the Tibetans and the Chinese; the Chin are related to peoples of nearby India; the Shan are related to Thais; and the Mon migrated to Burma from Cambodia. In general, these ethnic groups live in separate political states within Myanmar—the Kachin State, the Shan State, the Karen State, and so on; and for hundreds of years, they have warred against one another for dominance. Upon the withdrawal of the British in 1948, some ethnic groups, particularly the Kachins, the Karens, and the Shans, embraced the Communist ideology of change through violent revolution. Their rebellion against the government in the capital city of Yangon (the new name of Rangoon) had the effect of removing from government control large portions of the country. Headed by U Nu (U Aung San and several of the original government leaders having been assassinated shortly before independence), the government considered its position precarious and determined that to align itself with the Communist forces then ascendant in the People's Republic of China and other parts of Asia would strengthen the hand of the ethnic separatists, whereas to form alliances with the capitalist world would invite a repetition of decades of Western domination. U Nu thus attempted to steer a decidedly neutral course during the cold war era and to be as tolerant as possible of separatist groups within Burma. Burma refused U.S. economic aid, had very little to do with the warfare afflicting Vietnam and the other Southeast Asian countries, and was not eager to join the Southeast Asian Treaty Organization or the Asian Development Bank.

Some factions of Burmese society were not pleased with U Nu's relatively benign treatment of separatist groups. In 1958, a political impasse allowed Ne Win, a military general, to assume temporary control of the country. National elections were held in 1962, and a democratically elected government was installed in power. Shortly thereafter, however, Ne Win staged a military coup. (The military has controlled Burma/Myanmar ever since.) Under Ne Win, competing political parties were banned, the economy was nationalized, and the country's international isolation became even more pronounced.

Years of ethnic conflict, inflexible socialism, and self-imposed isolation have severely damaged economic growth in Myanmar. Despite an abundance of valuable teak and rubber trees in its forests, sizable supplies of minerals in the mountains to the north, onshore oil, rich farmland in the Irrawaddy Delta, and a reasonably well-educated population, in 1987 the United Nations declared Burma one of the least developed countries in the world (it had once been the richest country in Southeast Asia). Debt incurred in the 1970s exacerbated Myanmar's problems, as did the government's fear of foreign investment. Thus, by 1996, Myanmar's per capita income was less than $1,000 a year.

Myanmar's industrial base is still very small; some 70 percent of the population of 42 million make their living by farming (rice is a major export) and by fishing. Only 10 percent of gross domestic product comes from the manufacturing sector (as compared to, for example, approximately 45 percent in wealthy Taiwan). In the absence of a strong economy, black marketeering has increased, as have other forms of illegal economic transactions. It is estimated that 80 percent of the heroin smuggled into New York City comes from the jungles of Myanmar and northern Thailand.

Over the years, the Burmese have been advised by economists to open up their country to foreign investment and to develop the private sector of the economy. They have resisted the former idea because of their deep-seated fear of foreign domination; they have similar suspicions of the private sector because it was previously controlled almost completely by ethnic minorities (the Chinese and Indians). The government has relied on the public sector to counterbalance the power of the ethnic minorities.

Beginning in 1987, however, the government began to admit publicly that the economy was in serious trouble. To counter massive unrest in the country, the military authorities agreed to permit foreign investment from countries such as Malaysia, South Korea, Singapore, and Thailand and to allow trade with China and Thailand. In 1989, the government signed oil-exploration agreements with South Korea, the United States, the Netherlands, Australia, and Japan. Both the United States and the former West Germany withdrew foreign aid in 1988, but Japan did not; in 1991, Japan supplied $61 million—more than any other country—in aid to Myanmar.

POLITICAL STALEMATE

Despite these reforms, Myanmar has remained in a state of turmoil. In 1988, thousands of students participated in 6 months of demonstrations to protest the lack of democracy in the country and to demand multiparty elections. General Saw Maung brutally suppressed the demonstrators, imprisoning many students and killing some 3,000 of them. He then took control of the government and reluctantly agreed to multiparty elections. About 170 political parties registered for the elections, which were held in 1990—the first elections in 30 years. Among these were the National Unity Party (a new name for the Burma Socialist Program Party, the only legal party since 1974) and the National League for Democracy, a new party headed by Aung San Suu Kyi, daughter of slain national hero U Aung San.

The campaign was characterized by the same level of military control that had existed in all other aspects of life since the 1960s. Martial law, imposed in 1988, remained in effect; all schools and universities were closed; opposition-party workers were intimidated; and, most significantly, the three most popular opposition leaders were placed under house arrest and barred from campaigning. The United Nations began an investigation of civil-rights abuses during the election and, once again, students demonstrated against the military government. Several students even hijacked a Burmese airliner to demand the release of Aung San Suu Kyi, who had been placed under house arrest.

As the votes were tallied, it became apparent that the Burmese people were eager to end military rule; the National League for Democracy won 80 percent of the seats in the National Assembly. But the military junta refused to step down and remains in control of the government. Under General Than Shwe, who replaced General Saw Maung in 1992, the military has organized operations against Karen rebels and has so oppressed Muslims that some 40,000 to 60,000 of them have fled to Bangladesh. Hundreds of students who fled the cities during the 1988 crackdown on student demonstrations have now joined rural guerrilla organizations, such as the Burma Communist Party and the Karen National Union, to continue the fight against the military dictatorship. Among those most vigorously opposed to military rule are Buddhist monks. Five months after the elections, monks in the capital city of Yangon boycotted the government by refusing to conduct religious rituals for soldiers. Tens of thousands of people joined in the boycott. The government responded by threatening to shut down monasteries in the cities of Yangon and Mandalay.

The military government calls itself the State Law and Order Restoration Council (SLORC) and appears determined to stay in power. SLORC has vowed to keep Aung San Suu Kyi under house arrest. For several years, even her husband and children were forbidden to visit her. While under arrest, she was awarded the Nobel Peace Prize; in 1993, several other Nobelists gathered in nearby Thailand to call for her release—a plea ignored by

(Photo credit AP Laser-Photo)

In 1990, Myanmar's first elections in 30 years were held; a new opposition party, the National League for Democracy, headed by Aung San Suu Kyi, pictured above, won 80 percent of the seats in the National Assembly but she was never permitted to take office. Instead, she was placed under house arrest for several years. In 1991, Aung San Suu Kyi was awarded the Nobel Peace Prize.

SLORC. The United Nations has shown its displeasure with the military junta by substantially cutting development funds, as has the United States, which, on the basis of Myanmar's heavy illegal-drug activities, has disqualified the country from receiving most forms of economic aid.

But perhaps the greatest pressure on the dictatorship is from within the country itself. Despite brutal suppression, the military seems to be losing control of the people. Both the Kachin and Karen ethnic groups have organized guerrilla movements against the regime; in some cases,

GLOBAL STUDIES: JAPAN AND THE PACIFIC RIM

Burman people enter the Irrawaddy Valley from China and Tibet **800** B.C.

The Portuguese are impressed with Burmese wealth **1500s**

The First Anglo-Burmese War **1824–1826**

The Second Anglo-Burmese War **1852**

The Third Anglo-Burmese War results in the loss of Burmese sovereignty **1885**

The Japanese invade Burma **1941**

Burma gains independence of Britain **1948**

General Ne Win takes control of the government in a coup **1962**

Economic crisis; the pro-democracy movement is crushed; General Saw Maung takes control of the government **1980s**

Burma is renamed Myanmar (though most people prefer the name Burma) **1989**

1990s

The military refuses to give up power; Than Shwe becomes head of state

U Nu, first prime minister of modern Burma, dies in 1995 at age 87

Aung San Suu Kyi's activities remain restricted; Myanmar is granted observer status in ASEAN

they have coerced foreign lumber companies to pay them protection money, which they, in turn, use to buy arms against the junta. Opponents of SLORC control one third of Myanmar, especially along its eastern borders with Thailand and China and in the north alongside India. With the economy in shambles, the military appears to be involved with the heroin trade as a way of acquiring needed funds; it reportedly engages in bitter battles with drug lords periodically for control of the trade. To ease economic pressure, the military rulers have ended their monopoly of some businesses and have legalized the black market, making products from China, India, and Thailand available on the street.

Still, for ordinary people, especially those in the countryside, life is anything but pleasant. A 1994 human-rights study found that as many as 20,000 women and girls living in Myanmar near the Thai border had been abducted to work as prostitutes in Thailand. For several years, SLORC has carried out an ethnic-cleansing policy against villagers who have opposed their rule; thousands of people have been carried off to relocation camps, forced to work as slaves or prostitutes for the soldiers, or simply killed. Some 400,000 members of ethnic groups have fled the country, including 300,000 Arakans who escaped to Bangladesh and 5,000 Karenni, 12,000 Mon, and 50,000 Karens who fled to Thailand. Food shortages plague certain regions of the country, and many young children are forced to serve in the various competing armies rather than acquire an education or otherwise enjoy a normal childhood. Despite the lifting of martial law and some minor liberalization of the economy, it appears that it will be a long time before democracy will take hold in Myanmar.

THE CULTURE OF BUDDHA

For a brief period in the 1960s, Buddhism was the official state religion of Burma. Although this status was repealed by the government in order to weaken the power of the Buddhist leadership, or *Sangha,* vis-à-vis the polity, Buddhism, representing the belief system of 89 percent of the population, remains the single most important cultural force in the country. Even the Burmese alphabet is based, in part, on Pali, the sacred language of Buddhism. Buddhist monks joined with college students after World War II to pressure the British government to withdraw from Burma, and they have brought continual pressure to bear on the current military junta.

Historically, so powerful has been the Buddhist *Sangha* in Burma that four major dynasties have fallen because of it. This has not been the result of ideological antagonism between church and state (indeed, Burmese rulers have usually been quite supportive of Buddhism) but, rather, because Buddhism soaks up resources that might otherwise go to the government or to economic development. Believers are willing to give money, land, and other resources to the religion, because they believe that such donations will bring them spiritual merit; the more merit one acquires, the better one's next life will be. Thus, all over Myanmar, but especially in older cities such as Pagan, one can find large, elaborate Buddhist temples, monuments, or monasteries, some of them built by kings and other royals on huge, untaxed parcels of land. These monuments drained resources from the government but brought to the donor unusual amounts of spiritual merit. As Burmese scholar Michael Aung-Thwin explained it, "One built the largest temple because one was spiritually superior, and one was spiritually superior because one built the largest temple."

Today, the Buddhist *Sangha* is at the forefront of the opposition to military rule. Monks have joined college students in peaceful-turned-violent demonstrations against the junta. Other monks have staged spiritual boycotts against the soldiers by refusing to accept merit-bringing alms from them or to perform weddings and funerals. The junta has retaliated by banning some Buddhist groups altogether and purging many others of rebellious leaders. The military regime now seems to be relaxing its intimidation of the Buddhists, has reopened universities, and has invited some foreign investment. Although the Japanese have continued to invest in Myanmar throughout the military dictatorship, some potential investors from other countries refused to invest in a regime that is so obviously brutal and which gives little evidence of any desire to return the country to democracy.

DEVELOPMENT	FREEDOM	HEALTH/WELFARE	ACHIEVEMENTS

Primarily an agricultural nation, Myanmar has a poorly developed industrial sector. Until recently, the government forbade foreign investment and severely restricted tourism. In 1989, recognizing that the economy was on the brink of collapse, the government permitted foreign investment and signed contracts with Japan and others for oil exploration.

Myanmar is a military dictatorship. Until 1989, only the Burma Socialist Program Party was permitted. Other parties, while now legal, are intimidated by the military junta. The democratically elected National League for Democracy has not been permitted to assume office. The government has also restricted the activities of Buddhist monks and has carried out "ethnic cleansing" against minorities.

The Myanmar government provides free health care and pensions to citizens, but the quality and availability of these services are erratic. Malnourishment and preventable diseases are common, and infant mortality is high. Overpopulation is not a problem; Myanmar is one of the most sparsely populated nations in Asia.

Myanmar is known for the beauty of its Buddhist architecture. Pagodas and other Buddhist monuments and temples dot many of the cities, especially Pagan, one of Burma's earliest cities. Politically, it is notable that the country was able to remain free of the warfare that engulfed much of Indochina during the 1960s and 1970s.

70

New Zealand (Dominion of New Zealand)

GEOGRAPHY

Area in Square Kilometers (Miles):
268,680 (98,874) (about the size of
Colorado)
Capital (Population): Wellington
(148,000)
Climate: temperate; sharp regional
contrasts

PEOPLE

Population
Total: 3,407,300
Annual Growth Rate: 0.52%
Rural/Urban Population (Ratio):
14/76
Ethnic Makeup: 88% European; 9%
Maori; 3% Pacific islander
Major Languages: English; Maori

Health
Life Expectancy at Birth: 73 years
(male); 80 years (female)
Infant Mortality Rate (Ratio):
8.03/1,000
*Average Caloric Intake: 132% of
FAO minimum
Physicians Available (Ratio): 1/359

MAORI PRIDE

The 257,000 Maoris in New Zealand have, for the most part, been assimilated into white ("Pakeha") New Zealand culture. They speak English, worship in Christian churches, and actively participate in land speculation and
other commercial activities of the free-enterprise system. Some have inter-
married with whites, others with Japanese, and still others with Indians.
Yet, originally, Maoris enjoyed pride of place in their islands. Indeed, the
word *Maori* means "normal"; the 50 or so tribes began using the term only
after white contact to distinguish themselves from those who were so obviously different from the Maori norm. Today, pride in being uniquely Maori
is coming back.

Religions
81% Christian; 18% unaffiliated; 1%
others

Education
Adult Literacy Rate: 99%

COMMUNICATION
Telephones: 2,110,000
Newspapers: 32 dailies

TRANSPORTATION
Highways—Kilometers (Miles):
92,648 (57,441)

Railroads—Kilometers (Miles): 4,716
(2,923)
Usable Airfields: 120

GOVERNMENT
Type: parliamentary democracy
Independence Date: September 26,
1907
Head of State/Government: Chief of
State Queen Elizabeth II, represented
by Governor General Dame
Catherine Tizard; Prime Minister
Donald McKinnon
Political Parties: New Zealand
Labour Party; National Party;
Democratic Party; Socialist Unity
Party; New Zealand Liberal Party;
Green Party
Suffrage: universal at 18

MILITARY
Number of Armed Forces: 11,300
*Military Expenditures (% of Central
Government Expenditures):* 1.7%
Current Hostilities: none; disputed
territorial claim in Antarctica

ECONOMY
Currency ($ U.S. Equivalent): 1.46%
New Zealand dollars = $1
Per Capita Income/GDP:
$16,640/$56.4 billion
Inflation Rate: 1.6%
Natural Resources: natural gas; iron
ore; sand; coal; timber; hydropower;
gold; limestone
Agriculture: wool; meat; dairy
products; wheat; barley; potatoes;
pulses; fruits; vegetables; fishing
Industry: food processing; wood and
paper products; textiles; machinery;
transportation equipment; banking;
insurance; tourism; mining

FOREIGN TRADE
Exports: $11.2 billion
Imports: $10.4 billion

ITS PLACE IN THE WORLD

New Zealand, like Australia, is decidedly an anomaly among Pacific Rim countries. Eighty-eight percent of the population are of British descent, English is the official language, and most people, even many of the original Maori inhabitants, are Christians. Britain claimed the beautiful, mountainous islands officially in 1840, after agreeing to respect the property rights of Maoris, most of whom lived on the North Island.

New Zealand, although largely self-governing since 1907 and fully independent as of 1947, has always maintained very close ties with the United Kingdom and is a member of the Commonwealth of Nations. It has, in fact, attempted to re-create British culture—customs, architecture, even vegetation—in the Pacific. So close were the links with Great Britain in the 1940s, for example, that England purchased fully 88 percent of New Zealand's exports (mostly agricultural and dairy products), while 60 percent of New Zealand's imports came from Britain. And believing itself to be very much a part of the British Empire, New Zealand always sided with the Western nations on matters of military defense.

These efforts to maintain a close cultural link with Great Britain do not stem entirely from the common ethnicity of the two nations; they also arise from New Zealand's extreme geographical isolation from the centers of European and North American activity. Even Australia is more than 1,200 miles away. Therefore, New Zealand's policy—until the 1940s—was to encourage the British presence in Asia and the Pacific, by acquiring more lands or building up naval bases, to make it more likely that Britain would be willing and able to defend New Zealand in a time of crisis. New Zealand had involved itself somewhat in the affairs of some nearby islands in the late 1800s and early 1900s, but its purpose was not to provide development assistance or defense. Rather, its aim was to extend the power of the British Empire and put New Zealand in the middle of a mini-empire of its own. To that end, New Zealand annexed the Cook Islands in 1901 and took over German Samoa in 1914. In 1925, it assumed formal control over the atoll group known as the Tokelau Islands.

REGIONAL RELIANCE DEVELOPS

During World War II (or, as the Japanese call it, the Pacific War), Japan's rapid conquest of the Malay Archipelago, its seizure of many Pacific islands, and its plans to attack Australia demonstrated to New Zealanders the futility of relying on the British to guarantee their security. After the war, and for the first time in its history, New Zealand began to pay serious attention to the real needs and ambitions of the peoples nearby rather than to focus on Great Britain. In 1944 and again in 1947, New Zealand joined with Australia and other colonial nations to create regional associations on behalf of the Pacific islands. One of the organizations, the South Pacific Commission, has itself spawned many regional subassociations dealing with trade, education, migration, and cultural and economic development. Although it had neglected the islands that it controlled during its imperial phase, in the

(The Peabody Museum of Salem photo)

Maoris occupied New Zealand long before the European settlers moved there. The Maoris quickly realized that the newcomers were intent on depriving them of their land, but it was not until the 1920s that the government finally regulated unscrupulous land-grabbing practices. Today, the Maoris pursue a lifestyle that preserves key parts of their traditional culture while incorporating skills necessary for survival in the modern world.

arly 1900s, New Zealand cooperated fully with the United Nations in the islands' decolonization during the 1960s (although Tokelau, by choice, and the Ross Dependency remain under New Zealand's control), while at the same time increasing development assistance. New Zealand's first alliance with Asian nations came in 1954, when it joined the Southeast Asian Treaty Organization.

New Zealand's new international focus certainly did not mean the end of cooperation with its traditional allies, however. In fact, the common threat of the Japanese during World War II strengthened cooperation between Australia and the United States to the extent that, in 1951, New Zealand joined a three-way, regional security agreement known as ANZUS (for Australia, New Zealand, and the United States). Moreover, because the United States was, at war's end, a Pacific/Asian power, any agreement with the United States was likely to bring New Zealand into more, rather than less, contact with Asia and the Pacific. Indeed, New Zealand sent troops to assist in all of the United States' military involvements in Asia: the occupation of Japan in 1945, the Korean War in 1950, and the Vietnam War in the 1960s. And, as a member of the British Commonwealth, it sent troops in the 1950s and 1960s to fight Malaysian Communists and Indonesian insurgents.

NEW ZEALAND'S NEW INTERNATIONALISM

Beginning in the 1970s, especially when the Labour Party of Prime Minister Norman Kirk was in power, New Zealand's orientation shifted even more markedly toward its own region. Under Labour, New Zealand defined its sphere of interest and responsibility as the Pacific, where it hoped to be seen as a protector and benefactor of smaller states. Of immediate concern to many island nations was the issue of nuclear testing in the Pacific. Both the United States and France had undertaken tests by exploding nuclear devices on tiny Pacific atolls. In the 1960s, the United States ceased these tests, but France continued. New Zealand argued before the United Nations against testing on behalf of the smaller islands, but France still did not stop. Eventually, the desire to end test-

ing congealed into the more comprehensive position that the entire Pacific should be declared a nuclear-free zone. Not only testing but also the transport of nuclear weapons through the area would be prohibited under the plan.

New Zealand's Labour government issued a ban on the docking of ships with nuclear weapons in New Zealand, despite the fact that such ships were a part of the ANZUS security agreement. When the National Party regained control of the government in the late 1970s, the nuclear ban was revoked, and the foreign policy of New Zealand tipped again toward its traditional allies. The National government argued that, as a signatory to ANZUS, New Zealand was obligated to open its docks to U.S. nuclear ships. However, under the subsequent Labour government of Prime Minister David Lange, New Zealand once again began to flex its muscles over the nuclear issue. Lange, like his Labour predecessors, was determined to create a foreign policy based on moral rather than legal rationales. In 1985, a U.S. destroyer was denied permission to call at a New Zealand port, even though its presence there was due to joint ANZUS military exercises. Because the United States refused to say whether or not its ship carried nuclear weapons, New Zealand insisted that the ship could not dock. Diplomatic efforts to resolve the standoff were unsuccessful; and in 1986, New Zealand, claiming it was not fearful of foreign attack, formally withdrew from ANZUS.

The issue of superpower use of the Pacific for nuclear weapons testing is still of major concern to the New Zealand government. The nuclear test ban treaty signed by the United States in 1963 has limited U.S. involvement in that regard, but France has continued to test atmospheric weapons, and both the United States and Japan have proposed using uninhabited Pacific atolls to dispose of nuclear waste. In 1995, when France ignored the condemnation of world leaders and detonated a nuclear device in French Polynesia, New Zealand recalled its ambassador to France out of protest.

In the early 1990s, a new issue came to the fore: nerve-gas disposal. With the end of the cold war, the U.S. military proposed disposing of most of its European stockpile of nerve gas on an atoll in the Pacific.

The atoll is located within the trust territory granted to the United States at the conclusion of World War II. The plan is to burn the gas away from areas of human habitation, but those islanders living closest (albeit hundreds of miles away) worry that residues from the process could contaminate the air and damage humans, plants, and animals. The religious leaders of Melanesia, Micronesia, and Polynesia have condemned the plan, not only on environmental grounds but also on grounds that outside powers should not be permitted to use the Pacific region without the consent of the inhabitants there—a position with which the Labour government of New Zealand strongly concurs.

ECONOMIC CHALLENGES

The New Zealand government's new foreign-policy orientation has caught the attention of observers around the world, but more urgent to New Zealanders themselves is the state of their own economy. Until the 1970s, New Zealand had been able to count on a nearly guaranteed export market in the United Kingdom for its dairy and agricultural products. Moreover, cheap local energy supplies as well as inexpensive oil from the Middle East had produced several decades of steady improvement in the standard of living. Whenever the economy showed signs of being sluggish, the government would artificially protect certain industries to ensure full employment.

All of this came to a halt beginning in 1973, when Britain joined the European Union (previously called the European Community) and when the Organization of Petroleum Exporting Countries sent the world into its first oil shock. New Zealand actually has the potential of near self-sufficiency in oil, but the easy availability of Middle East oil over the years had prevented the full development of local oil and gas reserves. As for exports, New Zealand had to find new outlets for its agricultural products, which it did by contracting with various countries throughout the Pacific Rim. Currently, a third of New Zealand's trade is within the Pacific Rim. In the transition to these new markets, farmers complained that the manufacturing sector—intentionally protected by the government as a way of diversifying New

Socialized
medicine is
implemented
1941

New Zealand
becomes fully
independent
within the
Commonwealth
of Nations
1947

New Zealand
backs creation of
the South Pacific
Commission
1947

Restructuring of
export markets
1950s

The National
Party takes
power; New
Zealand forges
foreign policy
more
independent of
traditional allies
1970s

The Labour Party
regains power;
New Zealand
withdraws from
ANZUS
1980s

1990s

New Zealanders
consider
withdrawing
from the
Commonwealth

Maoris and white
New Zealanders
face economic
challenges from
other Pacific
Rimmers

New Zealand
recalls its
ambassador to
France in protest
of French
nuclear testing

Zealand's reliance on agriculture—was getting unfair favorable treatment. Subsequent changes in government policy toward industry resulted in a new phenomenon for New Zealand: unemployment. Moreover, New Zealand had constructed a rather elaborate social-welfare system since World War II, so, regardless of whether economic growth was high or low, social-welfare checks still had to be sent. This untenable position has made for a difficult political situation, for, when the National Party cut some welfare benefits and social services, it lost the support of many voters. The welfare issue along with a change to a mixed member proportional voting system that enhanced the influence of smaller parties threatened the National Party's political power. In order to remain politically dominant, the National Party in 1996 was forced to form a coalition with the United Party—the first such coalition government in more than 60 years.

In the 1970s, for the first time, New Zealanders began to notice a decline in their standard of living. Two decades later, the economy is only slightly improved. New Zealand's economic growth rate is the lowest of all Pacific Rim countries (only 2.6 percent per year, as compared to more than 9 percent in Thailand and Singapore); and its per capita income is lower than in Hong Kong, Australia, and Japan. Its inflation rate has dropped, however, to an encouragingly low 1.6 percent.

New Zealanders are well aware of Japan's economic strength and its potential for benefiting their own economy through joint ventures, loans, and trade. Yet they also worry that Japanese wealth may constitute a symbol of New Zealand's declining strength as a culture. For instance, in the 1980s, as Japanese tourists began traveling en masse to New Zealand, complaints were raised about the quality of New Zealand's hotels. Unable to find the funds for a massive upgrading of the hotel industry, New Zealand agreed to allow Japan to build its own hotels; it reasoned that the local construction industry could use an economic boost and that the better hotels would encourage well-heeled Japanese to spend even more tourist dollars in the country. However, they also worried that, with the Japanese owning the hotels, New Zealanders might be relegated to low-level jobs.

Concern about their status vis-à-vis nonwhites had never been much of an issue to Anglo-Saxon New Zealanders; they always simply assumed that nonwhites were inferior. Many settlers of the 1800s believed in the Social Darwinistic philosophy that the Maori and other brown- and black-skinned peoples would gradually succumb to their European "betters." It did not take long for the Maoris to realize that, land guarantees notwithstanding, the whites intended to deprive them of their land and culture. Violent resistance to these intentions occurred in the 1800s, but

Maori landholdings continued to be gobbled up, usually deceptively, by white farmers and sheep herders. Government control of these unscrupulous practices was lax until the 1920s. Since that time many Maoris (whose population has increased to about 260,000) have intentionally sought to create a lifestyle that preserves key parts of traditional culture while incorporating the skills necessary for survival in a white world.

Now, though, Maoris and whites alike feel the social leveling that is the consequence of years of economic stagnation. Moreover, both worry that the superior financial strength of the Japanese and newly industrializing Asian and Southeast Asian peoples may diminish in some way the standing of their own cultures. The Maoris, complaining recently about Japanese net fishing and its damage to their own fishing industry, have a history of accommodation and adjustment to those who would rule over them; but, for the whites, submissiveness, even if it is imposed from afar and is largely financial in nature, will be a new and challenging experience.

DEVELOPMENT

Government protection of manufacturing has allowed this sector to grow at the expense of agriculture. Nevertheless, New Zealand continues to export large quantities of dairy products, wool, meat, fruits, and wheat. Full development of the Maui oil and gas deposits could alleviate New Zealand's dependence on foreign oil.

FREEDOM

New Zealand partakes of the democratic heritage of English common law and subscribes to all the human-rights protections that other Western nations have endorsed. Maoris, originally deprived of much of their land, are now guaranteed the same legal rights as whites. Social discrimination against Maoris is much milder than with many other colonized peoples.

HEALTH/WELFARE

New Zealand established pensions for the elderly as early as 1898. Child-welfare programs were started in 1907, followed by the Social Security Act of 1938, which augmented the earlier benefits and added a minimum-wage requirement and a 40-hour work week. A national health program was begun in 1941. The government began dispensing free birth-control pills to all women in 1996 in order to reduce the number of abortions.

ACHIEVEMENTS

New Zealand is notable for its efforts on behalf of the smaller islands of the Pacific. In addition to advocating a nuclear-free Pacific, New Zealand has promoted interisland trade and has established free-trade agreements with Western Samoa, the Cook Islands, and Niue. It provides educational and employment opportunities to Pacific islanders who reside within its borders.

North Korea (Democratic People's Republic of Korea)*

GEOGRAPHY

Area in Square Kilometers (Miles):
120,540 (44,358) (slightly smaller than Mississippi)
Capital (Population): P'yongyang (2,694,000)
Climate: temperate

PEOPLE

Population
Total: 23,487,000
Annual Growth Rate: 1.78%
Rural/Urban Population (Ratio): 40/60
Ethnic Makeup: Korean
Major Language: Korean

Health
Life Expectancy at Birth: 67 years (male); 73 years (female)
Infant Mortality Rate (Ratio): 26.8/1,000
Average Caloric Intake: n/a
Physicians Available (Ratio): 1/370

Religions
Buddhism and Confucianism (now almost nonexistent)

Education
Adult Literacy Rate: 99%

FROM WHENCE THE KOREAN NATION?

According to Korean myth, in 2333 B.C., the god Hanul took human form and descended from heaven to Paektusan Mountain, in what is now North Korea. He was a god with three qualities: a teacher, a king, and a creator. He found tribes of people living on the Korean Peninsula and remained with them for 93 years, teaching them and creating the laws and customs of the Korean people. Eventually, he returned to heaven, but his influence was so powerful that until recent times, Korean dates and calendars were reckoned from the year of his arrival. At one time, the worship of Hanul was the primary religion of Korea, but that faith was replaced by numerous other religions, especially Buddhism. Under the Communists, the practice of *any* religion has become a rarity in North Korea.

COMMUNICATION

Telephones: 30,000 (available only to government officials)
Newspapers: 11

TRANSPORTATION

Highways—Kilometers (Miles): 30,000 (18,600)
Railroads—Kilometers (Miles): 4,915 (3,067)
Usable Airfields: 49

GOVERNMENT

Type: communist state
Independence Date: September 9, 1948
Head of State/Government: de facto President Kim Jong Il; Premier Kang Song San
Political Parties: Korean Workers' Party (only legal party, but others do exist)
Suffrage: universal at 17

MILITARY

Number of Armed Forces: 700,000
Military Expenditures (% of Central Government Expenditures): 20%–25% (est.)
Current Hostilities: continuing border conflicts with South Korea

ECONOMY

Currency ($ U.S. Equivalent): 2.15 wons = $1
Per Capita Income/GDP: $900/$21.3 billion
Inflation Rate: n/a
Natural Resources: hydroelectric power; oil; iron ore; copper; lead; zinc; coal; uranium; manganese; gold; salt
Agriculture: rice; corn; potatoes; soybeans; pulses; livestock and livestock products; fish
Industry: machinery; military products; electric power; chemicals; mining; metallurgy; textiles; food processing

FOREIGN TRADE

Exports: $1.02 billion
Imports: $1.64 billion

*Note: Statistics are generally estimated due to unreliable information.

A COUNTRY APART

The area that we now call North Korea has, at different times in Korea's long history, been separated from the South. In the fifth century A.D., the Koguryo Kingdom in the North was distinct from the Shilla, Paekche, and Kaya Kingdoms of the South. Later, the Parhae Kingdom in the North remained separate from the expanded Shilla Kingdom in the South. Thus, the division of Korea in 1945 into two unequal parts was not without precedent. Yet this time, the very different paths of development that the North and South chose rendered the division more poignant and, to those separated with little hope of reunion, more emotionally painful.

Beginning in 1945, Kim Il-Song, with the strong backing of the Soviet Union, pursued a hard-line Communist policy for both the political and economic development of North Korea. The Soviet Union's involvement on the Korean Peninsula arose from its opportunistic entry into the war against Japan, just 8 days before Japan's surrender. Thus, when Japan withdrew from its long colonial rule over Korea, the Soviets were in a position to be one of the occupying armies. Reluctantly, the United States allowed the Soviet Union to move troops into position above the 38th Parallel, a temporary dividing line for the respective occupying forces. It was the Soviet Union's intention to establish a Communist buffer state between itself and the capitalist West. Therefore, it moved quickly to establish the area north of the 38th Parallel as a separate political entity. The northern city of P'yongyang was established as the capital.

When United Nations representatives arrived in 1948 to oversee elections and ease the transition from military occupation and years of Japanese rule to an independent Korea, the Soviets would not cooperate. Kim Il-Song took over the reins of power in the North. Separate elections were held in the South, and the beginning of separate political systems got underway. The 38th Parallel came to represent not only the division of the Korean Peninsula but also the boundary between the worlds of capitalism and communism.

THE KOREAN WAR (1950–1953)

Although not pleased with the idea of division, the South, without a strong army, resigned itself to the reality of the moment. In the North, a well-trained military, with Soviet and Chinese help, began preparations for a full-scale invasion of the South. The North attacked in June 1950, a year after U.S. troops had vacated the South, and quickly overran most of the Korean Peninsula. The South Korean government requested help from the United Nations, which dispatched personnel from 19 nations, under the command of U.S. general Douglas MacArthur. (A U.S. intervention was ordered on June 27 by President Harry Truman.)

MacArthur's troops advanced against the North's armies and by October were in control of most of the peninsula. However, with massive Chinese help, the North once again moved south. In response, UN troops decided to inflict heavy destruction on the North through the use of jet fighter/bomber planes. Whereas South Korea was primarily agricultural, North Korea was the industrialized sector of the peninsula. Bombing of the North's industrial targets severely damaged the economy, forcing several million North Koreans to flee south to escape both the war and the Communist dictatorship under which they found themselves.

Eventually, the UN troops recaptured South Korea's capital, Seoul. Realizing that further fighting would lead to an expanded Asian war, the two sides agreed to cease-fire talks. They signed a truce in 1953 that established a 2.5-mile-wide demilitarized zone (DMZ) for 155 miles across the peninsula and more or less along the former 38th Parallel division. The Korean War took the lives of more than 54,000 American soldiers, 58,000 South Koreans, and 500,000 North Koreans—but when it was over, both sides occupied about the same territory as they had at the beginning. Yet, because neither side has ever declared peace, the two countries remain officially in a state of war. U.S. president Bill Clinton met with South Korean leaders in 1996 to propose peace talks, a move the North is considering. Yet the border between North and South remains one of the most volatile in Asia. The North staged military exercises along the border in 1996 and, breaking the cease-fire truce of 1953, fired shots into the Demilitarized Zone (DMZ). The South responded by raising its intelligence-monitoring activities to their highest level in years and requesting U.S. AWACS surveillance planes to monitor military movements in the North.

Scholars are still debating whether the Korean War should be called the United States' first losing war and whether or not the bloodshed was really necessary. To understand the Korean War, one must remember that, in the eyes of the world, it was more than a civil war among different kinds of Koreans. The United Nations, and particularly the United States, saw North Korea's aggression against the South as the first step in the eventual communization of the whole of Asia. Just a few months before North Korea attacked, China

(UPI/Bettmann photo by Norman Williams)

Pictured above are U.S. Marines with North Koreans captured during the Korean War.

had fallen to the Communist forces of Mao Zedong, and Communist guerrilla activity was being reported throughout Southeast Asia. The "Red Scare" frightened many Americans, and witchhunting for suspected Communist sympathizers—a college professor who might have taught about Karl Marx in class or a news reporter who might have praised the educational reforms of a Communist country—became the everyday preoccupation of such groups as the John Birch Society and the supporters of U.S. senator Joseph McCarthy.

In this highly charged atmosphere, it was relatively easy for the U.S. military to promote a war whose aim it was to contain communism. Containment rather than defeat of the enemy was the policy of choice, because the West was weary after battling Germany and Japan in World War II. The containment policy also underlay the United States' approach to Vietnam. Practical though it may have been, this policy denied Americans the opportunity of feeling satisfied in victory, since there was to be no victory, just a stalemate. Thus, the roots of the United States' dissatisfaction with the conduct of the Vietnam War actually began in the policies shaping the response to North Korea's offensive in 1950. North Korea was indeed contained, but the communizing impulse of the North remained.

COLLECTIVE CULTURE

With Soviet backing, North Korean leaders moved quickly to repair war damage and establish a Communist culture. The school curriculum was rewritten to emphasize nationalism and equality of the social classes. Traditional Korean culture, based on Confucianism, had stressed strict class divisions, but the Communist authorities refused to allow any one class to claim privileges over another (although eventually the families of party leaders came to constitute a new elite). Higher education at the more than 600 colleges and training schools was redirected to technical rather than analytical subjects. Industries were nationalized; farms were collectivized into some 3,000 communes; and the communes were invested with much of the judicial and executive powers that other countries grant to cities, counties, and states. To overcome labor shortages, nearly all women were brought into the labor force, and the economy slowly returned to prewar levels.

Today, many young people bypass formal higher education in favor of service in the military. Although North Korea has not published economic statistics for nearly 30 years, it is estimated that military expenses consume 20 to 25 percent of the national budget.

With China and the former Communist-bloc nations constituting natural markets for North Korean products, and with substantial financial aid from both China and the former Soviet Union in the early years, North Korea was able to regain much of its former economic, and especially industrial, strength. Today, North Korea successfully mines iron and other minerals and exports such products as cement, fish, and cereals. China has remained North Korea's only reliable ally; trade between the two countries exceeds $736 million a year. In one Chinese province, more than two thirds of the people are ethnic Koreans, most of whom take the side of the North in any dispute with the South.

Tensions with the South have remained high since the war. Sporadic violence along the border has left patrolling soldiers dead, and the assassination of former South Korean president Park Chung Hee and attempts on the lives of other members of the South Korean government have been attributed to North Korea, as was the bombing of a Korean Airlines flight in 1987. Both sides have periodically accused each other of attempted sabotage. In 1996, North Korea tried to send spies to the South via a small submarine; the attempt failed, and most of the spies were killed.

The North, seeing in the growing demand for free speech in the South a chance to further its aim of communizing the peninsula, has been angered by the brutal suppression of dissidents by the South Korean authorities. Although the North's argument is bitterly ironic, given its own brutal suppression of human rights, it is nonetheless accurate in its view that the government in the South has been blatantly dictatorial. To suppress opponents, the South Korean government has, among other things, abducted its own students from Europe, abducted opposition leader Kim Dae Jung from Japan, tortured dissidents, and violently silenced demonstrators. All of this is said to be necessary because of the need for unity in the face of the threat from the North; as pointed out by scholar Gavan McCormack, the South seems to use the North's threat as an excuse for maintaining a rigid dictatorial system.

Under these circumstances, it is not surprising that the formal reunification talks, begun in 1971 with much fanfare, have just recently started to bear fruit. Visits of residents separated by the war were approved in 1985—the first time in 40 years that an opening of the border had even been considered—but real progress came in late 1991, when North Korean premier Yon Hyong Muk and South Korean premier Chung Won Shik signed a nonaggression and reconciliation pact, whose

goal was the eventual declaration of a formal peace treaty between the two governments. In 1992, the governments established air, sea, and land links and set up mechanisms for scientific and environmental cooperation. North Korea also signed the nuclear nonproliferation agreement with the International Atomic Energy Agency. This move placated growing concerns about North Korea's rumored development of nuclear weapons and opened the way for investment by such countries as Japan, which had refused to invest until they received assurances on the nuclear question. In 1990, in what many saw as an overture to the United States, North Korea returned the remains of five American soldiers killed during the Korean War.

THE NUCLEAR ISSUE FLARES UP

The goodwill deteriorated quickly in 1993 and 1994, when North Korea refused to allow inspectors from the International Atomic Energy Agency (IAEA) to inspect its nuclear facilities, raising fears in the United States, Japan, and South Korea that the North was developing a nuclear bomb. When pressured to allow inspections, the North responded by threatening to withdraw from the IAEA and expel the inspectors. Tensions mounted, with all parties engaging in military threats and posturing and the United States, South Korea, and Japan (whose shores could be reached in minutes by the North's new ballistic missiles) threatening economic sanctions. Troops in both Koreas were put on high alert. Former U.S. president Jimmy Carter helped to defuse the issue by making a private goodwill visit to Kim Il-Song in P'yongyang, the unexpected result of which was a promise by the North to hold a first-ever summit meeting with the South. Then, in a near-theatrical turn of events, Kim Il-Song, at 5 decades the longest national office-holder in the world, died, apparently of natural causes. The summit was canceled and international diplomacy was frozen while the North Korean government mourned the loss of its "Great Leader" and informally selected a new one, "Dear Leader" Kim Jong Il, Kim Il-Song's son. Eventually, the North agreed to resume talks, a move interpreted as evidence that, for all its bravado, the North wanted to establish closer ties with the West. In 1994, North Korea agreed to a freeze on nuclear power-plant development as long as the United States would supply fuel oil, and in 1996, it agreed to open its airspace to all airlines.

THE CHANGING INTERNATIONAL LANDSCAPE

North Korea has good reason to promote better relations with the West, because the world of the 1990s is not the world of the

Kim Il-Song comes to power **1945**	The People's Democratic Republic of Korea is created **1948**	The Korean War begins **1950**	A truce is arranged between North Korea and UN troops **1953**	A U.S. spy boat, the *Pueblo*, is seized by North Korea **1968**	A U.S. spy plane is shot down over North Korea **1969**	Reunification talks begin **1971**

1990s

A nonaggression pact is signed with the South; North and South are granted seats in the UN

Fears of North Korea's nuclear-weapons capacity surge

Kim Il-Song dies and is succeeded by his son, Kim Jong Il

1950s. In 1989, for instance, several former Soviet-bloc countries cut into the North's economic monopoly by welcoming trade initiatives from South Korea; some even established diplomatic relations. At the same time, the disintegration of the Soviet Union meant that North Korea lost its primary political and military ally. Perhaps most alarming to the North is its declining economy; it was estimated to have dropped 3.7 percent in 1990 and 5.2 percent in 1991. Severe flooding in 1995 destroyed much of the rice harvest and forced the North to do the unthinkable: accept rice donations from the South. More than 100 North Koreans have defected to the South in the past 2 years, all of them complaining of near-famine conditions. With the South's economy consistently booming and the example of the failed economies of Central/Eastern Europe as a danger signal, the North appears to understand that it must break out of its decades of isolation or lose its ability to govern. Nevertheless, it is not likely that North Koreans will quickly retreat from the Communist model of development that they have espoused for so long.

Kim Il-Song, who controlled North Korea for nearly 50 years, promoted the development of heavy industries, the collectivization of agriculture, and strong linkages with the then–Communist bloc. Governing with an iron hand, Kim denied basic civil rights to his people and forbade any tendency of the people to dress or behave like the "decadent" West. He kept tensions high by asserting his intention of communizing the South. His son, Kim Jong Il, who had headed the North Korean military but was barely known outside his country, has taken over de facto control, but the delay in making his title official suggests internal dissent—dissent that is muddying the first dynastic power transfer in the Communist world. How the younger Kim will influence the direction of North Korea is unclear, but the somewhat more liberal authorities at his side know that the recent diplomatic initiatives of the South require a response. The North Korean government hopes that recent actions will bring it some badly needed international goodwill. But more than good public relations will be needed if North Korea is to prosper in the new, post–cold war climate in which it can no longer rely on the generosity or moral support of the Soviet bloc. When communism was introduced in North Korea in 1945, the government nationalized major companies and steered economic development toward heavy industry. In contrast, the South concentrated on heavy industry to balance its agricultural sector until the late 1970s but then geared the economy toward meeting consumer demand. Thus, the standard of living in the North for the average resident remains far behind that of the South. Unless a broader trading front is opened up, the North will continue to lag behind.

RECENT TRENDS

There is evidence that some liberalization is taking place within North Korea. In 1988, the government drafted a law that allowed foreign companies to establish joint ventures inside North Korea. Tourism is also being promoted as a way of earning foreign currency, and the government recently permitted two small Christian churches to be established. Nevertheless, years of a totally controlled economy in the North and shifting international alliances indicate many difficult years ahead for North Korea. Moreover, the bad blood between North and South would suggest only the slowest possible reconciliation of the world's most troubled peninsula.

Although political reunification seems to be years away, social changes are becoming evident everywhere as a new generation, unfamiliar with war, comes to adulthood, and as North Koreans are being exposed to outside sources of news and ideas. Many North Koreans now own radios that receive signals from other countries. South Korean stations are now heard in the North, as are news programs from the Voice of America. Modern North Korean history, however, is one of repression and control, first by the Japanese and then by the Kim government, who used the same police surveillance apparatus as did the Japanese during their occupation of the Korean Peninsula. It is not likely therefore, that a massive push for democracy will be forthcoming soon from a people long accustomed to dictatorship.

DEVELOPMENT

Already more industrialized than South Korea at the time of the Korean War, North Korea built on this foundation with massive assistance from China and the Soviet Union. Heavy industry was emphasized, however, to the detriment of consumer goods. Economic isolation presages slow growth ahead.

FREEDOM

Kim Il-Song's mainline Communist approach meant that the human rights commonplace in the West were never enjoyed by North Koreans. Through suppression of dissidents, a controlled press, and restrictions on travel, the long-time dictator kept North Koreans isolated from the world.

HEALTH/WELFARE

Under the Kim Il-Song government, illiteracy was greatly reduced. North Koreans have access to free medical care, schooling, and old-age pensions. Government housing is available at low cost, but shoppers are often confronted with empty shelves and low-quality goods.

ACHIEVEMENTS

North Korea has developed its resources of aluminum, cement, and iron into solid industries for the production of tools and machinery while developing military superiority over South Korea, despite a population numbering less than half that of South Korea.

Papua New Guinea (Independent State of Papua New Guinea)

GEOGRAPHY

Area in Square Kilometers (Miles):
461,690 (178,612) (slightly larger than California)
Capital (Population): Port Moresby (193,000)
Climate: tropical

PEOPLE

Population
Total: 4,294,800
Annual Growth Rate: 2.3%
Rural/Urban Population Ratio: 85/15
Ethnic Makeup: predominantly Melanesian and Papuan; some Negrito, Micronesian, and Polynesian
Major Languages: 715 indigenous languages; English; New Guinea Pidgin; Motu

Health
Life Expectancy at Birth: 56 years (male); 58 years (female)
Infant Mortality Rate (Ratio): 61.6/1,000
Average Caloric Intake: 85% of FAO minimum
Physicians Available (Ratio): 1/11,904

Religions
66% Christian; 34% indigenous beliefs

Education
Adult Literacy Rate: 52%

COMMUNICATION

Telephones: 70,000
Newspapers: 1

TRANSPORTATION

Highways—Kilometers (Miles): 19,200 (11,904)
Railroads—Kilometers (Miles): —
Usable Airfields: 505

GOVERNMENT

Type: parliamentary democracy
Independence Date: September 16, 1975
Head of State/Government: Prime Minister Sir Julius Chan; Governor General Wiwa Korowi
Political Parties: Pangu Party; People's Democratic Movement; People's Action Party; People's Progress Party; United Party; Papua Party; National Party; Melanesian Alliance
Suffrage: universal at 18

MILITARY

Number of Armed Forces: 3,200
Military Expenditures (% of Central Government Expenditures): 1.8%
Current Hostilities: civil strife

ECONOMY

Currency ($ U.S. Equivalent): 0.856 kina = $1
Per Capita Income/GDP: $2,200/$4.2 billion
Inflation Rate: 1.6%
Natural Resources: gold; copper; silver; natural gas; timber; oil potential
Agriculture: coffee; cocoa; coconuts; palm kernels; tea; rubber; sweet potatoes; fruit; vegetables; poultry; pork
Industry: copra crushing; palm oil processing; wood processing and production; mining; construction; tourism

FOREIGN TRADE

Exports: $2.4 billion
Imports: $1.2 billion

UNREST IN BOUGAINVILLE

In 1988, residents of the Papua New Guinea island of Bougainville revolted against a large Australian-owned, open-pit copper mine. The mine was closed, and the rebels declared Bougainville an independent nation. The government in Port Moresby responded by imposing an economic blockade and cutting off electricity service to the island. Later battles with government troops ended in death for many people. New Zealand sponsored peace talks between the rebels and the government, and a tentative agreement was reached in August 1990; the blockade was lifted and electricity restored. In early 1991 violence again erupted, and in mid-1992, the rebels killed the mediator who had negotiated a partial settlement. Three thousand people have died in confrontations so far; and, with the people of Bougainville increasingly divided into competing, tribal-based armies, it is likely that there will be many more victims before peace arrives.

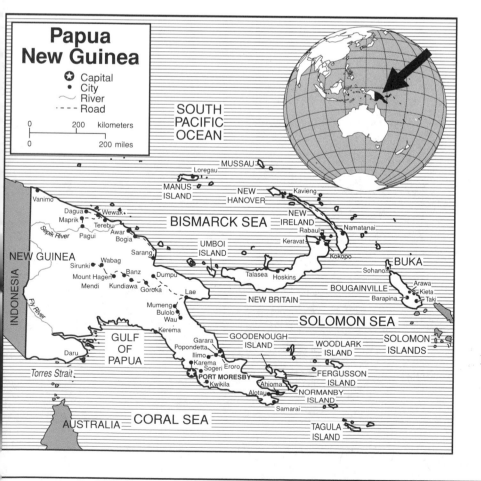

Papua New Guinea
* Capital
• City
~ River
- - - Road

0   200   kilometers
0   200 miles

SOUTH PACIFIC OCEAN
BISMARCK SEA
MUSSAU
Loregau
MANUS ISLAND
NEW HANOVER
Kavieng
NEW IRELAND
Rabaul
Namatanai
Keravat
Kokopo
BUKA
Sohano
BOUGAINVILLE
Arawa
Kieta
Barapina
Taki
Vanimo
Dagua
Wewak
Maprik
Terebu
Awar
Bogia
Pagui
Sepik River
Sarang
UMBOI ISLAND
Sirunki
Wabag
Banz
Dumpu
Talasea
Hoskins
Mount Hagen
Kundiawa
Goroka
Lae
NEW BRITAIN
SOLOMON SEA
SOLOMON ISLANDS
Mendi
Mumeng
Bulolo
Wau
Kerema
NEW GUINEA
INDONESIA
Fly River
GULF OF PAPUA
Daru
Garara
Popondetta
Ilimo
Karema
Sogeri
Eroro
GOODENOUGH ISLAND
WOODLARK ISLAND
PORT MORESBY
Kwikila
Ahioma
Alotau
FERGUSSON ISLAND
NORMANBY ISLAND
Torres Strait
AUSTRALIA
CORAL SEA
Samarai
TAGULA ISLAND

TERRA INCOGNITA

Papua New Guinea is an independent nation and a member of the British Commonwealth. Occupying the eastern half of New Guinea (the second-largest island in the world) and many outlying islands, Papua New Guinea is probably the most overlooked of all the nations in the Pacific Rim.

It was not always overlooked, however. Spain claimed the vast land in the mid-sixteenth century, followed by Britain's East India Company in 1793. The Netherlands laid claim to part of the island in the 1800s and eventually came to control the western half (now known as Irian Jaya, a province of the Republic of Indonesia). In the 1880s, German settlers occupied the northeastern part of the island; and in 1884, Britain signed a treaty with Germany, which gave it about half of what is now Papua New Guinea. In 1906, Britain gave its part of the island to Australia. Australia invaded and quickly captured the German area in 1914. Eventually, the League of Nations and, later, the United Nations gave the captured area to Australia to administer as a trust territory.

During World War II, the northern part of New Guinea was the scene of bitter fighting between a large Japanese force and Australian and U.S. troops. The Japanese had apparently intended to use New Guinea as a base for the military conquest of Australia. Australia resumed control of the eastern half of the island after Japan's defeat, and it continued to administer Papua New Guinea affairs until 1975, when it granted independence. The capital is Port Moresby, where, in addition to English, the Motu language and a hybrid language known as New Guinea Pidgin are spoken.

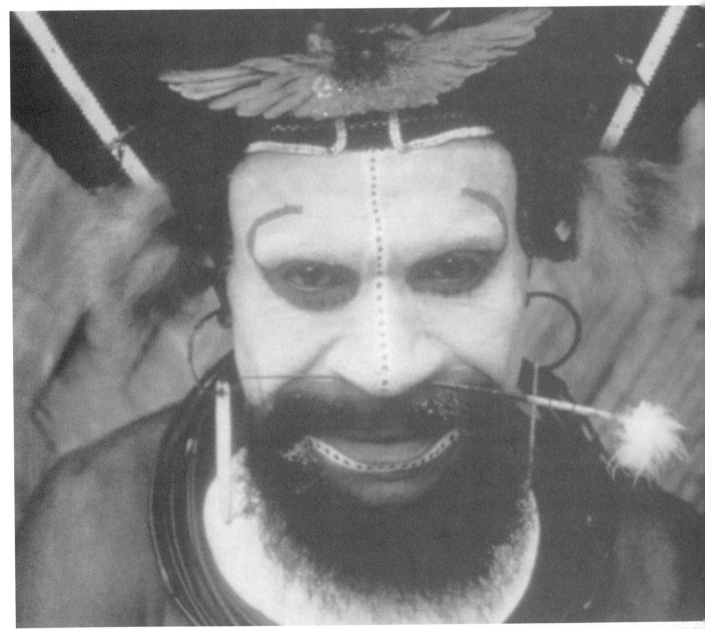

(UN photo)

Despite contact with the modern world because of mining and logging, many of the indigenous peoples of Papua New Guinea have retained their cultures, largely intact, that have existed for thousands of years.

| The main island is sighted by Portuguese explorers A.D. **1511** | The Dutch annex the west half of the island **1828** | A British protectorate over part of the eastern half of the island; the Germans control the northeast **1884** | Gold is discovered in Papua New Guinea **1890** | Australia assumes control of the British part of the island **1906** | Australia invades and captures the German-held areas **1914** | Australia is given the former German areas as a trust territory **1920** | Japan captures the northern part of the island; Australia resumes control in 1945 **1940s** | Australia grants independence to Papua New Guinea **1975** | A revolt against the government begins on the island of Bougainville **1988** |

1990s

An economic blockade of Bougainville is lifted, but violence continues, claiming 3,000 lives

600 army soldiers storm Parliament, demanding higher pay

Papua New Guinea joins APEC

STONE AGE PEOPLES MEET THE TWENTIETH CENTURY

Early Western explorers found the island's resources difficult to reach. The coastline and some of the interior are swampy and mosquito- and tick-infested, while the high, snow-capped mountainous regions are densely forested and hard to traverse. But perhaps most daunting to early would-be settlers and traders were the local inhabitants. Consisting of hundreds of sometimes warring tribes with totally different languages and customs, the New Guinea populace was determined to prevent outsiders from settling the island. Many adventurers were killed, their heads displayed in villages as victory trophies. The origins of the Papuan people are unknown, but some tribes share common practices with Melanesian islanders. Others appear to be Negritos, and some may be related to the Australian Aborigines. More than 700 languages, often mutually unintelligible, are spoken in Papua New Guinea.

Australians and other Europeans found it beneficial to engage in trade with coastal tribes who supplied them with unique tropical lumbers, such as sandalwood and bamboo, and foodstuffs such as sugarcane, coconut, and nutmeg. Rubber and tobacco were also traded. Tea, which grows well in the highland regions, is an important cash crop.

But the resource that was most important for the economic development of Papua New Guinea was gold. It was discovered there in 1890; two major gold rushes occurred, in 1896 and 1926. Prospectors came mostly from Australia and were hated by the local tribes; some prospectors were killed and cannibalized. A large number of airstrips in the otherwise undeveloped interior eventually were built by miners who needed a safe and efficient way to receive supplies. Today copper is more important than gold—copper is, in fact, the largest single earner of export income for Papua New Guinea.

A diplomatic flap between Papua New Guinea and Australia occurred in mid-1992, when Australian environmentalists complained about the environmental damage that a copper and gold mine in Papua New Guinea was causing. They called for its closure. The Papuan government strongly resented the verbal intrusion into its sovereignty and reminded conservationists and the Australian government that it alone would establish environmental standards for companies operating inside its borders. The Papuan government holds a 20 percent interest in the mining company.

The tropical climate that predominates in all areas except the highest mountain peaks produces an impressive variety of plant and animal life. Botanists and other naturalists have been attracted to the island for scientific study for many years. Despite extensive contacts with these and other outsiders over the past century, and despite the establishment of schools and a university by the Australian government, some inland mountain tribes continue to live much as they must have done in the Stone Age. Thus the country lures not only miners and naturalists but also anthropologists looking for clues to humankind's early lifestyles. One of the most famous of these was Bronislaw Malinowski, the Polish-born founder of the field of social anthropology who taught at both the University of London and at Yale. In the early 1900s, he spent several years studying the cultural practices of the tribes of Papua New Guinea, particularly those of the Trobriand Islands.

Most of the 4 million Papuans live by subsistence farming. Agriculture for commercial trade is limited by the absence of a good transportation network: Most roads are unpaved, and there is no railway system. Travel on tiny aircraft and helicopters is common, however; New Guinea boasts 505 airstrips, most of them unpaved and dangerously situated in mountain valleys. The harsh conditions of New Guinea life have produced some unique ironies. For instance, Papuans who have never ridden in a car or truck may have flown in a plane dozens of times. Given the differences in socialization of the Papuan peoples and the difficult conditions of life on their island, it will likely be many decades before Papua New Guinea, which joined the Asia-Pacific Economic Cooperation group in 1993, is able to participate fully in the Pacific Rim community.

DEVELOPMENT

Agriculture (especially coffee and copra) is the mainstay of Papua New Guinea's economy. Copper, gold, and silver mining are also important, but large-scale development of other industries is inhibited by rough terrain, illiteracy, and a bewildering array of spoken languages—more than 700. There are substantial reserves of untapped oil.

FREEDOM

Papua New Guinea is a member of the British Commonwealth and officially follows the English heritage of law. However, in the country's numerous, isolated small villages, effective control is wielded by village elites with personal charisma; tribal customs take precedence over national law—of which many inhabitants are virtually unaware.

HEALTH/WELFARE

Three quarters of Papua New Guinea's population have no formal education. Daily nutritional intake falls far short of recommended minimums, and tuberculosis and malaria are common diseases.

ACHIEVEMENTS

Papua New Guinea, lying just below the equator, is world-famous for its varied and beautiful flora and fauna, including orchids, birds of paradise, butterflies, and parrots. Dense forests cover 70 percent of the country. Some regions receive as much as 350 inches of rain a year.

Philippines (Republic of the Philippines)

GEOGRAPHY

Area in Square Kilometers (Miles):
300,000 (110,400) (slightly larger than Arizona)
Capital (Population): Manila (1,800,000)
Climate: tropical marine

PEOPLE

Population

Total: 73,266,000
Annual Growth Rate: 2.23%
Rural/Urban Population Ratio: 57/43
Ethnic Makeup: 95% Malay; 2% Chinese; 3% others
Major Languages: Pilipino (based on Tagalog); English

Health

Life Expectancy at Birth: 63 years (male); 68 years (female)
Infant Mortality Rate (Ratio): 51.9/1,000
Average Caloric Intake: 92% of FAO minimum
Physicians Available (Ratio): 1/1,062

THE RICH GET RICHER; THE POOR GET CHILDREN

Visitors to the Philippines' capital of Manila are often stunned by the stark contrast between the rich and the poor. The rich drive to their air-conditioned, high-rise offices in luxury cars, while alongside the highways are thousands of the poor living in tin shacks with no plumbing, few jobs, and inadequate food. Because the shantytowns are not conducive to the upscale image that Manila would like to show the world, white picket fences have been built alongside major thoroughfares to hide the squalor from the view of visiting dignitaries.

One quarter of the 1.8 million Manila residents are desperately poor squatters. Yet the Philippines continues to have one of the highest birth rates in Asia, and nearly 60 percent of the population are under age 20. The country's development plan, "Philippine 2000," has been criticized by the Catholic Church for promoting population control.

Religions

83% Roman Catholic; 9% Protestant; 5% Muslim; 3% Buddhist and others

Education

Adult Literacy Rate: 90%

COMMUNICATION

Telephones: 872,900
Newspapers: 234, of which about 32 are dailies

TRANSPORTATION

Highways—Kilometers (Miles): 160,700 (100,277)
Railroads—Kilometers (Miles): 800 (499)
Usable Airfields: 269

GOVERNMENT

Type: republic
Independence Date: July 4, 1946
Head of State: President Fidel V. Ramos
Political Parties: PDP-Laban; Struggle of Philippine Democrats; Nationalista Party; Liberal Party; the Philippine Communist Party has quasi-legal status
Suffrage: universal at 15

MILITARY

Number of Armed Forces: 85,800
Military Expenditures (% of Central Government Expenditures): 1.4%
Current Hostilities: dispute over the Spratly Islands with China, Malaysia, Taiwan, and Vietnam; claims the Malaysian state of Sabah

ECONOMY

Currency ($ U.S. Equivalent): 22.62 Philippine pesos = $1
Per Capita Income/GDP: $2,310/$161.4 billion
Inflation Rate: 7.1%
Natural Resources: timber; crude oil; nickel; cobalt; silver; gold; salt; copper
Agriculture: rice; coconut; corn; sugarcane; bananas; pineapple; mango; animal products; fish
Industry: food processing; chemicals; textiles; pharmaceuticals; wood products; electronics assembly; petroleum refining; fishing

FOREIGN TRADE

Exports: $13.4 billion
Imports: $21.3 billion

THIS IS ASIA?

The Philippines is a land with close historic ties to the West. Eighty-three percent of Filipinos, as the people of the Philippines are known, are Roman Catholics, and most speak at least some English. Many use English daily in business and government. In fact, English is the language of instruction at school. Moreover, when they discuss their history as a nation, Filipinos will mention Spain, Mexico, the Spanish-American War, the United States, and cooperative Filipino–American attempts to defeat the Japanese in World War II. The country was even named after a European, King Philip II of Spain. If this does not sound like a typical Asian nation, it is because Philippine nationhood essentially began with the arrival of Westerners. That influence continues to dominate the political and cultural life of the country.

Yet the history of the region certainly did not begin with European contact; indeed, there is evidence of human habitation in the area as early as 25,000 B.C. Beginning about 2,000 B.C., Austronesians, Negritos, Malays, and other tribal peoples settled many of the 7,107 islands that constitute the present-day Philippines. Although engaged to varying degrees in trade with China and Southeast Asia, each of these ethnic groups (nearly 60 distinct groups still exist) lived in relative isolation from one another, speaking different languages, adhering to different religions, and, for good or ill, knowing nothing of the concept of national identity.

Although 5 million ethnic peoples remain marginated from the mainstream, for most islanders the world changed in the mid-1500s, when soldiers and Roman Catholic priests from Spain began conquering and converting the population. Eventually, the disparate ethnic groups came to see themselves as one entity, Filipinos, a people whose lives were controlled indirectly by Spain from Mexico—a fact that, unique among Asian countries, linked the Philippines with the Americas. Thus, the process of national-identity formation for Filipinos actually began in Europe.

Some ethnic groups assimilated rather quickly, marrying Spanish soldiers and administrators and acquiring the language and cultural outlook of the West. The descendants of these mestizos (mixed peoples, including local/Chinese mixes) have become the cultural, economic, and political elite of the country. Others, particularly among the Islamic communities on the Philippine island of Mindanao, resisted assimilation right from the start and continue to challenge the authority of Manila. Indeed, the Communist insurgency, reported so often in the news and the focus of attention of former presidents Ferdinand Marcos and Corazon Aquino, is in part an attempt by marginated ethnics and others to regain the cultural independence that their peoples lost some 400 years ago.

As in other Asian countries, the Chinese community has played an important but controversial role in Philippine life. Dominating trade for centuries, the Philippine Chinese have acquired clout (and enemies) that far exceeds their numbers (fewer than 1 million). Former president Aquino was of part-Chinese ancestry, and some of the resistance to her presidency stemmed from her ethnic lineage. The Chinese-Philippine community, in particular, has been the target of ethnic violence—kidnappings and abductions—because their wealth, relative to other Filipino groups, makes them easy prey.

(United Nations photo by J. M. Micaud)

The Philippines has suffered from the misuse of funds entrusted to the government over the past several decades. The result has been a polarity of wealth, with many citizens living in severe poverty. Slums, such as Tondo in Manila, pictured above, are a common sight in many of the urban areas the Philippines.

Negritos and others begin settling the islands **25,000** B.C.		Malays arrive in the islands **2,000** B.C.		Chinese, Arabs, and Indians control parts of the economy and land **A.D.400–1400**		The islands are named for the Spanish king Philip II **1542**		Local resistance to Spanish rule **1890s**

FOREIGN INTEREST

Filipinos occupy a resource-rich, beautiful land. Monsoon clouds dump as much as 200 inches of rain on the fertile, volcanic soil. Rice and corn grow well, as do hemp, coconut, sugarcane, and tobacco. Tuna, sponges, shrimp, and hundreds of other kinds of marine life flourish in the ocean. Part of the country is covered with dense tropical forests yielding bamboo and lumber and serving as habitat to thousands of species of plant and animal life. The northern part of Luzon Island is famous for its terraced rice paddies.

Given this abundance, it is not surprising that several foreign powers have taken a serious interest in the archipelago. The Dutch held military bases in the country in the 1600s, the British briefly controlled Manila in the 1800s, and the Japanese overran the entire country in the 1940s. But it was Spain, in control of most of the country for more than 300 years (1565–1898), that established the cultural base for the modern Philippines. Spain's interest in the islands—its only colony in Asia—was primarily material and secondarily spiritual. It wanted to take part in the lucrative spice trade and fill its galleon ships each year with products from Asia for the benefit of the Spanish Crown. It also wanted (or, at least, Rome wanted) to convert the so-called heathens (that is, nonbelievers) to Christianity. The friars were particularly successful in winning converts to Roman Catholicism because, despite some local resistance, there were no competing Christian denominations in the Philippines and because the Church quickly gained control of the resources of the island, which it used to entice converts. Resisting conversion were the Muslims of the island of Mindanao, a group that continues to remain on the fringe of Philippine society but which signed a cease-fire with the government in 1994 after 20 years of guerrilla warfare (although sporadic violence continues, as in 1995, when 200 armed muslims attacked and burned the town of Ipil on Mindanao). Eventually, a Church-dominated society was established that mirrored in structure—social-class divisions as well as religious and social values—the mother cultures of Spain and Mexico.

Spanish rule in the Philippines came to an inglorious end in 1898, at the end of the Spanish-American War. Spain granted independence to Cuba and ceded the Philippines, Guam, and Puerto Rico to the United States. Filipinos hoping for independence were disappointed to learn that yet another foreign power had assumed control of their lives. Resistance to American rule cost several thousand lives in the early years, but soon Filipinos realized that the U.S. presence was fundamentally different from that of Spain. The United States was interested in trade, and it certainly could see the advantage of having a military presence in Asia, but it viewed its primary role as one of tutelage. American officials believed that the Philippines should be granted independence, but only when the nation was sufficiently schooled in the process of democracy. Unlike Spain, the United States encouraged political parties and attempted to place Filipinos in positions of governmental authority.

Preparations were under way for independence when World War II broke out. The war and the occupation of the country by the Japanese undermined the economy, devastated the capital city of Manila, caused divisions among the political elite, and delayed independence. After Japan's defeat, the country was, at last, granted independence, on July 4, 1946. Manuel Roxas, a well-known politician, was elected president. Despite armed opposition from Communist groups, the country, after several elections, seemed to be maintaining a grasp on democracy.

MARCOS AND HIS AFTERMATH

Then, in 1965, Ferdinand E. Marcos, a Philippines senator and former guerrilla fighter with the U.S. armed forces, was elected president. He was reelected in 1969. Rather than addressing the serious problems of agrarian reform and trade, Marcos maintained people's loyalty through an elaborate system of patronage, whereby his friends and relatives profited from the misuse of government power and money. Opposition to his rule manifested itself in violent demonstrations and in a growing Communist insurgency. In 1972, Marcos declared martial law, arrested

some 30,000 opponents, and shut down newspapers as well as the National Congress. Marcos continued to rule the country by personal proclamation until 1981 He remained in power thereafter, and he and his wife, Imelda, and their extended family and friends increasingly were criticized for corruption. Finally, in 1986, after nearly a quarter-century of his rule, an uprising of thousands of dissatisfied Filipinos overthrew Marcos, who fled to Hawaii. He died there in 1990.

Taking on the formidable job of president was Corazon Aquino, the widow of murdered opposition leader Benigno Aquino. Aquino's People Power revolution had a heady beginning. Many observers believed that at last Filipinos had found a democratic leader around whom they could unite and who would end corruption and put the persistent Communist insurgency to rest. Aquino, however, was immediately beset by overwhelming economic, social, and political problems.

Opportunists and factions of the Filipino military and political elite still loyal to Marcos attempted numerous coup d'état in the years of Aquino's administration. Much of the unrest came from within the military, which had become accustomed to direct involvement in government during Marcos's martial-law era. Some Communist separatists turned in their arms at Aquino's request, but many continued to plot violence against the government. Thus, the sense of security and stability that Filipinos needed in order to attract more substantial foreign investment and to reestablish the habits of democracy continued to elude them.

Nevertheless, the economy showed signs of improvement. Some countries particularly Japan and the United States and, more recently, Hong Kong, invested heavily in the Philippines, as did half a dozen international organizations. In fact some groups complained that further investment was unwarranted, because already-allocated funds had not yet been fully utilized. Moreover, misuse of funds entrusted to the government—a serious problem during the Marcos era—continued, despite Aquino's promise to eradicate corruption. A 1987 law, enacted after Corazon Aquino assumed the presidency limited the president to one term in office

A treaty ends the Spanish-American War
1898

The Japanese attack the Philippines
1941

General Douglas MacArthur makes a triumphant return to Manila
1944

The United States grants complete independence to the Philippines
1946

Military-base agreements are signed with the United States
1947

Ferdinand Marcos is elected president
1965

Marcos declares martial law
1972

Martial law is lifted; Corazon Aquino and her People Power movement drive Marcos into exile
1980s

1990s

Marcos dies in exile in Hawaii

The United States withdraws its military bases; Fidel Ramos is elected president

Typhoon Angela destroys 96,000 homes in Luzon

Half a dozen contenders vied for the presidency in 1992, including Imelda Marcos and other relatives of former presidents Marcos and Aquino; U.S. West Point graduate General Fidel Ramos, who had thwarted several coup attempts against Aquino and who thus had her endorsement, won the election. It was the first peaceful transfer of power in more than 25 years (although campaign violence claimed the lives of more than 80 people).

SOCIAL PROBLEMS

Ramos inherited the leadership of a country awash in problems. Inflation was nearly 9 percent per year, unemployment was above 11 percent, and foreign debt exceeded $30 billion. The 1991 eruption of Mount Pinatubo caused millions of dollars in damage. Under Ramos, conditions began to improve significantly, but one problem never seems to go away: extreme social inequality. As in Malaysia, where ethnic Malays have constituted a seemingly permanent class of poor peasants, Philippine society is fractured by distinct classes. Chinese and mestizos constitute the top of the hierarchy, while Muslims and most country dwellers form the bottom. About half the Filipino population of 73 million make their living in agriculture and fishing; but even in Manila, where the economy is stronger than anywhere else, thousands of residents live in abject poverty as urban squatters. Officially, 55 percent of Filipinos live in poverty. Disparities of wealth are striking. Worker discontent has been such that the Philippines

lost more work days to strikes between 1983 and 1987 than any other Asian country.

Adding to the country's financial woes in the early 1990s was the sudden loss of income from the six U.S. military bases that closed in 1991 and 1992. President Ramos had wanted the United States to maintain a presence in the country (indeed, U.S. war planes helped Aquino survive a dangerous coup attempt, and Ramos may have sensed the need for similar help in the future); but in 1991, the Philippine Legislature, bowing to nationalist sentiment, refused to renew the land-lease agreements that had been in effect since 1947. Occupying many acres of valuable land and bringing as many as 40,000 Americans at one time into the Philippines, the bases had come to be seen as visible symbols of American colonialism or imperialism. But they had also been a boon to the economy. Subic Bay Naval Base alone had provided jobs for 32,000 Filipinos on base and, indirectly, to 200,000 more. Moreover, the United States paid nearly $390 million each year to lease the land and another $128 million for base-related expenses. Base-related monies entering the country amounted to 3 percent of the entire Philippines economy. After the base closures, the U.S. Congress cut other aid to the Philippines, from $200 million in 1992 to $48 million in 1993. To counterbalance the losses, the Philippines accepted a $60 million loan from Taiwan to develop 740 acres of the former Subic Bay Naval Base into an industrial park. The International Monetary Fund also loaned the country $683 million—funds that have been successfully

used to transform the former military facilities into commercial zones.

CULTURE

Philippine culture is a rich amalgam of Asian and European customs. Family life is valued, and few people have to spend their old age in nursing homes. Divorce is frowned upon. Women have traditionally involved themselves in the worlds of politics and business to a greater degree than have women in other Asian countries. Educational opportunities for women are about the same as that for men; adult literacy in the Philippines is estimated at 90 percent. Unfortunately, many college-educated men and women are unable to find employment befitting their skills. Discontent among these young workers continues to grow, as it does among the many rural and urban poor.

Nevertheless, many Filipinos take a rather relaxed attitude toward work and daily life. They enjoy hours of sports and folk dancing or spend their free time in conversation with neighbors and friends, with whom they construct patron/client relationships. In recent years, the growing nationalism has been expressed in the gradual replacement of the English language with Pilipino, a version of the Malay-based Tagalog language.

DEVELOPMENT

The Philippines has more than $30 billion in foreign debt. Payback from development projects has been so slow that about 51 percent of the earnings from all exports has to be spent just to service the debt. The Philippines sells most of its products to the United States, Japan, Hong Kong, Great Britain, and the Netherlands.

FREEDOM

Marcos's one-man rule meant that both the substance and structure of democracy were ignored. The Philippine Constitution is similar in many ways to that of the United States. President Aquino attempted to adhere to democratic principles; her successor pledged to do the same. The Communist Party was legalized in 1992.

HEALTH/WELFARE

Quality of life varies considerably between the city and the countryside. Except for the numerous urban squatters, city residents generally have better access to health care and education. Most people still do not have access to safe drinking water. The gap between the upper-class elite and the poor is pronounced and growing.

ACHIEVEMENTS

Since the end of the Marcos dictatorship, foreign investment has been increasing in the Philippines. Inflation has eased somewhat. Most significant is the resumption of the peaceful transfer of political power.

Singapore (Republic of Singapore)

GEOGRAPHY

Area in Square Kilometers (Miles): 633 (244) (slightly less than 3½ times the size of Washington, D.C.)
Capital (Population): Singapore (2,334,400)
Climate: tropical

PEOPLE

Population

Total: 2,890,500
Annual Growth Rate: 1.06%
Rural/Urban Population (Ratio): almost entirely urban
Ethnic Makeup: 77% Chinese; 15% Malay; 6% Indian; 2% others
Major Languages: Malay; Mandarin Chinese; Tamil; English

Health

Life Expectancy at Birth: 73 years (male); 79 years (female)
Infant Mortality Rate (Ratio): 5.7/1,000
Average Caloric Intake: 134% of FAO minimum
Physicians Available (Ratio): 1/779

Religions

42% Buddhist and Taoist; 18% Christian; 16% Muslim; 5% Hindu; 19% others

Education

Adult Literacy Rate: 88%

COMMUNICATION

Telephones: 1,110,000
Newspapers: 7 dailies

THE PERANAKANS

Most ancestors of the 2.8 million contemporary Singaporeans moved to the island from various parts of China only about 150 years ago. A few Singaporeans, however, including former prime minister Lee Kuan Yew, can trace their origins back to the fifteenth century, when Chinese traders moved to the Malacca Strait, married local Malay women, and stayed to create a uniquely blended culture of Chinese and Malay traditions. Useful to their various European overlords as interpreters, these people, called Peranakans ("locally born"), became the backbone of Singapore's upper class.

TRANSPORTATION

Highways—Kilometers (Miles): 2,883 (1,799)
Railroads—Kilometers (Miles): 38 (23)
Usable Airfields: 10

GOVERNMENT

Type: republic within the British Commonwealth
Independence Date: August 9, 1965
Head of State/Government: President Ong Teng Cheong; Prime Minister Goh Chok Tong
Political Parties: People's Action Party; Workers' Party; Singapore Democratic Party; National Solidarity Party; Barisan Sosialis; Communist Party (illegal)
Suffrage: universal and compulsory at 20

MILITARY

Number of Armed Forces: 55,500
Military Expenditures (% of Central Government Expenditures): 6%
Current Hostilities: none

ECONOMY

Currency ($ U.S. Equivalent): 1.45 Singapore dollars = $1
Per Capita Income/GDP: $19,940/$57.0 billion
Inflation Rate: 3.6%
Natural Resources: fish; deepwater ports
Agriculture: rubber; copra; fruit; vegetables
Industry: petroleum refining; electronics; oil-drilling equipment; rubber processing and rubber products; processed food and beverages; ship repair, financial services; biotechnology

FOREIGN TRADE

Exports: $96.4 billion
Imports: $102.4 billion

Singapore

⊗ Capital
• City
〰 River
- - - Road

| 0 | 5 | kilometers |
| 0 | 5 | miles |

MALAYSIA

Johore Strait
Senoko
Woodlands
Sembawang
Kampong Kranji
Nee Soon
Punggol
PULAU UBIN
PULAU TEKONG BESAR
Bukit Panjang
Changi
Choa Chu Kang
Yan Kit
Bukit Timah Village
Toa Payoh
Pasil Panjang Village
Bedok
Jurong
SINGAPORE
Tuas
Queenstown
Singapore Strait
PULAU AYER CHAWAN
PULAU BRANI
SENTOSA
PULAU BUKUM
PULAU SEMAKAU
PULAU SENANG
INDONESIA
Main Strait

SINGAPORE

North Americans are well-off, it is often said, because they inhabit a huge continent that overflows with natural resources. This explanation for prosperity does not fit even remotely the case of Singapore. The inhabitants of this tiny, flat, humid island, located near the equator off the tip of the Malay Peninsula, must import even their drinking water from another country. With only 244 square miles of land (including 58 mostly uninhabited islets), Singapore is half the size of Hong Kong; however, it has one of the highest per capita incomes ($19,940) in Asia. With more than 11,000 people per square mile, one of the highest population densities in Asia, Singapore might be expected to have the horrific slums that characterize parts of other crowded areas. But unemployment in Singapore is less than 2 percent, inflation is only 3.6 percent, and most of its 2.8 million people own their own homes. Eighty percent of the residences are government-built apartments, but they are spacious by Asian standards and are well-equipped with labor-saving appliances.

Imperialism, geography, and racism help to explain Singapore's unique characteristics. For most of its recorded history, beginning in the thirteenth century A.D., Singapore was controlled variously by the rulers of Thailand, Java, Indonesia, and even India. In the early 1800s, the British were determined to wrest control of parts of Southeast Asia from the Dutch and expand their growing empire. Facilitating their imperialistic aims was Sir Stamford Raffles, a Malay-speaking British administrator who not only helped defeat the Dutch in Java but also diminished the power of local elites in order to fortify his position as lieutenant governor.

Arriving in Singapore in 1819, Raffles found it to be a small, neglected settlement with an economy based on fishing. Yet he believed that the island's geographic location endowed it with great potential as a transshipment port. He established policies that facilitated its development just in time to benefit from the British exports of tin, rubber, and timber leaving Malaya. Perhaps most important was his declaration of Singapore as a free port. Skilled Chinese merchants and traders, escaping racist discrimination against them by Malays on the Malay Peninsula, flocked to Singapore, where they prospered in the free trade atmosphere.

In 1924, the British began construction of a naval base on the island, the largest in Southeast Asia, which was nonetheless overcome by the Japanese in 1942. Returning in 1945, the British continued to build Singapore into a major maritime center. Today, oil supertankers from Saudi Arabia must exit the Indian Ocean through the Strait of Malacca and skirt Singapore to enter the South China Sea for deliveries to Japan and other Asian nations. Thus, Singapore has found itself in the enviable position of helping to refine and transship millions of barrels of Middle Eastern oil. Singapore's oil-refining capacities have been ranked the world's third largest since 1973.

Singapore is now the second-busiest port in the world (Rotterdam in the Netherlands is number one). It has become the largest shipbuilding and -repair port in the region and a major shipping-related financial center. Singapore's economy has been growing at rates between 6 and 12 percent for the past decade, making it one of the fastest-growing economies in the world. In recent years, the government has aggressively sought out investment from non-shipping–related industries in order to diversify the economy. In 1992, Singapore hosted a summit of the Association of Southeast Asian Nations in which a decision was made to create a regional common market by the year 2008. In order to compete with the emerging European and North American trading blocs, it was decided that tariffs on products traded within the ASEAN region would be cut to 5 percent or less.

A UNIQUE CULTURE

Britain maintained an active interest in Singapore throughout its empire period. At its peak, there were some 100,000 British military men and their dependents stationed there. The British military remained until 1971. (The U.S. Navy's Seventh Fleet's logistics operations have recently been transferred from the Philippines to Singapore, thereby increasing the number of U.S. military personnel in Singapore to about 300 persons.) Thus, British culture, from the architecture of the buildings, to the leisure of a cricket match, to the prevalence of the English language, is everywhere present in Singapore. Yet, because of the heterogeneity of the population (77 percent Chinese, 15 percent Malay, and 6 percent Indian), Singapore accommodates many philosophies and belief systems, including Confucianism, Buddhism, Islam, Hinduism, and Christianity. In recent years, the government has attempted to promote the Confucian ethic of hard work and respect for law, as well as the Mandarin Chinese language, in order to develop a greater Asian consciousness among the people. But most

(UPI/Corbis-Bettmann photo by Paul Wedel)
Singapore, one of the most affluent nations in Asia, features a booming financial district that overlooks the island state's boat harbor.

Singapore is controlled by several different nearby nations, including Thailand, Java, India, and Indonesia
A.D. 1200–1400

The Japanese capture Singapore
1942

The British return to Singapore
1945

Full elections and self-government; Lee Kuan Yew comes to power
1959

Singapore, now unofficially independent of Britain, briefly joins the Malaysia Federation
1963

Singapore becomes an independent republic
1965

Singapore becomes the second-busiest port in the world and achieves one of the highest per capita incomes in the Pacific Rim
1980s

1990s

Prime Minister Lee steps down; Goh Chok Tong is appointed

The U.S. Navy moves some of its operations from the Philippines to Singapore

Singaporeans seem content to avoid extreme ideology in favor of pragmatism; they prefer to believe in whatever approach works—that is, whatever allows them to make money and have a higher standard of living.

Their great material success has come with a price. The government keeps a firm hand on the people. For example, citizens can be fined as much as $250 for dropping a candy wrapper on the street or for driving without a seat belt. Worse offenses, such as importing chewing gum or selling it, carry fines of $6,000 and $1,200 respectively. Death by hanging is the punishment for murder, drug trafficking, and kidnapping, while lashing is inflicted on attempted murderers, robbers, rapists, and vandals. Being struck with a cane is the punishment for crimes such as malicious damage, as an American teenager, in a case that became a brief international cause célèbre in 1994, found out when he allegedly sprayed graffitti on cars in Singapore. Later that year, a Dutch businessperson was executed for alleged possession of heroin. The death penalty is required when one is convicted of using a gun in Singapore.

Political dissidents may be arrested, and the press cannot publish whatever it wishes without often generating the government's ire. Government leaders argue that order and hard work are necessities since, being a tiny island, Singapore could easily be overtaken by the envious and more politically unstable countries nearby; with few natural resources, Singapore must instead develop its people into disciplined, educated workers. Few deny that Singapore is an amazingly clean and efficient city-state; yet in recent years, younger residents have begun to wish for a greater voice in government.

The law-and-order tone exists largely because, after its separation from Malaysia in 1965, Singapore was controlled by one man and his personal hard-work ethic, Prime Minister Lee Kuan Yew, along with his Political Action Party (PAP). On November 26, 1990, Lee resigned his office (though he remains a powerful figure). Two days later he was replaced by his chosen successor, Goh Chok Tong. Goh had been the deputy prime minister and was the designated successor-in-waiting since 1984. The transition has been smooth, and the PAP's hold on the government remains intact.

The PAP originally came into prominence in 1959, when the issue of the day was whether Singapore should join the proposed Federation of Malaysia. Singapore joined Malaysia in 1963, but serious differences persuaded Singaporeans to declare independence 2 years later. Lee Kuan Yew, a Cambridge-educated, ardent anti-Communist with old roots in Singapore, gained such strong support as prime minister that not a single opposition-party member was elected for more than 20 years. Only one opposition seat exists today.

The two main goals of the administration have been to utilize fully Singapore's primary resource—its deepwater port—and to develop a strong Singaporean identity. The first goal has been achieved in a way that few would have thought possible; the question of national identity, however, continues to be problematic. Creating a Singaporean identity has been difficult because of the heterogeneity of the population, a situation that is likely to increase as foreign workers are imported to fill gaps in the labor supply resulting from a very successful birth control campaign started in the 1960s. Identity formation has also been difficult because of Singapore's recent seesaw history. First Singapore was a colony of Britain, then it became an outpost of the Japanese empire, followed by a return to Britain. Next Malaysia drew Singapore into its fold, and finally, in 1965, Singapore became independent. All these changes transpired within the lifetime of many contemporary Singaporeans, so their confusion regarding identity is understandable. Many still have a sense that their existence as a nation is tenuous, and they look for direction. In 1996, Singapore reaffirmed its support for a five-nation defense agreement among itself, Australia Malaysia, New Zealand, and Great Britain, and it strengthened its economic agreements with Australia.

DEVELOPMENT

Development of the deepwater Port of Singapore has been so successful that, at any single time, 400 ships are in port. Singapore has also become a base for fleets engaged in offshore oil exploration and a major financial center, the "Switzerland of Southeast Asia."

FREEDOM

Under Prime Minister Lee Kuan Yew, Singaporeans had to adjust to a strict regimen of behavior involving both political and personal freedoms. Citizens want more freedoms but realize that law and order have helped produce their high quality of life. Political opposition voices have largely been silenced since 1968, when the Political Action Party captured all the seats in the government.

HEALTH/WELFARE

Eighty percent of Singaporeans live in government-built dwellings. A government-created pension fund, the Central Provident Fund, takes up to one quarter of workers' paychecks; some of this goes into a compulsory savings account that can be used to finance the purchase of a residence. Other forms of social welfare are not condoned. Care of the elderly is the duty of children, not the government.

ACHIEVEMENTS

Housing remains a serious problem for many Asian countries, but virtually every Singaporean has access to adequate housing. Replacing swamplands with industrial parks has helped to lessen Singapore's reliance on its deepwater port. Singapore successfully overcame a Communist challenge in the 1950s to become a solid home for free enterprise in the region.

South Korea (Republic of Korea)

GEOGRAPHY

Area in Square Kilometers (Miles):
98,480 (38,013) (slightly larger than Indiana)
Capital (Population): Seoul (9,646,000)
Climate: temperate

PEOPLE

Population

Total: 45,554,000
Annual Growth Rate: 1.04%
Rural/Urban Population (Ratio):
26/74
Ethnic Makeup: homogeneous Korean
Major Language: Korean

Health

Life Expectancy at Birth: 68 years
(male); 74 years (female)
Infant Mortality Rate (Ratio):
20.9/1,000
Average Caloric Intake: 119% of
FAO minimum
Physicians Available (Ratio): 1/1,066

Religions

49% Christianity; 47% Buddhism;
3% Confucianism; 1% Shamanism
and Chondokyo

Education

Adult Literacy Rate: 96%

COMMUNICATION

Telephones: 13,276,000
Newspapers: 68 dailies

TRANSPORTATION

Highways—Kilometers (Miles):
63,201 (39,248)

Railroads—Kilometers (Miles): 6,763
(4,220)
Usable Airfields: 114

GOVERNMENT

Type: republic
Independence Date: August 15, 1948
Head of State/Government: President
Kim Young-sam; Prime Minister Yi
Hongku
Political Parties: Democratic Justice
Party; New Democratic Republican
Party; others
Suffrage: universal at 20

MILITARY

Number of Armed Forces: 750,000
*Military Expenditures (% of Central
Government Expenditures):* 3.3%
Current Hostilities: disputed
Demarcation Line with North Korea;
disputed Liancourt Rocks, claimed by
Japan

ECONOMY

Currency ($ U.S. Equivalent): 790.48
won = $1
Per Capita Income/GDP:
$11,270/$508.3 billion
Inflation Rate: 5.6%
Natural Resources: coal; tungsten;
graphite; molybdenum; lead;
hydropower
Agriculture: rice; root crops; barley;
vegetables; fruit; livestock and
livestock products; fish
Industry: textiles; clothing; footwear;
food processing; chemicals; steel;
electronics; automobile production;
shipbuilding

FOREIGN TRADE

Exports: $96.2 billion
Imports: $102.3 billion

WOMEN IN MODERN KOREA

According to the traditions of Confucianism, a woman had three people whom she was to obey throughout her lifetime: her father until she married; her husband after marriage; and her son after her husband's death. The subservience mandated by this ancient custom can still be seen throughout South Korean society at the interpersonal level, but times are changing in the public arena. Women may vote in Korea (more than 80 percent cast votes in presidential elections), and half a dozen women have been appointed to the cabinet at various times since 1948. Fifty-four women have served in the Legislature, and there are women judges, lawyers, and newspaper editors and reporters. Women account for about 35 percent of the South Korean workforce. Some 21 percent of all civil servants are women, but there has never yet been a woman president.

South Korea

- ★ Capital
- • City
- — River
- --- Expressway

0   50 kilometers
0   50 miles

EARLY HISTORY

Korea was inhabited for thousands of years by an early people who may or may not have been related to the Ainus of northern Japan, the inhabitants of Sakhalin Island, and the Siberian Eskimos. Distinct from this early civilization are today's Koreans whose ancestors migrated to the Korean Peninsula from Central Asia and, benefiting from close contact with the culture of China, established prosperous kingdoms as early as 1000 B.C. (legends put the date as early as 2333 B.C.).

The era of King Sejong, who ruled Korea from 1418 to 1450, is notable for its many scientific and humanistic accomplishments. Ruling his subjects according to neo-Confucian thought, Sejong taught improved agricultural methods; published books on astronomy, history, religion, and medicine (the Koreans were the first to invent movable metal type); and was instrumental in the invention of sundials, rain gauges, and various musical instruments. Of singular importance was his invention of *han-qul,* a simplified writing system that even uneducated peasants could easily learn. Before *han-qul,* Koreans used the more complicated Chinese characters to represent sounds in the Korean language.

REGIONAL RELATIONS

For most of its history, Korea has remained at least nominally independent of foreign powers. China, however, always wielded tremendous cultural influence and at times politically dominated the Korean Peninsula. Similarly, Japan often cast longing eyes toward Korea but was never able to control affairs successfully there until the beginning of the twentieth century.

Korean influence on Japanese culture was pronounced in the 1400s and 1500s, when, through peaceful trade as well as forced labor, Korean artisans and technicians taught advanced skills in ceramics, textiles, painting, and other arts to the Japanese. (Historically, the Japanese received most of their cultural influence from China via Korea.)

In this century, the direction of influence reversed—to the current Japan-to-Korea flow—with the result that the two cultures share numerous qualities. Ironically, cultural closeness has not eradicated emotional distance: Modern Japanese continue to discriminate against Koreans who live in Japan, and Japanese brutality during the years of occupation (1905–1945) remains a frequent topic of conversation among Koreans.

Japan achieved its desire to rule Korea in 1905, when Russia's military, along with its imperialistic designs on Korea, was soundly defeated by the Japanese in the Russo–Japanese War; Korea was granted to Japan as part of the peace settlement. Unlike other expansionist nations, Japan was not content to rule Korea as a colony but, rather, attempted the complete cultural and political annexation of the Korean Peninsula. Koreans had to adopt Japanese names, serve in the Japanese Army, and pay homage to the Japanese emperor. Some 1.3 million Koreans were forcibly sent to Japan to work in coal mines or to serve in the military. The Korean language ceased to be taught in school, and more than 200,000 books on Korean history and culture were burned.

Many Koreans joined clandestine resistance organizations. In 1919, a Declaration of Korean Independence was announced in Seoul by resistance leaders, but the brutally efficient Japanese police and military crushed the movement. They killed thousands of demonstrators, tortured and executed the leaders, and set fire to the homes of those suspected of cooperating with the movement. Despite suppression of this kind throughout the 40 years of Japanese colonial rule, a provisional government was established by the resistance in 1919, with branches in Korea, China, and Russia. However, a very large police force—one Japanese for every 40 Koreans—kept resistance in check.

One resistance leader, Syngman Rhee, vigorously promoted the cause of Korean independence to government leaders in the United States and Europe. Rhee, supported by the United States, became the president of South Korea after the defeat of the Japanese in 1945.

Upon the surrender of Japan, the victorious Allied nations decided to divide Korea

(Reuters/Bettmann photo by Tony Chung)

When Korea was divided, the South Koreans received large amounts of economic and military aid from the United States, which allowed them to follow the Japanese model of development. As the industrial base grew and they focused on specific markets, South Korea became an economic powerhouse. Workers in the Hyundai shipyards are pictured above.

into two zones of temporary occupation, for the purposes of overseeing the orderly dismantling of Japanese rule and establishing a new Korean government. The United States was to occupy all of Korea south of the 38th Parallel of latitude (a demarcation running east and west across the peninsula, about 150 miles north of the capital city of Seoul), while the Soviet Union was to occupy Korea north of that line. The United States was uneasy about permitting the Soviets to move troops into Korea, as the Soviet Union had entered the war against Japan just 8 days before Japan surrendered and its commitment to the democratic intentions of the Allies was questionable. Nevertheless, it was granted occupation rights.

Later, the United Nations attempted to enter the zone occupied by the Soviet Union in order to oversee democratic elections for all of Korea. Denied entry, UN advisers proceeded with elections in the South, which brought Syngman Rhee to the presidency. The North created its own government, with Kim Il-Song at the head. Tensions between the two governments resulted in the elimination of trade and other contacts across the new border. This was difficult for each side, because the Japanese had developed industries in the North while the South had remained primarily agricultural. Each side needed the other's resources; in their absence, considerable civil unrest occurred. Rhee's government responded by suppressing dissent, rigging elections, and using strong-arm tactics on critics. Autocratic rule, not unlike that of the colonial Japanese, has been the norm in South Korea almost ever since, and citizens, particularly university students, have been quick to take to the streets in protest of human-rights violations by the various South Korean governments. Equally stern measures were instituted by the Communist government in the North, so that, despite nearly a half century of Korean rule, the repressive legacy of the Japanese police state remains.

AN ECONOMIC POWERHOUSE

Upon the establishment of two separate political entities in Korea, the North pursued a Communist model of economic restructuring. South Korea, bolstered by massive infusions of economic and military aid from the United States, pursued a decidedly capitalist strategy. The results of this choice have been dramatic. Today, South Korea is often said to be the fastest-growing economy in the world; by the year 2010, it is expected that per capita income for Koreans will equal that of European economies. About 75 percent of South Korean people live in urban centers,

where they have access to good education and jobs. Manufacturing accounts for 30 percent of the gross domestic product. Economic success and recent improvements in the political climate seem to be slowing the rate of outward migration. In recent years, some Koreans have even returned home after years abroad.

North Koreans, on the other hand, are finding life unbearable. Hundreds have defected, some via a "safe house" system through China (similar to the famous "underground railroad" of U.S. slavery days). Some military pilots have flown their jets across the border to South Korea. Food shortages are increasingly evident, and some are predicting the total collapse of the North Korean economy.

Following the Japanese model, Korean businesspeople work hard to capture market share rather than to gain immediate profit—that is, they are willing to sell their products at or below cost for several years in order to gain the confidence of consumers, even if they make no profit. Once a sizable proportion of consumers buy their product and trust its reliability, the price is raised to a profitable level.

Many South Korean businesses are now investing in other countries, and South Korea is now a creditor rather than a debtor member of the Asian Development Bank— it is now in a position to loan money to other newly industrializing countries rather than to borrow from nations wealthier than itself. Given this kind of economic strength, some claim that Japan's towering economic powerhouse could be challenged by a unified Korea and that, therefore, Japan (which is separated from Korea by only 150 miles) is not interested in promoting reunification. The situation is not unlike European countries' concern about the economic strength of the reunified Germany.

SOCIAL PROBLEMS

Economically, South Korea is an impressive showcase for the fruits of capitalism. Politically, however, the country has been wracked with problems. Under Presidents Syngman Rhee (1948–1960), Park Chung Hee (1964–1979), and Chun Doo Hwan (1981–1987), South Korean government was so centralized as to constitute a virtual dictatorship. Human-rights violations, suppression of workers, and other acts incompatible with the tenets of democracies were frequent occurrences. Student uprisings, military revolutions, and political assassinations became more influential than the ballot box in forcing a change of government. President Roh Tae-woo came to power in 1987, in the wake of a mass protest against civil-rights abuses and other

excesses of the previous government. Students began mass protests against various candidates long before the 1992 elections that brought to office the first civilian president in more than 30 years, Kim Young-sam. Kim was once a dissident himself and was victimized by government policies against free speech; once elected, he promised to make major democratic reforms. The reforms, however, have not been good enough for thousands of striking subway workers, farmers, or students whose demonstrations against low pay, foreign rice imports, or the placement of Patriot missiles in South Korea have had to be broken up by riot police.

A primary focus of the South Korean government's attention at the moment is the several U.S. military bases in South Korea, currently home to approximately 43,500 U.S. troops. The government (and apparently most of the 44.6 million South Korean people), although not always happy with the military presence, believes that the U.S. troops are useful in deterring possible aggression from North Korea, which despite a collapsing economy, still invests massive amounts of its budget in its military. Many university students, however, are offended at the presence of these troops. They claim that the Americans have suppressed the growth of democracy by propping up authoritarian regimes—a claim readily admitted by the United States, which believed during the cold war era that the containment of communism was a higher priority. Strong feelings against U.S. involvement in South Korean affairs have precipitated hundreds of violent demonstrations, sometimes involving as many as 100,000 protesters. The United States' refusal to withdraw its forces from South Korea left an impression with many Koreans that Americans were hard-line, cold war ideologues who were unwilling to bend in the face of changing international alignments.

In 1990, U.S. officials announced that, in an effort to reduce U.S. military costs in the post–cold war era, the United States would pull out several thousand of its troops from South Korea and close three of its five air bases. The United States also declared that it expected South Korea to pay more of the cost of the U.S. military presence, in part as a way to reduce the unfavorable trade balance between the two countries. The South Korean government agreed to build a new U.S. military base about 50 miles south of the capital city of Seoul, where current operations would be relocated. South Korea would pay all construction costs—estimated at about $1 billion—and the United States would be able to reduce its presence within the Seoul metropolitan area, where many of

| The Yi dynasty begins a 518-year reign over Korea A.D. 935 | Korea pays tribute to Mongol rulers in China 1637 | Korea opens its ports to outside trade 1876 | Japan formally annexes Korea at the end of the Russo-Japanese War 1910 | Korea is divided into North and South 1945 | North Korea invades South Korea: the Korean War begins 1950 | Cease-fire agreement; the DMZ is established 1953 | President Park Chung Hee is assassinated 1979 | Democratization movement; the 1988 Summer Olympic Games are held in Seoul 1980s |

1990s

Reunification talks | A nonaggression pact is signed with North Korea; cross-border exhanges begin | President Kim Young-sam and Prime Minister Lee Yung Duk take office

the anti-U.S. demonstrations take place. Although the bases have been a focus of protest by students, surveys now show that about 90 percent of South Koreans want the U.S. military to remain in the country.

A second issue that has occupied the government for years is the question of reunification with North Korea. The division of the country has left many families unable to communicate with or visit relatives in the North, and the threat of a military incursion from the North has forced South Korea to spend large sums of its national budget on defense. Frequent charges of spying, counterspying, and other forms of subversive activities—not to mention the fact that the two nations have not signed a peace treaty since the Korean War, and that the North declared in 1996 that it would no longer recognize the 1953 armistice—have kept tensions high. High-profile meetings to discuss reunification have been held for several years, but with little concrete progress, despite a nonaggression and reconciliation pact and agreements on cross-border exchanges and other forms of cooperation. The impetus behind improvements in relations appears to be North Korea's loss of solid diplomatic and economic partners and thus its increasing isolation in the world economy, due to the collapse of the Soviet Union. Some South Koreans have estimated that it will cost $980 billion to reunify with the North.

South Korean government leaders have to face a very active, vocal, and even violent populace when they initiate controversial policies. Among the more vocal groups for democracy and human rights are the various Christian congregations

and their Westernized clergy. Other vocal groups include the college students who hold rallies annually to elect student protest leaders and to plan antigovernment demonstrations. In addition to the military-bases question, student protesters are angry at the South Korean government's willingness to open more Korean markets to U.S. products. The students want the United States to apologize for its alleged assistance to the South Korean government in violently suppressing an antigovernment demonstration in 1981 in Kwangju, a southern city that is a frequent locus of antigovernment as well as labor-related demonstrations and strikes. Protesters were particularly angered by then–president Roh Tae-woo's silencing of part of the opposition by convincing two opposition parties to merge with his own to form a large Democratic Liberal Party, not unlike that of the Liberal Democratic Party, which governed Japan almost continuously for more than 40 years.

Ironically, demands for changes have increased at precisely the moment that the government has been instituting changes designed to strengthen both the economy and civil rights. Under Roh's administration, for example, trade and diplomatic initiatives were launched with Eastern/Central European nations and with China and the former Soviet Union. Under Kim Young-sam's administration, 41,000 prisoners, including some political prisoners, were granted amnesty, and the powerful business conglomerates called chaebols were brought under a tighter rein. Similarly, relaxation of the tight controls on labor union activity gave workers more leverage in negotiating with man-

agement. Unfortunately, union activity, exploding after decades of suppression, has produced crippling industrial strikes—as many as 2,400 a year, and the police have been called out to restore order. In fact, since 1980, riot police have fired an average of more than 500 tear-gas shells a day, at a cost to the South Korean government of $51 million.

The sense of unease in South Korea has been tempered by the dynamism of the economy. Economic growth and democratization seem to be high on the agenda, although the latter has been exceptionally difficult to achieve. South Korea recently established unofficial diplomatic ties with Taiwan in order to facilitate freer trade. It then signed an industrial pact with China to merge South Korea's technological know-how with China's inexpensive labor force to build aircraft, automobiles, and even high-definition televisions. Relations with Japan have also improved since Japan's apology for atrocities during World War II and the visit of Kim Young-sam to the Japanese emperor Akihito in Tokyo in 1994.

DEVELOPMENT

The South Korean economy is booming. Construction of new homes and businesses is everywhere evident. Industrial workers have had to bear the brunt of the negative aspects of industrialization: low wages and long hours.

FREEDOM

Suppression of political dissent, manipulation of the electoral process, and restrictions on labor union activity have been features of almost every South Korean government since 1948. Martial law has been frequently invoked, and governments have been overthrown by mass uprisings of the people. Reforms have been enacted under Presidents Roh Tae-woo and Kim Young-sam.

HEALTH/WELFARE

Korean men usually marry at about age 27, women at about 24. In 1960, Korean women, on average, gave birth to 6 children; in 1990, the expected births per woman were 1.6. The average South Korean baby born today can expect to live to be about 70 years old, as compared to 75 for U.S. newborns.

ACHIEVEMENTS

In 1992, Korean students placed first in international math and science tests. South Korea achieved self-sufficiency in agricultural fertilizers in the 1970s and continues to show growth in the production of grains and vegetables. The formerly weak industrial sector is now a strong component of the economy.

Taiwan (Republic of China)

GEOGRAPHY

Area in Square Kilometers (Miles): 36,002 (22,320) (about the size of West Virginia)
Capital (Population): Taipei (2,720,000)
Climate: subtropical

PEOPLE

Population

Total: 21,500,600
Annual Growth Rate: 0.93%
Rural/Urban Population Ratio: 25/75
Ethnic Makeup: 84% Taiwanese; 14% Mainlander Chinese; 2% aborigine
Major Languages: Mandarin Chinese; Taiwanese and Hakka dialects also used

Health

Life Expectancy at Birth: 72 years (male); 79 years (female)
Infant Mortality Rate (Ratio): 5.6/1,000
Average Caloric Intake: n/a
Physicians Available (Ratio): 1/804

Religions

93% mixture of Buddhism, Confucianism, and Taoism; 4.5% Christian; 2.5% others

Education

Adult Literacy Rate: 92%

COMMUNICATION

Telephones: 7,800,000
Newspapers: 139

BAMBOO, A SYMBOL OF ASIA

In central Taiwan, near the city of Tai-chung, is a 6,000-acre forest research station, located approximately 4,000 feet above sea level. This forest is unique because its trees are mostly bamboo. Bamboo, of which there are some 200 species, is a member of the grass family, but some varieties grow to be more than 150 feet high and 1 foot in diameter. Some species have been known to grow nearly 2 feet a day.

With more than a dozen varieties of bamboo, the Hsitou Bamboo Forest preserves a plant that is now being slowly displaced by plastic and steel but which remains the single most useful building material throughout Asia and Southeast Asia. In Korea and elsewhere, bamboo is used as scaffolding on most construction jobs; in China, the small tips of new bamboo shoots are used as food in many dishes; in Japan, bamboo is fashioned into fans, flowerpots, water pipes, and a flutelike musical instrument called a *shakuhachi*. Chopsticks, baskets, and even paper are made from bamboo.

TRANSPORTATION

Highways—Kilometers (Miles): 20,041 (12,425)
Railroads—Kilometers (Miles): 4,600 (2,852)
Usable Airfields: 38

GOVERNMENT

Type: multiparty democratic regime
Head of State/Government: President Lee Teng-hui; Premier Lee Yuan-tseh
Political Parties: Nationalist Party (Kuomintang); Democratic Progressive Party; China Social Democratic Party; Labour Party
Suffrage: universal over 20

MILITARY

Number of Armed Forces: 400,000
Military Expenditures (% of Central Government Expenditures): 3.4%
Current Hostilities: officially (but not actually) in a state of war with the People's Republic of China

ECONOMY

Currency ($ U.S. Equivalent): 27.51 New Taiwan dollars = $1
Per Capita Income/GDP: $12,070/$257 billion
Inflation Rate: 5.2%
Natural Resources: coal; gold; copper; sulphur; oil; natural gas
Agriculture: rice; tea; bananas; pineapples; sugarcane; sweet potatoes; wheat; soybeans; peanuts
Industry: steel; pig iron; aluminum; shipbuilding; cement; fertilizer; paper; cotton; fabrics

FOREIGN TRADE

Exports: $93.0 billion
Imports: $85.1 billion

Taiwan

❂ Capital
● City
∼ River
--- Road

0   50   kilometers
0   50   miles

PEOPLE'S REPUBLIC OF CHINA

EAST CHINA SEA

TUNG-YIN TAO
LIANG TAO
PEI-KAN-T'ANG TAO
MA-TSU TAO
PAI-CH'UAN LIEH-TAO
P'ENG-CHIA YÜ

WU-CH'IU YÜ
Tan-shui
Chi-lung
★ TAIPEI
T'ao-yüan   Pan-ch'iao
I-lan
Hsin-chu
Miao-li   Su-ao
Taiwan Strait
QUEMOY OFFSHORE ISLANDS
Feng-yüan
T'ai-chung
Chang-hua   Hua-lien
Chung-hsing-hsin-ts'un
Nan-to'u
MA-KUNG   Cho-shui Hsi
Tou-liu
P'ENG-HU CH'ÜN-TAO (PESCADORES)
Chia-i
Hsin-ying
PHILIPPINE SEA
T'ai-nan
Pescadores Channel
T'ai-tung
Kao-hsiung   Feng-shan
P'ing-tung
LÜ TAO
Fang-liao
LUI-CH'IU YÜ
LAN YÜ

93

A LAND OF REFUGE

It has been called "beautiful island," "treasure island," and "terraced bay island," but to the people who have settled there, Taiwan (formerly known as Formosa) has come to mean "refuge island."

Typical of the earliest refugees of the island were the Hakka peoples of China, who, tired of persecution on the mainland, fled to Taiwan (and to Borneo) before A.D. 1000. In the seventeenth century, tens of thousands of Ming Chinese soldiers, defeated at the hands of the expanding Manchu army, sought sanctuary in Taiwan. In 1949, a third major wave of immigration to Taiwan brought thousands of Chinese Nationalists, retreating in the face of the victorious Red Chinese armies. Hosting all these newcomers were the original inhabitants of the islands, various Malay–Polynesian-speaking tribes whose descendants live today in mountain villages throughout the island.

Since 1544, other outsiders have shown interest in Taiwan, too: Portugal, Spain, the Netherlands, Britain, and France have all either settled colonies or engaged in trade along the coasts. But the non-Chinese power that has had the most influence is Japan. Japan treated parts of Taiwan as its own for 400 years before it officially acquired the entire island in 1895, at the end of the Sino–Japanese War. From then until 1945, the Japanese ruled Taiwan with the intent of fully integrating it into Japanese culture. The Japanese language was taught in schools, college students were sent to Japan for their education, and the Japanese style of government was implemented. Many Taiwanese resented the harsh discipline imposed, but they also recognized that the Japanese were building a modern, productive society. Indeed, the basic infrastructure of contemporary Taiwan—roads, railways, schools, and so on—was constructed during the Japanese colonial era (1895–1945). Japan still lays claim to the Senkaku Islands, a chain of uninhabited islands, which the Taiwanese say belong to Taiwan.

After Japan's defeat in World War II, Taiwan became the island of refuge of the anti-Communist leader Chiang Kai-shek and his 3 million Kuomintang (KMT, or Nationalist Party) followers, many of whom had been prosperous and well-educated businesspeople and intellectuals in China. These Mandarin-speaking mainland Chinese, called Mainlanders, now constitute about 14 percent of Taiwan's people.

During the 1950s, Mao Zedong, the leader of the People's Republic of China, planned an invasion of Taiwan. However, Taiwan's leaders succeeded in obtaining military support from the United States to prevent the attack. They also convinced the United States to provide substantial amounts of foreign aid to Taiwan (the U.S. government saw the funds as a way to contain communism) as well as to grant it diplomatic recognition as the only legitimate government for all of China.

China was denied membership in the United Nations for more than 20 years because Taiwan held the "China seat." World opinion on the "two Chinas" issue began to change in the early 1970s. Many countries believed that a nation as large and powerful as the People's Republic of China should not be kept out of the United Nations nor out of the mainstream of world trade in favor of the much smaller Taiwan. In 1971, the United Nations withdrew its China seat from Taiwan and gave it to the P.R.C. Taiwan has consistently reapplied for membership, arguing that there is nothing wrong with there being either two China seats or one China seat and one Taiwan seat; its requests have been denied. The United States and many other countries wished to establish diplomatic relations with China but could not get China to cooperate as long as they recognized the sovereignty of Taiwan. In 1979, desiring access to China's huge market, the United States, preceded by many other nations, switched its diplomatic recognition from Taiwan to China. Foreign-trade offices in Taiwan remained unchanged but embassies were renamed; the U.S. Embassy was called the American Institute in Taiwan. As far as official diplomacy with the United States was concerned, Taiwan became a non-nation, but that did not stop the two countries from engaging in very profitable trade, including a controversial U.S. agreement in 1992 to sell $4 billion to $6 billion worth of F-16 fighter jets to Taiwan. Similarly, Taiwan has refused to establish diplomatic ties, yet continues to trade, with nations that recognize the mainland Chinese authorities as a legitimate government. In 1992, for instance, when South Korea established ties with mainland China, Taiwan immediately broke off formal relations with South Korea and suspended direct airline flights. However, Taiwan continued to permit trade in many commodities. Recognizing a potentially strong market in Vietnam, Taiwan also established air links with Vietnam in 1992, links that had been broken since the end of the Vietnam War. In 1993 a Taiwanese company collaborated with the Vietnamese government to construct a $242 million highway in Ho Chi Minh City (formerly Saigon). Just over 30 states formally recognize Taiwan today, but Taiwan nevertheless maintains close economic ties with more than 140 countries.

AN ECONOMIC POWERHOUSE

Diplomatic maneuvering has not affected Taiwan's stunning postwar economic growth. Like Japan, Taiwan has been described as an economic miracle. In the past 20 years, Taiwan has enjoyed more years of double-digit economic growth than any other nation. With electronics leading the pack of exports, about 45 percent of Taiwan's gross domestic product

(UN photo by Chen Jr.)

Taiwan has one of the highest population densities in the world, but it has been able to expand its agricultural output rapidly and efficiently through a number of innovative practices. By terracing, using high-yield seeds, and developing adequate irrigation, Taiwanese can grow a succession of crops on the same piece of land throughout the year.

(UN photo by Chen Jr.)

Taiwan is described as an economic miracle. After World War II, it emerged as a tremendous source for labor-intensive industries, such as electronics and clothing. Many Western manufacturers moved their facilities to Taiwan to take advantage of the savings in labor costs.

comes from manufacturing. Taiwan has been open to foreign investment and, of course, to foreign trade. However, for many years, Taiwan insisted on a policy of no contact and no communication with mainland China. Private enterprises eventually were allowed to trade with China—as long as the products were transshipped through a third country, usually Hong Kong. In 1993, government-owned enterprises such as steel and fertilizer plants were allowed to trade with China, on the same condition. By the early 1990s, Taiwanese trade with China had exceeded $13 billion a year and China had become Taiwan's seventh-largest trading partner. The liberalization of trade between China (especially its southern and coastal provinces), Taiwan, and Hong Kong has made the region, now known as "Greater China," an economic dynamo. Economists predict that Greater China will bypass Japan's economy in the near future.

As one of the newly industrializing countries of Asia, Taiwan certainly no longer fits the label "underdeveloped." Taiwan holds large stocks of foreign reserves and carries a trade surplus with the United States (in Taiwan's favor) 4 times greater than Japan's, when counted on a per capita basis. The Taipei stock market has been so successful—sometimes outperforming both Japan and the United States—that a number of workers reportedly have quit their jobs to play the mar-

ket, thereby exacerbating Taiwan's already serious labor shortage.

Successful Taiwanese companies have begun to invest heavily in other countries where land and labor are plentiful and less expensive. In 1993, the Philippines accepted a $60 million loan from Taiwan to build an industrial park and commercial port at Subic Bay, the former U.S. naval base; and Thailand, Australia, and the United States have also seen inflows of Taiwanese investment monies. By the early 1990s, some 200 Taiwanese companies had invested $1.3 billion in Malaysia alone (Taiwan has now supplanted Japan as the largest outside investor in Malaysia). Investment in mainland China has also increased.

Taiwan's economic success is attributable in part to its educated population, many of whom constituted the cultural and economic elite of China before the Communist revolution. Despite resentment of the mainland immigrants by native-born Taiwanese, everyone, including the lower classes of Taiwan, has benefited from this infusion of talent and capital. Yet the Taiwanese people are beginning to pay a price for their sudden affluence. It is said that Taipei, the capital city of Taiwan (and the sixth most expensive city in the world for foreigners) is awash in money, but it is also awash in air pollution and traffic congestion. Traffic congestion in Taipei is rated near the

worst in the world. Concrete high-rises have displaced the lush greenery of the mountains. Many residents spend their earnings on luxury foreign cars and on cigarettes and alcohol, the consumption rate of which has been increasing by about 10 percent a year. Many Chinese traditions—for instance, the roadside restaurant serving noodle soup—are giving way to 7-Elevens selling Coca-Cola and ice cream.

Some Taiwanese despair of ever turning back from the growing materialism; they wish for the revival of traditional Chinese (that is, mostly Confucian) ethics, but they doubt that it will happen. Still, the government, which has been dominated since 1949 by the conservative Mandarin migrants from the mainland, sees to it that Confucian ethics are vigorously taught in school. And there remains in Taiwan more of traditional China than in China itself, because, unlike the Chinese Communists, the Taiwanese authorities have had no reason to attempt an eradication of the values of Buddhism, Taoism, or Confucianism. Nor has grinding poverty—often the most serious threat to the cultural arts—negatively affected literature and the fine arts, as it has in China. Parents, with incense sticks burning before small religious altars, still emphasize respect for authority, the benefits of harmonious cooperative effort, and the inestimable value of education. Traditional festivals dot each year's

Portuguese sailors are the first Europeans to visit Taiwan
A.D. 1544

Taiwan becomes part of the Chinese Empire
1700s

The Sino-Japanese War ends; China cedes Taiwan to Japan
1895

Taiwan achieves independence from Japan
1945

Nationalists, under Chiang Kai-shek, retreat to Taiwan
1947-49

A de facto separation of Taiwan from China; Chinese aggression is deterred with U.S. assistance
1950s

China replaces Taiwan in the United Nations
1971

Chiang Kai-shek dies and is succeeded by his son, Chiang Ching-Kuo
1975

The first two-party elections in Taiwan's history are held; 38 years of martial law end
1980s

Chiang Ching-Kuo dies; Lee Teng-hui is the first native-born Taiwanese to be elected president

1990s

Relations with China improve; the United States sells F-16 jets to Taiwan

China conducts military exercises to intimidate Taiwanese voters

calendar, among the most spectacular of which is Taiwan's National Day parade. Marching bands, traditional dancers, and a huge dragon carried by more than 50 young men please the crowds lining the streets of Taipei. Temples are filled with worshipers praying for health and good luck.

But the Taiwanese will need more than luck if they are to escape the consequences of their intensely rapid drive for material comfort. Some people contend that the island of refuge is being destroyed by success. Violent crime, for instance, once hardly known in Taiwan, is now commonplace. Six thousand violent crimes, including rapes, robberies, kidnappings, and murder, were reported in 1989—a 22 percent increase over the previous year, and the upward trend has continued since then. Extortion against wealthy companies and abductions of the children of successful families are causing a wave of fear among the rich.

There are also signs that the economy is heading for a slowdown. Labor shortages have forced some companies to operate at only 60 percent of capacity, and low-interest loans are hard to get because the government fears that too many people will simply invest in get-rich stocks instead of in new businesses.

POLITICAL LIBERALIZATION

These disturbing trends notwithstanding, in recent years, the Taiwanese people have had much to be grateful for in the political sphere. Until 1986, the government, dominated by the influence of the Chiangs, had permitted only one political party, the Nationalists, and had kept Taiwan under mar-

tial law for nearly 4 decades. A marked political liberalization began near the time of Chiang Ching-Kuo's death, in 1987. The first opposition party, the Democratic Progressive Party, was formed, martial law (officially, the "Emergency Decree") was lifted, and the first two-party elections were held in 1986. In 1988, for the first time, a native-born Taiwanese, Lee Teng-hui, was elected to the presidency. He was reelected in 1996 in the first truly democratic presidential election ever held in Taiwan. Although Lee has never promoted the independence of Taiwan, his high-visibility campaign raised the ire of China, which attempted to intimidate the Taiwanese electorate into voting for a more pro-China candidate by conducting military exercises and firing missiles just 20 miles off the coast of Taiwan. As expected, the intimidation backfired, and Lee soundly defeated his opponents.

It is still against the law for any group or person to advocate publicly the independence of Taiwan—that is, to advocate international acceptance of Taiwan as a sovereign state, separate and apart from China. When the opposition Democratic Progressive Party (DPP) resolved in 1990 that Taiwan should become an independent country, the ruling Nationalist government immediately outlawed the DPP platform. Recent high-level talks between the Taiwanese government and China on trade and tourism have further complicated the issue. Some believe that such talks will eventually result in Taiwan being annexed by China just as Hong Kong and Macau will be (although from a strictly legalistic viewpoint, Taiwan has

just as much right to annex China). Others believe that dialogue will eventually diminish animosity, allowing Taiwan to move toward independence without China's opposition. Opinion is clearly divided. Even some members of the anti-independence Nationalist Party have bolted and formed a new party (the New KMT alliance, or the New Party) to promote closer ties with China. As opposition parties proliferate, the independence issue could become a more urgent topic of political debate. In the meantime, contacts with the P.R.C. increase daily; Taiwanese students are now being admitted to China's universities, and Taiwanese residents by the thousands are now visiting relatives on the mainland. Despite complaints from China, Taiwanese government leaders have been courting their counterparts in the Philippines, Thailand, Indonesia, and South Korea. Moreover, President Lee has publicly promoted better relations with the People's Republic (the first president to do so), but China has vowed to invade Taiwan if it should ever declare independence. Under these circumstances, many—probably most—Taiwanese will likely remain content to let the rhetoric of reunification continue while enjoying the reality of de facto independence.

DEVELOPMENT

Taiwan has vigorously promoted export-oriented production, particularly of electronic equipment. In the 1980s, manufacturing became the leading sector of the economy, employing more than one third of the workforce. Ninety-nine percent of Taiwanese households own color televisions, and other signs of affluence are abundant.

FREEDOM

For nearly 4 decades, Taiwan was under martial law. Opposition parties were not tolerated, and individual liberties were limited. A liberalization of this pattern began in 1986. Taiwan now seems to be on a path toward greater democratization. In 1991, 5,574 prisoners, including many political prisoners, were released in a general amnesty.

HEALTH/WELFARE

Taiwan has one of the highest population densities in the world. Education is compulsory to age 15, and the country boasts more than 100 institutions of higher learning. Social programs, however, are less developed than those in Singapore, Japan, and some other Pacific Rim countries.

ACHIEVEMENTS

From a largely agrarian economic base, Taiwan has been able to transform its economy into an export-based dynamo with international influence. Today, only 20 percent of the population work in agriculture, and Taiwan ranks among the top 20 exporters in the world.

Thailand (Kingdom of Thailand)

GEOGRAPHY

Area in Square Kilometers (Miles):
514,000 (198,404) (slightly more
than twice the size of Wyoming)
Capital (Population): Bangkok
(5,833,000)
Climate: tropical

PEOPLE

Population
Total: 60,271,000
Annual Growth Rate: 1.24%
Rural/Urban Population Ratio: 80/20
Ethnic Makeup: 84% Thai; 12%
Chinese; 4% Malay and others
Major Languages: Thai; English;
dialects; others

Health
Life Expectancy at Birth: 65 years
(male); 72 years (female)
Infant Mortality Rate (Ratio):
35.7/1,000
Average Caloric Intake: 105% of
FAO minimum
Physicians Available (Ratio): 1/4,227

Religions
94% Buddhist; 4% Muslim; 2% others

Education
Adult Literacy Rate: 93%

COMMUNICATION

Telephones: 739,500
Newspapers: 23 dailies in Bangkok

TRANSPORTATION

Highways—Kilometers (Miles):
77,697 (48,328)
Railroads—Kilometers (Miles): 3,940
(2,442)
Usable Airfields: 105

THAILAND'S KING OF SWING

Thailand's revered, 70-year-old King Bhumibol Adulyadej has acquired a distinctly Western habit: he loves jazz. Born in Cambridge,
Massachusetts, and educated in Switzerland, King Bhumibol, who is
highly respected for his efforts to improve the lot of ordinary people in
Thailand, has his own jazz band and is an accomplished saxophonist
and composer. He holds jam sessions at the royal palace and has played
with such legends as Benny Goodman and the Count Basie Orchestra.
Says jazz great Lionel Hampton, "He is simply the coolest king in the
land."

GOVERNMENT

Type: constitutional monarchy
Independence Date: traditional
founding date: 1238 (never colonized)
Head of State/Government: King
Bhumibol Adulyadej; Prime Minister
Banharn Silpaarcha
Political Parties: Democratic Party;
Thai Nation Party; National
Development Party; New Aspiration
Party; Social Action Party; Liberal
Democratic Party; Solidarity Party;
Mass Party; Thai Citizens' Party;
People's Party; People's Force Party
Suffrage: universal at 21

MILITARY

Number of Armed Forces: 283,000
*Military Expenditures (% of Central
Government Expenditures):* 2.5%
Current Hostilities: boundary dispute
with Laos

ECONOMY

Currency ($ U.S. Equivalent): 25.07
baht = $1
Per Capita Income/GDP:
$5,970/$355.2 billion
Inflation Rate: 8.0%
Natural Resources: tin; rubber;
natural gas; tungsten; tantalum;
timber; lead; fish; gypsum; lignite;
fluorite
Agriculture: rice; cassava; rubber;
corn; sugarcane; coconuts; soybeans
Industry: tourism; textiles and
garments; agricultural processing;
beverages; tobacco; cement; electric
appliances and components;
electronics; furniture; plastics

FOREIGN TRADE

Exports: $46.0 billion
Imports: $52.6 billion

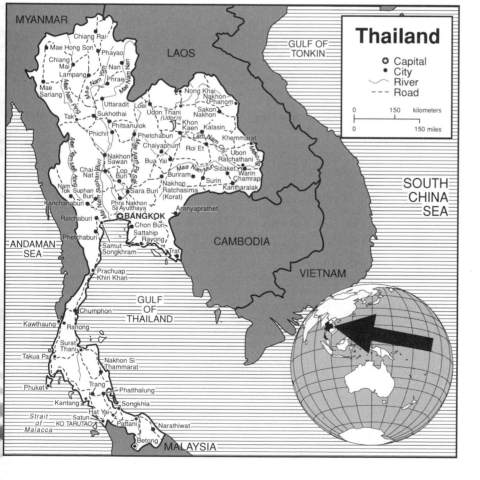

THAILAND'S ANCIENT HERITAGE

The roots of Thai culture extend into the distant past. People were living in Thailand at least as early as the Bronze Age; by the time Thai people from China (some scholars think from as far away as Mongolia) had established the first Thai dynasty in the Chao Phya Valley, in A.D. 1238, some communities, invariably with a Buddhist temple or monastery at their centers, had been thriving in the area for 600 years. Early Thai culture was greatly influenced by Buddhist monks and traders from India and Sri Lanka (Ceylon).

By the seventeenth century, Thailand's ancient capital, Ayutthaya, boasted a larger population than did London. Ayutthaya was known around the world for its wealth and for the beauty of its architecture, particularly its religious edifices. Attempts by European nations to obtain a share of the wealth were so inordinate that, in 1688, the king expelled all foreigners from the country. Later, warfare with Cambodia, Laos, and Malaya yielded tremendous gains in power and territory for Thailand, but it was periodically afflicted by Burma (present-day Myanmar), which briefly conquered Thailand in the 1760s (as it had done in the 1560s). The Burmese were finally defeated in 1780, but the destruction of the capital required the construction of a new city, near what, today, is Bangkok.

Generally speaking, the Thai people have been blessed over the centuries with benevolent kings, many of whom have been open to new ideas from Europe and North America. Gathering around them advisers from many nations, they improved transportation systems, education, and farming while maintaining the central place of Buddhism in Thai society. Occasionally royal support for religion overtook other societal needs, at the expense of the power of the government.

The gravest threat to Thailand came during the era of European colonial expansion. However, although both France and Britain forced Thailand to yield some of its holdings in Southeast Asia, Thailand—whose name means "Free Land"—was never completely conquered by European powers. Today, the country occupies a land area about the size of France.

MODERN POLITICS

Since 1932, when a constitutional monarchy replaced the absolute monarchy, Thailand (formerly known as Siam) has weathered 17 attempted or successful

(Photo credit United Nations/Prince)

Buddhism is an integral part of the Thai culture. Six hundred years ago, Buddhist monks traveled from India and Ceylon (present-day Sri Lanka) and built their temples and monasteries throughout Thailand. These newly ordained monks are meditating in the courtyard of a temple in Bangkok.

military or political coups d'état (most recently in 1991). The Constitution has been revoked and replaced numerous times; governments have fallen under votes of no-confidence; students have mounted violent demonstrations against the government; and the military has, at various times, imposed martial law or otherwise curtailed civil liberties.

Clearly, Thai politics are far from stable. Nevertheless, there is a sense of stability in Thailand. Miraculously, its people were spared the direct ravages of the Vietnam War, which raged nearby for 20 years. Despite all the political upheavals, the same royal family has been in control of the Thai throne for nine generations, although its power has been severely delimited for some 60 years. Furthermore, before the first Constitution was enacted in 1932, the country had been ruled continuously, for more than 700 years, by

often brilliant and progressive kings. At the height of Western imperialism, when France, Britain, Holland, and Portugal were in control of every country on or near Thailand's borders, Thailand remained free of Western domination, although it was forced—sometimes at gunpoint—to relinquish sizable chunks of its holdings in Cambodia and Laos to France, and holdings in Malaya to Britain. The reasons for this singular state of independence were the diplomatic skill of Thai leaders, Thai willingness to Westernize the government, and the desire of Britain and France to let Thailand remain interposed as a neutral buffer zone between their respective armies in Burma and Indochina.

The current king, Bhumibol Adulyadej, born in the United States and educated in Switzerland, is highly respected as head of state. The king is also the nominal head of the armed forces, and his support is critical to any Thai government. Despite Thailand's structures of democratic government, any administration that has not also received the approval of the military elites, many of whom hold seats in the Senate, has not prevailed for long. The military has been a rightist force in Thai politics, resisting reforms from the left that might have produced a stronger labor union movement, more freedom of expression (many television and radio stations in Thailand are controlled directly by the military), and less economic distance between the social classes. Military involvement in government increased substantially during the 1960s and 1970s, when a Communist insurgency threatened the government from within and the Vietnam War destabilized the external environment.

Until the February 1991 coup, there had been signs that the military was slowly withdrawing from direct meddling in the government. This may have been because the necessity for a strong military appeared to have lessened with the end of the cold war. In late 1989, for example, the Thai government signed a peace agreement with the Communist Party of Malaya, which had been harassing villagers along the Thai border for more than 40 years. Despite these political/military improvements, Army Commander Suchinda Kraprayoon led a coup against the legally elected government in 1991 and, notwithstanding promises to the contrary, promptly had himself named prime minister. Immediately, Thai citizens, tired of the constant instability in government occasioned by military meddling, began staging mass demonstrations against Suchinda. The protesters were largely middle-class office workers who used their cellular telephones to communicate from one protest site to another. The demonstrations were the largest in 20 years, and the military responded with violence; nearly 50 people were killed and more than 600 were injured. The public outcry was such that Suchinda was forced to appear on television being lectured by the king; he subsequently resigned. An interim premier dismissed several top military commanders and removed military personnel from the many government departments over which they had come to preside. Elections followed in 1992, and Thailand returned to civilian rule, with the military's influence greatly diminished.

The events of this latest coup show that the increasingly educated and affluent citizens of Thailand wish their country to be a true democracy. Still, unlike some democratic governments that have one dominant political party and one or two smaller opposition parties, party politics in Thailand is characterized by diversity. Indeed, so many parties compete for power that no single party is able to govern without forming coalitions with others. Parties are often founded on the strength of a single charismatic leader rather than on a distinct political philosophy, a circumstance that makes the entire political setting rather volatile. The Communist Party remains banned. Campaigns to elect the 360-seat Parliament often turn violent; in a recent election, 10 candidates were killed when their homes were bombed or sprayed with rifle fire, and nearly 50 gunmen-for-hire were arrested or killed by police, who were attempting to protect the candidates of the 11 political parties vying for office. The current prime minister has been under constant attack since 1995 due to a series of corruption scandals and alleged incompetence.

FOREIGN RELATIONS

Thailand is a member of the United Nations and of the Association of Southeast Asian Nations. Throughout most of its modern history, Thailand has maintained a pro-Western political position. During World War I, Thailand joined with the Allies; and during the Vietnam War, it allowed the United States to stage air attacks on North Vietnam from within its borders, and it served as a major rest and

(UN/photo by Saw Lwin)

Rice is Thailand's most important export. Its production utilizes a majority of the agricultural workforce. Today, the government is attempting to diversify his reliance on rice, encouraging farmers to grow a wider variety of crops that are not so dependent on world markets and the weather.

Possible horticulture in Thailand 10,000 B.C.	Migrants from China move into what is now Thailand 200 B.C.	The formal beginning of Thailand as a nation A.D. 1200s	King Sukhothai creates the Thai alphabet 1279–1299	Foreigners are expelled from Thailand 1688	Long-time rival Burma attacks Thailand 1760s

relaxation center for American soldiers. During World War II, Thailand briefly allied itself with Japan but made decided efforts after the war to reestablish its former Western ties.

Thailand's international positions have seemingly been motivated more by practical need than by ideology. During the colonial era, Thailand linked itself with Britain because it needed to offset the influence of France; during World War II, it joined with Japan in an apparent effort to prevent its country from being devastated by Japanese troops; during the Vietnam War, it supported the United States because the United States seemed to offer Thailand its only hope of not being directly engaged in military conflict in the region.

Thailand now seems to be tilting away from its close ties with the United States and toward a closer relationship with Japan. In the late 1980s, disputes with the United States over import tariffs and international copyright matters cooled the prior warm relationship (the United States has accused Thailand of allowing the manufacture of counterfeit brand-name watches, clothes, computer software, and many other items, including medicines). Moreover, Thailand found in Japan a more ready, willing, and cooperative economic partner than the United States.

During the cold war and especially during the Vietnam War era, the Thai military strenuously resisted the growth of Communist ideology inside Thailand, and the Thai government refused to engage in normal diplomatic relations with the Communist regimes on its borders. Because of military pressure, elected officials refrained from advocating improved relations with the Communist governments. However, in 1988, Prime Minister Prem Tinslanond, a former general in the army who had been in control of the government for 8 years, stepped down from office, and opposition to normalization of relations seemed to mellow. The subsequent prime minister, Chatichai Choon-

havan, who was ousted in the 1991 military coup, invited Cambodian leader Hun Sen to visit Thailand; he also made overtures to Vietnam and Laos. Chatichai's goal was to open the way for trade in the region by helping to settle the agonizing Cambodian conflict. He also hoped to bring stability to the region so that the huge refugee camps in Thailand, the largest in the world, could be dismantled and the refugees repatriated. Managing regional relations will continue to be difficult: Thailand fought a brief border war with Communist Laos in 1988. The influx of refugees from the civil wars in adjacent Cambodia and Myanmar continues to strain relations.

Part of the thrust behind Thailand's diplomatic initiatives is the changing needs of its economy. For decades, Thailand saw itself as an agricultural country; indeed, nearly two thirds of the workforce remain in agriculture today, with rice as the primary commodity. Rice is Thailand's single most important export and a major source of government revenue. Every morning, Thai families sit down on the floor of their homes around bowls of hot and spicy *tom yam goong* soup and a large bowl of rice; holidays and festivals are scheduled to coincide with the various stages of planting and harvesting rice; and, in rural areas, students are dismissed at harvest time so that all members of a family can help in the fields. So central is rice to the diet and the economy of the country that the Thai verb equivalent of "to eat," translated literally, means "to eat rice." Thailand is the fifth-largest exporter of rice in the world.

Unfortunately, Thailand's dependence on rice subjects its economy to the cyclical fluctuations of weather (sometimes the monsoons bring too little moisture) and market demand. Thus, in recent years, the government has invested millions of dollars in economic diversification. Not only have farmers been encouraged to grow a wider variety of crops, but tin, lumber, and offshore oil and gas production have also been promoted. Foreign investment in export-oriented manufacturing has been warmly welcomed. Japan in particular benefits from trading with Thailand in food and other commodities, and it sees Thailand as one of the more promising places to relocate smokestack industries.

(Photo credit United Nations/J. M. Micaud)

Industrialization in Thailand has drawn many people to the cities. The resultant overcrowding and strains on job availability have forced people into homelessness. These Thais are living under an elevated highway near Klong Toey Port in Bangkok.

| King Rama I ascends the throne, beginning a nine-generation dynasty **1782** | King Mongkut builds the first road in Thailand **1868** | Coup; constitutional monarchy **1932** | The country's name is changed from Siam to Thailand **1939** | Thailand joins Japan and declares war on the United States and Britain **1942** | Thailand resumes its historical pro-Western stance **1946** | Communist insurgency threatens Thailand's stability **1960s–1970s** | Student protests usher in democratic reforms **1973** | **1990s** |

A military coup attempt is thwarted

Chatichai Choonhavan replaces a former army general as prime minister

Chatichai is deposed in a military coup; mass demonstrations force a return to civilian rule

For its part, Thailand seems to prefer Japanese investment over that from the United States, because the Japanese seem more willing to engage in joint ventures and to show patience while enterprises become profitable. Indeed, economic ties with Japan are very strong. For instance, Japan is the largest single investor in Thailand and accounts for 41 percent of foreign direct investment (Taiwan, Hong Kong, and the United States each account for about 10 percent). About 30 percent of Thai imports come from Japan, and approximately 15 percent of its exports go to Japan.

Thailand's shift to an export-oriented economy is paying off. The growth rate of Thailand's gross domestic product has averaged about 10 percent a year—one of the highest in the world, and as high, or higher than, all the newly industrializing countries of Asia (Hong Kong, South Korea, Singapore, Taiwan, and China). Furthermore, unlike the Philippines and Indonesia, Thailand has been able to achieve this incredible growth without very high inflation; unemployment is about 6 percent.

SOCIAL PROBLEMS

Industrialization in Thailand, as everywhere, draws people to the cities. It is estimated that, by the year 2000, Bangkok will have a population of 10.7 million, making it one of the largest cities in the world. Numerous problems, particularly traffic congestion and overcrowding, already complicate life for Bangkok residents. An international airport that opened in 1987 near Bangkok was so overcrowded just 4 years later that a new one had to be planned, and new harbors had to be constructed south of the city to alleviate congestion in the main port. Demographic projections indicate that there will be a decline in population growth in the future as the birth rate drops and the average Thai household shrinks from the 6 people it was in 1970 to only 3 people by 2015. This will alter the social structure of urban families, especially as increased life expectancy adds older people to the population and forces the country to provide more services for the elderly. Today, however, a majority of Thai people still make their living on farms, where they grow rice, rubber, and corn, or tend chickens and cattle, including the ever-present water buffalo. Thus, it is in the countryside (or "upcountry," as everywhere but Bangkok is called in Thailand) that the traditional culture of Thailand may be found. There, one still finds villages of typically fewer than 1,000 inhabitants, with houses built on wooden stilts alongside a canal or around a Buddhist monastery. One also finds, however, unsanitary conditions, higher rates of illiteracy, and lack of access to potable water. Of increasing concern is deforestation, as Thailand's growing population continues to use wood as its primary fuel for cooking and heat. The provision of social services does not meet demand even in the cities, but rural residents are particularly deprived.

Culturally, Thai people are known for their willingness to tolerate (although not necessarily to assimilate) diverse lifestyles and opinions. Buddhist monks, who shave their heads and vow celibacy, do not find it incongruous to beg for rice in districts of Bangkok known for prostitution and wild nightlife. And worshippers seldom object when a noisy, congested highway is built alongside the serenity of an ancient Buddhist temple. (However, the mammoth scale of the proposed $3.2 billion, four-level road and railway system in the city and its likely effect on cultural and religious sites when it is completed in the late 1990s prompted the Thai cabinet to order the construction underground; but the cabinet had to recant, when the Hong Kong firm designing the project announced that it was technically impossible to build it underground.)

This relative openness has mitigated ethnic conflict among Thailand's numerous minority groups. The Chinese, for instance, who are often disliked in other Asian countries because of their dominance of the business sectors, are able to live with little or no discrimination in Thailand; indeed, they constitute the backbone of Thailand's new industrial thrust.

DEVELOPMENT

Two thirds of Thailand's workforce are small-plot or tenant farmers, but the government has energetically promoted economic diversification. Despite high taxes, Thailand has a reputation as a good place for foreign investment. Electronics and other high-tech industries from Japan, the United States, and other countries have been very successful in Thailand.

FREEDOM

Since 1932, when the absolute monarchy was abolished, Thailand has endured numerous military coups and countercoups, most recently in February 1991. Combined with the threat of Communist insurgencies, these have resulted in numerous declarations of martial law, press censorship, and suspensions of civil liberties.

HEALTH/WELFARE

About 2,000 Thais out of every 100,000 inhabitants attend college (as compared to only 200 per 100,000 Vietnamese). Thailand has devoted substantial sums to the care of refugees from Cambodia and Vietnam. The rate of nonimmigrant population growth has dropped substantially since World War II. AIDS has emerged as a significant problem in Thailand.

ACHIEVEMENTS

Thailand is the only Southeast Asian nation never to have been colonized by a Western power. It was also able to remain detached from direct involvement in the Vietnam War. Unique among Asian cultures, Thailand has a large number of women in business and other professions. Thai dancing is world-famous for its intricacy. In 1996, boxer Somluck Khamsing became the first Thai to win an Olympic gold medal.

Vietnam (Socialist Republic of Vietnam)

GEOGRAPHY

Area in Square Kilometers (Miles): 329,560 (121,278) (slightly larger than New Mexico)
Capital (Population): Hanoi (3,100,000)
Climate: tropical

PEOPLE

Population
Total: 74,393,400
Annual Growth Rate: 1.71%
Rural/Urban Population Ratio: 80/20
Ethnic Makeup: 90% Vietnamese; 3% Chinese; 7% Muong, Thai, Meo, and other mountain tribes
Major Languages: Vietnamese; French; Chinese; English; Khmer; tribal languages

Health
Life Expectancy at Birth: 64 years (male); 68 years (female)
Infant Mortality Rate (Ratio): 46.4/1,000
Average Caloric Intake: 91% of FAO minimum
Physicians Available (Ratio): 1/3,096

Religions
Buddhists, Confucians, and Taoists most numerous; Roman Catholics; Cao Dai; animists; Muslims; Protestants

Education
Adult Literacy Rate: 88%

COMMUNICATION

Telephones: 179,100
Newspapers: 4 dailies

TRANSPORTATION

Highways—Kilometers (Miles): approximately 85,000 (52,700)
Railroads—Kilometers (Miles): 3,059 (1,896)
Usable Airfields: 48

VU QUANG: A WILDLIFE PARADISE

Located on 65 acres of forested land near Laos in what was formerly North Vietnam is the Vu Quang Nature Reserve. Largely unspoiled despite decades of warfare, the area is proving to be a veritable paradise for natural scientists. Recently, as reported by Associated Press correspondent David Briscoe, a team of biologists from the World Wildlife Fund and the Vietnamese government found 62 kinds of known fish as well as 1 new tortoise species, 2 new species of birds, and a mammal with goatlike horns. The area is also home to tigers, leopards, and elephants. To protect the park from development (Vu Quang is only a 10-hour drive from Hanoi), the Ministry of Forestry has banned logging in the area and hopes to expand the boundaries of the park. Laotian officials have also been asked to declare adjacent land inside Laos a nature reserve as well. Unique in Southeast Asia, the reserve may add significant new chapters to humankind's knowledge of the animal kingdom.

GOVERNMENT

Type: Communist state
Independence Date: September 2, 1945
Head of State/Government: President Le Duc Anh; Prime Minister Vo Van Kiet; head of Communist Party: Do Muoi
Political Parties: Vietnam Communist Party
Suffrage: universal at 18

MILITARY

Number of Armed Forces: 940,000 (reductions have been announced)
Military Expenditures (% of Central Government Expenditures): 2.5%
Current Hostilities: boundary disputes with Cambodia; sporadic border clashes with China; other boundary disputes with China, Malaysia, Taiwan, and the Philippines

ECONOMY

Currency ($ U.S. Equivalent): 11,000 new dong = $1
Per Capita Income/GNP: $1,140/$83.5 billion
Inflation Rate: 15%–20%
Natural Resources: phosphates; coal; manganese; bauxite; chromate; offshore oil deposits; forests
Agriculture: rice; corn; potatoes; rubber; soybeans; coffee; tea; animal products; fish
Industry: food processing; textiles; machine building; mining; cement; chemical fertilizer; glass; tires; oil; fishing

FOREIGN TRADE

Exports: $3.6 billion
Imports: $4.2 billion

FOREIGNERS IN VIETNAM

Foreign powers have tried to control Vietnam for 2,000 years. Most of that time it has been the Chinese who have had their eye on control—specifically of the food and timber resources of the Red River Valley in northern Vietnam.

Most of the northern Vietnamese were ethnically Chinese themselves; but over the years, they had forged a separate identity for themselves and had come to resent Chinese rule. Vietnam was conquered by China as early as 214 B.C. and again in 111 B.C., when the Han Chinese emperor Wu Ti established firm control. For about 1,000 years (until A.D. 939, and sporadically thereafter by the Mongols and other Chinese), the Chinese so thoroughly dominated the region that the Vietnamese people spoke and wrote in Chinese, built their homes like those of the Chinese, and organized their society according to Confucian values. In fact, Vietnam (*viet* means "people" and *nam* is Chinese for "south") is distinct among Southeast Asian nations because it is the only one whose early culture—in the north, at least—was influenced more by China than by India.

The Chinese did not, however, directly control all of what constitutes modern Vietnam. Until the late 1400s, the southern half of the country was a separate kingdom known as Champa and was inhabited by people called Chams, who originally came from Indonesia. For a time, Champa was annexed by the north. However, between the northern region called Tonkin and the southern Chams-dominated region was a narrow strip of land occupied by Annamese peoples (a mixture of Chinese, Indonesian, and Indian ethnic groups), who eventually overthrew the Cham rulers and came to dominate the entire southern half of the country. In the 1500s, the northern Tonkin region and the southern Annamese region were ruled separately by two Vietnamese family dynasties. In the 1700s, military generals took power, unifying the two regions and attempting to annex or control parts of Cambodia and Laos as well.

In 1787, Nguyen-Anh, a general with imperial ambitions, signed a military aid treaty with France. The French had already established Roman Catholic missions in the south, were providing mercenary soldiers for the Vietnamese generals, and were interested in opening up trade along the Red River. The Vietnamese eventually came to resent the increasingly active French involvement in their internal affairs and took steps to curtail French influence. The French, however, impressed by the resources of the Red River Valley in the north and the Mekong River Delta in the south, were in no mood to pull out.

War broke out in 1858, and by 1863, the French had won control of many parts of the country, particularly in the south around the city of Saigon. Between 1884 and 1893, France solidified its gains in Southeast Asia by taking the northern city of Hanoi and the surrounding Tonkin region and by putting Cambodia, Laos, and Vietnam under one administrative unit, which it named *Indochina*.

Ruling Indochina was not easy for the French. For one thing, the region was comprised of hundreds of different ethnic groups, many of whom had been traditional enemies long before the French arrived. Within the borders of Vietnam proper lived Thais, Laotians, Khmers, northern and southern Vietnamese, and mountain peoples whom the French called Montagnards. Most of the people could not read or write—and those who could wrote in Chinese, because the Vietnamese language did not have a writing system until the French created it. Most people were Buddhists and Taoists, but many also followed animist beliefs.

In addition to the social complexity, the French had to contend with a rugged and inhospitable land filled with high mountains and plateaus as well as lowland swamps kept damp by yearly monsoon rains. The French were eager to obtain the abundant rice, rubber, tea, coffee and minerals of Vietnam but found that transporting these commodities to the coast for shipping was extremely difficult.

VIETNAMESE RESISTANCE

France's biggest problem, however, was local resistance. Anti-French sentiment began to solidify in the 1920s; by the 1930s, Vietnamese youth were beginning to engage in open resistance. Prominent among these was Nguyen ai Quoc, who founded the Indochinese Communist Party in 1930 as a way of encouraging the Vietnamese people to overthrow the French. He is better known to the world today as Ho Chi Minh, meaning "He Who Shines."

Probably none of the resisters would have succeeded in evicting the French had it not been for Adolf Hitler's overrunning of France in 1940 and Japan's subsequent military occupation of Vietnam. These events convinced many Vietnamese that French power was no longer a threat to independence; the French remained nominally in control of Vietnam, but everyone knew that the Japanese had the real power. In 1941, Ho Chi Minh, having been trained in China by Maoist leaders, organized the League for the Independence of Vietnam, or Viet Minh. Upon the defeat of Japan in 1945, the Viet Minh assumed that they would take control of the government. France, however, insisted on reestablishing a French government. Within a year, the French and the Viet Minh were engaged in intense warfare, which lasted for 8 years.

The Viet Minh initially fought the French with weapons supplied by the United States when that country was helping local peoples to resist the Japanese. Communist China later became the main supplier of assistance to the Viet Minh. This development convinced U.S. leaders that Vietnam under the Viet Minh would very likely become another Communist state. To prevent this occurrence, U.S. president Harry S. Truman decided to back France's efforts to recontrol Indochina (although the United States had originally opposed France's desire to regain its colonial holdings). In 1950, the United States gave $10 million in military aid to the French—an act that began a long, costly, and painful U.S. involvement in Vietnam.

In 1954, the French lost a major battle in the north of Vietnam, at Din Bien Phu, after which they agreed to a settlement with the Viet Minh. The country was to be temporarily divided at the 17th Parallel (a latitude above which the Communist Viet Minh held sway and below which non-Communist Vietnamese had the upper hand), and country-wide elections were to be held in 1956. The elections were never held, however; and under Ho Chi Minh, Hanoi became the capital of North Vietnam, while Ngo Dinh Diem became president of South Vietnam, with its capital in Saigon.

THE UNITED STATES ENTERS THE WAR

Ho Chi Minh viewed the United States as yet another foreign power trying to control the Vietnamese people through its backing of the government in the South. The United States, concerned about the continuing attacks on the south by northern Communists and by southern Communist sympathizers known as *Viet Cong,* increased funding and sent military advisers to help prop up the increasingly fragile southern government. By 1963, President John F. Kennedy had sent 12,000 military "advisers" to Vietnam. In 1964, an American destroyer ship was attacked in the Gulf of Tonkin by North Vietnam. The U.S. Congress responded by giving then-president Lyndon Johnson a free hand in

| China begins 1,000 years of control or influence over the northern part of Vietnam 214 B.C. | Northern and southern Vietnam are ruled separately by two Vietnamese families A.D. 1500s | Military generals overthrow the ruling families and unite the country 1700s | General Nguyen-Anh signs a military aid treaty with France 1787 | After 5 years of war, France acquires its first holdings in Vietnam 1863 | France establishes the colony of Indochina 1893 | Ho Chi Minh founds the Indochinese Communist Party 1930 | The Japanese control Vietnam 1940s | France attempts to regain control Post-1945 |

ordering U.S. military action against the north; before this time, U.S. troops had not been involved in direct combat.

By 1969, some 542,000 American soldiers and nearly 66,000 soldiers from 40 other countries were in battle against North Vietnamese and Viet Cong troops. Despite unprecedented levels of bombing and use of sophisticated electronic weaponry, U.S. and South Vietnamese forces continued to lose ground to the Communists, who used guerrilla tactics and built their successes on latent antiforeign sentiment among the masses as well as extensive Soviet military aid. At the height of the war, as many as 300 U.S. soldiers were being killed every week.

Watching the war on the evening television news, many Americans began to withdraw support. Anti-Vietnam rallies became a daily occurrence on American university campuses, and many people began finding ways to protest U.S. involvement: dodging the draft by fleeing to Canada, burning down ROTC buildings, and publicly challenging the U.S. government to withdraw. President Richard Nixon had once declared that he was not going to be the first president to lose a war, but, after his expansion of the bombing into Cambodia to destroy Communist supply lines and after significant battlefield losses, domestic resistance became so great that an American withdrawal seemed inevitable. The U.S. attempt to "Vietnamize" the war by training South Vietnamese troops and supplying them with advanced weapons did little to change South Vietnam's sense of having been sold out by the Americans.

Secretary of State Henry Kissinger negotiated a cease-fire settlement with the North in 1973, but most people believed that, as soon as the Americans left, the North would resume fighting and would probably take control of the entire country. This indeed happened, and in April 1975, under imminent attack by victorious North Vietnamese soldiers, the last Americans lifted off in helicopters from the grounds of the U.S. Embassy in Saigon, the South Vietnamese government surrendered, and South Vietnam ceased to exist.

The war wreaked devastation on Vietnam. It has been estimated that nearly 2 million people were killed during just the American phase of the war; another 2.5 million were killed during the French era. In addition, 4.5 million people were wounded, and nearly 9 million lost their homes. U.S. casualties included 58,000 soldiers killed and 300,000 wounded.

A CULTURE, NOT JUST A BATTLEFIELD

Because of the Vietnam War, many people think of Vietnam as if it were just a battlefield. But Vietnam is much more than that. It is a rich culture made up of peoples representing diverse aspects of Asian life. In good times, Vietnam's dinner tables are supplied with dozens of varieties of fish and the ever-present bowl of rice. Sugarcane and bananas are also favorites. Because about 80 percent of the people live in the countryside, the population as a whole possesses a living library of practical know-how about farming, livestock raising, fishing, and home manufacture. Today, only about 214 out of every 100,000 Vietnamese people attend college, but most children attend elementary school and 88 percent of the adult population can read and write.

Literacy was not always so high; much of the credit is due the Communist government, which, for political-education reasons, has promoted schooling throughout the country. Another thing that the government has done, of course, is to unify the northern and southern halves of the country. This has not been an easy task, for, upon the division of the country in 1954, the North followed a socialist route of economic development, while in the South, capitalism became the norm.

Religious belief in Vietnam is an eclectic affair and reflects the history of the nation; on top of a Confucian and Taoist foundation, created during the centuries of Chinese rule, rests Buddhism (a modern version of which is called Hoa Hao and claims 1 million believers); French Catholicism, which claims about 15 percent of the population; and a syncretist faith called Cao Dai, which claims about 2 million followers. Cao Dai models itself after Catholicism in terms of hierarchy and religious architecture, but it differs in that it accepts many Gods—Jesus, Buddha, Mohammed, Lao-Tse, and others—as part of its pantheon. Many Vietnamese pray to their ancestors and ask for blessings at small shrines located inside their homes. Animism, the worship of spirits believed to live in nature, is also practiced by many of the Montagnards. (About 400 Christianized Montagnards, incidentally, fought the Communists continually since 1975 and have only recently taken refuge outside of Vietnam.)

Freedom of religious worship has been permitted, and church organizational hierarchies have not been declared illegal. In fact, the government, sensing the need to solicit the support of believers (especially the Catholics), has been careful in its treatment of religions and has even avoided collectivizing farms in areas known to have large numbers of the faithful.

THE ECONOMY

When the Communists won the war in 1975 and brought the capitalist South under its jurisdiction, the United States imposed an economic embargo on Vietnam, which most other nations honored and which remained in effect for 19 years, until President Bill Clinton ended it in 1994. As a consequence of war damage as well as the embargo and the continuing military involvement of Vietnam in the Cambodian War and against the Chinese along their mutual borders, the first decade after the end of the Vietnam War saw the entire nation fall into a severe economic slump. Whereas Vietnam had once been an exporter of rice, it now had to import rice from abroad. Inflation raged at 250 percent a year, and the government was hardpressed to cover its debts. Many South Vietnamese were, of course, opposed to Communist rule and attempted to flee on boats—but, contrary to popular opinion, most refugees left Vietnam because they could not get enough to eat, not because they were being persecuted.

Beginning in the mid-1980s, the Vietnamese government began to liberalize the economy. Under a restructuring plan called *doi moi* (similar in meaning to Soviet *perestroika*), the government began to introduce elements of free enterprise into the economy. Moreover, despite the Communist victory, the South remained largely capitalist; today, with wages lower than almost every other country in Asia (about $1 a day; doctors earn about $22 per month and teachers make $15), an infra-

| The United States begins to aid France to contain the spread of communism **1950s** | Geneva agreements end 8 years of warfare with the French; Vietnam is divided into North and South **1954** | South Vietnam's regime is overthrown by a military coup **1961** | The United States begins bombing North Vietnam **1965** | Half a million U.S. troops are fighting in Vietnam **1969** | The United States withdraws its troops and signs a cease-fire **1973** | North Vietnamese troops capture Saigon and reunite the country; U.S. embargo begins **1975** | Vietnamese troops capture Cambodia; China invades Vietnam **1979** | Communist Vietnam begins liberalization of the economy **1980s** |

1990s

| U.S. and Vietnamese officials begin meetings to resolve the Cambodian war | The U.S. economic embargo of Vietnam is lifted | U.S. establishes full diplomatic relations in 1995; thousands of refugees are forcibly repatriated from around Southeast Asia |

structure built by France and the United States, and laborers who can speak at least some English or French, foreign nations are finding Vietnam a good place to invest funds. In 1991 alone, Australian, Japanese, French, and other companies spent $3 billion in Vietnam. After the embargo ended, firms poured into Vietnam to do business. By the end of 1994, more than 540 firms, especially from Singapore, Hong Kong, Japan, and France, were doing business in Vietnam, and some 70 other countries had expressed interest. The government's move toward privatization and capitalism, begun in 1986, was so successful that by the early 1990s, nearly 90 percent of the workforce were in the private sector, and loans from the World Bank, the Asian Development Bank, and the International Monetary Fund were flowing in to jumpstart national development.

Perhaps most significant is that the Vietnamese people themselves want to move ahead and put the decades of warfare behind them. Western travelers in Vietnam are treated warmly, and the Vietnamese government has cooperated with the U.S. government's demands for more information about missing U.S. soldiers. In 1994, after a 40-year absence, the United States opened up a diplomatic mission in Hanoi as a first step toward full diplomatic recognition. So eager are the Vietnamese to reestablish economic ties with the West that the Communist authorities have even offered to allow the U.S. Navy to lease its former port at Cam Ranh Bay (the offer has not yet been accepted). Diplomatic bridge-building between the United States

and Vietnam increased in 1990, when a desire to end the agony of the Cambodian conflict created opportunities for the two sides to talk together. Telecommunications were established in 1992, and in the same year, the United States gave $1 million in aid to assist handicapped Vietnamese war veterans. Finally, in 1995, some 20 years after the end of the Vietnam War, the United States established full diplomatic relations with Vietnam.

Despite this warming of relations, however, anti-Western sentiment remain strong in parts of the population, particularly the military. As recently as 1996, police were still tearing down or covering up signs advertising Western products and anti-open-door policy editorials were still appearing in official newspapers.

HEARTS AND MINDS

As one might expect, resistance to the current Vietnamese government comes largely from the South Vietnamese, who, under both French and American tutelage, adopted Western values of capitalism and consumerism. Many South Vietnamese had feared that after the North's victory, South Vietnamese soldiers would be mercilessly killed by the victors; some were in fact killed, but many former government leaders and military officers were instead sent to "reeducation camps," where, combined with hard labor, they were taught the values of socialist thinking. Several hundred such internees remain incarcerated 2 decades after the end of the war. Many of the well-known leaders of

the South fled the country when the Communists arrived and now are making new lives for themselves in the United States, Canada, Australia, and other Western countries. Those who have remained—for example, Vietnamese members of the Roman Catholic Church—have occasionally resisted the Communists openly, but their protests have been silenced. Hanoi continues to insist on policies that remove the rights to which the South Vietnamese had become accustomed. For instance, the regime has halted publication and dissemination of books that it judges to have "harmful contents." There is not much that average Vietnamese can do to change these policies except passive obstruction, which many are doing even though it damages the efficiency of the economy.

DEVELOPMENT

Vietnam is again a major exporter of rice. It also produces cement, fertilizer, steel, and coal. Aid and loans from other Asian nations are helping with the construction of roads and other infrastructure, but the average worker still earns only $1,140 a year.

FREEDOM

Vietnam is nominally governed by an elected National Assembly. Real power, however, resides in the Communist Party and with those military leaders who helped defeat the U.S. and South Vietnamese armies. Civil rights, such as the right of free speech, are curtailed. Private-property rights are limited. In 1995, Vietnam adopts its first civil code providing property and inheritance rights for citizens.

HEALTH/WELFARE

Health care has been nationalized and the government operates a social-security system, but the chronically stagnant economy has meant that few Vietnamese receive sufficient health care or have an adequate nutritional intake. The World Health Organization has been involved in disease-abatement programs since reunification of the country in 1975.

ACHIEVEMENTS

Vietnam provides free and compulsory schooling for all children, but the curricular content has been changed in an attempt to eliminate Western influences. New Economic Zones have been created in rural areas to try to lure people away from the major cities of Hanoi, Hue, and Ho Chi Minh City (formerly Saigon).

Articles from the World Press

Annotated Table of Contents for Articles

Topic Guide to Articles

TOPIC AREA	TREATED IN	TOPIC AREA	TREATED IN
Labor	3. Asia on the Brink 5. Vital and Vulnerable 7. Compass Swings	Security	1. Recipe for Asian Unity 4. Pacific Insecurity 8. Japan as an "Ordinary Country" 16. Cambodia: Will the Loser Take All? 17. Chinese Realpolitik 18. Giant Wakes 25. Stalemate on Bougainville 28. Taiwan's Balancing Act 29. Road to Capitalism
Linguistics	21. Empire of Uniformity		
Natural Resources	12. Lucky Country		
Nuclear Power	8. Japan as an "Ordinary Country"		
People	14. Aung San Suu Kyi 29. Road to Capitalism	Social Reform	7. Compass Swings 10. Welfare as Japan Knows It
Political Development	1. Recipe for Asian Unity 16. Cambodia: Will the Loser Take All? 22. Endgame in Indonesia? 29. Road to Capitalism	Social Unrest	5. Vital and Vulnerable 7. Compass Swings 10. Welfare as Japan Knows It 13. Myanmar's Mysterious Boom 15. Cambodia Struggles 24. Image Cracks 25. Stalemate on Bougainville 26. People Power, 1986–96
Political Unrest	13. Myanmar's Mysterious Boom 14. Aung San Suu Kyi 16. Cambodia: Will the Loser Take All?		
Politics	7. Compass Swings 8. Japan as an "Ordinary Country" 11. Fates Worse than Death 14. Aung San Suu Kyi 16. Cambodia: Will the Loser Take All? 22. Endgame in Indonesia? 29. Road to Capitalism	Standard of Living	5. Vital and Vulnerable 6. Rock Solid 10. Welfare as Japan Knows It 20. How Poor Is China? 24. Image Cracks 29. Road to Capitalism
		Suicide	11. Fates Worse than Death
Regional Relations	1. Recipe for Asian Unity 2. Global Forces Shape Asia 4. Pacific Insecurity 7. Compass Shifts 12. Lucky Country 16. Cambodia: Will the Loser Take All? 17. Chinese Realpolitik 18. The Giant Wakes 23. North Korea: Cold War Continues 28. Taiwan's Balancing Act	Taiwan Independence	7. Compass Swings 17. Chinese Realpolitik 28. Taiwan's Balancing Act
		Urban Life	6. Rock Solid 7. Compass Swings
		U.S. Involvement	1. Recipe for Asian Unity 3. Asia on the Brink 4. Pacific Insecurity 7. Compass Swings 8. Japan as an "Ordinary Country" 17. Chinese Realpolitik 23. North Korea: Cold War Continues
Rule of Law	15. Cambodia Struggles		
		Women	9. Japan's Feminine Falsetto 14. Aung San Suu Kyi
		Youth	6. Rock Solid 11. Fates Worse than Death

Article 1

Japan Echo, Winter 1995

Recipe for Asian Unity

Itō Kenichi

Born in 1938. Graduated from Hitotsubashi University, where he majored in law. Has served in the Ministry of Foreign Affairs, where his postings included the Japanese embassies in Moscow, Manila, and Washington. Is now president of the Japan Forum on International Relations and a professor at Aoyama Gakuin University. Author of Kokka to senryaku *(The State and Strategy),* Chō kindai no shōgeki *(The Impact of Postmodern Civilization), and other works.*

In the region known in the West as East Asia, and in Japan simply as Asia, we are today witnessing the rise of a tremendous dynamism, the birth of a new order, and the gathering of an energy capable of spearheading a new era in world history. It is a dynamism, an order, and an energy reminiscent of what was seen in Europe at the beginning of the modern age; one senses a truly momentous force at work. Yet while there can be no doubt as to the area's dynamism, the outlines of a new East Asian order have yet to be revealed in their entirety. We can be confident, however, that if the formation of this order proceeds in an appropriate direction, then just as Europe led the world into the modern age, East Asia will lead the way into a new era of world history.

From the seventh century until the final decades of the Qing Dynasty (1644–1912), East Asia existed in comparative peace under the loose economic and political order imposed by the Chinese Empire. This order, which we may call East Asia's Pax Sinica was destroyed by the incursion of the Western powers in the nineteenth century. Since then history has witnessed two failed attempts to establish a new order. Now a third attempt is under way.

The Failure of Imperialism

Before discussing this third attempt, let us briefly examine the nature of the two that preceded. After Columbus discovered the New World in 1492, the drive to spread Western ideas and power across the globe swelled into an irreversible tide that spared no region of the world. In the nineteenth century, Western imperialism found its way to Asia and ultimately overthrew the Pax Sinica. This "Western shock" was simultaneously the first attempt to rebuild the unity of the East Asian world.

Had the Western powers succeeded in completely colonizing East Asia and reorganizing it under the rule of Western civilization, the region might well have taken on a new and unified identity. Africa took on a coherent continent-wide identity only when it was colonized by the European powers. From Africa's experience we may infer that had East Asia been colonized in a similar fashion, its identity would have been defined by the values of Westerners eager to turn the region's inhabitants into "yellow Europeans."

The outcome of the Russo-Japanese War of 1904–5 was, I believe, what allowed East Asia to escape Africa's fate. Japan's victory was a decisive counterstrike by a native Asian force against the eastward expansion of the European imperialism. Were it not for this counterattack, East Asia would in all likelihood have been swallowed up by European civilization and its identity obliterated. At the very least, it would have been subject to the building of a new order on the basis of European intervention.

It is significant to note that this counterattack was carried out not by China, which had been the nucleus of the old order, but by a peripheral country, Japan. If we examine the process whereby China sank to the status of a quasi-European colony, it becomes evident that its own ethnocentrism was largely to blame. Within the Sinocentric worldview that had persisted through the ages, the Westerners were barbarians; the Chinese stubbornly refused to acknowledge and study the superior aspects of European civilization even after their country was defeated by Britain in the Opium Wars. This refusal is what turned Qing China from a sleeping giant into a dying giant.

Whereas the Chinese were unable to abandon their deep-rooted conviction that they existed at the center of the cosmos, the Japanese had no such illusions; they had been well aware of their peripheral position in world affairs ever since they had sent envoys to China during the Tang dynasty (618–906). Upon learning of the outcome of the Opium Wars, Japan's leaders quickly realized that the center of the world had shifted from China to Britain. They recognized that the key to the country's survival in the face of Western imperialism was to "enrich the country and strengthen the military" (*fukoku kyōhei*), and to that end it was necessary to forsake Asian civilization for that of Europe (*datsu-Anyū-ō*). That agile shift in consciousness was a major factor behind Japan's victory in the Russo-Japanese War.

Following through on this policy of Europeanization, Japan turned itself into a first-class imperialist power and adopted as its ultimate goal the creation of a Greater East Asia Coprosperity Sphere. This was the second at tempt to reunify East Asia. By 1942, at the height of World War II, Japan had extended its holdings to include Manchuria in the north, the Dutch East Indies in the south, Kiska and Tarawa islands in the east, and the British colony of Burma in the west. It was the most comprehensive unification of East Asia in history. Even China and all its tributaries had never covered a comparable amount of territory.

It was during this second attempt at unification that people of the region began for the first time to use the name "Asia" of their own accord, and in a positive sense. But the principles by which the Japanese sought to unify the region were both tyrannical and sadly lacking in universality—witness their insistence that colonial subjects daily face Tokyo and pay homage to the emperor. Exacted by force, this sort of obeisance was even more anachronistic than the ceremonial kowtowing performed by tribute-bearers at the Chinese imperial court.

Japan thus overreached itself as a peripheral country. Being on the periphery, the Japanese were cognizant of a larger world beyond their borders and even conceived the ambition of conquering. To succeed in this venture, however, they needed to master the principles of a rule based on universal values, something that their peripheral mind-set prevented them from understanding.

It has been said half-jokingly that through their postwar economic achievements the Japanese have secured the Greater East Asia Coprosperity Sphere that they failed to win through military conquest. Yet in this instance, too, they have proved themselves unable to overcome the limitations of a peripheral people. Their stubborn adherence to narrowly Japanese values and behavior patterns has once again caused other Asians to view them with suspicion and distrust.

Reemerging Identity

The forces that thwarted Japan's imperialist ambitions came not, for the most part, from within Asia (though Chinese resistance was a contributing factor) but from the West. More than anything else, it was American power that decided Japan's fate; the Soviets' last-minute entry into the war also played a role. The result was that the United States and Russia, two non-Asian nations, came to have a decisive voice in East Asian affairs after the war, and the internal pulse toward the creation of an autonomous regional order was nipped in the bud. The division of East Asia during the cold-war period was glaringly evident in its political polarization into "Eastern" and "Western" blocs on either side of the iron curtain and even more obviously in such armed conflicts as the Korean and Vietnam wars.

Even during this time, however, the historical evolution by which Asia would regain its identity and autonomy was proceeding, slowly but surely. In retrospect, we can identify a number of key events and developments in this process. First was the restoration of China to the status of major political power. This development was made manifest by the Sino-Soviet split that inevitably came to pass when Beijing made the decision to develop nuclear weapons in the teeth of fierce opposition from Moscow. Henry Kissinger's visit to China in 1971 as an envoy of U.S. President Richard Nixon marked the recognition by the world's greatest power that China was now a force to be reckoned with.

The second development was the relative decline of American power. In retrospect, we can see that the beginning of the end of America's absolute ascendancy was marked in the economic realm by the 1971 decision to end the convertibility of dollars into gold, and in the political and military realm by the fall of Saigon in 1975.

The third change was Japan's emergence as an economic superpower. Having chosen an economy-first policy under the so-called Yoshida doctrine, Japan eventually reached the point of "trading places" (the title of a book by Clyde Prestowitz) with the United States, racking up huge surpluses in bilateral trade and becoming "public enemy number one" in American eyes.

Fourth was the new regional economic dynamism that began with the rapid industrialization of South Korea, Hong Kong, Taiwan, and Singapore (the so-called four tigers); continued with the leaps in development seen in such countries as Indonesia, Malaysia, and Thailand (members, along with Singapore, of the Association of Southeast Asian Nations) and also in the coastal regions of China; and most recently shows signs of enveloping Vietnam and even Myanmar (Burma) in a phenomenon the World Bank has termed the "East Asian miracle."

Fifth was the collapse of the Soviet Union and the end of the cold war. The dismantling of the Soviet empire in 1991 left Russia as a second-rate power and vastly diminished its global influence. Today Russia has almost no voice in East Asian affairs.

The sixth was the growth of a new sense of political and cultural identity in the Asian nations that gained independence from European colonial control in the aftermath of World War II, coupled with the strengthening of regional solidarity through such groupings as ASEAN and the Asia-Pacific Economic Cooperation forum, as well as the region's progressive integration into the global economy through trade, investment, and technology transfers.

The seventh and final development that helped lay the groundwork for a third attempt at East Asian unification is the dominant role Asians have assumed in APEC. Of the 18 leaders attending the 1994 APEC summit in Bogor, Indonesia, 11 were Asian. By contrast, at the Washington Conference of 1921–22, where nine powers signed a treaty to deal with the China problem, the only Asians in attendance other than the Chinese were the Japanese. One cannot but feel that East Asia has come a long way since then.

All Eyes on China

Why is it that although unification proceeds apace in Western Europe, it seems an impossible dream in Eastern Europe? Surely one reason is that, while the countries of Western Europe sense no threat from a major regional power with hegemonic ambitions, the largest power in Eastern Europe has done nothing to allay its neighbors' suspicions on that score. Unification of Western Europe is feasible only to the extent that Germany's neighbors feel assured a unified Europe will not take the form of a German hegemony. In Eastern Europe, however, Russia's desire to dominate is so obvious that a unified setup embracing Russia is out of the question. The only unification option now under consideration by the smaller states of Eastern Europe is that of joining Western Europe with a view to avoiding Russian domination. Meanwhile, Russia, determined to prevent such an outcome, has taken foolishly to meddling in the foreign policy of its neighbors. This, of course, has only deepened these states' distrust.

East Asia, meanwhile, is embarking on its third attempt to rebuild unity since the collapse of the Pax Sinica. Needless to say, this unification effort must in no way emulate the earlier attempts of Western colonialism and Japanese militarism. At the same time, it obviously cannot be a resurrection of the ethnocentric order once imposed by the Chinese. East Asia at the end of the twentieth century is an animated arena in which a number of powerful players are jostling one another: not only political superpower China and economic superpower Japan, but also ASEAN as a regional power and Korea as a country that will eventually emerge as a unified contender. The question now is whether these various powers can build the framework for peace among themselves without the assistance of outside forces—whether, in other words, they can establish a balance of power and build a regional order to sanction it and guarantee its preservation.

The answer, I would submit, depends ultimately on China. If China remains wedded to an ethnocentric worldview and pursues policies premised on the idea of a China-centered regional order, the rest of the region will balk at the concept of a unified, autonomous East Asia. The region's hot spots currently form an arc hugging the Chinese mainland: the Korean Peninsula, the Taiwan Strait, and the South China Sea. Where the Koreas are concerned, the Chinese have played their hand closely, making it difficult to determine their true

motives, but in the other two problem areas they stand clearly on the side of altering the status quo.

A number of actions by China in recent years have helped lend credence to the notion of a "Chinese threat," notably, the enactment of a law unilaterally determining the extent of Chinese territorial waters, the firing of live missiles and shells into the waters around Taiwan, and the construction, over vigorous protests, of territorial markers and military installations on the Spratly Islands. Since 1989, Beijing has increased military spending at an average rate of over 10% a year, boosting the 1994 defense budget by a full 27%. It is only natural that China's neighbors be alarmed by this trend, continuing even as the major powers surrounding it—the United States, Japan, and Russia—have made deep cuts in defense spending.

To be sure, we must also acknowledge that Beijing has abandoned the "three worlds" doctrine that once lay at the heart of its international relations and embarked on a policy of international cooperation consistent with its recent emphasis on reforming and opening up the economy. At the same time, however, it appears that the Chinese, who have traditionally viewed their own country as the center of the East Asian order, are even now inclined to view China not as a part of East Asia but as East Asia itself. This is doubtless the reason they have been somewhat ill at ease with moves toward regional integration.

At the end of the 1970s, when Prime Minister Ohira Masayoshi came out with his Pacific Basin Cooperation Concept, Beijing viewed it skeptically as an attempt by Japan to extend its influence in the region. Subsequently, as China began shifting to a market economy and expanding its involvement in the global economy, it became a participant in the same trend toward regional cooperation. Beijing, however, has consistently limited its participation to the economic sphere, maintaining a wait-and-see approach to any cooperative framework encompassing politics or security.

No Unity on Security

Some sort of common security framework is a necessary condition for the rebuilding of a unified order for East Asia. However, the proposal for an East Asian framework modeled on the Organization for Security and Cooperation in Europe seems entirely unrealistic at this stage. For the most part, each country in the region faces separate security concerns and crises, not the sort of common concerns and crises that bound the countries of Western Europe together during the cold war.

Thus far, the only security mechanism that could be counted on has been the bilateral defense treaties between the United States and individual East Asian nations. From the American viewpoint, of course, these alliances created an extensive network fanning out from Japan and South Korea in the north to Australia in the south. It was a hub-and-spoke defense focused on a single target, the Soviet Union. Now that this single target has ceased to be a factor, the individual countries of the region are being forced to fundamentally rethink their defense strategies. They must now consider how much longer and to what degree they can put their trust in these bilateral alliances with the United States.

This is the context in which the ASEAN Regional Forum was launched in 1994, as a framework for the deliberation of intra- and extraregional security issues, with the participation of the foreign ministers of the six ASEAN member nations—Brunei, Indonesia, Malaysia, the Philippines, Singapore, and Thailand (to which Vietnam was recently added to make seven)—along with those from a number of non-ASEAN governments, including China, Japan, Russia, the United States, and the European Union. I am very skeptical, however, as to the possibility of this forum's evolving into something along the lines of an Organization for Security and Cooperation in Asia and ultimately an organization capable of working independently to settle regional conflicts.

The main reason is that China has continued to communicate its lack of enthusiasm for any sort of regional cooperation on political or security issues, indicating in stark terms that it intends to deal with the Spratly Islands issue through bilateral negotiations and will refuse to participate in multilateral talks. Confronted with this sort of attitude it is difficult to avoid the conclusion that now, as in the past, China sees itself not as a part of Asia but as Asia itself. Beijing's insistence on bilateral negotiations and its arrogant refusal to participate in multilateral talks suggests a mentality rooted in the old East Asian order, when the region's lesser nations were subjugated to China, which fancied itself the hub of the universe.

Whether or not one regards China as a threat, our method of dealing with China will determine the answer to the questions "What is the future of the region?" and "Can Asia exist as a distinct and coherent entity?" It is possible at this point to discern two possible approaches.

The first is a policy of "constructive engagement," that is, one of trying to integrate China into the global community. This means encouraging China to become an active participant in the global economy, the United Nations, and regional security frameworks and thereby inducing Beijing to adopt a more internationalist and cooperative foreign policy. This is presently the keynote of international policy toward China, and it should remain the basis of our policy.

The ideological problems raised by China's erstwhile affair with Marxism—Leninism and Maoism no longer stand in the way of such an approach. Instead, the problem, as I have already indicated, is the traditional ethnocentric Chinese worldview, which persists in influencing the thinking and behavior of the Chinese. This is what lies at the bottom of Beijing's "great nation" thinking and its obvious desire for power—a desire that was laid bare by its insistence on resuming nuclear tests last May, less than a week after China and other signatories voted to extend the Nuclear Nonproliferation Treaty indefinitely. It may be that China's big-power view of its own place in the world order is simply incompatible with the current concept of a global order as predicated on the equality of sovereign states and the willingness of individual nations to subordinate their sovereignty to multilateral agreements and decisions. If that is the case, a policy of constructive engagement, while fundamentally correct, may not provide all the answers.

This is where the second approach comes into play, one that may be characterized as a policy of "counterbalancing." China's emergence as a superpower is inevitable, and if this superpower, which is also the only country in East Asia that possesses nuclear weapons, should adopt a threatening posture and intimidating policies toward its neighbors in an attempt to create a modern version of the old tributary system, what would our options be? The only country in the region with anything resembling the ability to restrain China is Japan, but as a minor military power constrained by a war-renouncing Constitution, Japan is scarcely a protector its neighbors can count on.

Building a regional order will require the continued presence of the United States.

The recent decision to admit Vietnam into ASEAN can be interpreted in part as a move by small powers to combine forces against the "Chinese threat." By joining ASEAN, Hanoi hopes to strengthen its hand vis-à-vis Beijing, and by admitting Vietnam, ASEAN hopes to be able to use Vietnam as a bulwark against China. Yet it is one of the axioms of strategic theory since ancient times that such "alliances of the weak" are doomed to self-destruct. The fact is that achieving a balance of power just among the various forces within East Asia is virtually impossible. What this means is that building an acceptable regional order will require the continued presence of the United States. To put it another way, without the

U.S. presence, Asia in the twenty-first century is destined to revert to the China-centered order of the Pax Sinica.

However, with China's dynamism tempered by an appropriate American presence, East Asia will have the combination of ingredients it needs to lead the world into a new era. Washington, for its part, appears to be in the process of crafting a China strategy and an East Asia policy with these general ideas in mind. U.S. officials have been publicly emphasizing the need to integrate China into the global community while working steadily through a series of indirect measures—typified by the normalization of diplomatic ties with Vietnam last July—to ensure that China's power is adequately balanced in the region. Japan's role in the process will be to provide the conditions for the creation and maintenance of this delicate balance, for the good of the region and for the good of the world.

Translated from "Ajia' o saikō suru," in Shokun, October 1995, pp. 98–107; abridged by about one-third. (Courtesy of Bungei Shunjū)

Article 2　　　　　　　*Far Eastern Economic Review, 50th Anniversary Issue, October 1996*

Global Forces Shape Asia

John Naisbitt

Author of Megatrends Asia

We are living in the era of globalization, and while Asia will be the dominant player in the globalized 21st century, all parts of the planet will be profoundly affected.

One of the most striking things about globalization is that the bigger the global economy becomes, the smaller are its parts. The paradox I have formulated for this is:

The bigger the world economy, the more powerful its smallest players: countries, companies, right down to the individual. The tool to understanding how the world is changing is paradox. A paradox is seen when there are apparently contradictory phenomena which, on closer inspection, turn out to be true and not contradictory. The extraordinary complex world of the '90s has ushered in an era of paradox, an era of apparent contradictions. My advice is to make uncertainty your friend.

As the world integrates economically, the component parts are becoming more numerous and smaller and more important. At once, the global economy is growing while the parts are shrinking. The almost perfect metaphor for the movement from bureaucracies of every kind to small, autonomous units is the shift from the mainframe to PCs.

Globalization distinguishes competitiveness by swiftness to market and innovation. On those counts small companies right down to the individual can beat big bureaucratic companies 10 out of 10 times.

The mindset that in a huge global economy the multinationals would dominate world business could not have been more wrong. The bigger and more open the world economy becomes, the more small- and middle-sized companies will dominate. The world in turn will be dominated by person-to-person communications.

Last year, a record 1 million new companies were started in the U.S.

America and Asia have an entrepreneurial bond. They are the freest places in the world for entrepreneurs to be entrepreneurs. Hong Kong's greatest asset is its entrepreneurial class, its entrepreneurial leadership. Hong Kong must continue to nurture that asset. People in Hong Kong and Taiwan are sometimes preoccupied with the micro political issues on the ground. If they don't look up they could miss out on the chance for global leadership in whatever they do.

In Asia, it is millions and millions of entrepreneurs—bottom up—who have created the great new economies in this part of the world.

The economists seem to ignore the entrepreneurs. Fortunately, entrepreneurs always ignore the economists.

When people in the West began to speak of the "Asian Miracle," the hardworking Asian entrepreneurs did not identify with their efforts being called a "miracle." And now some in the West—not knowing much about Asia, either—call the "miracle" a "myth."

So here is my riddle:
"It is not a miracle, and the miracle is not a myth."

The '90s—and the beginning of the next century—is also the time of the entrepreneur. And entrepreneurs are increasingly building networks.

I would go so far as to say that Networks are replacing Nation States.

We have heard a lot of talk about the decline of the nation state, of a borderless world. But what replaces nation states? The answer is networks: the Chinese Overseas Network, the Korean Overseas Network, the Non-Resident Indian Network, plus Environmental Networks, Medical Networks, Women Networks, Financial Networks, and so on.

Networks are replacing nation states. As borders are erased, networks will become larger and more important. The place to start is the Chinese Overseas Network. (I am deliberately calling the Overseas Chinese the Chinese Overseas because 90% of these 57 million people are citizens of the countries in which they reside. "Overseas Chinese" suggests they are still part of China.)

The economy of the borderless Chinese Overseas is the third largest in the world. We are not used to thinking this way: counting the GDP of a network rather than the GDP of a country. If we counted the economic activity of all the Chinese Overseas as a country, all by itself it would be outranked only by the United States and Japan.

The Chinese Overseas Network is a lot like the Internet. If you know how the Internet works, you know how the Chinese Network operates. Just as the Internet is a network of about 25,000 networks, they have tens of thousands of networks networked together.

The number of networks and individuals on the Internet is not limited because the Internet is totally decentralized—and no one is in charge, just as no one is in charge of the Chinese Network. There are now more than 60 million individuals on the Internet. That number could reach one billion by the year 2000.

All powerful networks have one thing in common: each of the parts functions as if it were the centre of the network. When I am on the Internet in my home in Telluride, Colorado, sending and receiving messages with others all over the world, I experience being in the center, just as do each of the other 50 million people when they are on the Internet. That is very powerful.

Over the last several years entrepreneurs on mainland China have been joining the Chinese Overseas Network. To the world, it is China. But it is more than China. It is the global Chinese Network, and together they are driving the transformation of Asia.

I am more and more convinced that the Chinese network is the organizational model for the 21st century.

The World is moving from a collection of nation-states to a collection of networks. As borders are erased, paradoxically, national identity becomes more important. As we yield a little of our identity by becoming so economically interdependent, we seek a stronger cultural identity. Our roots, our nationality become more important. The paradox is that as nations become less important, nationality becomes more important.

And as the economic world moves from nation-states to networks, the Chinese are creating the first truly global, tribal network.

Networks have been around for a long time—Germany was a network before it became Germany; the difference today is that the revolution in telecommunications has elevated them to a new level.

The Indian counterparts of the Chinese Network are usually referred to as Non-Resident Indians (NRIs). They number about 10 million, with a combined income of an astonishing $340 billion, equivalent to the whole of India's 930 million people. As economic reforms settle in place in India these emigres are working with entrepreneurs in India,

much as the Chinese Overseas have done in China, and they will become a powerful force in India's ever so promising economic development.

Ethnic networks will be only part of the emerging global network of networks. Business-sector networks have begun to form: an architecture/construction network is being formed; a fashion network for designers, textile providers, and clothing manufacturers; automobile, travel, environmental, and of course, financial networks are being formed. It is an endless process as the importance of the political nation state yields to the economics of global networks.

Globalization has made the G-7 irrelevant. A Cold War relic. The Group of Seven Leaders fancy that they are responsible for the stewardship of the global economy. Who gave them that role? Most are doing a terrible job with their own economies. They represent a dwindling part of the world.

As economic considerations continue to overwhelm political considerations, Presidents, Prime Ministers, and Parliaments become less and less important. Add to this the vast and virtually universal privatization of government services. Every central government in the world is getting smaller. There is less and less for political leaders to do. A new kind of leadership is required.

The globalization of the world is being powered by the revolution in telecommunication.

Telecommunication is the driving force that is simultaneously creating the huge global economy and making its parts smaller and more powerful.

Global state-of-the-art telecommunications also means global transparency. Everyone can see and is aware of what everyone else is doing. Whatever the dynamics between Hong Kong and China in the coming years, we'll all be watching.

Globalization means that because everyone is watching everyone else and dealing with everyone else we will slowly begin to harmonize such things as taxes, accounting and pricing. Already most luxury goods cost the same whether you purchase them on Rodeo Drive in Los Angeles, on Avenue Montaigne in Paris or in the Landmark in Hong Kong.

Also to be harmonized in time will be the rules of behaviour, the appropriate

behaviour of politicians, of business people.

Globalization has meant that to be competitive countries of the West are trying to cut back on the welfare state that is now seriously burdening their competitiveness.

Globalization means everyone has to become world-class. Today in all the major centres of Asia world-class products and services are available, and soon that will be the case everywhere. If world-class goods and services are available in your neighbourhood, that means that to compete local goods and services have to be world-class.

Globalization is the phenomenon of the 21st century and the dominant region will be Asia. What is happening in Asia is by far the most important development in the world today. Nothing else comes close. Not only for Asians but the entire planet. The economic growth in Asia will drive the global economy to the benefit of us all as we move through the balance of this century. The modernization of Asia will forever re-shape the world as we move towards the next millennium.

In the 1990s Asia came of age. As we move towards 2000, Asia will become the dominant region of the world: economically, politically and culturally.

Up until the 1990s everything revolved around the West. The West set the rules. Japan played by those rules during its economic emergence. But now Asians—the rest of Asia—are creating their own rules and will soon determine the game as well. Even Japan will be left behind as the countries of Asia, led by China and the Chinese Overseas, increasingly hold economic sway.

The West now needs the East a lot more than the East needs the West.

When Macau returns to China at the end of this decade, the final chapter of Western dominance will have been written. For the first time in 500 years, every inch of Asian soil will be controlled and managed by Asians.

It will not be a smooth turn of the wheel—there will be setbacks, conflicts and disappointments—but 50 years from now it will be clear that the most momentous global development of the 1990s and into the next century is the modernization of Asia.

Asia was once the centre of the world, and now the centre is again returning to Asia.

Article 3

Across the Board, January 1996

Asia on the Brink

How Asian governments' hands-off policies have spurred the fastest economic growth in history.

Jim Rohwer

Jim Rohwer is director and chief economist for Asia in the Hong Kong office of CS First Boston. He is a former Asia correspondent and executive editor of The Economist *and the author of* Asia Rising: Why America Will Prosper as Asia's Economies Boom *(Simon & Schuster), from which this excerpt is taken.*

The economic rise of East and Southeast Asia in the half century since the end of World War II has been, if perhaps not precisely miraculous, nonetheless astounding. In 1945 most of these countries were at one of the lowest points in their long histories. Many of them were among the poorest countries in the world. For a century many had suffered colonization at the hands of various European powers, the Americans, and (in the cases of Taiwan and Korea) the Japanese. Almost all had endured the ravages of nearly two decades of probably the most destructive warfare in Asian history. A few, conspicuously Korea and Vietnam, were about to face yet more war; or in China's case, civil war, followed a decade later by mass starvation and a few years after that by a decade-long bout of near anarchy.

East Asia appeared to have almost no advantages as it began its struggle to enter the modern world. Its countries were generally poor in natural resources and seemed oversupplied with people who, to make matters worse, were largely illiterate (except in Japan, which had been modernizing for a century). Large numbers of East Asians had nothing. Millions were refugees, homeless and uprooted by war and civil war; many more millions were landless peasants, ground down by centuries of feudalism and decades of colonialism.

Out of these ashes rose the biggest and fastest economic improvement the world has ever seen. It took Britain, then the world's fastest-growing economy, almost 60 years to double per capita incomes after its economic takeoff in 1780. It took America almost 50 years to repeat that performance after 1840. Japan's per capita incomes doubled in 33 years after 1880. Then, after the war-torn first half of the 20th century had ended, came the great East Asian miracle. Indonesia's per capita incomes doubled in 17 years after 1965; South Korea's, in 11 years after 1970; and China's, in 10 years after 1978.

As that downward cascade of numbers suggests, modern Asia's breathtaking success has happened in part simply because it took advantage of changes in the world economy that over the past 200 years have made fast economic growth progressively easier to achieve. The world's stock of technology and economically productive ideas has been growing exponentially, both in size and in quality and sophistication. And the speed with which that stock of technology and ideas is added to and diffused throughout the world has constantly been accelerating.

These advantages of the modern economy are there to be seized by anyone; yet almost no other countries have pounced on them as quickly, comprehensively, and successfully as the rising economies of East and Southeast Asia. For decades these economies have vastly outstripped any others in successfully putting together the four elements of economic growth: labor, capital, human capital, and productivity. The reasons why Asia was able to do this are among the most complicated questions about human society in the second half of this century. But the complexities can be boiled down to a set of attributes widely shared by the East Asian success stories—attributes that, moreover, reinforce each other and reflect a consistent view of how a society and economy should be run.

No Safety Net for People—Or Companies

The nub of the Asian idea of public policy is that governments should not do much to temper the hazards of life, particularly the often harsh consequences of fast technological and economic change. Asia's governments have tended to offer little social protection, such as pay-as-you-go pensions, unemployment insurance, or state-provided health care. Government spending in Asia accounts for an unusually small share of economic activity; and, in comparison with Western countries, very little of Asian government spending goes for transfer payments from the pockets of one class of taxpayers into those of another class. Except in such places as India and the Philippines, even less of Asian governments' money goes for current spending on such things as civil servants' salaries. Conversely, Asian governments devote proportionally more of their more modest spending to investment, especially in education.

Although Asia's governments have been pro-business as well as small—meaning they leave much economic (and even social) decision making to the competitive interplay of businesses in marketplaces—these governments have in general been as reluctant to safeguard individual companies as they have been to protect individual people. It is true that whole industries in Asia, such as Japan's agriculture and its retail distribution system, sometimes receive impregnable protection from foreign competition. The more common practice is to force participants in the economy to live up to world standards of performance.

The Asian approach confuses many Westerners, who see (often rightly) a great deal of trade and other protection for Asian companies and therefore infer (usually wrongly) that the companies are being allowed an easy life. Some countries, such as Hong Kong, Taiwan, and (to a lesser degree) Thailand, allow competition to rage as unchecked as it does anywhere on earth.

Yet even the countries that pursue industrial policies and invoke the protectionism usually associated with them—South Korea is Exhibit No. 1—do so in ways that force the discipline of world competition on their companies even if world competitors are absent from the home market. When Korea's technocrats got some industrial policy wrong, as they often did, they quickly reversed themselves: The companies concerned were unhesitatingly stripped of whatever privileges they had been granted and told to fend for themselves. Throughout East Asia companies have tended to run scared.

So have people. In Hong Kong, the world's most free-market territory, few people have ever been shielded from the gusts of technological and market change that flow in from the whole world. From the days in the 1950s when industries like wig making rose and fell with extraordinary speed, Hong Kongers have come to expect to change jobs and even careers as matter-of-factly as they do clothes or cars. Yet even in as corporatist a country as Japan where company loyalty and lifetime employment have traditionally gone together at the big firms, most workers toil in establishments that boast nothing of that kind of job security.

Few people can cope on their own with unbridled change. But most of Asia has thrown the shock absorbing that an individual is bound to need onto the family, and the community and neighborhood networks associated with families, rather than onto public institutions. This is a policy that makes it extremely risky in Asian society to function as a maverick: Nobody, certainly not the government, will catch you if you fall.

A hands-off policy has deep consequences. If the family rather than the individual is the main unit of society,

individual freedom is undoubtedly reduced. Nobody, to take the principal example, however unhappy he or she is, ducks out of the obligations of marriage and children as readily in Asia as spouses do in the West. People are encouraged to work harder and save more; insecurity is a great spur to effort. Education is an even more worthwhile investment than it would otherwise be, since the parents providing it stand to gain from it almost as much as the children receiving it.

> *The refusal of Asia's governments to protect people is the main explanation of why Asian economies have grown so fast and why Asian social institutions are still so strong.*

This sort of policy makes for a harsh world; people without a social connection of some sort tend to be lost when they stumble. A society organized along these lines is utterly contrary to the spirit of modern Western Europe and mostly at odds with the assumptions introduced into America's public life during the New Deal and pushed far forward in the 1960s. Yet the refusal of Asia's governments to protect people is, I think, the main explanation of why Asian economies have grown so fast and why Asian social institutions are still so strong. It also is one of Asia's biggest advantages in a world of accelerating technological and economic change. A society organized along Asian lines is far better equipped than the average Western society to embrace and absorb change: If a powerful government will not conserve the patterns of the past on your behalf (and it is, eventually, futile to try), you learn quickly that you must cope with the future.

It stands to reason that Asia should have done well by its system of small government and strong society. Society, after all, is sunk a lot deeper in human nature than government is, and it is a more efficient regulator of people's behavior. The question now is whether Asia can continue to build on the substantial advantage of its social strengths.

The Next Step

Asia's trajectory over the next 25 years is unlikely to be a smooth continuation of the curve it has traced over the past 25. For one thing, the world's geopolitical structure has been completely transformed—especially the complicated Cold War balance among the Soviet Union, China, and Japan that allowed the United States to maintain a long period of unusual stability in Northeast Asia.

Second, the pace of technological change is accelerating, and with it the speed of transmission of new technologies throughout the world; like every other region, Asia is going to have much more change to absorb in the next quarter century than it did in 1970–95.

Third, Asia's relative economic weight in the world has grown so large that its further development cannot take place in the obscurity that it enjoyed during its fast ascent of 1970–95. China's rise has already provoked more controversy and more conflict with the United States than Japan's growth did until the Japanese were 10 times richer than the Chinese now are. Asia as a whole, and China in particular, will henceforth bulk much larger in the world both as an economic force and as a policy question, and this will change the character of its interaction with the West.

Asia is therefore about to enter a period when its long-term fate will be settled much more decisively than it was during its youthful and exuberant successes of the past quarter century. Asia is on the brink. Within another quarter century it will have become clear whether two-fifths of mankind was in 1995 on the brink of greatness, of world-changing (indeed history-changing) dimensions, or of failed early promise, failure in the worst case meaning the appalling destruction of large wars.

My view is that it will turn out to have been greatness. Whether I am right depends mainly on two things: on Asia's own success at strengthening its weak institutions: and on the willingness of the West in general (and of America in particular) to maintain a relatively free and open system of world trade, and of the United States to exert the role of great-power leadership that it alone is capable of playing. Asia's institutional weaknesses run the gamut from opacity of company governance to lack of political accountability to paucity of infrastructure to the historic inability of Asian countries to maintain the peace among themselves through their own balance of power

These weaknesses have done Asia very little damage so far—so little, indeed, that it could be argued they have been strengths. Modern Asia was a lot smarter than other parts of the poor world: Asia let its societies and economies run away with themselves at first rather than smothering them under government directives. Yet the imbalance in Asia between private strength and public weakness cannot last. If Asian firms are ever to function outside Asia—or eventually, even to compete successfully with Western firms in a modernized Asian economy—they will have to learn how to appraise and appease public concerns as well as they do private ones.

America's Opportunity

It will not be easy for Asia to rebalance itself this way. The rise of modern Asia has overwhelmingly depended on judgments (business and otherwise) based on personal trust and connections. Such a system, which is at its most intense and refined in the Chinese part of Asia, has many advantages, the greatest being speed and informality of decision making. But it makes transactions with those you do not personally know almost impossible. Moving to a more modern and objective institutional structure will be hard: There is an inherent conflict between loyalties based on personal ties and loyalties based on institutions.

Among Western companies, those of the United States are best positioned to profit from the rise of Asia and to compete on reasonably even terms with Japanese firms.

If things go reasonably well, during the first decade of the new millennium a belt of mostly middle-class societies—concentrated in a couple of dozen huge metropolises and their hinterlands—will run from South Korea (which by then could well include the whole of the Korean peninsula and, in an economic sense at least, a fair chunk of Russia's Far East), through Japan, all of coastal China, Java and Sumatra in Indonesia, the urban parts of Indochina, and the whole of the rest of Southeast Asia: a zone boasting a consumer class of about a billion people. To this should be added consumerist pockets in the Indian subcontinent, including another 200 million people. The people of this zone will be enjoying, in material terms, roughly the lives of average people in North America and Western Europe in the 1950s. They will make up the biggest middle class in history.

The spending power of this middle class will offer the West, and especially America, some of the most extraordinary business and financial opportunities ever. The rich world will probably account for half the worldwide growth of demand for most products and services in the next five years to 10 years, but it is extremely hard in the rich world to grab much market share from rivals unless you are in a brand-new industry.

The lion's share of the other half of worldwide demand growth will come from Asia, much of it from China. And, because Asia's markets are so new, most of that chunk of extra demand will be up for grabs by anybody. That is why Asian markets should prove so vital to any Western company that wants to grow fast.

Among Western companies, those of the United States are best positioned to profit from the rise of Asia and to compete on reasonably even terms with Japanese firms in their own backyard; and in the most advanced industries, where America is most competitive, American firms are in a position to do better even than that in the struggle for Asia's huge markets. This is one big reason

why the American government should be unstinting in its support of the open-world trading system and unhesitant about maintaining its role as the holder of Asia's balance of power. That America is today neither unstinting nor unhesitant poses the biggest single threat to Asia's continued prosperity.

In the case of trade, some American thinking about Asia is colored by America's experience with Japan. Leave aside the question whether that experience has been good or bad for the American economy and American business: the economic development of the great Asian landmass will not follow that of Japan. Even when Asia's fast-growing domestic markets have barriers to imports—and these vary widely across the continent—Asian countries are generally more receptive to foreign direct investment than Japan (or South Korea) has ever been.

For American firms, Asia's booming markets are an almost unalloyed blessing.

Politics and Society: Asia's New Millennium

I realized after living in Asia for a few years that probably the world's biggest intellectual gulf among highly educated people lay between Westerners and Asians on the subject of democracy. In the West democracy is generally thought to be the only form of government by which a civilized society should consider running itself. A few diplomats and academics will muse quietly, and in private, about the failures of representative democracy and the availability of alternatives, but the topic is essentially taboo.

This is understandable. In the West's experience for the whole of this century, the only alternative to democracy has seemed a horrible dictatorship that looted countries and brought war. In fact, this black-and-white perception is wrong. Some of the best-working political institutions in the West are deeply undemocratic: the most important being the central banks, some of which (notably Germany's) are also deeply popular with ordinary people. But the general assumption is, the more democratic the better

After the fall of the Soviet Union, the certitude in the West about democracy had reached the stage where some Americans were arguing that democracy should be considered a "fundamental human right" whose promotion was hence a proper ground for American military intervention abroad. The Clinton administration, while not putting the matter quite that strongly, was edging in the same direction both in its general pronouncements and in the specific matter of sending soldiers to Haiti to restore an elected government there.

By contrast, many thoughtful people living in Asia—including a lot who, unlike, say, Lee Kuan Yew [Singapore's former prime minister] do not have a personal interest in making the case for authoritarian government—are open to the idea, and sometimes argue it vigorously, that a certain kind of authoritarianism is better than a freewheeling democracy. This, too, is understandable. In modern Asia, unlike modern Europe, authoritarian government has often brought not hardship and war but instead peace, prosperity, and equality.

The authoritarians believe discipline is also needed—for a fundamental reason, in Lee Kuan Yew's view:

"Certain basics about human nature do not change. Man needs a certain moral sense of right and wrong. There is such a thing called evil, and it is not the result of being a victim of society. You are just an evil man, prone to do evil things, and you have to be stopped from doing them."

Lee himself admits that it will be a fight every step of the way to preserve what he thinks of as the basics of the Asian way: the family ("governments will come, governments will go, but this endures"), self-reliance, and enough freedom for people to make the best use of their talents but enough order to ensure that in exercising that freedom they do not deprive others of their rights to peace and security.—**J. R.**

Article 4   *Harvard International Review,* Spring 1996

Pacific Insecurity

Emerging Threats to Stability in East Asia

Jonathan D. Pollack

Jonathan D. Pollack is Senior Advisor for International Policy at RAND, where he specializes in East Asian political and security affairs.

East Asia is one of the world's primary arenas of international competition and collaboration in the post–Cold War era. Over the past century and a half, the region has experienced recurrent great power rivalries, military intervention, colonialism, revolutionary nationalism, and interstate as well as civil conflict. In recent decades, however, revolutionary upheaval has been supplanted by rapid and sustained economic growth, enabling the region to achieve unparalleled well-being and enhanced political stability. This unprecedented economic expansion has also allowed numerous states to augment their military power in pursuit of longer-range national security goals.

As the next century approaches, a pivotal question is whether the states of East Asia will be able to create a political and security structure commensurate with their economic success. Can the nations of the region define a satisfactory framework for interstate relations in pursuit of their separate national interests without inducing destabilizing geopolitical realignment or overt military hostilities? To some observers, the cessation of the US-Soviet global rivalry, the absence of a serious regional military crisis since the Sino-Vietnamese border war of 1979, and the nascent emergence of region-wide economic and political institutions suggest such a prospect.

However, these signs of stability may be misleading. Beneath a veneer of shared interests (especially related to economic development) loom deeper differences and potential incompatibilities that defy ready resolution. Although East Asia as a whole has achieved prosperity unimaginable several decades ago, the transition toward a more autonomous and powerful region is uneven, incomplete, and replete with uncertainty. As a consequence, the outlines of a more durable security order are barely discernible at present. Indeed, rather than guaranteeing a peaceful or stable regional system, East Asia's political and economic emergence could generate new patterns of competition and conflict that will shape some of the principal contours of the international system into the next century.

Potential for Crisis

Among the possibilities of a serious crisis, the prospects loom largest on the Korean peninsula, the one locale in global politics where the legacy of the Cold War remains largely intact. The latent potential for destructive military conflict in Korea has not diminished. North Korea is an embattled regime, heavily armed yet largely bereft of its previous sources of economic and security support, and many observers believe that the regime's days are numbered. Any internal unraveling in North Korea would affect the interests of all the major powers in the area, but first and foremost those of South Korea. Implosion, however, is not the only scenario. Under some circumstances, leaders in Pyongyang might yet opt to renew their truculence in relation to the outside world, even toward those whose assistance North Korea presently solicits. Therefore, all states in the region have an obvious incentive to work credibly with one another on the Korea problem, as none would be immune to the potential consequences of another Korean confrontation.

Quite apart from the antagonism between North and South Korea, the historical animosities between Korea and Japan remain profound. The early 1996 tensions between the two countries over the demarcation of their respective maritime boundaries could prove a portent of future trends. Indeed, despite Japan's stature as the world's second largest economy, Japan's political role, both regionally and globally, remains circumscribed and unsettled. Japan is not yet able to deal fully with its conduct in the Pacific war or its colonial record in Northeast Asia. Although Japan has moved somewhat closer to an acknowledgment of the legacy of its historical conduct, there is as yet no domestic consensus permitting a comprehensive judgment of Japan's past behavior toward its neighbors.

Moscow and Tokyo also have not fully addressed the legacy of the Pacific conflict. The two countries have yet to sign a peace treaty, and their economic interactions remain remarkably inconsequential. Russian military

(The White House)

Regional leaders must cooperate to define the East Asian security order.

power may no longer pose a direct threat to regional security, but the country's difficult transition to a market economy and democratic polity continues to stymie resolution of long-standing territorial disputes with Japan.

But there are other worrisome regional scenarios, primarily involving China. A possible confrontation or military conflict between China and Taiwan, or heightened maneuverings between China and another claimant to islands in the South China Sea loom especially large in this context. China has begun to emerge as a genuine major power intent on asserting and pursuing its longer-term political and security goals. China's sheer size and scale, its status as the region's only nuclear weapons state, and its continuing territorial disputes with neighboring states have all generated growing regional concern about the prospects for stable relations between China and its neighbors. The absence of clear institutional and legal constraints on the exercise of power and China's increasing reliance on nationalism as an integrative political force have reinforced this concern over the degree of China's commitment to the existing power relationships within East Asia.

The stakes and risks in relation to Taiwan seem especially high. In the summer of 1995 and again in the winter of 1996, China's political-military leadership responded to a perceived challenge to its vital national interests by visibly and volubly escalating military tensions in the Taiwan Strait. The pattern of Chinese military activities was presumably intended to convey to Taiwan the potential risks to the island's well-being should Taipei continue to pursue a strategy judged by Beijing to represent moves toward de jure official independence. Chinese leaders are aware that highly provocative moves could increase pressures for external political or military intervention, which would presumably dictate very carefully circumscribed military actions, intended more for psychological than military effect. But an internal political logic, perhaps abetted by the need to pre-empt further slippage in judgments, either domestic or external, about the resoluteness of China's senior policy makers, could prompt Chinese leaders to raise the stakes in the future. Should Chinese leaders deem Taiwan's behavior unacceptable, a larger use of force might well ensue, raising the possibility of a far more serious set of reconfiguring events.

Such a scenario, even if highly unlikely, vividly imparts the indeterminacy still prevalent in East Asian security. The region's unresolved historical antagonisms and the absence of a mature institutional framework—both in the context of rapidly changing power dynamics and appreciably heightened nationalism—loom as factors that could yet produce a destabilizing sequence of events for the region. Quite apart from the incentives for restraint and increased economic interaction, other imperatives could yet prove decisive in influencing leadership calculations.

These prospects underscore the challenge of building a more stable and effective regional security order. Such a framework would need to begin with existing relationships and understandings, but these relationships should better reflect the realities of post–Cold War East Asia. A more satisfactory security structure would need to ensure that no one state dominates the region or attempts to dictate its prevailing political and security norms. At the same time, regional actors and external powers must endeavor to realize a more normal and natural order for the region.

Lack of Structure

East Asia at present does not possess a fully developed security structure: a set of well-defined, broadly shared norms and relationships that govern conflict resolution and competition among the constituent states. To be sure, the Association of Southeast Asian Nations (ASEAN) is approaching universal membership within the Southeast Asian subregion, and the ASEAN Regional Forum (ARF) provides for an annual if modest set of security deliberations among the ASEAN member states, most of the countries of Northeast Asia, Australia, New Zealand, and extra-regional powers such as the United States. But even ASEAN's most fervent advocates would not describe these arrangements as a security structure. Rather, ASEAN has devised artifices that obscure the political and strategic differences among its members, while providing incentives for ASEAN's more powerful neighbors to the north to exercise restraint in their ties with the region. No multilateral security mechanism exists because the necessary internal and regional conditions that would permit it are lacking.

This problem is particularly relevant in Northeast Asia, where the dominant strategic patterns for the region as a whole will be largely determined by China and Taiwan, Japan, the United States, and Russia. Each of Northeast Asia's major powers possesses an economic, political, and strategic weight not found among the states of Southeast Asia, and Korean reunification would also have the potential to reconfigure regional political and strategic patterns.

Even in Southeast Asia, ASEAN's scope is limited. Australia is not a member of ASEAN, but it is a close ally of the United States and a military power of some consequence, and it has the capacity to help shape the subregional security environment. In the longer run, Vietnam and Indonesia also aspire to a more substantial regional voice and role. Short of the establishment of a means for collective action within Southeast Asia or the development of substantial security linkages between

Southeast Asia and an extra-regional power, ASEAN's field of vision will remain circumscribed.

The major limiting factors in regional security seem fairly straightforward. The differences in power between various states, unresolved historical issues, the existence of largely autonomous cultures unaccustomed to longer-term habits of association and interaction with their neighbors, and the recent extraordinarily rapid economic and social change have all constrained development of a more mature and institutionalized regional order within which states can pursue their political and security goals. The manifestations of these limiting factors are particularly evident throughout Northeast Asia.

Thus, despite the region's economic success and seeming stability, looming power asymmetries and conflicting national interests are likely to prove a long-term challenge. This is all the more true given the region's cultural predilection for hierarchy in power relations. Rapid economic growth and enhanced commercial and diplomatic ties between former adversaries (for example, between China and South Korea) have helped build a floor for political understandings, as well as create the potential for longer-term cooperation. Nearly all regional states also demonstrate a genuine awareness of the potential risks to their interests should commerce be impeded by the use of force, underscoring the primacy of development goals in national strategies. But international politics are event driven, and the region's resilience and stability have not been tested by a major challenge to the present equilibrium or by an outright crisis that undermines the status quo. Amid optimism about the region's extraordinary dynamism, deeper anxieties persist about the sustainability of the existing balance of power.

Given these conditions and uncertainties, the United States continues to occupy a pivotal position in regional security calculations. Nearly all East Asian states are loath to see the United States forgo its central role in regional security. The close bilateral security ties between the United States and Japan and between the United States and South Korea remain integral to regional stability, not so much because they are ideal instruments for ensuring peace, but because they have performed effectively in the past and because they seem decidedly preferable to any other policy alternative that is discernible at present. These alliance relationships provide a more realistic basis for ensuring collaboration outside the national security arena than would be the case in the absence of such ties.

This judgment, however, is too readily construed as an argument favoring maintenance of the status quo. Regional actors clearly seek reassurance about the continuity of US policy, and the Clinton Administration has emphasized the durability of its security obligations, as well as its commitment to maintain the forward deployment of 100,000 US military personnel in East Asia. However, even in the context of calls for predictability in US policy, the ground is shifting. Regional states are seeking a larger role in defining the terms of relations with the United States, including enhanced access to US defense technology. Although still generally desirous of US support, America's regional allies are far less vulnerable than in previous decades and more convinced of the need to develop indigenous concepts of their security needs. Even as the incentives for close relations with the United States persist, highly asymmetrical security ties are not viable over the long term.

> *At the moment, no credible evidence suggests that leadership sentiment in Japan is seriously inclined toward an autonomous security posture.*

These circumstances comport with US interests. US security policy is explicitly premised on a more equitable distribution of the defense burden between the United States and its increasingly prosperous regional allies, many of whom are now robust economic competitors as well as security partners. It is less a case of economics superseding security and stability in US policy calculations and more the need to reconfigure the balance of US interests without calling into question the durability of US security commitments. The United States is thus walking a fine line between assuming a disproportionate responsibility for regional security and prompting regional states to conclude that the United States is no longer prepared to fulfill a primary security role. Should the latter perception coalesce on a widespread basis, the region could prove far less hospitable to US interests as states plan for the longer term (for example, in their military acquisition programs) without an expectation of a continued, meaningful US security commitment.

Without the United States as a credible security guarantor, the most likely scenario would be security realignment configured on the basis of a longer-term competition between China and Japan, which would be almost certain to extend to an extensive Japanese weapons development program, which might well include the development of strategic weapons. This possibility

would in turn provoke major reactions on the part of Japan's neighbors, especially China and Korea. Any such outcome, therefore, would be highly deleterious to US interests, and this fact underscores the importance of the Clinton Administration's reaffirmation of US security commitments to Tokyo.

At the moment, no credible evidence suggests that leadership sentiment in Japan is seriously inclined toward an autonomous security posture. Even in the context of the growing discontent over various manifestations of the US military presence and increasing calls by Japan and Korea to renegotiate status of forces agreements, few voices have proffered an alternative to continued alliance with the United States. But the end of the Cold War has led many observers to conclude that, absent a major political-military adversary, the United States will not be prepared to uphold its position as a global power indefinitely. Any serious reconfiguration of the security environment in East Asia (especially on the Korean peninsula, given its singular significance in US regional defense planning) would almost certainly compel reassessment of the necessity of maintaining US forces at existing levels.

Despite the Clinton Administration's efforts to reiterate its current defense priorities in East Asia, these efforts will remain credible only so long as prevailing security circumstances require them. A more sustainable defense strategy in the region must simultaneously address three needs: first, maintaining capabilities to deter existing threats to the peace and to defeat them should deterrence fail (i.e., the threat of war on the Korean peninsula); second, redefining the basis of America's regional alliances to ensure their viability and relevance in the eyes of domestic publics on both sides of the Pacific; and third, achieving renewed political and strategic understandings with China that preclude the use of force or unilateral alterations of the status quo in the West Pacific. The credibility of a longer-term US security role seems likely to depend on how well these needs are met.

The East Asian Dynamic

The dynamics of East Asia are far too complex and varied to guarantee preferred long-range outcomes. This is especially true in view of the domestic transitions underway in a number of East Asian countries. Various states, including ones that are geographically contiguous with one another, find themselves on very different trajectories. Russia is a great power whose credentials and capabilities are much diminished at present, while China is a great power on the rise, even as it, too, confronts the inevitability of major societal and institutional transitions. North Korea is engaged in an effort to ensure regime survival, seeking to deflect pressures for accommodation and demilitarization in relation to South Korea, while simultaneously currying favor with the United States and Japan. Japan, South Korea, and Taiwan are all in the midst of internal political transitions that are redefining each system's domestic politics and their respective orientations toward immediate neighbors as well as the larger outside world. In Southeast Asia, Vietnam is trying to make up for decades of lost time, and all the states of ASEAN seek political and economic engagement with Beijing, even as they warily assess the implications of the development of a much more powerful and assertive China. For all of East Asia's dynamism, it is anything but stable and certain in its longer-term power configurations and relationships.

Under such complex and unpredictable circumstances, all regional actors are seeking to hedge against untoward developments, while endeavoring to preserve as much freedom of action as possible. The states of East Asia recognize that international politics—even in a much more interactive and collaborative era—remains a self-help system. A serious political or military crisis, though understandably of more immediate impact on particular states, could reconfigure regional politics as a whole. Thus, states have powerful incentives to manage the consequences of potentially destabilizing change, for it is in a crisis that the resilience and viability of existing relationships are tested. The stakes are too high for all involved nations not to invest energy and inventiveness in the creation of a durable regional political and security order that can better ensure stability as well as prosperity in the decades to come.

Article 5

LABOUR

Far Eastern Economic Review, May 23, 1996

Vital and Vulnerable

Asian countries are drawing in unprecedented numbers of migrant workers to feed industrial growth. But by leaving them in legal limbo, governments may be asking for trouble.

Gary Silverman in Dumai, Indonesia

It was a simple calculation, and the choice seemed obvious. But it has left Muhamad Zaki flat broke and 2,000 kilometres from home in the dreary Sumatran port of Dumai, a year of his life wasted.

Zaki, 26, comes from Lombok, the Indonesian island east of Bali, where he earned 85 cents a day as a motorcycle driver. When a friend told him he could earn 10 times as much in Malaysia, Zaki jumped at the chance. He entered Malaysia last year as a tourist, got a work permit and took a job as a rubber tapper at $9 a day. He figured he would work for a year and save enough money to buy a business back home.

Zaki's math was right on the money; he managed to save $1,375. But there was one variable he hadn't factored in. As a guarantee against running away, he was obliged to keep his papers and his savings with his boss. When his estate was raided as part of a crackdown on illegal immigration, the boss vanished with the money and Zaki was arrested. After a month's detention, he was deported to Dumai on Sumatra's east coast.

Now, he's Indonesia's problem, one of hundreds of deportees that Dumai officials house temporarily in their homes until they can be packed off to nearby saw mills. There, the salaries are as low as those in Lombok. "I have to work," Zaki says. "If I go home, I will be embarrassed."

But the shame isn't Zaki's—he merely crossed the border to increase the return on his human capital. The shame is that an arrangement making so much economic sense produced so much human hardship. And that's not only Zaki's problem—it's a problem for governments and societies in the region as well.

Like it or not, migrant workers have become part of the Asian economic miracle. Nearly 20% of workers in Singapore are foreign. The percentage could even be higher in Malaysia, if you could count all the illegal workers. When Thailand built a stadium in Chiang Mai for the Southeast Asian games, it had to bring in Shan workers from Burma.

Viewed from on high, this is simply a labour market at work. But in practice it's a market that doesn't work very well. To get their chance, migrants typically mortgage their human rights, take on crippling debts or simply become criminals by working illegally—leaving themselves open to exploitation from law-enforcers and employers. *(See box, "Slaves to the Law.")*

With migration hitting unprecedented levels around Asia, the tensions caused by the uses and abuses of imported workers could become a source of friction between states. Officials from the Association of Southeast Asian Nations acknowledge the risks-but they're having a hard time coming up with a solution. "This problem can very well get out of hand, if we don't find some way

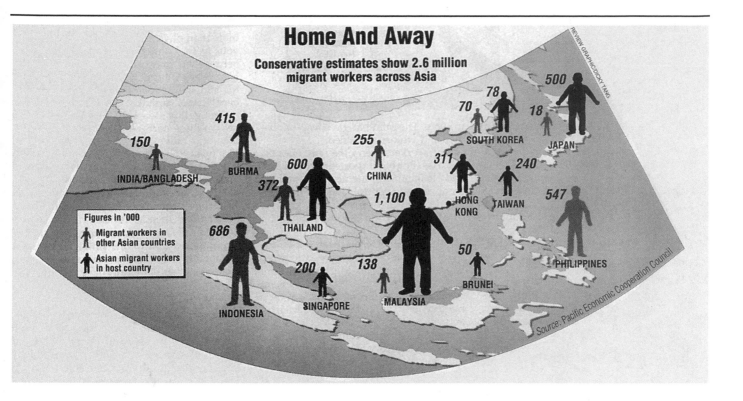

Home And Away

Conservative estimates show 2.6 million migrant workers across Asia

150 INDIA/BANGLADESH

415 BURMA

372 THAILAND
600 THAILAND

255 CHINA

70 78 SOUTH KOREA

500 18 JAPAN

311 HONG KONG

240 TAIWAN

547 PHILIPPINES

Figures in '000
Migrant workers in other Asian countries
Asian migrant workers in host country

686 INDONESIA

200 SINGAPORE

138

1,100 MALAYSIA

50 BRUNEI

REVIEW GRAPHIC/DICKY TANG

Source: Pacific Economic Cooperation Council

---

to regulate the flow," said a delegate to a recent closed-door Asean strategy session in Manila.

Labour migration is by no means new in Asia. Since the 1970s, millions of Filipinos, Indians and other Asians have worked in the Middle East. Javanese have been moving to Malaysia for centuries. Indonesia's Bawean island is known as the "Island of Women" because so many men migrate temporarily to Malaysia or Singapore. You're not a real man in Bawean until you work abroad; there are reports of women trying to divorce husbands for *failing* to leave.

But the current migration is unprecedented: More Asians are on the move, more are heading to Asian destinations—and experts say the numbers will keep going up. Exact figures are anyone's guess because of the large number of illegals. Malaysia says it has 650,000 registered foreign workers, but experts reckon there are at least as many illegals. A study by economist Charles Stahl of the University of Newcastle, in Australia, puts the number of migrants in East Asia at 2.6 million.

"The scale is startling," says Graeme Hugo, professor of geography at the University of Adelaide. "There is nothing to compare with the current movement."

The closest point of reference is the exodus from Indochina after the Vietnam War. Ironically, that chapter in the region's history of migration is now drawing to a close: Under an international agreement known as the Comprehensive Plan of Action, the camps that house the remaining few thousand Vietnamese boat people are to close by July 1. Branded economic migrants, the Vietnamese are being forced to go home, even as new waves of migrants are on the move across Asia.

This new migration is proceeding in a crazy-quilt pattern—some countries are importing migrants from poorer countries, while simultaneously sending workers to richer ones *(see table)*. For instance, Thailand is host to 600,000 migrants, but 372,000 Thai workers are spread across the region.

It's easy to see why the migration is taking place. Economic growth almost inevitably creates a demand for labour that some countries cannot meet from within. To cope with labour shortages, countries can automate factories or shift manufacturing abroad, but some jobs remain manual or stationary—on construction sites and plantations, for instance, or in homes, restaurants and brothels. Widening wage disparities between regions in Asia guarantee a steady supply of migrants prepared to do these jobs.

Malaysia's economic boom, for example, first encouraged plantation workers to find manufacturing jobs, leaving a vacuum in the countryside that was filled by migrants, mainly from Indone-

sia. More recently, the construction explosion in the cities has created even more jobs; and the growth in services has meant that, increasingly, migrants are minding shops, petrol stations and homes.

In countries such as Malaysia, employers have little alternative but to hire migrants. "It's not a gradual process where you can reconfigure your domestic labour supply," says Saskia Sassen, a professor of urban planning at Columbia University in New York and an expert on labour flows. "Speed is the key feature—the speed of investment and the need for an instantaneous labour force."

Many countries can't live without foreign workers—but don't want to live with them. The message to unskilled migrants is almost always: Get the job done and get lost. Citizenship is out of the question. "Countries are willing to admit workers; they are not willing to admit people," says Graziano Battistella, director of the Scalabrini Migration Centre in Manila.

That means migrant labour is tightly regulated labour. To make sure the foreigners will go home, they are kept separate and unequal. In Singapore, the work-but-don't-touch sentiment is bolstered by laws that can bar unskilled migrants from marrying citizens and oblige foreign maids to take pregnancy tests every six months.

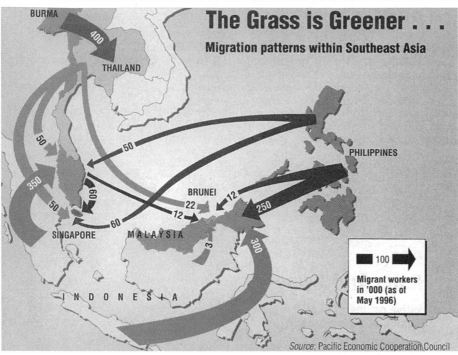

The Grass is Greener . . .

Migration patterns within Southeast Asia

BURMA
400
THAILAND
50
50
350
60
50
60
SINGAPORE
MALAYSIA
3
12
BRUNEI
22
12
250
300
PHILIPPINES
INDONESIA

100 → Migrant workers in '000 (as of May 1996)

Source: Pacific Economic Cooperation Council

(Review Graphic/Dicky Tang)

But Asia is growing so quickly that government efforts to control labour flows often backfire—and more rules mean more corruption. A subterranean migration industry has sprung up across Asia, to get workers where they want to go, by any means necessary. Migrants pay a price, pledging months of salary to finance their trips or putting their lives in the hands of smugglers. In the 1990s, 500 Indonesians have drowned trying to sneak into Malaysia by sea, says Human Rights Watch/Asia.

For Indonesians, the crossing to Peninsular Malaysia usually begins in Dumai and nearby islands of Riau province. These are at one and the same time smuggling centres and dumping grounds for migrants like Zaki. It's a three-hour ferry ride across the Strait of Malacca to Malaysia; most migrants cross illegally aboard wooden boats called *pompong,* after the sound of their outboard motors.

The vessels may look like refugee boats, but they are part of a highly efficient business in human cargo. Like any self-respecting Asian entrepreneur these days, Malaysian labour bosses, known as *towkay,* operate via mobile phone, calling in orders for workers to Indonesian smugglers, or *tekong.* The migrants are held in Riau safe houses—at one, a peek through a crack between the walls and ceiling reveals dozens of heads of black hair, packed together like chickens in a coop.

None of this would be possible without widespread corruption on both sides of the Malacca Strait, say tekong, migrants and human-rights workers. "It's impossible to go into Malaysia without the cooperation of the police," says one tekong.

The safety of the migrants is of little concern. For a trip across the strait, tekong typically load more than 100 migrants into vessels ill-equipped for the high seas—and some even prefer leaving on stormy nights for maximum cover. In one 1993 disaster, a tekong hit a sand bar as he neared Malaysia, and ordered 117 migrants to wade the remaining 400 metres to shore. The sand bar gave way—and 47 men and women drowned.

The workers aren't the only ones taking risks. For big importers like Malaysia and Thailand, tapping nearby supplies of cheap, easy-to-control labour can become an addiction that saps businesses' desire to progress beyond the sweatshop stage.

There are socio-political perils, too. Many societies are ill-prepared to accept so many foreigners. Migrants are perceived as a threat, particularly when a nation's self-image is based on racial homogeneity, as in Japan, or racial balance, as in Singapore and Malaysia. Says Stephen Castles, co-author of *The Age of Migration,* a history of modern population movements: "The idea of having a clearly bounded nation-state with a ho-

mogeneous identity could become unviable."

Migration also threatens to divide states. Thai officials worry that migrants pose a security threat; in Malaysia, they are seen as burdening social services. "I don't think we can import more," says Tengku Zaman Tengku Hariff, director-general of Malaysia's task-force on foreign workers. "The people are starting to complain. There is already overcrowding in medical facilities, in the schools."

But the Philippines and Indonesia are banking on migration. In the Philippines, the government says overseas workers remitted $2.6 billion in 1994—equivalent to nearly 20% of export earnings. In Indonesia, exporting labour was made a priority in the current five-year plan.

The nightmare scenario is an economic downturn in a major labour importer. At that point, foreign workers wouldn't be needed. Would they go home? "These are things governments never discuss," says Chandran Jeshurun, a fellow at the Malaysian International Affairs Forum. "But I am sure governments have contingency plans to ship them all out." He adds: "Logistically, it would be a nightmare."

Indeed, governments are hard-pressed to get rid of even small numbers of unwanted migrants. For instance, Malaysia sends Indonesian migrants like Zaki to Dumai, but cannot ensure that they won't return. Riau businessmen estimate that more than half the migrants deported from Malaysia go back.

This is easy territory to disappear in. Riau has 3,214 islands and the coasts are a mire of mangrove swamps, soggy peat-moss fields and mud so deep a grown man can sink to his knees. Policing the waterfront is tough and the challenge is more than physical. "If you want to clean your teeth, you have to go to Singapore because no one can open their mouth here," says Tabrani Rab, a hospital operator and newspaper publisher in Pekanbaru, Riau's capital.

Smuggling is a well-developed business in these parts—not only people, but logs and clove cigarettes are taken to Malaysia. The cargoes sometimes go together—people hidden under the logs, or shipped with cigarettes, which make handy bribes. Migrants are usually taken first from Dumai to nearby islands Rupat or Bengkalis then Malaysia.

A pair of tyre tracks cutting through a cassava field lead to one smuggling area in Dumai. A local fisherman says boats overloaded with migrants have been leaving here since 1974, but the pace has been picking up in recent months. Since the departures are usually at night, the fisherman says the smugglers disturb his sleep. "But we can't say anything," he says. "The people who bring the workers have high status."

Malaysia and Indonesia have tried to clean up the migration business without success. In Malaysia, the government has barred private labour recruiters—except those hiring maids—and set up a one-stop task force in their place. Its opposite number in Indonesia is Bijak, a labour agency owned by the Ministry of Manpower, which either supplies workers or farms out business to legal brokers.

But dealing with the bureaucracies can be maddening, says Thamrin Nasution, a labour broker and chairman of the Riau Chamber of Commerce. A would-be maid, for instance, has to take a literacy test, get a medical check-up, receive skills training, obtain a passport and wait two or three months for a Malaysian work permit. When prospective maids learn how long the process takes, Thamrin says, "they go to the illegal one—the tekong."

The tekong also offer competitive prices. Bijak charges workers about $400 to go to Malaysia, says Sidney Jones, executive director of Human Rights Watch/Asia. In Riau, tekong say they charge migrants $10 and $85 for the trip to Malaysia. A worker coming from clear across Indonesia would pay $100 to $280.

The prices may not seem like much, but they are significant because the migrants come from some of the poorest parts of Indonesia, East Java and West Nusa Tenggara, which includes Lombok.

Typically, the families of migrants sell property or go to loan sharks to raise the

---

Slaves to the Law

Gordon Fairclough in Ranong, Thailand

Crossing the border was easy, says Ko Ye. He made the short boat ride across the harbour from Burma's Victoria Point to the nearby Thai port city of Ranong in broad daylight. No one asked him any questions.

But Ko Ye knew getting to Bangkok—560 kilometres and several immigration checkpoints away—would be a different story. So he turned to the only people who could help him in this dangerous and unlawful enterprise: the police. For $100, a policeman drove Ko Ye all the way to the capital.

But Ko Ye's contact with the police didn't end there. Every few days, officers would shake him down for 200–300 baht ($8–12). Finally, he was arrested. The police pocketed all of his money and jewellery and packed him off to jail for four months.

There he saw what can happen to immigrants who have no legal protection. Men were beaten; women fared worse. "Sometimes, drunken policemen would come into the jail, take the women out of their cells and rape them," says Ko Ye. "No one dared help them. The police said they would shoot us."

In Thailand and across Asia corrupt officials profit enormously from the huge flows of workers crossing national borders. Not only do they help illicit job-seekers gain entry, but also they prey on them during their stay. This abuse of authority is made easier by governments that officially outlaw immigration while tacitly approving it.

Almost all illegal immigrants who make their way from Thailand's borders to cities deeper inside the country do so with the help of the police or the military. The standard fee, immigrants say, ranges from $100 to $200.

Those who want to make the trip but can't afford to pay become indentured servants. Nay Zar Htun, a 15-year-old from Moulmein in Burma's Mon state, ended her eight-hour journey from the border at the Bangkok residence of a former police general. A middle-aged Thai woman came and took her home to be a maid.

For a month, Nay Zar Htun worked 18-hour days, cooking, cleaning, doing the laundry, massaging her employers and sleeping on the floor in a storeroom. Then she asked for her salary. "The woman said that she had bought me for 5,000 baht, and that I would have to work five months with-

out pay," Nay Zar Htun says. She tried to get away once and was dragged back at gunpoint. A month later, she managed to escape.

Chalongphob Sussangkarn, who heads the Thailand Development Research Institute, says that by hiring illegal immigrants rather than Thais, employers save about 50 baht per person per day. Using a conservative estimate of the number of illegals in the country, this adds up to an annual windfall of more than $350 million.

A lot of this money ends up in the pockets of unscrupulous officials, who act as middlemen in the labour market and who extort protection money from the illegals and their employers.

Some Thai officials say the only way to end such abuses is to allow foreign workers to enter the country legally. "It's the only way we can keep the police from mistreating them," says Sira Chavanaviraj, the governor of Ranong. "If they're legal, they'll be much safer." But he admits changing the system won't be easy. "Too many people are making too much money."

money needed to send a son or daughter to Malaysia. "They sell everything," says Thamrin. "They sell their cows, their land, sometimes their house."

The burden is particularly heavy in the Philippines. Legally, recruiters can charge migrants 5,000 pesos ($192), but in fact charge up to 120,000 pesos for jobs in Japan or 100,000 pesos for Taiwan, says Cherry Padilla of the human-rights group Gabriela in Manila. Generally, Asian migrants pay three to four months of salary up-front, says Manello Abello, of the ILO's employment department in Geneva.

Still, migration is a strategy that works for many families. In East Flores in Indonesia, for example, there are villages where nearly every family has sent some one to Sabah in East Malaysia—and the are easy to spot, says Hugo of the University of Adelaide. The homes are made of brick and stone rather than wood and boast satellite dishes.

But while migrant workers are able to keep their families in some degree of comfort, they themselves find returning home difficult. Like Zaki, many set out hoping to make enough money to set up a business back home, but eventually find that investment opportunities are few and far between. The rich volcanic soil of East Flores would make it a good place to grow vegetables for export, but poor infrastructure makes that option unviable. As a result, remittances are more likely to be used for consumption. "I don't think there are going to be major regional benefits unless there is government involvement to create infrastructure for people to invest," says Hugo.

Without such opportunities, migrants have every reason to stay abroad—perhaps permanently. That's a scary proposition for importing countries that still see migration as temporary. Some countries are already looking for ways to reduce their dependence on foreign workers. In its recently released Seventh Five-Year Plan, Malaysia again emphasized automation and employing women as a way to phase out migrants.

But development alone doesn't end migration—and may spur it. Unskilled workers don't disappear in advanced economies: Office buildings need janitors, working women need maids. Meanwhile, in labour-surplus nations like Indonesia, the increasing use of fertilizers frees farm workers to migrate.

In countries like Malaysia and Thailand that are absorbing hundreds of thousands of migrants, it's inevitable some will put down roots, migration experts say. So it's probably a good idea for governments to make the best of the situation. Right now, workers across the region show up for work and wind up in jail—literally, for those like Zaki, or figuratively, for thousands of others imprisoned by debt or hemmed in by strict regulations.

Increasingly, migration experts are suggesting that the solution may be a lighter hand by government. "The impression we have from our analysis is that the systems governments have set up have unwittingly had a very exploitive aspect for the candidates for migration because they have to pay all the way," says Roger Bohning, chief of migration for the ILO's employment branch in Geneva.

How this would work is hard to say. Bohning says the ILO is working on recommendations and hopes to have them ready by late this year. ILO colleague Abello says his bias would be to "completely open up the market," allowing foreign employers to hire workers directly, perhaps posting a bond to make sure contracts are observed. That way workers escape the debt trap but someone takes responsibility. Hugo, at the University of Adelaide, says governments "need to regularize the system so that the vulnerability of the workers is reduced. The demand for labour is there. The system is in place to supply the labour. It's unfortunate the system is illegal."

There's no stopping the migrants now—they're on the move. "There are so many chances to work in Malaysia," Zak says with a smile as he sits in Dumai. "The work will find us."

The question for Asia is: Should that be a crime?

Article 6

Far Eastern Economic Review, December 5, 1996

YOUTH

Rock Solid

Asia's teens may strut their designer togs in trendy discos, but their beliefs remain staunchly conservative. If their world is so different from their parents', why are they still clinging to mom and dad's values?

By Simon Elegant in Bangkok and Margot Cohen in Jakarta. With reports from S. Jayasankaran in Kuala Lumpur, Bruce Gilley in Hong Kong, Charles Lee in Seoul and Murray Hiebert in Singapore.

With eyebrows tweezed razor-thin, lips painted plum and a black miniskirt barely sheathing her thighs, Ratna Sari Ismiati looks like a thoroughly modern maiden of the '90s. And so she should. The 23-year-old Indonesian holds one of the hippest jobs in town: She greets guests at the Fashion Cafe, the Jakarta branch of the restaurant and nightclub chain founded by four superstar international models. Two of these cover

queens, Naomi Campbell and Claudia Schiffer, graced the opening of the Jakarta restaurant—Asia's first—a few weeks ago. Not surprisingly, the restaurant has since been swamped by the city's trendiest young things.

Yet Ratna's personal goals reflect almost nothing of the glossy hype for which the Fashion Cafe stands. She may look like a siren, but as she tells her own story in between dashing back and forth to escort late lunch patrons, it's clear her family—and their traditional values—remains the focus of her life, just as it has been for countless generations.

Eight years ago, Ratna left her parents behind in Jakarta and went off to the West Java city of Bandung to attend a tourism academy. After graduation she found work at a Bandung hotel, but before long, she decided to move back home. "I wanted to be closer to my parents," she explains. "I'm happy at home. There's someone who takes care of my meals, keeps track of when I go to sleep." Ask her where she sees herself in five years, and the reply comes with no hesitation. "I want to get married as soon as possible. I just want a simple life—a husband, a home, children." And, despite the job at Fashion Cafe, Ratna says she doesn't feel drawn towards Western culture, which she defines as "free." "You express your opinions openly, we don't," Ratna says matter-of-factly.

Such are the contradictions of Asia's first children of plenty, its very own Generation X, teenagers and 20-somethings who have grown up knowing nothing but peace, dazzling economic growth and an ever-rising flood of consumer goods. Their elders complain that they are acquisitive, fickle and faddish, steeped in Western fashions and shallow consumer values. On the inside, though, most cling to the family as the bedrock of life; they are fiercely proud of their own countries and cultures and often reject what they see as the "individualism" of the West.

These broad generalizations are, of course, fraught with controversy, not least over the definition of what exactly constitutes "Western culture" or "Asian values." And, in a region as vast as Asia there are naturally many local variations, even complete exceptions. Politics, geography, a country's degree of economic development and unique cultural factors all affect the way a society's young people have reacted to the economic explosion of recent decades. In China, to take one example, the long years of isolation under communist rule followed by the shock of Deng Xiaoping's reforms has carved what the Chinese describe as a "ditch" between generations. On one side are the cautious elders inured to decades of capricious political campaigns and dependence on the state; confronting them are their brash, individualistic youngsters bent on making a million.

Still, whether conducting surveys or stumbling over anecdotal evidence, academic and private-sector analysts say the similarity of views expressed by Asia's Generation Xers is almost uncanny. In survey after survey, interviewees stress the importance of family, jobs, saving for the future, caring for older relatives and other such traditional values. Such supposed Western imports as individualism or a more relaxed attitude towards premarital sex are unequivocally rejected.

"We have been as surprised as anyone by the results of our research," says Jacks Pang, of the Hong Kong Federation of Youth Groups, which has been conducting extensive public-opinion surveys among young people in the colony for the last three years. "We always assume that youths will be nontraditional and nonconformist in their values," says the 30-ish Pang, himself youthfully attired in jeans. running shoes and a checked lumberjack shirt. "But one by one as we research the different topics we find one thing in common; that Hong Kong youths are quite traditional in the values they hold in areas like family, education, respect for elders, marriage."

Ben Tan is the assistant creative director of advertising agency Leo Burnett in Kuala Lumpur, and it is his job to find out what young people think—they are the focus of the ads. His conclusions are a virtual carbon copy of Pang's: "All our research with focus groups indicates that young Malaysians are pretty conservative. They value family life, parental consent, things like that. They may mimic American trends—music and fashion—but they aren't like American kids. They don't leave the home."

Many governments in the region don't seem to agree with that assessment, and often spend much time and effort attempting to head off what the Chinese official media dub "spiritual pollution" from the West. A state assemblyman in Malaysia recently sought to ban a Michael Jackson concert, blaming drug addiction among the country's young people on "the permissive lifestyles of foreign artists who promote outrageous hairstyles, wear earrings, shabby and torn outfits and indulge in illicit sex and drugs." And worries in Malaysia about the influence of "grunge" and "gangsta rap" fashions are such that the government bars ads that show teenagers wearing their baseball caps backwards, Leo Burnett's Tan notes.

To many researchers, though, a defining feature of the Asian Generation X is precisely the ease with which its members can reconcile global consumerism with loyalty towards home and community. "Gangsta rap is very popular in Malaysia," acknowledges Dave McCaughan, Asian consumer-insights director for the advertising agency McCann-Erickson, "but you've got to think about why. We had a focus group and one of the kids said, 'I love to wear this stuff because officially it's not approved. I wouldn't be seen dead in one of the government youth centres.' "

He adds: "These kids are sophisticated enough to understand that it is a symbol of rebellion. It annoys the hell out of government." McCaughan, who collates the insights provided by such focus groups from around the region, argues that most Malaysian teenagers sporting the baseball caps and baggy pants have no idea about the violent, anti-society message gangsta rap sometimes projects.

"Those baggy trousers, the kids don't know what they are wearing, or what it means," concurs Amata Luphaiboon, a 27-year-old Thai architect who keeps a keen eye on youth culture. "Just the way they wear a T-shirt with an 'X' on it but they don't know—or care—who Malcolm X is."

"Kids regard some of it as a bunch of crap," is the way Thai student Edpawin Jetjirawat—known to his friends as Eddie—describes the attitude his peers take towards aspects of Western culture ranging from individualism to more permissive attitudes towards sex and drugs. "You take the good parts and the rest you throw away," says the 18-year-old freshman at Bangkok's elite Thammasat University.

Increasingly, too, young Asians have an alternative to overseas imports that so irritate their governments: locally produced television shows, magazines, movies and music. And, be it the saccharine love songs of Canto-pop or the Malaysian soap operas that consciously project homespun virtues, there is little danger that the message they hear will erode traditional values. Quite the opposite in fact. Edwin Siregar, assistant editor of *Kawanku* ("My Friend"), a weekly magazine for teenage girls in Jakarta, says his magazine often runs stories profiling people who have succeeded through working hard so as to encourage readers to do the same.

But, if Eddie and his Asian peers are in no danger from home-grown media and can take or leave the Western cultural values their governments seem to fear so much, the question remains: What is it that makes them cling so tenaciously to highly conservative traditional values? After all, they undoubtedly have more freedom to rebel than any generation of Asians before them: more money, more free time, less parental supervision, fewer worries about the future. Nor is there any question that the societies they live in are much more open to the outside than those of 20 years ago.

Part of the explanation lies in what is any society's simplest—and strongest—binding forces, nationalism. "Maybe if you lived overseas you could be totally Westernized, but here in Thailand, you can't be like that," says Eddie. He happens to be wearing conspicuously baggy trousers himself, but is quick to point out that his multicoloured shirt is a traditional Thai design. "You still have to be Thai, the culture is in your life every day, its religion and values."

And yet, both sociologists and market researchers agree, it is the family—not society—that plays the dominant role in transmitting and sustaining traditional culture and values. Surveys consistently show that young Asians still look to their parents for instruction in most key areas of their lives. In Hong Kong, for example, an overwhelming majority of those interviewed said their parents should control what friends they chose, how hard they studied, how they treated family members and so on.

"There's no doubt that in Thailand traditional belief is still strong with young people because of the family, because of their upbringing," says Rawewan Prakobpol, who runs Acorn-Omnitrak, a market-research firm in Bangkok. "Superficially they may look Western, they may prefer their McDonald's or Kentucky Fried Chicken to Thai food, or watch the same programmes as their counterparts in the West. But inside they hold lots of values they get from their parents that are hard to change: respect for age, respect for the family, collective not individual action and so on."

"'What is imbibed from the parents is the whole concept of family," says Sanjay Kumar, an adviser to Indo-Ad, an Indonesian advertising agency that works in association with Ogilvy & Mather Worldwide. "The entire concept of family has not changed. If anything, it has become stronger." Kumar notes that fear of economic problems in the future tends to reinforce dependence on the family. Other such vaunted Asian values as saving a high proportion of one's income are also reinforced.

'Superficially they may look Western. . . . But inside they hold lots of values they get from their parents that are hard to change: respect for age, respect for the family. . . .'—Thai market-researcher Rawewan Prakobpol

If his peers are anything like Brandon Sta Maria, for instance, his generation can shrug off charges by elders that it is spendthrift. At 22 years old and one exam away from being an accountant, he saves a whopping 40% of his salary. Why? "Well," he shrugs, "it seems like a prudent thing do." And in Malaysia, it seems there are many Brandon Sta Marias. A unit trust recently set up by the government for Malaysians between the ages of 12 and 29 was swamped by

770,000 investors who deposited 1.4 billion ringgit ($560 million).

For the moment, then, it seems the children of Asia's boom are able straddle two worlds. But many observers wonder whether the persistence of those traditional values can survive the continued onslaught of urbanization, industrialization and Western consumerism. The pace of change is already so rapid, they argue, that even a few years can make a noticeable difference in attitude and values among young people.

Gary Chang, a 26-year-old designer in Taipei, says things are changing so fast that he is very much aware of the differences between his contemporaries and today's teenagers. "The views of 17- to 18-year-old 'little devils' are more open, even more different than our parents."

Thai architect Amata concurs. Just five years after graduating from Bangkok's premier university, Chulalongkorn, he says the students currently studying are "very different; even comparing them with my generation of students there is a big gap already." The current generation is much more materialistic, more interested in brand names, even more spoiled, he says.

"I don't think any society can stand still," says Rawewan of Acorn-Omnitrak, "unless you are a closed society like Burma. You don't want to lose your identity entirely, but it's very hard to resist change, the consumer culture, the influence of the West."

Others are more sanguine, though. Their argument: Every generation mellows as it matures, and culture is more powerful and deeply rooted than people might think. "It's a stage they're going through," says Kim Yong Ja, a consumer-economics professor at Sookmyung University in Seoul. "When they get older, they will inevitably return to what they learned from their parents. I also think the gap between the East and West is closing but that the two won't become the same. Culture just doesn't change that fast."

Article 7

The Economist, July 13, 1996

The Compass Swings: A Survey of Tomorrow's Japan

The road turns, at last.

Will the Japan of the new century be a full member of the global democratic family? Yes, says **Brian Beedham**—*provided it passes three tests*

The trouble with writing about Japan these days is that so many other people are doing it, too; and they could be writing about utterly different countries. On one side beam the optimists who say that by around 2010 Japan will in its politics, its economics and its foreign policy be much the same sort of place as the democracies of Europe and America. On the other side glowers a band of conspiracy theorists who think that a fundamentally non-western Japan is privately pursuing its own great-power agenda, and some of whom even seem to believe that any apparent evidence to the contrary (such as the only-just-ended four years of near-zero economic growth) is an ingenious piece of Japanese theatre, designed to deceive the onlooker.

No other great country, open to free inspection, produces such a clash of reactions from those who go to inspect it. A great deal—far more than the future of Japan itself—depends on which of those incompatible diagnoses is correct.

This survey will argue that the optimists are probably right, but only if the Japanese pretty soon take some decisions that their kind of government has in the past found it worryingly hard to take. The conspiracy theorists, though probably wrong in general, are therefore right to say that the world needs to take a closer look at the way the Japanese run their politico-economic life. The question about Japan is not just whether it wants to open up its economy, have a proper multi-party political system and shoulder a bigger share of the 21st century's foreign-policy burdens. It is whether Japan is organised in a way that will enable it to make up its mind about these things quickly enough. This is a question about the nature of Japanese society, and answering that question requires a delve into Japanese history. Reader, be patient.

The debate goes as follows. For a variety of reasons, Japan has preserved into the late 20th century a kind of society that has largely vanished from the rest of the world. The native religion of the Japanese people, Shinto, has always put great value on the loyalty that members of a family owe to each other. So do the ideas of Confucius, which Japan imported from China; and the Japanese soon Shintoised the non-family-minded Buddhism which had come to them from India. All this provided a powerful underpinning for the rules of feudal loyalty that grew up, in Japan as in other countries, during the time when warrior leaders commanded and protected their peasant followers.

The Past That Went On Too Long

The difference is that Japan, unlike those other countries, kept the feudal idea alive right up to the middle of the 19th century, by cutting itself off from the world for 250 years until Commodore Perry's warships sailed into Tokyo Bay in 1853. Neither the "first opening" of Japan, which followed Perry's bang on the door, nor the "second opening", the post–1945 American occupation, quite managed to remove this deeply rooted way of life. It is as if Bonnie Prince Charlie's Highlanders had fought off the English, waved the world goodbye and preserved the clan system into the electronic age.

Exchange rates		
End-June 1996		
$1	=	¥109.9
£1	=	¥170.4
DM1	=	¥72.1

The result is a Japan which, in the way its government and much of its economy are organised, still has a strangely archaic look. Chie Nakane, who in 1970 wrote an eye-opening book called "Japanese Society", drew a vivid picture of the semi-feudal structures within which many Japanese even then spent a large part of their daily lives. The country she described was a loose collection of semi-autonomous groups, each of which was held together by a powerful sense of communal loyalty but also granted a great deal of authority to the man at the top. It was a very clannish sort of place.

It still is, in many ways. The clannishness explains, among other things, why the Japanese still feel a far keener commitment than most other people to the place where they work—their car-making company, their investment bank, their government ministry. This loyalty gives each such organisation great strength. But it also has the consequence, as Ms Nakane pointed out, that the decision-making process in Japan is horribly slow. Each institution has to work out its own laborious internal consensus, and then those institutions whose interests overlap have to sit down together and hammer out a multi-sided compromise. It always took a long time for medieval barons to agree upon a new policy for their country as a whole. So with the baronial structures of today's Japan.

Yes, yes, say the optimists impatiently; this was no doubt true until deplorably recently; it may still be partly true; but it is at last changing.

Prosperity is breaking up Japan's old patterns of group loyalty. Urbanisation loosens the bonds of family. The Japanese tell you they love to keep in touch with their country cousins; but there is a limit to the survival of these country roots now that a fifth of all Japanese live in cities of more than 1m people and only 6% still work on the land. The strains of modern life are starting to eat into Japanese marriages; the divorce rate, though still low by western standards, has nearly doubled in the past 25 years. The links between parents and children are weakening; already, when asked whom they expect to look after them in old age, more than a third of Japanese say the state rather than their children, according to an opinion poll taken last year.

Perhaps even more important, as the Japanese get steadily richer the workplace ceases to be the chief focus of their communal loyalty. Now they can direct their enthusiasm into other sorts of group activity. They are soccer fans; they belong to music clubs; if female and young, they go and lay their collective hearts at pop stars' feet. Many of their new leisure-time activities, indeed, have nothing to do with groups at all; young Japanese go eating and dancing in couples, or sit down to the solitary pleasure of computer games. To have money to spend, and spare time to spend it in, was bound to melt the rigid old simplicities of Japanese society. The melting presumably goes even faster as more and more Japanese travel abroad (15m tourists went to foreign parts last year, 24 times as many as in 1970) and discover how much more relaxed life can be in other parts of the rich world.

Ms Nakane believes that in some ways the Japan of 1996 is no longer the place she described in 1970. The "periphery" of Japanese life, as she puts it, has broken free from the old patterns of behaviour. This periphery eye-catchingly includes the way younger Japanese behave when they are not at work. Look at the young fathers nonchalantly shouldering the baby while the wife walks untrammelled ahead, the parties of young women whooping it up over a restaurant dinner; things like this would have seemed astonishing even 25 years ago.

But the change is far from complete. What Ms Nakane calls the "core" of Japan—the bureaucracy, parliament, big business—still largely operates in the old style. It could take another 50 years, she depressingly thinks, before this core changes its ways. Ichiro Ozawa, the leader of the main opposition party, New Frontier, and just possibly Japan's next prime minister, is not as bleak as that, but he agrees that the breakthrough has yet to come. Japan still awaits, he says, a "revolution in consciousness".

The Coming Transformation, They Say

If and when that revolution comes, say the optimists, Japan will be transfigured. As the old order breaks up, it will be replaced by a radically new sort of society. Out of the late-feudal collectivism of the past 140 years will emerge a Japan based on the principles of individual enterprise and individual reponsibility. The Japanese are as capable as anybody else of running such a society, the optimists reckon; it is simply a matter of getting the door unlocked. Once the door does swing open, Japan will in this vital respect be no different from the democracies of Europe and America. This will be Japan's "third opening", and it will finish the job.

There is much to be gained if this happens, especially if it does not have to wait for another 50 years. The Japanese themselves will be better off. The big decisions ahead of them will be easier to tackle if they recognise that the machinery of state which drove them so triumphantly through the 1960s and 1970s will not work so well in the 2000s. If they do not recognise this, they will be less rich than they could have been; they will have no function in the world beyond the wielding of money; and their periphery and their core will increasingly wonder whether they belong to the same country.

But it is not just the Japanese who will benefit. This new sort of Japan will be a better partner for America and Europe in the business of trying to cope with the dangers of tomorrow's world. If the 21st century is to be peaceful and democracy friendly, America needs on the western side of the Pacific the sort of allies it already has on the eastern side of the Atlantic: people who share the same broad aims, who will if necessary fight for those aims, and whose decision-making processes are more or less comprehensible to their partners. Today's Japan passes none of those tests. A reformed Japan could take its place as a solid member of a durable, three-sided alliance of the democracies.

Above all, the emergence of such a Japan should put an end to the culture-war theory of history. The most acrimonious ideological debate of these post-communist days is the argument about "civilisations". Can the inhabitants of the different parts of the world eventually come to share the same ideas about how they ought to be governed, or are they condemned by their membership of different culture-areas to have different sorts of government?

The admirers of "Asian values" love to cite Japan as evidence for their belief that people in the Confucian culture-area will always give their rulers more power than people elsewhere want to give theirs. If the Asian-values advocates have their way, it will be a pity: because Japa-

nese (and other supposed Confucianists) will be less free than they might have been; because such arguments between different chunks of the world may become violent, and bring about that dreaded "clash of civilisations"; and because it will mean that mankind is not, in the end, a single band of brothers, just a bunch of suspicious neighbours. If Japan of all countries changes its ways, on the other hand, the Asian-values theory will have been proved wrong. The spectre of a culturally compartmentalised world will fade, and mankind can relax a little.

The test will come fairly soon. In the next few years Japan has to make up its mind whether to face, or to duck, some tricky questions about the future of its economy, the shape of its political system, and where it stands in the world. The answers it gives will show what sort of place it is. First the foreign-policy question, because it is the one the Japanese find hardest of all to face.

Between the Dragon and the Deep Blue Sea

A swelling China, a hesitant America: how to avoid a lonely Japan

By the start of the new century, two things could be changing the geopolitics of the western Pacific, Japan's home ground. There will have been a further growth in the power of China, and it will not be an amiable-looking growth; and there may have been a contraction of the comforting presence of the United States. Japan has barely started to think what the combination means for it.

About China, it is true, a distinct stir of apprehension can now be felt. The Japanese have woken up to the fact that the China of the early 21st century will probably have both the capacity for a rapid expansion of its military strength and a government with a powerful reason for using that strength in the service of a pugnacious foreign policy. The Chinese government reckons its economy will keep growing by about 8% a year into the new century. This means that within a decade it can roughly double its military spending without increasing the share of GDP allocated to defence (and China's one-party sort of government can probably expand that share without much difficulty). Even if that 8% growth rate proves too optimistic, the amount of extra money flowing into China's arms budget each year will still be formidable.

And China has a particularly worrying brand of one-party government. The Chinese Communists are trying to hold on to their monopoly of power even though they have abandoned much of the Leninist-Maoist ideology which they once used as the justification for that monopoly. They need a new justification. The likeliest substitute

is a chest-thumping nationalism, a claim that they are going to make China into a country the rest of the world will respect. The military instrument needed for this is "power projection". That means, among other things, the possession of a high-tech modern army and the sea power and air power needed to enable that army to fight outside China's borders. As China's noisy but unsuccessful show of force in the Taiwan Strait last March showed, it does not yet have power projection. It seems virtually certain that it will acquire it without further delay.

If Taiwan were the only target of that power, this might not seem too worrying: once the Taiwan issue had been settled one way or the other—with the island back inside a reunified China, or with China's acceptance of an independent Taiwan—the rest of the world could relax. But Taiwan may not be the end of it. If China's economic growth continues, so that a country of up to 1.5 billion people starts to develop middle-class tastes, its consumption of food and oil will rise spectacularly.

The way things look now, China will not be able to meet its needs for either of those things from within its present borders. One fairly cautious Chinese scientist says it will need to import 33m tons of food a year by 2020. As for oil, Kent Calder, of the Centre for Strategic and International Studies in Washington, DC, thinks that by 2010 the Chinese will each year be wanting to bring in from outside the equivalent of half of Saudi Arabia's total present production. They may hope to get some of this oil from the area around the Spratly Islands in the

South China Sea, whose ownership they claim (as do five other countries), or from a possible new oil field under the water between Taiwan and Okinawa, which the Japanese say belongs to them. Those are two possible uses for power projection.

There is another, even more disturbing. It is not impossible that China's need for oil may lead it into an alliance with some of the Muslim oil-producing countries of south-west Asia—Iran, Iraq and the ex-Soviet states east of the Caspian—in which China would offer these countries military protection in return for a guaranteed flow of oil and gas. This oil and gas would have to be brought to China either via a horribly expensive pipeline north of the Himalayas or by sea around India and South-East Asia, along sea-lanes China would then need to keep a military eye on. That would involve an even longer-range projection of Chinese armed strength.

Some of this may never happen. But even the most sober estimate of the possible growth of Chinese power will cause alarm in Tokyo when it is set alongside the entirely possible diminution of the American military presence in the region over the next decade or so. The Americans have said they will beep about 100,000 fighting men in the Asia-Pacific area, the same number as they propose to keep in Europe. But the 100,000 in Asia are much less securely dug in than their comrades in Europe.

For a start, the 20,000 American marines stationed on the Japanese island of Okinawa—not well loved by the locals these days—are there partly to dash to the help of South Korea if the North Koreans go mad and invade it. But Mike Mochizuki of the Brookings Institution in

Washington, DC, has pointed out that there are only enough suitable ships in the area to move about 3,000 of the marines at a time; and the Pentagon apparently reckons that the 37,000 American troops in Korea itself may be enough, with South Korea's own army, to win a fight there. As a senior Japanese politician recently observed, Japan pays roughly eight times as much per American serviceman stationed on its soil as Germany does. If the marines are to remain in Okinawa, they need a better strategic reason—and one the Japanese share—than they have now.

And what happens to those 37,000 Americans in Korea when the long horror story of North Korea comes to its preferably peaceful end? It might be nice for the general orderliness of the region if the government of a newly reunited Korea asked them to stay on. But it is far from certain that it will. The Americans have already given up their bases in the Philippines. After next year their warships will no longer find a welcome in Hong Kong. If and when Korea waves the boys goodbye, that promised 100,000-man presence in the Asian-Pacific region will look pretty hazy. The real American front line may one day be no farther west than Hawaii.

A physical American retraction is not the only thing nagging at Japanese minds. So is another awkward thought that is now beginning to register: that America's feelings about a newly powerful China might not be quite the same as Japan's.

Provided this new China respected the rules of global free trade—admittedly a large proviso—the Americans might decide that they could live with a China whose relationship to the rest of Asia was, as one man puts it, "like that of the United States to the rest of the Americas". America would not necessarily object if China occasionally clipped Vietnam's ear, required the Russians to be more co-operative in Siberia, or told India to shut up. But, from Tokyo, a China able to behave like that would look very different. A China wielding regional hegemony would, in that same caustic fellow's phrase, leave Japan as just "a higher-tech Canada" next to a giant much rougher than America. That is not how the Japanese want their 21st century to be.

You Help Me, I'll Help You

There is only one way—well, there is another, but it hardly bears thinking about—for Japan to avoid the risk of Canadaisation. It has to change its military relationship with America, so that America feels it is worth its while to keep its soldiers out there in Asia. At the moment, the basis of the American-Japanese arrangement is that Japan will do some of the job of protecting its own territory (though it would need American help against any serious attack), but America gets no Japanese help in any other fight. When communism was the global enemy, that was good enough for America. In post–communist days, when for many Americans Japan's trade surplus has become the new enemy, it is hard to see how so one-sided a bargain can endure.

The relationship between Japan and America has to become more like the one between Europe and America. The European allies of the United States now accept that, in return for continued American help in protecting their own lands, they will when necessary put their soldiers alongside America's in places farther afield; they are currently doing so in Bosnia. Japan has to start moving along a similar road.

The arguments against doing so are familiar, but with one exception no longer very convincing. A real alliance with America would fly in the face of Article 9 of the Japanese constitution, drawn up by the Americans after Japan's 1945 defeat. True, but Article 9 is a curious object; even the most cunning logic-chopper finds it hard to explain how the gleaming tanks and warships of Japan's current armed forces fit into the article's renunciation of "war as a sovereign right of the nation" and of the possession of all "land, sea and air forces". Such an alliance, it is also pointed out, would alarm Japan's second-world-war victims in Asia. . . .

The true obstacle is the fact that ordinary Japanese are understandably quite comfortable with the present arrangement (even though some feel like tearing the whole thing up when an Okinawan girl gets raped by American marines), and the lumbering processes of Japanese politics have not yet got round to explaining to ordinary Japanese why change is necessary.

A Matter of Redefinition

The straightforward way of dealing with the matter would be to change Article 9; but jaws in Tokyo drop at the thought of finding the necessary two-thirds majority of parliament, plus a majority in a referendum. The alternative is to go on gradually redefining what Article 9 permits. The Japanese love incremental reinterpretation. It is already agreed that Article 9 allows Japan to defend its own territory; since 1983, it has been accepted that American warships on their way to help Japan defend itself can themselves get Japanese help against an enemy attack; and, since President Clinton's visit to Japan last April, Japan can "in peacetime" provide fuel and other logistical aid to American forces engaged on problems outside Japan.

The next stages of the process might include, say, agreeing that Japan's fighting men can help to rescue Japanese and other civilians caught up in foreign crises, or under attack by terrorists abroad; letting Japanese minesweepers help clear mines off the coast of Korea (as they did almost unnoticed in 1951, during the Korean war); and saying that

American warships under attack can now be helped by Japanese ships and aircraft even if they are not actually pointing towards Japan when the attack happens. It should not take an interminable march down Redefinition Road before Japan discovers that its Article 9 is in fact compatible with Article 51 of the United Nations' charter, which accepts the right of collective self-defence—in short, before Japan joins the rest of the world in saying that self-defence does not have to wait until an invader actually clumps ashore on your beaches.

Put this to people in Tokyo, though, and you see why the machinery of Japanese government can be so bad at taking hard decisions. The man in the Ministry of Foreign Affairs agrees that America's demand for Japan to do more "must be squarely faced", but then falls silent. The man at the Defence Agency, having heroically dodged the question for ten minutes, says it "is our understanding" that the constitution prohibits collective defence. The Ministry of Finance veers down the side-road of what a change of policy might do to the budget. No ministry gives the impression of having made up its own mind, let alone sat down with the other ministries to discuss the matter.

Nor do the politicians provide much help. Some of the Liberal Democrats in the present government support an enlargement of Japan's military role, but are hamstrung by their party's coalition with the near-pacifist Socialists. Some members of the opposition New Frontier Party want a change, others passionately do not. It is an excellent example of how things can go adrift in Japan. Nobody says: "Here is a decision to be taken. Let us sit down and make up our minds."

The best hope of galvanising the system into action lies, curiously, in that barely thinkable alternative to a reworking of the American alliance. If Japan were one day to find itself without America and alongside a growing Chinese dragon, its only means of avoiding the bleakest sort of Canadaisation might be to go for the nuclear option. But building its own nuclear weapons would mean a terrifying confrontation with China; remember those Chinese missiles plopping down into the sea off Taiwan's ports last March, on much less provocation. It would meet intense opposition inside Japan. And because of Japan's special vulnerability to nuclear attack (about a third of its population and a solid chunk of its industry sit in that narrow, 350-mile strip of coastline between Tokyo and Osaka), the nuclear option would almost certainly need to be backed up by the acquisition of a protective anti-missile screen—the technological feasibility of which for Japan is still far from clear.

As alternatives go, this is the sort that makes the eyeballs roll. That is why, after Japan's coming election, which must be held by next summer, the assorted pieces of its policy-making apparatus may at last haul themselves together to give the country a serious role in the world. It will not be a moment too soon. Japan's armed forces, admirable though they are in many ways, are liv-

ing in a time-warp when it comes to the chief purpose of armed power....

The Deregimentation Job at Home

A new economy for the new century

When the bugler has blown [Reveille] outside the Ministry of Foreign Affairs, he can step a few yards up the road and do it again outside the Ministry of Finance. After the long, dark night—a GDP almost motionless from 1991 until last year, crashing home-loans companies and banks owed anything up to ¥100 trillion ($925 billion) in bad debts—Japan is this July opening its eyes to a scene very different from the decades when its economy looked like Superman and the bureaucrats who ran it felt pretty supermannish themselves.

For all the liveliness of the first new growth, the estimate in Tokyo these days is that the economy can hope to expand by an annual 2–3% in the next few years "if we do the right things" but not much above 1% if they don't. The men in the ministries now recognise how much some of the chief factors in the economic calculation have changed since the rip-roaring 1960s and 1970s. The greying of Japan, for instance, is well under way as the effect of past birth rates inexorably makes itself felt. The proportion of the population aged 65 and over, only 10% not many years ago, is soaring towards the 25% it is expected to reach by 2025, way above the figure for the United States and most of Europe.

This affects the calculations in two ways. The labour force will probably grow smaller, which means a smaller output unless productivity per man is improved by better education or by giving each worker more capital to use; and the money for both of those rescue devices will be harder to find if a rapidly ageing Japan consumes more and saves less of its annual income (though it has to be admitted that Japan's old-

sters are still surprisingly devoted savers). The other effect will be a large extra burden on the public-sector budget as the cost of pensions and old-age medical care rises. Since there may be other additions to the budget in coming years—more money for defence, for instance—the smaller number of people still at work will not enjoy either having to pay more tax or themselves getting less in state benefits.

The budget problem will be exacerbated if something is done about what has to be called the Squashing of Japan. The Japanese have in many ways escaped from the sort of economy they had a generation ago, when they were expected to produce heroically but consume very modestly; they now have most of the makings of a lively consumer society. The one glaring exception is the amount of living space available to them, and the concomitant inconveniences and deprivations of being squeezed so tightly together (see chart).

To a visitor from Europe travelling through the rabbit-hutch heartland of western Honshu between Tokyo and Osaka—even more to an appalled American—it seems obvious that the Japanese will before long have to start moving their homes out into those rugged, empty hills so close to the coast. The Japanese, admitting that they do not enjoy being squashed, in principle concur. But building earthquake-proof new towns on steep hillsides, and providing them with roads and railways and sewers and telecoms, is going to cost a lot of money—an extra 1% of GDP for some time ahead, on one qualified man's estimate. This will be another large claim on the amount of money the Japanese can lay their hands on for investment purposes.

The Japanese have also begun to recognise the cost of the cobweb of regulations and protectionism that still clings to so much of the economy. The gleaming efficiency of the country's big export industries conceals the Dickensian mixture of fusspottery and favouritism to be found elsewhere in Japan. The bureaucrats estimate that over 40% of the economy is still subject to a tangle of written regulations, and that does not count the array of unwritten conventions so readily used as weapons by Japanese in positions of authority. A lorry company has

A thrifty lot
Household savings rates as % of disposable income, 1995

France	
Japan	
Germany	
Britain	
United States	

Source: OECD

136

You're standing on my foot

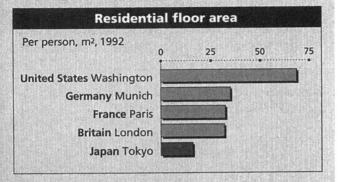

Residential floor area

Per person, m², 1992

| | 0 | 25 | 50 | 75 |

United States Washington
Germany Munich
France Paris
Britain London
Japan Tokyo

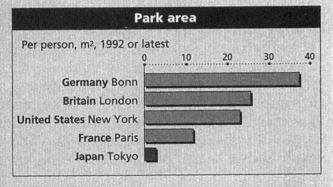

Park area

Per person, m², 1992 or latest

| | 0 | 10 | 20 | 30 | 40 |

Germany Bonn
Britain London
United States New York
France Paris
Japan Tokyo

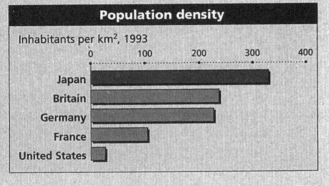

Population density

Inhabitants per km², 1993

| | 0 | 100 | 200 | 300 | 400 |

Japan
Britain
Germany
France
United States

Sources: UNCHS; World Bank; Japan Institute For Social and Economic Affairs; OECD

The Eyes Are Clearing

Most spectacularly, though, the events of the past few years have shaken Japanese faith in the men who are supposed to be steering the economy. The civil servants of the Ministry of Finance, the Ministry of International Trade and Industry and the Bank of Japan won a deservedly high reputation in the simpler days before 1980, when their task was to identify the industries that could beat foreign competitors, load them with cheap credit, point them at the export market and give the order to fire. Since 1980, the decisions have got trickier, and the supposed experts have made an unmistakable mess of the hyper-boom and consequent bust (see table) of the past dozen years.

First, they made sure the boom would get out of control by a half-hearted deregulation of Japan's financial system which failed to insist on some necessary competition between the different parts of the system, and also allowed the banks a dangerously inflationary definition of how much capital they possessed. The balloon continued to swell. Ordinary Japanese went on blowing into it, having been encouraged to believe that their government would never let a balloon go bang. The authorities made things worse by failing to raise interest rates soon enough, partly because they over-reacted to the jump in the value of the yen.

The balloon duly exploded. The men in the ministries thereupon compounded their first set of errors by making the opposite mistake: they kept interest rates higher than was justified for too long, and they did not increase public spending as much as they ought to have done (and claimed they were doing). The economy therefore stayed slumped longer than necessary.

No country's economic masters are blunder-free. But Japan's, who had begun to think they might be, now recognise that they got things outstandingly wrong in the 1980s and early 1990s.

A sobering contemplation of all this has produced various suggestions for improving the battered economy. Things being talked about are not necessarily things that will get done, least of all in Japan. But here are some of the more convincing ideas on parade in Tokyo.

1. The budget has to be reorganised. If Japan's savings rate continues to fall, it will eventually need more investment from abroad. Corporation tax and other imposts on business may therefore have to be cut from the present 50% to something more like the level foreign investors are willing to pay. As the economy thus becomes more internationalised, income tax will need to be cut, too. The revenue from direct taxes will fall steeply. But remember that demands on the budget will meanwhile be growing. The soaring number of over-65s will need more looking after; defence spending may have to rise;

a licence to operate within one prefecture, but has to do an expensive deal to work in the one next door; a former prime minister remembers that it took 37 trips to Tokyo to get permission for a traffic light in his home town to be moved; and so on.

The result of tens of thousands of such oddities is that prices are much higher than they would be in a freer system, and many Japanese continue to sit in comfortably unproductive jobs instead of moving to fill the gaps left by people of their father's generation now too old to work. Add the effect of the ingenious ways in which Japan still protects many of its domestic producers from foreign imports, and one guess is that regulation and protection between them make Japan something like a tenth poorer than it would otherwise have been.

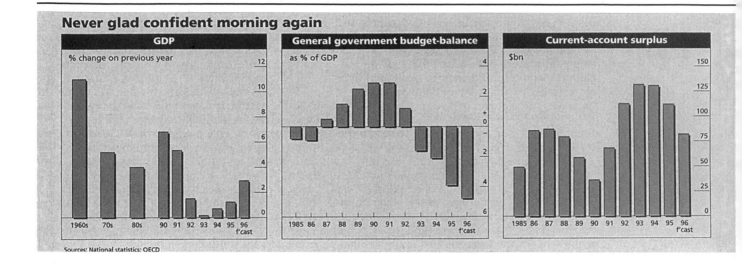

Never glad confident morning again

GDP — % change on previous year

General government budget-balance — as % of GDP

Current-account surplus — $bn

Sources: National statistics: OECD

giving the Japanese more square feet to live in will cost a lot of money. There is also a persuasive argument that the public-sector budget ought to run a sizeable surplus over the next decade or so in order to make sure that people now at work pay the cost of keeping themselves comfortable when they retire, and do not put the burden on the shoulders of what will then be a much smaller labour force.

It adds up to a sharp increase in indirect taxes. The consumption tax, Japan's equivalent of value-added tax, goes up from 3% to 5% next April. It may have to go quite a lot higher.

2. Education needs livening up. The present system worked well for the Japan of the 1960s; it produced large numbers of young people competent to deal with the fairly simple economy of those days. The harder task of the late 1990s—trying to keep up with an info-tech world—requires something sprightlier, a school system better at encouraging individual talent and a willingness to experiment.

Japan's schools are too uniform in what they teach and the way they teach it. The course lists of most of its universities look rather old-fashioned to visitors from the Anglo-American world. Improving things does not have to be impossibly expensive. Most of the extra money needed for higher education—America equips almost a third more of its young people with university degrees than Japan does—could come from a reform of the way the primary and secondary schools are run. If the heavy hand of the Ministry of Education were lifted, headmasters would have more independence, and parents' associations could make sure they used it efficiently. A more competitive school system would produce broader-minded and more inventive kids. But first somebody has to insert his hand into that ministerial hornets' nest.

3. The economy would benefit from more scientific research of the most basic sort. Japan's research-and-devel-opment record is in general good; the country spends proportionately more on R&D than America does, and much more of what it spends is privately financed, which on the evidence of several recent American studies stimulates productivity far more effectively than the government-financed sort. But Japan does not do enough basic research, the down-to-fundamentals slog which these American studies say is far and away the best productivity stimulant of all. A government committee last month recommended a large increase in research spending; if the budget can be made to afford it, that should stir up Japan's industrial productivity, which is on average well below America's.

4. More than anything else, a machete needs to be swung at the thicket of regulations which keep much of Japan's economy so unnecessarily inefficient. The areas in need of tidying up include some prestigious institutions. The various parts of the still-too-compartmental-ised financial system—the big "city" banks, the regional banks, the securities houses, the home-loans companies—should be given more freedom to compete with each other. The telecoms industry, though more competitive than it used to be, needs opening up still more if it is to cope with the Internet era. Most of the targets of the much-needed deregulation, though, are in territory less familiar to the outsider.

If you are a Japanese who wants a new job, you will be able to find only 29 kinds of employment through private employment agencies; for the rest, you have to go to the Ministry of Labour. If you wish to build a house or an office, the lobby organised by half a million little building firms has arranged with the Ministry of Construction an array of regulations which mean that you generally have to use dearer Japanese materials and designs rather than cheaper and often superior non-Japanese ones. When it comes to furnishing the house, you cannot find a store where you can buy at a reasonable price everything you need for every room, plus the garden; the retail-trade rules require you to tramp around town, getting chairs here, washbasins there, grass-seed the other place. The transport company that carries your furniture to the city where you plan to live will prove excessively expensive until it is able to get a multi-prefectural operating licence from the Ministry of Transport. And so the list runs on. It is the piling up of thousands of such petty, price-raising rules that makes the Japanese that tenth poorer than they ought to be.

When you put the question in Tokyo, you are assured that a serious assault on the regulatory jungle will soon begin; and, indeed, Japan's self-interest seems to demand it. Yet the doubts persist.

Who Will Say "This Way"?

Even the most worldly parts of the Tokyo bureaucracy—the Ministry of Foreign Affairs (which keeps a keen eye on the domestic economy), the Ministry of International Trade and Industry and the Ministry of Finance, in rough order of worldliness—are all happy little power centres whose power comes largely from operating the present system. Each has its own special links to business and to other parts of the civil service, and each feels itself in competition with the other top ministries. It is hard to

imagine them getting together of their own accord to take the painful decisions that are needed. And the lesser ministries are for the most part, almost by definition, defenders of things-as-they-are. Think how the Ministry of Labour and the Ministry of Construction and the Ministry of Transport will react to the self-disembowelling requirements [implicit in the last column on page 148]. As one senior civil servant puts it, "Each ministry is its own independent kingdom. Japan is a loose confederation of these kingdoms."

The case for hope is that more and more Japanese understand and admit the reasons why Japan needs to become economically more efficient—the dearer yen, the ageing workforce, the narrowing profit margins. Even so, it is by no means self-evident that this collection of semi-autonomous ministries, left to itself, will produce the necessary decisions. It needs a voice speaking from above. There needs to be, over the bureaucrats' heads, a higher region of decision-making where the problem is put, the different possible remedies are openly debated, and the solution preferred by a majority of Japanese emerges as the course of action the civil servants are required to follow.

In short, Japan needs something more like a proper multi-party system. It has not yet got one. This curious deficiency of Japanese democracy is the other big item on its turn-of-the-century agenda. . . .

The Nature Bestowed upon Men

Cheer up, Confucius and Luther were brothers after all.

From two parts of the world, there comes a by now crisply familiar answer to the question [whether or not the various parts of mankind all want to live in the same sort of political house]. No, say some serious people in the eastern part of Asia, it is a mistake to think that we East Asians want to import the system of politics you use in America and Europe; our whole background—our nature, even—is different, and so we need a different sort of politics. Quite so, say some learned men in the Muslim part of the world: good Muslims know that politics should be subject to God's will, and God's will is best interpreted by learned men, not by the moral anarchy you westerners call democracy. The Islamic objection and the Asian-values one start from very different premises, but they reach the same conclusion. For Europe and America to offer their western-invented democracy to everybody else in the world is at best condescending, and quite possibly a wicked neo-imperialist plot.

This survey is arguing that these Muslim and Asian-values conservatives are probably wrong, because they

are too pessimistic about the human condition. Of course, it would be folly for a western liberal to prescribe any particular version of democracy as the right one for any given country. The presidential model will work best in some places, the parliamentary one elsewhere; methods of voting will quite properly differ; not everybody is yet ready to start replacing the old-fashioned machinery of representative democracy with the cleaner-cut processes of direct democracy. But the idea underlying all the variations—the idea that the people should control the government, not the other way round, and that all sane adult human beings are equally entitled to share in the exercising of that control—is surely of universal application.

To believe otherwise is to believe that some parts of mankind will never be able to do what other parts can do. The advocates of universal democracy, rejecting that thought, assert the equality of mankind. That is why they plead not guilty of either condescension or imperialism.

The Past Is Not the Master

Those Japanese whose eyebrows rise when you say such things tend to reply as follows. Your western idea of democracy is based on a concept of individualism which we do not share, because our history and our culture have been different. Your view of individual responsibility as the foundation-stone of political and economic life is a product of the single-God religion of Jews and Christians, which has been the chief shaper of western culture. Anybody faced with the thought of a single, omnipotent God feels a sharpening of his own singularity, his special identity. It was this which produced the Reformation, that assertion of man's individual responsibility in his dealings with God, and it was the Reformation which led to the invention of democracy for men's dealings with each other.

We understand this, explain these Japanese. But it is different in the world of Buddhism and Confucianism and Shinto. For people brought up in such a culture, gods are a collection of relatively vague beings on the misty edge of life. What really matters in the ordering of people's conduct is the concept of the family. It is the family that gives a sense of continuity, as you pay your respects to the ancestors who shaped your children's bodies. Out of the family come the rules of what you may and may not do. And the family is not just father, mother, a couple of children and the hovering presence of those ancestors. It extends to a wider sort of family, once the feudal lord and his dutiful followers, now the captain of industry and his assiduous workforce.

All this helps to explain both why "loyalty" is such an important word in Japan, and why the head of any Japanese organisation commands so much authority. It also explains, conclude these Japanese, why the everybody-is-equal western notion of democracy may never take root in Japan.

Except for the last sentence, that is not a bad description of the undoubted differences which even at the end of the 20th century make Japanese and westerners scratch their heads about each other. But it does not add up to a reason for believing that they live in two permanently separate cultural capsules, and that Japan can never be what Europeans and Americans like to think of as a normal democracy.

There Was, and Will Be, Another Japan

For one thing, what this school of thought says about the effect of Buddhism and Confucianism is an over-simplification. Those two ideas also helped to shape much of the rest of north-eastern Asia, but they have not created in the other parts of the region a pattern of group loyalties as tightly organised as Japan's. The rest of the Confucian-Bud-dhist culture-area is relatively individualistic, and it currently seems to be producing, in Taiwan and Korea, infant multi-party democracies westerners can recognise.

More to the point, the argument deployed by these Japanese defenders of Japanese specialness is also an over-simplification of Japan itself. If you look at Japanese history—argue a number of vigorously counter-attacking Japanese such as Masakazu Yamazaki, of Osaka University, the author of "Individualism and the Japanese"—you will see that the country was not always such a sternly group-minded sort of place.

In the 15th and 16th centuries, in particular, a quite different Japan asserted itself. That was the time when the merchants of Kyoto and other towns, having made their fortunes by the individualist techniques of their trade, then spent some of the proceeds on encouraging the culture of the period. The culture they encouraged was not of a kind to appeal to roisterous feudal barons; it was contemplative poetry, the delicate formality of the tea ceremony, the calm privacy of the rocks-and-sand Japanese garden. Here was another Japan. The duties and loyalties of the family system are not the only force at work in the shaping of this country. There is an individualist side to the Japanese as well.

This individualist side is now reappearing, say the counter-attackers, as Japan emerges from its era of industrialisation and moves into a new period of its history. At work, Japanese will spend more of their time operating in small teams or in the do-it-alone processes of computerdom. After work, they will find that they have more money and longer leisure hours to put into the various interests—sports, music, dancing, eating and drinking—which they unmistakably share with the rest of the global consumer society. A more relaxed Japan, these optimists insist, will be a deregimented Japan, a country prepared to govern itself in new ways.

The other side of the Japan-is-special argument also has a hole in it. The defenders of the Japanese status quo are in effect saying that Euro-American democracy will work only for people who live in parts of the world shaped by the events that created the Euro-American culture—the birth of individualism in classical Athens, the rise of Christianity, the new waves of individualist change brought about by the Reformation and the Enlightenment. But this is plainly not true. One of the past half-century's most cheering sights has been the survival against great odds of democracy in India, the home of a very different culture. There are similar reasons for cross-fingers hope in South Africa, Turkey, Malaysia, Sri Lanka and other places dotted across the globe. This does not look like a one-culture phenomenon.

It seems much more likely that what is called the "western" idea of democracy in fact appeals to something people everywhere want to believe—that every human being is entitled to an equal say in how he is governed, and should not be denied it by others who claim that the business is best left to them. Perhaps it was merely good fortune which gave the West the first go at democracy. The West took its time about it, after all. The Reformation, the religious democracy which was the real start of the process, came pretty late in the West's 2,500-year history; and the political democracy which grew out of the Reformation had to wait until enough people had enough money in their pockets, and enough education in their minds, to insist on getting their democratic way.

It is a matter of timing, not of having to pass some curious cultural test. The demand for democracy exists everywhere, and demand begins to produce supply when enough independent-minded individuals feel able to look their governors in the eye and explain that from now on governing is something that everybody will do. It is striking that even in the Muslim world—the other chief centre of suspicion about "western" democracy—the spread of education and the growth of a new middle class may be starting to have the same effect. Some of the university-educated radicals of the Islamic revivalist movement now say that the interpretation of God's will should not be the monopoly of a more or less self-selected minority; every good Muslim's voice should be heard. If they say that about God's will, they can hardly insist that day-to-day government should be left in the hands of a minority.

The Time Could Hardly Be Better

But, if it is only a matter of timing, the Japanese are admirably placed to take the next step forward. They meet all the known conditions of full democratisation. They are among the richest people in the world, if you leave aside the squashed square footage they have to live in. They get a good basic education, even if they should be more adventurous in the way they teach their high-school and university students. And they are not at all, once you break through the surface politeness, a people without lively opinions of their own.

The Japanese, remember, are the inhabitants of a group of islands way out beyond the eastern end of the Eurasian land-mass. They were among the last Eurasians to feel the impact of the succession of philosophies and technologies to which that continent has given birth over the past 3,000 years. They were the last big country to open itself, only 130 years ago, to what modern America and Europe had to offer. They were, just a century ago, the last would-be imperial power in an already dying age of empires. If they come a little late to full democracy, it should be no surprise. It is part of a pattern; they take their time about these things.

There is also encouragement for Japan in something that seems to be happening inside the democracies of Europe and America. One of the reasons why many Japa-

nese have been reluctant to let go of their clannish approach to life, they explain, is that it provides a sense of belonging together, a comforting awareness that a man is not alone with his problems, that he has companions around him. Even liberal Japanese who accept that the time has come to move on to a more individualist-based system of politics and economics hope that it can be done without losing the spirit of community.

Quite a lot of Americans and Europeans are now prepared to say, with one qualification, that they see what these Japanese mean. There is no substitute for individual energy and individual decision-making as the engine of modern life. But this engine has to operate according to a set of generally accepted rules. Otherwise individualisation will become atomisation; and, in an increasingly urbanised world in which access to the means of consciousness-changing and the instruments of violence has become much easier than it used to be, atomisation is a frightening word.

Yes, says this sort of western liberal, the Japanese are right to want to preserve a sense of community. The one qualification is that so far the Japanese definition of "community" has been a group organised from the top down, in which the top man is offered much deference by those below him. That authoritarian definition will not work in the future. Tomorrow's community will have to be one in which the standards are defined, and freely agreed upon, by the community's members.

But this does not look like an insuperable problem. The Japanese liberal wants to move towards a more individualised Japan without letting go of a sense of community; these western liberals are trying to get back to the reassurance of community while holding on to the basics of individualism. They are, as it were, shuffling backwards towards each other.

The gap between Japan and the West may not be as wide as the pessimists have feared. Confucianism and Christianity are not the causes of two incompatible civilisations. The individual and the community may not be irreconcilable concepts. The old battle between authority and liberty continues, but in most places liberty seems to be on the advance. It was well put four centuries ago:

Foreign lands may differ from our own in manners and speech, but as to the nature bestowed upon men by heaven there cannot be any difference. Do not forget the common identity.

That was written by Seigwa Fujiwara, a Japanese who was a Buddhist priest and a Confucian scholar and who also wrote a book of rules for Japanese of his day who were setting out on voyages abroad. As their descendants embark on a new voyage, it is advice worth remembering on both sides of the water.

Article 8

Current History, December 1996

Japan as an "Ordinary Country"

Most American analysts ascribe an immutable inertia to Japan's security strategy. 'The United States–Japan alliance will never change unless there is a major external change in the security environment,' is a common refrain. This perspective, however, overlooks three fundamental transformations that are taking place inside the alliance. These transformations are in Japan's electoral system, its economy, and its military relations with the United States.

James Shinn

James Shinn is a senior fellow at the Council on Foreign Relations and the author of Weaving the Net: Conditional Engagement with China *(New York: Council on Foreign Relations Press, 1996).*

National security was barely mentioned in America's recent presidential contest; it figured even less in Japan's October 20 parliamentary election. But despite this inattention, the ground has shifted under the United States–Japan security alliance, a remarkably long-lived arrangement that may now be in slow-motion collapse—with profound consequences for the national security of both nations.

> *The most obvious result of Japan's October 20 election was a distinct bunching toward the center of the political spectrum.*

Most American analysts ascribe an immutable inertia to Japan's security strategy. "The United States–Japan alliance will never change unless there is a major external change in the security environment" is a common refrain. This perspective, however, overlooks three fundamental transformations that are taking place inside the alliance. These transformations are in Japan's electoral system, its economy and its military relations with the United States.

The evidence for some of these internal transformations is still spotty. Moreover, all three shifts are moving along different time frames. The transformation of Japan's electoral system was legislated three years ago, but only implemented with the October 20, 1996, election. The Japanese economy has been stalled for four years, but the underlying slowdown in long-term growth has been under way for a decade. The major military underpinnings of the United States–Japan alliance were knocked away with the collapse of the Berlin Wall, but political fault lines in the relationship had deepened well before 1989.

Rewriting the Electoral Rules

The most obvious result of Japan's October 20 election was a distinct bunching toward the center of the political spectrum. Candidates on the extremes were lopped off. Smaller parties took a drubbing; the exception was the Communists, who survived, but at levels so low as to be irrelevant. The once-powerful Socialists have been virtually wiped out.

Three major parties were left standing: the Liberal Democratic Party (LDP), headed by Prime Minister Ryutaro Hashimoto; the Shinseito (Renewal Party), headed by Ichiro Ozawa; and the Minshuto (Democratic Party) headed by Yukio Hatoyama and Naoto Kan. All three parties have their roots in the LDP's feuding intraparty factions known as *habatsu*. But for this election these three habatsu mutated into formally contesting political parties, feuding more on policies and less on personalities, and under very different rules of the electoral game.

Japanese voters did not suddenly cluster toward the center: the districts and the rules, not the voters, changed dramatically. Popular pressure for political reform has been building for years, culminating in the passage in

1993 of a new electoral law under Prime Minister Morihiro Hosokawa's cabinet that was put into practice this October. Under the new law 300 members were elected from single-seat, winner-take-all districts; 200 were elected from party slates in 11 nationwide districts.

The previous system of electing 511 members from multiple-seat districts had the perverse feature of pitting party members against each other in almost every electoral district. This corroded party solidarity and discounted the value of national party affiliation. The peculiar mathematics of the multiple-seat district system also left plenty of room for smaller parties to take Diet seats. The new system has created—in principle—more powerful national parties, with greater member loyalty and greater differentiation on national policy.

The new system has also ostensibly undermined the cohesion of the habatsu, whose constant jockeying and backbiting have dominated Japanese politics for decades. Under the old system a local candidate had limited faith in the national party, which was fielding at least one direct competitor in his district, so he relied instead on his habatsu connection to help raise funds and extract favors from the bureaucracy for his constituents. The candidate distinguished himself from his local opponents with "pork," not policy.

Stronger national parties should also retrieve authority from government bureaucrats, long viewed as their trusted agents. The Japanese term for these officials, kanryo, had none of the pejorative ring of "bureaucrat"—until recently. But today not only do the political parties no longer entrust policy to bureaucratic discretion, they also no longer trust the bureaucrats personally. Rival centrist parties mean alternating governments. The kanryo must therefore learn to serve two masters. The seeds of distrust were sown in the LDP during its months of bitter exile from power in 1993, when, as LDP veteran and former defense chief Koichi Kato told this author, "We were suddenly cut off from all power. The kanryo stopped returning our calls. We were nobodies."

Is there any evidence that the politicians are turning on the kanryo? All three centrist parties consistently bashed the bureaucrats during the campaign. Reform of the bureaucracy is one of the formal goals of Hashimoto's LDP. The co-head of the Minshuto, Naoto Kan, made his political name by tangling with and ultimately subduing the bureaucrats when he was health minister. And Ichiro Ozawa has had it in for the bureaucrats for years. The kanryo were given a shocking preview of this new political landscape when their leading candidate for the Ministry for International Trade and Investment (MITI) vice-minister post was publicly humiliated and fired in the early days of Prime Minister Hosokawa's term, allegedly at Ozawa's insistence. This unprecedented intervention was widely described as "killing a rooster to scare the monkeys."

Economic Slowdown and the Budget Squeeze

The second fundamental transformation underlying the October 20 election is Japan's lackluster economic performance. The economy has stalled for two reasons. One is long term, predictable, slow-moving, and inevitable; the second is short term, unexpected, fairly sudden, and entirely avoidable.

The long-term cause of the slowdown is economic maturation. Japan's labor force is rapidly aging and will soon begin to shrink. Japanese industrial investment has been consistently high for decades, to the point where the ratio of accumulated capital to output is more than three to one—the highest in the world. Shrinking marginal returns have triggered a tailing off of domestic investment and led to foreign direct investment (FDI) instead. Moreover, Japanese productivity growth has slowed to a snail's pace and is unlikely to accelerate; the rapid "catch-up" phase that relied on foreign basic technology is over. All this means that long-term growth rates for Japan over the next decade will hover around 2 to 3 percent at most—a staggering letdown from the 8 to 10 percent rates seen in the 1970s.

The short-term reason for Japan's slowdown is the macroeconomic equivalent of a deep ditch. The Japanese economy has been operating well below capacity for almost five years. The current gap between actual and potential GDP is between 2 and 3 percent (the so-called deflationary gap). This gap is due to cyclic shifts and poor financial regulation, which triggered a gut-wrenching asset deflation after a huge speculative run up from 1985 through 1993 created the "bubble economy."

Japan's deflationary gap was deepened by the pent-up pressures of adjusting to the international economy. As Japanese savings and investment poured offshore they created a consistent balance of payments surplus. This capital outflow was compounded by a thicket of Japanese nontariff barriers to imports. When the Japanese authorities were unable to consistently recycle these surpluses offshore, the yen soared, but because of the protectionist barriers, imports grew slowly. The yen stayed high and Japanese exports were hammered, with predictably dismal effects on business and consumer confidence.

Flat private sector demand left only government monetary or fiscal policy to pull the economy out of the ditch. But monetary policy has been singularly ineffective. Even though the Bank of Japan discount rate is at a record low it has failed to stimulate growth because the banking system is still incapacitated by the collapse of the bubble economy. The Finance Ministry estimated the sum of nonperforming loans for all financial institutions at 35 trillion yen (about $300 billion) as of mid-1996;

some private estimates run much higher. It will take the banking sector between three and five years to deal with the bad loan problem. In the meantime, the banking system is a fragile mechanism with which to stimulate aggregate demand.

The other remaining government policy tool is fiscal policy, in the form of deficit spending to reflate demand. The limited recovery in 1996 is due primarily to government spending on public works projects. But the Japanese government deficit is now 4 percent of GDP, enormously high by historical levels and more than twice that of the United States deficit in 1996.

The net effect of Japan's long- and short-term economic slowdown, combined with the aging population, is an enormous squeeze on government spending. The Ministry of Finance budgeters are awash in red ink and are looking to squeeze every item of government expenditure, including the "luxury" of national defense. There was ample evidence of this squeeze in the rancorous fiscal 1997 budgetary infighting that saw military spending capped at a 2.9 percent growth rate, not the 4.5 percent requested by the Japan Defense Agency (JDA).[1]

The Alliance Adrift

The third transformation in Japan—the slowest moving and longest in the making—is the loosening of the military alliance with the United States. The underpinnings of this alliance have been deeply eroded or eliminated by the post–cold war transition.

The Soviet military threat that sustained the American-Japanese alliance throughout the cold war is rusting away or being broken up for scrap. China's growing military muscle is a future threat currently far outmatched in equipment and training (if not in size) by the SDF, not to mention United States forces. The standoff on the Korean peninsula has been sustained for 40 years.

It is still possible that engagement rather than confrontation can bring China and perhaps even North Korea into the community of nations. In the absence of a clear and present danger, neither American nor Japanese citizens see the need for a heavily armed alliance. While poll data suggest that the Japanese public still believes the United States will defend Japan in the event of an attack, the Japanese public remains strongly negative about the presence of American troops. This deep inconsistency in popular views toward the alliance would be unimportant if Japanese politicians had invested political capital in "selling" the merits of the United States alliance to the public, but they have not.

The alliance has been marked by ambivalence and indirection in public discourse in Japan, and sustained with a series of commitments to appease pacifists and neutralists. LDP politicians have observed the so-called 1 percent de-

fense-ceiling rule (that is, defense spending cannot exceed 1 percent of GNP), strictly interpreted the Article 9 "renunciation of war" clause of the constitution, and split hairs over the legality of "collective security." The net effect has been not only to buy off the neutralists at home, but to neutralize American pressure on Japan to pay more of the cost and to increase its own defense efforts.

The advocates in the United States of forward deployment argue that Japan pays $5 billion toward the cost of stationing troops in Japan, and that it is cheaper for the United States to keep these troops there than to bring them home. And although Japan is far more generous in its burden-sharing contribution than the Europeans, it still does not pay for the real cost of American forces in Japan, such as personnel expenses, equipment, and research and development costs associated with these. This is, by any measure, a tremendous bargain for Japan.

Sensitivities about the inequity in burden sharing have been inflamed by accumulated trade friction, which has been aggravated by a huge bilateral trade imbalance. The American public perceives Japan as a closed market defended by truculent bureaucrats who respond only to pressure tactics. The mirror-image perception in Japan is of bullying, threatening, "crybaby" Americans who must be firmly dealt with by a Japan that can say "no."[2]

What will be the net effect of these three transformations on Japan's national security strategy? Japan must decide on five major aspects of its strategy: the roles and missions of the SDF; the level and nature of the country's defense spending; the standing of the JDA within the government; Japan's quest for a UN Security Council seat and role in UN peacekeeping missions; and, most delicately, the question of nuclear weapons.

Threats, Roles, and Missions

The electoral transformation will force party leaders to make clear pronouncements on Japan's national security—and threats to that security—rather than the carefully hedged platitudinous mumbling that has passed for official foreign policy statements. Leaders of the three centrist parties will make clearer statements because they need to differentiate themselves from one another on policy in order to get votes. They will also have less need to mollify the left, since it has been marginalized by the new electoral system.

A frank public discussion of Japan's national security concerns will probably fan Japan's latent nationalism. Ambitious politicians from the three centrist parties will likely play to this nationalism, cautiously but regularly, and to the potent sympathies of the Association of War Bereaved Families—one of Prime Minister Hashimoto's support groups. Over time, a prime minister's visit to the Yasukuni Shrine of the War Dead will be as commonplace as a United States president's visit to the Tomb of the Unknown Soldier.

A real policy debate means strong opinions. And because these strong opinions will be broadcast to the public, they will also be heard by Japan's allies and adversaries. This is likely to sharpen rhetorical exchanges with China and both Koreas. Americans may not like all of what they hear of this public debate.

Japan's economic transformation—especially the huge and growing stock of Japanese investment in Southeast Asia—will affect national security by pulling the SDF's role and missions farther south. Defense of the sea-lanes was the main argument used to justify the expansion of the SDF's mission under Prime Minister Zenko Suzuki in 1981. Japan's key sea-lanes run through Southeast Asia. The "Suzuki Sea-Lane Doctrine" discarded the concept of convoy defense in favor of sea routes, which has broadened to the defense of maritime space. Defending an area requires a far more sophisticated and aggressive military capability, which can now be linked with the protection of the 90,000 Japanese nationals and more than $60 billion of cumulative FDI in Southeast Asia (these figures exclude China and Korea but include Taiwan and Hong Kong).

Defense Spending

The ruling party may intervene in the budget process and push defense spending above the 1 percent GNP limit if the United States begins a force withdrawal, or if a serious security threat suddenly emerges in East Asia. The fiscal 1997 defense cap showed classic "incrementalism": every budget claimant received a marginal increase based on precedent, plus LDP log-rolling. But the incremental pattern may not hold, and the Finance Ministry may not call the shots. As Kent Calder has persuasively argued, LDP politicians have periodically stepped in to impose big changes on both budgets and agencies in periods of discontinuity or when challenges have been made to the governing system. "In times of political turbulence and flux, politicians take unusual initiative in policymaking, and stability-oriented bureaucrats and big businessmen defer to and even encourage such political initiative and preeminence."[3]

The ruling party would, however, encounter stubborn popular resistance. Polling data from 1985 through 1995 have been consistent on this point: about 60 percent of the Japanese public believe Japan's military spending is at the "right level"; 30 percent favor a "decrease," and 10 percent favor an "increase." Burden sharing is even less popular. The case for burden sharing, or for that matter the logical link between United States forces in Japan and America's security guarantee for Japan, has not been made persuasively to the Japanese public.

It will be easier for the ruling party to make the case for defense spending than for burden sharing. The opportunistic rebuttal in a public debate on burden sharing is likely to be that "if Japan must spend $5 billion on defense, then let's spend it on our own SDF, not on these increasingly unreliable and ungrateful American mercenaries." A public counterargument by the ruling party that $5 billion is a terrific bargain will open Japan to pressure from the Americans to pick up the full tab for United States forces. Either way, the burden-sharing issue is going to become even more controversial, and the odds of Japan's paying a larger share under the budget squeeze are slim.

Other aspects of Japan's economic transformation—epecially the FDI flood and the excess capacity of domestic manufacturing—will make weapons sales even more important to domestic contractors. However, a drive to increase arms production will collide with Japan's self-imposed "ban" on weapons exports. The arms export ban is even older than the 1 percent rule, and was introduced by Prime Minister Eisaku Sato in 1968 for reasons of political expedience. But exports are the fastest way to increase unit volumes without spending more defense dollars. If a public debate over Japan's national security justifies increased defense spending on the basis of potential security threats, then the moral onus of exporting weapons—and competing with the Americans and Europeans—is likely to fade quickly. The United States will restrict the re-export of United States-supplied defense technology, which means that Japan's weapons suppliers will test the market first with dual-use components and subsystems based on their own research and development.

A New Standing for the Defense Agency

The new parties will need contending platforms to stand on, and defense will be an area in which aspiring politicians from all three centrist parties can attempt to make their name. As a result, the JDA is likely to become a cabinet-level post, rather than a mere "agency." And as the Diet takes over more defense policy control from the Foreign Ministry, it is likely to peel away some of the layers of civilian bureaucrats with which the JDA has been muffled since its inception. The Ministry of Home Affairs—read the police—has had a strong hand in the JDA since its creation. Party elders like Masaharu Gotoda have used their long-time connection with the police to muzzle the SDF—for Gotoda was old enough to remember the military assassins of prewar Japan. But elders like Gotoda will soon pass.

The loosening of the alliance with the United States will probably act as the biggest boost to the standing of the SDF. From being a secondary arm of the United States armed forces, the SDF must reinvent itself as a credible military, capable of defending Japan against all threats. This will shock the SDF out of bureaucratic lethargy and into long-overdue reforms, such as a real joint military command (the SDF today has minimal interservice coordination).

Gaining a Security Council Seat

The centrist parties will support—and compete to take credit for obtaining—permanent seat for Japan on the UN Security Council. The price for this seat will be a clear statement that Japan will commit troops to UN peacekeeping efforts. The prestige of having a Security Council seat will overcome domestic resistance to dispatching troops for such operations. This resistance was finessed by legislation authorizing Japanese participation in UN peacekeeping operations that the Diet passed in June 1992, and ignored in fact by the broad use of Japanese troops in the UN's Cambodian peacekeeping operation. In any case, domestic resistance to peacekeeping came largely from the Komeito and from the Socialists, but Komeito is weakened and the Socialists are on the ropes.

Over the longer run, however, the mystique of the UN will wear off as Japanese peacekeeping troops come back in wooden boxes. Moreover, the economic squeeze will make Japan less willing to foot the bill for UN activities (Japan supplied 15 percent of UN funding in 1996), or at least more insistent on closely scrutinizing those activities it does bankroll.

With a seat on the Security Council, Japan will have to make tough choices under very bright lights. These choices will underscore Japan's increasingly independent diplomatic course from the United States. The most obvious divergence will likely be on problems in the Middle East, where Japan has always been uncomfortable with American support for Israel. This in turn will inject more tension into the United States–Japan military alliance, and will likely increase the distance.

Nuclear Power and Nuclear Weapons

Japan's huge nuclear power program will hit a brick wall because of the new electoral system. Plant siting is an election-district hot button, and MITI's ability to mollify anxious local residents will be weakened. The enormously expensive breeder-reactor program will probably go first. Japan will be on much higher moral ground when it presses for nonproliferation if it stops stockpiling plutonium (used to fuel reactors). The Japanese government currently holds over 4,800 kilograms of plutonium, a huge quantity by any measure.

Persistent Chinese nuclear testing and exports of nuclear technology (particularly to Pakistan) will provide a convenient rationale for Japan to cut off foreign aid to China. The rationale for this largesse—the belief that trade and investment with China will "civilize" or moderate China—is rapidly fading. According to Michael Green, "the core of Japanese strategic thinking on China has shifted from commercial liberalism to reluctant realism."[4] The budget squeeze will accelerate this shift: Why give scarce yen to a China that threatens us, rather than spend it on our own defense?

A reduction in conventional American forces will still leave a nuclear umbrella over Japan; without a trip wire of American soldiers on the ground, however, it will be less credible. Anxious Japanese defense planners will thus accelerate the development and deployment of ballistic missile defense systems.

Anti-missile defense is entirely consistent with Japan's nuclear "allergy" and the three nonnuclear principles (that Japan will not make, deploy, or allow nuclear weapons to pass through its territory). If Chinese officials are willing to threaten the United States, as they did during the 1996 Taiwan Straits incident, when there was talk about "turning Los Angeles into a lake of fire," they could also threaten Japan with nuclear blackmail at some point—perhaps deliberately, probably obliquely, possibly inadvertently—and this would galvanize Japan's anti-missile program. China's current arsenal of 300 warheads can easily reach Japan, whose population and industry are highly concentrated. If China uses missiles to intimidate either Taiwan or another Asian neighbor, or even if North Korea attempts to do the same, it could trigger a frenzied and sustained program of anti-missile defense in Japan.

What Kind of Japan—and the American Response

In the coming decades, Japan will be a harder edged actor in the international system. The leadership will take clearer policy positions, stake out Japan's vital interests, and make fewer but more credible commitments: "We will do this, we will not do that."

Japan as a harder edged ally will insist on clarifying some of the ambiguity of the current alliance with the United States: "We will assist in a second Korean War; we will sit on the sidelines in a Taiwan Straits War." The Japanese will insist on their rights to prior consultation and a conditional veto on the use of Japanese bases by American forces involved in regional conflicts.

The public debate about Japan's national security and the threats to that security, will further erode the deep-seated popular neutralism that is passing with time. World War II ended 50 years ago; a new generation is in charge in Tokyo with little memory, no guilt, and modest education about the war.

What do these changes in Japan's national security strategy imply for United States policy toward Japan? There is nothing inherently threatening about the military capabilities of a democratic and well-armed Japan, so long as doubts about Japan's strategic intent are satisfied. Public discussions of Japan's national security should be promoted between the United States Congress and the Diet, focusing on the intentions and capabilities of Japan's increasingly powerful military forces. Similar discussions should take place within multilateral security forums, such as the Association of Southeast Asian Nations Regional Forum. Japan can continue to be a model of transparency, nonproliferation, and confidence-building in Asia.

The United States should deepen its security dialogue with Japan on its commitment to Japan's defense and its expectations about Japan's role within the alliance. This is needed to eliminate the cloud of uncertainty that hangs over the relationship, a cloud that will inevitably darken as budgetary pressures build up over the next five years in both countries. This uncertainty could lead to accelerated Japanese rearmament and a more independent security posture, and thus trigger a dangerous arms race in East Asia.

It would be helpful to move away from the idea that United States security depends on a given level of troops forward deployed in Asia—or in Japan, for that matter. The current deployment of 100,000 troops is widely taken as a test of United States military resolve in the region. Instead, flexibility should be built into mutual expectations about force levels. At the same time, the United States should make clear that its security guarantee for Japan requires an American military presence here, and that it would be extremely expensive and risky to attempt to provide that guarantee "across the horizon" from Hawaii or Guam, with no bases in Japan. This is sometimes derided as a "magic carpet" strategy that calls for United States forces to show up instantly just as an invading force reaches Japan's shores.

Both sides must also tackle the issue of burden sharing. The United States should make it clear that cost pressures alone will accelerate a United States force withdrawal from Japan. The Japanese government will have to make some tough choices: either increase burden sharing; accept lower United States force levels; or replace United States troops with (even more expensive) Japanese SDF forces.

The United States should jointly negotiate with the Japanese government a clear understanding on responding to security contingencies in Asia; this would remove the kind of ambiguity that could result in another fiasco like Japan's delayed response to the Persian Gulf War. Without this clarification and underlying political commitment, United States military planners will have to leave the SDF out of contingencies, rather than risking dependence on Japanese support that may not be forthcoming. If American soldiers die in a nearby Asian action—such as armed conflict in Korea—and Japan does not support the United States, the alliance would probably be damaged beyond repair.

Americans should not worry too much about Japan's possible acquisition of offensive weapons systems or so-called power projection capability. Good sense, internal debate, and cold calculation of Japan's neighbors' reaction to such a capability will keep this in bounds. But the United States should seriously reconsider the scale of the current one-way flow of military technology to Japan, if only for reasons of declining leverage, its impact on industrial competitiveness, and its sheer inequity.

The United States should not badger the Japanese into adopting specific defense programs or drag them kicking and screaming into a strategy of "collective security"; Japanese statesmen and analysts are more than capable of thinking through the new realities of post–cold war security. They will have to build domestic public consensus on the strategy and sacrifices necessary to maintain the security of Japan as an "ordinary country," including the irreplaceable value of the United States–Japan security alliance. Such a public consensus in Japan will be a far more solid and sustainable foundation than the shifting sands on which the alliance stands uneasily today.

Notes

1. The JDA is the civilian agency that administers the Self-Defense Forces (SDF), which include the army, navy, and air force.

2. Ironically, Japan's trade surplus is plunging as a result of yen appreciation and the lagging consequences of Japan's foreign direct investment. The current account surplus peaked at about 15 trillion yen in 1993 and dropped to 10 trillion yen in 1995; estimates for 1996 are as low as 5 trillion to 6 trillion yen.

3. Kent Calder, *Crisis and Compensation: Public Policy and Political Stability in Japan* (Princeton: Princeton University Press, 1988), p. 448.

4. Michael Green and Ben Self, "The Changing Dynamics of Japan's China Policy: From Commercial Liberalism to Reluctant Realism," *Survival*, Spring 1996.

Article 9

The New York Times, December 13, 1995

Japan's Feminine Falsetto Falls Right Out of Favor

Nicholas D. Kristof

TOKYO, Dec. 12—Smiling beatifically at the restless shoppers, more like a saint than an elevator operator, Hiromi Saito opened her mouth to do her duty.

"I thank you from the bottom of my heart for favoring us by paying an honorable visit to our store," she said in The Voice. "I will stop at the floor your honorable self is kind enough to use, and then I will go the the top floor."

The Voice is as fawning as her demeanor, as sweet as syrup, and as high as a dog whistle. Any higher, and it would shatter the crystal on the seventh floor.

Most Japanese women cannot muster the Mount Fuji-like heights of Miss Saito's voice, but their voices regularly skirt the foothills. For a quick gauge of the status of women in Japan, just cock your ear and listen to Japanese women speak—or squeak.

European women no longer rearrange their bodies with corsets, and Chinese no longer cripple their daughters by binding their feet. But many Japanese women speak well above their natural pitch, especially in formal settings, on the phone or when dealing with customers.

"When slaves talk, they have their slave language," said Fujiko Hara, an interpreter in Tokyo. "Those girls are trained to be robots. With the elevator girls, you don't see a person but a doll."

Yet in a sign that the dolls are coming to life, women's voices in Japan are dropping significantly. Japan still has many squeakers, but a growing number of women speak in natural voices.

"When girls speak in really high voices, I just want to kick them in the head," said Mari Shimakura, a 15-year-old in Tokyo. "It's totally fake and really annoying. It gives me a headache. Mom tells me I speak in too low a voice, and that I should raise it. But I can't change it."

One standard-bearer of the changing times is Miyuki Morita, who was rejected when she first tried to enter broadcasting, as a disk jockey. "They said my voice was too somber, and they wouldn't hire me," Ms. Morita recalled. She eventually found a job with a television station in northern Japan, and she tried to imitate other female journalists who spoke in high voices.

"Then when I saw a video of myself, I saw my face, but it wasn't my voice," she said. "It didn't sound convincing. So I settled back to my voice."

That voice is now among the best known in Japan. Ms. Morita is the evening anchor of NHK News, the most popular television news program in the country.

Other evidence that women's voices are dropping comes from taped announcements on subway platforms in Tokyo. Older recordings are clearly higher pitched than the newer ones.

The pitch of female singers is also falling. Tadahiro Murao, professor of music at Aichi University of Education, has analyzed the frequency of 200 songs dating from the 1950's, and found a clear trend. "From the late 1980's, the pitch of female songs has dropped dramatically," Professor Murao said. "In fact, there was a popular duet last year in which the female vocalist sang the lower part, and the male sang the higher part."

Why have women traditionally spoken in high voices in Japan?

"Your voice in the office and your voice at home are totally different," said Harumi Yamamoto, who works at a computer company in Tokyo. "The point is that when you are with a customer, you want to be polite. If you're being courteous, your voice naturally rises."

Almost everyone agrees that high pitch is wrapped up in the Japanese preoccupation with courtesy. In polite conversation in Japan, people routinely denigrate themselves and try to sound unsure even about things they are certain of.

One technique women use to sound tentative, and therefore polite, is to raise their pitch and let their sentences trail off, the way Americans sometimes ask questions.

"A lower voice sounds too bullying, too aggressive, too manly," said Julie Saito, a reporter at Asahi Shimbun.

Ms. Saito said Japanese men seem attracted by high voices and girlish behavior, which some Japanese women then emulate. The attraction to young girls is known here as the Loli-con—short for Lolita Complex—and it is a Japanese phenomenon, the basis for endless psychoanalyses of the Japanese mind and libido.

"A high voice sounds more cute, more like a girlish image of women," Ms. Saito said. "In the United States I project more confidence, while in Japan I find I act in a more cute way."

Ms. Saito, like many bilingual women, speaks in a higher pitch in Japanese. Indeed, she said that when she returned recently from a visit to the United States, she telephoned her Japanese friends and they said, "Your voice sounds so low."

To be sure, in normal conversation at home or with friends, Japanese women sound normal to an American ear. But listen to the same woman apologizing to her boss on the phone, and her voice may go off the register.

"I have a lot of friends who visit me from Western countries, and although they don't understand Japanese, they told me that they'd noticed that Japanese women speak in shrill, infantile voices," said Hideki Kasuya, professor of speech science at Utsunomiya University, a male expert on the pitch of women's voices in Japan. "I had felt the same thing myself, and that is why I started my research."

Professor Kasuya has found that female television announcers in the United States speak in a significantly lower pitch than female Japanese announcers. But his latest measurements this year found that the voices of female Japanese announcers had dropped noticeably since his first survey four years ago.

In the meantime, Hiromi Saito and 18 other elevator operators continue to speak in falsetto as they announce the floors at the Mitsukoshi Department

Store in the Ginza district here. Miss Saito, as chief of the unit, trains the newcomers to raise their pitch.

"Girls with a lower pitch have a struggle when they come here to work at first," she said. "But after a month or so, you see a transformation. And after three months, they have a completely different voice."

Why do this?

"It may be hard for Americans to understand," said Sayori Iwata, a Mitsukoshi spokeswoman, "but in Japan, it's considered beautiful to sacrifice yourself for the service of others."

Article 10   *New York Times*, September 10, 1996

Welfare as Japan Knows It: A Family Affair

Nicholas D. Kristof

TOKYO, Sept. 9—Genially welcoming a visitor into his "home," the piece of cardboard on which he sleeps in the Shinjuku train station here, Katsuo Kawagoe drew deeply on a cigarette and recalled the times he had applied for public assistance from the Government.

"They just said, 'What do you want?'" he remembered. "They were not helpful. The only way you can get aid is if you're over 65 or if you're really sick and taken to the hospital."

"When I turn 65, I'll apply for welfare," Mr. Kawagoe, who is 53, added between racking, tubercular coughs. "But until then I've got no chance if I'm healthy."

Japan has a welfare system that in some ways makes even the new, dismantled American system seem a model of generosity. Applicants in Japan are obliged to get help first from their families, and a poor person physically able to work is not eligible for help—whether or not the person actually has a job.

From some perspectives, this system has worked brilliantly. The country's already strong family ties have been strengthened, and the main safety net is the family rather than the Government. The number of Japanese in the basic welfare program has declined sharply over the last half century, as people became better off and built up savings.

Today only 0.7 percent of the population receives benefits—compared with the 4.8 percent of Americans who get grants from Aid to Families With Dependent Children or the 9.7 percent who receive food stamps. About 2.3 percent of Americans receive grants through the Supplemental Security Income program, which serves the elderly, blind and disabled.

To be sure, Japan's welfare system operates in a very different milieu from America's. Only 1 percent of Japanese births are to unwed mothers. That compares with a percentage that keeps climbing in the United States and has now reached 30 percent.

Japan also has a far lower percentage of drug addicts than the United States has, a much lower unemployment rate, a much more egalitarian distribution of wealth, a greater sense of family obligation and an abiding sense of shame that colors almost every aspect of life.

Scholars say that the system in Japan almost never breeds dependence, and they suggest that the Japanese approach has emphasized the work ethic and the importance of family ties.

Caseworkers rigorously check applicants and drop by their homes regularly to make sure that they do not have banned luxuries like cars or air conditioners, and fraud seems extremely rare.

For all these reasons, the welfare system seems to have broad public support in Japan. In fact, instead of grumbling about welfare mothers in Cadillacs, people sometimes carp about how the authorities are too harsh to the poor.

"This system is financed by the taxpayers, so it's natural that we should be rigorous," said Tokuyuki Kase, an official in the Ministry of Health and Welfare in Tokyo. "Our standards are very strict."

Yet if the absence of a broad public safety net focuses people's minds on the need to stay on the tightrope, it is also clear that when some people inevitably do slip, there is often nothing to save them.

Last April, a 77-year-old woman and her disabled son starved to death in their Tokyo apartment. The local authorities apparently knew that the family was having trouble getting food, although it does not seem that they formally applied for welfare. After the bodies were found, the authorities discovered a diary kept by the woman, whose last entry read: "Every day is a struggle, and I want to die soon."

In another case, a 79-year-old widow was threatened with loss of welfare benefits unless she got rid of her air conditioner. She did, then collapsed in her apartment during the next heat wave and had to be taken to the hospital, where she spent six weeks recovering.

"This is a very cold society," said Yoshifumi Osaka, a homeless man who said he had forgotten his exact age but thought he was almost 80. Mr. Osaka ran away from his wife and children a year and a half ago, he said, "because they picked on me," and ever since has lived in a cardboard cocoon he built in Shinjuki station.

Like many homeless people, he says he has not applied for welfare benefits because he would never get them.

Japan does have two elements of a social welfare program that far surpass anything in the United States: universal medical care and comprehensive day care.

Everyone has access to doctors and hospitals at affordable prices, with the services free for the poor. And neighborhood nurseries throughout Japan provide excellent care for children from six months old to school age, if mothers work, for a modest fee that is waived for low-income families.

But while the United States offers a network of public assistance programs, Japan has no food stamps and relies principally on a single program of cash grants. Anybody who is poor is eligible, but only if the person has no family or assets and is unable to work.

"We go to financial institutions and check for savings accounts or other money," sid Kanji Tanaka, a welfare caseworker in Kawasaki, a city just south of Tokyo, "and we look up the family registrations to check if there are relatives, and then we contact them."

Mr. Tanaka also visits the applicant's home to insure that it is not too lavish and that it does not have anything regarded as a luxury.

An applicant who owns a home is normally advised to sell it and use the proceeds until the money runs out—and then to apply again. In May, a 96-year-old man was dropped from welfare because it came to light that he had $30,000 in savings. The caseworkers told him to use that up and then reapply.

A welfare worker has a caseload of about 60 in Japan, and there is time for regular, unscheduled visits to recipients' homes. The caseworkers have great discretion in handling cases, as well as considerable moral authority in advising recipients what to do.

Because able-bodied people are normally excluded on the ground that they could find work if they wanted to, the largest group of recipients is the elderly—many of them bedridden widows—amounting to 44 percent of households getting aid.

Households with a sick or handicapped person account for another 41 percent. About 9 percent are single mothers, but in Japan most of them are divorced or widowed, rather than never married.

Akemi Watanabe, a caseworker in Kawasaki, said 2 of the 60 recipients in her caseload were single mothers, both abandoned by their husbands. Both work part-time while receiving a supplementary welfare check.

Most single mothers in Japan do not get benefits, because they have parents or other family members who can support them. Because of this, single mothers are likely to live with their parents, so that the child grows up under the supervision of several adults.

The mothers are extremely reluctant to accept welfare.

"The Japanese have a tendency to regard it as extremely shameful to receive welfare, and so they are hesitant," said

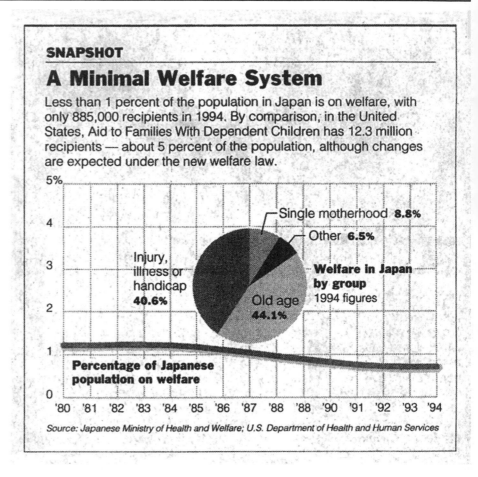

SNAPSHOT

A Minimal Welfare System

Less than 1 percent of the population in Japan is on welfare, with only 885,000 recipients in 1994. By comparison, in the United States, Aid to Families With Dependent Children has 12.3 million recipients — about 5 percent of the population, although changes are expected under the new welfare law.

Single motherhood 8.8%

Other 6.5%

Injury, illness or handicap 40.6%

Old age 44.1%

Welfare in Japan by group 1994 figures

Percentage of Japanese population on welfare

'80 '81 '82 '83 '84 '85 '86 '87 '88 '88 '90 '91 '92 '93 '94

Source: Japanese Ministry of Health and Welfare; U.S. Department of Health and Human Services

Toshio Hata, a senior welfare official in Kawasaki.

Mr. Hata led the way to a local welfare office nearby, on the sixth floor of a Government building. He showed the way to a separate, hidden elevator going directly to the sixth floor, so that welfare applicants need not be embarrassed by getting off a crowded elevator at the welfare floor.

"This is something we have to do, to avoid humiliating people," Mr. Hata said. "All the welfare offices in Kawasaki have a separate elevator so that visitors are not embarrassed."

Scholars say that many people who are eligible for welfare do not apply, because of this sense of shame.

"I could have used it, but I have too much pride," said Shiro Kitajima, 48, a homeless man with serious back problems who was encouraged by officials to apply for an $800-a-month stipend. "I got free medication for five months, and that was enough."

In interviews with homeless people—who only very rarely qualify for welfare—it was striking how little sense of entitlement there was. Even those who

said that they should be getting help quickly added that their neighbors did not deserve it.

"These people here who get up every few days and hunt in the garbage for food, they're just lazy," said a homeless male prostitute in his 30's, who would not give his name and did not think he should get assistance. "They shouldn't get help."

While dependency on welfare has not been a problem generally in Japan, one social group has more of a common profile with welfare recipients in the United States. This is a minority called the burakumin, who are ethnically indistinguishable from other Japanese but are descendants of those who had occupations considered "unclean," like skinning animals and burying the dead.

Burakumin are only a bit more than 2 percent of the Japanese population, but they have suffered discrimination for centuries and are disproportionately likely to abuse alcohol or drugs, to drop out of school, to have children out of wedlock and to qualify for welfare. About 5 percent of burakumin are on welfare, seven times the national average.

Burakumin community leaders say they worry not only about the impact of discrimination but also about these social problems, including excessive dependence on welfare. Still, these problems among the burakumin are diminishing rapidly as they start businesses and become more prosperous, and burakumin dependency on welfare is on the wane.

Article 11   *Far Eastern Economic Review,* February 29, 1996

Fates Worse Than Death

Schoolyard bullying, ijime, *is an old Japanese problem. But a rash of related suicides has made it a national issue.*

Sachiko Sakamaki in Tokyo

Hisashi Ito was a bright, sensitive 13-year-old living in Joetsu, a city 300 kilometres north of Tokyo. His friends often came round to play basketball at his home because he had a hoop in the garden. But one day, for no obvious reason, they turned against him. At first they merely ignored him, but the hostility later turned physical. At one point they stripped him naked in the school bathroom and poured water over him. Over time, they stole ¥5,000 ($50) from him. Eventually it became unbearable. On November 27, his father found him hanging by his neck from the basketball hoop.

"They took my life away from me," Hisashi wrote in a suicide note. "I don't want to live any more, so let me die."

His death would be horrible enough were it a singular event. But it's not. In the past 15 months, 14 Japanese students have committed suicide explicitly out of despair over *ijime,* the bullying that plagues most Japanese schools.

Schoolyard bullying is hardly unique to Japan, but there's a pervasive, insidious aspect to ijime that distinguishes it from similar behaviour elsewhere. That owes partly to the dearth of institutional redress that drives victims to such despair; and partly to the tacit consent of parents and teachers who tolerate ijime more as a troublesome cultural proclivity than as a social pathology.

However interpreted, ijime is emerging as the dark underside of Japan's much-vaunted educational system. Indeed, the latest suicides have created a sense of crisis that has moved the issue from the schoolyard to the highest levels of government. The newly installed prime minister, Ryutaro Hashimoto, used his inauguration speech to pledge a solution. The Education Ministry actually has a budget for ijime problems. It plans to triple it to ¥1.4 billion in the coming fiscal year, while increasing to 506 from 154 the number of schools throughout the country to which it sends counsellors. The recent deaths have also shaken up the Japan Teachers Union, which devoted much of its latest national convention to the problem.

It remains unclear just how big the problem is. For starters, is bullying actually on the rise, or is it just being reported more fully? The Education Ministry recorded 56,601 bullying incidents in 1994, up from 21,598 the previous year. But that partly reflects a change in accounting methods to include any student's bullying complaint, not just the officially confirmed cases reported in previous years. And no matter how you count, the ministry concedes, many cases are hidden by teachers and school administrators fearful of looking negligent.

More to the point, are ijime-related suicides on the rise? Though many people think so, it's hard to be sure. The number of reported child suicides has fallen since the 1980s, and of the 166 reported in 1994 only five were listed as ijime-related. But one thing is clear: More victims are leaving suicide notes naming ijime as the culprit.

Whether on the rise or not, even a single ijime-related suicide is one too many. The first step towards preventing more is explaining why bullying is so common to begin with. "There have been various analyses, but there's still no clear-cut answer," says Masanori Takahashi, who runs a national telephone helpline for ijime victims.

Education experts cite several possible causes. One is the educational system itself. From an early age, Japanese children are under immense pressure to succeed academically; many a Japanese childhood seems little more than a prologue to the ordeal of the university entrance exam. Academic pedigree is still the key measure of success in Japan, and most parents think getting into a top university requires a strict regime of juku, or cram classes. Kawaijuku, one of Japan's biggest cram-school operators, says 64.2% of students aged 12–15 attend jukus. The whole system, many think, cultivates pent-up hostilities that some children will inevitably vent against others.

"Children often tell me, 'I'm tired'," says Jun Kanno, a Waseda University psychology professor who counsels teenagers and their parents. "They are busy with school, cram-school and other activities—way beyond their natural limits."

What's more, many say, life in a juku world isolates children both from each other and from adults, hindering the development of social skills and sensitivities that would lessen the impulse to bully. Others say the workaholic ethos of Japanese adults deprives many children of the affection that's crucial at a young age. Students have been known to feign illness just to receive the attention of the school nurse. Some believe the shrinking Japanese family exacerbates the sense of alienation.

"They don't bond with others, so they feel isolated and useless," says Kanno. "When bullies make a child feel helpless, it often leads to suicide."

Many say the system puts excessive stress on discipline and conformity. Japanese education is strictly regulated—from the national curriculum to dress standards. Many foreigners admire the emphasis on order, but strict adherence to rules leaves little margin for error and sometimes allows lethal abuses.

In July, a teacher killed a high-school girl when he smashed her against a concrete wall in the course of an argument. In a notorious 1990 incident, a high-school teacher crushed a tardy girl to death in a school's heavy iron gates rather than give her a few more seconds to get through. (The first teacher was jailed; the second case is still pending.) Under such intense pressure, children who fail to shine often resort to abusing others, psychologists say.

Like it or not, such tragedies may be the logical result of policies adopted years ago, when, as professor Kanji Nishio says, "Japan chose equality at the expense of freedom." Postwar Japan, notes Nishio, of Tokyo Electric Communication University, was more concerned with uniform work force than with individual creativity, and that required precisely what the school system delivered: "a mass of mediocre workers."

Since the early 1980s, the Ministry of Education has tried to change things. High schools now have optional courses, an effort to encourage individuality; schools now take every Saturday off. But the ministry's critics claim nothing has really changed. Says Hiroto Kawai, vice-chairman of Kawaijuku: "Education doesn't change like the Japanese economy changes, because there are no trade disputes and so no outside pressure."

Perhaps the root cause of bullying lies much deeper than schooling. Japan is a largely homogenous society that is quick to marginalize the deviant, no matter how subtle their differences. An odd nuance of speech or appearance is enough to invite ostracism, and in a society where conformity is everything, no stigma weighs heavier than the curse of being different. Too fat or too short; too smart or too slow—all make inviting targets. Many Japanese children who have lived abroad deliberately perform poorly in, say, English classes so as not to stand out.

But these are long-standing national traits, and bullying itself is an old problem. The question vexing Japan now is: Why the apparent surge in ijime suicides? Some blame all the recent publicity. Hisashi chose to kill himself on the first anniversary of a widely publicized suicide by a 13-year-old boy near Nagoya. Tsukuba University professor Susumu Oda says sensational media coverage may be encouraging children to punish their tormentors with suicide notes.

Punishment, however, is something student bullies themselves rarely experience. The students who drove young Hisashi to suicide were questioned by police, but are today back in school as if nothing had happened. (In a rare gesture of social defiance, the parents of Yuhei Kodama, killed in a 1993 schoolyard-bullying incident, recently filed a $1.9 million lawsuit against both the assailants and school authorities.)

Last year, the Education Ministry ordered schools to protect victims and clamp down on bullying, but the message doesn't seem to have hit home. At a school in Narita, near Tokyo, children recently staged a drama about ijime and how to deal with it. In the play, one group of students bullies another, and the fictitious class discusses ways to stop it. Their conclusion was a rather left-handed concession to tolerance: Students who are different in some way deserve ridicule, but please try to constrain yourself.

"What the drama says is the bullied have something wrong so it's natural that you bully them," says Danece Stapleton, an American missionary and mother of a third-grade girl at the school. When her son was bullied several years ago, the teacher told her: "Your son peels tangerines in a strange way—and anyway, those boys that you say kicked him wouldn't do a thing like that."

Bullying doesn't stop at the school gates, but extends to the adult workplace. When psychiatrist Masao Miyamoto joined the Ministry of Health and Welfare after living in the United States for 11 years, he was ostracized for acting like a Westerner asking questions and demanding holidays. His boss told other officials to ignore Miyamoto and hide documents from him, even ordering tea ladies to skip him on their rounds.

"Bullying the weak is considered psychologically abnormal and a sign of immaturity in the West," Miyamoto wrote in *The Straightjacket Society,* a book about bullying in Japan's bureaucracy. But in Japan it's accepted."

That's why some educators now advocate counselling the bullies, who often lack any sense of remorse and responsibility. "The most crucial thing to prevent bullying is to deal with the bullies," educator and author Naoki Ogi recently wrote in the Yomiuri Shimbun. "Both the government and the public are obsessed with the victims, and this is a mistake."

For their part, teachers say there's usually no way to see an ijime-related suicide coming. They argue that they're busy with classwork, coaching and other chores that leave little time for one-on-one talks with distraught students. Many victimized children simply refuse to go to school: The number of 12- to 15-year-old truants increased to 51,365 in 1994 from 40,223 in 1990.

Others simply leave altogether. Midori Imai, 15, was an outgoing girl with lots of friends in a small town on Shikoku, an island off the coast of Kobe in western Japan. But one day in 1994, her school tennis club friends started ignoring her. It soon spread to her classmates, who handed her a note saying "You're a nuisance. Die."

The sudden hostility prompted lots of soul-searching and night-time walks in search of solace. Midori talked to the teacher, who got her classmates to write essays explaining why they bullied her, then read them to the class. This was disaster. The class simply used the opportunity to criticize Midori openly. The teacher told the parents—Midori's as well as the bullies'—that the students were simply on bad terms. She even suggested that Midori was to blame, because she supposedly ignored the other girls first. Eventually, Midori moved to another school.

"Teachers don't just ignore ijime," says her mother Yoko. "They justify it."

Article 12   *Far Eastern Economic Review,* April 11, 1996

The Lucky Country

Australia has lived for generations off a cornucopia of natural resources. But to remain competitive in the emerging global economy, it will need something more.

William McGurn in Sydney

From his office high above Sydney's Pitt Street, Richard Humphry looks out on a bustling city, sprawling in every direction. But as managing director of the Australian Stock Exchange—Asia's third largest behind Tokyo and Hong Kong—Humphry sees something even more alluring on the horizon: a 21st century of unbounded economic opportunity.

Humphry isn't the only one who sees a bright future for Australia. Politicians and bureaucrats of every stripe talk of moving closer to Asia and gaining access to its burgeoning markets. But Humphry thinks they have it backwards. If Australia really wants to be taken seriously in Asian markets, he says, it must first become competitive globally—which means getting things right at home.

If Australia is to compete, Asia-style, it needs to change. But it won't be easy to rebuild the economy. In the brave new world that beckons from Humphry's computer terminals, the increasing global premium on service and know-how spells trouble for an Australian economy whose wealth remains highly dependent on a base of natural resources that has witnessed steadily diminishing returns. Humphry is doing his small part: The Australian exchange launched an Asian Index, and is toying with the idea of 24-hour real-time trading. But to become the region's next tiger, the entire economy would need to make a tectonic shift.

"It's not about trying to be a part of Asia," says Humphry. "It's about making ourselves competitive in a world environment. And if you ask me what the biggest obstacle to that is, I'd say the culture."

This culture has its roots in radical 19th-century British egalitarianism, which has been sustained economically by the astounding wealth of natural resources that led historian Donald Horne in 1964 to dub Australia the "lucky country." Indeed, for most of its history, Australia prospered largely on what Providence had bequeathed it: staggering natural deposits of gold, silver, cop-

per, coal, iron ore, bauxite, uranium, lead, zinc, tin, nickel and natural gas, not to mention diamonds, sapphires and opals—and land perfect for sheep and cattle raising. As recently as 1951, wool accounted for 65% of Australia's exports. Although these resources made Australians the wealthiest people on earth for a time, it also kept them from developing a trading mentality like their hardscrabble Asian neighbours to the north.

Australia's dilemma now is that the kind of arrangements that made life so comfortable in the past—central wage management, protective tariffs and the high tax rates necessary to sustain them all—are today taking their toll on Australian competitiveness. And Australians are paying as their standard of living falls, relative to the rest of the world's. Though the World Bank still insists they are the world's richest people per capita (factoring in the value of the mineral reserves), Australians have seen themselves move steadily down the income rankings, dropping from No. 1 at the turn of the century to tenth place in 1970 to 18th today. In many ways it is the same drama being played out in other industri-

alized nations: the Great Society running smack into the Information Age.

"One of our big problems is that we went through a period where we could export anything we picked off the ground, and a job was whatever you decided to do," says Humphry. "Trade was taking a mountain and shipping it off to Japan."

In recent years this has begun to change. Today fully two-thirds of Australian exports go to Asia and only about a tenth to Europe, almost a complete reversal of the situation 40 years ago, when Australia was tied to British purse strings. Although former Prime Minister Paul Keating likes to take full credit for this shift himself, the changes largely reflect the hard economic realities imposed first by Britain's abandonment of the Commonwealth in favour of the European Community and second by the demands of global competition. What is fair to say is that the 13 years of the Keating era—first as finance minister, then as prime minister—corresponded with a greater awakening to the potential of Asia and serious moves to force open domestic markets that might not have been possible—at least without

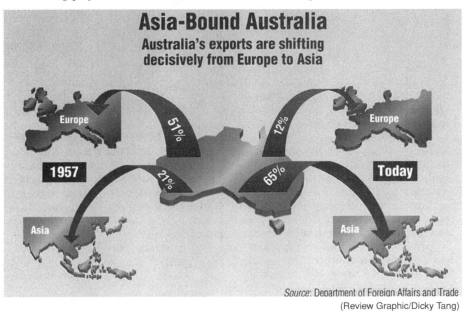

Asia-Bound Australia
Australia's exports are shifting decisively from Europe to Asia

Europe   51%   12%   Europe

1957   21%   65%   Today

Asia   Asia

Source: Department of Foreign Affairs and Trade
(Review Graphic/Dicky Tang)

provoking great labour unrest—under a non-Labor government.

The newly elected government of Liberal Party leader John Howard, for its part, suggests that the gains of the Keating era are overrated. Australia's total exports to Asia have indeed risen, Liberals concede, but that's because *everyone's* exports to Asia have risen. Hidden in those rising aggregates is the fact that Australia's *share* of exports to Asia is falling. Labor defenders counter that the loss is temporary and reflects the changing nature of Australian exports, which are moving from traditional commodities towards value-added products and services.

Both sides are probably right. Without doubt there is an emerging Australian business class that recognizes that the future lies beyond the country's borders and believes Australia's real comparative advantage lies in high value-added, knowledge-intensive areas. Take John McGarry. When recession hit Australia's construction industry in 1970, McGarry had no idea how to keep his engineering firm going. So he hopped aboard a flight to Jakarta, where he pounded the streets, searching for construction projects that might need engineers. He finally found one in the Hotel Borobudur, a 900-room structure begun under Sukarno but never completed. Within a year McGarry had 12 Australian engineers on site.

Today McGarry is chief executive officer of Transfield Construction Asia, a company that is increasingly looking northward for opportunity. Ten years ago, Transfield had only one or two projects in Asia, but today it operates in 10 countries throughout the Asia-Pacific region.

Dozens of other Australian businesses have also carved out their own Asian niches, whether it's Telstra providing Vietnam with telecommunications links or the Hotel Kurrajong, a new hotel school in Canberra hoping to train managers for the region's booming tourist trade.

Indeed, the education of Asian students has become a billion-dollar-a-year business. In the past decade or so, Australian universities have become the preferred destination for students from Singapore and Malaysia and second only to the U.S. and Britain for most other Asian nations. "I think it is going to prove Australia's 'secret weapon,' " says McGarry. "When they leave they will take a little piece of Australia with them. That's a terrific bonus for us."

It's a bonus Australia badly needs. In the last few months, the Department of Foreign Affairs and Trade has begun a "Market Australia" campaign to push

The White Man's Burden

Australians have never stood accused of mincing words. So when the immigration status of a Chinese couple named Wong came up in the federal parliament in 1947, the Labor minister for immigration, Arthur Calwell, responded in type. Arguing for deportation, Calwell cut to the chase. "Two Wongs," he said, "don't make a white."

This was more than an impolitic remark. Indeed, the concept of White Australia was long the cornerstone of national identity. It was the Australian Labor Party's very first plank, and its codification the first act of the newly independent Commonwealth of Australia in 1901. Until the 1960s, the nation's leading newsweekly, the *Bulletin*, carried the motto "Australia for the White Man."

But the country has changed, in ways that many outsiders have been slow to recognize. Australia's British identity began to erode with the post–war arrival of millions of immigrants from southern Europe. White Australia was formally abandoned in 1973, but the real change came in 1979, when the government of Malcolm Fraser agreed to open Australia's door to thousands of Vietnamese refugees. Since then Australia has adopted the most liberal immigration policy in the region, possibly the world.

"Maybe we haven't done all we need to do in terms of our economic competitiveness vis-a-vis Asia," says Greg Sheridan, editor of *Living With Dragons: Australia Confronts Its Asian Destiny.* "But White Australia is dead and buried."

In the process, Australia has transformed itself. Although America has the Statue of Liberty and a reputation as an immigrant country, today's Australia has three times the percentage of immigrants than the United States. Since 1945 Australia has taken in more than 5 million immigrants, and today 40% of Australians were either born elsewhere or have a parent who was. Increasingly they are coming from Asia. Nearly 40% of last year's 87,428 immigrants came from the region.

The demographic effects are obvious even in hitherto provincial outposts like Adelaide, home to Malaysian-born chef Cheong Liew's Grange Restaurant, a fusion of Asian and haute cuisine situated in the local Hilton.

Yet the real impact of Asian immigration goes far beyond the Australian palate. For White Australia was not exclusively, perhaps not even primarily, about prejudice. As the country's second prime minister, Alfred Deakin, argued: "It is not the bad qualities but the good qualities of these alien races that make them dangerous to us." White Australia was the political bedrock for a host of arrangements—from centralized wage setting to tariff protection—that kept out competition from its immediate neighbours.

Just how much this has changed was obvious at Hong Kong's Kai Tak Airport the day after Chinese New Year. A generation ago, most of those aboard Ansett Flight 888 for Sydney would not have been welcome; this day, a happy Cantonese din fills the air. "These passengers aren't just going to Australia," an Ansett stewardess explains. "They're going *home*."

William McGurn

Australia's advantages. But the campaign came about only after a survey of key Asian markets revealed a negative overall image towards Australian business. As the report bluntly put it: "Australia is simply not perceived to be a relevant player."

Such perceptions underline one of the many contradictions inherent in Australia's effort to become an Asian-style tiger. Unlike the business-driven economies of Asia, Australia's entry into the region has been government-led and schizophrenic. At the same time the Keating government beat the drums for involvement with Asia, it hardly created an open business environment back home. It castigated business leaders, let critical domestic reforms languish, and even reneged on an open-skies agreement with New Zealand. Political campaigns devolved into class warfare. Keating's government blamed budget shortfalls on wealthy Australians avoiding taxes; his critics said he should have focused on out-of-control spending. Before last month's election, the head of the Australian Council of Trade Unions, Bill Kelty, was threatening industrial action in the event of a Liberal victory.

Not by Bread Alone

Asa Wahiquist in Sydney

Quick, name a major Australian export that relies on hi-tech engineering and state-of-the-art market research. Bet you didn't say wheat. But Australia's exporters of wheat—for decades one of the country's top earners—are hustling to adapt to the sophisticated demands of the global marketplace, especially in Asia.

The shift is crucial if the A$3 billion ($1.9 billion) industry—which receives no subsidies—is to survive, says Trevor Flugge, chairman of the Australian Wheat Board. Twenty years ago, all the country's wheat was classified "fair average quality." Today, Australia produces more than 40 varieties, each with a highly specific endmarket in mind. As a result, Australia's wheat exports to Asia have increased to 50% of the 12.7 million tonnes it exports in an average year, up from 30% in 1989.

Indeed, Australia's focus on individual markets has kept the industry thriving even while the United States, a major global competitor, has poured out huge subsidies to help its exporters, says Flugge. For the long term, he adds, Australia's market-specific strategy "will give us the competitive edge in a changing market environment."

Australia is one of world's top five wheat exporters and is the most dependent on foreign markets. About 80% of total production is sold abroad, wheat perennially one of Australia's top-ten exports. Small wonder the industry is developing strains fit for Asian palates. Australia's white wheats, for example, are well suited to wheat-noodle production. Australian growers have capitalized on that: around one-third of Australia's wheat exports are now consumed as noodles.

Andrew Inglis, chairman of the Grains Research & Development Corp., says market research is becoming ever more precise. Taste tests of steamed buns, for instance, reveal a difference in preferences between native Koreans and Koreans who have spent more than seven years in Australia. "It's shown how conscientious you have to be to ensure the product you are developing meets the customer's requirement," says Inglis.

The rewards are potentially enormous. "In Japan consumption of instant noodles per person is 50 to 60 packets per year," notes Nigel Officer, who worked until recently at the wheat board's Hong Kong office. "While in China it is only five to six packets." In other words, there is plenty of untapped market out there.

And so the race is on to find the perfect instant noodle. West Australian researchers are studying colour stability in yellow alkaline, or Chinese-style, noodles. The Sydney Bread Research Institute is evaluating 52 wheat samples for northern-style Chinese steamed breads, while simultaneously working on a southern-style product. The institute is also developing a starch test that will help select varieties for yellow and white noodles and steamed bread.

Wheat growers are competing in other ways too. In Asia there is rising demand for stockfeed, a market now dominated by U.S. corn. Corn does not thrive in Australia, so wheat breeders have come up with a first-ever Australian wheat grown solely for feed.

Competition is only likely to increase, but Australian wheat growers are out to show they can cut it. In 1989 they lost their guaranteed minimum price when the domestic market was deregulated, though the wheat board retains its monopoly over exports and—until 1999—its access to government-backed borrowings that enable it to pay growers most of their earnings shortly after harvest. But there is pressure for further deregulation. Multinational grain traders are lobbying for an end to the wheat board's export monopoly, and the board itself is considering plans to privatize itself as a grower-owned entity.

Whatever its structure, it's clear that the future of Australian wheat will be largely determined by Asian bellies. As the wheat board's Flugge recently told a gathering of South Korean millers: "The future of our families is tied in together."

In the highly publicized push to join Asia, the connection between Australian trade and the need for Australia to become competitive was frequently lost. Energies—and money—were squandered on gimmicks like a new map showing Australia at the centre of East Asia, which Foreign Minister Gareth Evans distributed at last year's Asean meeting in Brunei.

"What Keating and Evans forgot is that in the end it's not Australia that trades with Asia," says John Stone, a former secretary to the treasury. "It's Australian businessmen that trade with Asian businessmen, and Australian companies trading with Asian companies."

Ironically, it is Australia's Asian-born citizens who are most sceptical about talk of transforming the country into an Asian-style tiger. On an early Sunday morning while the rest of Sydney is still sleeping, Peggy Wu, an immigrant from Shanghai who now works in a King's Cross laundromat, points to disincentives inherent in the Australian way of doing things. "Nice place to live, but bad for business," she explains as she pulls another load from a washer. "Do you know that if you make $100,000, the government takes 50%?"

That kind of thinking is alien to many of those steeped in an Australian ethos that looks askance at wealth and down on service. In egalitarian Australia, for example, passengers get in the front of cabs, lest they be thought guilty of putting on airs. There is even a name for it: the "tall poppy syndrome," meaning that anything that grows higher than its neighbours is immediately cut down to size. As the *Australian Financial Review* notes sadly, "entrepreneur" remains a dirty word in the Australian vocabulary.

All businesses complain about the nation's Unfair Dismissal Law, which is designed to make it difficult to fire someone unfairly but in practice has made companies reluctant to hire people—one reason for Australia's high (8.4%) unemployment rate. According to one survey, almost a third of Australian companies have been hit by an unfair dismissal claim, and one in seven say it has prompted them to hire temps and contract workers.

Whether Australia's Asian immigrants will help change this dynamic or succumb to it is still an open question. Thus far, however, there are signs of a shift. Greg Sheridan, foreign editor of *The Australian* and editor of *Living With Dragons: Australia Confronts Its Asian Destiny*, notes that the small-business bias of Asian immigrants is having an effect.

"Asian immigrants have played a big role in breaking down labour ri-gidities," says Sheridan. "The first shops allowed to open on Sundays in Sydney were in Chinatown." Indeed, even the fiercest Asian critic concedes that Sundays in Sydney now hum with commerce compared with just a few years ago.

Yet for all the changes of the past few years—a slash in tariffs, a float of the Australian dollar, a huge drop in private-sector union membership—Australia hasn't yet managed to shuck off a critical post–World War II legacy: centralized government control over key sectors in the economy. Ultimately the test of Australia's integration with the region will be not whether it belongs to this or that regional grouping but whether it succeeds in making its own economy competitive to the point where Asia can't do without what Australia brings to the table.

Alexander Downer, Australia's new foreign minister, believes this will be the real measure of acceptance in the region. Asian leaders, he says, "look at Australia with all the advantages Australia has had over just about any country on earth—social stability, rich as any country could be in natural resources, good education. But it's not a country dedicated to achieving any economic goals. And I think they think, 'Well, they could do better in Australia.'"

Article 13   *The Economist*, April 6, 1996

Myanmar's Mysterious Boom

YANGON

Scanning South-East Asia for the next "tiger" economy, many eyes have lighted on Myanmar (Burma). Always rich in resources, its government is now friendly to foreign businesses. Human-rights groups may carp at foreigners for dealing with an unpleasant military regime. But businessmen are scared of missing out on an economy that is now growing at tigerish rates.

When it seized power in 1988, the military junta running Myanmar inherited a closed, state-dominated economy, which it has opened up to market forces and foreign investment. Since then, GDP growth rates have caught up with the feverish regional norm. Figures just released by the government claim average growth of 8.2% over the past four years, which suggests that growth is picking up again (see chart).

The capital, Yangon, certainly looks like a boom-town. New tower blocks are poking above the faded colonial façades; streets that just a few years ago milled quietly with pedestrians, bicycles and the occasional pick-up truck now throb with Toyotas and Nissans. In one street, the pavement is stacked with cardboard boxes of Toshiba television sets. Well-groomed young couples dine in busy restaurants. Many see this as evidence that—whatever its other flaws—the junta has at least got the economy right.

Or has it? The opposition leader, Aung San Suu Kyi, thinks not. "The so-called boom is an artificial one," she declares. The economy, far from being the generals' saving grace, "will be their undoing." Since Miss Suu Kyi was released from six years of house arrest only last July, by a junta that still refuses to talk to her, she might reasonably be suspected of bias. But the opposition is not alone in seeing the appearance of new prosperity as in part a mirage.

Even the International Monetary Fund, in a report issued last October and praised by the government as "very sound", concluded that, on a per capita basis, "neither GDP nor agricultural output have yet recovered to the levels reached in the mid-1980s." The IMF acknowledges that "real economic activity has expanded strongly over the last three years." But it also identifies trends that make the government look less the prudent liberalisers of their own propaganda, more the spendthrift military dictators portrayed by their opponents.

Asian tigers tend to be noted for fiscal caution, small state sectors and high levels of investment. But Myanmar's budget deficit has been widening. Consumption has been increasing as a percentage of GDP at the expense of investment; and the private sector's share in that investment has actually been declining. Foreign-exchange reserves have been maintained at their current low level only by failing to pay back some foreign debt. Civil servants' wages and social services have been cut, while the junta has spent more on defence. The IMF estimates that defence expenditure accounts for 4% of GDP. Arcane book-keeping procedures, however, probably conceal an even greater amount.

The prescriptive part of the IMF's report has not been made public. The World Bank however, in a report also published last October, put reform of the currency, the kyat, at the top of its list of priorities. There is an official exchange rate of about 6 kyats to the dollar. But on the streets of Yangon, it takes 125 kyats to buy a dollar.

Myanmar insists it will need a lot of outside financial support to adjust the currency to market levels, if intolerable inflationary pressures are to be avoided. That is not true, or at least not for the person in the street, who already pays for imports at a realistic exchange rate. Rather, unifying the currency would encourage exports, and help with the budget deficit, by increasing revenues from import duties and sales tax.

The World Bank has a more convincing explanation for the government's re-

luctance to adjust the exchange rate—"the fear that influential groups in the population would lose as a result." That means those with access to imports at the official rate—government departments, the army and state enterprises, as

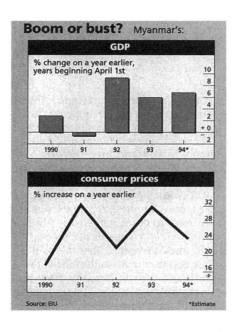

well as some individual civil servants and soldiers. The dual exchange rate robs the poor to give to the comfortably-off and the small but growing class of very, very rich.

It is also one reason why measuring Myanmar's economy is a guessing game. The use of the official rate hugely understates exports and imports, and distorts year-on-year comparisons. The government's figures probably underestimate the size of the economy, while exaggerating the growth rates.

Growth in Myanmar's economy has come largely from agriculture, which made up an estimated 62.6% of GDP in 1994, up from 57% in 1989. The gov-

ernment says farmers are doing nicely, thank you, and that savings in agricultural co-operatives are rising. Miss Suu Kyi says life is getting harder and harder in the paddy fields, even though the price of rice is soaring for consumers.

That, says Miss Suu Kyi, is why the government's economic failings will become obvious this year. But the foreign business delegations and conferences are multiplying. If the economy is such a mess, why are investors flocking in? The answer seems to be that there is a lot more looking than investing. The government likes to quote a figure of $3 billion for the foreign investment it has attracted. But less than a third of that has been disbursed. Actual investment has been concentrated in the oil and gas sector (41% in 1994–95)—almost all accounted for by one massive project to pipe gas to Thailand—and in hotel development. A third of disbursed investment in 1994–95 went into the plethora of new hotels, often financed from Singapore or Thailand, and built in anticipation of a surge of visitors as the country opens up.

Miss Suu Kyi argues that business optimism about the military junta is mistaken, because "you cannot do business with people who do not keep their word, who do not respect the law and who are not prepared to allow healthy competition." It is perhaps a characteristic of soldiers not to like competition, whether political or economic. But these ones face a dilemma. To suppress political competition, they are maintaining military spending at levels that are blowing holes in the state's finances. But they are also staking their future on economic growth. In which case, as one western observer puts it, they had better find a cheaper way of dealing with ethnic insurgency in the border regions, and social discontent just about everywhere.

Article 14   *Ms.*, January/February 1996

Aung San Suu Kyi

Through a private act of sacrifice, she helped keep her country's dream of democracy alive.

Gayle Kirshenbaum

Gayle Kirshenbaum is a writer based in New York City.

On April 5, 1989, Aung San Suu Kyi was walking down a road in the Burmese village of Danubyu when a group of soldiers stopped her. It wasn't the first time that she'd been harassed by Burma's repressive military regime while campaigning for the return of democracy there. But this time, six of the soldiers jumped out of a jeep, crouched down, and on the orders of their captain, aimed their guns at her and prepared to fire. Aung San Suu Kyi waved away her supporters and walked toward the soldiers alone. "It seemed so much simpler to provide them with a single target than to bring everyone else in," she later explained. At the last minute, the order to shoot was reversed.

Not long before that day in Danubyu, Aung San Suu Kyi had written that courage "comes from cultivating the habit of refusing to let fear dictate one's actions." She was reflecting on the bravery of her father, Aung San, who led the struggle against British colonial rule, and who was assassinated by a political rival just before Burma gained independence in 1948. Aung San Suu Kyi was two years old. She later took it upon herself to study his life, which came to foreshadow her own. Three months after her showdown with the army, she was placed under house arrest and was told she could gain her release only if she agreed to leave the country. She refused, and for the next six years was confined to her home in Rangoon.

Aung San Suu Kyi was finally freed unconditionally last July. The growing threat of an international economic embargo at a time when Burma is in dire need of foreign investment forced the generals to deal with their biggest public relations problem. We honor Aung San Suu Kyi, on the occasion of her release, as a woman whose commitment to her country's freedom has been complete and unwavering. She has displayed the bravery that she so admired in her own father, sacrificing her health and enduring a long, painful separation from her husband and children for the cause of democracy. Her quiet courage in the pursuit of nonviolent change puts her in the company of Mahatma Gandhi, Nelson Mandela, and Martin Luther King, Jr.

This courage was recognized in 1991 when Aung San Suu Kyi became only the eighth woman in history to receive the Nobel Peace Prize—an award she was unable to accept in person because of her confinement.

Her hard-won freedom now assured, Aung San Suu Kyi spoke with *Ms.* from her home in Rangoon, which is now truly a home and not a jail. "Those who don't like me use my gender against me," she says. The Burmese authorities have also repeatedly tried to use her marriage to a Westerner (British professor Michael Aris) to discredit her, having once gone so far as to put up posters around the country with sexual caricatures of her with her husband. More recently, the government has announced that anyone married to a foreigner should be barred from becoming president. Were she a man, "they probably would make less fuss," she says. "The feeling is always that the husband dominates the wife."

Aung San Suu Kyi had met Aris while studying at Oxford University in the mid-1960s. Anticipating that she might one day have to make a choice between her family and her father's legacy, she had tried to prepare Aris, writing presciently to him of the future: "Sometimes I am beset by fears that circumstances and national considerations might tear us apart." They later married, and made their home in Oxford, where they raised their two young sons while Aung San Suu Kyi studied for her doctorate in Burmese literature. Then, in March 1988, after receiving word that her mother had suffered a severe stroke, Aung San Suu Kyi left for Rangoon. Her return home coincided with the largest civilian uprising against the military government since it had seized power in 1962.

Her father's name was still a potent symbol of freedom, and Aung San Suu Kyi's home quickly became the nerve center of the nascent democracy movement. Shortly after her mother died in December 1988, Aung San Suu Kyi became the general secretary of the newly formed National League for Democracy. "If you ask whether we shall achieve democracy," she told one of her rapt audiences, "here is what I shall say: 'Don't think about whether or not these things will happen. Just continue to do what is right.'"

But while Aung San Suu Kyi and the nonviolent movement she represented continued to do what was right, the military stepped up its campaign of terror, gunning down demonstrators and killing thousands.

During her years of confinement, her sons, Alexander and Kim, who are now grown, lived with Aris in England. Although she was initially allowed sporadic visits and mail from her family, all contact was eventually banned. "Very obviously the plan was to break Suu's spirit by separating her from her children in the hope she would accept permanent exile," wrote Aris in a collection of essays by and about Aung San Suu Kyi that provided much-needed income during her detention. At times, her funds were so low that she had little to eat. As a result, her hair fell out, her eyesight worsened, and her spinal column began to deteriorate. "I kept thinking that I wished I had been put in at a younger age, so that after my release I would have a longer period to work," she later told *Vanity Fair* magazine.

Since her release she's been visited by her family, but refuses to leave the country for fear that she'll be prevented from returning. Although the threat of violent reprisals endures, Aung San Suu Kyi continues to speak out. In a videotaped speech delivered at the NGO (nongovernmental organizations) Forum on Women in China, she maintained that "it is time to apply in the arena of the world the wisdom and experience" that women have gained "in activities of peace over so many thousands of years."

Asked if she thinks of herself as a role model, she responds as if she had never before considered the notion. "I don't really know what that means," she finally replies. "There were many in Burma who did more, but the world doesn't know about them. I had the protection of my family name."

Aung San Suu Kyi acknowledges the exceptional natures of leaders like her father and Mahatma Gandhi. But of herself, she simply says, "I did what I felt I had to do."

Article 15   *The Christian Science Monitor*, July 12, 1996

EX-SOLDIER'S UNMET EXPECTATIONS

Cambodia Struggles To Overcome Legacy of Its Brutal Past

Cameron W. Barr

Staff writer of The Christian Science Monitor

PHNOM PENH, CAMBODIA
Poth Am fought in five armies to achieve this: A large, high-ceilinged room on the third floor of a grimy, garbage-strewn apartment complex in Cambodia's capital. Eight members of his family live here together, the space partitioned by plywood and cardboard. Bamboo latticework takes the place of window glass and most of the light comes from the doorway to a narrow balcony. A Buddhist altar dominates an open area where Poth Am's wife unrolls a plastic mat for visitors, and Poth Am sits cross-legged on the tile floor.

"Since the election, nothing has improved," he says, referring to the UN-supervised elections of 1993 intended to inaugurate an era of peace and reconstruction in Cambodia. "Everything is so complicated, there are no laws, there is so much corruption. Nobody cares."

'Poth Am admits he is a bitter man, but he is not alone. Cambodia's climb up from two decades of turmoil is proving to be a slow process riven with missteps and unmet expectations. Perhaps most distressing to a former soldier like Poth Am is that the rule of law remains an abstract concept in most of Cambodia.

"There are guns everywhere," he sighs. "If you don't believe me, just come around here at night. The government says we have laws, but no one respects them."

"What is called for is a thorough and massive and quick reform of the military and police forces," agrees Kao Kim Hourn, who views the problem from his more rarefied perch as the director of a government-backed think tank called the Cambodian Institute for Peace and Cooperation.

Mr. Kao knows these are just words. "We've been talking far too much. Our problem is implementation." Referring to men like Poth Am, he adds: "I think the people are losing confidence."

Road of Turmoil . . .

An apt metaphor for Cambodia's current situation is National Route 5, a highway linking Phnom Penh, the capital, with the country's second-largest city, Battambang, and continuing west to the city of Sisophon, near the Thai border.

'There are guns everywhere. If you don't believe me, just come around here at night. The government says we have laws, but no one respects them.'
—Ex-soldier Poth Am

At various times since the UN election, the road has been declared safe, but in recent months Khmer Rouge guerrillas have attacked villages near the highway and blown up a couple of small bridges. Banditry is a more pervasive problem, with soldiers routinely stopping vehicles in order to collect an unofficial toll of about a quarter or less.

The men assigned to guard Route 5's many bridges are poorly paid, and standing in front of an oncoming car holding an M-16 probably seems as good a way as any to augment one's income. Men of more obscure origins occasionally stop cars and rob travelers of more valuable possessions.

The condition of the highway itself varies from a fairly smooth two-lane blacktop to a rutted dirt road that still shows the signs of Cambodia's decades of civil strife. The poor condition of the roadway serves the criminals, since it is much easier to stop a vehicle traveling at 15 miles per hour than one doing 50.

The condition of Route 5 is "an indication of Cambodia still being a very weak state," says one diplomat in Phnom Penh.

... And of Progress

At the same time, the activity along the side of the road suggests more hopeful

OU NEAKIRY/AP

PHNOM PENH: *A Cambodian monk looks at street children sleeping in front of the entrance to an office building. Many hoped the 1993 UN-run election would bring peace and reconstruction. But recovery from two decades of turmoil is proving to be slow as the country lacks rule of law.*

things about the country's future. Route 5 is lined with houses on stilts, in the Cambodian fashion, some presiding over prosperous-looking rice fields. Others have been turned into roadside shops, and the variety of goods being carried on the backs of bicycles, motorbikes, and pickups show a healthy level of commerce.

But Poth Am is not in the mood to consider what the country has achieved in recent years. A wiry man with thinning black hair that flops over a squarish, lined face, he recounts the armies he has served as a paratrooper and medic. His last rank was lieutenant colonel.

After World War II, while in his late teens, he joined the Khmer resistance fighting against the French colonial administration. He served King Norodom Sihanouk after Cambodia received its independence in 1953. When the monarch was deposed in a right-wing coup in 1970, Poth Am joined the forces of the US-backed dictator, Gen. Lon Nol, and fought the communists trying to take over.

When the Khmer Rouge brutally took control in 1975, he hid his background as a soldier. The Maoist revolutionaries did not believe his stories of having been a farmer or a rickshaw driver and put him in prison for two years. Four of his 10 children died during Khmer Rouge rule in the late 1970s.

After the Vietnamese evicted the Khmer Rouge from Phnom Penh and installed another communist government, Poth Am and his family moved to the refugee camps on the Thai-Cambodian border.

For most of the 1980s and the early '90s he served in two rebel armies based along the border.

Given the crime and the scarcity of jobs, he says he sees little sign that life will improve, even for his children.

What he has left is Buddhism, he says, pointing to an electrified, colorful image of the Buddha that cost him $28—about what one of his daughters, a waitress, earns in a month.

If he is reincarnated, he says, he does not want to return as a Cambodian—better to be an American or a Frenchman.

Article 16

The World Today, March 1995

Cambodia: Will the Loser Take All?

Christopher Brady

Cambodia is a country where, more than anywhere else, things are not what they seem to be. Take the elections of May 1993, which to nobody's surprise resulted in a victory for the National United Front for an Independent, Neutral, Peaceful and Cooperative Cambodia (FUNCIN-PEC), led by Prince Norodom Ranariddh, over the Cambodian People's Party (CPP), led by Hun Sen. The other 18 contesting parties accounted for just 16 per cent of the vote. Of the 120 seats in the National Assembly, FUNCINPEC took 58 and CPP 51. But then, in part as a response to a secessionist attempt by Prince Chakrapong (CPP), Hun Sen and Ranariddh agreed to form a coalition government in which they would be Co-Premiers. A Constitution was drafted which included provision for a monarch, and on 23 September 1993 King Sihanouk returned to Phnom Penh to reign over a coalition government of the Kingdom of Cambodia.

Internal Divisions

But despite appearances—and the clear election results—power has predominantly remained in the hands of the minority CPP. This is especially true in the provinces where, irrespective of which party provides the governor, the bureaucratic structure beneath him remains that established during the 10 years when the State of Cambodia (SOC) government ruled Cambodia with Vietnamese support. In the government itself, CPP holds the Defence and Interior Ministries and, following a recent Cabinet reshuffle, it has added the Finance Ministry. The populist Sam Rainsy (FUNCINPEC) was sacked as Finance Minister and replaced by CPP's Keat Chhon. Rainsy claims that, with the National Bank also run by CPP, 'all the significant financial institutions are now in CPP hands'.[1] In addition to the main Ministries, the Royal Cambodian Armed Forces (RCAF) are also dominated by CPP. This is hardly surprising since the old SOC security apparatus remains largely intact. Thus the main pillars of government—finance, defence and interior—are controlled by the 'losing' party.

FUNCINPEC has recently been further weakened by the resignation of the popular Prince Sirivudh from his position as Foreign Minister. He resigned in order to voice his criticisms of the government but retains his position as General Secretary of FUNCINPEC and has denied speculation that he will form a new party.[2] Nevertheless, the damage a disaffected Sirivudh and the 14 Members of Parliament who support him are able to inflict on FUNCINPEC could be severe.

Despite its high degree of control, the CPP is not without problems. The attempted coup in July 1994, led by Prince Chakrapong, exposed divisions in the party. Explanations of the coup vary. According to some, the target was Hun Sen and the conspirators were the hardline wing of the party led by Chea Sim, the acting Head of State, and Sar Kheng, who as Interior Minister had control of the security police. Both have been accused of complicity in the events. In this scenario Chakrapong was just a convenient scapegoat. Another version sees the King's hand in the affair. According to this view, both Hun Sen and Ranariddh were to be assassinated, and consequently only one group could benefit—the trio of Sihanouk, Chea Sim and Sar Kheng. Perhaps the simplest explanation is that Chakrapong, having failed in his secessionist attempt, was encouraged to try again and was sacrificed when the coup failed. Whatever the explanation, the potential for division within CPP is obvious. Thus there are divisions within the parties as well as between them.

However, the coalition partners do seem to be united on pushing through new laws on the press, immigration and the judiciary, all of which have been criticised as repressive by a variety of non-government agencies. The local press has recently been subjected to assassinations (including that of the Editor of the *Voice of Khmer Youth,* Noun Chon), closure of offices, seizure of whole editions and generally repressive measures, allegedly government-orchestrated. The government's response to what it calls 'irresponsible press activity' has been to propose a draft law on the media which includes jail sentences of up to five years. The King and Prince Sirivudh have opposed this law, not least on the grounds that it sends the wrong signals to the international community.

By contrast, the draft immigration law has bipartisan support in the National Assembly but is opposed by human-rights groups and by Vietnam. Serge Ducasse of the United Nations High Commissioner for Refugees (UNHCR) argues that the law may be 'used as an instrument to expel out of the Kingdom of Cambodia a large number of non-Khmer people'.[3] There is disturbing evidence that Khmer-language tests have been conducted at entry points and also that ethnically-based surveys have resulted in the withdrawal of ID cards. Vietnamese border refugees are the group most at risk. The UN Centre for Human Rights in Cambodia has also attacked the laws affecting the judiciary which, contrary to the Constitution (Article 111), do not separate the executive from the judiciary and even give the Minister of Justice a prominent position on the Supreme Council of Magistry.[4]

A further constitutional wrangle over human rights concerns the amnesty for Khmer Rouge defectors. The government claims that it is an important and effective element of its strategy to defeat the KR. Human rights groups and foreign governments claim that it contravenes international law. The recent case of the self-confessed abductor of the Western hostages, Colonel Chhouk Rin, is a case in point. While Western governments call for his trial, he has been granted amnesty and allowed to retain his rank in the Cambodian armed forces. This has alienated Western sensibilities, but Co-Premier Hun Sen is guided by practical calculations, insisting that Chhouk Rin and his men 'must have the right to join the national community and to be ordinary citizens. We cannot take this chance to punish them as they have already left the Khmer Rouge to live with the national community. So this issue should be put aside.'[5]

And what of King Sihanouk in the political equation? He, as usual, is keeping his options open. He will return to Cambodia from Beijing, where he has been undergoing medical treatment, in the first half of this year. He and his followers, led by Prince Sirivudh, have been marginalised to a certain extent, but his influence should not be underestimated as he retains immense popular support. Sihanouk plans a public-relations spectacular when he returns, involving the cremation and reinterment of the Tuol Sleng skulls of the victims of the Khmer Rouge genocide in the 1970s.[6] His long absence in Beijing may have damaged his influence, but his past record demands that he should not be ignored in any political analysis.

The Regional Dimension

Although the domestic situation is complicated, foreign policy is relatively straightforward. The government's primary goal is to stabilise regional relationships, and that means In the first instance economic integration. The government's strategy is to join the Association of South-East Asian Nations (ASEAN) as quickly as possible. The new Foreign Minister, Ung Huot, has stated that joining ASEAN would mean 'cooperation, economic advantages, and friendship and the ability to find peace in

Cambodia'.[7] The hope expressed by the Chairman of the Foreign Affairs Committee, Om Radsady, is that 'as Vietnam and Laos join ASEAN, so then we cannot be isolated'.[8] Cambodia has been virtually assured of 'observer' status this year, just as Vietnam seems assured of full membership at the same time.[9]

In the runup to full membership, Cambodia is desperately seeking to attract foreign investment and aid. Huge amounts have been promised, for communications, power, irrigation and education projects. Also, the recently signed Mekong River Draft Pact will, when ratified, bring up to $750m for irrigation and hydroelectric projects.[10] There are many encouraging signs of this type, but less encouraging signs are also evident. The 'dumping' of banned and dangerous drugs onto an unregulated $40m-per-annum market is an example. There are now 150 legal and 450 illegal pharmacies in Phnom Penh alone. Under SOC rule there were 17 factories producing in-country drugs, now there is just one. As over-the-counter sales boom, so drugs supplied to state hospitals find their way into the pharmacies. Other areas attracting investment are luxury hotels, apartment blocks and casinos, none particularly necessary for infrastructural rebuilding.

For those interested in investing in the construction of roads, the privatisation of the rubber industry or indeed anything outside the cities, the problem is the still uncertain security situation. Since the government outlawed the Khmer Rouge on 7 July 1994, there has been a new security policy. Ranariddh has clearly stated that 'the Cambodian army will avoid set battle attacks in the forthcoming dry season, choosing instead to imitate the Khmer Rouge tactics of guerrilla-style harassment'.[11] There is a growing attachment to a campaign which combines a military and psychological approach. There will be an attempt to quarantine the large areas controlled by the KR while simultaneously encouraging defection and a clearance of the 'leopard spots'.[12] It is hoped this will eventually leave only the larger areas which by then may be vulnerable to a more heavily armed and better organised RCAF.[13] Simultaneously there will be a concerted effort to develop and stabilise the former Khmer Rouge areas.

To achieve its goals, the RCAF has agreed with donor countries to cut back from 130,000 men to 70,000 and to reform the 55/45 per cent ratio of officers to men, a factor alleged to be responsible for corruption, incompetence, factionalism and lack of loyalty. There are encouraging signs. Two recent successes, at Phnom Vour and Phnom Kulen, have produced hundreds of defectors and, in the case of Phnom Vour, control of a previously impregnable stronghold.[14] Soldiers at the front are reporting regular payment of salaries and the number of generals has been reduced from 2,000 to 600 in just six months.

The Khmer Rouge, for their part, are currently engaged in a series of large-scale abductions which may indicate a major offensive. The KR usually use 'abductees' as ammunition-porters and road-builders in advance of operations. However, recent reports have shown that many of the 'abductees' have been massacred when rice ransoms were not paid. This may point either to an increased level of economic sabotage or to the possibility that the current drought is seriously weakening the KR's food supplies. If these circumstances could be allied to genuine Thai efforts to close the border supply routes, the KR might be seriously threatened. The fact that 18 Thai companies are still reported to be operating illegally in Cambodia does not augur well for such a prognosis, but international pressure is being exerted on the Thais. However, even if there were to be a major KR offensive, the RCAF commanders are confident they could repel it, claiming that they have surmounted the problems which caused the embarrassing setbacks during the last dry season.

Future Prospects

On the political front, the dominance of the CPP, and Hun Sen within it, seems secure. There are undoubtedly divisions in the party, but not the schisms some commentators have suggested. By contrast, the morale in FUNCINPEC is low and Prince Sirivudh's resignation may develop into a leadership challenge that the party could ill afford. King Sihanouk's return may alter the balance of power against Ranariddh. The draft press, immigration and judiciary laws seem certain to pass through the National Assembly. How they are interpreted will partly determine the type of state Cambodia will become.

On security, the government seems committed to its new counter-insurgency tactics and is confident of dealing with any KR offensive. Success may depend on the consequences of proposed large-scale demobilisation. The usual problems associated with reducing forces are hugely magnified in Cambodia and easy solutions are not obvious. Plans to reduce the 150,000-strong civil service by 20 per cent will also exacerbate the situation.

Economically, Cambodia is set for expansion, either controlled or uncontrolled. ASEAN membership is assured, and despite security concerns investment and aid are being attracted. Although a majority of investment is not in the infrastructure, it is hoped that aid projects will compensate and that the expansion of the luxury end of the market will drag the rest of the economy with it. Also, if aid for such projects as the recently announced $215m five-year education plan can be found, it will provide a major social boost for Cambodia. There is a realisation that rapid economic growth may be achieved partly at the expense of human rights, but the increasing use of the rhetoric of 'cultural relativism' is designed to deflect human-rights criticisms.

The most difficult short-term-problem will undoubtedly be the projected rice shortage caused by the current drought. The need to import rice will damage the progress made in, reducing a 145-per-cent inflation rate to single figures in 12 months. More dangerously, it could also create the hardship and corruption upon which the Khmer Rouge thrive. Despite the myriad problems facing Cambodia, there is a remarkable atmosphere of optimism in the country. This optimistic mood may be based on the hope that Cambodia will sooner or later emulate the success of its neighbours. The country is unlikely to be resurrected as speedily as its people would want, simply because of the devastating effects of the past 25 years. No other nation has lost almost an entire generation of scientists, teachers and professionals, and it will take time to redevelop those talents, but it will happen. Cambodia may develop into a political autarky which Western sensibilities may find offensive, but the Asian view is that individual freedom prospers out of the stability and growth of the social structure, and that human rights follow in the wake of economic prosperity. This view seems to be increasingly influential in Cambodia.

Notes

1. In an interview with the *Phnom Penh Post*, 18 November–1 December 1994, pp. 4–5.
2. Interview with Prince Norodom Sirivudh, 9 December 1994.
3. In a speech at a public forum held at the Foreign Correspondents' Club of Cambodia, Phnom Penh, 3 August 1994.
4. Under pressure, the Minister has agreed not to attend but send a representative. This has not appeased the human-rights groups who argue that there should be no executive presence.
5. Phnom Penh Post, 4–17 November 1994, p.1.
6. The 'skull map' at the Tuol Sleng genocide museum erected by the Vietnamese has been a constant source of debate. It has been decided to cremate the skulls. King Sihanouk is likely to try to feature prominently in any ceremony.
7. Phnom Penh Post, 18 November–1 December 1994, p.1.
8. Ibid, p.7.
9. ASEAN's Secretary-General stated as much in a public forum organised in Phnom Penh by the Cambodia Institute for Cooperation and Peace. 8 December 1994.
10. The original Lower Mekong River Commission which began in 1957 consisted of Thailand, Cambodia, Laos and Vietnam. The intention is to add China and Myanmar.
11. *The Cambodian Times*, 27 November–3 December 1994.

12. 'Leopard spots' is the term used to designate the small pockets of KR-controlled territory dotted about the Cambodian countryside.

13. The RCAF expects to take delivery of 90 T55 tanks from Poland and the Czech Republic, plus 8 MIG 21s from China in addition to other armaments.

14. Phnom Vour is also alleged to have been achieved at the expense of the lives of the Western hostages. During mid-December, General Paet, a Khmer Rouge commander, launched an offensive to retake Phnom Vour and had, at the time of writing, been repelled with some difficulty. See Phnom Penh Post, 16–29 December 1994.

Article 17   *Foreign Affairs*, September/October 1996

Chinese Realpolitik

Thomas J. Christensen

Thomas J. Christensen is assistant professor of government at Cornell University and author of Useful Adversaries: Grand Strategy, Domestic Mobilization, and Sino-American Conflict, 1947–58 *from Princeton University Press. Research for this article was funded by the Asia Security Project at Harvard University's Olin Institute for Strategic Studies.*

Reading Beijing's World-View

Scholars and policy analysts seem almost obsessed with China's continuing rise toward the status of a great power. Debates rage about whether there is a "China threat" to East Asia or the United States, how to measure China's present military and economic power, and which trends best project China's growth into the next century. Less attention has been given to how Chinese government analysts view their own security environment. Because they influence the thinking of government decision-makers and are privy to their thoughts, an analysis of their views on security is valuable. By providing a better understanding of both China's baseline realpolitik view of international politics and two significant divergences from that baseline—Beijing's attitudes toward Japan and Taiwan—such a study can help contribute to a more prudent American East Asia strategy.[1]

China may well be the high church of realpolitik in the post–Cold War world. Its analysts certainly think more like traditional balance-of-power theorists than do most contemporary Western leaders and policy analysts.[2] For example, although China has not actively opposed multilateral humanitarian efforts, the rationales for international missions in Bosnia, Somalia, and Haiti are alien to the thinking of most Chinese analysts. They are also much less likely than their Western counterparts to emphasize political, cultural, or ideological differences with foreign countries. The United States considers the "en-

largement of areas of democracy" a core element of its grand strategy, but China has made almost no effort, with the possible exception of its relations with North Korea, to export its ideas about "market socialism."

China is not interested in pressing either allies or rivals to comply with global norms of human rights. On occasion, it will return fire when a country criticizes its human rights record, but this seems purely tactical. It is hard to believe that Chinese elites are truly concerned with the plight of Native Americans, African-Americans in south central Los Angeles, or Turkish guest workers in Berlin. Chinese analysts raise these topics only when defending China from attack on human rights grounds.

China's elites are suspicious of many multilateral organizations, including those devoted to economic, environmental, nonproliferation, and regional security issues. In most cases, China joins such organizations to avoid losing face and influence. But Beijing does not allow these organizations to prevent it from pursuing its own

[1] For this essay, I conducted dozens of interviews with military and civilian government analysts during three separate month-long trips to Beijing. These government think tank analysts are not decision-makers, but they advise and brief decision-makers in all relevant government organizations: the People's Liberation Army, the Foreign Ministry, the State Council, and the Chinese intelligence agencies. The research trips were hosted by the China Institute of Contemporary International Relations.

[2] I argue that, in general, Chinese security analysts think about their nation's security like Western scholars of realpolitik (e.g., E. H. Carr, Hans Morgenthau, and Henry Kissinger). One recent work argues that realpolitik thinking in China may have its roots in the dynastic era. See Alastair Iain Johnston, *Cultural Realism: Strategic Culture and Grand Strategy in Chinese History,* Princeton: Princeton University Press, 1995.

economic and security interests. Chinese analysts often view international organizations and their universal norms as fronts for other powers. Particularly in times of tension with the United States, such as mid-1995 when the United States allowed Taiwanese President Lee Teng-hui to visit, they view complaints about China's violations of international norms or laws as part of an integrated Western strategy, led by Washington, to prevent China from becoming a great power. Many analysts, particularly those in the military, believe that criticisms by foreign governments and nongovernmental organizations are plots to keep Beijing off balance and encourage domestic forces bent on the overthrow of the Chinese Communist Party or the breakup of the country.

China has not been cavalier in its attitudes toward multilateral organizations; it has been concerned and vigilant for reasons consistent with a hard-nosed view of international politics. For example, in 1994 Chinese analysts seemed wary of the Association of Southeast Asian Nations (ASEAN) and its new security forum, the ASEAN Regional Forum (ARF). Civilian and military experts were concerned that after Vietnam's acceptance into ASEAN, the organization might become an expanded, tacitly anti-Chinese alliance with links to the United States. They have argued against trying to create a formal security regime in East Asia to parallel the Organization for Security and Cooperation in Europe. Their fear seems to have been that in a more formal ARF, China might play Gulliver to Southeast Asia's Lilliputians, with the United States supplying the rope and stakes. If ARF were to adopt specific norms of transparency and rules on force deployment, it might enable the region to monitor and limit the growth of China's ability to project power.

China worries that a military buildup by Japan may be on the horizon.

China has participated fully in ARF activities since 1994, and its attitudes toward the organization have clearly softened on a range of issues. But Beijing still seems reluctant to use the multilateral forum to settle sovereignty disputes in the South China Sea, where islets, subject to overlapping territorial claims by the People's Republic of China, Taiwan, Malaysia, Vietnam, the Philippines, and Brunei are sprinkled across a vast stretch of seabed believed to contain rich oil and mineral deposits. Since China is the most powerful claimant, its wariness about the potential formation of a local anti-Chinese coalition is fully in accord with traditional balance-of-power politics.

Watching Japan

Chinese attitudes toward Japan mix elements of realpolitik with less antiseptic emotions rooted in China's bitter history of occupation by Japanese imperialists. Chinese security analysts, particularly military officers, anticipate and fear Japan's renaissance as a world-class military power in the early 21st century. These predictions are consistent with balance-of-power theories but not with the analysis of many Japan experts throughout the West, who believe that cultural pacifism after World War II, domestic political constraints, and economic interests will steer Japan away from such ambitions. Chinese analysts do not always dismiss these arguments out of hand, but many believe those obstacles will merely delay Japan's long-term military buildup. The two related and most important delaying factors, in the minds of these analysts, are the U.S.-Japan relationship, particularly the security alliance, and the political and economic stability of Japan. They believe that the United States, by reassuring Japan and providing its security on the cheap, fosters a political climate in which the Japanese public remains opposed to buildup and the more hawkish elements of the Japanese elite are kept at bay. If, however, the U.S.-Japan security alliance either comes under strain or undergoes a transformation in which Japan assumes a much more prominent military role, then, Chinese analysts believe, the ever-present hawks could more easily foment militarization.

Realpolitik would predict that the one-sided U.S.-Japan alliance will collapse after the demise of the common Soviet enemy. But Beijing's dread of various scenarios for change goes beyond the abstract logic of balance-of-power politics. According to that logic, China should be at least as concerned about coercion or attack by the world's only superpower, the United States, as about the remilitarization of Japan. As Secretary of Defense William Perry recently reminded China, America has by far the strongest military in the western Pacific. If one considers only military power, one might expect China to welcome the ejection of American forces from Japan and the rise of a new regional power that, in collaboration with China, might counter American regional hegemony. One might argue that Japan's geographic proximity alone would make a new regional power more of a threat to China than the more distant United States. But having lost hundreds of thousands of soldiers fighting the American military in the Korean War, China is unlikely to consider the United States a removed power. In any case, a conclusion about which nation poses a greater threat to China—a distant superpower or a local great power—cannot be reached by Chinese analysts or Western scholars weighing the international balance of power alone. It must be based largely on historical legacies and national perceptions.

If U.S.-Japan relations fray, China will want to quickly brace its arms.

The real reason that Chinese military and civilian analysts are so afraid of a breakdown or a fundamental change in the U.S-Japan alliance is a historically rooted and visceral distrust of Japan. Although they harbor suspicion toward the United States, they view Japan with even less trust and, in many cases, with a loathing rarely found in attitudes toward America. This is more a legacy of Japanese atrocities in the 1930s than a byproduct of contemporary Japanese power.[3] Like many other countries in the region, China seems grateful that America restrains Japanese militarization by guaranteeing Japanese security and replacing what would otherwise be Japanese aircraft carriers and marines with American ones. Although Chinese analysts are rarely so direct as to say that American forces should stay in Japan indefinitely, they are quick to say that they hope the United States will not leave anytime soon.

Through 1993 China's civilian and military analysts had similar takes on Japanese remilitarization. Japan's reemergence as a great power after World War II had been interpreted as the goal of a three-part grand strategy long pursued by the Liberal Democratic Party (LDP) leadership: first, become an economic superpower; next, a political superpower, by using increased economic aid and coercion and securing a Security Council seat; and finally, a significant military power that would vie for regional power and project force around the world. Many Chinese analysts were pessimistic about the ability of the U.S.-Japan security arrangement or domestic pacifism in Japan to prevent the timely completion of this long-term design.

In 1994 and 1995 this consensus seemed to break down in ways that may influence China's defense policy and international posture. Many analysts were influenced by Clinton administration pronouncements in 1994 and by the February 1995 Department of Defense East Asia strategy report, which underscored the importance for American post–Cold War strategy of the U.S.-Japan security alliance and the maintenance of at least 100,000 U.S. troops in the region. Some who had been skeptical about America's commitment to the region were reassured that the Soviet collapse and U.S. domestic politics were not going to render the remaining superpower isolationist and self-absorbed. Many Chinese analysts still agreed on the threat posed by the long-term goals of some Japanese elites, but the more liberal and moderate analysts in Beijing believed that, despite the domestic political shakeups in Japan, the desire for economic and social stability could dissuade Japan from launching any significant military initiatives, such as massive increases in defense spending or abrogation of the current Japanese ban on forces designed to project power more than 1,000 nautical miles from the home islands (e.g., aircraft carriers or aerial refueling planes). Also, these analysts seemed willing to believe that the U.S. military might be indefinitely engaged in the region, particularly in Japan.

Conservative Chinese analysts, many of whom are in the military, remained more skeptical about the durability of the American brake on Japan's military modernization. In 1993 and 1994, several of these analysts argued that the lack of a common enemy meant that Japan and the United States not only lost an incentive to cooperate in the western Pacific but gained an incentive to compete for economic and military influence in the region. They argued that the bilateral alliance would be poisoned by several factors: the effect of trade disputes and nationalist issues on domestic politics in both nations, the natural laws of international politics, and the zero-sum nature of Japanese and American rivalry in East Asia.

Since early 1995, Chinese security elites have found a new source of pessimism in the Clinton administration statements about "upgrading" or "strengthening" the U.S.-Japan defense relationship. If it were to occur, a U.S. withdrawal from Japan would still worry Chinese analysts most. However, America's presence in East Asia is only reassuring because it replaces—not strengthens—Japanese military forces. American efforts to improve Japanese defense technologies, introduce new weapons systems, and, most recently, encourage an expansion of Japanese roles in joint operations are perceived to undercut that role. The February 1995 Department of Defense East Asia strategy report received mixed responses from Beijing analysts. They seemed relieved that the United States set a formal floor for the size of its regional forces. However, they seemed worried by the suggestion that Japan and the United States might develop new weapons systems, including theater missile defense systems (TMD), that might counter China's deterrent capabilities against both Japan and Taiwan.

In the past, Chinese experts have worried about seemingly innocuous changes in Japan's defense policy, such as sending peacekeepers to Cambodia and minesweepers to the Persian Gulf. So the seemingly mild changes in policy that President Clinton and Prime Minister Ryutaro

---

[3] For the classic study of China's attitudes toward Japan, see Allen S. Whiting, *China Eyes Japan*, Berkeley: University of California Press, 1989.

Lansner/Black Star

Never let down your guard: A 1993 billboard promotes China's unsuccessful campaign to host the Summer Olympics in 2000.

Hashimoto announced in the April 1996 U.S.-Japan communiqué—e.g., increased Japanese logistic support for American missions in the region and consideration of future cooperation on theater missile defense systems—triggered strong negative responses from Beijing. Chinese analysts argue that unless the U.S.-Japan alliance were to turn sharply against Beijing and seek to contain China, little upgrading would be needed. Moreover, they believe that new roles for the Japanese military would only encourage independence from the United States and the development of Japan's force projection capabilities. One Chinese military analyst warned against American efforts to strengthen Japan's defense capabilities by citing a traditional Chinese expression, *yang hu yi huan,* which means, "When one raises a tiger, one courts calamity."

Whether or not they believe American abandonment or encouragement might spark Japanese militarization, few Chinese military or civilian analysts seem to believe that Chinese behavior could have much effect on the timing or intensity of a Japanese military buildup. Chinese analysts seem incredulous that Japan, given its history of aggression toward China dating back to the 1890s, could sincerely view China as a threat and alter its defense policy accordingly. If the current U.S.-Japan security relationship seems to be in trouble, there is likely to be a widening consensus among Chinese analysts that China should quickly build up its military power and settle various sovereignty disputes in the East and South China seas, by force, if necessary. Otherwise, China would have much less leverage against a Japanese navy and air force the is larger and could project power effectively into those areas. Chinese analysts realize that if Japan decided to strengthen its military capabilities its technological and economic base would allow it to do so quickly. They point to Tokyo's ongoing investment in defense-related technologies and to its defense

budget, which is small as a percentage of GNP but second only to America's in absolute size. Although outside observers might believe that China would be creating a self-fulfilling prophecy by anticipating an eventual Japanese buildup and threatening Japanese interests in the near term, most Chinese analysts do not believe China's behavior will affect Japanese policy. Consequently, Beijing is unlikely to factor Japanese fears of China into its policy equation.

Chinese analysts vary widely in their degree of pessimism about the likely pace and intensity of Japanese militarization, but there is a basic consensus that Japanese power would be more threatening than American power and that the status quo in the U.S.-Japan security arrangement—without upgrades—is desirable. This view is not immutable, however, and when the United States appears to be threatening core Chinese security interests, particularly the one-China policy barring Taiwanese independence, the U.S.-Japan alliance is perceived in a different light. In the summer of 1995, after Taiwanese President Lee Teng-hui's visit to Cornell University, Chinese analysts began to view the United States and Japan as collaborators in an attempt to break Taiwan away from the mainland. Suddenly American forces were not guarantors of Japanese restraint but instruments of tacit Japanese designs on China. The deployment of two U.S. aircraft carrier battle groups to Taiwan during Chinese missile exercises in March (including the *Independence,* based in Yokosuka, Japan) almost certainly affected Beijing's negative reaction to President Clinton's April trip to Japan and the resulting U.S.-Japan communiqué.

Worrying about Taiwan

Another area where realpolitik alone cannot account for Beijing's security attitudes is China's violent opposition to Taiwan's legal independence. China will almost certainly use force against Taiwan or Taiwanese interests (for example, shipping and offshore islands) if Taipei actively seeks independence. China will act even if it means damaging its profitable trade and investment relations with Taiwan, and it will do so regardless of the level of the U.S. military commitment to Taiwan's security. Since realpolitik would suggest attention to political realities, not legalities, it is puzzling why the change from de facto independence, which Taiwan has had since 1949, to legal independence would drive China to risk damage to its economy and war with the world's only superpower. But there is convincing evidence that China is prepared to do just that.

In China's century of humiliation, which began with a loss to the British in the Opium War and ended with the surrender of Japan in World War II, no event was more demeaning than the 1895 defeat at the hands of Japan, after which Taiwan was ceded to Tokyo. For the traditional Chinese state, it was degrading enough to be vanquished by "barbarians" from far-off lands like Britain and France. But given China's historical superiority to its tributary neighbors, succumbing to a local power was a much greater blow. Although Taiwan had little material value for China at the time, it became a symbol of this national tragedy. For Chinese, the return of Taiwan to China after World War II, as promised by the United States and Britain in the 1943 Cairo Declaration, was also a symbol of China's considerable contribution to the death of Japanese imperialism. Rectifying the century of humiliation is a core nationalist goal for any modern Chinese regime, and that means preventing the loss of Taiwan.

Preventing Taiwan's independence would be important to any Chinese regime, but it is a critical nationalist issue for the Chinese Communist Party government. The party has, by way of market reforms, all but obliterated the second of the two adjectives in its name. Almost no influential figure in Chinese government or society believes in communism anymore, and that has created a vacuum that nationalism, always a strong element in the party's legitimacy, is filling. As many analysts have noted, nationalism is the sole ideological glue that holds the People's Republic together and keeps the CCP government in power. Since the Chinese Communist Party is no longer communist, it must be even more Chinese.

China's military wants to regain the pride it lost at Tiananmen.

As continuing economic reforms and exposure of the Chinese people to Western ideas and international news cut ever more deeply into CCP legitimacy, there are few issues left that do not trigger debate and exacerbate tensions between the state and society. Yet in all sectors of politically aware Chinese society a consensus remains on the legitimacy of using force, if necessary, to prevent Taiwan's independence. On that issue one is almost as likely to hear a hawkish reaction from scholars who protested in Tiananmen Square in 1989 as from a military officer who fired on them.

Chinese leaders will go to extraordinary lengths to prevent Taiwan's independence in part because they fear a national breakup. Chinese analysts believe that national integrity would be threatened by an uncontested declaration of Taiwanese independence, especially because of the decades of propaganda about Taiwan's unbreakable

links to the motherland. They subscribe to a domestic domino theory in which the loss of one piece of sovereign territory will encourage separatists elsewhere and hurt morale among the Chinese forces who must defend national unity. Their most notable concerns are with traditionally non-Han regions such as Tibet, Xinjiang, and Inner Mongolia.

Not surprisingly, People's Liberation Army officers are even more hawkish than civilian analysts on sovereignty issues, particularly Taiwan. To justify increasing military budgets after the collapse of the Soviet Union, which was regarded as China's main military threat, the army needs a mission, and defending sovereignty is not a hard sell. On political grounds, tensions with Taiwan make the military even more important in the succession struggles that will follow the death of Deng Xiaoping. Although few China experts in the West expect a military coup, almost all believe that the military will play kingmaker. Gaining early military support and avoiding opposition from the military should prove critical to any leader hoping to succeed Deng.

PLA leaders, particularly the influential officers living in and around Beijing, also desperately want to regain their social standing after the Tiananmen massacre. Almost all PLA officers believe that the pro-democracy protests should have been suppressed forcibly, but several expressed embarrassment over the level of force used and the damage to the military's image. Chinese military officers, like professional soldiers around the world, take pride in their work. The chance to show that their main mission is defending national integrity, not shooting unarmed civilians, will not be forfeited lightly.

One may get the impression that civilian leaders will grapple with Taiwan as a central issue if there is a succession struggle following Deng's death. Although attempts to endear themselves to the military and hard-liners may make economically oriented technocrats more macho and nationalistic, the jockeying is more likely to manifest itself in their attitudes toward the defense budget, the Spratly Islands disputes, or Western criticism of Chinese human rights violations than in their opposition to Taiwan's independence. Strong differences of opinion apparently have formed between more moderate and more hawkish Chinese over the wisdom of using military exercises to deter Taiwan from pursuing independence. Many elites apparently had strong reservations about the last and most provocative round of exercises in March, before the Taiwanese elections. But these differences would likely disappear if Taiwan appeared to be on the brink of declaring independence. In that case a broad consensus, including dovish liberal technocrats as well as hawkish conservatives, would likely form around a hard-line policy.

Democracy is served by having Taiwan remain nominally part of China.

Succession struggles are not meaningless, however. The political process may make China more sensitive about what constitutes a significant move toward independence by President Lee Teng-hui's government. Taiwan's self-styled "pragmatic diplomacy" has been presented publicly as a bid to increase the island's diplomatic space and recognition without abandoning the one-China principle that Taipei has so strongly adhered to since 1949. But Beijing believes that Lee is tacitly pursuing independence. Chinese analysts say that Lee has not said so in public for purely pragmatic reasons, the most important of which is the threat of violent retaliation from the mainland. When nerves are raw in Beijing and succession politics are under way, Taipei must be very careful not to take actions that might seem mild in Taipei and elsewhere but might be interpreted in Beijing as significant advances toward independence.

Implications for U.S. Policy

By keeping American forces in Japan, the United States can simultaneously reassure Japan and its major potential rival, China, and thereby stabilize the region. Washington should do more than stay engaged; it should reassure Japan and other regional powers publicly and often that it intends to do so indefinitely. Any suggestion that the United States might withdraw its forces from Japan may set off an arms race, escalating tensions, and self-fulfilling prophecies about Japanese militarization, all of which will destabilize the region. Chinese security analysts watch closely what the United States says about its relationship with Japan, and the division between Chinese conservatives and moderates is most visible in predictions about the hardiness of the current U.S.-Japan defense arrangement. Anything that underscores America's long-term commitment to protect Japan with American forces will have a positive impact on China and helps the moderate analysts sell their message of stability and optimism to CCP leaders. Anything that suggests either fragility or fundamental reform in the U.S.-Japan security relationship has a negative impact on China and helps conservative, hard-line analysts sell their portrayal of a threat from Japan and prescriptions for a tougher Chinese security posture. For example, any linkage of the U.S.-Japan security arrangement with reduction of America's trade deficit with Japan would be irresponsible because it would quickly be interpreted in Beijing

as an omen of discord in the U.S.-Japan alliance. Encouraging Japan to take on more military roles also may not be a good short-term strategy. For example, the United States should weigh carefully the political cost of U.S.-Japan TMDs against their military benefits. The political implications should be taken at least as seriously as the political costs of ballistic missile defenses and scrapping the Antiballistic Missile Treaty for America's Russia policy. Since China, like Russia, is in a transition period, U.S.-Japan TMD should be considered using a similar type of cost-benefit analysis.

The United States should make a clear distinction between its general goal of spreading democracy and its policy on Taiwanese sovereignty. Taiwanese democracy and Taiwanese independence are logically and morally separate issues. The United States should support the former and distance itself from the latter. Indeed, if the United States wants to spread democracy, it should encourage Taiwan to remain nominally part of China. When Taiwan claims to be both Chinese and democratic, it puts the lie to Beijing officials' claim that Chinese culture and Western-style democracy do not mix. In the "enlargement" strategy of the United States, China is a prize 55 times larger than Taiwan. American idealists should not be myopic and settle for current Taiwanese independence at the expense of future Chinese democracy.

Until tensions settle down, both in relations between Taipei and the mainland and in the succession politics of Beijing, Washington should discourage President Lee from aggressively pursuing his pragmatic diplomacy agenda. For example, Washington should not only refuse to support Taiwan's bid for entry into the United Nations, it should discourage Taipei from vigorously pursuing that goal in the near term. The United States should provide a guarantee of support for Taiwanese security, including direct American intervention if necessary, but this guarantee should be conditional: Taiwan's democracy will be assisted only if it does not provoke an attack by moving toward formal independence.

Taiwan should not provoke an attack just to transform a de facto reality into a legal one.

Even generally hawkish military and civilian analysts in Beijing have firmly stated that the current Chinese government would never attack Taiwan out of the blue, so it would be fair to deduce that a reversal in this policy would carry grave implications. A China that would launch an unprovoked, military reunification campaign that violates its own economic and political interests would have to be a radically more aggressive China. The United States would have to contain such a China vigorously or expect to face it in battle soon. For either of those tasks, Taiwan is a better platform than most.

If, however, Taiwan takes provocative diplomatic steps toward a more independent legal status, the United States should let Taiwan know unequivocally that it will also stand alone in security matters. Taiwan and the United States stand to lose too much in a fight against the mainland, particularly for the mere purpose of transforming a de facto reality—Taiwan's independence—into a legal one. If Taiwan declared independence and was then attacked by the mainland, one could not draw conclusions about Beijing's expansionist designs any more than one could draw conclusions about American expansionism from the northern states' reaction to the South's secession. If Taiwanese independence provokes the attack, Taiwan could hardly be portrayed as China's Sudetenland, and American aloofness could not be compared to Chamberlain's appeasement at Munich.

Some American security analysts believe that Taiwan is a logical place for Washington to draw the first unconditional containment line around any potential Chinese aggression. Taiwan is, as MacArthur said long ago, an unsinkable aircraft carrier, and it has a strong military and economy with which the United States could join forces. But if the United States were to draw a line in the Taiwan Strait now and offer unconditional assurances to Taiwan, this would encourage Taiwanese independence and spark hypernationalism in China, creating just the kind of expansionist, hard-line regime in Beijing that America and everyone else in the region fear.

On military grounds alone, Washington should recognize that, while Taiwan may be an unsinkable aircraft carrier, it is also an immovable one. Although China probably could not invade Taiwan successfully even if America stood on the sidelines, the United States can do little to defend Taiwan from attacks that, though a far cry from invasion, would devastate its economy. China can use force effectively against Taiwan without the slightest pretense of a D-Day–style invasion. The mere announcement that shipping around Taiwan was no longer safe from assault would cripple Taiwan's trade-dependent economy. If a few missiles landed in Taipei, the stock market there would likely crash. The drop in Taipei stocks from the first P.R.C. missile exercises last July to the last round of exercises preceding this year's March 23 elections testifies to the danger of even limited threats, let alone force.

In March the Clinton administration may have finally found a balance in its policy toward the dispute over Taiwan. Although the current leadership in Beijing was almost certainly not preparing to attack Taiwan even if America stood idly by, Washington's deployment of two carrier battle groups to the area sent a long-term signal to any hypernationalists in Beijing who might vie for power after Deng's death: the cost of an unprovoked attack on Taiwan will likely be high. At the same time, the United States avoided the politically provocative and militarily imprudent option of placing carrier battle groups in the Taiwan Strait itself.

Although it received far less news coverage than the deployment of the carriers, an equally important message was apparently sent to Taiwan through back channels and carefully worded public statements by high-level administration officials: Washington supports Taiwan's security conditionally, and it expects Taipei to avoid provoking the mainland. While the United States cannot and should not dictate policy to the democratically elected government of Taiwan, it should stress the dangers and costs of certain options so that Taiwanese officials do not base their strategic policies on misperceptions and false hopes of unconditional U.S. support.

The United States should not limit its regional role to helping Taiwan defend against unprovoked attack. Instead, it should continue to commit itself to the peaceful settlement of the sovereignty disputes in the South China Sea. The United States need not and should not take sides there, but it should guarantee peaceful resolutions. By doing so, the United States is not "containing" China, it is protecting international sea-lanes in the region.

This policy is more prudent than a containment policy and an unconditional commitment to Taiwan's security. Beijing's claim to the Spratly Islands does not carry the same emotional baggage as its claim to Taiwan. By adopting a neutral stance on the sovereignty disputes, the United States would reduce the risk of appearing imperialistic and fueling Chinese hypernationalism. Most important, the United States would be taking actions with the express purpose of protecting Japan's sea-lanes. A large percentage of Japan's trade and the majority of its oil imports from the Middle East pass through those international waters, and keeping them open and safe is a vital security interest for Japan. If the United States explained to China and all other regional actors that the alternative to U.S. Navy patrols would be Japanese navy patrols, the message probably would not fall on deaf ears.

America has huge stakes in the political transitions of China and other East Asian nations. By remaining engaged in the region and rejecting short-sighted strategies such as a Cold War–style containment policy toward China, the United States will improve the odds that China's next generation of leaders will be moderate at home and abroad. As the differences between Deng Xiaoping and Mao Zedong make clear, leadership matters, especially in nondemocratic countries. Chinese elites' current realpolitik tendencies are infinitely preferable to the messianic versions of Chinese nationalism that might come to the fore if the United States, Japan, or other powers treat Beijing as an enemy. By engaging China and encouraging its participation in multilateral forums and confidence-building regimes, over the long term the United States may help soften China's skepticism about these institutions, which could help stabilize East Asia.

Article 18   *Harvard International Review,* Spring 1996

The Giant Wakes

The Chinese Challenge to East Asia

Gerald Segal

Gerald Segal is a Senior Fellow at the International Institute for Strategic Studies, Director of Britain's Pacific Asia Program, and Co-Chairman of the European Council for Security Co-operation in Asia Pacific.

The rise of China undeniably poses a problem for East Asian security. Those who suggest that there is not a problem are either strategically myopic or have prematurely capitulated to the notion of a Sinified East Asia. The real question is how to define the nature and extent of the Chinese challenge. Although China is often compared to the Soviet Union, a more appropriate comparison might be to Japan or Germany in the 1930s. China is undergoing far-reaching and destabilizing social and economic reform, while its authoritarian leadership is losing its ability to control China's rapidly changing social, economic and political system. Meanwhile, China is spending increasing amounts (in absolute terms) on its armed forces. Most importantly, China, like 1930s Germany or Japan, is a non-status quo, increasingly nationalistic power that seeks to change its frontiers and to reorder the international system. These trends do not necessarily prove that China is a threat. But it is instructive that these are precisely the characteristics of great powers in the past century that have posed the biggest challenge to their neighbors and to international order.

If these fundamental features of China are not cause enough for concern, consider China's past and present weight. For centuries China was the world's greatest civilization. It is still the world's longest lasting empire. Until 1850 it was the world's largest economy. In short, there is nothing extraordinary about the current rise of China, for in fact it is the re-rise of China. As a result, there is nothing especially odd about the people who live close

to China deciding that when China is strong, they must accommodate rather than confront their giant neighbor.

During the past 150 years East Asians had grown used to a weaker and divided China. While China was tearing itself apart, other East Asian nations achieved remarkable economic success. Now that China too is on the rise, East Asians have to decide if they wish to allow China to regain its suzerain status in the region, or whether they wish to constrain Chinese behavior. If China is to be constrained, then it will have to be while it is still vulnerable to being tied into the international system.

Before the notion of "constrainment" is misread as "containment," it should be noted that China, as has already been suggested, is not very much like the Soviet Union during the Cold War. China's military is not poised to thrust through the Asian equivalent of the German plains. China is far more interdependent in the global market economy than the USSR ever was, and it is becoming even more so. China has abandoned its support for revolutionary Communist movements in East Asia, and its ruling Communist Party has abandoned Marxism-Leninism in all but name. But accepting that China is not to be contained like the Soviet Union should not mean abandoning all notion of constraining China's international behavior. It is important to avoid over learning the lessons of the Cold War and forgetting the lessons of earlier struggles against unstable and unsatisfied great powers.

Territorial Ambitions

China has territorial disputes with most of its neighbors and has refused to forswear the use of force to regain lost land. While its disputes with India are not a problem at the moment, this is only because India has essentially recognized the current lines of control, and China claims no Indian land beyond what it now holds. China and Russia have made some progress in delineating frontiers, and China has apparently abandoned its wider claims for territory seized by Czarist forces. Interestingly, Russia is the only resident power in East Asia with military power superior to that of China. China also claims islands currently held by South Korea and Japan but has put these issues aside while it seeks the economic benefits of good relations with these two countries.

The current focus of Chinese territorial ambition i[s] further south. In 1984, China obtained the agreement of the United Kingdom to return Hong Kong and its six million people to Chinese control in 1997. China clearly could have taken Hong Kong whenever it wanted to, but it saw the benefit of receiving a Hong Kong in decent economic shape, and this required a modicum of cooperation with Britain. That deal is now done, and as 1997 approaches China has shown ever more clearly that [it] feels unconstrained in molding Hong Kong to suit its interests. China promised to safeguard Hong Kong under the slogan of "one country-two systems," but it is already apparent that there will be one system for all.

The fate of Hong Kong is being watched by the 21 million people of Taiwan. The Taiwanese government once claimed to be the rightful government of all China, but it has now abandoned such a pretense. The rulers in Beijing have done no such thing. They view the signs of increasing support for self-determination in Taiwan as a fundamental threat to Chinese sovereignty and see no reason why they should eschew the use of force to prevent such a trend. In 1995 and again in 1996, China closed air and sea lanes in East Asia in order to "test-fire" missiles as a sign that it was still prepared to use force to crush even a democratically-elected government in Taiwan committed to self-determination.

Few doubt the sincerity of Beijing's threats, and therefore no East Asian government is prepared to suggest that it might be sympathetic to the Taiwanese people's calls for assistance in exercising their democratic right of self-determination. Only the more distant Western powers, especially the United States, remain less equivocal. They tell China that it should not use force to settle this dispute, but stop short of giving Taiwan a blank check to declare independence and trigger just the kind of crisis that everyone hopes will somehow go away. Many hope that Taiwan and China can reach some sort of pragmatic accommodation, perhaps in a loose federal structure, but even if such an accord could be reached, it would be a long time in the future.

Just as East Asians do not doubt China's determination to regain Taiwan, so they do not doubt China's desire and eventual ability to take the disputed islands, shoals, and rocks of the South China Sea. In the 1970s, China claimed and eventually took the more northerly Paracel islands. In the 1990s, it is working its way through the Spratly islands, taking all it can, albeit in a relatively cautious manner. In 1995, China took on a member state of the Association of Southeast Asian Nations (ASEAN) for the first time, seizing territory claimed by the Philippines. China has agreed to be bound by the United Nations Law of the Sea Convention, but only on the basis of Chinese sovereignty over the disputed territory. Thus China promised to allow freedom of navigation, but was determined to take and to hold the territory and the resources that might lie in its vicinity. East Asians know that everything China takes, it keeps. They also know that China is a threat in the sense that it is taking what they once thought was theirs. But they feel China cannot be stopped and, in any case, China has no desire to take their main territory.

A Chinese Order

Even if China satisfies its territorial ambitions in Hong Kong, Taiwan, and the South China Sea, and persuades Japan and South Korea to surrender their islands, it will not necessarily become a satisfied power. What China, like the Soviet Union during the Cold War, seems to want is a predominant voice in managing regional international relations.

Consider Chinese policy toward the most important regional security issue where China is not a direct protagonist: the Korean conflict. China is a neighbor of North Korea—indeed, it is North Korea's only ally. While China was flexible enough to open economic relations with South Korea, much to the chagrin of its ally in Pyongyang, it only normalized diplomatic ties when it was the last major power without decent relations with South Korea. In short, China's natural inclination was to take what economic benefit it could get from the relationship with the South, while not budging on political issues until it was too embarrassed to be so isolated.

As for security issues, China's behavior throughout the tension surrounding North Korea's nuclear program in 1993–1994 was at best passive and at worst obstructive of international efforts to force North Korea to comply with the International Atomic Energy Association (IAEA). China did not want a nuclear-armed North Korea, but it also did not want North Korea to be bullied into submission by the United States and its Western allies. So China equivocated. It declined to press North Korea to make concessions and most often claimed to be without influence in Pyongyang. Western negotiators remain uncertain about whether China did anything through private channels, but they certainly decline to say China was being helpful.

The 1994 agreement with North Korea accorded almost perfectly with Chinese desires, as North Korea was both

hored up with Western assistance and not forced to capitulate. Pyongyang was allowed to remain ambiguous
about whether it had diverted enough nuclear material
into a weapons program. Japan and South Korea were
persuaded that China would not cut off food and fuel
supplies to North Korea so there was no point in seeking
sanctions, with all the attendant risks of conflict. Thus
the outcome of the Korea negotiations demonstrated that
China was the major power in Northeast Asia—quite a
change from earlier in the century when Russians and
Japanese could pillage Chinese territory in Northeast
Asia at will.

The lessons of the Korean nuclear crisis suggest that,
while China is prepared to talk about regional security,
it will seek to, and often can, win the result most favorable to its own national interests rather than to the interests of general security. Much the same lesson can be
drawn from China's approach to regional security in East
Asia as a whole. East Asians are only at the earliest stage
of building what might someday be worthy of the name
"regional security." East Asia made abortive attempts to
establish regional security structures during the Cold
War, but by the time the Soviet Union collapsed and its
regional allies deflated, there was little left of regional
security thinking, let alone any formal structures. The
only formal multilateral arrangement in East Asia was a
leftover of the British empire, the Five Power Defense
Arrangements.

When East Asians began to think seriously about formal multilateralism, they began with the only half-way
serious regional institution, ASEAN. ASEAN itself is
more of a mutual confidence-building club, and it is certainly not an intrusive organization designed to constrain
national security policy. Thus, when ASEAN formed the
ASEAN Regional Forum (ARF), it did so with the dual
recognition of its limited ability to constrain national security policy, even well into the future, and the need to
accommodate the main post-Cold War feature of regional
security—the rise of China. The combination of these two
notions gave China a de facto veto over the development
of regional security.

If China were committed to interdependence of security, openness, transparency, and confidence building
measures, it could have seized the initiative by setting
the ARF on a dynamic course of building regional security. China's actual behavior was quite the opposite and
quite understandable from the Chinese point of view.
China, and probably most of its neighbors, felt that it
was natural for China to dominate regional security and
saw no reason why Beijing should encourage the
strengthening of international forces that would merely
constrain China's ability to act as it sees fit.
So far, the result of this attitude has been predictable.
The ARF is little more than a gentleman's dining club.

The non-governmental partner of the ARF, the Council
on Security and Cooperation in Asia Pacific (CSCAP) has
not moved much further, largely because China is blocking any attempt to have Taiwanese representation in
CSCAP. Neither the ARF nor CSCAP will discuss the Taiwan question. The South China Sea issue was raised in
the ARF, but China made no change to its position regarding sovereignty. China has agreed to consider publishing a report on its military, but China's record on
publishing accurate military information is abysmal. In
sum, there is no regional security in East Asia that is not
Chinese security.

Shaping Regional Order

One might well ask whether there [is] anything necessarily wrong with China taking the territory that it wants
and ordering the international relations of East Asia in
its own image, so long as China leaves us alone to live
in peace. However, while China may become a satisfied
and cooperative power when it has what it wants and
its neighbors know their place, the logic of an increasingly interdependent East Asia suggests that such a future is not likely.

> *China's policies and the ASEAN response suggest that China is not willing to accept the constraints of economic interdependence. As China grows strong and incorporates Hong Kong, its economic clout will be such that it can drive most of its neighbors into submission.*

For example, China has already made it clear that it
will tell its neighbors what policies they should have toward Taiwan. ASEAN states provoke Chinese wrath

when Taiwanese officials visit for vacations, and Beijing even tells Japan which Taiwanese officials can visit without causing a diplomatic row. China also tells East Asians and others how they should handle visiting Chinese dissidents or the Dalai Lama. Even journalists and academics are told that they should stop writing critical things about China, or else they will be denied visas. When the writers remain uncowed, China then goes after the investors and even charities that support such freedom of expression by threatening to close access to the Chinese market.

Indeed, Chinese behavior on trade issues also suggests that it sees nothing wrong with hegemonic behavior in economic affairs. When Japan's trade surplus with China began to grow very large, Chinese officials instructed the Japanese government to restore a better balance, and China's brow beating succeeded where US threats of trade retaliation had failed. It is quite possible that China may soon demand the transfer of technology from the developed states of East Asia, even technology banned by the United States and the European Union (EU).

Not surprisingly, China is resistant to being constrained by the rules of the World Trade Organization (WTO), and Chinese negotiators still reject the idea that it should be subject to the WTO dispute settlement mechanism. Most ASEAN states have already accepted the Chinese argument, but Japan remains quietly supportive of US and EU demands that China be bound by the rules. China's policies and the ASEAN response suggest that China is not willing to accept the constraints of economic interdependence. As China grows strong and incorporates Hong Kong, its economic clout will be such that it can drive most of its neighbors into submission. China is unlikely to accept the kind of constraints that the United States accepted in joining the North American Free Trade Agreement.

The notion of China engaging in free trade in East Asia is so far in the future that there is little point in prolonging the discussion. But before moving on to considering responses to the Chinese challenge, consider a few other problems China might pose in the future. For instance, there is the possibility that if Russia collapses even further, China will seek to solve its dependence on foreign energy by taking the Russian Far Eastern territories. After all, China once claimed these territories as its own. China might also take a more active role in defense of beleaguered ethnic Chinese in Southeast Asia. Should Indonesia or Malaysia suffer internal struggles where ethnic Chinese are the targets of discrimination or worse, China would not sit idly by. Even if China does not use force to intervene, the ASEAN states would still find that

their domestic affairs are ordered in part by the fear of what China might do.

Constraining China

Whether there is a will in East Asia to constrain China is unclear. The current conventional wisdom is that China should be "engaged." Of course it should. Few could argue with the noble goals of the ARF and of expanding economic relations. The problem is that engagement is a necessary but not sufficient condition of successful policy. All too often those who suggest that something more than engagement is necessary are dismissed as supporters of "containment" who oppose engagement. But engagement alone does not constrain China, especially an increasingly nationalistic China that sees talk of interdependence as a challenge to Chinese sovereignty.

If East Asians want [to] formulate a policy of "constrainment," they must start with a determination of interests. Most East Asians do not want China to take Taiwan or the South China Sea, but they feel there is little they can do to stop it. This legacy of Sinification is a major psychological affliction, as it tends to become a self-fulfilling prophecy. The assumption that nothing can be done means that those in the United States, Australia, Japan, Indonesia, Malaysia, the Philippines, and Thailand who might wish to build a de facto deterrence of China are not given the support to try. Hence US troops find it hard to establish bases. We are left with talk of "virtual alliances" and a "virtual American presence" in East Asia. That is a virtual policy.

If China is to be constrained, it will have to be told what others do not want it to do. It will have to be deterred from doing so. And if it persists, it will have to be compelled to cease. To some extent such a firm policy has only recently been adopted by the United States regarding Chinese threats to Taiwan. The United States can be firm if it wants to.

Constraining the Soviet Union was a tall order during the Cold War, and the current international conditions are far from propitious for constraining China. What is far more likely is a pre-Cold War type of international relations, in which timid powers shy of confrontation appease rising nationalists. Should this scenario come to pass, China will dominate East Asia and take what it wants. But if East Asians want to prevent Chinese domination and defend the freedom of action that they still have, they will have to recognize that the challenge posed by China's growing power is real and demands a firm response.

Article 19   *The Economist*, August 17, 1996

A Funny-Looking Tiger

What can the Asian tigers tell us about the future of China?

For almost 20 years China has had the fastest growing economy in the world. Even so it is easy to find people deeply pessimistic about the country's future. Western academics speculate about political turmoil, hyperinflation and national disintegration. In China itself, many intellectuals share some of this western pessimism and base their worries on the cyclical features of Chinese history, in which dynasties rise and fall and periods of prosperity and strength are followed by periods of weakness and chaos.

If you are looking for optimists, however, the people to talk to are overseas-Chinese businessmen in the rest of Asia. They were the first to spot what was happening in China after the start of Deng Xiaoping's economic reforms in 1978, and the first to invest. After the Tiananmen Square massacre of 1989, the overseas Chinese retained their faith and continued to invest, while westerners pulled back. Even today, investors from Hong Kong, Taiwan and South-East Asia have bigger stakes in China than have American or Japanese multinationals. Nothing seems to shake their confidence. Just months after China was threatening to invade Taiwan, Formosa Plastics, one of the island's largest firms, announced plans to invest $3.8 billion in new power plants on the mainland.

The overseas Chinese base their optimism on the belief that China is just the latest and largest in a series of Asian economic miracles. To them, the lessons for China of the tiger economies—Hong Kong, Malaysia, Singapore, South Korea, Taiwan, and Thailand—are twofold. First, that growth of the sort that China has had for two decades can be maintained for many years yet. Second, that political turmoil of the sort experienced by China in 1989 need not prevent growth. Indeed, for many tigers, a massacre seems to have been a sort of bloody rite of passage to economic adulthood.

Much of the debate about the future of China involves, in one way or another, this parallel with Asia's tiger economies. If the optimists are right, China is just another tiger and its future

is clear: there will be decades more of supercharged growth, probably accompanied by gradual political liberalisation, as the market economy breeds a more pluralistic society. For many of the pessimists, however, the things that distinguish China from the tigers are more striking than the similarities.

Economically, they say, China has not yet overcome the legacy of central planning. Internationally, it faces more uncertainties than other countries in the region that have sheltered under America's security umbrella. At home, China's dictatorship is in its own league when it comes to the brutalities it has inflicted upon its people, and its political problems still run deep; no one knows what will happen after the death of Mr Deng. Above all, there is the country's size. China's population is now over 1.2 billion, and 70% live in the countryside. In contrast, the two tiger economies to have made it into the club of rich countries—Hong Kong and Singapore—are city-states, and the largest of the middle-income tigers, South Korea, has 40m people—the size of a middling Chinese province.

So who is right? The answer depends on economics, politics and the international environment in which China will develop.

The Economic Parallels

On the economic arguments, the optimists seem, for the most part, justified. Take long-term growth rates. The experience of the other tigers shows that annual growth of 8–10% can be sustained for many years. South Korea is now growing at almost 8% a year, even though its GDP per head is now more than $10,000. Singapore is an even more spectacular case. Its GDP per head is now almost the same as that of America—and its economy has lately been growing at rates of up to 10% a year.

Moreover, some of the factors that were crucial to the growth of the tigers also seem to obtain in China. High savings, for example, have permitted very high levels of investment. In China, at 40% of GDP, the savings rate is even

higher than the thrifty East Asian average (see chart).

The fact that Asian governments consume a relatively small share of GDP has also been important to growth. Remarkably, despite being run by a Communist Party, the Chinese government's share of GDP is tiny. Officially, government spending was just 11.6% of GDP last year, compared to around 20% in the Asian tigers (see chart). Off-the-books revenue-raising schemes by local governments may mean that the Chinese state's take is twice the officially stated level. Even so, the basic point remains that the Chinese government's share of national income is comparable to those of the tigers.

In one respect, China is arguably better off. The enormous size of its labour force should mean that it will take much longer for China to experience upward pressure on wages as a result of labour shortages.

A final parallel with the tigers which supports the optimists' case is the extent to which China's economic dynamism is linked to success in manufactured exports. Though the tigers are now experiencing difficulties as their rate of export growth slows, it is clear that, in the long run, a determination to export has helped East Asia's most successful economies to increase productivity and to embrace international standards in technology and product development. China is following the pattern. In 1978 its exports totalled a mere $9.8 billion. By 1994, they were $121 billion, making China the eighth largest exporter of manufactured goods in the world.

On the other hand, the structure of Chinese exports provides the pessimists with their first reason for caution over the country's prospects. Though the growth of China's exports compares well with that of the tigers, the country is unusually dependent on foreign investors to make them. While foreigners account for just 2% of China's manufactured output, they account for 30% of its exports—and this proportion is growing, not shrinking.

The East Asian experience has been that the efficiency of foreign investors

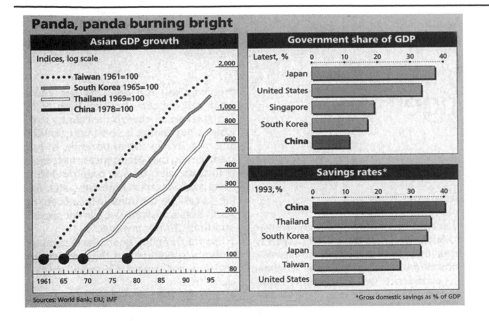

Panda, panda burning bright

Asian GDP growth
Indices, log scale

•••• Taiwan 1961=100
—— South Korea 1965=100
—— Thailand 1969=100
—— China 1978=100

Government share of GDP
Latest, %

Japan, United States, Singapore, South Korea, **China**

Savings rates*
1993, %

China, Thailand, South Korea, Japan, Taiwan, United States

Sources: World Bank; EIU; IMF

*Gross domestic savings as % of GDP

will rub off on domestic producers. But that does not seem to be happening in China. Nicholas Lardy, an expert on Chinese foreign trade, reckons that "To some extent export industries appear to be enclaves." He worries that "Over the longer term it will be difficult for China to sustain the growth of exports at anywhere near that of the past decade, unless there is widespread industrial restructuring." The recent decline in Chinese exports suggests that Mr Lardy's pessimism may be being borne out.

Doubt over the future of Chinese exports points to the fact that, despite similarities to the tigers, the legacy of central planning has left China with some unique problems. Two big and related difficulties have still to be overcome: a financial system which is not yet run on market lines, and the country's huge number of loss-making state-owned enterprises. These are the two main economic planks in the pessimists' case.

One legacy of central planning is that China has more than 100,000 state-run companies, employing two-thirds of the urban workforce. This means that the unusually low figure for state spending as a share of GDP does not capture the full extent of government involvement in the economy. The government admits that almost half the state-sector firms are losing money and that the proportion is rising.

Anxious about creating mass unemployment in the cities, the government is committed to keeping these sinking firms afloat. As a result state banks—which are meant to lend on commercial lines—are, in reality, under pressure to keep extending credit to state firms. The

consequence is that a mass of unpaid debts is undermining the financial system. So, while the Chinese may save a great deal, a lot of that saving is wasted. Something like 70% of bank loans to industry still go to the state sector, which produces just 34% of industrial output. The pressure on the government to provide fresh credits to state-run firms also means that China is still vulnerable to bouts of inflation.

The pessimists are right to draw attention to these weaknesses in the economy, but the question is whether they can be dealt with. On this, economists are increasingly hopeful. The private sector is growing so fast that the state's share of production and employment is falling steadily. According to Fan Gang, one of China's leading economists, the number employed by state industries has fallen by 10m to 90m in the past year alone. The growth of private firms, alongside the quasi-private economy of China's so-called "township and village enterprises" (companies set up by local governments but run on market lines), may mean that withering of the state sector can be managed smoothly. That in turn should allow more resources to be shifted to the private sector, increasing China's potential for growth.

Similarly, while China has far to go before establishing a market-based financial system, the central bank is now saying the right things—and even doing some of them. A recent surge in inflation (which hit 27% in 1993) was reined in without provoking a crash, in marked contrast to the boom-bust cycles of the 1980s. This suggests that the govern-

ment is developing better tools for managing the economy.

Certainly, few western economists watching China are predicting that growth will slow any time soon. Pieter Bottelier, head of the World Bank's office in Beijing, thinks that China's current growth is sustainable for another 20 years. But, if that is to happen, he concedes, much will depend on continuing stability in domestic politics and international affairs. Neither can be relied upon.

The Political Questions

Asian businessmen were much less fazed by the killings in Tiananmen Square than westerners. After all, many had witnessed similar events in their own countries—and seen them prosper.

In 1980 the South Korean army killed thousands of civilians in Kwangju; the decade of military rule that followed saw GDP grow by 177%. In 1976 the Thai army killed hundreds of students at Thammasat University, Bangkok; the Thai military was only dislodged from power 20 years later, having seen output rise by 235% over the period. The rule of both the Kuomintang (KMT) in Taiwan and President Suharto in Indonesia was established after massacres of thousands. They too became tigers.

Clearly, bloodshed and repression do not preclude an economic miracle. Nor do they preclude a subsequent move towards democracy. Three of these countries—Taiwan, Thailand and South Korea—are now among the most democratic in East Asia.

Since many Asian businessmen put the killings in China in 1989 in the context of the development of the rest of East Asia, they were less quick to assume that Tiananmen was a harbinger of economic disaster. But dismissing the events of 1989 as just a regrettable blip, typical of Asian miracles, may be too glib. In politics, the pessimists have good grounds for worrying that China's problems run much deeper than those of the rest of East Asia.

Unlike the tigers (though like Vietnam), China is having to make the transition to a market economy under Communist-Party rule. That seems to make the country's historical burden the more onerous. One of the more sinister aspects of modern China is that Mao Zedong, a man responsible for the deaths of more of his compatriots than Stalin, is still an official national hero. There is little discussion of the terror and brainwashing of the Cultural Revolution

1966–76); none of the Mao-made famine of the Great Leap Forward (1959–61). It is as if Russia still banned discussion of the Great Terror and gulags, or as if Germany had never undergone denazification. China's reckoning with its own history is likely to be far more painful and destabilising than anything that the tigers have endured. Whereas South Korea has been able to pin blame for the Kwangju killings on the generals who ran the country at the time, in China an entire system—built around the Communist Party—will be at stake.

China's leaders may hope to take heart from the case of Taiwan. The ruling KMT operated a Leninist one-party system, but managed to preserve its grip on power, while moving towards democracy and allowing a limited reassessment of history. But the KMT, while no softies, were not responsible for the deaths of millions. Nor do Taiwanese leaders fear, as the mainland Chinese do, that liberalisation may unleash separatism in the country. In that respect, the position of China is more like that of sprawling Indonesia, which, significantly, has also not made any substantial moves towards political liberalisation.

The fact is that China's immense size continues to haunt its politics. Great disparities of income divide the rich coastal regions from the poorer inland provinces. This makes the Communist Party reluctant to loosen the reins of power for fear of losing control, while simultaneously making central control harder to maintain. The more growth widens the disparities, the greater the dilemma. The reluctance of the central government to delegate power also makes it harder to collect taxes and maintain law and order—in short, to govern.

None of this means that political liberalisation is impossible—or even unlikely—in China. But it does suggest that, when change does happen, it may be more violent and destabilising than anything that occurred in South Korea or Taiwan.

Outside the Middle Kingdom

One last difference could distinguish China's political and economic path from that of the rest of East Asia, and gives the pessimists further cause for worry. This is the international context.

Indonesia apart, the tigers are small and unthreatening; and they have all been closely allied to the United States. This has had two consequences. The first is that America has generally seen the growing prosperity of the tigers as in its own strategic interest. As a result it has been more inclined to open its markets to goods produced by "our friends" in East Asia.

The second consequence is that, at crucial points, America has been able to give liberalisation a shove in the right direction. In 1987, when the South Korean regime was faced with mass demonstrations and may have been contemplating another Kwangju, the fact that this would have gone down badly in Washington—and might have cost the country the 1988 Olympic Games—helped persuade the military to hold their fire. Similarly in Taiwan in 1990, the KMT must have wondered whether holding the island's first free election was really such a good idea. Knowing that moves towards democracy would bolster support for Taiwan in Washington was crucial in keeping the party honest. Most dramatic of all, America pulled the plug on Ferdinand Marcos in the Philippines in 1986—even providing a helicopter to fly him out of the country.

How does China compare? China's leaders are convinced—or profess to be convinced—that America is out to thwart their country's development. And it is true that America is less inclined to compromise in trade disputes with China because China is a potential adversary. All the same, on trade, China is not so different from the tigers. Though America has protectionists aplenty, on China they appear to be outweighed by others—notably multinational firms and the diplomatic establishment—pushing for accommodation.

The real difference between China and the tigers may well be that American voices will matter much less when China's political crisis comes than they did in Taiwan, South Korea or the Philippines. Unlike South Korean generals, the Chinese will not be listening to diplomats in the American embassy counselling restraint. No American helicopters are on standby to whisk China's president off to retirement in Hawaii. More's the pity.

In the Forests of the Night

One day crowds may again be on China's streets demanding change, but it is hard to imagine such a confrontation ending with the government's quick retreat, still less with its leaders being rescued by American marines. The optimists are therefore making a leap of faith when they think of China as just another tiger. Tiger it may be, but certainly no ordinary one: domestic political uncertainty looms over the country far more than in any of its smaller neighbours. You cannot say of China, as some do of the tigers, that "the economy is all that matters; growth can survive any political upheaval."

On the other hand, China seems to have enough tigerish characteristics for growth to continue; it has an emerging middle class with a stake in stability; and, though its rulers may be capable of mucking up development, that is a far cry from saying they are bound to do so. The contrast between economic opportunity and political worries is familiar all over Asia. It is sharper in China than elsewhere and the worries are greater. But on balance, optimism seems better grounded than the alternative.

Article 20   *The Economist,* October 12, 1996

How Poor Is China?

New research suggests that poverty in China is more widespread, and the economy much smaller, than previously thought.

In recent years it has become accepted wisdom that China is an economic superpower in the making. Reputable economists have predicted that the Chinese economy could be the largest in the world by 2001. Businessmen have panted at the potential of a market of 1.2 billion consumers. The World Bank has lauded China's achievements in reducing the proportion of its population living in poverty to less than a tenth.

There is only one snag. Many of the numbers on which these claims were based appear to have been wrong. A recent World Bank report, "poverty in China; what do the numbers say?", has substantially revised the statistics put out in other Bank publications. The new figures reduce estimates of the size of the Chinese economy by over 25%. And the Bank has also decided that the proportion of the Chinese population living in poverty is closer to a third, rather than the 7% or so that was commonly cited until recently.

These revisions do not mean that the Chinese economic miracle is a mirage. Chinese growth rates remain among the highest in the world. The country's trade and official reserves continue to swell impressively. But the new figures do suggest that China is further behind the developed countries than had been widely assumed.

The world of statistics can often seem faintly unreal. But the estimates put out by the World Bank and others matter because they affect the real world. China's international rehabilitation after the Tiananmen massacre of 1989 was significantly influenced by awe at the Chinese boom. Disgust at the killings was balanced by respect for the government's increasingly well publicised achievement of lifting hundreds of millions of people out of poverty. Respect of a different sort was created by the idea that China might be the dominant economic power of the next century. And the lure of Chinese markets has created a business lobby keen to get on with China.

If some of the gloss is now taken off the Chinese miracle, will that damage China internationally? Not necessarily. Indeed in some ways it might now suit China to be "poor" rather than "rich". One of the biggest international issues facing today's China is the question of the terms on which it will join the World Trade Organisation. The richer it is seen to be, the faster America and other members will expect it to liberalise its trade rules. So a reminder that much of China remains very poor is actually quite helpful to the Chinese authorities.

Lies and Damned Lies

In its recent poverty report, the World Bank has made two important changes. First, it has raised the income level below which a Chinese is deemed to be poor from $0.60 cents a day to $1.00 a day. This has had the effect of increasing the number of Chinese deemed to be poor from fewer than 100m to well over 300m. Second, the report has lowered estimates for Chinese income per person, measured on a purchasing-power-party (PPP) basis, which adjusts for the local cost-of-living. The Bank's 1996 *World Development Report* puts Chinese GDP per person, measured on a PPP basis, at around $2,500 in 1994. The new report puts the figure at $1,800.

This change shrinks the estimated size of the Chinese economy dramatically. For example, writing in 1992, Lawrence Summers, who was then chief economist at the World Bank, argued that the size of the Chinese economy was already "greater than that of Germany or Japan". At that time he put Chinese GDP per person at $2,500 on a PPP basis. Extrapolating America's and China's current economic growth rates into the future, Mr Summers went on: "If this growth differential continues, Chinese total output will exceed American total output in 11 years." Unsurprisingly, such a bold prediction from such an eminent source excited much comment. "The Rise of China", a bullish bestseller by William Overholt, a banker, picked up on Mr Summer's prediction, as did *The Economist.*

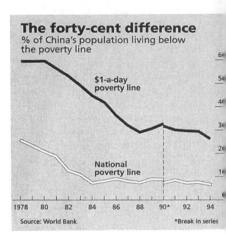

The forty-cent difference
% of China's population living below the poverty line

$1-a-day poverty line

National poverty line

1978 80 82 84 86 88 90* 92 94

Source: World Bank   *Break in series

The new figures, however, put the date when China becomes the world's largest economy further into the future. At current growth levels, it would now take about 20 more years. In any event using PPP for extrapolations of this sort as Mr Summers and others have done may be misleading. Adjusting income for purchasing power is crucial for gauging relative poverty, because it shows how a nominal income of a few hundred dollars—which would mean destitution in America—can translate into an acceptable standard of living in China.

But when it comes to buying western goods, or indeed companies, it is Chinese wealth measured at the real exchange rate, not at PPP, which is of concern to businessmen. Similarly, to extrapolate PPP-based estimates of GDP is probably misleading because rapid economic growth in China, combined with flourishing exports, will almost certainly lead to an appreciation of the Chinese currency, which will narrow the gap between GDP measured on a PPP and on a nominal basis.

It may be for this reason that some Bank officials now seem to be eschewing PPP as a basis for the politically loaded business of measuring the relative sizes of the Chinese and American economies. Pieter Bottelier, the head of the World Bank office in Beijing, makes a back-of-an-envelope calculation using current

United Nations photo

n recent years, China's economy was predicted to become the preeminent world's leader. More recent estimates, based on more balanced assessments of Gross Domestic Product per person, find that China realistically has much further to go to effectively become part of the world economy. Poverty in China is spread much wider than at first thought, and manual labor is still the driving force behind a vast part of their economy.

exchange rates. This suggests that China's economy is now roughly 10% of America's and may catch up in about 40 years' time.

The poverty report is fairly mysterious about the basis on which it has revised the PPP figures, simply citing "better data". When it comes to measuring the numbers of poor Chinese, however, it argues that both the new and the old figures are "right" in different ways. The 60-cents poverty line is a Chinese standard, the $1-a-day line is better for international comparisons.

Maybe so. But in the past, the Bank was not always shy about using the Chinese figure as the basis for international comparisons. For example, in a report on poverty in Vietnam issued in 1995, the Bank observed, "Poverty is considerably higher in Vietnam (51%) than in China (9%), Indonesia (15%), the Philippines (21%) or Thailand (16%)." To some people these figures always seemed implausible. They entailed believing, for example, that, although GDP per person in Thailand (measured on a nominal basis) was five times that in China, the proportion of people living in poverty in Thailand was double that in China. Anybody who had looked around in the two countries would have found that hard to swallow.

Back in the real world, that a third of the population of China is still living in poverty poses more than a humanitarian problem for the Chinese government. Whichever yardstick you use for measuring poverty, the statistics seem to show that the biggest inroads were made in the early 1980s, just after private farming was allowed. For the past decade, the reduction of poverty has slowed. Meanwhile, as a manufacturing-led boom has taken hold on the coasts, the gap between the booming east ern cities and the poorer inland areas has widened. That gap may prove to be the biggest economic and political challenge now facing the Chinese government.

Article 21

Discover, March 1996

Empire of Uniformity

With its vast area and long history of settlement, China ought to have hundreds of distinct languages and cultures. In fact, all the evidence indicates that it once did. So what happened to them all?

Jared Diamond

Jared Diamond is a contributing editor of DISCOVER, *a professor of physiology at the* UCLA *School of Medicine, a recipient of a MacArthur genius award, and a research associate in ornithology at the American Museum of Natural History. Expanded versions of many of his* DIS-COVER *articles appear in his book* The Third Chimpanzee: The Evolution and Future of the Human Animal, *which won Britain's 1992* COPUS *prize for best science book and the* Los Angeles Times *science book prize.*

Immigration, affirmative action, multilingualism, ethnic diversity—my state of California pioneered these controversial policies, and it is now pioneering a backlash against them. A glance into the classrooms of the Los Angeles public schools, where my sons are being educated, fleshes out the abstract debates with the faces of children. Those pupils speak more than 80 languages in their homes; English-speaking whites are in the minority. Every single one of my sons' playmates has at least one parent or grandparent who was born outside the United States. That's true of my sons also—three of their four grandparents were immigrants to this country. But the diversity that results from such immigration isn't new to America. In fact, immigration is simply restoring the diversity that existed here for thousands of years and that diminished only recently; the area that now makes up the mainland United States, once home to hundreds of Native American tribes and languages, did not come under the control of a single government until the late nineteenth century.

In these respects, ours is a thoroughly "normal" country. Like the United States, all but one of the world's six most populous nations are melting pots that achieved political unification recently and that still support hundreds of languages and ethnic groups. Russia, for example, once a small Slavic state centered on Moscow, did not even begin its expansion beyond the Ural Mountains until 1582. From then until the late nineteenth century, Russia swallowed up dozens of non-Slavic peoples, many of whom, like the people of Chechnya today, retain their original language and cultural identity. India, Indonesia, and Brazil are also recently political creations (or re-creations, in the case of India) and are home to about 850, 703, and 209 languages, respectively.

The great exception to this rule of the recent melting pot is the world's most populous nation, China. Today China appears politically, culturally, and linguistically monolithic. (For the purposes of this article, I exclude the linguistically and culturally distinct Tibet, which was also politically separate until recently.) China was already unified politically in 221 B.C. and has remained so for most of the centuries since then. From the beginnings of literacy in China over 3,000 years ago, it has had only a single writing system, unlike the dozens in use in modern Europe. Of China's billion-plus people, over 700 million speak Mandarin, the language with by far the largest number of native speakers in the world. Some 250 million other Chinese speak seven languages as similar to Mandarin and to each other as Spanish is to Italian. Thus, while modern American history is the story of how our continent's expanse became American, and Russia's history is the story of how Russia became Russian, China's history appears to be entirely different. It seems absurd to ask how China became Chinese. China has *been* Chinese almost from the beginning of its recorded history.

We take this unity of China so much for granted that we forget how astonishing it is. Certainly we should not have expected such unity on the basis of genetics. While a coarse racial classification of world peoples lumps all Chinese people together as Mongoloids, that category conceals much more variation than is found among such (equally ill-termed) Caucasian peoples as Swedes, Italians, and Irish. Northern and southern Chinese, in particular, are genetically and physically rather different from each other: northerners are most similar to Tibetans and Nepali, southerners to Vietnamese and Filipinos. My northern and southern Chinese friends can often distinguish each other at a glance: northerners tend to be taller, heavier, paler, with more pointed noses and smaller eyes.

The existence of such differences is hardly surprising: northern and southern China differ in environment and climate, with the north drier and colder. That such genetic differences arose between the peoples of these two regions simply implies a long history of their moderate isolation from each other. But if such isolation existed, then how did these peoples end up with such similar languages and cultures?

China's linguistic near-unity is also puzzling in comparison with the linguistic *dis*unity of other parts of the world. For instance, New Guinea, although it was first settled by humans only about 40,000 years ago, evolved roughly 1,000 languages. Western Europe has by now about 40 native languages acquired just in the past 6,000 to 8,000 years, including languages as different as English, Finnish, and Russian. Yet New Guinea's peoples are spread over an area less than one-tenth that of China's. And fossils attest to human presence in China for hundreds of thousands of years. By rights, tens of thousands of distinct languages should have arisen in China's large area over that long time span; what has happened to them? China too must once have been a melting pot of diversity, as all other populous nations still are. It differs from them only in having been unified much earlier: in that huge pot, the melting happened long ago.

A glance at a linguistic map is an eye-opener to all of us accustomed to thinking of China as monolithic. In addition to its eight "big" languages—Mandarin and its seven close relatives (often referred to collectively as Chinese), with between 11 million and 700 million speakers each—China also has some 160 smaller languages, many of them with just a few thousand speakers. All these languages fall into four families, which differ greatly in their distributions.

At one extreme, Mandarin and its relatives, which constitute the Chinese subfamily of the Sino-Tibetan language family, are distributed continuously from the top of the country to the bottom. One distinctive feature of all Sino-Tibetan languages is that most words consist of a single syllable, like English

it or *book*; long, polysyllabic words are unthinkable. One could walk through China, from Manchuria in the north to the Gulf of Tonkin in the south, without ever stepping off land occupied by native speakers of Chinese.

The other three families have broken distributions, being spoken by islands of people surrounded by a sea of speakers of Chinese and other languages. The 6 million speakers of the Miao-Yao family are divided among five languages, bearing colorful names derived from the characteristic colors of the speakers'

clothing: Red Miao, White Miao (alias Striped Miao), Black Miao, Green Miao (alias Blue Miao), and Yao. Miao-Yao speakers live in dozens of small enclaves scattered over half a million square miles from southern China to Thailand.

The 60 million speakers of languages in the Austroasiatic family, such as Vietnamese and Cambodian, are also scattered across the map, from Vietnam in the east to the Malay Peninsula in the south to northeastern India in the west. Austroasiatic languages are characterized by an enormous proliferation of

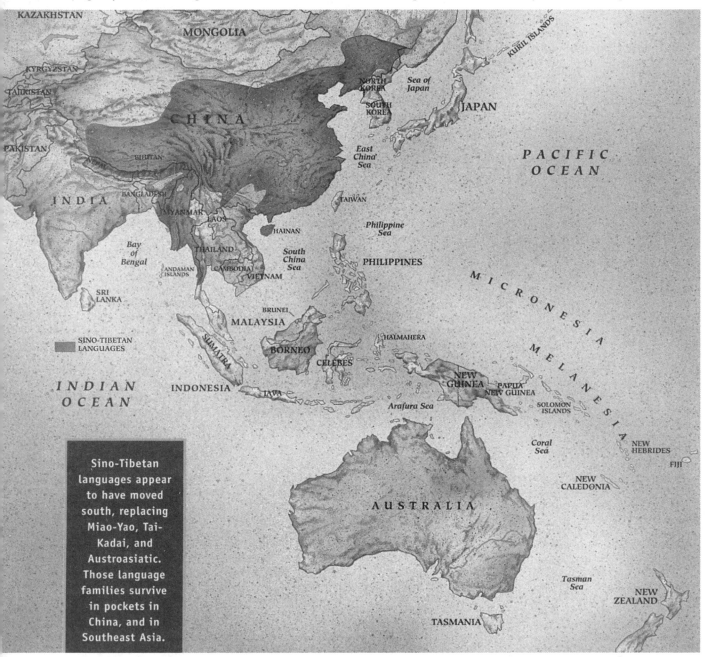

Sino-Tibetan languages appear to have moved south, replacing Miao-Yao, Tai-Kadai, and Austroasiatic. Those language families survive in pockets in China, and in Southeast Asia.

vowels, which can be nasal or nonnasal, long or extra-short, creaky, breathy, or normal, produced with the tongue high, medium high, medium low, or low, and with the front, center, or back of the tongue. All these choices combine to yield up to 41 distinctive vowel sounds per language, in contrast to the mere dozen or so of English.

The 50 million speakers of China's fourth language family, Tai-Kadai, are scattered from southern China southward into peninsular Thailand and west to Myanmar (Burma). In Tai-Kadai languages, as in most Sino-Tibetan languages, a single word may have different meanings depending on its tone, or pitch. For example, in Thai itself the syllable *maa* means "horse" when pronounced at a high pitch, "come" at a medium pitch, and "dog" at a rising pitch.

Seen on a map, the current fragmented distribution of these language groups suggests a series of ancient helicopter flights that dropped speakers here and there over the Asian landscape. But of course nothing like that could have happened, and the actual process was subtractive rather than additive. Speakers of the now dominant language expanded their territory and displaced original residents or induced them to abandon their native tongues. The ancestors of modern speakers of Thai and Laotian, and possibly Cambodian and Burmese as well, all moved south from southern China and adjacent areas to their present locations within historical times, successively inundating the settled descendants of previous migrations. Chinese speakers were especially vigorous in replacing and linguistically converting other ethnic groups, whom they looked down on as primitive and inferior. The recorded history of China's Chou Dynasty, from 1111 B.C. to 256 B.C., describes the conquest and absorption of most of China's non-Chinese-speaking population by Chinese-speaking states.

Before those relatively recent migrations, who spoke what where? To reconstruct the linguistic map of the East Asia of several thousand years ago, we can reverse the historically known linguistic expansions of recent millennia. We can also look for large, continuous areas currently occupied by a single language or related language group; these areas testify to a geographic expansion of that group so recent that there has not been enough time for it to differentiate into many languages. Finally, we can reason conversely that modern areas with a high diversity of languages within a

(Maps by Susan Johnston Carlson)

given language family lie closer to the early center of distribution of that language family. Using those three types of reasoning to turn back the linguistic clock, we conclude that speakers of Chinese and other Sino-Tibetan languages originally occupied northern China. The southern parts of the country were variously inhabited by speakers of Miao-Yao, Austroasiatic, and Tai-Kadai languages—until they were largely replaced by their Sino-Tibetan speaking neighbors.

An even more drastic linguistic upheaval appears to have swept over tropical Southeast Asia to the south of China, in Thailand, Myanmar, Laos, Cambodia, Vietnam, and peninsular Malaysia. It's likely that whatever languages were originally spoken there have now become extinct—most of the modern languages of those countries appear to be recent invaders, mainly from southern China. We might also guess that if Miao-Yao languages could be so nearly overwhelmed, there must have been still other language families in southern China that left no modern descendants whatsoever. As we shall see, the Austronesian family (to which all Philippine and Polynesian languages belong) was probably once spoken on the Chinese mainland. We know about it only because it spread to Pacific islands and survived there.

The language replacements in East Asia are reminiscent of the way European languages, especially English and Spanish, spread into the New World. English, of course, came to replace the hundreds of Native American languages

not because it sounded musical to indigenous ears but because English-speaking invaders killed most Native Americans by war, murder, and disease and then pressured the survivors into adopting the new majority language. The immediate cause of the Europeans' success was their relative technological superiority. That superiority, however, was ultimately the result of a geographic accident that allowed agriculture and herding to develop in Eurasia 10,000 years earlier. The consequent explosion in population allowed the Europeans to develop complex technologies and social organization, giving their descendants great political and technological advantages over the people they conquered. Essentially the same processes account for why English replaced aboriginal Australian languages and why Bantu languages replaced subequatorial Africa's original Pygmy and Khoisan languages.

East Asia's linguistic upheavals thus hint that some Asians enjoyed similar advantages over other Asians. But to flesh out the details of that story, we must turn from linguistics to archeology.

As everywhere else in the world, the eastern Asian archeological record for most of human history reveals only the debris of hunter-gatherers using unpolished stone tools. The first eastern Asian evidence for something different comes from China, where crop remains, bones of domestic animals, pottery, and polished stone tools appear by around 7500 B.C. That's no more than a thousand years after the beginnings of agriculture in the Fertile Crescent, the area with the ldest established food production in the world.

In China plant and animal domestication may even have started independently in two or more places. Besides differences in climate between north and south, there are also ecological differences between the interior uplands (which are characterized by mountains like our Appalachians) and the coastal lowlands (which are flat and threaded with rivers, like the Carolinas). Incipient farmers in each area would have had different wild plants and animals to draw on. In fact, the earliest identified crops were two drought-resistant species of millet in northern China, but rice in the south.

The same sites that provided us with the earliest evidence of crops also contained bones of domestic pigs, dogs, and chickens—a livestock trinity that later spread as far as Polynesia. These animals and crops were gradually joined by China's many other domesticates. Among the animals were water buffalo (the most important, since they were used for pulling plows), as well as silkworms, ducks, and geese. Familiar later Chinese crops include soybeans, hemp, tea, apricots, pears, peaches, and citrus fruits. Many of these domesticated animals and crops spread westward in ancient times from China to the Fertile Crescent and Europe; at the same time, Fertile Crescent domesticates spread eastward to China. Especially significant western contributions to ancient China's economy were wheat and barley, cows and horses, and to a lesser extent, sheep and goats.

As elsewhere in the world, food production in China gradually led to the other hallmarks of "civilization." A superb Chinese tradition of bronze metallurgy arose around 3000 B.C., allowing China to develop by far the earliest cast iron production in the world by 500 B.C. The following 1,500 years saw the outpouring of a long list of Chinese inventions: canal lock gates, deep drilling, efficient animal harnesses, gunpowder, kites, magnetic compasses, paper, porcelain, printing, sternpost rudders, and wheelbarrows, to name just a few.

China's size and ecological diversity initially spawned many separate local cultures. In the fourth millennium B.C. those local cultures expanded geographically and began to interact, compete with each other, and coalesce. Fortified towns appeared in China in the third millennium B.C., with cemeteries containing luxuriously decorated graves juxtaposed with simpler ones—a clear sign of emerging class differences. China became home to stratified societies with rulers who could mobilize a large labor force of commoners, as we can infer from the remains of huge urban defensive walls, palaces, and the Grand Canal—the longest canal in the world—linking northern and southern China. Writing unmistakably ancestral to that of modern China is preserved from the second millennium B.C., though it probably arose earlier. The first of China's dynasties, the Hsia Dynasty, arose around 2000 B.C. Thereafter, our archeological knowledge of China's emerging cities and states becomes supplemented by written accounts.

Along with rice cultivation and writing, a distinctively Chinese method for reading the future also begins to appear persistently in the archeological record, and it too attests to China's cultural coalescence. In place of crystal balls and Delphic oracles, China turned to scapulimancy—burning the scapula (shoulder bone) or other large bone of an animal, such as a cow, then prophesying from the pattern of cracks in the burned bone. From the earliest known appearance of oracle bones in northern China, archeologists have traced scapulimancy's spread throughout China's cultural sphere.

Just as exchanges of domesticates between ecologically diverse regions enriched Chinese food production, exchanges between culturally diverse regions enriched Chinese culture and technology, and fierce competition between warring chiefdoms drove the formation of ever larger and more centralized states. China's long west-east rivers (the Yellow River in the north, the Yangtze in the south) allowed crops and technology to spread quickly between inland and coast, while their diffusion north and south was made easy by the broad, relatively gentle terrain north of the Yangtze, which eventually permitted the two river systems to be joined by canals. All those geographic factors contributed to the early cultural and political unification of China. In contrast, western Europe, with an area comparable to China's but fragmented by mountains such as the Alps, and with a highly indented coastline and no such rivers, has never been unified politically.

Some developments spread from south to north in China, especially iron smelting and rice cultivation. But the predominant direction of spread seems to have been the other way. From northern China came bronze technology, Sino-Tibetan languages, and state formation.

The country's first three dynasties (the Hsia, Shang, and Chou) all arose in the north in the second millennium B.C. The northern dominance is clearest, however, for writing. Unlike western Eurasia, with its plethora of early methods for recording language, including Sumerian cuneiform, Egyptian hieroglyphics, Hittite, Minoan, and the Semitic alphabet, China developed just one writing system. It arose in the north, preempted or replaced any other nascent system, and evolved into the writing used today.

Preserved documents show that already in the first millennium B.C. ethnic Chinese tended to feel culturally superior to non-Chinese "barbarians," and northern Chinese considered even southern Chinese barbarians. For example, a late Chou Dynasty writer described China's other peoples as follows: "The people of those five regions—the Middle states and the Jung, Yi, and other wild tribes around them—had all their several natures, which they could not be made to alter. The tribes on the east were called Yi. They had their hair unbound, and tattooed their bodies. Some of them ate their food without its being cooked by fire." The author went on to describe wild tribes to the south, west, and north indulging in equally barbaric practices, such as turning their feet inward, tattooing their foreheads, wearing skins, living in caves, not eating cereals, and, again, eating their food raw.

So overwhelming was the Chinese steamroller that the former peoples of the region have left behind few traces.

States modeled on the Chou Dynasty were organized in southern China during the first millennium B.C., culminating in China's political unification under the Chin Dynasty in 221 B.C. China's cultural unification accelerated during that same period, as literate "civilized" Chinese states absorbed or were copied by the preliterate "barbarians." Some of that cultural unification was ferocious: for instance, the first Chin emperor condemned all previously written historical books as worthless and ordered them burned, much to the detriment of our understanding of early Chinese history. That and other draconian measures must have helped spread northern China's Sino-Tibetan languages over most of China.

Chinese innovations contributed heavily to developments in neighboring regions as well. For instance, until roughly 4000 B.C. most of tropical Southeast Asia was still occupied by hunter-gatherers making pebble and flake stone tools. Thereafter, Chinese-derived crops, polished stone tools, village living, and pottery spread into the area, probably accompanied by southern Chinese language families. The southward expansions from southern China of Laotians, Thai, and Vietnamese, and probably Burmese and Cambodians also, completed the "Sinification" of tropical Southeast Asia. All those modern peoples appear to be recent offshoots of their southern Chinese cousins.

So overwhelming was this Chinese steamroller that the former peoples of the region have left behind few traces in the modern populations. Just three relict groups of hunter-gatherers—the Semang Negritos of the Malay Peninsula, the Andaman Islanders, and the Veddoid Negritos of Sri Lanka—remain to give us any clue as to what those peoples were like. They suggest that tropical Southeast Asia's former inhabitants may have had dark skin and curly hair, like modern New Guineans and unlike southern Chinese and modern tropical Southeast Asians. Those people may also be the last survivors of the source population from which New Guinea and aboriginal Australia were colonized. As to their speech, only on the remote Andaman Islands do languages unrelated to the southern Chinese language families persist—perhaps the last linguistic survivors of what may have been hundreds of now extinct aboriginal Southeast Asian languages.

While one prong of the Chinese expansion thus headed southwest into Indochina and Myanmar, another headed southeast into the Pacific Ocean. Part of the evidence suggesting this scenario comes from genetics and linguistics: the modern inhabitants of Indonesia and the Philippines are fairly homogeneous in their genes and appearance and resemble southern Chinese. Their languages are also homogeneous, almost all belonging to a closely knit family called Austronesian, possibly related to Tai-Kadai.

But just as in tropical Southeast Asia, the archeological record in the Pacific shows more direct evidence of the Chinese steamroller. Until 6,000 years ago, Indonesia and the Philippines were sparsely occupied by hunter-gatherers. Beginning in the fourth or fifth millennium B.C., pottery and stone tools of unmistakably southern Chinese origins appear on the island of Taiwan, which is in the straits between the southern Chinese coast and the Philippines. Around 3000 B.C. that same combination of technological advances spread as a wave to the Philippines, then throughout the islands of Indonesia, accompanied by gardening and by China's livestock trinity (pigs, chickens, and dogs). Around 1600 B.C. the wave reached the islands north of New Guinea, then spread eastward through the previously uninhabited islands of Polynesia. By 500 A.D. the Polynesians, an Austronesian speaking people of ultimately Chinese origin, had reached Easter Island, 10,000 miles from the Chinese coast. With Polynesian settlement of Hawaii and New Zealand around the same time or soon thereafter, ancient China's occupation of the Pacific was complete.

Throughout most of Indonesia and the Philippines, the Austronesian expansion obliterated the region's former inhabitants. Scattered bands of hunter-gatherers were no match for the tools, weapons, numbers, subsistence methods, and probably also germs carried by the invading Austronesian farmers. Only the Negrito Pygmies in the mountains of Luzon and some other

Philippine islands appear to represent survivors of those former hunter-gatherers, but they too lost their original tongues and adopted Austronesian languages from their new neighbors. However, on New Guinea and adjacent islands, indigenous people had already developed agriculture and built up numbers sufficient to keep out the Austronesian invaders. Their languages, genes, and faces live on in modern New Guineans and Melanesians.

Even Korea and Japan were heavily influenced by China, although their geographic isolation from the mainland saved them from losing their languages or physical and genetic distinctness. Korea and Japan adopted rice from China in the second millennium B.C., bronze metallurgy in the first millennium B.C., and writing in the first or early second millennium A.D.

Not all cultural advances in East Asia stemmed from China, of course, nor were Koreans, Japanese, and tropical Southeast Asians noninventive "barbarians" who contributed nothing. The ancient Japanese developed pottery at least as early as the Chinese did, and they settled in villages subsisting on Japan's rich seafood resources long before the arrival of agriculture. Some crops were probably domesticated initially or independently in Japan, Korea, and tropical Southeast Asia. But China's role was still disproportionately large. Indeed, the influence of Chinese culture is still so great that Japan has no thought of discarding its Chinese-derived writing system despite its disadvantages for representing Japanese speech, while Korea is only now replacing its clumsy Chinese-derived writing with its wonderful indigenous Hangul alphabet. The persistence of Chinese writing in Japan and Korea is a vivid twentieth-century legacy of plant and animal domestication that began in China 10,000 years ago. From those achievements of East Asia's first farmers, China became Chinese, and peoples from Thailand to Easter Island became their cousins.

Article 22   *The World & I,* December 1996

Endgame in Indonesia?

James Clad

James Clad, a former staff correspondent for the Far Eastern Economic Review, *is research professor for Southeast Asian studies at Georgetown University. His latest book is* After the Crusade: American Foreign Policy for the Post-Superpower Era *(Madison, 1995).*

Jakarta. Each visit to this eight-million-strong coastal city—the name comes from the Sanskrit words *jaya karta,* meaning the place of glorious deeds—disorients a traveler who first grew familiar with Indonesia's capital in the 1970s.

Huge bank buildings and shopping plazas dot flat expanses that only a few years ago were rice fields and swamps. Traffic snarls the main avenues as thoroughly as in Bangkok or Manila. Each day, commuters traveling to office jobs clamber aboard the elevated railway that circles the huge city, reading glossy magazines bulging with advertisements.

Make no mistake: Indonesia—the world's fourth-largest country in population, the largest Muslim nation, a member of the Organization of Petroleum-Exporting Countries, an industrializing textile and electronics exporter, and the primary prop of Southeast Asia's prosperous stability—is one country that matters. Consider:

• It sits astride two of the world's most strategic waterways: the Straits of Malacca and Lombok.

• It supplies Japan with much of the cleaner fuels it needs to stay in business.

• Its brand of Islamic devotion ranges from the highly orthodox to the merely casual, and the Suharto regime exerts a restraining influence on both the Non-aligned Movement (over which Suharto now presides) and the 42-nation Islamic Conference.

• Foreign multinationals increasingly choose to locate their factories in Indonesia, where profits from manufacturing firms (from Motorola chips to Nike shoes) now contribute the largest source of export earnings.

This sprawling country of 13,600 islands and 200 million people now seems set, if it carefully manages a crucial and inevitable transition, to become another of Asia's economic "tigers" by the first decades of the twenty-first century. What is that transition, and what might derail this picture of forward movement and steady growth?

The awarding in October of the 1996 Nobel Peace Prize to Carlos Felipe Belo, a Roman Catholic bishop, and Jose Ramos-Horta, an aggrieved freedom fighter, points to one answer. The men, both of them "Indonesians" in the eyes of the Jakarta government, seek the dissolution of the forcible union of their homeland, the former Portuguese colony of East Timor, with Indonesia in 1975.

In addition, three months before the Nobel prizes, unprecedented riots in Jakarta on July 27 also focused attention on another lingering problem: the reluctance of its president, a Javanese general named Suharto, to leave office after 30 years at the helm.

For these and many other reasons, Indonesia seems certain to figure prominently in world news reports right up to the end of the century.

Both the nagging problem of East Timor and the jolt of the July riots have increased pressure on the 75-year-old Suharto (Indonesians, especially the majority Javanese people, often use but one name), but he is playing a clever holding game, alternating repression and crackdowns with new maneuvers to outflank his disunited adversaries.

The Suharto Dilemma

The wily, quiet-spoken old soldier is now in his sixth five-year term. There seems little doubt that, if he chooses to do so, he can stay in office indefinitely. If he truly wants to win another term, he can easily activate the machinery to make this happen.

An election to select a new parliament will occur next year. In 1998, the parliament will join a group of handpicked government appointees to select Indonesia's supreme leader. Unless the shrewd president decides otherwise, he will again win that endorsement—just as he has each time since 1967.

The July 1996 riots resulted from the regime's surprisingly flat-footed efforts to marginalize the daughter of Suharto's charismatic predecessor and Indonesia's first president, a man named Sukarno. Megawati Sukarnoputri had sought to take over a tame, government-created alternative party named the Indonesian Democratic Party (PDI). For a time, she acted as a focus for many disparate forces yearning for change.

Steadily over the year, the regime moved to marginalize Megawati, blocking her efforts to build up a serious PDI organization ahead of parliamentary elections in May 1997.

The government decided, just two days after U.S. Secretary of State Warren Christopher and other Western foreign ministers had left Jakarta after a meeting of the Association of Southeast Asian Nations, to have Megawati's followers evicted from the PDI headquarters in Jakarta. This ignited two days of riots, causing at least five deaths, many burned buildings (notably businesses owned by ethnic Chinese families), and a dramatic quickening of the political tempo.

Does repression of these yearnings for change work? Sidney Jones, a longtime Indonesia watcher and director of the New York-based Human Rights Watch, says that "in Asia, violence by governments has almost always served to strengthen the opposition.... Violence against the political opposition is almost always a sign of weakness and declining legitimacy."

She has a point: The crushing of a popular uprising in Burma has led to Aung San Suu Kyi's "near-holy status," as Jones puts it, while repression by Philippine dictator Ferdinand Marcos only hastened his demise. Some Thai army leaders lost power in 1992 after shooting down demonstrators in Bangkok's streets.

Even though it took July's riots to focus renewed attention on the "succession issue," as it is known in Indonesia, Suharto's political longevity fascinates the disparate country he rules.

Excepting Cuba, no country on the planet—neither China nor Iraq nor Libya—comes anywhere near Indonesia's preoccupation with one man's temperament and liabilities. And nowhere else will the departure of a single man so decisively close an era.

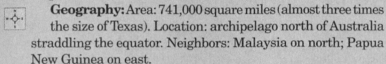

Indonesia

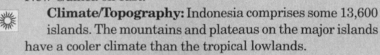

Official Name: Republic of Indonesia

Capital: Jakarta

Geography: Area: 741,000 square miles (almost three times the size of Texas). Location: archipelago north of Australia straddling the equator. Neighbors: Malaysia on north; Papua New Guinea on east.

Climate/Topography: Indonesia comprises some 13,600 islands. The mountains and plateaus on the major islands have a cooler climate than the tropical lowlands.

People: Population: 200 million. Ethnic groups: Javanese, 45 percent; Sundanese, 14 percent; Madurese, 7 percent; Malay, 7 percent. Principal languages: Bahasa Indonesian, or Malay (official), English, Dutch, Javanese.

Religion: Muslim, 87 percent.

Education: Literacy: 85 percent.

Economy: Industries: food processing, textiles, cement, light industry. Chief crops: rice, coffee, sugar. Minerals: nickel, tin, copper, oil, bauxite, natural gas. Crude oil reserves: 10.7 billion barrels. Arable land: 8 percent.

Government: Republic.

SOURCE: *THE WORLD ALMANAC*, 1995

In Indonesia, Suharto's "New Order" regime came to power in a confusing, Machiavellian putsch in 1965. Now, the end of that aging New Order and of that aging general may be in sight. In today's Indonesia, the circumstances in which Suharto leaves his job will have profound consequences.

Indonesia Up Close

The Republic of Indonesia groups together an archipelago that stretches a distance equal to that from California to New York. For any ruler, archipelagic unity depends on a separation of government from the islands' predominant religion, Islam. Although 87 percent of Indonesians are Muslims, their orthodoxy varies considerably.

In the "outer islands" (those away from Java and Bali), people tend to be more religiously observant and more mindful of traditions. As a general rule, people living along Indonesia's coastline also profess a stricter mode of Islam than those dwelling in the interior, be it on Java, Borneo, Sumatra, or other large islands.

By contrast, especially the interior of Java remains influenced by earlier Hindu and Buddhist influence. Sometimes described as "nominal Muslims,"

these more easygoing adherents of Islam number in the tens of millions. Their approach to religion is more syncretic, borrowing here from the Hindu pantheon and there from Islamic mysticism.

Strong spiritual movements, collectively known as *aliran kebatinan* ("streams of inwardness") continue to influence religious and civic life. Suharto leans toward this type of religious temperament.

Another theme in Indonesian life flows directly from the first. The military, known by its Indonesian acronym ABRI, has special roots in Java, and its outlook remains decidedly, even aggressively, secular. While large organizations group tens of millions of Indonesian Muslims under one banner, all Indonesian social groups must accept a special brand of secularism found in the government's *pancasila* (pronounced PAHN-cha-SEE-la) ideology.

This five-point mantra, memorized by schoolchildren, can be considered Indonesia's "mother and apple pie" shortlist: In addition to humanitarianism, social justice, consensual politics, and a belief in constitutional process, a "belief in one God" completes the list. This belief may be expressed in Muslim, Buddhist, Christian (Protestants and Catholics re-

ceive separate recognition), or Hindu observance.

Christians live in pockets of believers, the flowering of earlier missionary work, often on remote islands, while Indonesia's Hindus live almost entirely on Bali.

Traditions Old And New

Dating back to before the Christian era, the Hindu-Buddhist traditions originated in various South Indian kingdoms, a subcontinental culture that spread over many centuries across the East Indies, with commerce as the engine of expansion. A thousand years later, Islam followed the same leisurely course of conversion through these islands. While northern Sumatra had embraced Islam by the seventh century, the last Hindu-Buddhist kingdom in central Java did not capitulate until the 1400s.

Some among Indonesia's 180 million Muslims would dearly like to impose Sharia (Islamic religious law) across the country. But political Islam has always failed to reach a panarchipelagic critical mass.

A major reason lies in the special place Indonesia's armed forces have in their society. It even has a name: *dwi fungsi*, or "dual function." It means that the military both has a defense role and occupies a uniquely special place in society—and in the economy—to ensure "national resilience."

Since the 1960s, the Javanese-dominated military has widened the country's frontiers, not always very gently, in various places in the eastern half of the archipelago. Two disputes still defy Jakarta's total control, however.

The first problem arises from the forcible incorporation of East Timor, the eastern half of an island sleepily administered by Portugal for 350 years until 1974.

The second conundrum arises from the bullying takeover in 1969 of the Dutch-administered, predominantly Melanesian territory of West New Guinea (now renamed Irian Jaya).

As a rule, the Javanese and other Malay peoples of the archipelago despise the darker-hued Melanesians, whose physical traits become gradually more prevalent the further east one travels in the archipelago. (The near-universal dislike of ethnic Chinese, about 4 percent of the population, results from other factors—chiefly a complex web of envy and loathing arising out of the overwhelming Chinese predominance in business, finance, and trade.)

Powerhouse Pacific Archipelago

- Indonesia is the biggest, most powerful cog in the Association of Southeast Asian Nations' economic machine.

- Its per capita gross domestic product has rocketed from $90 to over $1,000 in two decades.

- It is highly influential in the international Nonaligned Movement and the 42-nation Islamic Conference.

- Indonesia controls two strategic straits through which much of the world's oil traffic must pass.

- Its main problems stem from confusion over who will succeed the aging President Suharto, and unrest as a result of repression in the largely Christian areas of East Timor and Irian Jaya.

The unrest and separatist yearning in East Timor, described by Indonesian Foreign Minister Ali Alatas as "that pebble in my shoe" and showing every sign of renewed resilience after the Nobel Peace Prize announcement, simply refuse to go away.

Indonesian abuses in East Timor resulted in as many as 200,000 deaths from 1975 to 1978. The United Nations has yet to recognize the territory's legal incorporation into Indonesia, and the issue has become the blackest blot on the country's international reputation.

These problems aside, Jakarta has also made significant diplomatic contributions to Southeast Asian peace. They include brokering the Cambodian peace accord of 1991, smoothing competition by China and Southeast Asian countries over territorial claims in the South China Sea, and mediating a peace pact between the Philippine government and Muslim rebels.

Depoliticizing Politics

If this were not enough, the regime, with the military behind it, frowns on such activist politics as environmentalism, human rights monitoring, and efforts to improve labor conditions. Many analysts see Suharto as trying his best to "depoliticize" all politics in Indonesia.

And a great many Indonesians—even the growing middle class—seem to have bought the argument for heavy-handed

stability. This argument rests on Indonesia's superabundant pluralism—ethnic, religious, linguistic, and cultural. Its 27 provinces contain 366 distinct ethnic groups. Over 80 discrete language groups exist outside of the Melanesian bastion of Irian Jaya.

Even after Suharto departs, walking tall or recumbent, Indonesia will probably remain a rather autocratic country. During the nation's 51 years of independence, regionally based rebellions and communist challenges have reinforced the habit of centralized rule from Jakarta.

Other pressures favoring the status quo include a political culture of elaborate deference, a patrimonial system fueled by natural-resource-based corruption, and nepotistic manipulation of licensed monopolies. Oil sales and timber concessions top the list of extravagantly corrupt activities.

This tendency to corruption made the news recently with allegations of influence peddling by the Lippo Group, an Indonesian financial and real estate behemoth run by the billionaire Riady family, which has close ties to President Clinton. Three Lippo-connected people in the United States have funneled millions of dollars to the Democratic National Committee. It is alleged that Clinton agreed to a quid pro quo to soften human rights policy on Indonesia in exchange for the contributions.

The year 1965 marked the greatest chasm in Indonesian life. The New Order regime in effect traded political participation for economic progress. In just the last decade, the country has witnessed a huge growth of export-led manufacturing in industrial zones located on Java and Sumatra.

Besides becoming self-sufficient in rice production, Indonesia has reinvested in rubber and palm oil, broadening the spread of export revenues. Whereas as recently as the late 1970s Indonesia relied on oil exports for three-quarters of its export income, today that dependence has dropped to just over 20 percent, with manufactured goods and agricultural products (including the value-added products from the rapid felling of Indonesia's huge tropical forest reserves) making up the rest.

Per capita gross domestic product has risen from $90 to over $1,000 in two decades, a tremendous improvement. Jakarta's boom is like a magnet to rural migrants, who come to Java by the thousands each day.

Looking Backward, Looking Forward

The peace achieved and the wealth generated in most of Southeast Asia since the 1960s, and increasingly in Indochina after 1989, owe much to the peace and prosperity that Suharto's authoritarian rule has brought to Indonesia's 3,000-mile reach across four time zones, from the Indian to the Pacific Oceans. And Southeast Asia's ability to resist pressure from an emerging China depends on the regional stability that is Indonesia's handiwork more than any other country's.

Southeast Asia's ability to resist pressure from an emerging China depends on the regional stability that is Indonesia's handiwork more than any other country's.

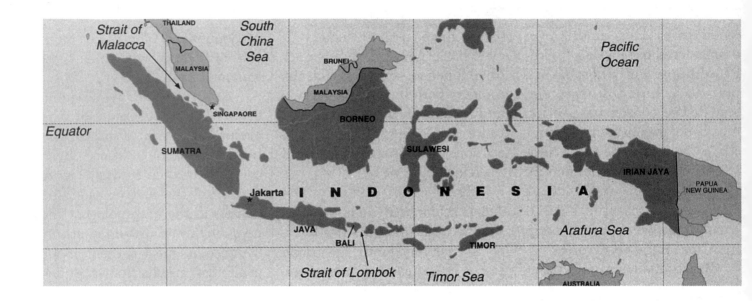

Further afield, others are also watching Suharto's endgame with varying degrees of concern:

• Japan receives much of its energy supply from Indonesia, especially natural gas.

• American oil companies have a large stake in that business.

• Other U.S. firms hold a respectable slice of a swiftly growing manufacturing sector financed mainly by foreign investment.

• U.S. naval access through Indonesian straits is at issue. Washington defines the waterways as "high seas," but Jakarta claims they are "archipelagic" (and therefore territorial). U.S. access depends on a tacit agreement that both countries may hold differing views while routine naval passage occurs.

Nor should we discount the anxious memories that Indonesia's southern neighbor, Australia, or northern neighbors Malaysia and Singapore still retain of past Indonesian turbulence. Periodically (most recently in a 1990 parliamentary white paper), these fears have prompted the identification of Indonesia as Australia's principal long-term threat.

Switching tack, however, Canberra in December 1995 entered into a surprise mutual security pact with Jakarta that provides for joint consultations on "matters affecting common security." The motivation appears to be, in part, concern over China's ambitions.

Will the transition to post-Suharto rule be managed well? Given the turbulent history of 1965, no one can be entirely sure that Indonesia's next turn of the political wheel will be as orderly as the proponents of order demand, especially since the strange atmosphere of politics-without-politics has pervaded Indonesia for three decades. Yet the smell of *fin de regime* hangs over the huge metropolis of Jakarta like monsoon clouds, piled up, cloud upon cloud, in the humid air.

This is the country to watch in the remaining years of our century.

Article 23   *Current History*, December 1996

North Korea: The Cold War Continues

It is a supreme irony that North Korea, faltering economically and practically abandoned by its Russian and Chinese partners, hopes to survive with the help of its enemies: the United States and its allies. That beggars can't be choosers does not seem to apply to North Korea.

Manwoo Lee

Manwoo Lee is a professor of political science at Millersville University. He is the author of The Odyssey of Korean Democracy *(Westport, Conn.: Praeger, 1990) and coeditor of* The Changing Order in Northeast Asia *(Boulder, Colo.: Westview, 1993).*

Kim Il-sung's embalmed body may lie in the Kumsusan Memorial Palace, but his ghost reigns over North Korea. More than two years after the North Korean leader's death in June 1994, pictures of Kim appear almost daily in the North Korean media, and official functions are held in front of his enormous portrait. This life-in-death state of affairs has left North Korea watchers puzzled: when will the Central Committee of the Korean Workers Party and the Supreme People's Assembly meet to elect Kim's son, Kim Jong-il, party chief and state president? Groomed since the early 1970s to be his father's successor, Kim Jong-il remains the commander of the Peoples Army and chairman of the National Defense Commission, posts he assumed in 1991 and 1993, respectively. His position in the party is still unclear; he is called the Great Ryongdoza—Great Leader—of the party and the people, but North Korea continues to emphasize the leadership of the late Kim.

Kim Jong-il has not appeared often in public since his father died. When he does he is usually surrounded by military men, giving credence to those who see the rising influence of generals in North Korea. Most North Korea watchers, however, believe Kim Jong-il is in charge, albeit not firmly. Still, it is clear that the younger Kim does not enjoy his father's status and is not powerful enough to assume the top posts. Perhaps he is unwilling to take over the leaking ship of state. Or perhaps the ruling elites in Pyongyang are in a state of paralysis, unable to settle the succession crisis because they believe it too risky either to finalize the succession or to oust Kim Jong-il. Nevertheless, it appears that there is no person or group powerful enough to topple him.

Biting the Hand that Feeds It?

According to the Bank of Korea, North Korea's GNP last year was $22 billion; per capita GNP was $957 (in contrast, South Korea's GNP was $452 billion and its per capita GNP about $10,000). The North Korean economy has posted a negative growth rate—a 25 percent decline in terms of GNP—for the sixth consecutive year. Moreover, since the dissolution of the former Soviet Union, North Korea's foreign trade has sharply declined.

To make matters worse, floods last year inundated nearly 75 percent of the country, causing an estimated $15 billion in damage, equivalent to about 70 percent of North Korea's GNP. The floods were the worst in a hundred years, wiping out 40 percent of the north's arable land and causing food production to fall to 4.2 million tons, 2.59 million tons short of the country's needs. This year, too, many parts of North Korea were hard hit by floods in late July.

Reports from defectors to the south confirm widespread food shortages and even starvation in North Korea. International organizations have expressed grave concern about the status of flood victims; it is reported that approximately 130,000 people have not received food rations for several months and are on the brink of famine. The United States, Japan, China, and South Korea are among the nations that have come to the aid of North Korea. South Korea itself supplied North Korea with 150,000 tons (worth $237 million) of emergency rice at no charge.

However, the politics of rice aid has degenerated into another inter-Korean skirmish. In 1995 North Korea forced a South Korean freighter carrying the first batch of rice aid to hoist the North Korean flag when entering a northern port. That same year, another South Korean freighter and its crew were taken into custody and charged with spying. Angered by North Korea's hostile attitude, Seoul refuses to acknowledge that a famine exists in North Korea and has withheld further food aid, arguing that North Korea is sitting on large military stockpiles of grain and needs no further assistance.

But reports of serious unrest among North Koreans grown desperate in the face of hunger cannot be ignored. United Press in Seoul reported this March that some 7,000 North Koreans had fled to Yangbian, an autonomous Korean province in China, because of worsening economic conditions. And several North Korean defectors to the south have told horror stories of the current situation in the north, detailing food shortages, malnutrition among children, and corruption in the ruling circles. It has also been reported that North Korea has purchased from the West large quantities of riot control equipment—tear gas launchers, synthetic rubber bullet guns, cellular phones and radio pagers, gas masks, shields and billy clubs—indicating the existence of civil disturbances.

To divert internal attention from worsening living conditions, Pyongyang has sharply escalated its anti-South Korean rhetoric. In July 1996, Marshal Kim Kwang-jin, the first deputy minister of the North Korean People's Army, accused South Korea of treating the north's food crisis as an opportunity to invade the north and spread rumors about its collapse. Moreover, South Korea recently attempted to prevent the United States, Japan, and other nations from providing economic assistance to North Korea unless North Korea accepted four-way talks on the inter-Korean problems involving Seoul–Washington and Pyongyang–Beijing; North Korea considers this an act of war.

South Korea and the United States hold sharply different attitudes about the food shortages in North Korea. A May 21, 1996, *New York Times* editorial accused South Korea of using food as a diplomatic weapon and urged the Clinton administration to put hunger above politics. It lamented the spectacle of President Kim Young Sam discouraging economic aid to his fellow countrymen in the north. But South Korea does not understand why the north bites the hand that wants to feed it.

Pyongyang's High-Risk Diplomacy

Pyongyang's main concerns—national security and the economy—require it to negotiate simultaneously with Seoul and Washington. But it has chosen to exclude Seoul. In Pyongyang's view, economic development is important, but not as important as ending the state of war with Washington. North Korea believes that a peace treaty with Washington that excludes Seoul is essential to its survival. In this regard Pyongyang's foreign policy has been consistent for the past two decades. As early as 1974 North Korea attempted to pursue contacts with the United States to formally end the Korean War. Washington, however, simply ignored these efforts.

With the end of the cold war, North Korea's desperation has become more apparent. A declining defense

budgets, currently about one-sixth the size of South Korea's projected 1997 defense budget of $17.6 billion, is also a serious concern for the north. South Korea's establishment of diplomatic relations with Moscow and Beijing in the early 1990s was a major blow to the north and it responded ominously by raising the specter of a nuclear weapons program. To the north's dismay, South Koreans openly discussed absorbing North Korea. North Korea, under extreme pressure from the United States, South Korea, and the international community to abandon its nuclear program but without any security guarantees, surprised the world on March 13, 1993, when it announced that it would withdraw from the nuclear Non-Proliferation Treaty (NPT). This decision reflected North Korean frustration and insecurity in dealing with South Korea and its allies.

In dealing with the United States, North Korea has skillfully employed a high-risk strategy—renouncing obligations under the NPT and the International Atomic Energy Agency (IAEA) safeguards agreement, threatening to destroy Seoul, and withdrawing from the Military Armistice Commission that oversees the demilitarized zone between the two Koreas. These strategies have created intense frustration among United States negotiators and South Korean policymakers, but their effectiveness has often been demonstrated by American eagerness to have high-level talks in response to North Korea's threats.

Americans returning from North Korea do not talk about North Korea preparing for invasion; only defectors to the south and South Korean officials say that it is.

In this manner North Korea has extracted security-related concessions from the United States, such as cancellation of the Team Spirit military exercises by South Korean and American troops and a guarantee that nuclear weapons would not be used on the Korean peninsula. Though North Korea has yet to secure a peace treaty or diplomatic recognition, it believes it can achieve these aims by promoting tension on the peninsula.

North Korea apparently believes that the October 21, 1994, Geneva accord—a historic agreement negotiated between the United States and North Korea to bring the latter into the international community in return for the freezing of North Korea's nuclear programs—is one or two steps below an eventual peace treaty with and diplomatic recognition by the United States. For more than 40 years Washington's North Korea policy was based on the assumption that the country was so dangerous and untrustworthy that its behavior had to be punished. The Geneva accord reverses this stance and rewards a rogue state for promising to become a responsible member of the international community.

The Geneva accord, if successfully carried out, will enable North Korea to escape a German-style absorption by South Korea. The accord's timetable allows for a minimum of five years before inspections begin to determine how much weapons-grade plutonium North Korea has diverted in past years. Furthermore, it is expected to take eight to ten years to remove North Korea's 8,600 plutonium-laden fuel rods.

In accordance with the Geneva accord, North Korea first must freeze its nuclear weapons program, then the United States and its allies will provide Pyongyang with alternative sources of energy. In return for the freeze, the United States and its allies must begin work on the first of two light-water reactors for North Korea. Projected to cost over $4 billion, they are to be financed mainly by South Korea and Japan. The Korean Peninsula Energy Development Organization (KEDO), a multinational consortium that assigns a central role to Seoul for this project, was established in March 1995.

The assignment of a key role to Seoul in KEDO revived North Korea's high-risk strategy however. Rejecting South Korean-financed light-water reactors, it warned Washington that it would resume operations at its Yongbyon nuclear complex. In June 1995, Washington and Pyongyang agreed that although South Korea would play a central role in providing the light-water reactors, North Korea would not get light-water reactors with the label "Made in South Korea." And on July 11, 1996, North Korea and KEDO signed a protocol in New York on privileges, immunities, and consular protection for the KEDO staffs in North Korea.

Problems remain, the most important being how to share the rising reactor costs—which could easily exceed $5 billion or even $6 billion because of inflation and transportation costs. The United States is unable to contribute any money because of Congress's refusal to endorse the commitment to finance the project; this could complicate KEDO talks in the future.

The accord's second phase depends on progress by KEDO. In this phase North Korea must allow international monitors to inspect the two nuclear waste sites that were off limits to inspectors in the past. In the third and final phase, North Korea must dismantle its 5-megawatt Yongbyon nuclear reactor and destroy its partially finished 50-

and 200-megawatt reactors. In exchange, the United States and its allies are to complete the construction of the second light-water reactor.

The accord offers the potential to accommodate North Korea's desire for economic development and national security. It contains provisions that could jump-start the North Korean economy since trade with the United States, Japan, and other Western nations would eventually link the north to the world market. The construction of the light-water reactors will take ten years and North Korea has earned enough time to reform its system, if it is willing to do so.

The agreement also helps restore equilibrium on the Korean peninsula, which has been lacking since the end of the cold war. South Korea's normalization of relations with Russia and China—unaccompanied by North Korea's normalization of relations with the United States and Japan—has created disequilibrium in the East Asian balance of power. But the Geneva accord has had the effect of restoring that balance since the prospects for cross-recognition are brighter than they have ever been. The deal between the United States and North Korea is thus more than a resolution of the nuclear issue; it signals the end to a half-century of enmity between the United States and North Korea.

Frustration and Discontent

Vacillating between their impulse to strangle North Korea and their wish to provide it assistance, South Koreans are uncomfortable with the Geneva accord's incomplete resolution of the north's nuclear program. South Koreans have grown frustrated in dealing with North Korea because their efforts seem to carry less weight with the north than those of former United States President Jimmy Carter, Robert Gallucci (who negotiated the Geneva agreement), and President Bill Clinton. They are angry because their bid to be the prime mover in the resolution of the nuclear crisis and other inter-Korean matters has proved futile: Washington gets the credit and Seoul shoulders the major financial burden in constructing the expensive light-water reactors in the north.

A triangle involving the United States, South Korea, and North Korea increasingly favors North Korea. North Korea's campaign to isolate South Korea has been fairly effective. Though officially Washington and Seoul maintain a kind of solidarity toward Pyongyang, growing Washington-Pyongyang contacts have changed Washington's perception of North Korea. The image of North Korea as a Stalinist regime bent on invading South Korea has changed to that of an economic basket case trying without much success to open itself to the outside world.

This image change is quite dramatic. In the past the North Korean threat was taken seriously because of the memory of the Korean War, the capture of a United

States spy ship, the brutal murder of American service-men at Panmunjom in the mid-1970s, and the downing of a Korean Airlines plane to sabotage the Olympic Games in Seoul in 1988. Today North Korea is viewed as a dying country that has lost the race with South Korea for legitimacy. The change in American attitudes toward North Korea is the result of numerous contacts between the two nations over the last eight years. Both the Reagan and Bush administrations encouraged a modest initiative aimed at ending North Korea's isolation from the mainstream of the East Asian region. Pyongyang's perception of America has also changed significantly. North Korea began with the perception that the United States, along with South Korea, was determined to destroy it, but today Pyongyang is increasingly relying on the United States to guarantee its survival.

American officials tend to take a relatively benign view of North Korea's hostile behavior toward South Korea. They emphasize North Korea's defensiveness rather than its bellicose nature. Unlike South Korean officials, who emphasize the possibility of a North Korean invasion, they believe the likelihood of war is very low. A recent assessment by the United States Defense Intelligence Agency (DIA) shows that North Korean military activity is directed at enhancing internal control; the assessment also notes that its ability to conduct large-scale military operations continues to erode. Both the CIA and the State Department concur with a DIA view that North Korea is complying with the Geneva accord to freeze its nuclear project. These agencies reason that worsening economic conditions in North Korea make compliance more likely because North Korea knows that smooth relations with the United States are essential to its survival. Americans returning from North Korea do not talk about North Korea preparing for invasion; only defectors to the south and South Korean officials say that it is.

South Koreans have little faith in the ability of American officials to deal with "deceptive" North Koreans. Seoul wasted no time in discrediting the Clinton administration's moderate attitude toward North Korea when a spy submarine entered the south in September. The infiltration sparked a massive manhunt during which most of the agents either committed suicide or were killed. The incident gave South Korea an opportunity to reaffirm its view of North Korea as a rogue state that has not abandoned its policy of undermining South Korea. South Korean officials firmly believe that North Korea's unceasing effort to drive a wedge between the south and Washington is also designed to create division and turmoil in the south and undermine the government.

North Korea hopes that expanded United States–North Korean contacts and its calculated efforts to humiliate the Kim Young Sam government will erode public confidence in the southern governments ability to

manage inter-Korean affairs. North Korea's ultimate purpose is to bring about significant policy differences between Seoul and Washington that would create an attractive context for North Korean peace proposals. North Korea, for example, no longer emphasizes the withdrawal of American troops as the necessary condition for a peace accord with Washington. South Koreans, pushed to the sidelines, sleep with the worst scenario, in which units of the 80,000-strong North Korean Special Operations Force arrive via boats, submarines, and light planes to attack Seoul and create chaos.

Juche Junked?

It is a supreme irony that North Korea, faltering economically and practically abandoned by its Russian and Chinese partners, hopes to survive with the help of its enemies: the United States and its allies. That beggars can't be choosers does not seem to apply to North Korea. The quickest way to revive North Korea's economy and improve its standard of living would be through direct talks with South Korea and serious economic reform. But the North Korean government fears that such a course of action would be suicidal, since it would expose North Koreans to the freedoms of the south. North Korea will only discreetly transact with South Korea. The current arrangement of maintaining separate United States–North Korea, United States–South Korea, and South Korea–North Korea tracks is disappointing to South Korea, but not to North Korea. Washington's view that a North Korea with nuclear weapons constitutes the most serious threat to peace and stability on the Korean peninsula and in all East Asia has given North Korea an opportunity to confront the superpower and get something from it—official contacts, light-water reactors, interim energy supplies, the possibility of trade, and even diplomatic recognition pending the fulfillment of the Geneva accord. Pyongyang has skillfully exploited Washington's eagerness to discuss important issues—freezing the nuclear program, American soldiers missing-in-action from the Korean War, Pyongyang's missile sales to terrorist states in the Middle East, and the food shortages—and has used these discussions to drive a wedge between Washington and Seoul. This method of conducting business will continue.

Though no one can rule out the collapse of North Korea (in fact, President Kim Young Sam believes that it soon will occur), there are a number of factors pointing toward its holding out a few more years, if not indefinitely. First, there is consensus in the international community that North Korea must be integrated into it. Second, no nation, including South Korea, wants to see the collapse of North Korea. The four major powers—the United States, Japan, China, and Russia—fear the preictable negative consequences of such a collapse: refugees, killing, and chaos. And while South Koreans might feel satisfaction if North Korea collapsed and they achieved German-style unification, they know that such a scenario would be extremely dangerous.

Though South Koreans are angry at North Korea's intransigent behavior, they remain willing to help their fellow countrymen. If the Seoul government permitted it, South Korean businessmen would invest in the Rajin-Sonbong free-trade area, which has business links to mainland China, Russia, Japan, the United States, Canada, and other countries (trade between the two Koreas amounted to several hundred million dollars in 1995, making South Korea North Korea's third-largest trade partner after China and Japan, and a major source of North Korea's hard currency). Seoul boycotted an investment seminar in the free-trade area held this September because the north refused to invite South Korean officials and journalists. The seminar was a major attempt by Pyongyang to link up with the outside world; some 550 business and media representatives, mostly from Japan, the United States, and China, attended. Various agreements were reached involving tourist promotion and the construction of hotels, a hospital, a motorcycle plant, and telecommunications system.

Despite its official *juche* ("self-reliance") ideology, North Korea appears to have committed itself to the Chinese model. Moreover, the pace of economic reform in North Korea may accelerate when it obtains

a peace treaty with the United States. North Korea's problem may be largely psychological. Without a peace treaty, it feels too insecure to embark on serious economic reform.

To dramatize the need for a peace treaty, North Korea has employed with the United States the double-edged tactics of courtship and nuclear brinkmanship. North Korea may think that its strategy and tactics have been effective gambits for a peace treaty with the United States. But the country's long-term security cannot be guaranteed by a peace agreement with the United States alone. Its survival depends on economic development, political stability and the goodwill of South Korea and its allies.

The key problem is engaging the two Koreas in direct negotiations. At present, Seoul, despite its economic superiority, has no magical power that can change North Korea's attitude. Perhaps only the United States and Japan can open up North Korea through the normalization of relations. If and when North Korea is opened, it may acquire attitudes more compatible with Seoul's worldview. Then it may talk to the south. But for the present, South Korea vehemently rejects this option, saying it is incompatible with its domestic politics. The infiltration of the North Korean spy submarine in September is a clear reminder that the cold war continues on the Korean peninsula, undermining all the efforts Washington and Pyongyang have made to reach the Geneva accord. North Korea knows not only how to hurt its southern neighbor, but also how to hurt itself.

Article 24

Far Eastern Economic Review, February 29, 1996

The Image Cracks

A shootout in Pyongyang and defections by ranking cadres could indicate that the regime's control has slipped enough to make its eventual collapse a matter of when, not how.

Shim Jae Hoon in Seoul

Something is rotten in North Korea, though the Stalinist curtain that shrouds the country makes it hard to say precisely how far the rot has set in. More and more often these days, however, weird incidents flash through the veil to give outsiders glimpses of a society gone horribly wrong.

The latest occurred at half past five in the morning of February 14 in Pyongyang, when hardly a soul moved on the broad Mansudae boulevard opposite the

official residence of North Korean leader Kim Jong Il. According to the Russian Itar-Tass news agency, a North Korean soldier in his twenties jumped over the walls of the sprawling Russian embassy compound nearby. Spotted by North Korean guards, he fired a pistol at them, killing three and wounding another. Then he dashed to the embassy's trade mission building, demanding asylum and safe passage to Moscow.

After a 30-hour standoff with North Korean soldiers inside the compound,

the intruder was shot and killed. The Russian Foreign Ministry announced that Cho Myong Gil, a corporal, committed suicide by shooting himself in the head. The official Korean Central News Agency in Pyongyang, however, claimed he was alive and "undergoing treatment for mental disorder."

"A situation like this could have been hardly imagined before, as it happened in an area crowded with major government buildings and watched by armed security agents at all time[s]," says Kang

Myong Do, a North Korean defector who arrived in Seoul in May 1994. Kang, one of the highest-ranking northerners to defect to Seoul, ought to know. As son-in-law of North Korean Premier Kang Song San, he was privy to the mood at the top of the northern power hierarchy.

On the surface, the embassy incident could be seen merely as a case of a soldier who cracked. But that it could happen to a member of one of the more pampered sections of North Korean society, the army, might indicate that the regime's facade of control is also cracking. Indeed, Itar-Tass said Pyongyang was angry the incident had been broadcast to the outside world. The North Koreans protested to Moscow, calling the report a provocation.

To South Korean officials, however, the bizarre early-morning shoot-out raises the disturbing spectre of the Pyongyang government wobbling to a collapse because of a variety of factors, among them acute food shortages and a breakdown in state control. Coming as it does in the wake of a series of defections by troops and members of other relatively better-off sections of society, the shoot-out also points to growing disillusionment among the power elites in Pyongyang.

The North Korean populace is tightly insulated from the outside world, while those at the top who know what's going on tend in the main to stick together, holding on to their privileges. Still, most experts agree that while the Kim Jong Il regime may not collapse immediately, it is showing signs of steady unravelling. One consequence, intelligence experts in Seoul believe, is that what was once a small trickle of North Korean defectors could turn into a flood.

"I don't think the North is going to collapse immediately," says Kim Young Kwang, formerly a top intelligence analyst at South Korea's Agency for National Security Planning, "but the current rush for defection could well be its prelude." Suh Jae Jean, the chief North Korea analyst for Seoul's National Unification Board, agrees with many other analysts that a weakening in the North's leadership structure because of the power vacuum created by the death of President Kim Il Sung in 1994 could have dangerous implications.

Though Suh says "we should be careful not to over-read the message" of the shoot-out in Pyongyang, he too believes it might be an indication of "more and more people losing confidence in their system." And this, says Lee Jung Min, a Rand Corp. specialist on Korea, "raises

the question of who's actually in control in Pyongyang."

The Russian embassy incident has delivered a monumental blow to the prestige of Kim Jong Il, who has been anxious to project the image of a North Korea solidly united behind his ascension to power. The shoot-out, the first such case reported to the outside world, came just two days before the nationwide celebration of Kim's 54th birthday on February 16. State media, including Radio Pyongyang, gave effusive coverage of rallies across North Korea celebrating the anniversary, calling Kim "Great Leader" and referring to him as commander in chief of the People's Armed Forces.

But the media gave no clue as to when Kim would assume the formal titles of state president or party general secretary. Recent defectors have said it was unlikely he would assume those honorifics until after the third anniversary of his father's death, which will be in July 1997, in deference to the Confucian observance of a three-year mourning period.

The question titillating North Korea watchers in Seoul is whether Kim can last that long. Meanwhile, intelligence specialists have begun warning the Seoul government to be prepared for any emergency north of the Demilitarized Zone.

The Russian embassy incident followed another recent embarrassment for Kim. His first wife and former actress Sung Hye Rim, mother of his eldest son and heir-apparent, Kim Jong Nam, has vanished from her apartment in Moscow. Sung Hye Rim, who had been receiving medical treatment in the Russian capital, disappeared with her sister and niece. According to a report in Seoul's Chosun Ilbo newspaper, they were hiding in France and considering making Seoul their final destination. If that happened, the defectors could provide inside clues to the workings of Kim's mind, besides indicating whether he has been successful in his bid to consolidate his power.

There is little question that there has been a dramatic spurt in the number of high-profile North Korean defectors disenchanted by their system. In early January, three North Koreans slipped into the South Korean embassy in Lusaka, Zambia, asking for asylum. They brought to 110 the number of North Korean defectors since 1990, far more than the 49 who escaped between 1980 and 1989. "Everybody in the North is convinced that there's no way out of economic difficulties short of profound policy changes," Hyon Song Il, a third sec-

retary at the North Korean embassy i[n] Zambia, said at a news conference i[n] Seoul on February 13.

With the Pyongyang government u[n-] able to remit money to the embass[y] since last August, Hyon said, he and h[is] wife were reduced to a subsistence-lev[el] existence. Embassy staff and the amba[s-] sador quarrelled frequently, and all su[f-] fered from severe emotional strai[n.] Hyon's wife later said she fled to th[e] South Korean embassy in Lusaka afte[r] the ambassador struck her for refusin[g] to sweep the office floor. Hyon said h[e] too decided it was time to flee when th[e] ambassador ordered him to kill his wi[fe] at a meeting arranged by Zambian off[i-] cials to confirm her intention to defec[t.]

Whatever their motives, the swe[l-] ling number of North Korea[n] streaming to the South by cros[s-] ing from the Demilitarized Zone, deser[t-] ing their work sites in China, easter[n] Europe and Africa or escaping from lo[g-] ging camps in Siberia is forcing Seoul [to] review its refugee resettlement pr[o-] gramme. In 1993 South Korea revised i[ts] law governing asylum-seekers, cuttin[g] down on the cash rewards and lavis[h] subsidies instituted during the Cold Wa[r] years. Under the new law, cash subsidie[s] for defectors have been cut from an ave[r-] age of 45 million won ($57,600) per ye[ar] to 16 million. Similarly, the size of th[e] average government-provided apar[t-] ment has been reduced from 50 squa[re] metres per person to 30.

The diminishing hospitality is provo[k-] ing howls of protest from the recent a[r-] rivals, especially the unskilled worke[rs] who form the majority of the defector[s.] Unused to the individualistic lifestyl[e] of a competitive capitalist society, the[y] find it difficult to adapt to new ord[er] based on cash and personal initiativ[e,] says Kim Chang Hwa, who arrived [in] Seoul in 1988 by way of China. "It tak[es] time for them to realize how importa[nt] money is in a capitalist society," sa[ys] Kim, who runs a restaurant with th[e] help of five other defectors. "By the tim[e] they learn how valuable it is, it's ofte[n] too late." However, those who can[e] with professional training or higher ed[u-] cation have fared better, finding caree[rs] as entertainers, doctors, engineers an[d] consultants advising business firms [on] investment in the North.

Preparing for a worst-case scenario [in] which a massive influx of refugees fo[l-] lows a government collapse in Pyong[y-] ang, the Seoul government has set up a[n] inter-ministerial committee to deal wi[th] the problem. A special refugee resettl[e-] ment programme now under discussion envisages raising the budget for resettlement and programmes for social inte-

gration, job training, even the setting up of large-scale tented camps in coastal areas for emergency accommodation.

Most South Koreans hope things won't come to such a pass that the tents will be filled.

Article 25   *New Asia–Pacific Review*, Vol. 3, No. 1, 1996

Stalemate on Bougainville

James Griffin

It is now nearly eight years since sabotage at the huge Panguna copper mine initiated the secessionist rebellion on Bougainville and with it the worst violence seen in the Southwest Pacific since the Second World War. It has effectively destroyed what was in 1988 the most prosperous and best governed province of Papua New Guinea.

However, this is a war not just between rebel guerrillas and the Papua New Guinea Defense Force (PNGDF) but between Bougainvilleans themselves—between the Bougainville Revolutionary Army (BRA) and the Bougainville "Resistance". The situation is further confused in that many "Resistance" members favor eventual secession but are not prepared to accept an outcome in which the rebel political arm, the Bougainville Interim Government (BIG) and the BRA, both led by Nasioi language speakers from the central mainland, emerge as the ruling coterie.

At the time of writing (late August 1996), the Papua New Guinea government led by Sir Julius Chan recently called off a search and destroy campaign in the central area aimed at wiping out at least the rebel leadership. Operation High Speed, as it was known, had been made possible by the temporary presence of both PNGDF battalions (1,400 strength) in what would normally be a garrison changeover.

On past indications, the undisciplined, ill-equipped, undermanned, logistically under serviced and unpredictable PNGDF was never going to succeed. So the question arises, why this campaign was launched at this time. Two years ago (July 1994) the present commander of the PNGDE, Brigadier-General Singirok, then a battalion commander, indicated clearly that a military solution was not possible. Against his better judgment, he had to lead his troops to the Panguna heights. They were not re-

sisted, but found, as he expected, that they were unable to hold on without reserves and adequate supplies. On the downward trek, his squad encountered sniper fire, and he was wounded. Leaving aside invincibly poor judgment, one can only assume that the PNGDF received new optimistic intelligence or that High Speed was being driven by the prime minister's need for a show of strength as parliament moves into its 1997 election mode—and that he wildly miscalculated.

Two serious problems reemerged before the central military thrust began. PNGDF squads, both in boats and in an Iroquois helicopter, again breached the Bougainville Straits border and engaged in crossfire with the Solomon Islands field force. As a result, the Solomons prime minister, Solomon Mamaloni, instructed his United Nations envoy to seek help from the United Nations Secretary General, Dr. Boutros Boutros-Ghali, to forestall an incipient conflict. Port Moresby, however, pleaded grave provocation. Over the years, BRA members have continually crossed the border not just for medical supplies and refuge but to procure material and essential supplies.

The PNGDF saw itself as doing what it futilely objected to in the past on the Irian Jaya border when Indonesian troops engaged in "hot pursuit" of the OPM. Solomons politicians, especially from its Western provinces, have been openly sympathetic to the rebels. They share a conspicuously black pigmentation with Bougainvilleans, and traditional affinities persist. Until it was recently burnt down and its director expedited to the Netherlands a BIG external office, in continuous radio contact with the BRA, was tolerated in Honiara. The complexity of the secession issue and the extent of its support do not seem to have been understood there. Further border intrusions by the PNGDF have the potential to damage Papua New Guinea's cause internationally and even

provoke Honiara into some form of recognition of Bougainville independence.

Moreover, Australia has to be concerned about the border forays in view of its substantial backing of the PNGDF in terms of subsidy, supplies, and training. While, on the one hand, it has constructed and supported Papua New Guinea's territorial integrity, on the other hand it will not intervene to guarantee it. When giving four Iroquois helicopters to the PNGDF in 1988–89, Australia stipulated they were not to be used offensively or mounted with guns but were for purposes of transportation, medical evacuations and surveillance. But they were permitted to return fire in self-defense. This was the loophole; abuses occurred. Human rights groups in Australia are pressuring Canberra to exert sanctions for breaches of the agreement. In the heat of battle, the PNGDF is confused, even outraged, by such nicety. The issue underlines the limits to Australia's alleged hegemony in the region. In fact, Canberra has been made to appear muddled and even impotent.

Attempts have been made to end hostilities. A ceasefire in March 1990 was followed by the withdrawal of all Papua New Guinea security forces from the Bougainville mainland and Buka Island leaving the BRA in control. However, Port Moresby then imposed a blockade on supplies and services, which in turn was met with a unilateral declaration of independence (UDI) on May 17 and the formation of the BIG. The result was chaos as the BRA in its turn terrorized those not openly supportive and the BIG proved totally incompetent. A peace conference in late July-August on a New Zealand ship off Bougainville between delegates from Port Moresby led by "the father of the nation", Sir Michael Somare, and BIG representatives produced an agreement that foundered immediately, implicitly on the intractable issue of sovereignty.

In late August, leaders on Buka Island who had set up their own Liberation Front against BRA groups, which were often led by Nasioi language speakers from the central mainland, invited the PNGDF to return. A further conference in Honiara in January 1991 resulted in another impractical accord after which even the BIG signatories were repudiated by their president who did not attend. In April the PNGDF crossed to the mainland, adopting then a strategy of moving south only when invited by local leaders. By 1992 the PNGDF had a presence in, though not control of, most of the province, the BRA-central heartland excepted.

After the last election in mid-1992, the newly elected prime minister, Mr. Paias Wingti, a Highlander influenced by maverick Australian mining advisers, opted for greater aggression than his gradualist predecessor, Rabbie Namaliu, was prepared to use. Even if the whole BRA could not be subdued, Wingti was persuaded that a cordon sanitaire could be imposed around the mine that had yielded, in 1988, 17 percent of national revenue and 40 percent of foreign exchange. Such a blow was expected to dispirit BRA/BIG leaders; the revolt would then struggle to an end. The wounding of General Singirok in 1994 provided a temporary lesson. Soon after, in August, Chan replaced Wingti; peace on Bougainville was to be his first goal. He met the supremo of the BRA, Sam Kauona, in the Solomons, flattered him with the title "General" and initiated a peace conference in the main Bougainville town of Arawa, which took place in October under the surveillance of a multinational South Pacific force financed by Australia. Rebel leaders, however, refused to attend, ostensibly distrusting Chan's guarantees of safety. Still, "Resistance" and noncombatant leaders from most parts of the province did so, but Chan, indignant at the rebel boycott, brought the conference to a peremptory end and denounced rebel leaders as "criminals" to be hunted down, although officially he kept the ceasefire in place.

The greatest bonus for peace making was the defection from behind BRA lines, before the Arawa conference, of Theodore Miriung, a former acting judge of the Supreme Court, and a legal adviser to the BIG since 1990. He brought with him followers from the North and South Nasioi areas and the immediate hinterland of Arawa. Miriung remained, in principle, a secessionist, rejecting as immoral the imperial carve-up that had severed Bougainville from the rest of the Solomons archipel-

ago. However, realizing now that neither the U.N. nor outside states were prepared to recognize Bougainville as an independent state, he was prepared, on pragmatic grounds, to accept Papua New Guinea's sovereignty.

A united Bougainville could not be subdued indefinitely by Papua New Guinea's security forces and a failure to grant a meaningful degree of autonomy (as prior to 1989) would strengthen a demand for self-determination.

Chan's dire post-conference threats did nothing to reduce guerrilla terrorism even in reputedly safe areas. The PNGDF reciprocated with undisciplined and sometimes undiscriminating sorties. Neither side could eliminate the other. In September and December 1995, Miriung's efforts brought about two Australia-sponsored peace conferences in Cairns, North Queensland, with Chan's approval. The second was attended by Kauona, Joseph Kabui (premier in 1987 to 1990 and a minister in the BIG), members of the BTG led by Miriung, the province's four national MPs, and "exiled" leaders from Port Moresby. Especially significant was the presence of representatives of the U.N. Secretary-General and the Commonwealth Secretariat to act as chairmen and observers from the Unrepresented Nations and Peoples Organization (UNPO) and the International Commission of Jurists (ICJ).

The meeting was amicable. Miriung tried to persuade rebel representatives that Papua New Guinea sovereignty was an insuperable fact and

Comsec and U.N. representatives pointed out that an act of self-determination was not available. However, with the ICJ representative seeming to cast doubt on this, Kabui, for example, felt that attrition was in favor of the rebels and that Port Moresby would eventually find the war too expensive of lives and resources. A tabled letter from his cultic leader, Francis Ona, "President, Republic of Bougainville", indicated the irrationality on which this hope and faith were built. Ona declared that he spoke "in the Name of the ever-living God and the powers of the Holy Spirit," that he was "fully supported by 99 percent of the total population of Bougainville" and that his army "controls 95 percent of the total land area." He was looking forward to "taking full control over all island (sic) very soon," and he assured delegates that "you are all mine, and I love each one of you, and I wish [you] to share with me the promises of our new nation of Mekamui" (a Nasioi word meaning "sacred land").

.As with the first Cairns conference, the second was followed not by a lull in the fighting but an increase such that in March, with nearly twenty PNGDF and police killed since New Year, Chan called off the official cease-fire. Even Buka's defenses were briefly breached by the BRA. The schedule of further negotiations planned at Cairns has lapsed. The immediate future is uncertain. However, even if Chan's offensive had succeeded in subduing the BRA, it is difficult to see Bougainvilleans as a whole submitting to the new centralized regime now imposed elsewhere in the place of the previously elected provincial governments. Provincial government had been granted to Bougainville in 1976 in return for the withdrawal of its first UDI (September 1, 1975) which was proclaimed just before Independence. In the interests of uniformity it was extended to all other provinces, whereas accepting Bougainville as a special case with a separate constitutional status now appears to have been a better option. It must surely be clear now that at least a united Bougainville could not be subdued indefinitely by Papua New Guinea's security forces and a failure to grant a meaningful degree of autonomy (as prior to 1989) would strengthen a demand for self-determination. In any case, without acceptance by locals, it will be impossible to restart the mine. (Not that this is the province's sole asset as it is agriculturally rich, having in 1988 provided 45 percent of the country's cocoa and some 20 percent of its copra, and its Exclusive Economic Zone is substantial.)

If the possibility that there can be military intervention on behalf of Port Moresby by Australia or Indonesia, or that the U.N. will insist ultimately that an act of self-determination be enjoined by a multinational force is dismissed, there is only one alternative to a continuing impasse. That is for Port Moresby to forego its desire for administrative uniformity and for rebel leaders to join with Miriung in a compromise that restores at least the status quo antebellum in national-provincial relations, as well as ensuring rehabilitation, amnesties, and pardons. This should be the more acceptable to Bougainvilleans insofar as the outsiders who flocked in from other parts of Papua New Guinea ("redskins," as the jet black, Bougainvilleans call them) have long been "repatriated," and administrative controls could ensure that they return only as required for specific work. Moreover, for future resource exploitation, a package readjusting royalties and equity was offered by Prime Minister Namaliu in May 1989 and could be offered again, even expanded. That much seems to be the bottom line. The fear in Port Moresby of some domino effect in stimulating separatist tendencies elsewhere simply has to be outfaced. Except in the outer part of the islands region (New Britain, New Ireland, and Manus), there is no need to take secessionist threats seriously; and even in the islands they will be more the result of Port Moresby's policies and maladministration than, in the case of Bougainville, a stubborn reluctance to integrate.

Nevertheless, there are factors suggesting that Bougainville may bleed for the foreseeable future and the solution left until one side wearies of the conflict. Self-sufficient in basic food, Bougainville will not be starved into submission, and the lack of education and outside contacts will make it easier to keep young people under cultic influence. Rebel leaders will be attentive to complaints of the cost to the nation of persevering with the war and continue to hope for a withdrawal of the PNGD, after which they can intimidate or eliminate the "Resistance". However, in spite of this cost and the body bags bringing home dead soldiers and police, the Bougainville quagmire makes relatively little political impact, elsewhere in Papua New Guinea. It will not be a decisive issue in the 1997 elections, although the conduct of the war could be one factor in the choice of prime minister. Port Moresby has so far withstood the drain on its resources and should be able to do so indefinitely, pending some resolution, which must entail in the first instance a substantial degree of autonomy for Bougainville under the sovereignty of Papua New Guinea.

About the Author:
Emeritus Professor James Griffin was Professor of History at the University of Papua New Guinea and is now an author and consultant.

Further Reading:
Douglas, Oliver, 1991. *Black islanders: A Personal Perspective of Bougainville 1937–1991*, University of Hawaii Press, Honolulu; May, R. J. and Spriggs, Matthew (eds.), 1990. *The Bougainville Crisis*, Crawford House Press, Bathurst.

Article 26

Far Eastern Economic Review, February 29, 1996

People Power, 1986–96

It hasn't failed. It hasn't been tried.

On paper the Philippines is a wealthy country. Providence has bequeathed it many advantages over richer neighbours such as Taiwan and South Korea, including an almost inexhaustible supply of natural resources: gold, iron ore, copper, cement, salt, granite, marble. Its soil is rich and its produce bountiful, including rice, sugar, coconuts, bananas and avocados. It boasts a hardworking, educated and English-speaking citizenry. In the late 1950s and 1960s, it was second only to Japan among Asian countries in economic performance.

It is worth keeping these assets in mind on this 10th anniversary of the People Power Revolution. No doubt President Marcos did much to ruin the country he fled in such ignominious circumstances. But the lessons his rule affords have still to be drawn. As the hundreds of millions of dollars former South Korean Presidents Chun Doo Hwan and Roh Tae Woo siphoned off for themselves should remind us, executive corruption—however lamentable—need not be a barrier to development. Where Mr. Marcos really failed the Philippines was in centralizing both political and economic authority, a process that turned a nation full of promise into an Asian also-ran. In the gallery of rogues should also be included the bilateral and multilateral lending institutions that still have not explained why they kept the money flowing. All contributed to the debilitating belief that wealth is something that needs to be managed rather than created.

Corazon Aquino may have changed how those who preside over this process are elected, but she left the equation intact. Only now has a much-heralded privatization programme begun to reduce the power of government cartels. The Americans were booted out under the premise that the Philippines no longer faced any external threat, an interesting premise in light of Manila's recent appeals after China's actions in the Spratlys. Indeed, successive Philippine governments have been unable to meet the two top responsibilities of any state: securing the borders against outside intruders, and protecting the public against crime and anarchy.

Yet the failure that has done the most to discredit People Power is a constitution whose economic sections would have been more at home in Sukarno's Indonesia or even Ho Chi Minh's Vietnam. The result is the strangling of badly needed business initiatives, most recently the second attempt to sell off the Manila Hotel. In other words, Marcos-era big government continues. This is a reminder that revolutions are not made in the streets, and democracy requires more than voting. If the promise was government of the people, by the people and for the people, then most Filipinos are still waiting. Indeed, without secure property rights and well-defined limits on government meddling, elections simply politicize the economy, leaving the most basic rights of life, liberty and property secure only for the well-connected.

Despite the strides made by President Fidel Ramos, the idea somehow still reigns that business decisions are better made by politicians than by the people. In recent weeks, for example, a Senate committee passed a bill that would require all employers, including those in the private sector, to give married male employees seven paid days of paternity leave. Instead of blasting such a regulation as the kind of excess the Philippines can hardly afford, President Ramos gave it his blessing. Likewise the recent decision in a country where unemployment remains stickily high to boost the minimum wage by 20 pesos (77 cents) per day, which now puts it about double the rate in China and four times the rate in Vietnam.

Customs is widely regarded as more corrupt than the police; bureaucracies like the Bureau of Textile Export Promotions seem to spend all their time searching for someone who might have committed a trade without permission; and the Philippines is now in danger of becoming the only country in the World Trade Organization to fail to meet tariff-reduction commitments agreed to in the Uruguay Round of trade talks. At least in China, notes a frustrated business acquaintance, they don't hit you for the exports. Yet instead of concluding that the problem is too much government, the government declares there are too many Filipinos. How ironic an end for a movement that started out under the banner of People Power.

For those who recall the great promise of the Philippines only a generation ago, the lost opportunities are especially bitter. Indeed, our own view is that Philippine leaders are setting their sights too low. Instead of trying to catch up with the rest of Asia, they should have their eye on leading. The only obstacles are all man-made. Filipinos have had plenty of governments that have tried to help them. Ten years after their "revolution," they still wait for one that will let them help themselves.

Article 27   *The World & I,* May 1996

In Pursuit of Democracy

The government party faces well-organized challenges from three opposition parties.

John Kie-chiang Oh

John Kie-chiang Oh is professor of politics and a former academic vice president at the Catholic University of America, in Washington, D.C. He is the author, among numerous publications, of Korea: Democracy on Trial *(Cornell University Press, 1970).*

Two suspenseful political dramas are unfolding simultaneously in South Korea today. Both will have significant impact on an important presidential election to be held next year.

The first drama is the general elections for the 299 members of the National Assembly. These elections take place in the wake of the first full-fledged local government elections in Korea, held on June 25, 1995, in which the ruling party of President Kim Young Sam suffered a decisive defeat by all accounts. This year's assembly elections are also the very first legislative contests under the duly elected civilian government of President Kim, which displaced over 30 years of military-dominated regimes.

The second drama is the unprecedented court trials of two former generals-turned-presidents, Chun Doo Hwan and Roh Tae Woo, for (1) slush fund scandals involving over a billion dollars of illicit funds amassed while in office and (2) military insurrection and treason as well as massacring innocent citizens demanding democracy in Kwangju in 1980. Chun and Roh may be sentenced to long prison terms and heavy fines for the first. The possible sentences for the second include death.

If the first drama represents the forces of a brighter democratic future for Korea, the second embodies the darkest past of a military dictatorship that corrupted absolutely. Several heads of business-industrial conglomerates who "donated" astronomical amounts of money to these unabashedly greedy military dictators are also being tried. In a sense, the Republic of Korea's perennial contest between democratizing aspirations and the deeply rooted authoritarian force that tends to corrupt is continuing.

Most important, these two dramas are taking place while the nation awaits an important presidential election set for December 1997. In Korea, as in so many countries, the presidency constitutes the center of all political and administrative authority.

In Korean politics, each chief executive has played defining roles in his period. Each "republic" (for example, the Seventh Republic of Korea under President Kim) represents each president's tenure in office—with the exception of the Fourth, which signified a fundamental change in policy under President Park Chung Hee.

Executive-Legislative Relations

The National Assembly has had its ups and downs in prestige and power. It has exercised a relatively greater influence under "democratic" chief executives, particularly under Premier Chang Myon of the short-lived Second Republic, 1960–61. In fact, during the Second Republic, the only period when Korea had a cabinet system of government, the National Assembly was indeed supreme.

The National Assembly's position is inversely related to the power of the chief executive. Under a strong or dictatorial president, the assembly has often become an "automatic voting machine," dutifully endorsing the presidential will. However, with a democratically elected president such as Kim Young Sam, the assembly has been more of a partner with the executive branch. Many important pieces of legislation are the product of this executive-legislative collaboration.

An exceptional situation was created in the first years of the Sixth Republic, 1988–1993, under President Roh, when a situation known as *yoso-yadae* (literally, a small ruling party vs. a large opposition) occurred in the National Assembly. This created an executive-legislative deadlock that was resolved only when Roh's ruling party merged in early 1990 with two opposition parties. One was led by Kim Young Sam, who had been denouncing Roh as a military dictator. The other was headed by Kim Jong Pil, who was the closet ally of Gen. Park Chung Hee when he executed the first successful military coup in 1961.

Out of this strange "marriage of convenience," Kim Young Sam managed to emerge as the successful presidential candidate of the ruling party by 1992. Though the prestige of the National Assembly has waxed and waned, it has nevertheless remained a visible focus of national attention. Numerous politically ambitious Koreans aspire to join its ranks and wear the "golden badge" of honor.

Extraordinary attention is focused on the April election. It is generally expected that the 15th Assembly will be a partner with President Kim and the president to be elected in 1997, instead of a handmaiden to the president.

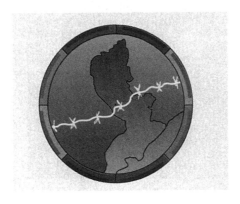

The 14th Assembly elections took place in March 1992, the last year of President Roh's five-year term. He spent astronomical sums from his mammoth slush fund to assure an overwhelming victory for his Democratic Republican Party. The lineup in the 14th Assembly was as follows:

The Democratic Republican Party— 149 seats, 49.8 percent;

The (opposition) Democratic Party— 97 seats, 32 percent;

The (minority) United People's Party—31 seats, 10.4 percent;

Independents—21 seats, 7 percent; and

The Party for New Political Reform— 1 seat, 0.03 percent.

Hard as Roh, Kim Young Sam, and Kim Jong Pil tried, a three-party merger could not produce two-thirds of the Assembly seats, the magic number that permits amendment of the constitution. Amending the constitution to adopt a cabinet system of government was a secret compact that did not remain secret very long after the three-party merger took place among the strange bedfellows of Roh and the two Kims.

When Kim Young Sam was inaugurated in 1993 as the first civilian president in 32 years, his government carried out a series of long-overdue reforms. Among other matters, the military was systematically removed from positions of governmental power, the real-name financial transaction system was inaugurated to minimize the possibilities of corruption by the use of borrowed or false names, and at least three important pieces of reform legislation were enacted in 1994.

These laws were (1) an integrated election and election malpractice prevention act to assure clean, fair, and violence-free elections, (2) a political fund law to minimize corruption and maximize transparency in raising and using political funds, and (3) a local autonomy act, which institutionalized local elections and governments.

The 1995 Local Government Elections

President Kim had an approval rating of over 80 percent in the first year of his five-year term, when he was busily carrying out and institutionalizing democratic reforms. However, toward the end of his second year, he seemed to be running out of ideas for what some cynics already called his "surprise shows." The regime appeared to falter as conservative resistance to his reform measures gradually stiffened.

When numerous people clamored for punishment of those involved in the Kwangju massacre of 1980, clearly implicating Chun and Roh, President Kim stated vaguely that "history should be their judge" and did not initiate any moves against them. His regime then decided to send shiploads of rice to the North Koreans, who were said to be starving; when a South Korean ship entered North Korean waters it was given insulting treatment by the North, which demanded that the ship fly a North Korean flag. What was intended as a praiseworthy humanitarian gesture suddenly turned sour, and Kim's popularity rating plummeted.

Under the circumstances, some in the Kim regime evidently attempted to postpone the local government elections, but the maneuver failed. By early 1995, Kim Jong Pil, a partner in the 1990 merger of Roh's party and Kim Young Sam's, was unceremoniously ousted from the ruling party. Kim Jong Pil promptly formed a new party, the United Liberal Democrats, in opposition to President Kim. Yet another Kim, Kim Dae Jung, the most consistent nemesis of military dictatorship and a political rival of Kim Young Sam, was a power behind the scenes of the major opposition Democratic Party.

In any case, the local elections of 1995 represented the first test of reform legislation enacted in 1994. By all accounts, the elections were generally fair, clean, and violence-free. Of a total of 1,120 local government officials elected, the outcome was once again decidedly yoso yadae, with a small ruling party vs. a larger opposition:

The (ruling) Democratic Liberal Party under President Kim—361 seats;

The (opposition) Democratic Party largely identified with Kim Dae Jung—443 seats;

The (new opposition) United Liberal Democrats under Kim Jong Pil, ousted from the ruling party—110 seats; and

Independents—206 seats.

Thus the government party managed to elect only 32 percent of the total of local government posts in 1995. In the 1992 National Assembly elections, during which the ruling party had the advantage of an incumbent president possessing an enormous slush fund, the government party occupied nearly 50 percent of the National Assembly seats. The ruling party's 1995 percentage was even lower than the plurality of 41 percent that Kim Young Sam received in the 1992 presidential election, when his opponent Kim Dae Jung garnered 33 percent.

Trials of Two Former Presidents

The ruling party and President Kim appeared stunned and tried to minimize the significance of the impact of the local election returns. It must have been clear that if they did not reverse the adverse trend, their political future was bleak. Significantly, the ruling party sought to change its image by changing its name to the New Korea Party.

In October 1995, when the dust from the local elections was settling, the real-name financial transaction system began to detect what many had long suspected. The public learned that Roh and Chun were attempting to convert some of their huge but frozen false-name accounts to real-name entries so they could access the hidden money

The prosecutor's office has traditionally been under the president's influence. Former President Roh was questioned in person on November 1 and was detained several weeks later for alleged corruption while in office. By December 3, former President Chun had been arrested.

President Kim's previous stance that "history should be their judge" was evidently reversed. As his unpopular

predecessors were put on trial, his popularity rating shot up to over 50 percent, according to a recent survey.

As the trials continue to reveal dark deeds, however, the former presidents are turning into a couple of potential "time bombs" that may explode in the face of President Kim and his party. The most critical question is the extent to which Kim benefited from the illicit largesse of the former generals, particularly Roh, who was president when Kim became the government party's presidential candidate.

Roh had already testified that he dispensed a large amount of his slush fund during the 1992 presidential election. Surprisingly, Kim Dae Jung, Kim Young Sam's opposition presidential candidate in 1992, admitted that he too received some $2.5 million from Roh, but President Kim has simply stated to this date that he did not receive any money directly and personally from Roh. An inescapable deduction is that the bulk of Roh's money went to support the ruling party, whose presidential candidate was Kim Young Sam.

Some Prospects

During the 1992 National Assembly elections, Roh's ruling party was greatly advantaged. The government party that is now bound by its own election and political fund legislation faces well-organized challenges from three opposition parties in the 1996 Assembly elections.

Shortly after the local government elections last year, the most tenacious politician, Kim Dae Jung, a three-time presidential candidate, formed a new opposition party, the National Congress for New Politics. It now constitutes the major opposition group, with a stable regional following in his native province of Cholla and also in the vote-rich Seoul area. The old opposition Democratic Party is still the second-largest group in the Assembly. Kim Jong Pil's United Liberal Democrats is the third powerful opposition party in the Assembly. This party also has a committed following in Kim Jong Pil's native region of Ch'ungch'ong and among numerous conservatives disgruntled with President Kim's showy reform moves.

A notable phenomenon that may erode the ruling party's votes is that 475 of 1,352 candidates are independents. This is twice the number of independents who ran in the 1992 Assembly elections, according to the Central Election Management Commission.

Thus it is probably unlikely that any one party, including the ruling New Korea Party, will gain a majority of seats in the next Assembly in a four-party contest. The government party will probably occupy more than 32 percent of the Assembly seats, the percentage the ruling party captured in the local elections last year when the Kim government's approval rate was at the nadir.

Kim Dae Jung's National Congress is hopeful of capturing about 100 out of 299 seats. Should the opposition parties be able to unite on certain issues, President Kim will find the Assembly a difficult partner for the remaining 22 months of his lame-duck presidency.

The trials of the two former presidents will drag on for months. The second public trial of Chun was conveniently postponed to April 15, preventing any revelation acutely embarrassing to Presi-

> ## The Political Scene
>
> - The duly elected civilian government of President Kim Young Sam displaced 30 years of military-dominated regimes.
> - The outcome of the trials of Roh Tae Woo and Chun Doo Hwan will greatly affect the political future of Korea.
> - Kim Dae Jung, a veteran "fighter for democracy," will be a serious challenger to Kim Young Sam in the 1997 presidential elections.

dent Kim from being made before the Assembly elections. The 1997 presidential election may be a different story.

In the end, both Chun and Roh will receive prison terms and fines for corruption while in office. Either Chun or both of them may actually be sentenced to death for military insurrection and massacre, but President Kim will probably commute the sentences in the last months of his presidency. This may be the only remaining card President Kim still holds that may prevent Chun and Roh from totally embarrassing him with their testimonies.

The presidential race in 1997 will largely depend on the results of the Assembly elections this year. If the National Congress for New Politics does well, say capturing 100 or more seats,

Kim Dae Jung will run a fourth time for president.

If the United Liberal Democrats actually receive nearly all disaffected conservative votes, Kim Jong Pil may also run for president. Kim Dae Jung will be 72 and Kim Jong Pil 71 in 1997. The government party may field younger candi-

dates for a refreshing "generational change," for instance Yi Hwoe-ch'ang, 62, formerly a staff prosecutor who later served as prime minister under President Kim.

The possibility still remains that Chun and/or Roh may explode a time bomb by revealing enough about President

Kim Young Sam's past collusion with the military-dominated regime. But even without such exposures, in any three-way contest among the two Kims and Yi, Kim Dae Jung, a lifetime "fighter for democracy," may emerge as the heavyweight. However, in politics, many surprises may occur in a year and a half.

Article 28   *New Asia-Pacific Review*, Vol. 3, No. 1, 1996

Taiwan's Balancing Act: Growth or Democracy?

Asia Pacific Profiles is the authoritative annual review of regional economies by the ANU's Asia Pacific Economics Group. In this survey **Heather Smith** *examines the dilemma facing the "other China."*

Stable political and economic relations with China will be crucial to Taiwan achieving its development objectives. Although 1995 began in China with Jiang Zemin's New Year speech hinting at more relaxed cross-straits relations, by years' end relations had deteriorated considerably. Beijing was infuriated by President Lee Teng-hui's six-day trip to the United States in June to attend a Cornell University alumni reunion. Although unofficial, the visit was perceived by China as a major step toward raising Taiwan's international profile.

After the visit, Beijing suspended semi-official functional talks. Political relations then sunk to a new low when Beijing followed up its verbal protests by staging two rounds of missile tests and a large-scale military drill off Taiwan between July and November last year. In the run-up to Taiwan's March 1996 elections China's aggression toward Taiwan continued to unnerve the world, with live missiles landing within twenty kilometers of Taiwan's shores. President Lee Teng-hui calmly went on electioneering. But he now has a delicate balancing act to perform.

Despite President Lee's resounding victory in March, his governing party, the Kuomintang (KMT), has a less secure mandate to govern than at any time since it fled to Taiwan. While portraying itself as the party of moderation and sta-

bility, the KMT still suffers from a severe image problem, being identified with corruption and money politics. Its biggest asset is that it is seen as standing for the maintenance of the status quo vis-à-vis mainland China, seeking neither early reunification nor formal independence—a sentiment shared by a majority of voters in Taiwan.

> *. . . domestic reform issues can often carry more weight with Taiwan's electorate than the intimidatory actions of China.*

Contrary to outside perceptions of Taiwan politics, domestic reform issues can often carry more weight with Taiwan's electorate than the intimidatory actions of China. Issues such as corruption, inadequate infrastructure, environmental pollution, health care, economic performance, the accountability of government, and the excessive influence of big

business are of increasing concern to the electorate and will need to be addressed by all political parties. For its part the KMT faces the difficult task of formulating a policy toward unification with China and carrying out major domestic reforms at home while adroitly juggling the demands of the electorate for greater international recognition for Taiwan.

Meanwhile, Taiwan's government has big plans to reinvent the economy. Taiwan's goal is to develop a competitive services sector, shift its economic structure toward products embodying a high degree of technology and skill, and at the same time build a social infrastructure worthy of a middle-income industrialized economy. In large part hopes to meet this challenge are resting on three major government policies. The first aims to upgrade Taiwan's infrastructure through construction projects; the second focuses on modernizing and internationalizing laws and regulations in order to turn Taiwan into a regional operations centre; and the third is the "Go-South" investment policy, which encourages investors to target Southeast Asian countries. Taiwan's 10-year economic plan beginning in 1997 envisages annual growth of 6 to 7 percent. Attaining this growth rate depends largely on how successfully Taiwan carries out these policies.

Since the 1950s, Taiwan has experienced sustained strong growth and dramatic transformation. Its strong economic performance has taken in its stride over the past eight years' far-reaching political change and considerable democratization. This year's March presidential elections mark the last stage in Taiwan's transition to a fully-fledged democracy. The opening of economic relations with the mainland in 1987 has led quickly to the People's Republic becoming the largest destination for direct foreign investment and, with Hong Kong, the largest market for exports.

Taiwan's economy is now entering a new phase of development. Real economic growth is slowing gradually as the economy matures. After growing at an average annual rate of 6.5 percent between 1990 and 1995, and by 9 percent between 1985 and 1989, the economy is now entering a period of moderate growth. The substantial restructuring and industrial relocation that has taken place since the mid-1980s is reflected in the changing structure of Taiwan's economy. Industry's share of GDP has fallen from 51 percent in 1985 to 36 percent in 1995. Services' share of GDP has grown rapidly to 60 percent, from 43 percent in 1985. Taiwan's economy has not hollowed out as far as Hong Kong's, but complementarities between the three Chinese economies mean Taiwan is investing more in industrial production on the mainland.

The recent cross-straits tensions are an example of the growing significance of mainland China's influence over Taiwan's economic fortunes. China's missile test affected consumer and business confidence and crimped Taiwan's growth during the second half of last year and in early 1996. While Taiwan's growth last year of 6.1 percent was respectable, it was well below government expectations and was the lowest annual rate since 1990. Cross-straits tensions saw Taiwan's stock market fall 27 percent during 1995, making it the worst performing market in East Asia. But domestic factors also affected confidence. The depressed state of Taiwan's property market has caused problems in the banking sector, where balance sheets have been looking unhealthy, with record overdue loans and high bad check ratios.

A series of financial scandals and political uncertainties surrounding elections also played a part. while falling asset prices subdued Taiwan's domestic economy, strong external demand provided the main impetus for growth in 1995. Taiwan's merchandise exports grew at their highest rate (20 percent) since 1988. Buoyant world trade and sustained growth in China has fueled demand for Taiwan's goods. The ap-

preciation of the yen against the NT$ during the first half of 1995 increased Taiwan's export competitiveness in Japan and in other markets and has encouraged Japanese direct investment in the country.

The most ambitious of Taiwan's plans is the recasting of its economy into an Asia-Pacific regional operations center by early next century. Formally approved in January 1995, the plan envisages the development of a regional hub in six areas: financial services, telecommunications, air transport, sea transport, manufacturing, and media services. The goal is to make Taiwan both a base for domestic enterprises and a stepping stone for multinational businesses to invest in and develop Asia-Pacific markets. The plan involves a range of policy adjustments, such as lowering tariffs, reducing restrictions on the employment of foreign specialists, and opening Taiwan's financial markets. Between ten and twenty new high-tech industrial parks are scheduled to be developed in Taiwan over the next two decades. By upgrading the investment environment during the next five years, the government seeks both to attract foreign investment in upgrading industrial technology industries and to persuade local firms to invest more at home.

The government, in aiming to lift Taiwan to the same rank as the regional financial centers in Hong Kong and Singapore, is counting on capturing financial business that may be diverted from Hong Kong after the transfer to China in 1997. Taiwan has made progress in opening its financial markets since 1995, being driven at least in part by plunging stock prices, which prompted authorities to seek an infusion of foreign capital. But attempts to turn Taiwan into a regional operations center seem likely to be delayed by the government's reluctance to liberalize the financial sector. The hope, though, is that the plan will lock in Taiwan's own liberalization, drawing attention to restrictions on the flow of capital and goods in and out of Taiwan.

Taiwan has many advantages: a solid manufacturing base, an abundant supply of high-tech manpower, a geographically convenient position, and a well-developed industrial network of local enterprises. Yet it seems improbable that Taiwan will be able to make itself attractive as a significant regional center unless it is also prepared to open its domestic markets to foreign business at a faster pace. Transnational companies face higher taxation and greater restrictions on the movement of

capital there than in Singapore and Hong Kong. Customs laws and regulations are a primary obstacle to plans for the air and sea transport industries and to the establishment of telecommunications and media industries. Better trade and transportation links with China will also be critical to Taiwan's goal of becoming a regional business and finance centre.

As past experience with the six-year infrastructure plan (1991–96) shows, Taiwan's planning process is sometimes unrealistic. There is a big difference between opening up to the outside world and becoming a regional center. Success of the ambitious plan appears to depend on the government itself. The most frequently cited problem is the government's failure to reduce its own inefficiency in the regulatory and legal systems. A streamlining and internationalizing of laws and procedures is urgently needed.

Taiwan ranks among the top four investor nations in Thailand, Malaysia, the Philippines and Vietnam.

Taiwan's government is particularly keen to encourage inward foreign investment in large-scale enterprises that have the scope for undertaking significant research and development. Yet more than 95 percent of Taiwan firms are small-and medium-sized enterprises (SMEs), and the success with which they carry out restructuring in response to both domestic and global pressures will be crucial to Taiwan's future industrial development. Since the mid 1980s, increasing production costs have seen Taiwan's predominantly labor-intensive SMEs gradually lose their international competitiveness. While flexible in meeting market demand, the SMEs have few brand name products and labor-intensive technologies and are thus largely incapable of conducting intensive R&D. Unlike in Korea, where the bottleneck to further industrial upgrading of SMEs is access to capital, in Taiwan the main bottleneck lies in the acquisition of design and processing technology. To date, the SMEs have adopted the following strategies in seeking to overcome these limitations:

overseas mergers, investment abroad in China and Southeast Asia, joint efforts for the upgrading of technology; and technology alliances in acquiring design and processing technology.

Outward investment in particular is playing a major role in the restructuring and liberalizing of Taiwan's domestic economy while at the same time fostering extensive links in China and Southeast Asia. Many firms are still looking to offshore locations for their lower value-added activities as the cost of labor and land increases—the price of land in Taiwan has risen by more than five times since 1987.

Initiated three years ago, Taiwan's "Go-South" policy of encouraging firms to invest in Southeast Asia was a response to government concerns that Taiwan's economy was becoming too closely linked to mainland China by the billions of investment dollars going across the Taiwan Straits. To date, more than 4,000 Taiwan manufacturers have invested in Southeast Asia. Acute labor shortage, skyrocketing real estate prices, stricter environmental protection rules, and insufficient infrastructure have been among the main reasons that have led firms to shift their operations abroad. Priority targets are Indonesia, Vietnam and the Philippines, with Malaysia and Thailand already well established as Taiwan investor destinations. The officially approved investment totals nearly US$25 billion, but actual accumulated investment in Southeast Asian economies is much larger. Taiwan ranks among the top four investor nations in Thailand, Malaysia, the Philippines, and Vietnam.

In spite of the recent cross-straits tensions, economic links between Taiwan and the mainland have continued. While investment dropped in August after China's military exercises, indirect investment in mainland China maintained double-digit growth. In 1995, some 490 Taiwanese investment projects in China worth US$1.1 billion were approved, a rise of nearly 14 percent. Some 25,000 Taiwan businesses are operating in China with investment totaling US$20-30 billion. Mainland China reports more than 30,000 contracted investment projects had been approved, worth US$27 billion.

In an historic symbol of the redirection of trade, in May 1995 mainland China plus Hong Kong became a bigger market for Taiwan than the United States. The pace of trade has been remarkable given political uncertainties. In 1995, two-way trade across the Straits totaled US$21 billion, with Taiwan enjoying a trade surplus of US$15 billion, a rise of nearly 15 percent. A study by Taiwan's Council for Economic Planning and Development concluded that if mainland China-Taiwan trade stopped, Taiwan's growth rate would fall by nearly 2 percent, unemployment would increase by 0.5 percent, and Taiwan would suffer a 7.1 percent decline in exports.

Although political relations remain in a state of flux, economic contacts looks set to increase. In July last year, shortly after China began its missile tests, Taiwan's government announced that state-owned enterprises would engage in indirect commercial relations with mainland companies beginning early 1996. Taiwan continues to expand its list of approved imports permitted from the mainland. One reason for the increase is Taiwan's fear that an increasing trade surplus may give rise to trade conflicts. While current dialogue has been stymied by political squabbles, both sides are keen to facilitate direct postal and communication links, including the laying of a direct undersea fiber-optic cable, as well as cooperation on direct telecommunications by cable and satellite.

Taiwan is also beginning to deal with the implications of Hong Kong's return to China in 1997. In July last year, Taiwan signed a five-year agreement to allow Hong Kong's Dragon air and Air Macau to carry passengers from Taiwan to China with only a touchdown in Hong Kong or Macau, provided the flight number is changed after the touchdown. This is the first time since 1949 that "direct" flights have been allowed. Hong Kong is a key factor in sustaining the country's economic growth. At least 70 percent of all Taiwan-made goods bound for Hong Kong are transshipped to the mainland. A large portion of these shipments consist of machinery, industrial components or raw materials used by the thousands of Taiwan factories in mainland China. Many goods are nominally shipped to Hong Kong but proceed directly to China. For this reason, Hong Kong is a much more important destination for Taiwan exports than Taiwan is a source for Hong Kong imports (for re-export or otherwise).

Meanwhile, implementation of Taiwan's cross-straits shipping initiative is at a standstill, reflecting recent strains. The proposed offshore transshipment center in Taiwan's southern port of Kaohsiung was to be the first step towards the establishment of direct transportation ties. Under the proposal, foreign and foreign-registered cargo ships are permitted to sail directly between Taiwan and the mainland—but the ships involved will only be able to carry goods being shipped between foreign countries and the mainland via Taiwan.

For the foreseeable future, Taiwan's diplomacy will continue to be dominated and constrained by mainland China. Through its saber rattling, China has succeeded in frustrating Taiwan's search for greater international recognition. Taiwan's economic future is irrevocably tied to the mainland, and is becoming even more so. The effect of cross-straits tensions on Taiwan's economy, especially the financial sector, during 1995 was real enough. Effects on the real economy were more pronounced in the first quarter of 1996. Missile tests and war exercises affected business confidence in the lead up to the March presidential election. Demand for U.S. dollars and gold increased before the election on rumors that the government would freeze foreign currency deposit accounts in order to check the outflow of capital. Plans for new capital investment have been falling since October 1995, and some Taiwan firms have been delaying or scaling back investment plans on the mainland. Ongoing political instability would prove a major setback to government plans to turn the island into a regional financial hub.

The Taiwan government is forecasting average growth of 6.5 to 7 percent over the next five years and 6 to 6.5 percent for the period 2001–2005, aimed at achieving per capita income of US$20,000 by 2000 and US$28,000 by 2006. Taiwan's maturing economy means that trend growth in the range of 5 to 6.5 percent until the year 2000 and 5 to 6 percent from 2001 to 2205 is more realistic. Achieving this depends upon Taiwan's productivity growth from the structural adjustment strategies currently being adopted—namely policies to attract inward investment to upgrade the high technology sector and outward investment in fostering production links with Southeast Asia and China. A related challenge will require greater streamlining of Taiwan's domestic regulatory regimes and faster liberalization of the financial sector. In its transition to full democracy, popular demands for a higher quality of life, better public services and a cleaner environment pose new challenges for Taiwan's government. In listening to these voices, the government will need to strike a balance between these demands, its own ambitious plans to transform Taiwan's economy, and the financing constraints both of these considerations will place upon it. Huge spending on infrastructure, defense procurement, and recently launched social welfare programs will keep government finances in the red for several more years.

The appearance of democracy will now be an increasingly important factor in Taiwan's relations with China. Mainland China will continue to dominate much of Taiwan's trade and investment policy, and increasingly its transport and communications policy. While it is likely that any concrete steps by Taiwan toward declaring itself independent would trigger military action by China, such a declaration is improbable. The most extreme scenario—military confrontation—would have an impact far beyond Taiwan's financial sector and would seriously damage Taiwan's real economy and growth prospects. The

most probable scenario will see Taiwan's President Lee Teng-hui tone down calls for greater international recognition of Taiwan and reiterate Taiwan's commitment to the goal of unification with China. In maintaining the status quo, Taiwan's strategy will then be to wait until significant democratic reforms take root in China before unifying with the mainland. When the time comes, reunification might be symbolic more than real. Both Beijing and Talpei have time on their side, if both are prepared to recognize it.

About the Author:
Dr. Heather Smith is Postdoctoral Fellow in the Northeast Asia Program in the Research School of Pacific and Asian Studies at the Australian National University. She is Associate Director of the PAFTAD (Pacific Trade and Development) Secretariat and was

Australia's academic representative at the APEC Next Generation's meeting in Seattle in 1995.

For Further Reading:
Schive, Chi, 1995. *Taiwan's Economic Role in East Asia,* The Center for Strategic and International Studies, Washington D.C.; Ranis, Gustav (ed.), 1992. *Taiwan: From Developing to Mature Economy,* Westview Press, Boulder; Galenson, Walter (ed.), 1979. *Economic Growth and Structural Change in Taiwan,* Cornell University Press, Ithaca; Kuo, S., Ranis, G. and Fei, J., 1981. *The Taiwan Success Story: Rapid Growth with Improved Distribution in the Republic of China, 1952–1979,* Westview, Boulder; Li, K. T., 1988. *The Evolution Behind Taiwan's Development Success,* Yale University Press, New Haven and London.

Article 29   *The Economist,* July 8, 1995

The Road to Capitalism

Make Money, Not War

After half a century of war and poverty, Vietnam is set for success,
writes **Edmund Fawcett.**

"Then we had to fight," the Vietnamese colonel says, offering more shrimp in banana leaf. "Now we have to make something to hand on to the next generation, and not just subsidies." A hero of the Viet Cong's Tet Offensive in 1968 and a lifelong communist, the colonel owns and runs a hotel in Hue with help from a smiling niece.

From warfare to hotel-keeping might sound a letdown, from communism to capitalism a climbdown. But pity would be wasted on Colonel Nguyen Quoc Khanh. He is as resilient as a bronze pot and has an eye for gauging slim chances. Military virtues, yes, but qualities suited also to the get-rich imperatives of present-day Vietnam. Nor is the colonel a type to lie awake at night agonising over old ideals: for him and his family, what is making money but a continuation of nation-building by other means?

There are lots more like the colonel. Meet them in number, and it is easy to conclude that the French and Americans in Vietnam never stood a chance. Ten years ago the Vietnamese found themselves in an economic cul-de-sac. They coolly reversed out, and are now roaring off—on scooters. If they turn out to be half as good at making money as they were at making war, Vietnam's people have a bright future.

A proud lot, the Vietnamese do nothing to puncture the notion that they are special. They like to play up the David-and-Goliath mystique for the benefit of foreigners, and half-believe it themselves. How else would they have dared take on France, America and China? And had they thought the normal rules applied to them, would they not have paused in 1979 before invading Cambodia and getting sent to Coventry by most of the world?

Perhaps it is living next to China that has led the Vietnamese, like kid brothers everywhere, to prefer negative attention to none. Whatever the reason, Vietnam, like Mexico or Ireland, has more stage-presence than you would guess from the size of its population (75m), its wealth (annual income: $200 a head) and its military prowess (an ageing army and a few torpedo boats).

If Vietnamese pride were just cockiness, ahead would lie hubris, not riches. But Vietnam's self-assurance comes also from a down-to-earth feel for reality, from being able to look blunders in the eye and to start over. "Face", it is said, matters in Asia. Not in Vietnam, where being seen to be weak or wrong matters less than really being weak or wrong.

And reality cruelly supports the Vietnamese belief in being special: Vietnam stands out by coming bottom in East Asia.

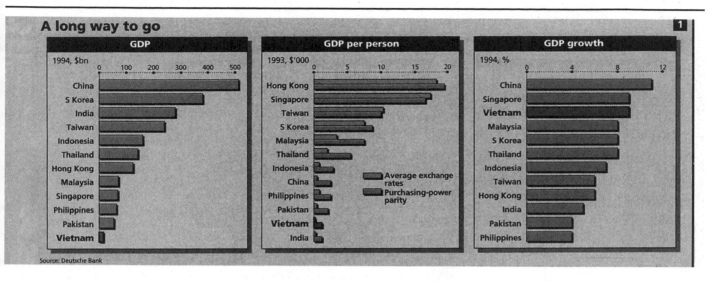

A long way to go

Source: Deutsche Bank

Economically it is behind China, much poorer than Thailand or Malaysia and in a distant league from the Asian "tigers".

Historically, the torments of Vietnam's recent past are not so odd for the region. In the backwash of world war and Japanese occupation, almost every land around it also had fratricidal wars: Burma, China, Indonesia, Korea, Malaya. Each reached statehood under a nationalist banner—anti-colonial, anti-Japanese, pro-communist, or some motley thereof. All were poor at mid-century and have got far richer. The difference with Vietnam—whose wars killed perhaps 3m–4m people—is that it all took so much longer.

Late developers can have terrible luck with timing. When Vietnam's communists triumphed in 1975 after 30 years of war, it was too early for them not to Sovietise the south of Vietnam, but too late to avoid the planetary recession of communism. Vietnam won the 19th-century ideal of national unity and independence at a point in the 20th century when global money, commerce and culture seemed to be putting sovereign identities into doubt.

But late developers can also learn from mistakes, especially their own. Be it a waiter asking the difference in English between "in the air" and "in the open", or a central banker wanting to know how Algeria or Zaire handles the Paris lenders' club, the Vietnamese show a rage to learn.

That is a boon for Vietnam on its bold new course, which could without condescension be called "Learning Neighbourhood Norms". Vietnam has won deserved credit, enjoys widespread goodwill and shows huge promise. But it is starting late, and from a low base. Four doubts need resolving. One: is Vietnam really one country now? Two: how durable is "market Leninism", Vietnam's mix of capitalist economics and communist politics? Three: how swiftly can Vietnam move from socialism and subsistence? And four: for Vietnam—due to join the Association of South-East Asian Nations (ASEAN) on July 28th—is "friends everywhere" a reliable foreign policy?

One Nation, Indivisible, Under Our Ancestors

Vietnam is growing together again.

"All men are created equal. They are endowed by their creator with certain inalienable rights, among these are life, liberty and the pursuit of happiness." These words open the Declaration of the Democratic Republic of Vietnam, dated September 2nd 1945. It was written by Ho Chi Minh, revolutionary leader and president of communist Vietnam until his death in 1969.

With minor changes, Vietnam's founding father was quoting Thomas Jefferson. His choice of an anti-colonial slave-owner from 18th-century Virginia instead of a scientific socialist from the 19th-century Rhineland underlines two things about modern Vietnam. One is the particularity of the home-brew known as Marxism-Leninism-Ho Chi Minh Thought. The other is the outstanding importance of national identity.

To anyone used to viewing North and South Vietnam as two countries, one democratic and backed by the Americans, the other communist and supported by China and the Soviet Union, "national identity" may sound like a lure. That North and South were reunited in 1975 by communist arms, after which 2m southerners fled and thousands more were sent to "re-education" camps, hardly strengthens the claim that Vietnam is one cohesive nation.

Yet time heals. Three-fifths of Vietnam's people are under 25, too young for their own experience of the war. A vivid scene in the anti-heroic novel, "The Sorrow of War" by a Hanoi writer, Bao Ninh, is the American bombing of a bridge over the Ma River at Thanh Hoa, a railhead for communist troops and equipment moving south to the Ho Chi Minh Trail. But few signs of war are now to be seen, apart from a giant message carved into the limestone hillside which roughly translates into English as "Never give up". How often was the rickety steel-truss bridge rebuilt? Teenage boys working on the rail-line laugh. "How should we know? That was too long ago. We're the post–war generation."

Nations recuperate. Split them, conquer them, devastate them in civil war: true nations come back whole. It may be a test that they are nations, not just geographical entities. Some countries, Pakistan, say, and maybe Czechoslovakia, break up for good. Others, Italy for example, teeter forever. A third sort are impossible whole, impossible in pieces: Yugoslavia. A fourth kind lasts: America, Germany, Korea probably, Spain. Vietnam is the enduring sort.

As nations go, Vietnam is old. Land-hungry Viets spilled out of the crowded Red River valley round Hanoi before the 15th century. Having defeated the Cham people on the central coast, they colonised the south in the 17th and 18th centuries. A Vietnamese sense of identity was honed in resistance to French rule (1883–1954), to American support for the

A thousand years of history		3
10th century	Independent Vietnamese kingdom in Red River valley	
14th-18th century	Vietnamese expansion south, conquest of Cham people and Mekong Delta	
1802	Vietnam unified under emperors of Nguyen dynasty	
1883-1940	French rule	
1940-45	French administration under Japanese occupation	
1945-54	War of independence against France	
1954	Vietnam divided at 17th parallel into communist Democratic Republic of Vietnam (north) and American-backed Republic of Vietnam (south)	
1965-73	American armed forces support South Vietnam	
1973	Paris peace accords	
1975	Fall of Saigon	
1976	Vietnam formally reunified	
1979	Vietnamese troops invade Cambodia; Chinese ones invade Vietnam	
1986	Economic reform begins	
1991	Free-market economy confirmed	
1993	Full resumption of western aid	
1995	Vietnamese and American rapprochement. Vietnam joins ASEAN	

government of South Vietnam (1965–75) and to China's ever-present attentions and interferences, friendly or unfriendly. A highlight of the Historical Museum in Hanoi is its record down the centuries of Vietnamese triumphs over invading Chinese armies.

China also shaped Vietnam peacefully, imparting attitudes the Vietnamese were classically taught to prize. These included "Confucian", "male" values—respect for hierarchy, order and rules, a taste for learning, a sense of decorum and a regard for sincerity, courage and perseverance—and, for balance, "Buddhist", "female" ones: compassion, flexibility, a feel for equality. Whether this ethical cocktail was suited to independence and national renewal was a hobby horse among the Vietnamese intellectuals of a century ago wondering why Vietnam had fallen to cruel or lazy French planters. Some blamed their country's decline on outmoded Confucian-Buddhist values, some on modern, western ones. Few questioned whether the cocktail was typically Asian, let alone Vietnamese.

Three people who know Vietnam and the Vietnamese—a foreigner, a southerner and a northerner—stress their sense of nationhood. Ulrich Golaszinski works for the Friedrich Ebert Foundation, a German social democratic think-tank. Before Hanoi, he had been in Africa. "Compared with many countries there, the Vietnamese have a real sense

of national feeling," he says. Nguyen Xuan Oanh, a former governor of South Vietnam's central bank and now a consultant in Ho Chi Minh City (formerly Saigon), does not pause when asked what red thread holds Vietnam together: "National identity". Dang Nghiem Van, a communist professor of religion at Hanoi University, puts it more vividly: "If the world is a sea in which countries have dissolved like salt, then there's nothing, nothing," he says vehemently. "No, what remains in a world of global markets is the nation."

Though northerners tease southerners about their lazy consonants—"Shaigon" for "Saigon"—the two speak one language. The country is ethnically homogeneous, too, even though it has 54 recognised ethnic minorities, living scattered in central-highland pockets, the far north and deep in the Mekong Delta. Most of these minorities are poor, and some of their villages have not changed much in two centuries. But the most recent census says they make up less than 15% of the population.

From the Jungle to the Beach

Too much is made of the north-south divide. Vietnam was not split into two until 1945, when the job of disarming Japan's army in the north was given to Nationalist Chinese troops and in the south to British ones. Colonial Vietnam came in three parts, themselves carry-

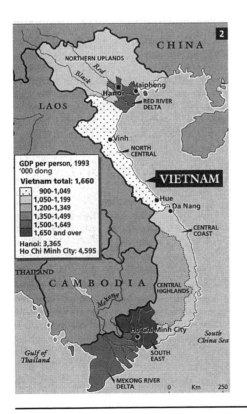

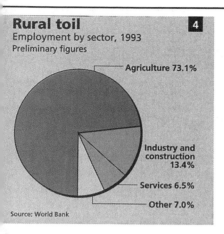

Rural toil
Employment by sector, 1993
Preliminary figures

Agriculture 73.1%

Industry and
construction
13.4%

Services 6.5%

Other 7.0%

Source: World Bank

everywhere. The province produces people who want to change things one way or another: scholars, soldiers and rebels. Schoolchildren from Nghe An do well in national exams. Ho Chi Minh came from there. General Giap, who bested the French and the Americans, was from nearby. Vietnam's present masters worry not so much that the south will outstrip the north economically, as that jobless people from provinces such as Nghe An will flood towns in both north and south.

The Wounds of Peace

National healing is not complete. After the People's Army of Vietnam took Saigon in April 1975, the communists decided to cow and collectivise the south. Economic change has brought a kind of reconciliation since, and the preferred official term for the fall of South Vietnam is now "unification", not "liberation". But many thousand, some say a million, southern soldiers, officials and intellectuals were sent to "re-education" camps. Of the 2m people who went, or were driven, into exile, a few were killers and torturers. Others were businessmen, "third-road" sympathisers of southern communists in the National Liberation Front, writers, ethnic Chinese or simply economic refugees.

These Viet Kieu or Overseas Vietnamese are organised, particularly in America, and by Vietnamese standards they are rich. Somebody has calculated that they earned $17 billion after tax last year—rather more than all the Vietnamese in Vietnam produced. Vietnam's rulers have mixed feelings about the Viet Kieu. They are both a source of money sent to relations in Vietnam and of irritating complaints about human rights.

Among those who left were many writers who could not stick the cultural shutdown imposed by Cromwellians from the north. These were not cheerleaders of the corrupt, exhausted regime of President Thieu, South Vietnam's president during 1967–75. But they saw no future either in a Sovietised Vietnam.

Writers such as Nguyen Huy Thiep and Bao Ninh, whom the authorities just about tolerate, work on in Hanoi. Frowned-upon books are not, strictly speaking, censored but put out in tiny runs and left to be sold as pirated photocopies. For publication in Vietnam, Bao Ninh's war novel had to be renamed "The Sorrow of Love". He is shy to talk about a new book long in the making. "There are good and bad seasons to publish," he explains.

Another loss to the nation were many of Saigon's Chinese traders, swept out in 1977–78 by a wave of anti-capitalism and xenophobia. In the otherwise bustling Cholon district of old Saigon their bolted shops can still be seen. To the victims of this chauvinistic folly it was little consolation that Hanoi's communists were re-enacting a scene from history: in the early 19th century Vietnam's Nguyen emperors, groping for national unity after civil war, had shackled commerce and harassed Chinese traders in the same way.

As Vietnam's poverty worsened late in the 1970s, people in boats set off across the South China Sea where winds or tides took them: south towards Singapore, north to Hong Kong. Thousands have since been sent back under controversial "orderly repatriation programmes". But the persecution they feared does not seem to have come about.

Home beckons. Not all Cholon Chinese left, and even many who did regularly drop back on business. Some exiles, or their children, are returning. When Henri Bac Lo left Saigon in 1975 with his parents, two sisters and a brother, he was 11. His father had owned a fruit plantation. As refugees they fell to earth in Paris, where the father pumped petrol and the mother cleaned house. The children studied hard and became professionals. Henri travels to Hanoi from Paris, a go-between for foreign bankers and businessmen. He feels French and not French, Vietnamese and not Vietnamese. One day, he says, he might think of returning to Vietnam.

vers: a protectorate in the north, a emi-protectorate in the centre, and a olony in Cochin China (the south).

The contrast is overdone, too, between Hanoi, an austere city of communist lerks, and Ho Chi Minh City, a raunchy lace of brothels and crooked entrepreneurs reverting to the sinful ways of old aigon. Huynh Son Phuoc, an editor of *uoi Tre,* Vietnam's "youth" paper, talks f "the people of the beach"—pampered outherners—and "the people of the jungle"—puritan warriors from the north. He is offering both stereotypes for aughs. Hanoi is also spreading fast, and ollar rents there are among the world's ighest. New private housing is hardly planner's dream in either place, but Hanoi's style is the zanier of the two.

A more striking gap is that between he cities and the countryside. Hanoi's acome per head in 1994 was around 500 a year, Ho Chi Minh City's $800. conomically Hanoi is growing nearly s fast as old Saigon. Income per head the two poorest regions is a quarter r at best a third of that in or near the wo big cities (see map 2).

Nghe An, between Hue and Hanoi, is typical poor province. As Doan Nam f its foreign-relations department explains, its income per head is half the national average. The capital, Vinh, nows scant signs of America's heavy ombing, but scars of backwardness are

The Contradictions of Market Leninism

Can one party ever be enough?

y rights the Communist Party of Vietnam (CPV) ought to have fallen apart. nder its leadership, ten years ago Vietnam was up against a wall. Whole prov-

inces were starving. The party's ideology was bankrupt. China had given a brutal lesson in its brief but devastating invasion of six northern provinces in

1979. The CPV's most loyal patron, the Communist Party of the Soviet Union, was dying. After a brief attack of vertigo, Vietnam's Communists got their

Poor, but not wretched

Social indicators | 5

	Population growth, annual average %, 1985-93	Life expectancy at birth, 1992	Infant mortality per 1,000 live births, 1992	Adult literacy rate, %, 1992	Female labour force, % of total, 1993	Doctors per 100,000 people, 1990	Televisions per 100 people, 1990	Telephones per 100 people, 1990
Algeria	2.6	67	55	60.6	10	43	7.4	4.7
Vietnam	**2.4**	**67**	**36**	**88.6**	**47**	**35**	**3.9**	**0.3**
Philippines	2.3	65	40	90.4	31	12	4.8	1.7
Turkey	2.1	67	54	81.9	34	79	17.4	20.3
Thailand	1.6	69	26	93.8	44	20	11.4	3.1
Cuba	1.0	76	10	94.5	32	370	20.7	5.7

Sources: World Bank; UNDP

nerve back and gambled on a deal: rising incomes for political stability, which was code for one-party rule. Party purists could recall Lenin's market-minded New Economic Policy. A more recent and obvious precedent, though not one to stress in public, was China.

For now, Vietnam's Communists look unassailable. Of the National Assembly's 395 members, 92% belong to the CPV and the rest have been vetted by the party. Almost all army officers and a third of the rank and file are Communists. Mass organisations for workers, women, youth and so on are gathered under a Communist-held umbrella, the Fatherland Front.

Why does the CPV live on? An obvious answer is that Vietnam has not had multi-party elections. Yet, as post–communist Eastern Europe shows, communists can win at the polls. Vietnam's Communists—both words need stressing—command support. Though membership fell after the Soviet Communist Party was banned, making the Vietnamese one seem a less attractive career prospect, it has since risen again, officials say. The party, indeed, is enjoying a peace-and-prosperity bonus. Most Vietnamese are better off than before and the silent majority generally has more reason to be content than a decade ago. Religion is not just tolerated, but making a comeback. Opposition has no visible focus. The few brave voices of dissent—Buddhist monks, lone writers—are commonly silenced by jail or by being confined to a native town or village: Vietnam's way of sending people to Siberia.

Even before, Vietnam's Communist Party had over the years banked genuine popular capital. It voiced a common yearning for equality and betterment. Few communist parties so harnessed themselves to national ideals. Its cruelty might have been feared, but its daring and tenacity for a cause most Vietnam-ese supported—national independence—was admired.

The Strong Shall Be Weak

Success came partly by default. Unlike those in India, Indonesia or Malaysia, the only nationalists who spoke for all Vietnam were communists. Religion was no obstacle. There were few Muslims. Catholics made up 5–10% of Vietnam's population, but they were untypical of a rural majority whose faith was a mix of Taoism, Buddhism and Confucianism. South Vietnam's leader from 1955 to 1963, Ngo Dinh Diem, a Catholic, did not have even passive support in village society. Ethnic minorities were no pivot of resistance, and Vietnam's national-minded middle class was weak.

Failures by the communists' foreign enemies helped. America's President Roosevelt was not far out when in 1944 he told his secretary of state Cordell Hull, that Vietnam at that point was worse off than when the French had come 100 years earlier. Even pro-French Vietnamese had begun to waver in 1940–45 when Vichy France dutifully ran Vietnam for its Japanese occupiers. By the 1950s France, like Britain, had tired as a colonial power.

Although 58,000 Americans died in Vietnam there is some truth to the proposition that the Americans lost a war without losing a major battle, almost none to the claim that politicians cheated soldiers of victory. The American people were never fully committed to the war, rightly sensing that their leaders did not know what America was fighting for. American leaders could not grasp the appeal, or sincerity, of Ho Chi Minh's nationalism.

Theirs was a failure of intellect, not will, and at mid-century it was an easy mistake for them to make. America's leaders saw themselves as defending freedom and democracy against their polar opposite, world communism. Vietnam's communists surely could not be genuine patriots because they were beholden to Moscow, or perhaps to Beijing—the argument got a little confused here. And indeed once Germany's Nazis were gone, patriotism and anti-communism did merge in Soviet-occupied Eastern Europe. Yet the precedent was fatally misleading. The Americans did not register till too late that most Vietnamese might put up with communists to get rid of foreigners.

Four Trumps?

Vietnam's Communists these days are courting America and seem eager not to gloat over past successes. Huu Tho, the editor of *Nhan Dan*, the party's daily newspaper, instead lists the CPV's present virtues as he sees them: collective leadership, willingness to admit mistakes, relative freedom from corruption and, with the exception of Ho Chi Minh, rejection of the cult of personality. "Once the party is isolated from the people," he says, "they won't support it." Yet as Vietnam gets richer and citizens less ready to take government on trust, are these not wasting assets?

The party holds together at the top partly because losing arguments does not cost careers, let alone lives. Indeed who argues what is often unclear to outsiders, making work for jobless Kremlinologists in Hanoi. As one-party officials go, the Vietnamese are talkative and frank. But public records are thin, and a Vatican-like obscurity hangs over big decisions in Vietnam's recent past: arming guerrillas against South Vietnam at the beginning of the 1960s, launching the Tet uprising in 1968, invading the South in 1974 and then, after formal unification in 1976, Sovietising its economy. Accounts of recent economic rows also sound schematic.

In this collective environment, Vietnamese politics is full of second acts.

The politburo is remarkably stable. No more than 30 people served on it from the CPV's first congress in 1935 to its seventh in 1991. Truong Chinh (a nom-de-guerre meaning "Long March") was general secretary in 1941–56, Le Duan in 1960–86. Pham Van Dong was prime minister in 1953–87: long service, no long knives.

The last of the charter generation retired at the sixth party congress in 1986. New members were added to the politburo at the seventh congress in 1991, and more changes may be made at the eighth, probably in the summer of 1996. Some Vietnamese say it is vital for economic reform that Vo Van Kiet, Vietnam's current prime minister and a moderniser, should use the coming congress to wrest full control from the old hands and take over as general secretary from Do Muoi. But others are in contention, too.

In fact, who is general secretary probably matters less in Vietnam than it did, say, in the Soviet Union. The labels, besides, are tricky. Do Muoi, a central planner, is now an apostle of renovation. The more important question is how fast a younger, more market-minded generation finds a voice in the middle reaches of the party. Only three members of the central committee are under 50. Market thinking is a rarity among older party members, even economic reformers. Economics to them is about production, not selling, other countries more geopolitical chessmen than competitors in international trade.

Unprintable

The practice of party "self-criticism" is not just a gruesome charade. In the mid-1950s it caused the authorities to modify a brutal land reform. *Doi moi*, Vietnam's economic reform policy, was launched with the admission that Sovietising the South had been a blunder. But a more reliable critic would be a freer press.

Ly Quy Chung, a newspaper editor in Ho Chi Minh City, argues that Vietnam's press is better than it is given credit for. There are, to be sure, four "untouchables", he says. "You cannot discover anything about the life of Ho Chi Minh at variance with the official biography. You cannot question the truth of socialism, or attack members of the politburo. You cannot question national defence policy." Prodded, he adds that you must be careful about Buddhist protests. It sounds, he admits, like a lot of don'ts. But Vietnam's press, he insists, is a lot freer than it used to be.

Yet foreign reporters are discouraged from working outside big cities without a friendly (and expensive) interpreter-minder; and the official press prefers good news to bad. Page one of a recent issue of the English-language *Vietnam News* comes up with an example:

No one was hurt but inhabitants of Cat Linh Street in Hanoi were terrified yesterday morning when a gale felled an old tree in front of a row of shops selling toiletries and construction materials.

Tucked away on page three is a report on "Scaffold Deaths": not executions, but three people dead and four badly injured on a building site in Saigon.

Ancestor worship and anti-Chinese historical propaganda are no lasting substitutes for a sellable ideology.

Press attacks on corrupt officials do not, perhaps, require much courage, as an official campaign against corruption is on. But corruption can mean many things. In Vietnam the mandarin tradition of the scholar-gentleman lives on. Top Communists do not live ostentatiously as they did, say, in East Germany. Mandarins, it is true, took no vow of poverty; but they were not hurt either by an air of austere dedication, and so it is with older Vietnamese Communists.

Even so, an energy minister is in jail for taking kickbacks from power-line constructors. One rotten apple or an unlucky scapegoat? Party people, certainly, use government connections to get loans to start a business or turn part of some state enterprise into a joint venture with foreigners. Customs men ask higher tariffs for imports made by non-state firms than by state ones, but will apply the lower rates for a consideration. Rice traders evade export rules, with police help, and sell rice in China where prices are higher. Policemen moonlight as enforcers of commercial contracts. They shake down motorists in the street. In one notorious incident three years ago, a policeman

shot and killed a motorist who refused to pay a bribe. When crowds rioted at his light sentence, a review was ordered. In March the policeman was executed, the first time in ten years that capital punishment was used.

By world standards, corruption in Vietnam is hardly grave. But it is, or seems, new and faces the party with a painful dilemma. A certain probity was part of its authority, and nakedly corrupt officials put that at risk. On the other hand, much "corruption" is really private enterprise by another name: cracking down on it risks a backlash from the traders and businessmen on whom a better economy depends.

The rule against the cult of personality allows one exception: Ho Chi Minh. A disrespectful visitor to the mausoleum in Hanoi where Ho's grandfatherly corpse lies may wistfully recall that "Ho Chi Minh"—one of many aliases—means, roughly, "the Enlightener". Ho himself, like Lenin, wanted to be cremated, not venerated. But to his successors he was too handy an object of worship. Taken one way, the Ho cult is as crudely exploitative as the cult of Stalin, Mao or Kim Il Sung. Seen another way, it is a natural extension of a cultural tradition. The Vietnamese—Catholics and Communists included—light incense sticks to dead relatives or past heroes as a form of prayer. Ho Chi Minh is not alone among revered historical ancestors.

If you are driven from Vinh to Hanoi—driving yourself is perilous on the laneless roadlet known as National Highway One—you can visit both Ho Chi Minh's native village at Kim Lien, where no mention of Marx or Lenin is to be seen, and shrines to earlier national heroes. At Hoa Lu, the ancient Vietnamese capital, is a shrine to Emperor Dinh Tien Hoang, whose generals beat the soldiers of the Sung Chinese, and not far off one to Nguyen Trai (1380–1442), a scholar, diplomat and speech-writer who advised Emperor Le Loi in his campaigns against the armies of China's Ming dynasty.

In Search of an Ideology

Ancestor worship and anti-Chinese historical propaganda are no lasting substitutes for a sellable ideology. Vietnamese Communists seem aware of the void. One response is that of the practical-minded political manager. Ask Truong Tan Sang, the chairman of the People's Committee (ie, mayor) of Ho Chi Minh City, whether communist politics and capitalist economics are compatible, and he will tell you that theorists must work this out. Pressed, the mayor begins to sound like a social democrat: markets are needed for economic growth, he believes, but should not throw up extremes of wealth and poverty. Taiwan, he adds intriguingly, is a capitalist country where income gaps are not too wide.

Pham Chi Lan, the chairwoman of the Chamber of Commerce and Industry of Vietnam in Hanoi, has a shrewd answer to the question whether market economics does not inevitably loosen social ties and encourage individualism: "Individuals cannot be successful on their own. Young businessmen may try to succeed by themselves. But they learn to discuss, to share, to make associations."

The second response to the need for an ideology comes from the theorists. There are less pleasant ways to spend a morning than discussing the meaning of socialism over green tea and watermelon at the Institute for the Study of Marxism-Leninism-Ho Chi Minh Thought in Hanoi. Its vice-director, Vu Huu Ngoan, responds deftly to all attempts to expose his institute as a temple of post-Marxist revisionism.

Does the economic base of society determine the political superstructure? "Not quite; they influence each other." If history is a sequence—slavery, feudalism, capitalism, socialism—are we now going backwards? "No, there must be a higher form of society than capitalism." Will it be classless? "No. But friction between classes will be greatly reduced." And what, besides rising incomes, will hold classes together? "The nation." On saying farewell, the professor mentions with a twinkle that his institute is also studying party systems from all over the world, a hint perhaps that Vietnam's one-party system may yet evolve.

Strong Party, Weak State

At present, then, Vietnam's Communist Party is playing it by ear under the slogan, "A rich, strong and stable Vietnam." The more enlightened members seem to hope the party system can evolve—by becoming more representative and open rather than by moving to multi-party competition in one bound. But there is a second, perhaps more pressing, contradiction in market Leninism: between a strong party and a weak state.

Vietnam's fourth constitution, in 1992, ditched most of the revolutionary exhortation of earlier ones dated 1946, 1960 and 1980. The new constitution shows signs of compromise. Vietnam is called

a "Socialist Republic". Article four makes the CPV "the leading force" in Vietnamese society. The right to free speech and public trial are subject to restriction by law. Yet the socialist goals outlined in various articles might better be called social-democratic and would not look out of place in, say, the German *Grundgesetz*. The Vietnamese government's job is no longer to build socialism but to supervise the administration. Article 58 underpins the right of citizens to own property.

Without countervailing powers, it is tempting to dismiss Vietnam's constitution as just a piece of paper. But that would be wrong. Not the least of its virtues is that it points to how government in Vietnam might grow less monolithic. It makes the National Assembly a place for argument and point of correction to executive fiat. These powers are being used with growing zest. Debate is more genuine. Bills are discussed in newspapers and get altered in draft. In June 1994 the labour code was changed. In October 1994 the health and education ministers were grilled. Last April the state-enterprise code and a bill on administrative courts were heavily altered. "It's not a theatre," says Mr Golaszinski of the Friedrich Ebert Foundation. "If you ask people with a stake in legislation, they don't know the outcome any longer. It's a more open game."

Vietnam's rulers realise that a market economy cannot work by command politics alone. One party there may be, but public administration has to apply suppler methods than giving orders. The sway of party minders in ministries has been reduced. Ideally the legal vacuum in the lower layers of Vietnamese government needs filling. Vo Van Kiet declared 1995 the year of administrative reform, but finding tools of government besides fly-whisk or hammer is not easy, especially in a society where an odd mix of government edict and popular participation can sometimes work.

Take the Tet Offensive of 1995. Last January residents of Hanoi were asked to sign a promise to their local watch—the police committee assigned to their block—that they would not let off fireworks during Tet celebrations at the lunar new year. In 1994 these had caused deaths and injuries as well as two days of noise. Big-booted government? Perhaps not. Almost 90% of the city's residents signed, some no doubt out of prudence, but many presumably because they too were fed up with Tet fireworks.

Or take Hanoi's dykes. For centuries they have kept back the Red River.

They are both a treasured public good and irresistible real estate. Under Vietnam's opaque land law, nobody knows who, if anyone, owns the ground they occupy. In 1990 the government forbade houses on them for safety reasons. That did not stop private building on the dykes, apparently with the city's encouragement, a direct challenge to the national government. Three months ago, lacking subtler means, an exasperated prime minister sent troops to tear the fronts off offending dwellings to make them unusable.

Vietnam is run by a Leninist party that favours free markets, and normally economic competition brings the political sort in its wake.

The dyke story illustrates the unsuitability of current regulation. Old administrative codes were intended for a socialist economy with different conditions. They impede the wealth-creation the government now wants to promote. In the countryside, the absence of clear legislation on the ownership of land has to some extent been corrected. Land is deemed public, but people can buy and sell long agricultural leases. Even so, the prime minister's office recently stepped in to forbid, by decree, the use of leased rice-land for building.

Pagodas of Power

The dyke tale shows up even more sharply the imperfect meshing of the different levels of government. Vietnam has 50 provinces and three urban municipalities: Hanoi, Haiphong and Ho Chi Minh City. Provinces are run by People's Committees, dominated by a local boss. Though normally Communists, they cannot just be parachuted in from Hanoi. Jealous of prerogatives, they fight for high rankings in foreign-investment league tables. Typical is Nguyen Van Me, Hue's deputy mayor, who proudly touts his city's attractions. Its Buddhist pagodas and its imperial citadel and tombs are a draw for Vietnam's 1m foreign visitors a year, not to mention low wages and land prices.

There is no shortage of ideas for untangling lines between province and centre. Most of them seem designed to make it easier for ministers in Hanoi and for foreign investors to decide whether province or centre holds the key. But Vietnamese democracy would get a bigger boost from more widely representative local assemblies.

Welfare too has suffered from Vietnam's weak state. The market has arrived in health care and schooling. Many doctors and nurses practise privately. Good health care may soon be out of the reach of the poor. Medicines have to be paid for; the same is true for many schoolbooks. Communist Vietnam spent well on schools and health. The country needs a modern tax system to continue paying for them.

Vietnam, to sum up, is run by a Leninist party that favours free markets. Normally economic competition brings the political sort in its wake. That is the first contradiction of market Leninism: between party and people. The second is between a strong party and a weak state. Government needs to rely more on law, less on party fiat. Enlightened CPV members accept that public administration needs to be improved, but not that people need more power. Not yet....

Looking for Security

China will always be there.

China's invading army had been captured and the victorious emperor of Vietnam, Le Loi, was urged to have the prisoners killed. No, counselled his adviser, Nguyen Trai: the Chinese would simply send a bigger army next time. Better to make peace and apologise for the Vietnamese victory to the Chinese emperor. Le Loi not only took Nguyen Trai's advice but pressed horses and ships on the Chinese troops to be sure they went home.

The main determinant of Vietnam's foreign relations is the same now as in 1427. Other countries—France, America—come and go. China is always there. In Vietnam's long period of relative independence between the 10th century and the arrival of the French 900 years later, a new Vietnamese ruler's first act was to beg recognition from the Chinese court. Whether China plays Vietnam's absent father, its kind uncle or its brother enemy, it routinely gets the bigger part and the last word.

This makes the Vietnamese feel insecure. They admire Chinese culture, to the point of having Vietnamised many of China's ways. But they fear China's power, and see no alternative to uneasy coexistence. They have always known that China is too vast and strong for Vietnam to gain from endless conflict, even if hardy soldiers and clever tactics could hold off Chinese invaders. Vietnam's rulers, besides, have often needed Chinese help in putting down rebels or in getting rid of foreigners.

Those People Next Door

The Vietnamese have felt safest with the Chinese in three sets of circumstances: when China itself was weak or divided; when China was preoccupied with its "northern barbarians", the Russians; and when Vietnam was at peace with its smaller neighbours and on good terms with the rest of the world. Now seems to be the third sort of time. "Friends everywhere" is how Tran Quang Co, a deputy foreign minister, sums up Vietnam's current priorities in foreign policy.

Vietnam is courting diplomats and investors from across the world. It is due to join ASEAN at its meeting in Brunei on July 28th, a big step with promising strategic implications for the region. Further afield, the Vietnamese earlier this year initialled a co-operation agreement with the European Union and, with American trade reopened since February 1994, are hoping that any day the United States will restore full diplomatic ties.

Boringly normal stuff, you might think. For ordinary countries, yes. But less than a decade ago Vietnam was a far-from-normal country, spurned by much of the world. Vietnam's recent return to international grace, like its fall, has been sensationally swift.

In Paris in 1973, the Vietnamese communists and their southern allies in the communist-dominated National Liberation Front signed agreements with the Republic of (South) Vietnam and its protector, the United States, ending the Second Indochina War. This was a victory in all but name for Communist Vietnam, which won respect, if not affection, across the world.

Vietnam was recognised as one country. Who should rule it was to be settled by talk, not war. But that question had been fought over since France's defeat in the First Indochina War in 1954. South Vietnam could not defend itself without America's presence. And beyond supplying weapons, America wanted no

further part in the war. Northern troops were not even made to leave the south. Ho Chi Minh's goal, one country under communist leadership, was at last within reach.

But near-victory went to the Vietnamese Communists' head. China's dying leaders, Mao Zedong and Zhou Enlai, advised them to relax, to savour the moral advantage over a corrupt, tottering south and to put their war-torn economy in order, but the advice was ignored. In late 1974 party leaders and soldiers met at the army guesthouse on Pham Ngu Lao Street in Hanoi to plan the military "liberation" of the south. The attack began in March 1975. Saigon fell on April 30th.

Its fall appeared to close a chapter, particularly among Americans for whom, after America's rapprochement with China, Vietnam suddenly seemed not to matter. But Vietnam was not so soon forgotten. In 1978 it signed a 25-year friendship treaty with the Soviet Union, including naval rights at Camh Ran Bay, making China, encouraged by America, keen to put Vietnam in its place and to frustrate a Soviet ally. Vietnam gave China its opening on Christmas Eve 1978 by invading Cambodia and soon afterwards capturing its capital, Phnom Penh. To Vietnam, the world's outcry came as a shock. Ha Van Lau, then Vietnam's UN representative, told a diplomat from Singapore that Cambodia would be "forgotten in a fortnight." He was repeating what his masters in Hanoi seem sincerely to have believed. In judging "the correlation of forces", they got it spectacularly wrong. Instead of welcoming Vietnam for ridding Cambodia of Pol Pot's murderous tyranny, the world condemned it for breaking the first rule of states: keep off

each other's turf. No matter that Vietnam was hitting back after Khmer Rouge massacres of Vietnamese villagers. No matter that Pol Pot's government had murdered on a genocidal scale. With American acquiescence, China sent 85,000 troops into Vietnam for a 16-day "pedagogical" war. Vietnamese defenders bloodied China's nose. But China had noses to throw away. It replaced their commander and captured five provincial capitals, including Lang Son, which it flattened. Then it withdrew.

Sent to Coventry

An alignment of America, China, Japan and ASEAN states punished Vietnam by diplomatic isolation and commercial sanctions, including loss of foreign borrowing. The Khmers Rouges were given sanctuary in Thailand and could harry the Vietnam-backed government from there. Cambodia was plunged back into civil war. The morale of Vietnam's army in Cambodia slumped. For the soldiers and their families, the Third Indochina War became Vietnam's own Vietnam.

By 1989 the country had cracked. The Soviet Union, its lone ally, was foundering, and Vietnam wanted to concentrate on economic reform. It withdrew its main forces in September of that year, although a UN-sponsored settlement in Cambodia was not reached until October 1991. Despite claims that Vietnamese soldiers lingered on as settlers, Cambodia since has faced its problems alone. Vietnam once again became acceptable in polite society. Normal ties were restored with China, Japan, ASEAN and Western Europe, and a thaw with America began. Access to foreign lending was reopened. Market reform won widespread support, although complaints continued about Vietnam's summary treatment of political critics.

From lionisation to ostracism and most of the way back: the Vietnamese

have lived through it with their customary mixture of realism and hurt pride. They smart at the hypocrisy of nations but see, too, that they blundered: "We miscalculated the world's response and the harshness of our isolation," Tran Quang Co admits.

Acceptance is balm for now, and Vietnam seems reconciled to a normal life in the neighbourhood. Yet its historic sense of vulnerability has been merely assuaged, not cured. There is a fair-weather sound to any "friends-everywhere" foreign policy: fine if everyone wants to be friends, but whom does Vietnam turn to in the next storm?

Asked about threats to Vietnam's national security, the editor of *Quan Doi Nhan Dan*, the army daily, has a surprisingly domestic answer. "There are four," he says: "Our economic backwardness; social tensions from rapid economic change; corruption; and peacetime damage from hostile foreign forces—drugs and pornography, for example."

Vietnam, in the post-Soviet era, faces a resurgent China, an opportunistic Japan, and a reluctant America, not much of a choice for a country always on the lookout for a strong protector.

The splendours and miseries of foreign policy do matter less to Vietnam than catching up economically. But surely Vietnam must have interests to defend? Turn the talk as you may, Vietnamese soldiers or diplomats will not budge from their declared faith in negotiated solutions, regional co-operation and the United Nations. In this eirenic mood, they sound like the Vietnamese

that Roosevelt must have been thinking of when he assured Stalin at Yalta: "The Vietnamese are small people: they're not at all warlike."

Three Sorts of Security

Vietnam does have security concerns and points of friction with neighbours. China, Taiwan and Vietnam have competing claims for jurisdiction in the South China Sea over the Spratly Islands and other scattered bits of disputed marine real estate. Crestone, an American oil company, has explored for oil on China's behalf in a spot claimed by the Vietnamese. Brunei, the Philippines and Malaysia have partial claims to the Spratly Islands. China and Vietnam say they will settle the dispute by talk, not force, but have made no visible progress. China's tactic is evidently to pick off other Spratlys claimants one by one. The China-Vietnam land border is also in question at points.

Vietnam and Thailand, by contrast, have acted to ease tensions between them. They have discussed setting up a military hotline between Hanoi and Bangkok. With Cambodia and Laos, the two have agreed to "sustainable development" of the Mekong River under the United Nations Development Programme. There is talk of confidence-building measures, preventive diplomacy and conflict resolution mechanisms in South-East Asia. All to the good. But ASEAN is not a security alliance and Vietnam belongs to none.

Vietnam, in fact, has little manoeuvring room. On the rosiest economic assumptions it will be at most a middle-sized power, though one which before long could well shift the regional balance of power within ASEAN. Even so, once feared as the Prussia of South-East Asia, Vietnam is now cast in a less threatening role, having in effect abandoned its old ambition of mastering Indochina.

Vietnam must, as ever, make the best of its weaknesses. In the post–Soviet era it faces a resurgent China, an opportunistic Japan and a reluctant America, not much of a choice for a country always on the lookout for a strong protector.

Three paths suggest themselves. Vietnam could modestly settle into becoming a more populous Asian Finland, in the shadow of a powerful neighbour and on the margin of geopolitics. Alternatively, it might seek a more active but riskier part in the coming struggle for mastery of Asia either as China's junior partner or, turning openly against its old "brother enemy", as Japan's ally or even Russia's.

Vietnam would probably find most security in a third course: growing richer fast and working with its neighbours to strengthen ASEAN. While not wanting China to boss them about, today's Vietnamese, like the Emperor Le Loi, will want to keep in mind which country is bigger.

A Story with Three Endings

Cross your fingers for the one that will work.

Vietnam, on a closer look, is one country. Despite civil war, regional disparities and growing differences of wealth, its national identity is strong. Useful as nationalism was for Vietnam in its recent heroic period, it is going to be less help—particularly in its anti-foreigner guise—in Vietnam's present struggle to overcome poverty and catch up with richer, less backward neighbours.

Vietnam's one power, the Communist Party, looks unbudgeable, but not unchangeable. Despite the name, it has scrapped pure communism and, like China, is pursuing market Leninism: a mixture of capitalist economics and communist politics. In the end this combination cannot work. The question is how and when it will end.

Publications gratefully plundered for this survey of Vietnam include:
"Vietnam at the Crossroads", by Michael Williams, Chatham House-Pinter, 1992
"Vietnam to 2005, Advancing on All Fronts", by Adam Fforde and Anthony Goldstone, The Economist Intelligence Unit, 1995
"Dictionary of the Modern Politics of South-East Asia", by Michael Leifer, Routledge, 1995
"Brother Enemy: A History of Indochina since the Fall of Saigon", by Nayan Chanda, Collier, 1986

It might be that, at the cost of new isolation for Vietnam and lower living standards for its people, command politics could be saved by restoring command economics. But the market has probably already gone too far to be easily or peacefully abandoned. A second path would be for the Communist Party to risk a popular convulsion by resisting the demands for political change which economic freedom usually brings. The Communist Party would then either crack apart or, more likely, crack down, as Chinese troops did in Tiananmen Square or Burmese ones in the streets of Yangon (Rangoon).

A third, less melancholy, possibility is that Communist rule could evolve, as national and local assemblies got more

(Wide World Photo)

Vietnam experienced five decades of war and poverty. Today three-fifths of the population is under the age of 25, too young to have had personal experience with war. The contrast of the old with the young is evident on the faces pictured above: the older people have long suffered and sacrificed, while the young are optimistic about their future.

say, as something resembling a rule of law spread down through courts and the administration, and as the Communist Party grew more representative of Vietnam's young majority, its women and its business people.

The chances are that by early next century a Vietnam of perhaps 120m people will have grown into a handsome striped dragon.

So long as enlightened Communists go on winning the argument and the party keeps a nose for public opinion, this path seems the likeliest. Suppler

one-party government under laws would not be democracy. But it would be a step towards it, and not unusual for the region. For now, it looks the most desirable of Vietnam's available options—though there is a proviso.

When Vietnam's Communists first embraced the market, all they had to do to make the economy flourish was to step aside. Now they must cherish and foster the market more actively. Do they know how? Building physical infrastructure—roads, power-lines—is something communists understand. But the market infrastructure Vietnam urgently needs—financial intermediaries, a regulatory framework, a competitive environment for enterprises—is something they are still groping towards. For market liberals such as the prime minister, Vo Van Kiet, winning the argument against the economic old guard—or against simple inertia—is not enough. A new offensive is needed to keep market reform on track.

Silence those Doubts

The ifs and buts mount up. Pile them on Vietnam's tiny GDP, and it can look as

though hopes for Vietnam are all faith and no evidence. True, Vietnam has had over 40 years of war since 1945, counting Cambodia, during most of which north and south were subsidised dependencies. But that historic excuse for penury is weakening all the time.

David Hume, an 18th-century philosopher, urged sceptics to question their doubts as well as their convictions. Economically, most of Vietnam's now-thriving neighbours came from nowhere. Before its economic miracle South Korea in 1960 was scarcely richer than Vietnam. Vietnam's GDP has risen by over 8% a year since 1992 and is expected to go on growing fast. The Vietnamese are well-educated and hard-working. They may baffle Americans and Europeans, but Chinese and Japanese investors take them seriously. Vietnam may have more oil and gas than it lets on. And the country is sitting in the middle of the world's most economically buoyant region. The chances are that by early next century a Vietnam of perhaps 120m people will have grown into a handsome striped dragon.

Credits

Sources for Statistical Reports

U.S. State Department, *Background Notes* (1996).

C.I.A. *World Factbook* (1996–1997).

World Bank, *World Development Report* (1996).

UN *Population and Vital Statistics Report* (January 1997).

World Statistics in Brief (1996).

Statistical Yearbook (1996).

The Statesman's Yearbook (1996–1997).

Population Reference Bureau, *World Population Data Sheet* (1996).

World Almanac (1997).

Demographic Yearbook (1996).

Glossary of Terms and Abbreviations

Animism The belief that all objects, including plants, animals, rocks, and other matter, contain spirits. This belief figures prominently in early Japanese religious thought and in the various indigenous religions of the South Pacific.

Anti-Fascist People's Freedom League (AFPFL) An anti-Japanese resistance movement organized by Burmese students and intellectuals.

ANZUS The name of a joint military-security agreement originally among Australia, New Zealand, and the United States. New Zealand is no longer a member.

Asia Pacific Economic Cooperation Council (APEC) Organized in 1989, this body is becoming increasingly visible as a major forum for plans about regional economic cooperation and growth in the Pacific Rim.

Asian Development Bank (ADB) With contributions from industrialized nations, the ADB provides loans to Pacific Rim countries in order to foster economic development.

Association of Southeast Asian Nations (ASEAN) Established in 1967 to promote economic cooperation among the countries of Indonesia, Malaysia, the Philippines, Singapore, Thailand, and Brunei.

British Commonwealth of Nations A voluntary association of nations formerly included in the British Empire. Officials meet regularly in member countries to discuss issues of common economic, military, and political concern.

Buddhism A religious and ethical philosophy of life that originated in India in the fifth and sixth centuries B.C., partly in reaction to the caste system. Buddhism holds that people's souls are endlessly reborn and that one's standing with each rebirth depends on one's behavior in the previous life.

Capitalism An economic system in which productive property is owned by individuals or corporations, rather than by the government, and the proceeds of which belong to the owner rather than to the workers or the state.

Chaebol A Korean term for a large business conglomerate. Similar to the Japanese *keiretsu*.

Chinese Communist Party (CCP) Founded in 1921 by Mao Zedong and others, the CCP became the ruling party of the People's Republic of China in 1949 upon the defeat of the Nationalist Party and the army of Chiang Kai-shek.

Cold War The intense rivalry, short of direct "hot-war" military conflict, between the Soviet Union and the United States, which continued from the end of World War II until approximately 1990.

Communism An economic system in which land and businesses are owned collectively by everyone in the society rather than by individuals. Modern communism is founded on the teachings of the German intellectuals Marx and Engels.

Confucianism A system of ethical guidelines for managing one's personal relationships with others and with the state. Confucianism stresses filial piety and obligation to one's superiors. It is based on the teachings of the Chinese intellectuals Confucius and Mencius.

Cultural Revolution A period between 1966 and 1976 in China when, urged on by Mao, students attempted to revive a revolutionary spirit in China. Intellectuals and even Chinese Communist Party leaders who were not zealously communist were violently attacked or purged from office.

Demilitarized Zone (DMZ) A heavily guarded border zone separating North and South Korea.

European Union (EU) An umbrella organization of numerous Western European nations working toward the establishment of a single economic and political European entity. Formerly known as the European Community (EC).

Extraterritoriality The practice whereby the home country exercises jurisdiction over its diplomats and other citizens living in a foreign country, effectively freeing them from the authority of the host government.

Feudalism A social and economic system of premodern Europe, Japan, China, and other countries, characterized by a strict division of the populace into social classes, an agricultural economy, and governance by lords controlling vast parcels of land and the people thereon.

Greater East Asia Co-Prosperity Sphere The Japanese description of the empire they created in the 1940s by military conquest.

Gross Domestic Product (GDP) A statistic describing the entire output of goods and services produced by a country in a year, less income earned on foreign investments.

Hinduism A 5,000-year-old religion of India that advocates a social caste system but anticipates the eventual merging of all individuals into one universal world soul.

Indochina The name of the colony in Southeast Asia controlled by France and consisting of the countries of Laos, Cambodia, and Vietnam. The colony ceased to exist after 1954, but the term still is often applied to the region.

International Monetary Fund (IMF) An agency of the United Nations whose goal it is to promote freer world trade by assisting nations in economic development.

Islam The religion founded by Mohammed and codified in the Koran. Believers, called Muslims, submit to Allah (Arabic for God) and venerate his name in daily prayer.

Keiretsu A Japanese word for a large business conglomerate.

‌‌‍‍‌

‌‍‍‌

Khmer Rouge The communist guerrilla army, led by Pol Pot, that controlled Cambodia in the 1970s and continues to attempt to overthrow the UN-sanctioned government.

Kuomintang The National People's Party (Nationalists), which, under Chiang Kai-shek, governed China until Mao Zedong's revolution in 1949; it continues to dominate politics in Taiwan.

Laogai A Mandarin Chinese word for a prison or concentration camp where political prisoners are kept. It is similar in concept to the Russian word *gulag.*

Liberal Democratic Party (LDP) The conservative party that ruled Japan almost continuously between 1955 and 1993 and oversaw Japan's rapid economic development.

Martial Law The law applied to a territory by military authorities in a time of emergency when regular civilian authorities are unable to maintain order. Under martial law, residents are usually restricted in their movement and in their exercise of such rights as freedom of speech and of the press.

Meiji Restoration The restoration of the Japanese emperor to his throne in 1868. The period is important as the beginning of the modern era in Japan and the opening of Japan to the West after centuries of isolation.

Monsoons Winds that bring exceptionally heavy rainfall to parts of Southeast Asia and elsewhere. Monsoon rains are essential to the production of rice.

National League for Democracy An opposition party in Myanmar that was elected to head the government in 1990 but that has since been forbidden by the current military leaders to take office.

New Economic Policy (NEP) An economic plan advanced in the 1970s to restructure the Malaysian economy and foster industrialization and ethnic equality.

Newly Industrializing Country (NIC) A designation for those countries of the developing world, particularly Taiwan, South Korea, and other Asian nations, whose economies have undergone rapid growth; sometimes also referred to as newly industrialized countries.

Non-Aligned Movement A loose association of mostly non-Western developing nations, many of which had been colonies of Western powers but during the cold war chose to remain detached from either the U.S. or Soviet bloc. Initially Indonesia and India, among others, were enthusiastic promoters of the movement.

Opium Wars Conflicts between Britain and China in 1839–1842 and 1856–1866 in which England used China's destruction of opium shipments and other issues as a pretext to attack China and force the government to sign trade agreements.

Pacific War The name frequently used by the Japanese to refer to that portion of World War II in which they were involved and which took place in Asia and the Pacific.

Shintoism An ancient indigenous religion of Japan that stressed the role of *kami,* or supernatural gods, in the lives of people. For a time during the 1930s, Shinto was the state religion of Japan and the emperor was honored as its high priest.

Siddhartha Gautama The name of the man who came to be called the Buddha.

Smokestack Industries Heavy industries such as steel mills that are basic to an economy but produce objectionable levels of air, water, or land pollution.

Socialism An economic system in which productive property is owned by the government as are the proceeds from the productive labor. Most socialist systems today are actually mixed economies in which individuals as well as the government own property.

South Pacific Forum An organization established by Australia and other South Pacific nations to provide a forum for discussion of common problems and opportunities in the region.

Southeast Asia Treaty Organization (SEATO) A collective-defense treaty signed by the United States and several European and Southeast Asian nations. It was dissolved in 1977.

Subsistence Farming Farming that meets the immediate needs of the farming family but that does not yield a surplus sufficient for export.

Taoism An ancient religion of China inspired by Lao-tze that stresses the need for mystical contemplation to free one from the desires and sensations of the materialistic and physical world.

Tiananmen Square Massacre The violent suppression by the Chinese Army of a prodemocracy movement that had been organized in Beijing by thousands of Chinese students in 1989 and that had become an international embarrassment to the Chinese regime.

United Nations (UN) An international organization established immediately after World War II to replace the League of Nations. The organization includes most of the countries of the world and works for international understanding and world peace.

World Health Organization (WHO) Established in 1948 as an advisory and technical-assistance organization to improve the health of peoples around the world.

Bibliography

GENERAL WORKS

Mark Borthwick, *East Asian Civilizations: A Dialogue in Five Stages* (Cambridge: Harvard University Press, 1988). The development of philosophical and religious thought in China, Korea, Japan, and other regions of East Asia.

Richard Bowring and Peter Kornicki, *Encyclopedia of Japan* (New York: Cambridge University Press, 1993).

Commission on U.S.–Japan Relations for the Twenty-First Century, *Preparing for a Pacific Century: Exploring the Potential for Pacific Basin Cooperation* (Washington, DC: November 1991).
Transcription of an international conference on the Pacific with commentary by representatives from the United States, Malaysia, Japan, Thailand, Indonesia, and others.

Susanna Cuyler, *A Companion to Japanese Literature, Culture, and Language* (Highland Park, NJ: B. Rugged, 1992).

William Theodore de Bary, *East Asian Civilizations: A Dialogue in Five Stages* (Cambridge: Harvard University Press, 1988).
An examination of religions and philosophical thought in several regions of East Asia.

Syed N. Hossain, *Japan: Not in the West* (Boston: Vikas II, 1995).

Seijiu Naya and Stephen Browne, eds., *Development Challenges in Asia and the Pacific in the 1990s* (Honolulu: East-West Center, 1991).
A collection of speeches made at the 1990 Symposium on Cooperation in Asia and the Pacific. The articles cover development issues in East, Southeast, and South Asia and the Pacific.

Edwin O. Reischauer and Marius B. Jansen, *The Japanese Today: Change and Continuity* (Cambridge: Belknap Press, 1995).
A description of the basic geography and historical background of Japan.

NATIONAL HISTORIES AND ANALYSES

Australia

Boris Frankel, *From the Prophets Deserts Come: The Struggle to Reshape Australian Political Culture* (New York: Deakin University [St. Mut.], 1994).
Australia's government and political aspects are described in this essay.

Herman J. Hiery, *The Neglected War: The German South Pacific and the Influence of WW I* (Honolulu: University of Hawaii Press, 1995).

David Alistair Kemp, *Society and Electoral Behaviors in Australia: A Study of Three Decades* (St. Lucia: University of Queensland Press, 1978).
Elections, political parties, and social problems in Australia since 1945.

David Meredith and Barrie Dyster, *Australia in the International Economy in the Twentieth Century* (New York: Cambridge University Press, 1990).
Examines the international aspects of Australia's economy.

Brunei

Wendy Hutton, *East Malaysia and Brunei* (Berkeley, CA: Periplus, 1993).

Graham Saunders, *A History of Brunei* (New York: Oxford University Press, 1995).

Nicholas Tarling, *Britain, the Brookes, and Brunei* (Kuala Lumpur: Oxford University Press, 1971).
A history of the sultanate of Brunei and its neighbors.

Cambodia

David P. Chandler, *The Tragedy of Cambodian History, War, and Revolution since 1945* (New Haven: Yale University Press, 1993).
A short history of Cambodia.

Michael W. Doyle, *UN Peacekeeping in Cambodia: UNTAC's Civil Mandate* (Boulder: Lynne Rienner, 1995).
A review of the current status of Cambodia's government and political parties.

Craig Etcheson, *The Rise and Demise of Democratic Kampuchea* (Boulder: Westview Press, 1984).
A history of the rise of the Communist government in Cambodia.

William Shawcross, *The Quality of Mercy: Cambodia, Holocaust, and Modern Conscience; with a report from Ethiopia* (New York: Simon & Schuster, 1985).
A report on political atrocities, relief programs, and refugees in Cambodia and Ethiopia.

Usha Welaratna, ed., *Beyond the Killing Fields: Voices of Nine Cambodian Survivors* (Stanford, CA: Stanford University Press, 1993).
A collection of nine narratives by Cambodian refugees in the United States and their adjustments into American society.

China

Julia F. Andrews, *Painters and Politics in the People's Republic of China, 1949–1979* (Berkeley: University of California Press, 1994).
A fascinating presentation of the relationship between politics and art from the beginning of the Communist period until the eve of major liberalization in 1979.

Ma Bo, *Blood Red Sunset* (New York: Viking, 1995).
A compelling autobiographical account by a Red Guard during the Cultural Revolution.

Jung Chang, *Wild Swans: Three Daughters of China* (New York: Simon and Shuster, 1992).
An autobiographical/biographical account that illuminates what China was like for one family for three generations.

Kwang-chih Chang, *The Archaeology of China,* 4th ed. (New Haven: Yale University Press, 1986).

___, *Shang Civilization* (New Haven: Yale University Press, 1980).
Two works by an eminent archaeologist on the origins of Chinese civilization.

Qing Dai, *Yangtze! Yangtze!* (Toronto: Probe International, 1994).
Collection of documents concerning the debate over building the Three Gorges Dam on the upper Yangtze River in order to harness energy for China.

John King Fairbank, *China: A New History* (Cambridge: Harvard University Press, 1992).
An examination of the motivating forces in China's history that define it as a coherent culture from its earliest recorded history to 1991.

David S. G. Goodman and Beverly Hooper, eds., *China's Quiet Revolution: New Interactions between State and Society* (New York: St. Martin's Press, 1994).
Articles examine the impact of economic reforms since early 1980s on the social structure and society generally, with focus on changes in wealth, status, power, and newly emerging social forces.

Richard Madsen, *China and the American Dream: A Moral Inquiry* (Berkeley: University of California Press, 1995).
A history on the emotional and unpredictable relationship the United States has had with China from the nineteenth century to the present.

Suzanne Ogden, *China's Unresolved Issues: Politics, Development, and Culture* (Englewood Cliffs: Prentice Hall, 1992).
A complete review of economic and cultural issues in modern China.

Hong Kong

"Basic Law of Hong Kong Special Administrative Region of the People's Republic of China," *Beijing Review*, Vol. 33, No. 18 (April 30–May 6, 1990), supplement.

Ming K. Chan and Gerard A. Postiglione, *The Hong Kong Reader: Passage to Chinese Sovereignty* (Armonk, NY: M. E. Sharpe, 1996).
A collection of articles about the issues facing Hong Kong during the transition to Chinese rule after July 1, 1997.

Berry Hsu, ed., *The Common Law in Chinese Context* in the series entitled *Hong Kong Becoming China: The Transition to 1997* (Armonk, NY: M. E. Sharpe, Inc., 1992).
An examination of the common law aspects of the "Basic Law," the mini-constitution that will govern Hong Kong after 1997.

Benjamin K. P. Leung, ed., *Social Issues in Hong Kong* (New York: Oxford University Press, 1990).
A collection of essays on select issues in Hong Kong, such as aging, poverty, women, pornography, and mental illness.

Jan Morris, *Hong Kong: Epilogue to an Empire* (New York: Vintage, 1997).
A detailed portrait of Hong Kong that gives the reader the sense of actually being on the scene in a vibrant Hong Kong.

Mark Roberti, *The Fall of Hong Kong: China's Triumph and Britain's Betrayal* (New York: John Wiley & Sons, Inc., 1994).
An account on the decisions Britain and China made about Hong Kong's fate since the early 1980s.

Frank Welsh, *A Borrowed Place: The History of Hong Kong* (New York: Kodansha International, 1996).
A presentation on Hong Kong's history from the time of the British East India Company in the eighteenth century through the Opium Wars of the nineteenth century to the present.

Indonesia

Amarendra Bhattacharya and Mari Pangestu, *Indonesia: Development, Transformation, and Public Policy* (Washington, DC: World Bank, 1993).
An examination of Indonesia's economic policy.

Frederica M. Bunge, *Indonesia: A Country Study* (Washington, DC: U.S. Government, 1983).
An excellent review of the outlines of Indonesian history and culture, including politics and national security.

Philip J. Eldridge, *Non-government Organizations and Political Participation in Indonesia* (New York: Oxford University Press, 1995).
Examination of Indonesia's nongovernment agencies (NGOs).

Audrey R. Kahin, ed., *Regional Dynamics of the Indonesian Revolution: Unity from Diversity* (Honolulu: University of Hawaii Press, 1985).
A history of Indonesia since the end of World War II, with separate chapters on selected islands.

Hamish McConald, *Suharto's Indonesia* (Australia: The Dominion Press, 1980).
The story of the rise of Suharto and the manner in which he controlled the political and military life of the country, beginning in 1965.

Susan Rodgers, ed., *Telling Lives, Telling Histories: Autobiography and Historical Immigration in Modern Indonesia* (Berkeley, CA: University of California Press, 1995).
Reviews the history of Indonesia's immigration.

David Wigg, *In a Class of Their Own: A Look at the Campaign against Female Illiteracy* (Washington, DC: World Bank, 1994).

GLOBAL STUDIES: JAPAN AND THE PACIFIC RIM
Looks at the work that is being done by various groups to advance women's literacy in Indonesia.

Japan

Michael Barnhart, *Japan and the World since 1868* (New York: Routledge, Chapman, and Hall, 1994).
An essay that addresses commerce in Japan from 1868 to the present.

Marjorie Wall Bingham and Susan Hill Gross, *Women in Japan* (Minnesota: Glenhurst Publications, Inc., 1987).
An historical review of Japanese women's roles in Japan.

John Clammer, *Difference and Modernity: Social Theory and Contemporary Japanese Society* (New York: Routledge, Chapman, and Hall, 1995).

Mark Gauthier, *Making It in Japan* (Upland, PA: Diane Publishers, 1994).
An examination of how success can be attained in Japan's marketplace.

Paul Herbig, *Innovation Japanese Style: A Cultural and Historical Perspective* (Glenview, IL: Greenwood, 1995).
A review of the implications for international competition

Harold R. Kerbo and John McKinstry, *Who Rules Japan? The Inner-Circle of Economic and Political Power* (Glenview, IL: Greenwood, 1995).
The effect of Japan's politics on its economy is evaluated in this essay.

Hiroshi Komai, *Migrant Workers in Japan* (New York: Routledge, Chapman, and Hall, 1994).
Focus on the abundance of the migrant labor supply in Japan.

Solomon B. Levine and Koji Taira, eds., *"Japan's External Economic Relations: Japanese Perspectives,"* special issue of *The Annals of the American Academy of Political and Social Science,* January 1991.
An excellent overview of the origin and future of Japan's economic relations with the rest of the world, especially Asia.

E. Wayne Nafziger, *Learning from the Japanese: Japan's Pre-War Development and the Third World* (Armonk, NY: M. E. Sharpe, 1995).
Presents Japan as a model of "guided capitalism," and what it did by way of policies designed to promote and accelerate development.

Nippon Steel Corporation, *Nippon: The Land and Its People* (Japan: Gakuseisha Publishing Co., 1984).
An overview of modern Japan in both English and Japanese.

Korea: North and South Korea

Chai-Sik Chung, *A Korean Confucian Encounter with the Modern World* (Berkeley, CA: IEAS, 1995).

Korea's history and the effectiveness of Confucianism are addressed.

Donald Clark et al., *U.S.–Korean Relations* (Farmingdale, NY: Regina Books, 1995).
A review on the history of Korea's relationship with the United States.

James Cotton, *Politics and Policy in the New Korean State: From Rah Tae-Woo to Kim Young-Sam* (New York: St. Martin's, 1995).
The power and influence of politics in Korea are examined.

James Hoare, *North Korea* (New York: Oxford University Press, 1995).
An essay that addresses commerce in Japan between 1868 and the present.

Dae-Jung Kim, *Mass Participatory Economy: Korea's Road to World Economic Power* (Landham, MD: University Press of America, 1995).

Korean Overseas Information Service, *A Handbook of Korea* (Seoul: Seoul International Publishing House, 1987).
A description of modern South Korea, including social welfare, foreign relations, and culture. The early history of the entire Korean Peninsula is also discussed.

___, *Korean Arts and Culture* (Seoul: Seoul International Publishing House, 1986).
A beautifully illustrated introduction to the rich cultural life of modern South Korea.

Callus A. MacDonald, *Korea: The War before Vietnam* (New York: The Free Press, 1986).
A detailed account of the military events in Korea between 1950 and 1953, including a careful analysis of the U.S. decision to send troops to the peninsula.

Christopher J. Sigur, ed., *Continuity and Change in Contemporary Korea* (New York: Carnegie Ethics and International Affairs, 1994).
A review of the numerous stages of change that Korea has experienced.

Laos

Sucheng Chan, ed., *Hmong: Means Free Life in Laos and America* (Philadelphia: Temple University Press, 1994).

Arthur J. Dommen, *Laos: Keystone of Indochina* (Boulder: Westview Press, 1985).
A short history and review of current events in Laos.

Joel M. Halpern, *The Natural Economy of Laos* (Christiansburg, VA: Dalley Book Service, 1990).

___, *Government, Politics, and South Structures of Laos: Study of Traditions and Innovations* (Christiansburg, VA: Dalley Book Service, 1990).

___, *The Natural Economy of Laos* (Christiansburg, VA: Dalley Book Service, 1990).

220

Macau

Charles Ralph Boxer, *The Portuguese Seaborne Empire, 1415–1825* (New York: A. A. Knopf, 1969).
A history of Portugal's colonies, including Macau.
W. G. Clarence-Smith, *The Third Portuguese Empire, 1825–1975* (Manchester: Manchester University Press, 1985).
A history of Portugal's colonies, including Macau.

Malaysia

Mohammed Ariff, *The Malaysian Economy: Pacific Connections* (New York: Oxford University Press, 1991).
The report on Malaysia examines Malaysia's development and its vulnerability in world trade.
Richard Clutterbuck, *Conflict and Violence in Singapore and Malaysia, 1945–1983* (Boulder: Westview Press, 1985).
The Communist challenge to the stability of Singapore and Malaysia in the early years of their independence from Great Britain is presented.
K. S. Jomo, ed., *Japan and Malaysian Development: In the Shadow of the Rising Sun* (New York: Routledge, 1995).
A review of the relationship between Japan and Malaysia's economy.
Gordon Means, *Malaysian Politics: The Second Generation* (New York: Oxford University Press, 1991).
R. S. Milne, *Malaysia: Tradition, Modernity, and Islam* (Boulder: Westview Press, 1986).
A general overview of the nature of modern Malaysian society.

Myanmar (Burma)

Michael Aung-Thwin, *Pagan: The Origins of Modern Burma* (Honolulu: University of Hawaii Press, 1985).
A treatment of the religious and political ideology of the Burmese people and the effect of ideology on the economy and politics of the modern state.
Aye Kyaw, *The Voice of Young Burma* (Ithaca, NY: Cornell SE Asia, 1993).
The political history of Burma is presented in this report.
Chi-Shad Liang, *Burma's Foreign Relations: Neutralism in Theory and Practice* (Glenview, IL: Greenwood, 1990).
Mya Maung, *The Burma Road to Poverty* (Glenview, IL: Greenwood, 1991).

New Zealand

Bev James and Kay Saville-Smith, *Gender, Culture, and Power: Challenging New Zealand's Gendered Culture* (New York: Oxford University Press, 1995).
Patrick Massey, *New Zealand: Market Liberalization in a Developed Economy* (New York: St. Martin, 1995).
Analyzes New Zealand's market-oriented reform pro-grams since the Labour government came into power in 1984.
Stephen Rainbow, *Green Politics* (New York: Oxford University Press, 1994).
A review of current New Zealand politics.
Geoffrey W. Rice, *The Oxford History of New Zealand* (New York: Oxford University Press, 1993).

Papua New Guinea

Robert J. Gordon and Mervyn J. Meggitt, *Law and Order in the New Guinea Highlands: Encounters with Enga* (Hanover: University Press of New England, 1985).
Tribal law and warfare in Papua New Guinea.
David Hyndman, *Ancestral Rainforests and the Mountain of Gold: Indigenous Peoples and Mining in New Guinea* (Boulder: Westview Press, 1994).
Bruce W. Knauft, *South Coast New Guinea Cultures: History, Comparison, Dialectic* (New York: Cambridge University Press, 1993).

The Philippines

Frederica M. Bunge, ed., *Philippines: A Country Study* (Washington, DC: U.S. Government, 1984).
Description and analysis of the economic, security, political, and social systems of the Philippines, including maps, statistical charts, and reproduction of important documents. An extensive bibliography is included.
Manual B. Dy, *Values in Philippine Culture and Education* (Washington, DC: Council for Research in Values and Philosophy, 1994).
James F. Eder and Robert L. Youngblood, eds., *Patterns of Power and Politics in the Philippines: Implications for Development* (Tempe: AZ: ASU Program, SE Asian, 1994).
A review of the impact of politics and its power over development in the Philippines.

Singapore

Lai A. Eng, *Meanings of Multiethnicity: A Case Study of Ethnicity and Ethnic Relations in Singapore* (New York: Oxford University Press, 1995).
Paul Leppert, *Doing Business with Singapore* (Fremont, CA: Jain Publishing Co., 1995).
Singapore's economic status is examined in this report.
Hafiz Mirza, *Multinationals and the Growth of the Singapore Economy* (New York: St. Martin's Press, 1986).
An essay on foreign companies and their impact on modern Singapore.
Nilavu Mohdx et al., *New Place, Old Ways: Essays on Indian Society and Culture in Modern Singapore* (Columbia, MO: South Asia, 1994).

South Pacific

C. Beeby and N. Fyfe, "The South Pacific Nuclear Free Zone Treaty," Victoria University of Wellington *Law Review,* Vol. 17, No. 1, pp. 33–51 (February 1987).
A good review of nuclear issues in the Pacific.

William S. Livingston and William Roger Louis, eds., *Australia, New Zealand, and the Pacific Islands Since the First World War* (Austin: University of Texas Press, 1979).
An assessment of significant historical and political developments in Australia, New Zealand, and the Pacific Islands since 1917.

Taiwan

Joel Aberbach et al., eds., *The Role of the State in Taiwan's Development* (Armonk, NY: M. E. Sharpe, 1994).
Articles address technology, international trade, state policy toward the development of local industries, and the effect of economic development on society, including women and farmers.

Bih-er Chou, Clark Cal, and Janet Clark, *Women in Taiwan Politics: Overcoming Barriers to Women's Participation in a Modernizing Society* (Boulder: Lynne Rienner Publishers, 1990).
Examines the political underrepresentation of women in Taiwan and how Chinese culture on the one hand and modernization and development on the other are affecting women's status.

Stevan Harrell and Chun-chieh Huang, eds., *Cultural Change in Postwar Taiwan* (Boulder: Westview Press, 1994).
A collection of essays that analyzes the tensions in Taiwan's society as modernization erodes many of its old values and traditions.

Dennis Hickey, *United States–Taiwan Security Ties: From Cold War to beyond Containment* (Westport: Praeger, 1994).
Examines U.S.–Taiwan security ties from the Cold War to the present and what Taiwan is doing to ensure its own military preparedness.

Chin-chuan Lee, "Sparking a Fire: The Press and the Ferment of Democratic Change in Taiwan," in Chin-chuan Lee (ed.), *China's Media, Media China* (Boulder: Westview Press, 1994), pp. 179–193.

Robert M. Marsh, *The Great Transformation: Social Change in Taipei, Taiwan, since the 1960s* (Armonk, NY: M. E. Sharpe, 1996).
An investigation of how Taiwan's society has changed since the 1960s when its economic transformation began.

Robert G. Sutter and William R. Johnson, *Taiwan in World Affairs* (Boulder: Westview Press, 1994).
Articles give comprehensive coverage of Taiwan's involvement in foreign affairs.

Thailand

Medhi Krongkaew, *Thailand's Industrialization and Its Consequences* (New York: St. Martin, 1995).
A discussion of events surround the development of Thailand since the mid-1980s with a focus on the nature and characteristics of Thai industrialization.

Ross Prizzia, *Thailand in Transition: The Role of Oppositional Forces* (Honolulu: University of Hawaii Press, 1985).
Government management of political opposition in Thailand.

Susan Wells and Steve Van Beek, *A Day in the Life of Thailand* (San Francisco: Collins SF, 1995).

Vietnam

Chris Brazier, *The Price of Peace* (New York: Okfam Pubs. U.K. [St. Mut.], 1992).

Ronald J. Cima, ed., *Vietnam: A Country Study* (Washington, D.C.: U.S. Government, 1989).
An overview of modern Vietnam, with emphasis on the origins, values, and lifestyles of the Vietnamese people.

Chris Ellsbury et al., *Vietnam: Perspectives and Performance* (Cedar Falls, IA: Assn. Text Study, 1994).
A review of Vietnam's history.

D. R. SarDeSai, *Vietnam: The Struggle for National Identity* (Boulder: Westview Press, 1992).
A good treatment of ethnicity in Vietnam and a national history up to the current involvement in Cambodia.

PERIODICALS AND CURRENT EVENTS

The Annals of the American Academy of Political and Social Science
c/o Sage Publications, Inc.
2455 Teller Rd.
Newbury Park, CA 91320
Selected issues focus on the Pacific Rim; there is an extensive book-review section. Special issues are as follows:
"The Pacific Region: Challenges to Policy and Theory" (September 1989).
"China's Foreign Relations" (January 1992).
"Japan's External Economic Relations: Japanese Perspectives" (January 1991).

The Asian Wall Street Journal, Dow Jones & Company, Inc.
A daily business newspaper focusing on Asian markets.

Canada and Hong Kong Update
Joint Centre for Asia Pacific Studies
Suite 270, York Lanes
York University

4700 Keele St.
North York, Ontario M3J 1P3, Canada
A source of information about Hong Kong emigration.

Current History: A World Affairs Journal
Focuses on one country or region in each issue; the emphasis is on international and domestic politics.

The Economist
25 St. James's St.
London, England
A newsmagazine with insightful commentary on international issues affecting the Pacific Rim.

Indochina Interchange
Suite 1801
220 West 42nd St.
New York, NY 10036
A publication of the U.S.–Indochina Reconciliation Project. An excellent source of information about assistance programs for Laos, Cambodia, and Vietnam.

The Japan Foundation Newsletter
The Japan Foundation
Park Building
3-6 Kioi-cho
Chiyoda-ku
Tokyo 102, Japan
A quarterly with research reports, book reviews, and announcements of interest to Japan specialists.

Japan Quarterly
Asahi Shimbun
5-3-2 Tsukiji
Chuo-ku
Tokyo 104, Japan
A quarterly journal, in English, covering political, cultural, and sociological aspects of modern Japanese life.

The Japan Times
The Japan Times Ltd.
C.P.O. Box 144
Tokyo 100-91, Japan
Excellent coverage, in English, of news reported in the Japanese press.

The Journal of Asian Studies
Association for Asian Studies
1 Lane Hall
University of Michigan
Ann Arbor, MI 48109
Formerly *The Far Eastern Quarterly;* scholarly articles on Asia, South Asia, and Southeast Asia.

Journal of Southeast Asian Studies
Singapore University Press
Singapore
Formerly the *Journal of Southeast Asian History;* scholarly articles on all aspects of modern Southeast Asia.

Korea Economic Report
Yoido
P.O. Box 963
Seoul 150-609
South Korea
An economic magazine for people doing business in Korea.

The Korea Herald
2-12, 3-ga Hoehyon-dong
Chung-gu
Seoul, South Korea
World news coverage, in English, with focus on events affecting the Korean Peninsula.

The Korea Times
The Korea Times Hankook Ilbo
Seoul, South Korea
Coverage of world news, with emphasis on events affecting Asia and the Korean Peninsula.

Malaysia Industrial Digest
Malaysian Industrial Development Authority (MIDA)
6th Floor
Industrial Promotion Division
Wisma Damansara, Jalan Semantan
50490 Kuala Kumpur, Malaysia
A source of statistics on manufacturing in Malaysia; of interest to those wishing to become more knowledgeable in the business and industry of the Pacific Rim.

News from Japan
Embassy of Japan
Japan–U.S. News and Communication
Suite 520
900 17th St., NW
Washington, D.C. 20006
A twice-monthly newsletter with news briefs from the Embassy of Japan on issues affecting Japan–U.S. relations.

Newsweek
444 Madison Ave.
New York, NY 10022
A weekly magazine with news and commentary on national and world events.

The New York Times
229 West 43rd St.
New York, NY 10036
A daily newspaper with excellent coverage of world events.

Pacific Affairs
The University of British Columbia
Vancouver, BC V6T 1W5
Canada
An international journal on Asia and the Pacific, including reviews of recent books about the region.

South China Morning Post
Tong Chong Street
Hong Kong
Daily coverage of world news, with emphasis on Hong Kong, China, Taiwan, and other Asian countries.

Time
Time-Life Building
Rockefeller Center
New York, NY 10020
A weekly newsmagazine with news and commentary on national and world events.

U.S. News & World Report
2400 N St., NW
Washington, D.C. 20037
A weekly newsmagazine with news and commentary on national and world events.

The World & I: A Chronicle of Our Changing Era
2800 New York Ave., NE
Washington, D.C. 20002
A monthly review of current events plus excellent articles on various regions of the world.

Index

Ministry of International Trade and Industry (MITI), 34, 143
Minshuto Party. *See* Democratic Party
Miriung, Theodore, 196, 197
missiles, "test-fire," 172, 203
Montagnards, 104
Morita, Miyuki, 148
Murao, Tadahiro, 148
music, religious practices in Indonesia and, 57
Myanmar, 8, 10, 111, 156–157, 158–159; overview of, 67–70

Nakane, Chie, 131, 132
National Bank, 161
National Day parade, of Taiwan, 96
National Front, of Malaysia, 65
national identity, lack of, in Pacific Rim, 7
National League for Democracy, 69, 158
National Liberation Front, 207, 211
National Party, of New Zealand, 73, 74
National United Front for an Independent, Neutral, Peaceful and Cooperative Cambodia (FUNCINPEC), 161, 163
National Unity Party, of Myanmar, 69
nationalism, 129
nation-states, replacement of, by networks, 114–115
natural resources; Japan and, 11; of Indonesia, 57; resource-rich developing countries and, 8, 9
Naura Phosphate Corp., 15
Nauru, 15, 40
Ne Win, 68
nerve-gas disposal, in Pacific, 73
New Caledonia, 16
New Economic Policy (NEP); of Malaysia, 65–66
New Frontier, 132, 135
New Guinea, 180
New Korea Party, 200
New Order, of Indonesia, 58, 186
New Party, of Taiwan, 96
New Territories, 53
New Zealand, 16, 122; overview of, 71–74
newly industrializing countries (NICs), 8, 9
Nga'dha peoples, 57
NGO Forum on Women in China, 159
Nguyen ai Quoc, 103–104, 204
Nguyen-Anh, 103
Nihonjin-ron, 27
Nishio, Kanji, 152
Nixon, Richard, 111
Non-Proliferation Treaty (NPT), 190
Non-Resident Indians (NRIs), 115
North Korea, 5, 91, 92, 120, 172–173, 189–195; overview of, 75–78
nuclear weapons, 15, 73, 77, 111, 113, 121, 135, 146, 172, 173, 191

Oanh, Nguyen Xan, 206
obligation, in Japan, 26–27
oil: in Brunei, 42; in China, 133–134; in Indonesia, 57, 187, 188
Okinawa, 134
Ona, Francis, 196
Operation High Speed, 195

opium, 53
Opium War, 53, 110
Organization for Security and Cooperation, 112, 113
organizations, multilateral, 164–165
overpopulation, 5–6, 47, 82
Overseas Vietnamese, 207
Ozawa Ichiro, 132, 142, 143

Pacific Basin Cooperation Concept, 112
Pacific Islands, 13–17
Pacific Rim, as term, 3
pancasila ideology, 186
Papua New Guinea, 40, 195–197; overview of, 79–81
Papua New Guinea Defense Force (PNGDF), 195, 196, 197
Paracel Islands, 172
Parhae Kingdom, of North Korea, 76
Park, Chung Hee, 77, 199
Parliament, of Japan, 33
party faction system, in Japan, 33–34
Pathet Lao, 61
Patten, Chris, 54–55
Pax Sinica, 110, 112, 114
penal colony, Australia as, 37
"people of the beach," 207
"people of the jungle," 207
People Power, of Philippines, 84
People Power Revolution, 197, 198
People's Army of Vietnam, 207
Peranakans, 86
Perry, William, 165
"Philippine 2000," 82
Philippines, 6–7, 128, 134, 179, 197–198; overview of, 82–85
phosphate mining, on Mauru, 15, 40
Pithecanthropus erectus, 57
Pol Pot, 44, 45, 211, 212
Political Action Party (PAP), of Singapore, 88
Polynesia, 13, 14
population-growth policies, 5–6, 47, 82
Portugal, 20, 57, 63
Poth Am, 159–160
pragmatism, in Japan, 26
Prem Tinslanond, 100
prevention, in Japan, 26
prime minister, of Japan, 33
Pygmy language, 182

racial classification, in China, 180
Raffles, Stamford, 87
Rahman, Abdul, 65
railway system, in Japan, 24
Rainsy, Sam, 162
Rajin-Sonbong free-trade area, 193
Ramos, Fidel, 85, 198
Ramos-Horta, Jose, 185
Ranariddh, Prince Norodom, 161, 162, 163
Ratni Sari Ismiati, 128
rats, Hmong immigrants in U.S. and, 59
Recruit Scandal, 24
Reformation, 140, 141

refugees, 3–4; North Korean, 194–195; Vietnamese, 207
religion: in China under communism, 51; in Hong Kong, 54; in Indonesia, 7; in Japan, 32–33; music in Indonesia and, 57; in Vietnam, 104
Renewal Party, of Japan, 142
research and development: in Japan, 138; in Taiwan, 202
resource-rich developing nations, 8, 9
Rhee, Syngman, 90, 91
rice: in Cambodia, 163; in Indonesia, 187; in Japan, 35; in Thailand, 99, 100
Rise of China, The (Overholt), 178
Roh Tae-woo, 91, 92, 198, 200, 201
Roman Catholicism, Philippines and, 82, 83, 84
Royal Cambodian Armed Forces (FCAF), 161, 162
Russia, 111, 112, 113, 120–121, 122, 123

Saisuri Chutikul, 121
Saito, Hiromi, 148, 149
Saito, Julie, 148
Samoa, 16, 17
samurai, 20–21
Sangha, 67, 70
Sar Kheng, 161
Sato, Eisaku, 145
savings, in Japan, 25
Saw Maung, 68–69
"Scaffold Deaths," 209
scientific research, in Japan, 138
Sejong, king of Korea, 90
Self-Defense Forces (SDF), 145, 147
"7-11 husbands," 19
Shang Dynasty, 47, 183
Shans, 68
Shilla Kingdom, of South Korea, 76
Shintoism, 20, 33, 131, 140
shoguns, 19
Sihanouk, Norodom, king of Cambodia, 44, 45, 161, 162
Singapore, 111, 113, 175; overview of, 86–88
Singirok, 195, 196
Sinification, legacy of, 174, 184
Sino-Tibetan language, 182, 183
Sirivudh, Prince, 161, 162, 163
slash-and-burn farming, in Laos, 60
Soares, Mario, 63
"Socioeconomic National Development Plan," of Laos, 60
Solomon Islands, 195
Somare, Michael, 195
Sony Corporation, 11, 25
Sorrow of Love, The (Bao), 207
Sorrow of War, The (Bao), 205–206
Souphanouvong, prince of Laos, 61
South China Sea, 4
South Korea, 5, 9, 10, 11, 76–77, 111, 113, 116, 117, 118, 120, 176, 177, 191, 192, 193, 194, 198–201; overview of, 89–92
South Pacific Bureau of Economic Cooperation, 15
South Pacific Commission, 15
South Pacific Forum, 15